Medieval
Western Civilization
and the
Byzantine and Islamic Worlds

Medieval Western Civilization
and the
Byzantine and Islamic Worlds

INTERACTION OF THREE CULTURES

Deno J. Geanakoplos

Yale University

D.C. HEATH AND COMPANY
Lexington, Massachusetts   Toronto

Maps and charts by Norman C. Adams

Photo Credits
p. 1, Museum of Fine Arts, Boston; p. 163, Editorial Photocolor Archives, Alinari/Scala; p. 413, Museum of Fine Arts, Boston; title page: Charlemagne and Anastasis, Cliché des Musées Nationaux-Paris; Islamic relief (detail), The Metropolitan Museum of Art, Rogers Fund, 1938

International Standard Book Number: 0–669–00868–0

Library of Congress Catalog Card Number: 78–52827

PREFACE

The purpose of this book is to provide a complete, enriched, and balanced view of medieval Western civilization from 300 to 1500 by presenting it in the broader context of the *entire* medieval world—the Byzantine and Islamic East, as well as the Latin West. An accurate account of the evolution of the medieval West must acknowledge the centuries-long impact the neighboring Byzantine and Islamic cultures had upon it. This work, therefore, while focusing primarily on the internal developments in the medieval West, also traces Western interaction with the Byzantine Empire and the Islamic Caliphates of Baghdad and Cordova, Spain.

Medieval Western Civilization and the Byzantine and Islamic Worlds is intended mainly for a college course in medieval history or civilization. Because of its comparative approach (an approach now increasingly favored by historians), the book will also be important to the layman interested in the development of medieval Western culture and the contributions to the West from its Muslim and Byzantine neighbors. It also provides insight into the medieval background of present-day differences between the West, the Slavic East, and the Arab nations.

Within its unique three-culture framework, the text reflects recent scholarly interpretations in Latin, Byzantine, and Islamic political history. I have also incorporated new material on institutions and social themes—demography, epidemics, economic depression—and on the treatment of minority groups such as women, Jews, heretics, and homosexuals. Life styles of the various classes in Western and Eastern societies are discussed along with theological questions pondered in the major centers of Constantinople, Cordova, Rome, and Paris. Where appropriate, I have compared intellectual and artistic achievements in the Latin, Byzantine, and Muslim worlds—in literature, philosophy, and science, as well as in painting, architecture, and music. For example, one aspect that is usually overlooked is the formative impact of late Byzantine humanism and painting on later Medieval (that is, Early Renaissance) Western culture. The Slavs (including early Russians), the Turks, and other latecomers to medieval Europe are discussed. This book gives fuller treatment than most medieval civilization texts do to the critical fourteenth and fifteenth centuries in the West. During this time a strengthening of certain medieval institutions and ideals coexisted with the more secular qualities of the emerging early modern world.

Finally, I show that the chief beneficiary of the age-old interaction of the three major societies is our own modern Western civilization. The roots, early development, and promise of this civilization are the focus of this book.

To make it easier for the reader to follow simultaneous events in all three societies, the book includes comparative chronologies, maps, photographs, charts, and annotated bibliographies. All of these features are designed to provide an up-to-date account of the evolution of the Latin West in the context of the three interacting cultures of the medieval world.

It would be difficult to list all those who have contributed in one way or another to the final version of this book. I mention first the principal one, Professor Charles Wood of Dartmouth College, to whom I am deeply indebted for a critical reading of all the Western portions of the manuscript. I wish also to thank Professor Fred Donner of Yale for reading the Islamic portions, Professor John Boswell of Yale for reading Chapter 11 on Medieval and Eastern social history, Professor Paul Bushkovitch, also of Yale, for going through the Slavic section, and Professor Archibald Lewis of the University of Massachusetts for perusing parts dealing with the West. Finally, I express my genuine appreciation to the following persons who, as assistants of mine at Yale at various times, contributed valuable help: Andrew Cappel, David Coles, James Forse (now professor at Ball State University), and Edward Manciewicz. I also want to thank my secretary, Ruth Kurzbauer.

D.J.G.

CONTENTS

PART II
The High Middle Ages

PART III

The Later Middle Ages: The Early Renaissance

MAPS AND CHARTS

Maps

Charts

PART I

The Early
Middle Ages

PROLOGUE

The Three "Successor Civilizations": Western, Byzantine, and Islamic

Out of the vast structure in late antiquity of the one Christian Roman Empire three "successor civilizations" emerged—the Latin, the Byzantine, and later the Islamic. Each of these civilizations drew heavily on elements of the classical Greco-Latin culture of the Roman world, although each developed in a different way and came to fruition at a different time. After an almost continuous cultural decline from the fifth to the early eleventh century (the so-called Dark Ages), the transmission of ancient Greek philosophy and science to the Germano-Latin West from the Arabs of Spain (themselves inheritors of Hellenistic culture from the Arabs of the East) gave the first decisive impulse to the emergence in the West of a more sophisticated intellectual tradition.

By contrast Byzantine civilization was from the start shaped by the blending of Hellenistic Greek culture, the Roman legal and administrative tradition, and especially Orthodox Christianity. Ancient Greek culture, too, played a role, though more limited, in the development of important aspects of Islamic civilization. In the Arab Caliphates of Baghdad and (subsequently) Spanish Cordova, the influence of Greek learning on the foundation of Islamic culture, the Koranic teachings, stimulated the development of Islamic philosophy and science. Both these Byzantine and Islamic civilizations were long to exert influences on what was for centuries the more retarded Western world.

But by the early twelfth century the West, having completely assimilated the "barbaric" Germanic element into its Latin Christian cultural tradition, began to catch up with and in later centuries even surpass the civilizations of Byzantium and Islam. The development of Latin society and culture in the medieval period, culminating in the emergence in many areas of a complex urban society, resulted not only from the West's own internal ferment, but also from beneficial cultural influences flowing in from its two great neighbors, Byzantium and Islam. This evolution of medieval Western civilization, together with the West's interaction with the Byzantine and Muslim worlds, will be the primary focus of this book.

3

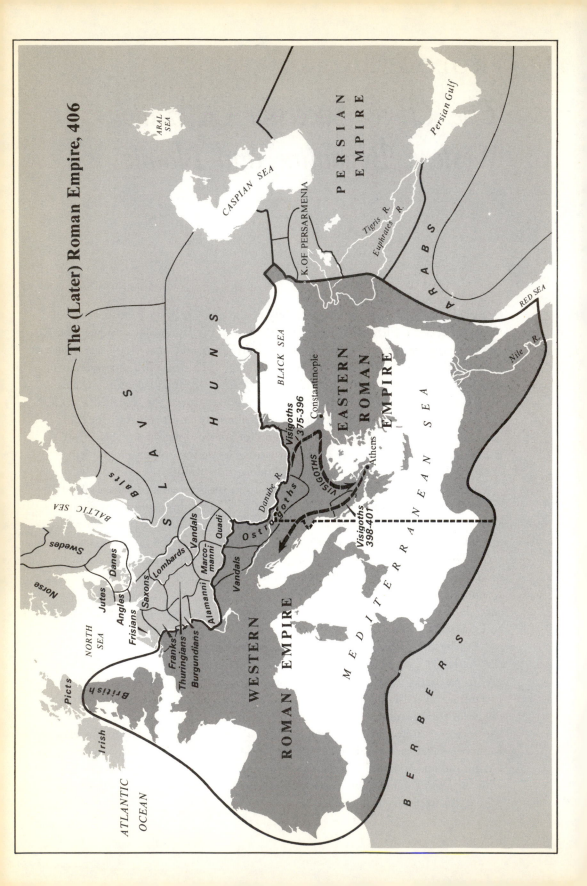

The (Later) Roman Empire, 406

ATLANTIC OCEAN

NORTH SEA

BALTIC SEA

Norse

Swedes

Danes

Jutes

Angles

Frisians

Picts

Irish

British

Saxons

Franks

Thuringians

Burgundians

Alamanni

Lombards

Marco-
manni

Quadi

Vandals

Vandals

Vandals

S L A V S

Baits

H U N S

Ostrogoths

Danube R.

WESTERN
ROMAN EMPIRE

ARAL SEA

CASPIAN SEA

BLACK SEA

Constantinople

Athens

Visigoths
375-396

VISIGOTHS

Visigoths
398-401

EASTERN
ROMAN
EMPIRE

MEDITERRANEAN SEA

BERBERS

PERSIAN
EMPIRE

Persian Gulf

K. OF PERSARMENIA

Tigris R.

Euphrates R.

A R A B S

RED SEA

Nile R.

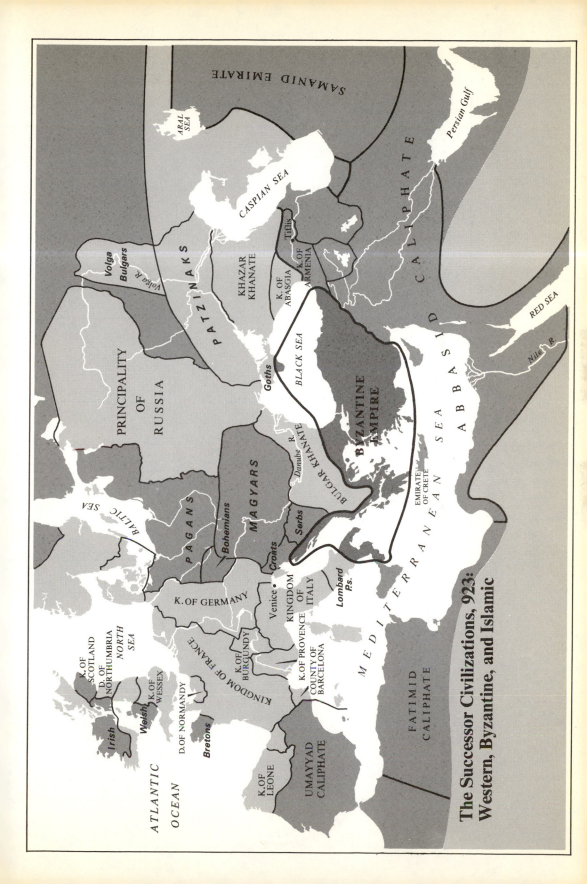

The Successor Civilizations, 923:
Western, Byzantine, and Islamic

PART I *The Early Middle Ages*

Western World	Byzantine and Slavic World	Islamic World
313 Constantine's Edict of Milan tolerating Christianity	325 First Ecumenical Council, Nicaea: Arianism condemned	No Arabs except in Arabian peninsula; no Slavs in Balkans
	330 Constantine founds Constantinople	
	378 Battle of Adrianople: Germans break into "Byzantine" Empire	
	381 Second Ecumenical Council, Constantinople	
395 Definitive triumph of Christianity: Division of Roman Empire into East and West	395 Definitive triumph of Christianity: Division of Empire into East and West	
410 Visigoths sack Rome		
430 St. Augustine dies in North Africa	431 Third Ecumenical Council, Ephesus	
	451 Fourth Ecumenical Council, Chalcedon: Monophysites declared heretical	
451 German-Roman alliance crushes Huns at Châlons		
455 Vandals sack Rome		
466 Visigoths establish first German state on Roman soil		
476 End of Roman Empire in the West		

481–511 King Clovis is ruler in Frankish Gaul
489 Ostrogoths enter Italy

529 St. Benedict founds Monte Cassino under Benedictine Rule

568 Lombards invade Italy

590–604 Pontificate of Pope Gregory the Great
591 Gregory of Tours writes *History of the Franks*; Boethius in Italy; Isidore in Spain

491–518 Anastasius reforms Byzantine coinage; tries to placate Monophysites
527–565 Reign of Justinian: Reconquest of parts of West; Justinian codifies Roman law; First "Golden Age" of Byzantine art (St. Sophia); Akathistos Hymn written

540 Persians sack Antioch (Syria) and, shortly after, Jerusalem

582–602 Creation of Exarchates of Ravenna and Carthage

610–641 Emperor Heraclius crushes Persians; fails to placate Monophysites

626 Persians and Avars besiege Constantinople

570–632 Life of Muhammad

622 Muhammad's flight to Medina

632 First Arab Caliph, Abu Bakr
636 Syria falls to Arabs

PART I *The Early Middle Ages*

Western World	Byzantine and Slavic World	Islamic World
		639–642 Byzantine Egypt falls to Arabs
		661 Umayyad Caliphate established in Damascus
668 Theodore of Tarsus, Archbishop of Canterbury		
673–735 Venerable Bede		
		711–714 Arabs overrun Spain
	717 Leo III overcomes Arab blockade of Constantinople	717 Arabs defeated at Constantinople
	726 Leo III issues decree on Iconoclasm	
732 Arab advance into Western Europe stopped at Tours		
		750 Fall of Umayyad Caliphate; Abassid Caliphate established
		c.750–900 Arabs translate ancient Greek philosophy and science at Baghdad
751 Byzantine Ravenna falls to Lombards	751 Byzantine Ravenna falls to Lombards	
		755 Independent emirate of Cordova (Spain) established
756 Pepin's "donation" of Ravenna Exarchate to Pope		
		763 Abassid Caliphate moved to new capital, Baghdad
		786–809 Caliph Harun al' Rashid
	787 Icons restored by Empress Irene (7th Ecumenical	

813–833 Caliph Al-mamun

827–902 Arabs conquer Sicily

861–870 Turkish mercenaries take power in Baghdad

---

c.826 Arabs take Sicily and Crete

843 Final triumph of icons: "Feast of Orthodoxy"

c.850 Higher school ("University") refounded in Constantinople

860 First Rus attack on Constantinople

862 Oleg takes Kiev: becomes Rus capital
863 Cyril and Methodius' mission to Moravia
864 Conversion of Bulgars
867 Photius becomes patriarch: Schism of Greek and Roman churches

---

c.788–800 Donation of Constantine forged
800 Charlemagne crowned emperor of "restored" Roman Empire in West

843 Treaty of Verdun: Charlemagne's empire divided into future France, Germany, and Italy
850–1000 Invasions of Arabs, Vikings, and Magyars into Western Europe
858–867 Pope Nicholas I and his claims to Roman primacy

911 Norse given "Normandy" as permanent possession by King of France

PART I *The Early Middle Ages*

Western World	Byzantine and Slavic World	Islamic World
955 Magyars settle in Hungarian plain		956 Seljuk Turks embrace Islam
	957 Rus princess Olga baptized, probably in Constantinople	969 Fatimid Caliphate established in Egypt
	969 Liudprand's mission to Constantinople	
	976–1025 Macedonian dynasty: Empire's apogee	
	989 Vladimir and Rus nation converted by Byzantium	Late 10th century: Philosopher Avicenna active
c.1000 End of Arab, Viking, and Hungarian invasions		
	1030 Normans begin conquest of Byzantine south Italy	

The modern world with its considerable emphasis on the secular, material aspects of life seems to be far more similar to the classical Greco-Roman than to the religious-oriented medieval world. But, paradoxically, some of the most important characteristics of modern life and institutions are an outgrowth, directly or indirectly, of medieval practices and developments. The ideology of the Papacy as an international power, the idea (particularly American) of complete separation of church and state, the development of vernacular languages, the origins of representative institutions such as parliamentary assemblies and city councils, and even the present rivalry between the two worlds of East and West find their roots in developments of the medieval period (or sometimes as a reaction against them). The epoch of the Middle Ages is therefore worthy of

CHAPTER 1

The Legacy of the Ancient World: Latin and Greek

study not only for itself, but also for insights into the origins and development of modern institutions and ways of thinking.

Historians disagree about dates for the beginning and end of the Middle Ages. All scholars, however, concur that there was a period of transition from the ancient Greco-Roman world, after which three civilizations emerged in both East and West whose natures, by the eighth century, had become something quite different from those of classical Greece and Rome. Modern medieval historians have been too often oriented exclusively toward the West, forgetting or neglecting the significance of developments in the Christian East and related developments in the Islamic world. My primary focus here will remain on the West, but I shall also survey events taking place in the Greek East with its somewhat different Christian civilization, and at certain points concentrate entirely on Eastern Christendom. The Greek East (and somewhat later the Islamic Empire) was culturally so advanced over the West, particularly during the early medieval period of the so-called Dark Ages, that it is appropriate to label the centuries from the fourth to the mid-eleventh the period of the "dominance of the East."

Within this broad panorama of both East and West, what date marks the beginning of the Middle Ages? Most Western-oriented authorities have traditionally fixed on an obvious one, A.D. 476, the year a German chieftain deposed the last Roman emperor in the West. However, Byzantinists, those who emphasize the history of the Christian East, prefer 330, the year that Emperor Constantine dedicated the city of Constantinople as the "new Rome," the new capital of what was henceforth to be the *Christian* Roman Empire. Other scholars stress the growing division between East and West. They have selected the year 395, after which, save for a brief period in the sixth century, the two great halves of the Roman Empire split apart, each under its own Roman emperor. Still another view—again with emphasis on the West but also on Islam—is that one cannot truly speak of the emergence of the medieval period until about the mid-eighth century, when the rise of Islam led to the emergence for the first time simultaneously in European history of three fundamental institutions important for the history of the medieval West: vassalage, the Papacy, and the Islamic Caliphate.

Whatever date may be chosen—and there is justification for each—no doubt exists that sometime between the fourth and the ninth or tenth centuries a new cultural synthesis was taking shape in *both* Eastern and Western Christian Europe, as well as in the Near East. The synthesis in the West was essentially a blend of three basic elements: 1) the old Greco-Roman (more Roman than Greek) institutions and traditions, 2) an emerging Christianity, and 3) a strong Germanic component. The East Roman (or Byzantine, as we call it today) cultural synthesis shared the first two elements with the West, although the Greek heritage was far stronger than the Latin and its form of Christianity somewhat different. In place of the Germanic component the Greek East was influenced by an oriental heritage from ancient connections with the Near East —Persia, Syria, Anatolia, and the Hebrews. The first two elements of the new cultural syntheses—the Greco-Roman tradition and the emergence of Christianity—will be the focus of this chapter.

The backdrop in both East and West for the emergence of these elements was the great political structure of the Roman Empire, extending from the Pillars of Hercules (Gibraltar) in the West to the Euphrates river (in Mesopotamia) in the East. To evaluate the Western medieval synthesis accurately, then, we must first examine the cultural milieu of the late Roman world in which Christianity developed and into which, in the West, the Germanic component was introduced.

A word about terminology: Medieval people (Latin, Byzantine, or Arab) were of course never cognizant of living in a "middle" period between the ancient world and the modern. The term *Middle Ages* was first used, derogatorily, by Italian humanists of the late fourteenth and early fifteenth centuries. For them the entire thousand-year period preceding their own age of the Renaissance was a long step backward, a Dark Age, for in their view Western culture had lost the chief ingredient necessary for cultural validity: Greco-Roman thought and learning. The terms Early, High, and Later Middle Ages, as well as Early Renaissance, as used in this book are of course borrowed from Western usage and applied primarily to a Western frame of reference. They are employed here, however imperfectly, to apply to chronological divisions for all three civilizations—Western, Byzantine, and Islamic—because the development of Western culture will engage most of our attention and in the end will profit most from the interaction of the three great medieval societies.

The Greco-Roman Tradition

In contrast to the sharp political divisions of modern Europe, the Roman world of the first and second centuries A.D. was remarkably unified. The entire Mediterranean world from Spain across North Africa to Mesopotamia and parts of Armenia—including most of Western and Eastern Europe as they are today—constituted one vast political organism, the Roman Empire.

To be sure, the Germanic peoples situated across the Rhine frontier or in the Scandinavian areas were not included in the empire; nor, farther eastward, were the Slavs of what is now Poland and most of European Russia. The Hungarians had not yet entered Europe, the Balkans were entirely free of Slavic peoples, and Asia Minor was still largely Greek in population, no Turks having penetrated into Anatolia. Nor had the Arabs emerged from their primitive homeland in Arabia. The entry of all these peoples and the changes they wrought in Europe and the Middle East was to be a phenomenon of the Middle Ages.

Beneath the vast, unified political structure of the empire there were, however, significant regional variations. The old Hellenistic areas—Egypt, Palestine, Syria, Asia Minor, and of course Greece—were essentially Greek in culture, at least among the upper classes. These areas constituted the eastern, Greek-speaking half of the Roman Empire. The western half, including Gaul, Spain, Britain, North Africa, and Italy, was essentially Latin-speaking and Latin in culture.*

The international citizenship of the Roman Empire, the feeling of all its citizens that despite racial differences they belonged to one great unified world-state, together with the existence of the *pax Romana* (Roman peace), which, remarkably, prevented the outbreak of any major conflict for over two centuries, enabled the citizen of even the most obscure corner of the empire to reap the benefits of Greco-Roman civilization. Indeed, despite the subsequent destruction of the Roman state in the West, the legacy of Rome—cultural, political, or otherwise—was not entirely lost, and the recollection of imperial unity remained an ideal to which both East and West aspired.

Classical Literature and Philosophy

The Romans made their most original contributions to civilization in such practical fields as law and engineering. In the cultural sphere Rome made few original contributions, being for the most part satisfied with imitating Greek efforts in art, architecture, literature, and philosophy. Vergil's great Latin epic poem, the *Aeneid*, was essentially an imitation of Homer's *Iliad* and *Odyssey*, and the eclectic Cicero and the Stoic Seneca based their philosophy largely on that of the Greeks. Roman architectural orders were Greek, as were Rome's sculpture and art in general, although Roman portrait sculpture with its greater realism made an advance on the Greek. In both East and West, however, by the fourth or fifth centuries, the realistic Greco-Roman style of art was giving way to the sacred, symbolic representation characteristic of the Christian Middle Ages.

In literature the Latin tradition was able to survive in the West, although partially lost and barbarized. Latin remained the language of the Western Church, of scholars, and, up to at least the fifteenth century, of most official documents. Vergil, Ovid, Cicero, and others continued to be read by a few; but as time went on, with the adoption of Christianity, the original pagan meaning of their work was lost. What little science the West retained was inherited from

* The terms *Greek* and *Latin*, unless otherwise indicated, have a primarily cultural connotation in this book.

ancient Greece and Hellenistic Alexandria, but gradually even this became diluted and superstition-ridden. Almost all of Aristotle, except for his elementary treatises on logic, was lost to the West until its recovery in the mid-twelfth and thirteenth centuries. Plato fared somewhat better, at least initially, since certain Latin Fathers of the Church, notably Augustine, incorporated Neoplatonic ideas into their theological works. Nevertheless, despite the transmission of certain aspects of Platonic thought from the ancient to the medieval world, almost all Greek learning and culture in its original Greek form was lost to the Western world by the end of the sixth century. Even knowledge of the Greek language itself, with rare exceptions, died. (The modern scholar Étienne Gilson has, in fact, attributed the decline of Western learning to its loss of most of Greek literature and philosophy.) Yet it must be emphasized that what little philosophical or theological speculation was carried on in the West in the medieval period utilized the method of classical philosophical schools. In this respect Greco-Roman philosophical ideas must be ranked next to Christian beliefs as molders of Western medieval thought.

Roman Law and the "State"

The last Roman emperor in the West, Romulus Augustulus, was deposed in 476 by Odovacar, a Germanic chieftain of Italy. However, Odovacar and almost all the early Germanic kings more or less maintained the legal fiction that they ruled as agents or clients of the Roman emperor sitting in Constantinople. So strongly did this old ideal of Roman unity persist that as late as 800, when the great German ruler Charlemagne was crowned emperor of a restored Roman Empire, both he in the West and the Byzantine emperor in Constantinople claimed to rule over the entire empire, and each refused to recognize the legitimacy of the other.

Another legacy of Rome to the medieval world, probably its greatest contribution, was Roman law. The original law code of the city of Rome, applying only to Roman citizens, consisted of a rigid set of rules of narrow scope called the Law of the Twelve Tables. But as Rome extended its rule over the Mediterranean world, particularly as it came into contact with the more cultured Greek and Semitic East, Roman law began to be leavened by Greek philosophic ideas. The law was influenced, for example, by the Stoic concept that all men have a spark of the divine within them, hence all men are basically brothers. Such views tended to improve the treatment of slaves and, in general, to be conducive of a greater sense of equality of the various classes before the law. The result of all this was the development of a new and more flexible legal code that could cover a greater variety of cases and had a wider philosophic base. This, together with the gradually evolving concept of the autocratic authority of the emperor, served to broaden Roman law. The expanded code was also fundamental to the extension of Roman citizenship (A.D. 212) to all free men within the empire, regardless of race or class.

A standard system of jurisprudence now gradually came to be applied to all areas and citizens of the empire. It is important to note that Roman law was predicated on the concept of the state as a sovereign power with authority to legislate directly for all its citizens. This concept of the state soon disappeared in the medieval West, not to reappear until many centuries later. Roman law, too, was greatly weakened; indeed it virtually disappeared in the West in the early Middle Ages. But Roman law nevertheless left certain traces in the Germanic law codes. In the later medieval period its revival became, ultimately, after undergoing certain changes, the most widespread code of law in modern Western and Eastern Europe.

Traces of the Latin cultural tradition remained in the West, although Western culture became Germano-Latin after the coming of the Germans. The culture of the East, on the other hand, became more and more Greco-Oriental. The Latin language, which had been restricted largely to the court circles in Constantinople, fell into disuse in the East sometime in the sixth century. This cultural division between East and West was to become more and more pronounced as the medieval period progressed.

The Eastern or Byzantine half of the Roman Empire was legally and politically a continuation of the old empire with the capital transferred from Rome to Constantinople. There, in contrast to the West, Roman law remained in force, although it was modified to reflect changes in social conditions. Furthermore, again in contrast to the West, the Greek East retained its knowledge of ancient Greek and Hellenistic culture. Greek continued to be the language of the upper class and much of the lower. Students read Homer, and historians carried on the tradition of Herodotus and Thucydides. The East, which escaped the main force of the Germanic invasions, was, culturally speaking, to remain for centuries far advanced over the West.

In both East and West, however, the two elements of the ancient tradition were modified by the addition of an even more important element, Christianity, which emerged in the context of the political, social, and religious conditions of the Roman Empire.

The Emergence of Christianity

Christianity was doubtless the most important element in the medieval cultural synthesis. It became the molder of virtually all thought and expression in East and West up to the period of the Renaissance. Before examining its fusion with classical culture, however, it is important to investigate how such an initially insignificant, even despised, religion was able to triumph over and displace the established paganism of the empire.

Most Roman citizens of the late empire had little concern for politics. However, a great part of their thought and energy was directed toward religion. This emphasis on religion was partly the result of the decline in political, economic, and social freedom brought about by the growing intrusion of the state into private life—especially under certain reforms instituted by Emperor Diocletian. It was also a result of a growing cosmopolitanism that made belief in the old anthropomorphic gods such as Jupiter and Juno appear ridiculous.

Through religion an individual could better appreciate his own personal worth, if not in this life at least in the hereafter. Thus among the upper, educated classes certain "philosophical" religions became popular, such as Stoicism and, to a lesser degree, Epicureanism. Both tried to explain the meaning of life and how to achieve happiness. While Epicureanism preached that man should seek happiness by avoiding pain and seeking what gives him pleasure (not physical but intellectual gratification, the highest form of pleasure), Stoicism taught that man could achieve true happiness only by conforming freely to his destiny, by schooling himself to remain unperturbed by passions and desires, and by fostering a love of justice. A tenet of Stoicism, which in the long run influenced Christianity more than did Epicureanism, was that a spark of the divine exists in all men, and in this sense, then, all men are brothers.

Despite the morally elevated qualities of both philosophical systems, they were not true religions and could not provide the emotional satisfaction necessary for the religious craving of the period. Many inhabitants of the empire, in despair over the conditions they faced, needed to believe that a personal god was vitally interested in them. Abstract principles of philosophy offered little consolation for life's imperfections, and, seeking some hope for a better existence if only in the afterlife, many turned to Oriental mystery cults, religions with roots reaching deep into the age-old traditions of the East. Thus in the city of Rome itself many aristocrats became devotees of the cult of Cybele, the great earth goddess of Asia Minor; of the Egyptian Isis; of the Syrian Baal; or of the Persian god Mithras, who was especially popular with the Roman army. The cults were tolerated by the government, with some Romans even being devotees of two or more at the same time. They were similar in many important respects, and, of course, all were assimilated into the general framework of Greco-Roman thought.

These religious cults appealed to individuals regardless of race or class, and they all offered salvation. Each had an elaborate ritual through which the worshipers could identify themselves with a god and, by means of secret ceremonies, believed themselves fused with the god's divine nature, able to partake of the god's immortality. Hence the term *mystery cults*. An example of such ritual is the taurobolium, in which the worshiper secured the vital quality of Mithras by being covered with the blood of a slaughtered bull representing the god.

In this milieu of the mystery cults that strove for something to mitigate the worsening psychological and social conditions of life, Christianity developed. In the beginning, in fact, many Romans looked upon Christianity as simply another mystery cult.

The Development of Early Christianity

In the development of Christianity the central figure is, of course, Jesus Christ. But despite the four accounts of his life included in the New Testament (no two of which are in complete accord), the facts are not entirely clear. Most authorities agree that he was recognized by John the Baptist as the Christ, the Jewish Messiah prophesied to come and lead the Hebrews to freedom and victory. But to Jesus, the Kingdom of God awaited by the Jews meant less an earthly monarchy than a spiritual kingdom. To enter it one had to be reborn in the spirit. For Christ, inward thought was more important than the

This manuscript illumination from the Irish Lindisfarne Gospel shows St. Luke, one of the four Evangelists, holding a manuscript. (Reproduced by Courtesy of the Trustees of the British Museum, Harley ms. 2788, f. 13v)

outward observance of the Mosaic law. It was in part because of his attack on the sacred Jewish traditions and vested Jewish interests that Jesus was put to death by the Romans, crucified (*c.*A.D. 29) in the manner of a common criminal.

Three of the four Gospels—Matthew, Mark, and John—were evidently written by Jews, and the fourth, Luke, by a Greek (or at least, Greek-speaking) physician. Yet it should be noted that all four, in the earliest texts we possess, are written not in the spoken language of the Jews (Aramaic), but in the common, spoken Greek (Koine) of the period, current among all cultured people in the East. Although the four accounts differ in detail, they agree on the main points. Whatever the accuracy of the four Evangelists (and inaccuracies were inevitable, given the time elapsed after the actual events and the probability that the Evangelists, except possibly Matthew or Mark, were not actual witnesses), these Gospels constitute the basic text of Christianity. As such they were to exert a tremendous influence on the molding of medieval thought.*

The ancient Dead Sea Scrolls manuscripts were discovered in 1947 and later in an area northwest of the Dead Sea. They deal largely with the Essenes, a brotherhood of Jews that in the first century B.C. practiced celibacy and extreme asceticism and engaged in communal living. Some of the beliefs of the Essene sect—purification through baptism and immortality of the soul, for example—were also held by the Christians.

Christianity was born among the Jews, but it was first nurtured among the Greeks. The Twelve Apostles apart, the first community to which the term *Christian* was applied was the Greek city of Antioch in Syria. Paul, a Greek-speaking Jew who converted to Christianity, projected the new religion as a universal one. At this time there were two main obstacles to the universal appeal of Christianity and to the unity of the Christian Church. First, Jewish Christianity was confined to the Jews, offering no message of salvation for the Greeks and other Gentiles. Second, the early Christian Jews insisted that all believers in the new religion follow the law of the Old Testament to the letter. To some of the Christian Gentiles, parts of the law were unacceptable. As a result a rift existed between the Christian Jews and the Christian Gentiles, and the only way to resolve the issue was to free the Christian belief from the strictures of Judaism. Paul found the way. Through his zealous work as preacher and missionary and through his writings—epistles to converts or would-be converts in widespread areas—he not only freed the Christian Church from the requirements of Judaism, but cast the new religion in the mold of a mystery cult in which Christ promised salvation to *all* believers. Paul's Epistles were incorporated by the Church into the official canon of the New Testament as a funda-

---

* Since at least the time of Renan in the nineteenth century, scholars have sought to establish the character and personality of the historical Jesus unobscured by the traditional overlay of later centuries.

mental source for Christian doctrine and belief. So important was Paul's role in the development of early Christianity that he is ranked with the Twelve Disciples as an Apostle.

Why Christianity Prevailed

Christianity was able to prevail over the pagan mystery cults, despite the considerable similarity between them for several reasons. First, in contrast to some of the cults, the story of Jesus was compellingly beautiful to many. Moreover, he was believed to have come to redeem *all* people, rich and poor, men and women, peasant and intellectual. Jesus' ethical teachings were simple and direct, not borrowed from complex philosophical systems intelligible only to the learned.* And of course the long Judaic tradition, with its uncompromising loyalty to a single god, provided Christianity with an exclusiveness of belief that was a source of great strength. Thus a Christian, unlike the worshipers of the mystery cults, could not be a member of another religion as well. The organization of the Christian Church, in contrast to that of the mystery cults and decaying paganism, was far stronger and more compact. Finally, the unity of the Roman Empire and the relative ease of communication from one area to another were two factors that helped the rapid spread of Christianity throughout the East and, later, to the West.

When Christianity first emerged, the imperial government took little notice, considering it merely a kind of Jewish heresy. This was important because for some time the Jews had enjoyed a privileged position in the empire. Because of their monotheistic belief, they alone were not required to make obeisance to the state by casting incense before the statue of the emperor or the goddess Roma. If a citizen refrained from this act of allegiance, he was not permitted to participate in any of the activities of Roman political and social life.

But Christianity, freed by Paul from the narrow nationalistic emphasis of the Jews, rapidly became more international in scope and thus appeared to pose a danger to the empire. Not only did their monotheism prevent the Christians from "pledging their allegiance" to the state by making obeisance to the emperor's image, many of the earliest followers of Christ were also pacifists and refused to serve in the army. It is not surprising therefore that the Roman state soon undertook to destroy so hostile a group. Eventually, merely to be a Christian was evidence of treason.

At first persecution was local and sporadic, the most serious episode occurring in A.D. 64 when Nero used the Christians as scapegoats for the burning of Rome. But the fervor and sincerity of Christians as they went to their deaths in the arena had the effect of converting some pagan spectators, which may in

---

* John the Evangelist's gospel depends on some Greek philosophic thought.

part account for the proselytizing power of early Christianity. Persecution increased as the sect grew. But it was not until 250 that the Emperor Decius undertook, more or less systematically, to destroy Christianity. Several emperors continued this policy, notably Diocletian (284–305), who sought to revitalize the collapsing empire by the adoption of authoritarian methods. Not tolerating any kind of disobedience to the state, he issued a series of edicts calculated to give the *coup de grâce* to the Christian religion. A blood bath ensued, but in the long run all his measures failed. Under Diocletian's successor, the Emperor Constantine the Great (306–337), Christianity was not only tolerated, but even became the favored religion of the empire.

It has been estimated that the number of Christians at this time did not exceed one-tenth of the citizens of the empire. Why, then, did Christianity survive? Despite their small number, the Christians were well organized; even more important, they had an acute sense of mission in the world.

Constantine the Great and the Early Church

Although the Greeks claim Constantine as their own, ranking him, in the Byzantine tradition, "equal to the Apostles," he was Latin by birth. He was the son of Constantius I, known as Chlorus, one of the Caesars who ruled Gaul, and of Helena, who was later to be proclaimed a saint for her discovery of the True Cross. At the abdication of Diocletian in 305, Constantine's father succeeded in the West as senior emperor, the Caesar Galerius receiving the East. For some time Galerius had been suffering from what may have been intestinal cancer. In the belief that the disease was due to divine retribution for his persecution of the Christians, he issued, in 311, an edict of toleration to all religions, including Christianity. This edict was in force only in the East and, though important, it is overshadowed by the Edict of Milan (313), issued jointly by the newly enthroned Western and Eastern Emperors Constantine and Licinius. This measure, however, only legalized Christianity; it did not make it the official religion. It was a significant step, for throughout the empire Christianity was placed on the same level as paganism.

Constantine's adviser, the ecclesiastical historian Bishop Eusebius of Caesarea, described the emperor's famous conversion, which resulted in reversing the Roman religious policy of centuries. In 312, just before the crucial battle of the Milvian bridge against his rival Maxentius for mastery of Rome and all of Italy, Constantine and his army, according to Eusebius, saw a blazing cross in the sky superimposed on the sun and bearing the motto *in hoc signo vinces* ("in this sign conquer"). The next night Christ appeared to Constantine in a dream and bade him adopt the labarum as a standard for his armies. The symbol was subsequently used on the shields and standards of the soldiers of the Byzantine Empire and became the emblem of the empire. Whether these visions were actual occurrences, the result of an overworked imagination, a meteorological phenomenon (as one scholar maintains), or even fabrications by Eusebius, after his triumph over Maxentius, Constantine favored the Christian religion.

Historians have heatedly debated the motivation for Constantine's remarkable conversion, an event that decisively altered the course of world history. Was he a political opportunist, a man of expediency who sought to use Christianity to bind together the decaying empire? Was he completely sincere? It seems more likely that he was a combination of both: a man representative of the spiritual age in which he lived but who, at the same time, wanted to use Christianity for political purposes. In any event Christianity seemed to bring him victories over his enemies.

Constantine granted freedom of worship to all Christians, educating his own children in this religion. He showed partiality to Christians in public office and began to concern himself with dogma and faith. He recognized the Christian Church as a legal body before the law, a fact that meant the Church could not only hold property but accept bequests and have its own ecclesiastical courts. All these developments were to influence the subsequent history of both East and West during the medieval period.

Yet Constantine did not entirely disestablish paganism; for himself he retained the pagan Roman title of *pontifex maximus* ("highest priest"). Roman paganism, unlike Christianity, had no priestly caste as such; the emperor, as the highest civil official, merely donned the robes of high priest when the occasion demanded it. Constantine's retention of the title and function of pontifex maximus was one of the factors that led in the East to the great degree of imperial control over the Church. Constantine himself continued to be worshiped by the pagans as the divine emperor. He was not baptized, in fact, until he was virtually on his deathbed. Perhaps he sought thereby to avoid the possibility of committing further sin, for many Christians then believed that no sin could be forgiven if committed after baptism.

Besides establishing Christianity as a legally recognized religion, Constantine in 330 dedicated a new capital for what came to be called the "Christian Roman Empire." The capital was established on the site of the old Greek town of Byzantium, which he renamed *Constantinople* ("the city of Constantine"). From the start it was meant to be a purely Christian city, the "new Rome." With its strategic geographical location and defenses—surrounded on three sides by water and on the fourth by a huge, virtually impregnable wall—Constantinople controlled the entrances to the Aegean and Black seas and stood astride both Europe and Asia. As noted earlier, the foundation of Constantinople as the capital of the Christian Roman Empire marks the beginning of the medieval period for Byzantinists. It signified the union of two of the most important cultural elements of the Middle Ages, the classical Greco-Roman tradition and the new religion of Christianity. The Germanic element, which was to complete the

A gold coin (c. 323–330) depicting the head of Emperor Constantine the Great. Born in England, Constantine changed the course of history in both West and East by accepting Christianity. As founder of Constantinople, the new Christian Roman capital in the East, he is considered the first "Byzantine" Emperor. (Courtesy Museum of Fine Arts, Boston)

medieval cultural synthesis in the West, was essentially absent from the Byzantine East, where the Oriental influences of Persia, Syria, the Jews, and others were felt instead.

The Final Triumph of Christianity

Despite the adoption of Christianity as a legitimate religion, it was centuries before paganism completely disappeared from the empire. But now, with the triumph of Christianity, an ironic reversal of the earlier imperial policy occurred: the emperors began to persecute paganism, or at least the more pernicious aspects of it, using the machinery of the state. With the new *rapprochement* of Christian church and state, certain changes now inevitably occurred in Christianity itself.

The growth of Christianity was remarkable. Beginning as an obscure sect in the first century, it had, in the second century, aroused in the government increasing hostility; in the third it had become so strong that organized persecution against it proved ineffective; and finally, in the fourth century, Christianity became the official religion of the state. This last phase occurred mainly under the sons and successors of Constantine (from 337 to the death of Theodosius I in 395). Yet in the ascendancy of Christianity one important though futile attempt to curb this advance should be noted. The Emperor Julian (361–363), called the Apostate, successor to the sons of Constantine, supported the ancient philosophy of Hellenism and made a determined effort to restore paganism of the higher, philosophic type. Borrowing certain attributes of Christianity

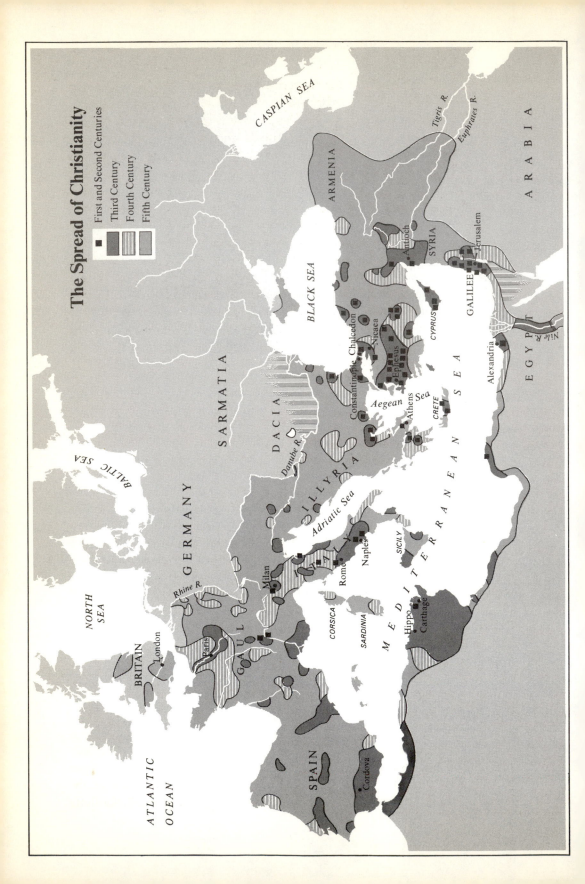

The Spread of Christianity

First and Second Centuries

Third Century

Fourth Century

Fifth Century

CASPIAN SEA

ARMENIA

ARABIA

Tigris R.

Euphrates R.

Antioch

SYRIA

Jerusalem

GALILEE

CYPRUS

Chalcedon

Nicaea

Constantinople

Ephesus

Aegean Sea

Athens

CRETE

Alexandria

EGYPT

Nile R.

BLACK SEA

SARMATIA

DACIA

Danube R.

ILLYRIA

Adriatic Sea

MEDITERRANEAN SEA

Milan

Rome

Naples

SICILY

CORSICA

SARDINIA

Hippo

Carthage

BALTIC SEA

GERMANY

Rhine R.

GAUL

Paris

NORTH SEA

BRITAIN

London

ATLANTIC OCEAN

SPAIN

Cordova

—emphasis on the priesthood, the delivery of sermons to the congregation, liturgical services—he sought in effect to graft a kind of Christian organization onto
pagan beliefs. Most disruptive to the Christians was his edict that only pagans
could teach the classical works to children in the schools. But the emperor's campaign failed, evidence of the great vitality of Christianity. Yet paganism, though
defeated, died a lingering death, existing in certain rural areas as late as the sixth
century. (One view holds that the word *pagan,* from the Latin *paganus,* a rustic,
refers to the rural population, which was among the last to be Christianized.)

After Julian's death Jovian re-established Christianity, but he was tolerant
of the pagans and even of the Arians (whom I shall discuss shortly). In the
reign of Theodosius the Great (379–395) the more or less definitive triumph of
Christianity occurred. Theodosius prohibited pagan sacrifices, and many temples were destroyed, including the Serapeum at Alexandria, with its famous
library. In a later phase of this struggle the celebrated Neoplatonic woman
philosopher Hypatia was torn to pieces by a Christian mob consisting largely of
fanatical monks. Theodosius not only crushed paganism, but also attacked the
Christian heresy of Arianism. His aim was a united church in a united empire.

Two incidents during Theodosius' reign demonstrate the rising power of
the Church. In the first, Ambrose, bishop of Milan, refused communion to
Theodosius until the latter did penance for a massacre he had ordered to be
carried out in Thessalonica. Later, Ambrose again refused Theodosius communion until he revoked his orders to rebuild a Jewish synagogue and to punish
the Christian rioters who had been responsible for burning it. These two events
set an important precedent that later reached full culmination in the West: the
Church, in the person of the bishops, could exert its authority over secular power
when matters of faith and morals were concerned. Another incident should be
added that symbolizes the final triumph of Christianity. In the old Senate house
of Rome a pagan altar had stood for centuries dedicated to victory, a veritable
symbol of the paganism of the old empire. Despite the appeals of Symmachus, a
leading political and literary figure of the time, the Emperor Gratian refused to
permit the restoration of the altar, which earlier, in 357, had been removed by
Constantius. The speech of Symmachus requesting restoration of the altar has
been called "the swan song of dying paganism."

The Organization of the Early Church

The question of how the early Church became organized, in particular how the bishops first emerged as leaders of the various communities, cannot
be fully answered. But the evidence indicates that during the period of the
Apostles and shortly thereafter, the Church was composed of small, far-flung

groups of Christians whose primary means of communication was through missionaries such as Peter and Paul. Each of these communities was at first administered by a board of elders, headed by a president or priest (from the Greek *presbyter,* "older man"). As the Christian communities grew, the presidents began to assume administrative functions over larger areas, not only over a whole city, but also over the surrounding regions as well. Because of their increasing functions, they were called bishops (from the Greek *episcopos,* "overseer"). At first the bishops dispensed the sacraments of baptism and communion with the aid of deacons, although in larger areas this function may well have been shared by the priests, whose primary responsibility was always the parish. One of the foremost tasks of the bishops was to settle disputes arising within their Christian congregations.

Actually, there seems to have been no uniform system of episcopal organization during this very early period. A criterion, however, for determining the legitimacy or rank of bishops soon became generally accepted—whether or not a bishop had received consecration through a succession of previous bishops traceable back to an Apostle. Such a bishop was considered to be in the "Apostolic Succession," his power having been passed down to him through each succeeding bishop of that see (from Latin *sedes,* "seat"). In the Roman Catholic, Orthodox, and Anglican churches the bishops are in the Apostolic Succession.

The Five Patriarchates

Each major city of the empire came to have its own bishop. Indeed, the Church adopted an organization patterned almost exactly after the administrative system of the empire developed by Diocletian. Above the bishops in the capital city of each province were archbishops, sometimes in the Greek East called metropolitans. And above the archbishops, at the very top, were the patriarchs. At first there were only three patriarchs, one in Rome, Antioch, and Alexandria. With the foundation of Constantinople in 330 as the new capital of the empire, a patriarch later emerged there as well. Still later, in 451, Jerusalem was officially added to the list, making a total of five patriarchates.

The question of the increasing importance of the patriarchates in the early Church has led to conflicting modern views of the Pope's authority by the Roman Catholic and Greek Orthodox churches. (The name *pope* originally had no special attachment to Rome, meaning simply "father" or "little father," and as such is a title—*papas*—still applied to all Greek priests.) The Greek Orthodox believe that by the fifth century, at the latest, the five great patriarchs headed the Church in a pentarchy (five heads). All were essentially equal, although it was generally believed that, as the original capital of the empire, Rome held a position of *honorary* primacy, "the first among equals." This meant, for example, that the Pope (as the patriarch and bishop of Rome) or his representatives should speak first at councils. But, the Orthodox affirm, the Roman see possessed no jurisdictional authority (the right to appoint and depose bishops, and so forth) over the other patriarchates. Roman Catholics, on the contrary, believe that from the very beginning the bishop of Rome held a position of jurisdictional authority over the other patriarchs. This view is based on what is known as the Petrine theory of Papal authority—the theory that Peter was the chief of the Apostles because Christ, according to Matthew, said to Peter "Thou art Peter and on this rock [*petra* in Greek] I will build my church." As first bishop of Rome, Peter is said to have passed on his primal authority to his successors in Rome. The Greeks object to this view on at least two grounds: that all the Apostles were essentially equal, thus emphasizing Christ as the head of the Church; and that before founding the bishopric of Rome, Peter had, as is historically authenticated, already established the bishopric of Antioch in the Greek East.

In the fourth and fifth centuries the patriarchs became adamant rivals, jealous of each other's prestige. In the jockeying for position Rome chose almost from the beginning to ally itself with Antioch or Alexandria against what it considered upstart Constantinople, the city that had supplanted it as capital of the empire.* The Second Ecumenical Council (381) pronounced Constantinople second to Rome in dignity, and later the Council of Chalcedon (451) pronounced the city the equal of Rome because "it is the new Rome." Despite Constantinople's increasing prestige, however, its patriarch had little scope for independent action, as he was closely situated under the thumb of the emperor. Indeed, in Byzantium the Church was to become almost a department of state, though with certain qualifications that I shall note later.

An important fact to remember in tracing the rivalry among the patriarchs, especially between those of Rome and Constantinople, is that the West had only one patriarch, the patriarch of Rome, whereas the East had four. With no ecclesiastical rival nearby, patriarchal authority in Rome could develop more freely, whereas in the East it was to remain divided for centuries. Even before the deposition of the last Roman emperor in the West (476), the Pope did not have an emperor residing in the same place who might dominate him.

Although the patriarchate of Rome may have claimed control over the patriarchates of the East, in the early period the Pope had trouble even exerting his authority over the various churches in the West. Thus in 445 an imperial edict had to be issued by the Western Emperor Valentinian III declaring all the Western churches to be under the control of the Roman bishop, even though, at the Council of Sardica in 342, the Pope had already been vested with supreme

---

* According to Orthodox tradition it was St. Andrew, one of the Twelve Apostles, who founded the see of Constantinople, thereby making it, too, an apostolic see. Of course, in his time Constantinople was still called Byzantium, its original name.

judicial powers over these same churches. As imperial power continued to decline in the West with the German settlement, the Popes not only were able to increase their ecclesiastical authority, but even to assume many functions formerly belonging to the Roman civil officials. With the development of a power vacuum after the fall of the Western Empire, the Popes and other leading Latin bishops stepped in to fill it. Such vigorous Popes as Leo I (440–461) and Gregory the Great (590–604) inherited, as it were, the mantle of the Roman Empire. As more and more political and moral authority devolved on Rome, its bishop viewed himself as the supreme head of the Church and even assumed the former imperial title of pontifex maximus.

Monasticism

While Christianity was becoming organized administratively, other developments were also taking place. Widespread conversion en masse was the trend in the fourth century—a conversion often only skin-deep and carried out with an eye toward avoiding the state's penalties against paganism or gaining the new pragmatic advantages of being a Christian. As a result, Christianity in many areas lost its original fervency and became watered down to the level of the masses.

In the meantime the Church was becoming very wealthy, with slaves and other bequests granted to it from all sides. Many churchmen were criticized as being more interested in their temporal activities than their spiritual duties. St. Jerome (340–420), in his letters, and the presbyter Salvianus of Marseilles, in his *On the Governance of God,* gave a vivid picture of the growing worldliness of the clergy. Jerome acidly refers to "fat, sleek priests flattering rich matrons in the hope of securing rich bequests." Disturbed by this growing laxity within Christianity, many devout Christians demanded more rigorous adherence to the ideals of the early Church. Partly to satisfy their needs a new institution emerged: monasticism.

Monasticism (from the Greek word *monachos,* "alone") was a way of life for those who wished to devote themselves exclusively to the salvation of their souls. Abandoning home and family, such persons would lead a celibate life. Their life styles included fasting, frequent prayers, solitary living in the wilderness, and sparse clothing. It was believed that this self-denial or self-mortification, asceticism, would cleanse the spirit and enable the monk to reach nearer to God.

Christian monasticism, according to tradition, first appeared at the end of the third century in southern Egypt. The first monk was St. Anthony, who for years lived as a hermit practicing austerities in the burning Egyptian desert. Attracted by his piety, many monks followed his example. Because such monks lived in solitude they were called anchorites, from the Greek word meaning "to go away." Some monks, however, did not want to live in complete isolation. Instead they built their dwellings around a famed ascetic to gain the benefit of his instruction and example. Such a group of dwellings was called a laura.

Greek and Latin Monasticism

The first truly monastic establishment was founded by Pachomius, a converted Egyptian. After living as a hermit, he realized the demands of such a life would tax the strength of most ascetics beyond endurance. He founded the coenobium—a community living together in one house and under one rule. Members of such a community are called cenobitic monks, or cenobites, from the Greek word meaning "common." Unlike the anchorites and the monks of the laura, the cenobites worked as well as prayed, following a prescribed schedule for common worship, private meditation and devotions, and manual labor. At the time of his death Pachomius supervised a group of eleven houses. By the end of the fourth century there were 7,000 Pachomian monks in Upper Egypt who felt that within the larger church of the world they were creating an inner group more assured of attaining salvation because of their greater purity.

A painting showing Syrian anchorite monks living in their desert caves. Note that one perches on top of a column, like Simeon Stylites. (Courtesy Vatican Museum)

Extreme asceticism seemed to appeal to the people of the East; the number of Christian anchorite monks who went into the desert to practice austerities increased rapidly. The most famous of these was St. Simeon Stylites of Syria. Living atop a column for over thirty years, he acquired such a reputation for sanctity that many came to solicit his advice. His example, however, fostered vanity in some anchorites, who tried to surpass their fellows in feats of asceticism.*

St. Basil the Great, a fourth-century Greek Father of the Church who came from Asia Minor, is widely recognized as the founder of the most enduring form of Eastern monasticism. He formulated a rule for the organization of monastic institutions on the basis of hard work, charity, and communal life. He advised his followers that they could better serve God by leading a cenobitic life than by living as purely ascetic hermits. His rule was to become the standard Byzantine system and is still followed today in the Orthodox East—in Greece, Syria, and among the Slavs of the Balkans and Russia.

Monasticism originated in the East, then spread to the West. It is often asserted that St. Athanasius introduced the anchorite type of monasticism to Rome in the early fourth century. But although it found some early adherents, the extreme austerity of the anchorites did not take root in the West, for Eastern practices of austerity were often incompatible with the more rigorous climate of the West. Among famous early Western monks John Cassianus, who came from the Greek East, founded the monastery of St. Victor at Marseilles (c.415) and composed a monastic rule that influenced early Western monasticism. An even more famous monastery that came under Cassianus' influence was the one on the nearby island of Lérins, founded (c.410) by St. Honoratus.

The most famous early Western monk was St. Martin, bishop of Tours in the fourth century. Martin, as we know from the notable biography written by his follower Sulpicius Severus, spent his life combating the surviving remnants of paganism in Gaul. Severus' biography, recounting the many miraculous deeds of St. Martin, became the model for a Western literature of saints' lives.

Important as the work of these men was, the system established by the Italian monk Benedict of Nursia became standard in the West. According to tradition, Benedict was born near Naples and educated in Rome. As a young man he was attracted by the ascetic ideal, went into the savage mountains near Rome, and spent several years living alone in a cave. He had to constantly struggle to conquer human desires—by practicing austerities, meditating, and reading the Bible. As his fame spread, others gathered around him, electing him to head their community. In 529, according to tradition, Benedict founded a monastery at Monte Cassino (situated midway between Rome and Naples) on the

---

* Standing atop his pillar, Simeon Stylites, as was once counted, bowed down and touched his head to the stone over 1,200 times.

ruins of an ancient pagan temple. There he drew up his famous Benedictine Rule, which was based in part on (or at least inspired by) the tradition of Basil and Cassianus. The essence of the rule may be summarized in the motto, *laborare est orare* ("to work is to pray"). It was Benedict's belief that if a monk carefully followed his rule he would, in the end, be conquered by love of God and would be free of fear.

Before entering the monastery the novice had to cut off all ties with the outside world. After a trial period of a year, certain vows were to be taken. The vow of obedience to the abbot, the superior of the monastery, was the most fundamental. Also to be observed, at least by implication, were the virtues of chastity and poverty. Benedict's ideal was the subordination of each monk's personality to the welfare of the group. The monks were not allowed to own anything—even the clothing of a monk who died was passed on to another—and all property of the monastery was administered by the abbot. Certain religious duties and observances were prescribed. Scripture reading accompanied meals, which the monks ate in a common dining room. Stress was placed on manual labor, which took up most of the time. A certain amount of individual Bible reading was to be done, though Benedict did not stress this requirement. Later the common monastic practice of copying manuscripts developed. For this purpose a special room, the scriptorium, was set aside in the monastery. To divorce itself further from the outside world, the monastery was to be economically self-sufficient.

A typical day in a Benedictine monk's life follows. Rising at dawn, he would gather with the others for the religious service called Matins. He would work until 6 A.M., at which time he would again assemble with the monks for another prayer service. Work would then continue until 9 A.M., either in the fields, the numerous workshops, or, in a later period, in the scriptorium, after which still another service would be held. At noon the monk would take his first meal of the day, resuming work until three, when he would attend a fourth prayer service. He returned to work until sunset, and then would go to Vespers. There was dinner, and just before bedtime all of the monks would gather again for the Compline (completion). Finally, at two in the morning the monks would arise for the service known as Nocturns.

There is no doubt that the Benedictine Rule was admirably suited to the conditions of the period, as it provided the organization for a closely knit, economically self-sufficient, self-governing body amidst the turmoil and insecurity of life in the West. Within two or three centuries it had spread almost everywhere except to Ireland, which, for a time, remained under the influence of Eastern monastic ideals. The Benedictine Rule was also socially significant. With the increasing numbers of monastic organizations the Western clergy generally became divided into two classes: the regular clergy or monks who followed a monastic rule (*regula*), and the secular clergy (bishops, priests,

One of the greatest Greek church fathers, St. Basil in the fourth century was the true systematizer of Byzantine monasticism. (Courtesy of the Dumbarton Oaks Collection, Washington, D.C.)

deacons) who served the Church in the outside world. Benedict's type of monasticism had a profound impact on the religious and intellectual life of Western medieval man.*

The Development of Christian Doctrine

As long as the Church remained underground, so to speak, the difficulties of communication among its adherents and the lack of strong supervision over them gradually produced certain differences in the interpretation of doctrine and belief. Moreover, as the more educated classes were converted, they

---

* Benedict was known in the Greek East through a Greek translation of his life and miracles by Pope Gregory the Great.

began to demand more rational explanations of Christian dogma. Contradictions often arose between the more rational Greco-Roman philosophical views of certain thinkers and the original simple tenets of the Christian faith. This dilemma produced a great crisis in the development of Christian thought.

The Apologists

To answer the attacks on Christianity by pagan Greco-Roman thinkers a group of Apologists, or defenders of Christianity, emerged in the second century. They began to draw upon Greek philosophical concepts to buttress the beliefs of Christianity. The Apologists used the methods and a good deal of the learning of older philosophical schools such as Platonism. Against the objections raised by classical philosophies, Christianity could defend itself only by developing its own rational exposition of the faith. Because of confusion caused by the false assumptions of many pagans, this was imperative if Christianity was to be accepted by the more learned classes. Most of this work of creating and refining a Christian philosophy, or theology, was accomplished in the Greek East.

In the second century the initial attempts to combine philosophy and Christian dogma backfired in one of the major crises faced by the early Church. The Gnostics, a far from homogeneous group, maintained that man could reach God exclusively through knowledge (*gnosis*). But this knowledge was an almost irrational, eclectic mixture of genuine philosophical speculation and strange pagan, mythological beliefs. The body was considered evil. Christ they declared to be simply a kind of intermediate being and not truly God. Had Gnosticism triumphed, Christ would have become simply another "aeon," an inferior spirit in the Gnostic cosmology.

In the process of combating this Gnostic danger Christianity underwent certain significant developments in both organization and doctrine. Compelled to clarify and crystallize its beliefs, orthodox Christianity now closed ranks by adopting the concept of Apostolic Succession discussed earlier, which enabled certain bishops to be recognized both as legitimate heads of the various churches of the empire and as caretakers of the orthodox tradition. Moreover, to combat attacks on dogma by the Gnostics—who claimed that they alone possessed the secret, oral teachings of the Apostles—the accepted canon of Scripture, the New Testament, was developed. Interestingly enough, certain works, such as the Shepherd of Hermas, which according to some scholars had as valid a claim to canonicity as some of the accepted Scriptures, were discarded as apocryphal because they were feared to have been of Gnostic inspiration.

The most important Apologists of this period were Clement and Origen, two Greeks living in Alexandria in the late second and early third centuries. Both taught in a catechetical, or theological, school, and both contributed a great deal toward the blending of Christian thought and Platonic philosophy. Their aim was to provide Christianity with a rational "scientific" framework.

Origen

Origen may be considered the greatest creative thinker ever produced by the Christian Church. He was the first to pose and offer answers for virtually all of the basic questions of dogma that occupied generations of succeeding theologians—problems dealing with salvation, free will, the nature of God, the divinity of Christ, the Incarnation, and so on. He was primarily responsible for developing for Christianity the allegorical method of biblical exegesis—the method of interpreting every passage in the Bible allegorically as well as literally. He also set forth the relation between the famous Greek philosophic concept of the logos and Christ, the Son of God. The Greek word *logos* has several meanings, the most basic being "reason," or "word." Ancient Greek philosophical schools such as Stoicism and Platonism taught that reason (logos) was the all-pervading force in the universe, an attribute of both God and man. Elaborating on the basis of the identification of the logos with Christ found in the Gospel of John—"In the beginning was the Word [logos], and the Word was with God, and the Word *was* God"—Origen was able to appropriate a good deal of Greek thought. This was a development that served to open the way for acceptance of Greek philosophical speculation—a fundamental step in the creation of a systematic Christian theology. Because of his formative influence on Christian thought, in particular his attempt to reconcile Greek philosophy and Christian faith, Origen has been called the father of speculative theology. The period of the Apologists, especially their remarkable work of reconciling Christian belief with Greek philosophy, is now recognized as one of the most creative periods, philosophically speaking, in the history of the Western world.

Other theologians began to use Origen's speculative method. But differences of interpretation inevitably resulted and soon produced schisms in the doctrinal unity of the Church. So serious were some of these that the need arose for a standardized dogma that would be acceptable to the entire Church. One dogmatic point of difference in particular, the question of the relationship of Christ to God the Father, was so controversial during the reign of Constantine that, in 325, he had to convoke the so-called First Ecumenical Council at the city of Nicaea in Asia Minor. This controversy, more than any other, was creating acute disunity in the Church and threatening to make Christianity a divisive rather than a unifying force within the empire.

The Arian Controversy

The issue arose over a difference of views on the doctrine of the Holy Trinity, the concept of one God in three persons—God the Father, God the Son, and God the Holy Ghost—and the relationship among the three in the Godhead. Arius, a Greek priest of Alexandria, and his followers, called Arians, fervently maintained that Christ the Son was not fully God. As they put it, he was not of exactly the same substance as the Father. He was, rather, a being *created* by God the Father for the creation of the world, and hence inferior to the Father. Arius' opponent, Athanasius, bishop of Alexandria, insisted with equal fervor that if one could not believe that Christ was fully God (as well as fully man), then Christ's death on the cross for mankind was in vain, and hence man could not be truly saved. The conflict turned on two Greek words: *homoousios*, "of the same substance," and *homoiousios*, "of similar substance." (The difference between them of only one letter—the Greek *i*, *iota*—reminds one of the modern saying "not an iota of difference.") Had Arius' views—which were more in the Greek philosophical tradition than those of Athanasius— prevailed, they would have cut the heart out of the Christian doctrine of salvation.

The Early Ecumenical Councils.   The First Ecumenical Council was attended by 318 bishops from the empire, most of whom came from the East, a few from the West. Constantine was the chief influence at the sessions; he may even have presided. His convocation of the council set a precedent for later Byzantine emperors in the Greek East, later to be transformed in the West into the Pope's claim to have the sole authority to convoke councils. Under the influence of his adviser, Bishop Hosius of Cordova, and perhaps because he was unable to understand fully the theological subtleties involved, Constantine at first supported Athanasius. He later came to prefer a compromise between the two extremes.

Although its most radical doctrines were defeated at Nicaea, Arianism was not yet dead. During the reigns of Constantine's successors the controversy continued to rage. For a time it even appeared as if the whole Eastern part of the empire would become Arian. To settle the controversy, further definitions had to be made. The Second Ecumenical Council held in 381 at Constantinople found a solution to the problem. It defined more precisely the nature of the third person of the Trinity, the Holy Ghost, as being also of the same substance as the Father and the Son. It thus propounded the doctrine that the three distinct persons, the Father and the Son and the Holy Ghost, united in the Godhead, are each of exactly the same substance. Hence after years of heated debate the Arian controversy was finally settled. The accession of Emperor Theodosius I (379–395) put an end to the threat of Arianism. Relentlessly persecuted by Theodosius, it managed to survive only among the barbarian Goths.

It is important to observe that the Creed, which begins "We believe in One God, the Father Almighty...and in One Lord Jesus Christ, the only-begotten Son of God...and in the Holy Ghost," first propounded at Nicaea in 325 and completed at Constantinople in 381, is still accepted by all the major

Christian churches of both East and West, by Roman Catholics, Greek Orthodox, and many Protestants.

Another fundamental theological controversy soon arose—the question of
the relationship between the divine and human natures in Christ. How is it
logically possible for there to be such a union in one person? Theologians of
Alexandria, later called Monophysites, took the position that Christ, in effect,
possessed a single nature, the divine, which had absorbed the human. Rival
theologians of Antioch seemed to stress the human nature of Christ over his
divine nature. These were called Nestorians after their leader Nestorius, a monk
and popular preacher of Antioch, who later became for a time patriarch of
Constantinople. The Third and Fourth Ecumenical Councils were called to deal
with this question, at Ephesus in 431 and at Chalcedon in 451. The official doctrine decided upon at these councils was that the two natures of Christ, the
divine and human, are distinct but joined in the one person of Christ. The
dogma obviously did not permit logical explanation; it was a mystery that had
to be accepted on faith alone.

As a result of the Councils of 431 and 451, first the Nestorians and then the
Monophysites were declared heretics. Many of the persecuted Nestorians of the
empire, especially those in Syria and Armenia, fled to Persia or what later
became Arab-dominated areas. With them they carried not only their religion,
but also Greco-Byzantine culture. I shall discuss in Chapter 5 the considerable
influence they exerted on the development of Arabic civilization. The Monophysites, on the other hand, remained within the empire; they were for some time
a constant center of resistance to the unity of the Church.

The different views in dogma of this period were taken very seriously,
certainly far more so than religious questions are taken today. A Greek Father
of the Church, Gregory of Nyssa, said in Constantinople during the period of
the Second Ecumenical Council in 381,

> Everything is full of those who are speaking of unintelligible things
> —streets, markets, squares, crossroads. I ask how many *oboli* I have
> to pay; in answer they philosophize on the born or unborn; I wish
> to know the price of bread; one answers: "The Father is greater
> than the Son;" I inquire whether my bath is ready; one answers,
> "The Son has been made out of nothing."

In the acrid disputes over dogma, political and ecclesiastical rivalries of the
various patriarchates also played a part, each jockeying for position against its
rivals; first Alexandria against Antioch, then Alexandria against Constantinople, Rome against Alexandria, and finally, Rome against its most enduring
rival, Constantinople. Once again, however, it is important to stress that in the
early Church, until far into the medieval period, there was only one orthodox,

catholic Church. Several administrative heads, to be sure, existed in the persons of the five patriarchs, but all felt they belonged to the one, undivided, Christian Church.

The Fathers of the Church: Eastern and Western

By the end of the fourth century certain ecclesiastics, because of the special weight of their authority in doctrinal and other matters, were honored with the title "Father of the Church." Of these, we now discuss four Eastern, three Latin from North Africa, and three from Western Europe.

The Eastern Orthodox Church has singled out three Fathers, considering them the three Hierarchs of the Church: St. Basil of Caesarea, mentioned earlier in connection with Greek monasticism; the theologian Gregory of Nazianzus; and, perhaps the most famous, John Chrysostom, the preacher. The first two, along with Gregory of Nyssa, Basil's brother, the fourth Greek Father, are important for their work in helping to solve the doctrinal problem presented by Arianism. Basil's views on reconciling the ideals of Greek literature and philosophy with Christianity are also significant, since he believed that pagan Greek literature, because of its noble thoughts, could be conducive to living the better Christian life. Chrysostom, whose name means "golden-mouthed," was a priest of Antioch who later, in 398, became patriarch of Constantinople. He is best known for his stirring sermons, some of which were delivered against members of the imperial court itself. These sermons, incidentally, were among the favorites of Erasmus, the great sixteenth-century humanist.

The cradle of Western theology was not Rome but North Africa. There, before the four great Latin Fathers of the Church, two Africans had been primarily responsible for the emergence of Latin theology. Tertullian was educated for the law and became converted to Christianity in A.D. 195–196. His rigorous approach to the concept of the Trinity set the tone for later Latin theology. Tertullian's near contemporary, Cyprian, bishop of Carthage, insisted that Christians could not be saved unless they were members of the Church. Cyprian affirmed that the presence of the Apostolic bishop in each area best manifested the legitimacy of the Church. In contrast to Eastern theologians, who were most concerned with the element of salvation in Christianity, these two theologians stressed its legal and moral aspects.

The first imperial intervention in Church disputes took place in North Africa, also. In the earlier phase of his reign, Constantine, as emperor of the West, had become alarmed by the Donatist controversy in North Africa. The Donatists (much like Wycliffe and Huss a millennium later) denied the efficacy of the sacraments unless they were administered by a priest of good moral character. They were particularly opposed to priests and bishops who, under the threat of persecution, had at one time abandoned the Church and therefore, in the opinion of the Donatists, had lost the authority to administer the sacraments. The Donatist position threatened to undermine the whole sacramental system of the Christian Church. How could one be sure that a priest, at some time in his life, had not sinned? Moreover, how could one be sure that any sacrament, even though administered by a priest who was not in a state of sin, was actually efficacious as the Church affirmed? These rigoristic African Donatists became so serious a threat to the organized institution of the Church that Constantine had to use the power of the state in an attempt to suppress them. His action, coupled with imperial intervention at the Council of Nicaea, marked the beginning of the perennial problem of the relationship between the power of the state and that of the church.

The chief Latin Fathers, several of whom corresponded with the Greek Fathers, were several decades younger than the latter. One of the most authoritative figures in the early Western Church was St. Ambrose, the great bishop of Milan (d.397). As is the case with the Greek Fathers, Ambrose's life in thought and action reflects the typical conflict between paganism and Christianity. Ambrose was born in Gaul. After his studies in Rome he became a lawyer and advanced in his career in the civil service. As governor of north Italy he earned the people's confidence through his firm and wise conduct. In 374, during a conflict between Arian and Nicene Christians over the election to the episcopal throne of Milan, Ambrose, as governor, attempted to quiet the unruly congregation. Suddenly a voice was heard, "Let Ambrose be bishop," and the crowd, so tradition has it, insisted on electing Ambrose, even though he had not yet been baptized. As bishop, Ambrose's episcopal administration of Milan was exemplary. Through his eloquence he converted many of the Arians. He was important in shaping medieval ethics. His theological treatises on the allegorical meaning of the Scriptures, influenced in part by Neoplatonic thought, had great influence on subsequent Western speculative theology. His spiritual authority as bishop was so highly regarded that he twice dared to reprove the Emperor Theodosius, thereby setting a Western precedent—in matters of faith bishops are superior even to the emperor.

St. Jerome was perhaps the first important scholar to be canonized by the Roman Church. Educated in Rome, he learned the Latin classics and loved them deeply—to the point of sin, he thought. So strong was their lure that he could not altogether turn away from them despite the fact that each time he relapsed into the study of Cicero and Vergil he suffered agonizing pangs of guilt. An earnest seeker of truth, Jerome journeyed to the Greek East to study. At Antioch in 375 an emotional dream in which Christ accused him of being a "Ciceronian, not a Christian" drew him from the classics and turned him more zealously to the "books of God." Ascetically inclined, he lived for a while in the desert near Antioch, devoting himself to studying the Scriptures and learning Hebrew. He returned to Antioch in 378, was ordained priest there, and then went to Constantinople, where he studied biblical interpretation under Gregory of Nazianzus, the Greek Father. Summoned to Rome by the Pope to assist in Eastern matters, he remained as Papal secretary. Disturbed by the laxness of the Christian clergy, he became so outspoken in his criticism that some of the clergy threatened to drown him in the Tiber. His neurotic temperament and controversial attitude involved him in many disputes with other theologians during his lifetime.

At the Pope's request Jerome undertook a complete revision of the translation of the Scriptures into Latin, as the previous translation was defective. The result of his work was the celebrated Vulgate version of the Bible (in the "vulgar," that is, the spoken Latin of the period), which has, with little modification, remained the official Roman Catholic version of the Bible. But although he used Greek manuscripts for the New Testament and secured the help of learned Jews for the Old Testament (preferring that to the standard Greek Septuagint version), his work could not, of course, achieve the accuracy possible in modern biblical, textual scholarship. Jerome also wrote lives of certain of the saints, a type of literary genre that was becoming very important in the early medieval period. Through his various writings he played a significant role in explaining Christian doctrine and popularizing the developing institution of monasticism. In sum, he became a fountainhead of Christian scholarship in the West.

The greatest of the Latin Fathers and the most important creative thinker in the development of Christian thought in medieval Western Europe was Augustine. Early in life he developed a passion for Latin literature and style and eventually became a professor of rhetoric. But Augustine had a natural bent for religion. His search for religious truth is described in his famous autobiography, the *Confessions* (*c*.400). Although his mother was a Christian, Augustine himself at first needed more certitude in religion than he thought Christianity could provide. He turned to Manichaeism, a religion possessing both an evil god and a good god—a simple explanation for the existence of evil in the world. Later he rejected Manichaeism for Neoplatonism. It was through this more spiritual Greek philosophy (as well as his belief in the overriding importance of divine grace) that he accepted Christianity. One result of this conversion was his remarkable synthesis of Platonic and Christian thought. Augustine's conversion was marked, however, by a genuine spiritual crisis, much like the crises experienced by St. Paul and by Martin Luther. Indeed, like the latter, Augustine found the certitude he was seeking in Paul's Epistle to the Romans, in the passage reading "You shall be saved by faith alone." Augustine was ordained bishop of the North African city of Hippo. He died there in 430, during the Vandal siege of the city.

Augustine's importance for the Middle Ages lies, in part, in his philosophical interpretation of the universe; it served to establish the basic framework for the entire Western medieval outlook. His masterpiece is the stupendous *The City of God,* whose theme is salvation, and in which he discusses every kind of theological question. The work was written primarily to answer the criticism of pagans and the pleas of troubled Christians about why Rome, after standing for a thousand years, was suddenly sacked (410) by the semi-barbaric Visigothic Germans. The pagans' charge was that the adoption of Christianity had weakened the empire. Augustine's answer was that there are two states (or cities) in the universe: first, the City of God, which is eternal and in which all the saved reside or will reside; and second, the City of Earth, which is corrupt and will ultimately be destroyed, and of which the Roman Empire is a part. The fundamental point is that the aim of all life is salvation (that is, to attain the City of God) and that what happens in this sinful City of Earth (the Roman Empire) does not really matter in the light of God's grand design of salvation or damnation for all mankind. Augustine did not say so explicitly, but he implied that the Church represents the City of God on earth—hence the tremendous authority of the Church over mankind and the development of the medieval Western view that the clergy held the keys to salvation.

In *The City of God* Augustine proposed a genuine theory of history, one based largely on the Judaic ideas of creation and on God's purpose for the existence of the world. This theory, so different from certain pagan Greek views that reflected a cyclical interpretation of history (and often emphasized the eternity of the world and of matter), established the framework for all subsequent medieval religious and philosophical thought in the West and culminated, in the thirteenth and early fourteenth centuries, in the great works of St. Thomas Aquinas and Dante.

Most of Augustine's views were accepted by the Western Church. The one notable exception was his theory of predestination, the idea that some men are chosen by God to be saved, others to be damned, and that man can do nothing to help himself. His great opponent on this question was Pelagius, a theologian from the British Isles. Pelagius maintained that man had complete freedom of will, attacked the doctrine of original sin, and denied the need for divine grace to be saved. Actually a compromise view (sometimes called semi-Pelagianism) triumphed in the Western Church—that is, that God's will (grace) and good works on the part of man, who could himself take the first step, together are conducive to salvation. The Eastern view is similar.

Augustine was most responsible intellectually for removing man from the center of the Greco-Roman universe and replacing him with God. Indeed, his theological ideas were to dominate Western thought until the twelfth century. In view of all these basic contributions, it is little wonder that he has been considered the prime architect of the Western medieval world view.

The fourth great Father of the Church in the West was Pope Gregory I, called the Great. Gregory lived in the sixth century, nearly two hundred years later than the other three Western Fathers referred to above; since his contributions lie mainly within the sphere of the development of Papal authority, I shall discuss him later in this context.

FOR FURTHER READING

Augustine, *The City of God* * (many editions). The most influential work in the field of Western political thought and intellectual development up to the thirteenth century.

Augustine, *Confessions** (many editions). The famous autobiography of St. Augustine.

Bettenson, H., ed. *Documents of the Christian Church,* 2nd ed.* (1963). Useful collection of Christian documents and texts.

Brown, P., *Augustine of Hippo* (1967). Fine biography.

Bury, J. B., *A History of the Later Roman Empire,* 2 vols.* (1957). The best work in English on the early period of Byzantine history from 395 to 565.

Cochrane, C. N., *Christianity and Classical Culture** (1944). A penetrating analysis.

Eusebius, *The History of the Church: From Christ to Constantine,* trans. G. Williamson* (1966). The first ecclesiastical history, by the adviser to Constantine the Great.

Goodenough, E. R., *The Church in the Roman Empire* (1931). A brief but accurate study of the spread of Christianity in the Roman Empire.

Jedin, H. and Dolan, J., eds., *Handbook of Church History,* vol. 1 (1965). Best work on early Christian church.

Jones, A. H. M., *Constantine and the Conversion of Europe** (1948). An objective approach to the problem of Constantine and Christianity.

Jones, A. H. M., *The Decline of the Ancient World* * (1966). [A summary of his longer work on the same period—*The Later Roman Empire 284–602: A Social, Economic and Administrative Survey,* 2 vols., 1964.] A survey by a leading scholar in the field.

Laistner, M. L. W., *Christianity and Pagan Culture in the Later Roman Empire** (1967). An interesting work.

Lietzmann, H., *A History of the Early Church,* trans. B. L. Woolf, 2 vols.* (1961). A standard scholarly treatment emphasizing the theology of the early Church.

McGiffert, A. C., *A History of Christian Thought,* 2 vols.* (1932–1933; 1953). A noteworthy distillation of the thought of Western and Eastern Church Fathers, by a Protestant. Volume I deals with the early Eastern period.

* Asterisk indicates paperback edition available.

Rand, E. K., *Founders of the Middle Ages** (1928; 1957). A thorough discussion of the Western Church Fathers, especially their roles as transmitters of classical ideals to the barbarian West.

Sulpicius Severus et al., *The Western Fathers, Being the Lives of Martin of Tours, Ambrose, Augustine of Hippo, Honoratus of Arles and Germanus of Auxerre,* ed. and trans. F. O. Hoare* (1954). The lives of some of the important Western Fathers, by their contemporaries.

Taylor, H. O., *The Classical Heritage of the Middle Ages** (1958). [Formerly *The Emergence of Christian Culture in the West,* 1911.] A well-known work by a distinguished scholar.

In the previous chapter I discussed in some detail two basic elements in the formation of a new cultural synthesis in the East and in Western Europe —first, the old Greco-Roman institutions and traditions, and second, Christianity. The third element added to the Western cultural synthesis was the Germanic. This Germanic component, for the most part absent in the East, accounts to a considerable extent for the differences between Western and Byzantine cultures. And it was, along with certain other factors, the conquest and occupation of the West by German tribes that led to the "fall" of the Roman Empire in the West.

Among the various Germanic peoples who penetrated the Western half of the Roman Empire from about 400–600, one group, the Franks, played a supremely important role in the development of Europe. The Franks became

CHAPTER 2

The Barbarian Germans

rulers of a great kingdom, which at its height under Charlemagne included much of Western Europe. Under their rule a fusion of the Roman and Germanic peoples and of the two cultures, which had been gradually taking place over several centuries, was finally achieved. The addition of this third element in the West completes what may be referred to as the cultural synthesis of the Western Middle Ages.

The Germans and the Fall of the Empire in the West

Historians once believed that the Germanic peoples living beyond the Rhine-Danube frontier of the Roman Empire suddenly and inexplicably (except that perhaps they were being pressured from behind by Asiatic nomads) crossed the frontier, bringing about the fall of the Roman Empire in the West. These historians said the result was the destruction of classical culture and the onset of the Dark Ages. Such a simple thesis is of course no longer accepted by reputable scholars. It is now clear that the Roman Empire, although attacked from without, had decayed from within as well. The question of the fall of the Roman Empire in the West is a celebrated one, still not completely solved. But it is certain that since about 180 a decline had set in not only in the formerly vital "civic spirit" of the upper- and middle-class Roman citizens, economic life, and institutions in general, but also in connection with the moral decay of Roman society. (Gibbon believed that the adoption of Christianity with its emphasis on humility was largely responsible for Rome's fall!) The German invasions merely gave the *coup de grâce* to a disintegration long in process. Roman civilization in the West, however, was not entirely destroyed by the invaders. Some remnants of it—certain practices and ideals—endured, though in shreds.

In examining the movement of the Germanic invasions, two basic questions should be kept in mind: 1) How did the Germans penetrate into the empire in sufficient strength to make it possible for them to overthrow the Roman government? 2) To what extent did the Germans absorb Latin culture once they had entered the empire?

The Early Germans

The Germans, in the first two or three centuries A.D., were only one group of various European frontier peoples surrounding the empire. The Celts, residing in what is present day Britain, France, and parts of the Spanish penin-

An Anglo-Saxon box lid from the seventh century depicting a battle scene. (Reproduced by Courtesy of the Trustees of the British Museum)

sula, although already largely living within the Roman Empire, were not completely Latinized. In Eastern Europe, the Slavs, residing primarily in present-day Poland, Russia, and Czechoslovakia (but not as yet in the Balkans), had no effective contact with the Roman Empire.

The Germanic peoples who played the paramount role in Western Europe were first heard of in lands bordering the Baltic Sea, particularly in Scandinavia. Knowledge of them comes from archaeological evidence (burial mounds, for example), from later medieval accounts, and from the *Germania,* a short tract written in the last decade of the first century A.D. by the Roman historian Tacitus. In his account Tacitus described the habits and character of the German tribes he knew: "The Germans have no taste for peace; renown is easier won among perils, and a large body of companions cannot be maintained except by violence and war." It is not an objective account, however, for Tacitus was a moralist as well as a historian. Elsewhere he extravagantly praises the simplicity of the Germans and their supposedly high moral standards, judgments that were intended to point up, by contrast, the corruption, depravity, and loose morality of the Romans of his time.

According to Tacitus the Germanic peoples lived in a land of "wild forests and dirty swamps." But they were not savage. Organized into tribes, they lived in village communities. They practiced agriculture, hunted, herded livestock—cattle, horses, and swine—and knew how to work in iron and gold. The Germans, Tacitus reports, were divided into several social classes: hereditary nobles, warrior chiefs, freemen (the main body of warriors), freedmen, and slaves. Freedmen were not much better off than slaves.

The German peoples had a tradition of government by assembly of all freemen. The chief, or king, of each tribe was elected to office by the adult males of military age, who met in the tribal assembly. All questions of importance were discussed and decided upon in the assembly presided over by a council of chiefs.

Historians, especially the nineteenth-century Germans, have stressed (perhaps unduly) the early Germanic love of freedom. Each family within the tribe had a duty to protect the rights of its members and was, in turn, responsible for the actions of its members. Blood-feuds were common, since there was no state government, as we know it, to preserve order. It was possible, however, for an injured family to take a complaint to the tribal assembly. The accused could prove his innocence only through recourse to primitive ordeals or by oaths taken in his behalf by friends. Nearly all crimes, including murder, could be compensated for by the payment of money.

Among the peculiarly Germanic institutions was the *comitatus* (from the Latin *comes*, "companion"). This was a small unit of young men attracted to the service of a strong military chief who provided them with food and weapons. In exchange, the chief's followers swore to serve him with absolute fidelity, considering it a disgrace to survive him in battle. Tacitus put it succinctly: "The dignity of a [German] prince was according to the strength and fidelity of his comitatus." The comitatus is important insofar as it may have led to the emergence of the medieval institution of vassalage (see Chapter 4).

In general, however, loyalty to institutions or ideas as such—a hallmark of a more sophisticated civilization—was lacking among the early Germans. Since they had no notion that authority, for example, could be exercised other than by one man over another, they could not delegate power; thus the effectiveness of a prince depended upon his military strength alone. This inability to conceive of political relationships on any basis other than one of personal loyalty was a basic weakness that several Germanic kingdoms subsequently founded in Western Europe never entirely overcame.

This, then, is a picture of the Germanic peoples in the early period. In the third century, to be sure, under the influence of Rome, some of the Germans became more advanced in political and economic organization, either as a result of increased contact with Roman traders or through service as mercenaries in the Roman army. In war, however, the Germans learned most readily; in the fifth century German generals were quite the equals of their Roman counterparts. This growing Romanization of the Germans is significant because it makes the thesis held by many scholars more intelligible—that, far from wishing to destroy Roman civilization, the Germans as a whole were eager to benefit from its advantages.

The main channel of early German infiltration of the empire was through service in the Roman army. The army, which never exceeded 600,000 or 700,000 men (in a total population estimated at between 70 and 120 million people), was constantly in need of new recruits. The generally sophisticated Mediter-

Rider from Stabio. Originally decorating a shield, this bronze plaque gives some idea of the barbarians that the Roman troops faced along most frontiers. (Museum of History, Berne, Switzerland)

ranean peoples were, as a rule, either unwilling to fight or physically unfit for military life. Hence the Germans, and others from the frontier areas, were taken into service. Attracted by the pay of a military career or by the allure of Roman civilization, the Germans at first entered the empire, as individuals, to join the army. Later they began to come in groups. By the fourth century entire German tribes were incorporated into the Roman army as *foederati*, or allies, serving under their own commanders or, increasingly, under Roman generals. By the fifth century even the supreme commanders in many cases were Germans who had become Romanized and trained in Roman methods of warfare. In the battles of the fourth and early fifth century it was not uncommon to see a "Roman" army, composed of and commanded by Germans, fighting against armies of other "barbarian" Germans. Both Attila the Hun and Alaric the Visigoth (who sacked Rome in 410) were at one time mercenaries of this type. In most battles that took place probably not many more than 20,000 Romans faced an equal number of German troops. As for the size of each German tribe (the figures are always exaggerated by the chroniclers) it probably did not exceed 80,000 to 100,000 persons.

Mass Germanic tribal migration into the Roman Empire took place at the end of the fourth century and continued throughout the fifth century. Whole tribes settled down in Western Europe and North Africa. The reasons for this migration are various. Sometimes economic necessity was the direct cause; pasture land for herds was needed. Increased population made it necessary to acquire a large extent of land. Moreover, poor agricultural methods exhausted the soil. Often the tribes came in search of better homes and easier living conditions. Sometimes they came just to plunder. Frequently tribes were driven into the empire by pressures of other barbaric peoples. Many were freely admitted by the Romans to colonize vacant lands or to serve as a buffer against other, more barbarous tribes.

The Visigoths—the western (some scholars would say "wise") Goths—were the first important German people to move southward from Scandinavia. Jordanes, the Latin historian of the Goths, tells us something of this migration in his *Gothic History*. After settling for a time in northern Germany, in the third century they again moved southward, approaching the Roman territory of Dacia (modern Romania). When they came in contact with the old Greek population of southwestern Russia (the great land bridge for migration between Asia and Europe), the Goths learned how to build a fleet of ships and soon were raiding and pillaging the famous old cities of mainland Greece and along the coasts of the Aegean Sea. Conquering all of Dacia from the Romans, the Visigoths established themselves there.

The Ostrogoths—the eastern (some scholars interpret this term as "brilliant") Goths—occupied the land north of the Black Sea. This area had from early antiquity been settled by various peoples, the Greeks in particular, whose colonies made the Black Sea coast, especially the Crimea, virtually an extension of Greece. Another people found here were the Sarmatians (Iranians), famous for their horsemanship. Some historians maintain that the Sarmatians may have brought with them two devices unknown to the Greeks and Romans, the stirrup and spurs, which allowed the horseman greater agility in handling his steed and thus hastened the development of a heavy-armed cavalry. The Goths of the area may have adopted these practices from the Sarmatians. At any rate, the Gothic horseman may in a sense be considered a precursor of the Western medieval knight.

As their contact with the Romans increased, the Visigoths and Ostrogoths began to undergo Romanization. Most significant was their conversion to Christianity in the fourth century. This was not a conversion to the Nicene faith but to Arianism, which was dominant in the Greek East under Constantine's sons, but was soon pronounced heretical (see Chapter 1).

According to tradition, the Visigothic conversion is attributed to the work of the missionary Ulfilas, who was probably a German. (Some historians, however, maintain he was half Greek.) He learned Greek and Latin in Constantinople, possibly as a hostage. Consecrated an Arian missionary bishop (341), Ulfilas moved into the areas settled by the Goths and converted them. An important contribution to history was his translation of most of the Bible into Gothic, for which he invented an alphabet based on Greek letters. This work is still today our chief basis for the study of the early Germanic languages. Partly as a result of Ulfilas' efforts, Arian Christianity began to spread from the Visigoths to other Germanic peoples outside the empire. All the important German invaders, with the notable exception of the Franks, became Arian Christians, a development of tremendous political consequences. Since the lands the Germans invaded were peopled by orthodox Catholics, their Arian Christianity was an almost insuperable barrier between the Germans and the Romans that retarded the fusion of the two races.

Establishment of the Visigothic Kingdom

The key date for the breakthrough of the Germans into the Roman Empire is 378, when the Roman army was defeated by the Visigoths at the Battle of Adrianople. The advance of the Huns started the confrontation between the Roman government and the Germans that culminated in this battle. Related to the Mongols, the Huns came from the great plateau of Central Asia. They were remarkable horsemen: to speed their advance they even slept in the saddle. Moving westward from Mongolia as the first of a long series of Asian nomads, the Huns collided with the Ostrogoths (c.370). Jordanes describes the terrifying impression they made upon the Goths: "With small, foul, shaggy faces, seamed with scars, with their clothes rolling on them, wearing helmets on their heads of the skins of wild rats, they ate their food raw, warming the meat by carrying it between their thighs and the backs of their horses." If food were unavailable on a forced march, the Hunnic horsemen, according to Jordanes, would draw blood for sustenance from the veins of their horses.

The Ostrogothic kingdom in southern Russia collapsed before the onslaught of the Huns. The Ostrogoths were pushed back precipitously on the Visigoths, who were then occupying Dacia. Terrified in turn, the Visigoths humbly asked permission of the Emperor Valens to cross the Danube frontier. Valens hesitated at first, contemplating perhaps the large number to be permitted to cross into Roman territory—variously estimated at from 35,000 to the improbable figure of 1 million. Finally, however, he agreed to permit their entry, requiring them first to surrender their weapons and give hostages.

The Roman troops treated the Visigoths shamefully: they sold food to them at exorbitant prices, robbed them, and raped the women. Incensed, the Visigoths, with any means at their disposal, revolted. At the Battle of Adrianople, partly as a consequence of surprise, ambush, and lack of Roman discipline, the Gothic cavalry defeated the vaunted Roman infantry in one of history's most decisive battles. The Emperor Valens himself was killed. The East now lay exposed. Valens' successor, Theodosius, who, as a commander of German troops understood the Germans, managed to impose a Roman policy of conciliation. His skillful diplomacy eventually transformed the Visigoths from enemies into useful mercenaries of the empire.

After the death of Theodosius in 395 the empire, which he had reunited, was again divided. One of Theodosius' sons, Honorius, ruled the West from Ravenna, and his second son, Arcadius, ruled the East from Constantinople. After Theodosius' death and up to the year 476 in the West the actual powers in the empire were the *magistri militum* ("commanders in chief of the troops"), themselves often semibarbarian Germans. Despite the power they exercised, however, never once did a German take the final step of mounting the imperial throne. A non-Latin emperor would have been unimaginable to the Romans and Germans alike. Thus the Germans usually contented themselves with appointing Latins as puppet emperors. During the reign of Honorius, the real master of the West was the Vandal General Stilicho. Intrigue was rampant among civil as well as military officials, a situation that brought Alaric, king of the Visigoths, to the fore.

Alaric was then serving as a mercenary of the Romans. Angered at the meagerness of pay, and motivated also by personal ambition, he led his people to war against Stilicho. After plundering Greece they moved westward.

Honorius, meantime, executed Stilicho ostensibly for treason and fled to the marshes of Ravenna for safety. This left the West in chaos. Unhindered, Alaric was able to ravage Italy. In the year 410 the Visigoths sacked Rome. The sack of their city was a tremendous shock to the Romans, evoking the famous response of St. Augustine's *City of God,* yet as a military event it was far less momentous. Although for three days the Visigoths pillaged Rome, they left untouched most of the main buildings, especially the churches. Alaric then moved southward in the direction of Africa, probably in search of food for his people, but in southern Italy he died. A river was diverted from its course, Alaric and his treasures were buried in its bed, and the river allowed to flow again over the grave.

Under Alaric's successors, Athaulf and Wallia, the Visigoths abandoned Italy and passed over to Gaul and thence to Spain. From approximately 412 Spain and southern Gaul were held by the Visigoths. They did not, however, establish a state as such until the reign of King Euric (466–484). This was the first Germanic state established on Roman soil.

The Ostrogothic State in Italy

Having settled on the banks of the Danube after their defeat by the Huns, the Ostrogoths posed a serious problem for the Eastern emperor by their ravaging of the Balkans. The Emperor Zeno devised a scheme to rid himself not only of the Ostrogothic menace, but at the same time of another German chieftain, the Herul Odovacar, who had conquered much of Italy. Indeed in 476 Odovacar had deposed the last Roman emperor in the West, Romulus Augustulus, and sent his insignia of imperial office to the Eastern Roman emperor Zeno, in Constantinople. So in 489 Zeno sent the Ostrogothic King Theodoric to conquer Italy and rule it in the emperor's name.

After four years of fighting, Theodoric defeated Odovacar. The Ostrogothic kingdom he then founded in Italy became culturally the most advanced of all the Germanic realms. Theodoric had spent many years as a hostage in Constantinople, where he acquired a deep regard for Roman culture. He tried to preserve Roman civilization in Italy. Under his rule the Ostrogothic state achieved considerable political stability, economic prosperity, and intellectual advancement, evidenced by the presence at his court of such scholars as Boethius and Cassiodorus (see Chapter 3). This state of affairs did not survive long after Theodoric's death. Under his successors the hostility generated among the orthodox Catholic subjects by the Ostrogothic preference for Arian Christianity, together with the internecine struggles of the Gothic nobles, weakened the Ostrogothic kingdom. Finally, the troops of the Eastern Emperor Justinian, after twenty years of bitter fighting (from 535 to c.556), were able to subdue the entire kingdom and thereby restore Italy to the jurisdiction of the East. Once again, one emperor ruled most of the Roman world.

Vandals, Huns, and Anglo-Saxons

Meanwhile, still another Germanic tribe, the Vandals, had in 406 crossed the Danube frontier, now left virtually undefended. Sweeping through Gaul they crossed the Pyrenees into Spain, where a memento of their passage remains in the name of (V)Andalusia. The Visigoths, however, defeated the Vandals, and as we have seen, approximately 80,000 Vandals then crossed over into North Africa at the invitation of the Roman governor. Gaiseric, the Vandal king and one of the ablest of the German rulers, then proceeded to take over all of Africa; it was during his siege of Hippo that the great St. Augustine, discussed in the previous chapter, died.

From their kingdom in North Africa the Vandals now dominated the Mediterranean with their ships. In 455 they even sacked Rome. The destruction they are believed to have wrought everywhere has given rise to the term *vandal-*

Germanic Kingdoms and the East Roman Empire 481

ism, "senseless destruction." But recent scholarship has shown that the Vandals were less plunderous, perhaps less intolerant, and more commercially inclined than has been believed. The Vandal kingdom depended too much on the abilities of Gaiseric, however, and with his death the kingdom rapidly declined. Vandal Africa was reconquered with little difficulty by the troops of the Eastern Emperor Justinian in the sixth century.

A number of other Germanic tribes also wandered and marauded in this period, but they did not settle and establish independent states. The Burgundians, whose original home was east of the Oder, did move into the valleys of the Rhone and Saône rivers and in *c.*443 established a principality there. But the name of the Burgundians later came to be associated with several different political entities: one a Merovingian kingdom, much later a French duchy, and third, a "free county" in the Holy Roman Empire.

After crushing the Ostrogoths in southern Russia, the Huns built up a huge, loosely knit empire stretching from the Rhine to the Caspian Sea; it included as subjects both Slavs and Germans. At this time, except for occasional service as *foederati,* the Huns had little contact with the Romans. Under their great warrior Attila (433–453), however, they began to plunder the empire. Ravaging the Balkans, the Hunnic hordes advanced to the very gates of Constantinople. But the capital held out, and Attila turned toward the West.

The destruction and slaughter wrought by the Hunnic army as it swept through Gaul earned for Attila his reputation as the "Scourge of God." In 451 a coalition of Roman and German armies met the Huns at Châlons in central Gaul, and after a great carnage Attila withdrew. The Romans could not claim a clear-cut victory, but for the first time they had checked the Hunnic advance.

Descending into Italy, Atilla sacked Aquileia in 452. Refugees from the city fled to the marshy area at the mouth of the Po River and there founded a settlement that became the city of Venice. Meanwhile, after plundering Milan and Pavia, Attila turned toward Rome. The circumstances are not completely clear, but it seems that an embassy headed by Pope Leo I met Atilla and negotiated his withdrawal from the area. Contemporaries, however, attributed the repulse of the terrifying Huns to divine intervention through the instrumentality of the Pope—a belief that helped to enhance the growing political prestige of the Papacy.

Soon thereafter Atilla's army was racked by famine and disease. There is some reason to believe that the Hunnic king himself became ill at this time, since only a few months later he died of a broken blood vessel. After the death of Atilla, upon whom the cohesion of the empire primarily depended, the great Hunnic kingdom rapidly fell to pieces.

At the beginning of the fifth century, during the barbarian invasions of the Roman Empire, Britain was abandoned by the Roman army. The least Romanized of imperial territories, Britain now saw the final vestiges of its Roman civilization destroyed by an invasion of three north German tribes, the Angles, Saxons, and Jutes.

Raids by barbarian Picts and Scots from the north had already been increasing when the Angles and Saxons, two tribes that had had less contact with Rome than any of the other Germanic peoples, began their invasion of the island. After their initial raids, the invaders brought their dependents and settled in the areas conquered from the native Celts. During the struggle with the Angles and Saxons (*c.*500) the Celts, under the leadership of Artorius, gained a temporary victory. His exploits against the invaders may have given rise to the famous Arthurian legends.

The primitive culture of the Germanic conquerors and their relatively rapid assimilation of the native population resulted in the virtual disappearance of Roman civilization in Britain. Since the Anglo-Saxons were pagans (not even Arian Christians like their Visigothic and Ostrogothic contemporaries), Christianity was able to survive only in very isolated areas of the island. A few centuries later Britain virtually had to be re-Christianized by Irish monks and by missionaries sent by the Pope.

By the end of the sixth century the Anglo-Saxons had pushed the native Britons into the mountains of Wales and established several petty tribal kingdoms: Kent, Essex, and Sussex in the southeast; Mercia, East Anglia, and Northumbria in the Midlands and the north; and Wessex in the southwest. None of these Anglo-Saxon kingdoms was as large or as powerful as the other kingdoms of Western Europe: Frankish Gaul, Visigothic Spain, or Ostrogothic Italy. The only form of political unity among the Anglo-Saxons was a shadowy kind of overlordship, sometimes claimed by one king over all of the others. Unlike the barbarian rulers of the Continent, the Anglo-Saxon kings made no attempt to preserve Roman institutions. The history of Anglo-Saxon Britain from its conquest until about the ninth century is, in fact, mainly the attempts of these petty kingdoms to gain supremacy over their neighbors.

Frankish Gaul

The real founders of the new Europe that emerged from the ruins of the Western Empire were the Franks. A west Germanic tribe, the Franks were divided into two branches, the Salians (dwellers by the sea: perhaps from the Latin word *sal,* "salt"), who originally dwelt along the North Sea, and the Ripuarians, who dwelt along the banks of the Rhine (their name perhaps derived from the Latin *ripa,* "river bank"). Distinguishing truth from fiction in the early history of the Franks is difficult. The main sources of information include archaeological evidence, such as graves in which each warrior was buried with a German battle-axe, the *francisca,* and the work of the Gallo-Roman historian Gregory, bishop of Tours, who lived during the latter part of the sixth century. His *History of the Franks,* one of the most important narratives of the early medieval period in the West, must be consulted with caution, however, for it is not an impartial account: his aim was to exalt his heroes, especially the Frankish King Clovis, and to show that the victories of the Franks against the Arians were won because of their orthodox Catholic faith.

The earliest Frankish king of whom we have mention is Merovech, the legendary founder of the famous Frankish dynasty of the Merovingians. He and his people, one of the numerous Salian tribes, had fought as Roman *foederati* against the Huns at the Battle of Châlons in 451. His grandson, the famous Clovis (reigned 481–511), was the real creator of Merovingian power.

Clovis, in fact, may be considered the greatest figure in Gaul in the eight-century period between Caesar and Charlemagne.

Clovis, King of the Franks

Clovis began his drive to power by defeating Syagrius, the last of the Roman governors, at Soissons, thereby extending Salian territory to the Loire river. He moved his headquarters from Tournai to Soissons. Soon he was acknowledged the ruler of northern Gaul, perhaps with the aid of some Gallo-Roman bishops, despite the fact that he was a pagan. Gregory of Tours provides insight into Clovis' primitive character, his cruelty and bloodthirstiness, by describing how the Frankish king calmly crushed the skull of one of his warriors after the latter had smashed a vase—considered by the soldier to be part of his booty—which Clovis had demanded of him.

Clovis next waged a campaign against the Alamanni, a confederation of Germanic tribes drawn from the Rhine Valley. This war is of special significance because it was connected with Clovis' conversion to Christianity. At the Battle of Tolbiac he and his Ripuarian allies were on the verge of being defeated by the Alamanni. As Gregory of Tours tells us, the threat of defeat caused Clovis to think of Christ, the God of his wife, Queen Clotilda, who had repeatedly urged her husband to convert to Christianity. Believing that his own gods had forsaken him, Clovis now invoked the name of Christ and promised to adopt Christianity if victory were granted him. He triumphed and kept his promise; he and 3,000 of his warriors were baptized in the Roman Christian faith.

Recent scholarship has challenged the chronology of certain events related by Gregory. More important, his account of Clovis' conversion is probably oversimplified. Was Clovis really sincere? Or was it rather that through conversion he hoped to curry favor with the Gallo-Roman bishops, the most influential social group in all Gaul? In any event, his conversion and baptism at Reims constitute for Western Europe an event of paramount significance. As a result he won the support of the large Catholic population of the greater part of Gaul, thus encouraging a more rapid fusion between the Gallo-Roman and Frankish elements. (Because of their Arianism, such a fusion was a far more difficult process for the Visigoths in Spain and southern France and the Burgundians of the Rhone valley.) Besides securing for Clovis an alliance with the bishops, his conversion also served to bring him into a more direct relationship with the Papacy.

Clovis then became conveniently sensitive to the Arianism of his Visigothic and Burgundian neighbors, using their heresy as a pretext to attack them. Moving against the Visigothic kingdom in southern Gaul, where the Catholic bishops tended to favor him, Clovis captured the Visigothic center of Toulouse

Baptism of the Frankish King Clovis in 496, illustrated long after the event in a manuscript history (Vie de St. Denis) *of the French kings. Legend held that a dove, symbol of the Holy Ghost, brought from heaven the vessel of holy oil with which Clovis was anointed.* (*Bibliothèque Nationale, Paris*)

and pillaged its rich treasury. The Visigoths were now forced to withdraw to Spain, where they established a capital at Toledo. Under their hegemony and its subsequent Islamic masters, Toledo became one of the most flourishing cities of the peninsula. After his election as king of the Ripuarian and Salian Franks and his destruction of the Visigothic holding in southern Gaul, Clovis again moved his capital southward, from Soissons to Paris. But he was never able to extend his rule to the Mediterranean. Provence continued to be held by Theodoric, the Ostrogothic king of Italy. The great western Mediterranean ports of Ostrogothic Marseilles and Visigothic Barcelona also remained out of Clovis' reach.

Clovis' conversion and baptism had little influence on his morals. He had both relatives and rival kings killed when he deemed it necessary for the maintenance of his authority and the expansion of his kingdom. Gregory of Tours, by implication, seems to condone, or, at the very least, understate Clovis' crimes, emphasizing instead his generosity and his support of the Frankish Church.

Clovis did grant many privileges and gave great estates to the bishops and abbots of his realm. Yet at the same time he saw to it that the Church remained strictly under his own control.

Like most Germanic rulers in the West, Clovis respected the Roman tradition of the empire. Although he was a semibarbarian and was independent of Roman authority, he was eager to gain recognition from the emperor in Constantinople, who conferred upon him the exalted title of consul. As with Theodoric the Romans maintained the fiction of a German chieftain acting as an agent in the governing of an old Roman province.

The importance of Clovis to early medieval history cannot be overemphasized. He may be considered the distant founder of modern France and, through his conquest of the territory of the Alamanni, of Germany as well. Most significant of all, his was the only Germanic kingdom in the West to survive on the European continent.

The Merovingian Dynasty

At Clovis' death in 511, in accordance with Frankish custom, his kingdom was divided among his four sons. Seldom have the members of a ruling family hated each other so bitterly—the history of the Merovingians is studded with assassination, intrigue, treachery, and all manner of violence. Their campaigns against each other and the constant division of the kingdom served to bring the realm to near anarchy. Nevertheless, the Franks somehow managed to avoid losing territory to foreign rulers. When circumstances demanded, the Merovingian kings occasionally managed to get together to fight outside aggressors and seize new lands. Clovis' sons were able to take Burgundy and later, when the Italian Ostrogothic kingdom collapsed under the attacks of the Emperor Justinian, the rich area of Provence.

Under the Merovingians there were no political institutions, properly speaking, except the monarchy. The realm belonged to the king, who looked upon it as his private property, to be disposed of at his death as he decided. The monarchy became absolute and despotic. The tribal assembly, which once had served as a check on power, ceased to meet. The old Frankish nobility, who also had served as a check, disappeared for several generations. Aristocrats, if they can be called such, were men in the king's service who retained authority only as long as the king desired. They, of course, enjoyed no hereditary rights. (Inevitably, a nobility later re-emerged, and service to the king, with the privileges it entailed, became hereditary.) The Gallo-Roman aristocracy, however, did survive, not as a political power but as a social class. Their status and welfare were dependent entirely on the king's favor. Bishops, too, were subservient to the king.

The Merovingian king rendered no services to his subjects. He was interested only in hoarding a vast treasury for the purpose of maintaining his authority and bribing a rival's followers. We are told that one Merovingian king withdrew from circulation all the metal specie he could lay hands on and deposited it in his private treasury. As one modern historian has so aptly put it, Merovingian administration was simply the "exploitation of his subjects by the king." The notion of public welfare, in the modern sense, had completely disappeared.

Since no distinction was made between the office of the king and the person of the king, the officials of the central administration were merely his personal servants. Among these were the keeper of the stable (constable), the keeper of the treasury, the army commander, and the *major domus,* the official in charge of the royal household and estates, who by the seventh century became the powerful mayor of the palace and eventually master of the king. There was no clear-cut division of functions; an official could be called to perform a duty that was actually the responsibility of another. The king himself served as chief judge in cases involving the palace personnel.

Under the Merovingians, then, the efficient, centralized administration developed by the Roman Emperor Augustus and his successors disintegrated. By the end of the fifth century the provinces had disappeared. There remained only the bare outlines of the *civitates,* or municipalities. To administer the local areas the king now appointed a count who was given full powers of administration, jurisdiction, the military, and finance. Later there appeared the dukes, who were essentially responsible for providing military leadership. Under Clovis' rule every Frank was obligated to serve in the army at his own expense. If he failed to meet the obligation he was subject to a heavy fine. Under Clovis' sons compulsory army service was extended to the other subjects. Given the smaller Frankish population in Gaul, the army soon came to be composed largely of Gallo-Romans.

The system of a direct tax on land, so elaborately devised by Diocletian and Constantine, virtually disappeared by the middle of the seventh century. On the other hand, indirect taxes—such as tolls on bridges and roads, on river ports and markets—multiplied. In addition to these revenues, the king swelled his coffers with judicial fines, "presents" demanded of the nobility, and of course with war booty and income from the royal estates.

In this transition from ancient to medieval society the fusion of the Gallo-Roman population with the Franks was a fundamental ingredient. For a considerable time, however, fusion was retarded by the fact that Franks and Gallo-Romans each followed a separate code of law. Nevertheless, from an early date personal relations between the aristocrats of both peoples were amicable. A community of interests, economic and otherwise, tended to bring the upper classes together. Mixed marriages, for example, frequently took place. Although the long process of the fusion of the two peoples cannot be documented with any

Germanic Kingdoms and the East Roman Empire 526

real degree of accuracy, most historians affirm that it was more or less completed by the seventh century.

By the seventh century the royal power was noticeably weakening. The Frankish and Gallo-Roman nobles, both lay and ecclesiastic (archbishops, bishops, and abbots), angered by the despotism of the monarchy, were raising their voices in bitter protest. In 614 they took action. Under the leadership of the mayor of the palace, they obliged the king to issue an edict that limited royal authority. The main provision of the edict stipulated that henceforth the nobles of each area were to appoint the mayors of the palace in the three major kingdoms that had emerged in Frankish Gaul. These kingdoms, the result of the Frankish custom of dividing the inheritance, were Austrasia, the northeastern part of Gaul to the Rhine; Neustria, west of Austrasia and extending to Brittany in the west and to the Loire in the south; and Burgundy, south of Austrasia.

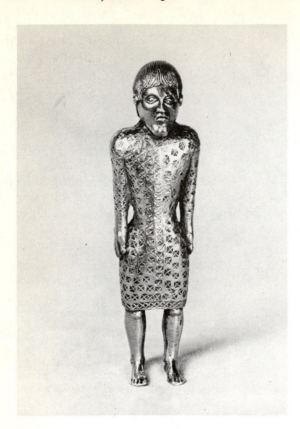

A gold statuette from the late fourth to fifth century of a man from Gaul. (Courtesy of the Dumbarton Oaks Collection, Washington, D.C.)

The signing of the edict may be considered the turning point for Merovingian loss of royal power. The Merovingian kings had become weak in mind and body from debaucheries. As a result they became useless nonentities, mere puppets in the hands of the mayors of the palace, who ruled the country. These last Merovingians have gone down in history as *Rois Fainéants,* "do-nothing kings."

Of all the Germanic kingdoms established in the West, Merovingian Gaul was the only one on the Continent to survive. There were several reasons for this. First, as noted earlier, the Merovingians, having adopted the orthodox Catholicism of the conquered Gallo-Romans, were given firm support by the Gallic church, which thus served as an effective unifying force. Second, unlike the Visigoths and Vandals, the Franks had not been uprooted from their habitat in northern Gaul. They expanded rather than migrated—and therefore could more easily draw on their original reservoir of manpower to replace men lost in battle. Third, its more distant location in the north shielded Merovingian Gaul from attacks from the east (that is, Constantinople) and later from the Arab incursions from the south. Finally, even the constant division of the realm had its immediate advantages. During this period Gaul was too extended a kingdom for one ruler to govern well. In fact, Merovingian Gaul was often weakest when the lands were united under a single ruler.

The Church in the Germanic Kingdoms

In the early years of the Romano-Germanic kingdoms, German and Roman lived side by side, each according to his own law. While the army usually consisted of Germans, Romans ordinarily served in the civil administration. A significant point of contact between the two peoples was the Church, which, with the disappearance of Roman civil rule, came into ever-increasing prominence. Nevertheless, in Spain, Italy, and southern Gaul the Arianism of the Goths retarded their fusion with the Latin people. Although all of the Western areas settled by Germans saw the emergence of what have been termed "national" churches, it was only the church of "Catholic" Gaul that had close relations with the Papacy. Indeed, it was many generations before the Papacy and the Catholic Church in general could overcome the obstacles created by the Goths' adherence to Arianism.

Although for two centuries the Visigoths refused to be converted to the Nicene faith, they were, nevertheless, fairly tolerant of Catholics. In the early seventh century, however, conflict between the Goths and the local Catholic population broke out. The result was the persecution of the Catholics by the king. It was not until the late sixth century under King Reccared, whose brother had been martyred, that the Visigoths were converted to Catholicism.

The Catholic bishops of Spain, hitherto in a subordinate position, now began to acquire considerable influence in state affairs. Some light is cast on their influence by the acts of the Council of Toledo (589) and the chronicles of Isidore, bishop of Seville (*c.*570–636). Ecclesiastical assemblies in this period functioned not only as religious councils, but also as a kind of parliament, in which king, prelates, and laymen all participated. The growing authority of the Spanish bishops seems to have produced a considerable amount of dissension within the realm. Indeed, some historians affirm that it was the disunity created by the substitution of the more divisive authority of the various bishops for royal authority that made it impossible for the Visigoths, under their last king, Rodriguez, to put up effective opposition to the Arab invaders of the early eighth century.

In North Africa the Arian Vandals were only intermittently tolerant of the native Catholic population. Indeed certain Catholic churches, especially those around Carthage, were converted to Arian worship quite early, and some persecution of Catholics took place there. We have a legendary account of the martyrdom of St. Victor, which describes how Catholics were put into leaky boats, towed out to sea, and left to drown. Yet, despite the internal dissension that resulted, the Vandal kingdom prospered for a time. The daring of Vandal fleets struck terror into the peoples living on the Mediterranean shores.

The Vandal kingdom existed until 533, when it was destroyed by the conquests of the Byzantine Emperor Justinian. Deprived now of the vigorous leadership that Gaiseric had given them, the Vandals were able to put up only weak resistance. The opinion of certain historians that the "enervating climate" of Africa made the Vandals "effete" is questionable. Nor can we be certain that the ill-feeling resulting from the sporadic Catholic persecution was a contributing factor. Whatever the case may be, the Vandals vanished from history in the sixth century.

The Ostrogoths of Italy were more tolerant toward the Catholics of their realm, permitting them, for the most part, to handle their own religious affairs. Theodoric refused to intervene in papal elections, even though he was requested to do so by the Catholic prelates. Theodoric's patience, however, wore thin when, near the end of his reign, he discovered (or so he thought) certain of his Catholic subjects plotting with Constantinople to overthrow his rule. Among those he executed was the famous philosopher Boethius, one of his ministers. Theodoric died in 526, and soon after the troops of Justinian invaded Italy. But, as noted earlier, the Ostrogoths were stubborn. Only after a struggle of twenty years were they finally subdued. Some of them then crossed the Alps to Gaul; the rest were soon entirely absorbed by the native population of Italy.

In the Byzantine reconquest of Italy, as might be expected, the Catholic clergy and nobles supported the restoration of the legitimate Roman (that is, Byzantine) rule. The large Jewish colonies of southern Italy, however, owing to the Byzantine policy of intolerance, supported Gothic domination, for Theodoric had respected the old Roman laws granting the Jews certain privileges, especially exemption from participation in public rites.

Gregory of Tours

Gregory of Tours' *History of the Franks* (finished *c.*591) reflects the semibarbarized, highly credulous mentality of Gaul in this period, particularly that of the clergy. Gregory may have been shocked at the crimes of the Merovingians, but he glossed them over in appreciation of their generosity to the Church. Desperately afraid of hellfire, the Merovingian kings endowed the churches, and particularly the monasteries, with lavish gifts to expiate their many crimes. In contrast to Visigothic Spain where the Catholic bishops increasingly secured a large measure of control over the state, the Merovingian kings were able to keep their bishops subservient. The constant strife and intrigue that went on among the Merovingian heirs with the resulting shifting of borders brought about a nearly complete destruction of the old diocesan system and the degradation of the Gallic church and its hierarchy as well. Many of the clergy and the people became illiterate. Many priests in Gaul could not even understand the Latin they recited in the mass. The excessive superstition of the time is demonstrated in the belief, reported by Gregory of Tours, that if one of the faithful were to run his tongue around the railing of St. Martin's tomb at Tours, he would be cured of disease. For Gregory this manifested the true piety of the people.

The Lombard Conquest of Byzantine Italy

The last Germanic people to settle in the West were the Lombards. Considered by contemporary historians to be the most ferocious of the German peoples (Pope Gregory the Great labeled them, as Attila the Hun had been labeled, the "Scourge of God"), the Lombards came down into Italy in 568 from the northeast, taking from the Byzantines much of what the latter had only recently taken from the Ostrogoths. A good deal of information about the early Lombards in the period before their invasion of Italy comes from the Lombard historian Paul the Deacon, who lived in the late eighth century. Like other writers of the period, Paul's theme was the ultimate victory of Catholicism and the gradual Latinization of the Lombard people.

Before the Lombards invaded Italy, they had migrated southward from Scandinavia to Pannonia (present-day Hungary). According to Paul, these early Lombards were fierce pagans given to blood feuds. In approximately 500, after coming into contact with Arian missionaries, they became Christianized, though, like other Germans, only superficially at first. The primitiveness of their life at this time is revealed by Paul's story of Alboin, the Lombard's first important king. Alboin, allied with the Avars, a tribe of Asian nomads, and following in the footsteps of the Huns, had crushed and destroyed a rival Germanic tribe called the Gepidae. Alboin's share of the booty was the beautiful Rosamund, daughter of the slain Gepid king. At a banquet Alboin brought forth a cup made of the skull of Rosamund's father and ordered her to "drink with your father." In revenge Rosamund managed to have Alboin killed, and, fleeing to Ravenna, she placed herself under the protection of the Exarch, the Byzantine governor of Italy.

What drew the Lombards down into Italy was probably a combination of factors: pressure from the Avars, love of plunder, and the perennial problem of finding new food sources. After their conquest of much of Italy, the Lombards

Germanic Kingdoms and the East Roman Empire 570

remained very suspicious of the Romans, keeping apart from them as much as possible. Unlike other Germans the Lombards did not systematically appropriate a share of the land for themselves; they took over estates only if the Roman owners died without heirs. It was their usual practice, in connection with the land, only to demand a tribute of produce.

The Lombards maintained their language and their identity as a people longer than any of the other Germanic tribes dwelling in the midst of a Latin-speaking population. But gradually, owing to political conditions and the influence of Pope Gregory the Great, they too began to be assimilated. Gregory, however, was unable to convert them en masse. This was not accomplished until much later in the seventh century. The process of conversion was in fact so slow that the Lombards long retained their reputation of being enemies of the faith.

In 568, as the Lombards moved into Italy, they first occupied the region now called Lombardy, making Pavia their capital. Although the Byzantines ruled the rest of Italy, the Lombards managed to conquer Tuscany, and, farther south, to establish duchies in Spoleto and Benevento. The rest of the peninsula remained Byzantine, especially the principal cities and surrounding territories of Rome, Ravenna, Venice, and southern Italy. The so-called Lombard kingdom was not therefore one contiguous territory. It consisted, rather, of semi-independent principalities or duchies. This almost mosaic division of Italy between Lombard and Byzantine territories was to last for over two centuries. In the eighth century the Lombard "kingdom" was finally destroyed by Charles the Great (Charlemagne), though Lombard principalities continued to exist in the south.

Despite all the havoc caused in the West by the Germans, some historians believe that no really fatal blow to civilization resulted from the Germanic invasions. As noted earlier, the empire in the West was already a decaying political organism, and it was perhaps inevitable that it would break up into smaller units. To be sure, the Germanic penetration had considerable effect in weakening the Western political and social organization, the culture of which was geared to more sophisticated, urban peoples. Whatever damage may have been done to classical civilization, there is no doubt that a genuine fusion of the Germans and the Christianized Romans eventually took place, and that this fusion in time led to the birth of a new civilization.

True, most of the German states failed to survive. Several factors were responsible for this: the Germans were few in number; many tribes were too dependent on the talents of an individual leader. Of the Germanic kingdoms on the Continent, only Frankish Gaul survived. In Britain, the Angles, Saxons, and Jutes took over almost the whole island.

Having discussed the dismemberment of the Roman Empire in the West by the Germans, a brief examination of the reasons for the survival of the empire in the East is appropriate. The eastern half of the empire suffered for a shorter period from German attacks, although it did see some German settlement. At the same time, however, the Eastern Empire had greater success in bringing to its aid other barbarian peoples—the Isaurians of Asia Minor, for example—to counterbalance the influence of the Germans. There were far fewer German invaders in the East. It has been suggested that the East had a more uniform, integrated culture than the West—most inhabitants of the East were Greek-speaking—but the significance of this factor in connection with the invasions is difficult to evaluate. There is some evidence, however, that the greater variety of the East's economic structure—a greater number of urban and industrial centers, fewer great estates, and a more stable coinage—combined to give this half of the empire a healthier economic base, especially after the Emperor

Anastasius in the early sixth century reformed the currency by establishing a definite ratio of gold to silver and to copper coins. By this time a scarcity of hard currency was beginning to be felt in the West, a circumstance that would later be one factor in the emergence of almost a barter economy.

Of primary importance also is that in the West the invasions disrupted communications, rendering the Western emperors unable to raise revenues and recruit troops effectively, while the emperors at Constantinople continued to possess undisturbed the rich province of Asia Minor from which they could collect taxes, recruit soldiers, and thus carry out the administrative functions so necessary to the well-being of the empire. Finally, the role of contingency and chance should not be overlooked. While the East enjoyed a series of capable and experienced rulers, the West in the same period was too often ruled by weak puppets, fools, or scoundrels.

FOR FURTHER READING

Benedict, *The Rule of St. Benedict,* ed. J. McCann (1952). The guide for the constitution of all Western monasteries after the seventh century.

Bury, J. B., *The Invasion of Europe by the Barbarians** (1967). A rapid survey, accurate and well-written.

Dawson, C., *The Making of Europe** (1932). A scholarly account by a Catholic historian.

Dill, S., *Roman Society in Gaul in the Merovingian Age* (1970). The best study of Merovingian society and history available in English.

Dill, S., *Roman Society in the Last Century of the Western Empire,* 2nd ed. (1921). Important for social developments.

Drew, K. F. (trans.), *The Lombard Laws* (1973). Good translation of important barbarian law codes.

Duckett, E. S., *The Gateway to the Middle Ages,* 3 vols.* (1938; 1961). A good, popular account.

Gregory of Tours, *History of the Franks,* trans. O. M. Dalton, 2 vols.* (1969). A primary source for the history of Merovingian Gaul; especially important for the conversion of Clovis.

Jones, A. H. M., *The Decline of the Ancient World* * (1966). Perceptive analysis.

Jordanes, *The Gothic History,* ed. Ch. Mierow, trans. of Jordanes' Abridgement of Cassiodorus (1960). English version.

Lot, F., *The End of the Ancient World and the Beginnings of the Middle Ages,* trans. P. and M. Leon* (1931; 1961). A classic work on the bridge between the ancient and medieval worlds.

---

* Asterisk indicates paperback edition available.

Stenton, F. M., *Anglo-Saxon England,* 2nd ed. (1947). Now the standard account on the subject.

Sullivan, R., *Heirs of the Roman Empire** (1960). A short, general survey of the successor states in East and West.

Tacitus, *On Britain and Germany,* trans. H. Mattingly of Tacitus' *Agricola* and *Germania* (1960). A basic source for the life of the early German peoples.

Thompson, E. A., *The Goths in Spain* (1969). Recent and informative; best work in English.

Venerable Bede, *Ecclesiastical History of the English Nation* (1954). Adequate English version.

Wallace-Hadrill, J. M., *The Barbarian West: The Early Middle Ages, A.D. 400–1000** (1952; 1962). A good, brief survey of political and social life in the early medieval West.

Wallace-Hadrill, J. M., *Early Germanic Kingship in England and on the Continent* (1971). Important for fresh views.

Renaissance humanists, deploring what seemed to them the almost complete loss of the classical tradition in the West following the Germanic invasions, called the entire thousand-year period from about 400 to 1400 the "Dark Ages." Scholars no longer accept this view. With proper qualification there is indeed reason for considering the period from about 500 to 1000 a Dark Age, but not because there was no glimmer of learning whatever during these five centuries. Charlemagne in the late eighth and early ninth centuries, for example, attempted a revival of education, and here and there isolated scholars like Gerbert (d. 1003) occasionally appeared. What is significant about the period, however, is that the Western European "mind," when compared with the Byzantine and Arabic "minds" of the same time, became virtually sterile and incapable of

CHAPTER 3

The Latin West Before and After Charlemagne

any original conceptual thought, the basic requirement of any intellectual development.

In contrast to Byzantium and Islam, lay education in the West was nearly nonexistent except in certain areas of Italy. Generally, the only education available was provided by the monastery or later, by an occasional cathedral school. But even here the primary purpose was not education per se but the training of clergy to perform the duties of ecclesiastical office. Even educational conditions of the clergy became so bad by the eighth century that Charlemagne had to issue an edict stating that henceforth clerics celebrating mass had to understand the meaning of the Latin words that they recited.

As discussed earlier, the decline in Western civilization cannot be attributed solely to the destruction wrought by the Germans, inferior though their cultural standards were. Henri Pirenne, the celebrated Belgian historian writing just before the Second World War, preferred to attribute this decline to the advance of the Arabs in the seventh and eighth centuries. According to Pirenne's pioneer thesis, the collapse of Western civilization was brought about primarily by the depredations of the Arabs, especially their conquest of all the main islands of the Mediterranean (Sicily, Sardinia, Corsica, Crete, and Cyprus). These conquests in effect closed off the West to long-range sea trade with the East. The Arab conquests, combined with a new wave of invasions from the east and north—Hungarians and the Vikings, particularly—laid waste the West from one end to the other, turning it in upon itself. Finally, what is known as a closed, or barter, economy resulted.

Pirenne's thesis, revolutionary in many respects, created a sensation among historians. After forty years there is still something to be said for it, but the theory has been greatly qualified. Historians now know, for example, that not all relations between East and West were severed. In the East the Byzantines still controlled the Aegean Sea (they recovered Crete in 962), and southern Italy and Venice never really ceased to engage in trade with Byzantium. In the tenth century merchants from the great Greek emporium, Constantinople, were already trading with Scandinavia through Varangian intermediaries, Swedish Vikings who had settled in the Ukraine area of southern Russia. A trading link was thereby forged between the eastern Mediterranean and northern Europe. Pirenne underestimated that despite German admiration for Roman civilization and their attempts to live in harmony with the old Gallo-Roman population of the West, German social and economic institutions, especially in law and political organization in the main prevailed when the fusion of Germanic and Roman peoples was completed.

In this chapter I shall first discuss the Germanic law, which came to be substituted for Roman law during this period. I shall also examine the decline of cultural standards, especially the conscious attempts on the part of certain Romans to stem the loss of classical learning. In this connection Charlemagne, in the late eighth and early ninth centuries, attempted a revival of civilization, only to have it wrecked or possibly driven underground by the advent of what has been sometimes termed exaggeratedly, the "Second Dark Age." At this time —the latter part of the ninth century—a new and even more destructive wave of invasions swept over Western Europe. Continuing well into the tenth century, they turned the West into a shambles, bringing it culturally, socially, and economically to the lowest point of its existence since the pre-Roman period. The changes that necessarily came about in Western institutions to permit the West to survive these new onslaughts will be discussed in the next chapter.

Germanic Law

A good indication of the level of any society and culture is its law. Law is what binds society together, and the more equitably and philosophically based the law is, the higher is the cultural standard. By this criterion, society in Western Europe, as is clear from the law imposed by the Germanic tribes during the early Middle Ages, was very primitive, indeed almost barbaric.

Unlike the Romans, the Germans had no real concept of the state. They had kings, to be sure, but there was no sense of duty to the abstract principle of the nation as a whole. Thus the concept, implicit in Roman law, that a crime against an individual was a crime against the state as well tended to disappear. When murder or lesser crimes were committed, it was the duty of the individual and his *family* to seek revenge. No public prosecutor stepped in, as would happen today.

The Germans did have available certain fifth-century Roman collections of law, and, to a certain degree, a few of the Germanic codes were affected by them. But in general the Germans lacked the ability to master the concepts of Roman law; nor was their society sufficiently advanced even to apply such concepts. In the early period Romans living in the Germanic kingdoms were, as a rule, permitted to retain their Roman law, but as fusion of the two peoples began to take place (a process completed in about the seventh century) Germanic law prevailed. With the passing of time, the various local customs, themselves evolving primarily out of earlier Germanic practices, came to have the force of law. This *customary* law, as it was called, applied only to the specific area in which it had developed. Thus in the same kingdom there was a veritable patchwork of differing customary laws. In time the highly developed Roman legal system was completely supplanted in the West by local, semibarbarian practices.

The main concern of Germanic law was to regulate violence, not to govern in the sense of furthering the public welfare. Fines were imposed for most offenses. Virtually every crime had its price; the compensation for murder was called *wergild* ("man-money").

The method of trial was particularly primitive. In case of conflict between two persons, the defendant, who was considered guilty until his innocence was demonstrated, had several ways of proving the truth of his position. If he were a high-ranking person he could sometimes clear himself by taking an oath on holy relics, such as bones of saints, or on the Bible. If one perjured himself while thus invoking divine aid, it was considered a certainty that he would be eternally damned. Moreover, if he hesitated or made a slip of the tongue during his recitation of the oath, it was often taken as an indication of perjury.

To fortify his oath the defendant's friends might be called upon to swear that he was telling the truth. Such character witnesses were not required to have personal knowledge of the case in question, but only to attest to the defendant's good character. This procedure was called *compurgation*. The number of compurgators varied with the social rank of the accused, the crime committed, and sometimes local custom. If a noble or high-ranking person had slain another, seven compurgators were required. If the victim was a freeman, four. In one case an accused queen proved the legitimacy of her newborn son by having several bishops and no less than three hundred nobles take an oath in her behalf!

More common than compurgation for the upper class was the resort to physical tests, called *trial by ordeal*. A typical ordeal was to have the accused pick up a red-hot iron and carry it a few paces. If his hands healed cleanly within a specified period of time, it was believed that God had adjudged him innocent. Or the accused would be made to plunge his bare arm into boiling water. Such barbaric trials by ordeal had become common practice in the West by the ninth century. They continued even after they were condemned by the Pope at the Fourth Lateran Council in 1215.

Longer lived than the ordeal, and obviously more appealing to the warlike German upper class, was the *judicial duel*, or trial by combat (which only became a "trial" later with the advent of feudalism—see Chapter 4). It was usually resorted to in cases of disputed land inheritance. One could sometimes avoid other types of trial by challenging one's accuser—including even the judge—to single combat. Women and children did not fight, of course, but engaged a champion to defend their rights. This warlike form of judgment, with the subsequent development of feudal society, became very popular among the nobles; such occasions even became times of festivity. Non-nobles—primarily peasants—had no recourse to trial by combat.

There is no reason to suppose that these various methods of proof produced just decisions except perhaps by accident. A feeling of guilt might induce nervousness in the accused—as may be demonstrated by the use of the lie detector today. When liars were thought to be consigned to hellfire, such nervousness must have been induced quite easily. Perjury, nevertheless, was not uncommon; later medieval writers often bitterly denounced the taking of an oath as a method of proof. In any event, the real merit of this Germanic system of law, which spread throughout Western Europe and hardened into local feudal custom, was that it often stopped feuds. Western society had fallen to a very low condition especially when compared with the societies of the contemporary Arab world and the Byzantine East where the precepts of Roman law continued to prevail.

Western Culture and Learning in the Early Middle Ages

Just as we today are aware that our world is constantly changing because of technological improvements, so in the fifth and sixth centuries a few Western intellectuals were acutely aware that their society was being transformed by the Germanic invasions. These scholars feared, in particular, that classical learning would entirely perish in the West. Thus certain of them made a conscious effort to preserve what they could of the Latin, and especially the Greek, classical works. Because of their activities these men have been termed "transmitters" of learning.

Boethius, Cassiodorus, Isidore, Gregory of Tours

Among the most important transmitters was the philosopher Boethius. A minister at the court of the Ostrogothic King Theodoric, Boethius conceived the grand design of translating into Latin the complete works of Plato and Aristotle, as he knew that few Westerners could any longer read Greek. He was not able to advance very far with his task, but he did complete a commentary on Porphyry's *Introduction to the Categories of Aristotle,* a translation of Aristotle's *Elementary Logic,* and several other works of Aristotelian logic, which unfortunately were lost until the eleventh century. The two works named, however, were to become important handbooks during the medieval period. Indeed, they were virtually all of Aristotle that was known in the West for half a millennium. Even such leading eleventh- and early twelfth-century figures as St. Anselm, archbishop of Canterbury, and the French philosopher and teacher Abelard, had to base their philosophic speculations on them. Boethius' most famous original work was *The Consolation of Philosophy.* He wrote it in prison, where he had been committed, perhaps on false charges, for involvement in a treasonable plot to restore Byzantine rule to Italy. In this work, within the broad framework of the Christian faith, he dealt with concepts of classical Greek philosophy, thus in a sense juxtaposing those basic Christian and Greek philosophic elements whose relationship would be so fundamental to all subsequent medieval speculative thought.

Another member of Theodoric's court, his secretary Cassiodorus, was also a significant transmitter. His importance lies primarily in the inspiration for learning that he imparted to the Benedictine monastic houses in the West. Benedict's Rule placed no special emphasis on learning. Founding a monastery on his estates in southern Italy, Cassiodorus stressed the copying of manuscripts and an education focusing on what came to be called the seven liberal arts, based on the learning of the ancient Roman world. But for him *all* learning, classical and Christian alike, was to be subordinated to the leading of a good Christian life. Here was, then, a union of the Christian monastic ideal and that of classical learning. The idea of the fusion of monastic life with scholarly pursuits soon became an inspiration to other monasteries. The inspiration of Cassiodorus helped to make monasteries oases of learning in the West until the early eleventh century.

Monastic intellectual activities were largely restricted, however, to the copying of manuscripts. Every monastery came to have a special room, called the scriptorium, where manuscripts were preserved, copied, and often carefully illuminated. When a monkish scribe encountered a Greek passage, he would usually write, *Graecum non legitur,* "Greek, it can't be read." (Consider our saying, "It's Greek to me.")

Another representative of the meager learning of the period is the seventh-century Bishop Isidore of Seville, in Visigothic Spain. Isidore's best-known work is the *Etymologies,* a kind of encyclopedia or dictionary—a single volume sufficient to contain all knowledge then known in the West! Isidore believed that the essence of a thing could be revealed by its name; hence his work is actually a long series of definitions and commentaries, often extremely fanciful. For example, Isidore wrote that man (*homo* in Latin) is so called because according to the Bible he is "made of earth" (*humus*). Isidore possessed little critical insight; he usually compiled snippets of information, much of it taken from earlier writings, which he frequently misunderstood. His ideas of political theory were somewhat less elementary. Despite his many faults he, like Boethius and Cassiodorus, was in his own way trying to enlighten an extremely uninformed society.

In sixth-century Gaul the leading literary figure was Gregory, Bishop of Tours (see Chapter 2). His major work, the *History of the Franks,* written in barbarized Latin, may be said to exemplify the low level of education and culture of his time. Gregory himself lamented that he could "find no one who can read Latin in all Gaul." Gregory also wrote a popular work on the miracles of St. Martin of Tours, a collection of stories reflecting the credulity of the times about miracles. These stories explained all sorts of events of a remarkable nature for which there was no apparent rational explanation. Gregory's work, besides providing invaluable information about the Merovingians, is also significant for revealing the very low level of social and intellectual life in that period.

Brief mention must also be made of the Latin Fathers Jerome, Augustine, and Ambrose. Although much of their work was developing Christian doctrine, these theologians, using ancient Greek (that is, non-Christian) philosophical notions, passed on to later thinkers a certain amount of ancient philosophy. Indeed, Augustine was the major source for almost all subsequent Western formulations of Christian theology from the later fifth to the thirteenth century. The Neoplatonic concepts in his works inspired later intellectuals such as Anselm and Abelard. Another Latin Father, Pope Gregory the Great, also considered a transmitter of ancient learning, will be discussed in Chapter 4.

England and Ireland

Before the withdrawal of the Roman army in the early fifth century, Britain had produced several important theologians, including Pelagius, the great opponent of St. Augustine on the question of predestination. Pelagius, in contrast to Augustine, did not believe in the doctrine of the transmission to all men of Adam's "original sin," nor in the inability of man to contribute to his own salvation.

After the Roman legions left, the Angles and Saxons invaded, and England became barbarized. As for Ireland, it had never been conquered by the Romans, although we know that the Romans made an attempt to Christianize the island. The legend of St. Patrick's conversion of the Irish is well known. Patrick (*c.*389–461), who was born in Britain, was a monk at the Greek-oriented monastery of Lérins, founded by the Eastern monk Cassian on an island near present-day Marseilles. Captured by pagan Irish pirates, Patrick was later inspired, because of his experience, to go to Ireland as a missionary.

With the Anglo-Saxon conquest of England, Ireland was for a long time cut off from relations with the Continent. Thus an Irish ecclesiastical organization developed that was somewhat different from the rest of the West. In the first place, the early Irish Church was completely monastic. Abbots ruled the Church; the bishops were subordinate to them. Other variants from continental Church tradition concerned the question of the chronology of Easter (the Irish used the Greek calendar), the type of tonsure (head shaving), and, as in the East, a greater emphasis on austerity in the monastic life. It may well be that the apparent influence of Eastern ecclesiastical customs on Ireland came, at least in part, from the monastery at Lérins. It is also possible, on the other hand, that these influences by way of Lérins merely strengthened the much earlier development of native Celtic Christianity already existent in Britain.

In the sixth and seventh centuries both Irish and so-called Roman monks sought to Christianize the Anglo-Saxons. The Romans had come with the monk Augustine, a missionary dispatched in 596 to heathen Kent by Pope Gregory the Great. The Irish monks moved from north to south, the Roman monks in the opposite direction. A conflict between these two groups broke out in the early seventh century, revolving primarily around the method of calculating the date of Easter. Prolonged by the firm resistance of the remnants of the old Celtic Church, the differences were not resolved until 664 at the Council of Whitby. There Rome triumphed, but many of the Irish, unwilling to give up their convictions and practices, withdrew to the Continent, where Irish missionary establishments—many founded earlier among the Germans of Gaul, in the Lowlands, and even in northern Italy—served as places of refuge.

These Irish monks were possessed by a wanderlust and a fervor to convert the heathen. One of the most famous was Columba, founder in 563 of the monastery of Iona off the Scottish coast. But the greatest Irish missionary was Columbanus (585–615), who reconverted many lapsed Christians in Gaul and later converted the Alamanni of the middle Rhine and the Lombards of north Italy. He, too, founded some important monasteries.

St. John holding his Gospel. From a masterwork of Irish Celtic art, the Book of Kells. (*The Board of Trinity College, Dublin*)

Historians believe that in the sixth and seventh centuries many Irish scholars and clergy were highly educated, knowing Latin and, some maintain, even having some knowledge of Greek. Evidently they preserved learning from the Romans in earlier centuries or from contacts with Lérins and St. Victor's. Many of the Irish monasteries founded on the Continent in this period, such as Luxeuil in Gaul (*c.*590), St. Gall in Switzerland (*c.*750), and Bobbio in northern Italy (612), remained centers of learning throughout the Middle Ages.

The rule of these Irish monasteries was more ascetic and austere than that of the Benedictines. But in the early eighth century, mainly through the efforts of the English missionary monk Boniface, the Continental monasteries of Irish foundation were forced to accept the Rule of Benedict or be turned over to the Benedictines. Nevertheless, the importance of the Irish influence on the Continent continued to be significant. Although it is uncertain that many Irish monks really knew Greek (the philosopher John Scotus Erigena of the ninth century is one of the very few historians are certain about), it cannot be denied that for three centuries they focused a bright intellectual beam on Scotland, England, and the Continent—a light dimmed only by the Viking invasions of the ninth century.

The Anglo-Saxons of southern England had been converted to Christianity by the monk Augustine. In 668 Pope Vitalian consecrated a Greek monk, Theodore of Tarsus, archbishop of Canterbury, and sent him to the island to perfect its ecclesiastical organization and to bring the English Church more closely under the control of Rome. It was Theodore who established Canterbury as the primatial see of England. The use of a Byzantine in Papal service indicates that the Eastern and Western branches still constituted one undivided Church. Under Theodore, Canterbury became the most important center of learning in England, reflecting at this time a certain Greek influence.

Anglo-Saxon monks continued the missionary work of the Irish on the Continent, bringing these areas, however, under the allegiance of the Pope. The Anglo-Saxon missionaries Willibrord (658–739), the "Apostle of Frisia," and especially Boniface, the "Apostle of Germany," reached beyond the Rhine. Boniface reorganized the then corrupt Frankish Church of Gaul and in addition labored to Christianize those Germans who were still heathen. Appointed the first archbishop in Germany by the Pope, Boniface established the connection of Germany with Rome. He converted the Germans, or at least a large number of them living east of the Rhine, thereby bringing them into the orbit of Western European culture.

The foremost scholar and literary figure of the early Middle Ages was the Venerable Bede (*c.*673–735), as he is always called. An Anglo-Saxon monk at the monastery of Jarrow in northern England, his scholarship was in the Irish tradition of learning. Bede had a knowledge of both Greek and Latin, remarkable for his time. But, like Cassiodorus, he tried to subordinate his interest in classical literature to the ideal of Christian education. Our system of dating from the birth of Christ is largely due to his essay on chronology (the monk Dionysius Exiguus of the sixth century and the Byzantine ecclesiastic Eusebius of the fourth century had earlier contributed to this convention). His *Ecclesiastical History of the English People* ranks as the best history written in the West between the sixth and twelfth centuries. Composed in a good Latin style, the work also exhibits a genuine historical sense. Bede almost invariably cites his sources of information; yet, typical of the age in which he lived, the work is also full of accounts of miracles. For Bede, as for Gregory the Great, the miracle was an event in the natural world, but out of its established order it became a phenomenon brought about by the intervention of divine power.

This, then, was the culture of Western Europe in the early Middle Ages (the so-called Dark Ages) and its representatives in Italy, Spain, Gaul, and England. This culture was closely connected with monasticism and missionary activity. On the whole, learning was very limited. Most of the writings, except for those of Bede, were mere collections of previous writers imperfectly understood and diluted by the beliefs and superstitions of the age.

In this period of the gradual and seemingly endless decline of Western Europe, the reign of Charles the Great (768–814), usually referred to as Charle-

The Anglo-Saxon Benedictine monk, Venerable Bede (d. 735), known in his day as the most learned man of Western Europe. Miniature from Life of St. Cuthbert, 12th century. (The Master and Fellows of University College, Oxford)

magne, stood out above all. Charlemagne's rule brought to an end the first phase in the transformation of European civilization. During his reign and those of his successors we can begin to distinguish among what were to become three of the modern nations of Western Europe: France, Germany, and Italy. For a time it appeared that Charlemagne might even be able to arrest the seemingly inexorable process of decline and dissolution. But the stability he gave Western Europe was only temporary, and at the end of the ninth century Western society almost completely collapsed under the impact of a second, more devastating, series of invasions. It is in this period of near anarchy that the most basic institutions of the medieval age proper emerged in Europe.

Origins of the Carolingian Dynasty

In the seventh century the Frankish kingdom of the Merovingians, "that bankrupt and accursed house," as Einhard, the friend and biographer of Charlemagne, put it, seemed to be disintegrating as had the earlier Germanic realms. With the continual division of their territory and despite all their efforts to the contrary, the Merovingian kings had been steadily losing power to the Frankish magnates. Indeed, after the reign of Dagobert (628–639), the last effective Merovingian monarch, the kings became *les rois fainéants* ("do-nothing kings"), and the real ruler of each of the three Frankish provinces was the mayor of the palace. For about fifty years after Dagobert's death civil wars between Austrasia, Neustria, and Burgundy were carried on by the mayors of the palace. Finally, the mayor of Austrasia, Pepin of Heristal (680–714), managed to prevail over his rival mayors and reunited the whole realm under his rule, partly as a result of an alliance with the ecclesiastics.

Pepin's successor as mayor was his bastard son, Charles (later surnamed Martel, "the Hammer"), the grandfather of Charlemagne. Under Charles Martel's control the royal authority declined even further. As Einhard put it, "Now the Merovingian kings had nothing to call their own but the empty title of king." Charles Martel's wars extended his power over Swabia in southern Germany and Aquitaine in southwestern France. But the achievement for which he is most remembered was his halting of the Arab invaders at the Battle of Tours in 732. At this time, in order to procure the heavy-armed cavalry he so desperately needed to oppose the Arab invaders, he appropriated certain lands of the Church. These he then handed over to magnates of the realm in exchange for promises of military service, though it appears that the Church retained some sort of claim to revenue. This action of Charles Martel has been viewed by some scholars as constituting an early step in the development of the fief, a feudal institution to be discussed in Chapter 4.

Although the significance of the Battle of Tours has sometimes been exaggerated, Charles's triumph did constitute a decisive check to the Muslim advance in the West. The Pope was impressed. Partly as a result of the victory he later turned to Charles for aid against the Lombards then attacking Rome. (On the parallel Byzantine triumph over the Arabs at the siege of Constantinople in 717, see p. 141.) Since Byzantium was occupied in the East in a grave struggle against the Arabs and unable to defend Italy against the Lombards, the Papacy seemed to need to form an alliance with the Franks, the strongest military and political power in the West. Actually, the Papal-Frankish alliance came about as a result of the Lombard King Aistulf's capture, in 751, of Ravenna, the Byzantine capital of Italy. It was certainly not coincidence that at this very moment an embassy came from Charles Martel's son and successor, Pepin the Short, inquiring if the Pope considered it right that one person hold the Frankish royal title while another exercised the royal power. The Pope replied (as Pepin doubtless hoped) that it was against all justice. A great Frankish assembly was thereupon convoked and Pepin was elected king of the Franks. His predecessor, the last Merovingian, was sent off to a monastery.

In 754 an apparently minor incident occurred, which in the long view of history has great significance. The Pope suddenly appeared at Pepin's camp seeking aid against the Lombards. After the fall of Ravenna to the Lombards, the Byzantine emperor had instructed the Pontiff to go to the Lombard capital, Pavia, and negotiate the return of the exarchate to Byzantium. But, on his own initiative, the Pope contravened his instructions by proceeding farther northward to see Pepin at Paderborn. There, at the Frankish camp, the Pope, following the ancient ritual of the Hebrews, anointed Pepin king of the Franks, and conferred on him at the same time the title of *patricius Romanorum* (in effect, "protector of Rome"). Actually, the Byzantine emperor alone, not the Pope, had the legal authority to award this title. In return for these titles Pepin promised the Pope that the Franks would conquer the old exarchate of Ravenna from Aistulf and then bestow it on the Pope, not on the Byzantine emperor.

The Pope's alliance with Pepin resulted in a reorientation of European politics. The Pope repudiated his traditional overlord and protector, the Byzantine emperor in Constantinople, and turned instead to the Franks. Pepin conquered the exarchate and, in 756 in an act known to history as the "Donation of Pepin," presented the lands to the Pope. Thus the Papal States, the area stretching between Rome and Ravenna, came into being.

Charlemagne

After Pepin's death (768), in accord with Frankish custom, the kingdom was divided between his two sons, Charles and Carloman. At Carloman's death, three years later, the kingdom was reunited under Charles. Charles's accession in 768 marks the enthronement of the greatest figure in early Western medieval history.

In his biography Charles's friend and secretary Einhard has left a fascinating description of that monarch:

> Charles was large and strong, and of lofty stature, though not disproportionately tall (his height is well known to have been seven times the length of his foot); the upper part of his head was round, his eyes very large and animated, nose a little long, hair fair, and face laughing and merry. Thus his appearance was always stately and dignified, whether he was standing or sitting, although his neck was thick and somewhat short, and his belly rather prominent; but the symmetry of the rest of his body concealed these defects. His gait was firm, his whole carriage manly, and his voice clear, but not so strong as his size led one to expect.

Einhard goes on to relate that Charles was fond of hunting, eating, and had a predilection for women. He also had a bent for letters. According to Einhard he was "such a master of Latin that he could speak it as well as his native tongue; but he could understand Greek better than he could speak it." In addition he liked to discuss rhetoric, dialectics, and astronomy. But despite all this outward evidence of learning, the Frankish king could read only with difficulty and learned to write by keeping tablets "in bed under his pillows so that at leisure hours he might accustom his hand to form the letters."

Charlemagne's (that is "Charles the Great's") most remarkable quality was tremendous energy, which enabled him to wage constant military campaigns. His first campaign, in 774, was against the Lombards, who were trying to retake their former lands. Charlemagne deposed the Lombard king, renewed the Donation of Pepin, and declared himself king of the Lombards.

During most of his reign, Charlemagne was occupied with his war against the pagan Saxons of northern Germany, whose conquest extended the territory of the Frankish state all the way to the Elbe. The terms of victory required the fierce Saxons to be baptized en masse or be put to the sword. This fate actually befell 4,500, who were beheaded in one day during a revolt of the Saxons in 782. After subjugating Bavaria and crushing the Avars, Charlemagne moved against Muslim Spain. But if he had it in mind to capture Spain, the campaign was generally a failure. He was able only to establish the Spanish March, a long strip of territory situated across the Pyrenees from France, the main center of which was Barcelona. On the return journey the rear guard of his army, under his commander Roland, was ambushed and massacred by Christian Basques at the pass of Roncesvalles (778). This incident later became immortalized in the *Chanson de Roland,* an outstanding example of medieval epic poetry.

An incident of enormous significance for medieval history now occurred, the revival of the Roman Empire in the West. The background to this event was an interplay of factors among the Lombards, the Papacy, the Franks, and Byzantium.

As was not infrequent in the medieval period, the Pope of the time, Leo III, was in conflict with the lay aristocracy of Rome. In the course of it Leo was seized by the nobles, cast into a dungeon, and, according to legend, was blinded and had his tongue cut out. An angel restored both, says the Papal source, the *Liber Pontificalis*. Leo escaped and fled to Charles in Germany, but at the same time the nobles sent Charles a grave indictment of crimes allegedly committed by Leo. Thereupon Charles the Great, who had inherited the title of *patricius Romanorum* from his father, descended on Rome with his army and there convoked a synod to decide the dispute. Presiding over the synod, Charles had Leo cleared by having the Pope take an oath swearing his innocence on the Bible.

The Revival of the Roman Empire in the West

Shortly thereafter, on Christmas day of the year 800, after the solemn celebration of mass at St. Peter's and while Charles knelt praying at the altar, the Pope suddenly placed a diadem on his head. The throng gathered in the church then began to shout in the Roman (that is, Byzantine) fashion, "To Charles, Augustus, crowned by God, great and pacific Emperor [of the Romans], life and victory!" Once again the West had a "Roman" emperor.

According to Einhard, Charles was taken completely by surprise by the coronation, later declaring that he would never have set foot that day in St. Peter's had he "foreseen the design of the Pope." However, this account is not convincing; the stage seems to have been set too carefully for the scene to have been spontaneous. Examination of the points of view of the various protagonists involved can shed some light here.

One thing seems certain. There must have been some previous agreement between the Pope and Charles regarding the restoration of the empire. To be sure, there already was a Roman emperor in Constantinople, but the throne was now occupied by a woman, Irene, and according to Frankish (Salic) law women could not inherit the throne. Hence in the eyes of the Franks the Roman throne may have been considered vacant. In the view of the Westerners the imperial title had been transferred to the West when Charles was crowned.

The ideal of a universal Roman Empire undoubtedly had never completely left the minds of men in the West. With the enormous expansion of his territory, the ambitious Charlemagne himself must have noted the physical similarity between his realm and that of the Western half of the old Roman Empire. For him, therefore, the assumption of the imperial title was, perhaps, logical.

From another point of view: what motives did the Pope have in crowning

Charles? The Pope had no such authority under Roman law. If, therefore, as reported by Einhard, Charlemagne appeared displeased, it was probably because the coronation was made to appear the result of Papal initiative. The Pope probably wanted to free himself even symbolically from subordination to Byzantium and perhaps at the same time to exalt his own authority. By his placing the crown on Charlemagne's head, the Pope doubtless made it appear that Charlemagne owed him fealty. It is of considerable interest that when Charles later had his own son, Louis, crowned, he took care to perform the ceremony himself, without the participation of the Pope.

Historians have not entirely clarified the problem of the "translation of empire" from the Byzantines to the Germans, as this celebrated event has been called. We do know, however, that it is central to the development of medieval history. The Byzantines were, of course, deeply outraged and considered Charles and his successors, whom they called rex ("king"), out-and-out usurpers. Later, owing to political pressure, the Byzantines for a time and with qualification acknowledged Charles as co-Roman Emperor. The coronation of Charles the Great marked the beginning of the famous centuries-long conflict, a veritable

A contemporary bronze stat-uette believed to represent the Emperor Charlemagne. Note the orb he carries as symbol of imperial office. (Louvre)

political schism between the two empires of East and West—a conflict that was to continue until 1453.

More significant than this, however, was the impact the "translation of empire" had on the subsequent relations between Pope and Western emperor. For it was, at least in part, a result of Charlemagne's policy toward the Church that events later led to the famous investiture conflict between Pontiff and emperor.

Under Charles the institutions and concepts of church and state were blurred and, in some respects, even fused. Not that ecclesiastics were no longer a clearly defined group differentiated from laymen. One person, however, the emperor, seemed in effect to control *both* church and state. It was Charlemagne's ideal to be the ruler of the one Christian society (*unum corpus*), whatever forms its various institutions might take. The ultimate aim of his rule was to guide his subjects in leading a good, moral life on earth that would be rewarded by salvation in the afterlife. Because of this policy of controlling both church and state, Charles has been termed more "caesaropapistic" than the Byzantine emperors. His capitularies (edicts) dealt indiscriminately with both secular and ecclesiastical affairs. As shown in the *Libri Carolini,* he even tried to legislate for the Frankish Church, leaning toward a policy of iconoclasm, or destruction of images, in opposition to the Pope. And when he sent out his agents, the *missi dominici,* to inspect his administration in the outlying areas, an ecclesiastic usually accompanied a layman, both being involved in what we would term secular, administrative work.

This blurring of the two institutions, church and state, was, on the part of the Church, derived from the Old Testament ideal of the consecrated priest-king ruling the Hebrews and from the more recent influences of Augustine and Ambrose. On the part of the state, it stemmed from Charles's continuation of the policies of the earlier Carolingians and perhaps from his emulation of Constantine and the succeeding emperors of the Byzantine East. The Hebrew influence is reflected in Charlemagne's being nicknamed David by his friends at court. Byzantine emperors were, among other things, acclaimed by the people as another "David," after the biblical King David.

In the Western ceremony of consecration the emperor became the anointed of God and protector of the Church, and, to Charlemagne's way of thinking, he was thus authorized by implication to interfere in the affairs of the Church (although, like the Merovingians, he had before this time freely interfered). But Charles always had the best interest of the Church at heart. He constantly strove for the appointment of able, high-minded ecclesiastics. And indeed the Papacy, at this time, made no objection because Charles was its patron and protector. Charles, too, gained by the use of ecclesiastics in his administration. They alone possessed some education; and some of them may even have retained, albeit vaguely, the concept of the state. They were usually of a higher morality than the lay aristocracy, an important requisite for spiritual advisers responsible for the moral conduct of the people. Finally, through his policy of appointing to ecclesiastical office Charles had the opportunity to exploit the Church's lands if he wished to do so.

Charles's policy, then, was not simply a subordination of church to state as some authorities have maintained, but rather a systematic blurring or confusion of the two spheres, in which political considerations were merged with over-all religious ends. As a result of this policy, however, the state would later find that it had fallen into real difficulties. For as the state became assimilated into the broader Christian society, with its pervasive Christian ideals, the Church could ultimately claim the right to *direct* that society and state. There is no doubt that the Church profited greatly during Charles's reign, not least through the Pope's claim that he had the right to crown and, by implication, even to approve the choice of emperor.

Administration Under Charlemagne

Like his early Merovingian predecessors, Charles himself commanded the Frankish army, administered justice, and, as I have shown, controlled the Church. He did not make laws in the old Roman imperial fashion. Rather, to issue a capitulary (roughly, an edict) he assembled a body of advisers, which counseled him—though to be sure, his will always in the end prevailed. It was difficult to impose one law on the many far-flung areas of the realm, as Rome had done. The capitularies could deal only with the larger, more general problems of the empire or, on occasion, with comparatively minor matters. Left in force in each area was the "customary" German law that had been developing there. By now the distinction between Roman and German law had completely disappeared. Except perhaps in Italy, all free men were considered Franks and eligible for military service. The officials of the administration were the emperor's personal servants: a chamberlain, a seneschal to manage the royal estates, a constable to command the army, a chaplain to draw up legal documents. None of these officials, it should be emphasized, had been trained as professional bureaucrats.

As his agents in the provinces Charlemagne appointed the counts and, to handle military matters in the strategic border areas called "marches," strong officials called dukes. Keeping check on the distant counts was a problem; Charlemagne made personal inspections, often leaving Aachen, his favorite residence, to travel around the realm. Or he dispatched the *missi dominici* as inspectors, one layman usually traveling with an abbot or bishop.

Of direct taxation, such as the Romans had had and as we have today, only vestiges remained. The raising of revenue for supporting the army tended, for example, to become the function of the lordly class in society. Charles derived the revenues for carrying on his government from his own personal estates, for he was the greatest landowner in the empire. His famous capitulary *de villis*—concerning his villas, or estates—provided remarkably detailed instructions to his various stewards for the management of his lands.

Economically, Western European society from the third century onward had been becoming progressively less urban. Manufacturing tended to disappear along with townsmen and traders. There was no longer any middle class. What little manufacturing remained was done almost exclusively on the great estates. In view of the increasingly chaotic conditions, trade, except perhaps during Charles's reign, was also drying up and becoming more and more restricted to local areas. Western Europe was on its way to becoming a fairly closed, almost entirely agrarian economy.

The Revival of Learning Under Charlemagne

Perhaps Charlemagne's greatest service to Europe was his interest in the revival of education and his support for reform in the Church. Education in the dark period of the early Middle Ages had, as we have seen, sunk to a very low state in the West, although under Byzantine rule conditions in southern Italy and Sicily (the latter fell to the Arabs in 826) were far superior. (Indeed, up to the start of the twelfth century, southern Italy should be considered to belong, culturally at least, to the Byzantine East rather than the Latin West.) Charles, observing the deplorable condition of culture in his realm, centered his attention on the development of his so-called Palace School in Aachen, to which he tried to attract the best minds of Western Europe. He took an active interest in the school, often observing the students at work. According to one source, Charlemagne became agitated if he saw the pupils shirking their duties at school: "[He watched] the lazy sons of the nobility with fire in his eyes, uttering terrible words, which seemed thunder rather than human speech." And he would shout, "By the King of Heaven, I take no account of your noble birth!" A poem written by one of the students of the court school relates that he was even beaten by Charlemagne because of his mistakes in grammar.

Over this school he placed as supervisor the noted Anglo-Saxon scholar Alcuin. Alcuin, who was in the tradition of Bede and the Irish monks, had directed the cathedral school at York. Under his administration many learned men from all corners of Western Europe were now brought to Aachen. The result of their work has been called, with some exaggeration, the Carolingian Renaissance. Although the school was interested in the seven Roman liberal arts, its main purpose was to prepare candidates for clerical office and to help them better understand the Bible. With the exception of some poetry composed in Latin, the scholarship of this circle was not, as a whole, creative: the works produced for the most part sought rather to imitate or to interpret the Bible, the works of the Fathers of the Church, or certain of the Latin classics. An example of such imitation is the famous life of Charlemagne by Einhard, who, using the style, organization, and sometimes the very phrases of the ancient Roman Suetonius as a model, wrote the most remarkable biography of the early medieval period.

Other notable scholars were Paul the Deacon, the monk of Monte Cassino who wrote a history of the Lombards; Peter of Pisa, the grammarian; and Theodulf the Visigoth, a poet interested in Latin literature. A basic problem for all these men was the apparent incompatibility between devotion to Christianity and a love of the pagan classics—only the Latin classics, however, since Greek had been virtually forgotten. The solution of Alcuin and his school to this question was that if one so wished, he could read the Latin classics, but only for the purpose of helping one lead the better Christian life. One could *use* the classics but not *enjoy* them (*utor non fruor*). Of course such a figure as Theodulf must have found it difficult to avoid taking at least some pleasure in perusing Ovid, Vergil, or some other refined Latin poet.

This cultural revival, then, had its literary aspect, but it was basically theological in its emphasis. In order to raise the educational level of the clergy, Charles (or his son Louis, as a result of Charles's influence) issued a capitulary directing each cathedral in the empire to set up a school for the training of its clergy. At the palace, among the scholars assembled, theological questions were frequently under discussion, though, to be sure, with no great degree of philosophical speculation. These involved questions concerning the significance of the Eucharist (the sacrament of the Lord's Supper), the doctrine of predestination, and the cult of the icons (images)—holy pictures of Christ, the Virgin, and saints. Charles leaned toward iconoclasm, whereas the Pope opposed it. (On Iconoclasm in the Byzantine East see Chapter 5.)

One original philosophic mind did appear in this period, that of the Irish monk John Scotus Erigena. John, however, worked mainly in the court of Charlemagne's grandson, Charles the Bald. Inspired in part by certain Byzantine works sent from Constantinople to the court of Charles, John wrote his important *On the Division of Nature,* which has a distinctly Neoplatonic, almost pantheistic, cast. He also translated into Latin the works of the great Eastern mystic, the pseudo-Dionysius, with the commentaries of the Byzantine theologian Maximos the Confessor—works which would have an enormous effect on subsequent Western mystical thought. But his philosophic views and his independence of judgment, remarkable for this early period, had little effect.* Although he may be considered the culmination of the Carolingian theological revival, Erigena remained an isolated figure whose views were not entirely understood among his contemporaries and who therefore left no influential followers.

* Consider, for example, his view, remarkable for the time, that in matters of dispute reason should prevail over authority.

Gold Carolingian book cover with jewels (eighth century). Note its eclectic nature, with Christ portrayed in Italo-Byzantine style while the decorative border style is Irish. (The Pierpont Morgan Library)

The real contribution of this so-called Carolingian Renaissance was a technical one: its assembling and copying of the scattered fragments of the classical Latin inheritance permitted the re-establishment of a common Western culture in which the German elements could now participate on an equal plane with the Roman. Indeed, we owe most of the classical Latin works we now possess to the scribes of this period. To Alcuin and his followers we also owe a debt of gratitude for the development of the Carolingian miniscule—a system of writing employing lower-case letters as opposed to all capital letters.

Many rulers in history have been called "Great," but perhaps only in the case of Charlemagne has the word become an integral part of his name. He failed to create a lasting government largely because of social-economic conditions that favored the development of localism, but some of his work did endure. The progressive decline that had been going on since the third century was halted, and the foundations were laid for a new Europe. The distinction between Roman and German was no longer made. True, soon after his death, with the new invasions Western Europe fell into an even more troublesome period—at the end of his reign Charles himself was already beset by troubles—but the impetus provided by Charles enabled Europe finally to surmount even this terrible new calamity. Free of the ancient world at last, Western Europe could now begin to evolve a new and original civilization of its own.

The Successors of Charlemagne

Under the weak reigns of Charlemagne's successors his great empire collapsed internally. Even the imposing personality of Charles had sometimes found it difficult to control counts in remote areas (Einhard says that they were all dishonest). Not that all his successors were without ability; divisive internal strains, combined with invasions from without, were simply too much for them.

Charles's heir was his son Louis the Pious. Well educated, he was however extremely religious and tended to be more susceptible than Charles to the wishes of his ecclesiastical advisers and the Pope. Disobeying his father's injunction, he had himself recrowned emperor by the Pope although his father had already crowned him. He thereby strengthened the theory of the necessity of Papal coronation for the Western emperor. But Louis's chief problem was how to divide his empire among his three sons and still retain some kind of political unity. In order to provide economic support for each of his sons, he apportioned the realm into thirds, all to be subordinate to the eldest son, Lothair, who would inherit the imperial title. Because of family disagreements, especially as a result of the remarriage of Louis and his desire to provide for a new heir, the three older sons revolted against their father. A violent civil war broke out; but the only persons to profit from it were the nobles, who, in return for their support of one or the other faction, extracted concessions in land.

After Louis the Pious died, Charles the Bald and his brother Louis, both in opposition to their brother Lothair, reached an agreement at Strasbourg in 842. There they made a public promise to aid each other, each taking an oath in the vernacular tongue commonly used by the other's troops. Charles signed in German and Louis in what was to become French. The so-called Strasbourg Oath provides the first written example of the dialects that were to develop into modern French and German.

The alliance of the two brothers forced Lothair to come to terms, and in 843, by the Treaty of Verdun, the empire was divided into three parts. Lothair, with the title of emperor, secured the largest territory, a long central strip extending from the mouth of the Rhine south to Rome. Lacking any geographic, political, or linguistic unity, it was strictly an artificial state destined soon to fall apart. Louis, called "the German," got all the territory east of the Rhine, and Charles the Bald, the western areas. The Treaty of Verdun is of fundamental

Charlemagne's Empire

- Charlemagne's Empire, 814
- Tributary States Under Charlemagne

TREATY OF VERDUN, 843
- Area East of This Line Went to Louis
- Area West of This Line Went to Charles
  Italy and Area Between Lines Went to Lothair

TREATY OF MERSEN, 870
- Division of East and West Frankish Kingdoms

significance, for it pointed, if indirectly, to the ultimate formation of three nations: France, Germany, and Italy.

Although the eastern and western kingdoms retained a superficial integrity, Lothair's realm broke into many fragments, some of which went to his sons, some to his brothers and their successors. Further wars occurred, particularly over possession of the imperial title. With the passing of only seventy-five years, from Charlemagne's coronation in 800 to 875, the imperial title had become worthless. Once, however, under Charles the Fat, all the Carolingian territories were again briefly united. But Charles was utterly incompetent and in 887 was deposed. Much like the Merovingian house, the line of Charlemagne had become enervated, and in place of such nicknames as "the Hammer" (Martel) and "the Great," the later Carolingians earned the names "the Fat," "the Stammerer," and "the Simple." Carolingian power was no longer effective. Near anarchy prevailed in northern Europe, and the Carolingian dynasty itself finally came to an end in Germany in 911 and in France in 987.

The New Invaders: Arabs, Northmen, and Magyars

After Charles's death in 814 the difficult problems of government his remarkable personality had masked became clear. Internally the empire was too large, communications too difficult. Thus the fatal disease of localism began to take hold everywhere. Added to this was the personal weakness of his successors, who were either unwilling or unable to maintain the security of the empire. Externally a new wave of barbarian invasions made almost impossible the task of maintaining central authority.

In the later ninth and tenth centuries Western Europe became almost entirely ringed by three peoples: the Saracens (Arabs), the Northmen (Vikings), and the Magyars (Hungarians). With light ships or swift cavalry, one or another of these peoples raided almost every region, from England to Sicily to the Black Sea. They plundered and stole everything they could lay their hands on and slaughtered thousands. The sheer task of defense against them was almost insurmountable.

The Arabs came first, doing the least damage although they raided for the longest period. Checked in their main advance into Gaul by Charles Martel, they continued to plunder the coastal areas of Italy and southern France. They were able to take all the principal islands of the Mediterranean, including Sicily, Sardinia, Corsica, and even Crete, thus making much of the Mediterranean, especially the western part, unsafe until the eleventh century, since the Carolingians had no fleet. From their great base in southern Italy the Arabs destroyed the monastery of Monte Cassino and in 847 even sacked St. Peter's in Rome. The Arab danger ended only gradually near the end of the tenth century, when Western rulers and the Byzantines united briefly against them. Byzantium was able to retake southern Italy and Crete. Subsequently in the early eleventh century the Italian mercantile cities of Pisa and Genoa reconquered Sardinia and Corsica, and a half century later the Normans were to take Sicily from the

Arabs. Thus it was not until the late eleventh century that most of the Mediterranean was again open to Christian trade.

More destructive were the Northmen (or Vikings), whose activities ranged from Spain all the way to Russia, though their worst plundering was in Britain and France. (Of the obscure early life of these Northmen little is known, except for the evidence provided by recent archaeological finds, especially in Sweden.) The population of Scandinavia had evidently increased from the fifth century onward, and many emigrated to northern Germany and elsewhere. These heathen Vikings were superb sailors, daring in the extreme as they sailed in their open boats far from land. They went to Greenland, and it is now generally accepted that they came to the North American continent, where in about the year 1000 they founded settlements.* They therefore preceded Columbus, but, unlike Columbus, they were followed by no permanent settlement. In Western Europe the Vikings were chiefly attracted by the wealth of Christian churches and monasteries, which they delighted to loot and destroy, slaughtering their victims, as the Western sources put it, "with cold fury."

Danish Vikings raided England, Ireland, and Frisia from the end of the eighth century onward. Soon they established permanent bases, often in the mouths of great rivers such as the Seine, Thames, and Loire, from which they made incursions into the interior. Their small ships, holding twenty to forty men, could navigate all the important rivers in Europe.

The peak of Viking activity came in the mid-ninth century. The Danes, from the late seventh to the early eleventh century, held all or part of England, which was for a time ruled by a Danish king. Danish place-names from the occupation still exist in England. Meantime, the Norse invaded Ireland. Danish Vikings sacked many French areas and in 886 even besieged Paris. Some Vikings finally reached the Mediterranean.

In the early tenth century the Carolingian king of the territory now comprising much of France saw his inability to protect that area against the Northmen. So in 911 he granted to their leader, Rollo, an area on both sides of the mouth of the Seine River. This territory came to be called, after the Northmen, Normandy. Within a century the Northmen there had become assimilated and adopted the French language, manners, and institutions. Under the leadership of their dukes, who showed real talent for government, Normandy had become one of the most advanced areas administratively in Western Europe by the mid-eleventh century.

Besides the Danes and Norse, a third group of Northmen, the Swedes, moved eastward into today's Soviet Union. The story of their colonization and close connections with the Byzantine East will be discussed in Chapter 12.

---

* The so-called Vinland Map, probably made in the fifteenth century and recently much publicized, was believed for a time to corroborate what had long been known to modern scholars.

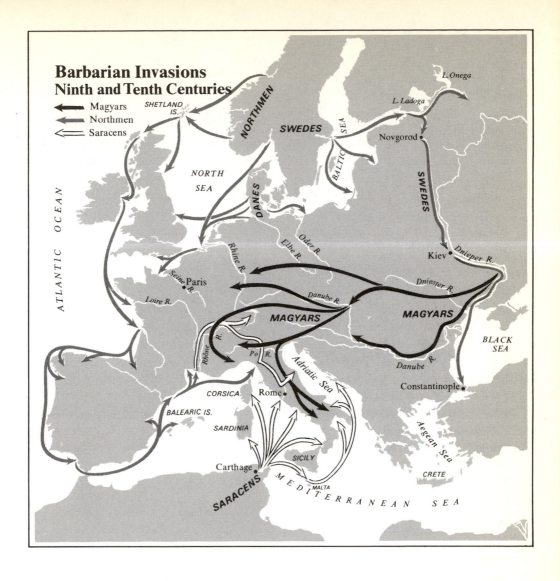

Barbarian Invasions
Ninth and Tenth Centuries

← Magyars
← Northmen
← Saracens

SHETLAND IS.

NORTHMEN

SWEDES

BALTIC SEA

L. Onega

L. Ladoga

Novgorod

SWEDES

NORTH SEA

DANES

ATLANTIC OCEAN

Rhine R.

Oder R.

Elbe R.

Kiev

Dnieper R.

Seine R. Paris

Loire R.

Danube R.

Dniester R.

MAGYARS

MAGYARS

BLACK SEA

Rhone R.

Po R.

Adriatic Sea

Danube R.

CORSICA Rome

Constantinople

BALEARIC IS.

SARDINIA

Aegean Sea

Carthage

SICILY

CRETE

SARACENS

MALTA

MEDITERRANEAN SEA

To add to the misery and devastation of the Carolingian territories, as the danger from the Northmen began to subside new invasions began from the East. Coming from Asia, the Magyars, a people related linguistically to the Turks and the Finns, poured into the Danube Valley. Nomads like the Huns (a few scholars still think they are related), the Magyars were great horsemen, ferocious and merciless. Uniting with the Avars, they devastated the eastern territory of the Carolingian Empire. Their main damage was to Germany, northern Italy, and the Rhone Valley. But the force of their attacks rapidly decreased. They lacked manpower, and after their decisive defeat at Lechfeld in 955 by the German King Otto I, the Magyars settled down on what is today the plain of Hungary. The principal consequence of their invasion was to drive a wedge between the two great groups of Slavs, the Poles and Czechs of the west and the Serbs and Croats of the south.

By about the year 1000 this new phase of invasions was at an end. Europe had survived its most critical period. Many areas of the West were depopulated and in ruins, but a new Europe was taking form, different even from that of Charlemagne. A new type of government, feudalism, was emerging from the crucible of the desperate ninth and early tenth centuries. As can be imagined, because of the chaotic conditions out of which feudalism arose, it was not a coherent, logical system. Feudalism in fact was an improvisation of the times, an attempt by the people of each local area to protect themselves and to provide the rudiments of government. These factors should be kept in mind during the detailed discussion of the feudal system in the next chapter.

FOR FURTHER READING

Arbman, H., *The Vikings* (1961). On Viking art and archaeology.

Blair, P. H., *The World of Bede* (1970). General introduction.

Boethius, *The Consolation of Philosophy,* trans. W. Anderson (1963). Translation of Boethius' greatest work.

Brondsted, J., *The Vikings** (1963). Best recent work on the Vikings.

Bullough, D., *The Age of Charlemagne* (1977). Fine general study.

Duckett, E. S., *Alcuin, Friend of Charlemagne* (1965). A rare study (in English) on the head of Charlemagne's palace school.

Einhard and Notker the Stammerer, *Two Lives of Charlemagne,* trans. L. Thorpe (1969). Sources for Charlemagne's career by Einhard and Notker.

Fichtenau, H., *The Carolingian Empire: The Age of Charlemagne,* trans. from the German* (1957, 1964). One of the best studies on Charlemagne and his reign.

Isidore of Seville's History of the Goths, Vandals, and Suevi, trans. G. Doni and G. Ford (1970). Original source in English.

Laistner, M. L. W., *Thought and Letters in Western Europe, A.D. 500–900* * (1957). Good discussion of Carolingian Renaissance and the cultural developments behind it.

Latouche, R., *Birth of the Western Economy,* trans. E. Wilkinson (1961).

Pirenne, H., *Mohammed and Charlemagne* (1955). Highly controversial thesis, now in large part unacceptable. Very well written.

Sawyer, P., *The Age of the Vikings* (1962). Good recent study.

* Asterisk indicates paperback edition available.

In the period described in the last chapter—the period of the progressive decline of Western civilization from about 500 to *c*.950—the institutions that are generally called medieval emerged in Western Europe. The period was one of disorder and anarchy, in some regions of complete chaos, and for this reason the institutions that arose, though similar, were not exactly the same everywhere. Institutions of England, for example, were somewhat different from those of France, and even more so from those of northern Italy. Yet the institutions that emerged in the various areas had a good deal in common.

It is impossible to trace with exactitude the development of each of the major Western medieval institutions. Indeed, few scholars would completely agree on many of the points at issue. But the fact is that at a time when central authority (that of Charlemagne's successors in particular) had broken down,

CHAPTER 4

*W*estern Feudalism, Manorialism, and the Papacy

and when Arabs, Northmen, or Magyars might at any moment pounce on a village, the most fundamental need was security and the maintenance of order. Not only was it defense against the marauding invader; more often it was self-protection against a neighbor who found that merely to survive he, too, had to be aggressive. But not everyone in society had lost all sense of morality. Some people, especially the monks, deplored the breakdown of ethical values. Nevertheless, in the period of the tenth century even some abbots, to protect their monasteries or perhaps at the request of their superiors, rode into battle at the head of their troops. Such a society, predatory and very insecure, came to exist in almost all areas of Western Europe. In this context, where the strong usurped authority over the weak and law and order could not be maintained, the institutions of "feudalism" slowly emerged.

The Development of Feudalism

There are various interpretations of the meaning of the term *feudalism*. Some historians have defined it in a very broad sense to refer to the entire social and institutional structure of Western Europe from the late ninth to the thirteenth or fourteenth century. A much more restrictive, legalistic, and judicious use of the term (which is employed here) is: a *method or system of government* in which the essential political functions of the "state" are carried out by means of private contracts or agreements between *individuals,* not between a sovereign government and its subjects. This use of the term feudalism applies primarily to the life and social history of the upper or "feudal" class of Western society in the period. The term "manorialism," as used in this book, refers primarily to the agricultural or the economic system, the system involving the peasants, the workers on the land.

Today the government of each "state" (or nation) possesses sovereignty, the ultimate authority to control every citizen directly. More specifically, the state has the power to make laws governing all, the right to tax directly, and the authority to police its citizens and raise an army to protect the nation from attack. Imagine a society in which the governmental authority of the state, as we know it, has almost completely disappeared—a society such as in early medieval Frankland. There, instead of one central government that all must answer to, hundreds of little "governmental" organizations came into being. Each was virtually an independent territory, though vaguely connected by a kind of hierarchy or loose network of personal agreements among the local dukes, counts, or simple knights. This "particularism," with its extreme fragmentation of power (in direct contrast to the ancient Greco-Roman and the modern concept of the state), must be understood first to even begin to understand Western political institutions in the period of the Early and High Middle Ages.

Vassalage and the Feudal Contract

As I have noted, what each person primarily sought was protection, and obviously this could be gained only from someone stronger—perhaps from the counts or dukes, descendants of Charlemagne's officials, or from a bishop or a strong abbot. (Towns, as commercial nuclei, had by this time virtually disappeared in northwestern Europe, though urban centers remained in southern Italy, which was part of the Byzantine world.) Thus the custom developed of placing oneself in a dependent relationship to a more powerful person. In this relationship, termed in medieval law, *vassalage,* the superior came to be called the lord (or the suzerain) and the inferior, the vassal. Vassalage is the key relationship in the development of feudalism and was probably the first feudal institution to emerge.

Scholars disagree over the influence exerted on the development of vassalage by previous Roman and German institutions. It seems probable that the Germanic institution of *comitatus* (see Chapter 2) had some influence; for instance, in Merovingian times prominent men had bands of private retainers resembling the *comitatus.* Other scholars believe, instead, that medieval vassalage reflected the influence of the ancient Roman *clientela,* a group of socially inferior persons dependent on the favors of an influential patron. Certainly by Carolingian times freemen were in the habit of "commending" themselves to more powerful individuals to secure protection and maintenance in return for definite services. An example of this phenomenon of *commendation* is in the so-called *Formulae Turonenses,* a seventh-century charter of Tours in which the mutual obligations of the protector and the protected are set forth:

> To the magnificent Lord *so-and-so,* I *so-and-so*: Since it is known to all and sundry that I lack the wherewithal to feed and clothe myself, I have asked of your pity, and your goodwill has granted to me, permission to deliver and commend myself into your protection.... You have undertaken to aid and sustain me in food and clothing, while I have undertaken to serve you.... And for as long as I shall live I am bound to serve you and respect you as a free man ought, and during my lifetime I shall not have the right to withdraw myself from your authority.... I must on the contrary be for the remainder of my days under your power and protection.

Individuals commended in the above manner to the Carolingian kings came to be called vassals (from the Celtic *gwassawl,* "one who serves"). In the practice of commendation the surrender of one's land to the lord was normal. By Carolingian times a vassal who was to serve the king in some political or military capacity would be granted royal lands in return for his services. The income from these lands, indeed the lands themselves, went to benefit the vassal. Such a grant of land was known as a *beneficium* (benefice, in English). By the end of the eleventh century, however, the term *beneficium* was replaced by the term *feudum,* or *fief,* meaning a grant of land from a lord to a vassal in exchange for certain services, usually military. Other great landowners, including bishops and abbots with their vast ecclesiastical estates, also found it advantageous to grant large tracts of land (even to laymen) in return for administrative or military services. The legal arrangements for the granting of all such holdings, or *benefices,* involved contracts stipulating both services to be rendered by the lord or landowner and services owed by the vassal or landholder.

In the general disruption accompanying the devastating invasions of the ninth and tenth centuries, military service came to be the most important service a vassal could provide his lord. The uncertainty of the times, together with the weakness of the old governmental machinery and a need for a certain continuity, resulted in the tendency for the fiefs to be turned into hereditary possessions. Thus, at the death of the vassal his heir had to take an oath of fealty and pay the lord an "inheritance tax" called *relief,* sometimes equivalent to a year's revenue from the fief. In the developing feudal system, then, the fief came to be "owned" by one noble, while the income from it was usually enjoyed by his vassal. Use of the land and title to it were then in the hands of two different persons.

During the turmoil of the ninth and tenth centuries the function of governing fell largely into the hands of the local lords and their vassals. This system of "local" government, functioning in a framework based on private contracts between individuals, developed out of necessity to replace the eroding civil authority of the Roman state. From the political and economic standpoint we may say that feudalism developed in the holding of the fief by the vassal from his lord; socially and legally it developed through the private feudal courts, that is, the administration of justice by the individual lord in cases involving his vassals (as well as his peasants, as I shall show later). If these private courts retained any sense of "public" welfare at all, it was inherited from the Carolingian period. When all these considerations—political, economic, social, and legal—converged sometime before 1000 the formation of the institution of feudalism was completed. (Yet the process of evolution, as I have pointed out, differed somewhat in the various areas of the West.)

In this welter of thousands of individual governmental units all over Western Europe, each consisting of a lord and his vassals with their own lands, there existed nevertheless a vague sort of unity. For where there was a king, he was considered theoretically to be the highest lord of the realm with the great lords as his vassals, though royal authority over them was for a long time only nominal.

The Feudal "Pyramid"

Feudalism, then, at least when it became crystallized by the early eleventh century, was a system of government in which the direct authority of the state over its subjects was replaced by contractual agreements between lords and vassals. The system was arranged in a more or less hierarchical system with the king at the apex of what has been termed the *feudal pyramid*. The symbol of a pyramid with its implications of orderliness and unity is of course a gross oversimplification. The feudal "system" never really achieved such symmetrical form, despite the efforts of the lawyers of the thirteenth century who tried to impose some measure of uniformity. The heterogeneous development of long centuries could not be easily overcome, even by the efforts of lawyers. The accompanying chart illustrates the simplified feudal pyramid.

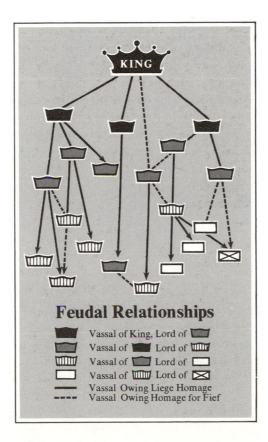

Feudal Relationships

Vassal of King, Lord of
Vassal of   Lord of
Vassal of   Lord of
Vassal of   Lord of
—— Vassal Owing Liege Homage
---- Vassal Owing Homage for Fief

The system of feudal contracts applied only to the noble class, which included, besides the king and the lords, the higher clergy and their vassals. It should be noted that there was no stigma attached to being a vassal. Even the king of England, after 1066, in his capacity as Duke of Normandy, was the vassal of the king of France; later, in the twelfth and thirteenth centuries, such kings as John of England and Roger II of Sicily became vassals of the Pope. The vast bulk of the population, however, comprising mainly the peasants working the land, was non-noble and outside the feudal system proper.

In the organization of feudalism a noble could be simultaneously a vassal and a lord with his own vassals. As shown in the chart, the top of this irregular feudal pyramid was the king, the highest lord, having under him his own powerful vassals. Each suzerain, or lord, including the king, had the authority to command, that is, to make demands (strictly defined by the feudal contract, which was based on the local "customs" of each area) only on the vassals immediately under him—on those, that is, who held their lands directly from him, usually in exchange for military service. In most areas the lord (England after 1066 being a notable exception) could not command the vassals of his vassals, called his rear vassals, until as late as the fourteenth or fifteenth centuries. This is a basic difference between the "sovereignty" of a modern state, where the central government has *direct* authority over each subject, and medieval Western feudalism, where the contractual relationship was generally limited only to a lord and his *immediate* vassals.

Each vassal retained part of his fief (the lands he received from his lord) for his personal use, to be worked by his peasants. A fief usually contained many farming villages. In order to ease the task of administering so much land, and, even more important, to secure military service, the vassal in turn would break up his fiefs and allot portions of his lands to vassals of his own. This process of dividing fiefs into smaller units and granting them in turn as fiefs to one's own vassals is called *subinfeudation.*

Homage and Fealty

As early as the late eighth century the ceremony of *homage* developed among the Franks to symbolize the vassal's dependence on his lord and the lord's tie to his vassal. The ritual included several steps. First came the act of homage. Kneeling before his lord, the vassal placed his hands between those of his superior and declared himself the lord's man. Next came the oath of *fealty,* sworn by the vassal on the Bible or sacred relics (often the bones of saints). Finally, there was the *investiture.* The lord handed the vassal a clod of earth or some other object as a symbol of the transfer of the fief from lord to vassal. The tie thus created between lord and vassal was regarded as sacred, and

This medieval medallion depicts the Western act of homage (usually part of the vassalage ceremony) in which a vassal put his hands inside those of his lord thereby becoming personally bound to him. (Bibliothèque Nationale, Paris)

it was a major crime in feudal law for a vassal to defy his lord or to fail to carry out his duties.

What happened if a vassal held lands of two or more lords, as by the twelfth century sometimes occurred in the rather hit-or-miss growth of this system? To meet this contingency the feudal system developed the concept of *liege homage* —multiple vassalage to various lords but primary allegiance to only one particular lord. Service, especially military, would be owed to that lord before all others.

Here is the oath of fealty sworn in June 1196 by Baldwin IX, Count of Flanders and Hainaut, to his lord King Philip Augustus of France. It shows that, despite his allegiance to several other lords, Baldwin owed primary allegiance to one liege lord, the king of France:

> I, Baldwin, Count of Flanders and of Hainaut, make known to all men present and to come that I have agreed and sworn to my liege lord Philip, the illustrious King of France, to give him aid, openly and in good faith, all the days of my life, against all mortal men; and moreover to aid him for my land of Hainaut both against my lord

the Bishop of Liège, if he should ever seek to trouble the king or if the king should wish to proceed against the said bishop, and also against the [Holy Roman] Emperor [who, along with the Bishop of Liège, controlled lands in Flanders]; and I will never withhold or withdraw such aid from the King of France as long as the said lord king shall be ready to do right to me in his court and to let me be judged by those who ought to be my judges in the court of the King of France.

Obligations of Lord and Vassal

What specific services were to be rendered to the lord by the vassal according to the terms of the feudal contract (this was not a written charter for centuries), and what services in exchange could the vassal expect of the lord? As noted above, the lord provided protection and sustenance. He was also obligated to see that justice was done in his feudal court in case of conflict between vassals. It was common practice for the lord, at stated intervals or for special purposes, to summon his vassals to his court (attendance at the court was called, technically, *suit to court*), at which time justice would be meted out and problems common to the lord and his vassals discussed. The meeting of the vassal at his lord's court in order to give counsel and consent to problems affecting both parties was called *concilium*.

Each noble was entitled to the "judgment of his peers," that is, the right to be tried by his fellow vassals in the court summoned by the suzerain. The judgment was rendered according to the "custom of the area"—the traditional usages handed down from generation to generation. When convicted, a defendant could often appeal to the decision of a judicial duel, that is, to personal combat with his accuser (or, in France at least, with one of his judges!). The practice of judicial duel might be used at the first hearing of a case. In the judicial duel it was believed that God would defend the right. The procedure, of course, applied only to the noble class, not to the peasants.

The primary duty of a vassal was to render military service. He was required to come to the aid of his lord with whatever military forces he possessed for as long a time as local custom demanded, usually about forty days a year. In addition, the vassal had to render *feudal aids,* special payments often paid in money on specified occasions: the knighting of the lord's eldest son, the marriage of his eldest daughter, the undertaking of a crusade by the lord, or the ransoming of the lord when captured by an enemy. Besides the feudal aids the vassal was obliged to provide *hospitality* (room and board) for his lord and his frequently not small entourage. (Lords, in fact, sometimes purposely lived off their vassals.) A more important obligation of the vassal (which led to frequent abuse in the form of a demand for excessive payments) was the *relief,* the "inheritance tax" that the heir of a vassal had to pay to the lord.

These demands of the lord on his vassal were more or less clearly specified in all regions. They were the results of long-term developments and as such came to be considered part of the "customary" law of the area, any change being looked upon per se as illegal. (Paradoxically, customary law, by its very nature, could never be truly static; social, economic, and other changes would ultimately be reflected in such law.) If a vassal failed to carry out the terms for the services required by his feudal contract, his lord could declare him a *contumacious* (disobedient) vassal and confiscate his fief. Conversely, if the lord infringed on the contract, the vassal had the right to resist. Indeed, to such a degree did the lords and vassals identify their interests with "customary" feudal privileges and arrangements of their particular area, that any infringement of such privileges was looked upon as an infraction of the rights of private property. If disagreement arose between vassal and lord, battle usually ensued, its outcome depending on the military strength each could bring against the other. Of course in that age of violence, if a lord was too weak to defend his fief others would be tempted to seize his lands.

At first glance the system of feudalism seems rather impractical, even illogical. But despite its negative features, especially the constant warfare it seemed to foster, certain important political benefits did undeniably accrue from it for the civilization of Western Europe. Moreover, where rulers, especially from the twelfth century onward, were very competent, the feudal governments they created were stronger than any political units that had existed since the fall of Rome. Feudal government itself, requiring the services of no trained officials, was very simple and inexpensive. It demanded minimum services and payments in kind—a real advantage in this period of scarce money.

It is now more clear why feudalism has been referred to as "political organization reduced to its lowest terms." It may well have been the only type of government that could fill the void caused by the collapse of the Roman state. Feudalism did, after all, render certain services to the governed, something that the Merovingian rulers did very little of, if at all. Under feudalism, landholding entailed a certain political responsibility, something not true even today. Chapter 8 shows that from the base of feudal government England and France ultimately developed into the modern nation-states we know today. Certainly some of our modern notions of government—the definition and limitation of its powers (recall the feudal contract); parliaments (the germ of which is in the lord's *concilium*); and perhaps trial by jury (which in the modern sense resembles the vassal's trial by his peers, although some scholars believe that trial by jury came, rather, from the Scandinavians)—derive in larger part from the Western medieval feudal tradition than from the institutions of the ancient world.

Western Feudal Warfare

The principal activity of the feudal lord was fighting. From earliest youth the lord's ambition was to become a brave knight, one who in pitched battle or single combat could skillfully handle his horse and weapons: shield, lance, sword, battle-axe, and mace (spiked club). War was considered a noble profession. If ambitious lords were not fighting the king's war, they were carrying on private wars for various reasons: to gain revenge, glory, and rich material rewards; or in extreme cases, just to keep a man in good mettle.

The nobles at first lived in unfortified dwellings, which, however, soon developed into strong fortresses, or castles as barbarian invasions intensified. Before the tenth century castles were made of wood; later they were constructed of stone. Entry to the castle was by drawbridge over a protective moat. A castle was important not only as a residence but as a means of continuing a battle; if a pitched battle had been lost, a noble and his army could retreat to the castle and make a last stand in the donjon tower.

With the addition of thicker stone walls and high turrets, castles were stronger, and siege warfare became an important military development. From the turrets the defenders would pour boiling water or pitch upon the attackers, push over the enemy ladders with long forked poles especially designed for this purpose, and shower the attackers with rocks, arrows, and spears. To storm the castle various siege weapons were developed. Battering rams and catapults were used to breach or crumble the walls and break down the gates. Techniques such as tunneling, mining, and sapping were employed. The technique of sapping consisted of inserting timbers under castle walls temporarily while the foundations were removed; then the timbers were set on fire, causing the walls to collapse. In the last analysis, of course, starvation was the most potent weapon against the medieval castle, which eventually became almost impregnable to assault.

During the course of time the arms and armor of the lord were improved. In the Carolingian period the warrior wore only a simple leather coat and carried a shield, a lance, and a club. Over the course of two or three centuries a major development was the coat of mail, armor consisting of thousands of metal links all woven into one piece. Such mail offered effective protection against sword, dagger, and arrow, but because of its flexibility it offered only slight protection against a crushing blow with a club. To overcome this disadvantage, in the twelfth century metal plate was applied to various parts of the armor, especially at the shoulders and joints. By the fourteenth century heavy, all-plate armor replaced the coat of mail. Plate armor was so heavy, however, that the knight had to be hoisted into his saddle with a winch; if he was unhorsed he was virtually helpless. Plate armor was very expensive, and, partly because of this, the poorer nobles who were unable to afford such costly protection lost some of their military importance.

This thirteenth-century copy of a tenth-century manuscript illumination depicts military life in Spain during the early "Reconquista." The slaughter of Muslim prisoners is shown at the bottom. (The Pierpont Morgan Library)

By modern standards feudal armies were usually quite small, a large one consisting of only a few thousand men. The chief branch of the army was the cavalry with its mounted knights. Until the thirteenth century the infantry usually was employed only in extensive siege operations or to "mop up" after a cavalry charge. Military tactics were rather simple, each force trying to gain the more advantageous position—the command of the heights of a hill, for example. The opposing armies assumed a position facing each other. At command, the mounted knights charged, and the battle was joined. Small wonder that up to the thirteenth and fourteenth centuries the foot soldier was of little importance. For what foot soldier could stand up to a head-on charge of heavily armored knights? In the late Middle Ages, however, the effectiveness of the cavalry charge was severely challenged by several innovations in military infantry warfare: the pike, a long pole with a pointed metal head, and the longbow, a weapon powerful enough to penetrate plate armor.

Although feudal warfare was almost continuous in some areas, there were respites. In the first place, the standard term of service for a vassal, consisting of about forty days a year, limited the waging of an extensive campaign. Moreover, during the time of spring planting or fall harvesting, the lords might choose to stay at home rather than fight. Weather conditions, which even today may impede military action, were naturally a major factor in the campaigns of the medieval period. War was usually not waged during the winter months; most campaigns were limited to the months of June, July, and August. Finally, the Church sought to mitigate the evil effects of war and to limit fighting by imposing restrictions. In the late tenth century the Church proclaimed the Peace of God, whereby all who used violence on noncombatants—women, children, the clergy, and peasants—did so under pain of excommunication. The Truce of God, pronounced in the early eleventh century (originally in honor of the passion, death, and resurrection of Christ), forbade the fighting of private wars from Friday morning to Sunday evening. Later, fighting was prohibited from Wednesday evening to Monday morning during Lent and on specified holy days. These two institutions were not always observed, but they did help somewhat to mitigate the violence and excesses of feudal warfare.

The Western Manorial System

Thus far I have concentrated on the political significance of Western feudalism, that is, as a system of government. Now I shall examine the economic system of Western medieval society. This system, usually termed *manorialism,* was perhaps even more fundamental to medieval life than was feudalism. The key to understanding the economic and in many ways social history of the Middle Ages, manorialism has to do primarily with the life of the vast bulk of the population, the peasants, who lived on the manor and worked the land.

The antecedents of manorialism (originally from the Latin word *manere,* "to stay," that is, "to reside"; later it referred to a unit of land, the *mansus*) are in certain respects found earlier in the great estates (*latifundia*) of Roman Gaul. The tenants who tilled the lands of these Roman estates were slaves, or *coloni,* semidependent farmers bound by law to the proprietor and hence to his land. This kind of estate continued to exist in Charlemagne's period and, some scholars maintain, forms the basis for the medieval manor. Another view affirms that the medieval manor was descended from the ancient German free village community, whose people, because of the prevailing anarchy, were gradually reduced to serfdom. It would be interesting to know what proportion of the peasants, who constituted the vast mass of medieval population, had originally

Labors of the month. This twelfth-century miniature shows activities of farmers for each month. Harvesting in August was an innovation of the eighth century that enabled production of two harvests a year. (Chapelle de Pritz à Laval)

been German freemen subsequently depressed to a status of serfdom because of their need for security. Or, as society crystallized into two distinct groups—nobles and non-nobles—how many German freemen merged with slaves and serfs and were dragged socially and economically down to their level. Still another view of the origin of the manor—and probably the most valid one—holds that the manor is of Roman-German origin, mixed with vestigial remains of earlier agricultural village practices, particularly those of the Celts; hence the manor may be considered as primarily a fusion of Roman and German elements. The problem is, of course, made difficult by the scarcity and obscurity of the source material.

In a typical manor, the village was an agglomeration of thatched cottages huddled close together. Attached to each hut was a small plot of land for a vegetable garden, a chicken yard, and possibly a stable. A stream with a mill pond or marsh at the end ran through the area; beyond was a meadow and beyond that woods and wasteland. The best farmland of the area might be fairly close by, belonging to the feudal lord of the manor, though his land was normally mixed with that of the villagers. Situated on a hill overlooking the village, as if on guard over all, was the lord's castle.

The villagers' fields or strips might be a half mile or so from the village. Whereas the ancient world and the early Germans utilized what is called the two-field system—the division of all arable land into two large fields—in the eighth century or thereabouts the three-field system was introduced in the West. (Possibly it was first used in Boniface's monasteries at Fulda and elsewhere.) The economic advantage of the new three-field system was that crops could be sown twice a year, in autumn and spring, while the third field could lie fallow to give the soil a chance to recover. In this manner it was possible to increase the yield, perhaps by as much as a third, and at the same time produce a greater variety of crops.

In both two- and three-field systems each peasant's holding consisted of strips scattered throughout the fields. (In certain areas of Western Europe this custom still survives.) By this system, land could be more equitably distributed among the peasants so that each possessed both fertile and less fertile strips. The size of the strips was determined largely by the work of the plows. An acre, one day's work with a plow, was the unit of cultivation. The length and narrowness of the strip resulted from the long furrows made by the plow. The villagers worked cooperatively, with everyone plowing, sowing, or reaping at the same time. In harvest time the villagers were supposed to harvest the lord's crops first, even if their own crops were ruined in the meantime. Together the villagers sometimes allotted strips, built a market hall, and set boundaries for common wasteland and woods.

Every manor was virtually self-sufficient, producing or manufacturing most of its necessities. The carvings next to the doors of the northern French cathedral of Amiens show typical scenes of smithies, millers, workers of leather, and weavers of woolen and linen cloth. Much of the work was done by women, though special skills such as those of blacksmith and miller were reserved to men.

The size of a manor might vary greatly. Few records survive, but it seems that the typical medieval manor was much bigger than most modern farms, able to support at the very least ten families of peasants. Perhaps some manors reached the size of 1,000 acres. Each lord possessed at least one manor, and a great duke or count might have hundreds in his fief. The Church and the monasteries possessed thousands of manors, not all contiguous.

The manor was administered by several officials: the steward, the general overseer of all his lord's manors; the bailiff, who was stationed permanently on a manor; and the bailiff's subordinates. The peasants often chose one of themselves to act as their representative before these officials. Usually the bailiff and the peasants' representative together allotted strips and supervised cultivation. They also distributed rights in the woodland, wasteland, meadow, and pasture —all of which were held in common with the lord. One of the duties of the steward (or the bailiff) on behalf of the lord was to hear the cases of the peasants

*Man pruning vines. This sculpture by Benedetto
Antelami in the Baptistry of Parma, Italy, is a
good example of Romanesque art in Italy.
(Parma Italia—Via Mistrali)*

in the manorial court. He was the final authority, but usually he took into consideration the findings of the peasants who might serve as a kind of board of inquiry.

The Peasantry

It is difficult to distinguish the various types of social status of the peasants because the manorial system was not uniform throughout Western Europe; it varied in custom and practice in different regions and at different times. The peasants can, however, be roughly divided into three types: the *serfs,* the *villeins,* and the *freeholders.* Originally there was also a class of slaves who were mere chattel to be bought and sold at the lord's whim. Slavery, however, gradually diminished in the West and by the year 1000 had become negligible; slaves were often given parcels of land and raised to the status of a serf.

All the inhabitants of the village belonged to the peasant class. The lowest type of peasant on the manor was the serf, who as a rule was bound to the land and could not leave it without the lord's consent and the payment of a fine. On the other hand, the lord could not dispossess the serf, nor could he separate him from his wife and children. Many, if not most, of the peasants up to the late twelfth century were serfs. A higher type of peasant was the villein who paid a type of rent for his land and was not bound to the manor. He was, perhaps, a descendant of one of the class of small, free landowners who had surrendered their land to the lord in return for protection and had later sunk to a state of dependence. The highest type of peasant was the freeholder, who owned his own land, but was in some cases subject to the local lord's jurisdiction.

The life of the peasant was hard. He worked long hours, usually in the fields, from before sunrise almost to sunset. His wife usually tended to the hut and family or might, if necessary, also work in the fields. He was at the beck and call of the lord, though certain rules, "customs" of the manor as they were called, were supposed to limit the demands of the master. But the lord could easily circumvent these restrictions, especially by invoking the *corvée,* a kind of forced labor that reverted to Roman times. When the lord, for example, demanded that his peasants build a new trail or repair a bridge, they had to respond to his call at once.

The peasants' homes were damp, dirty, and dark. There was little artificial light; candles were expensive. The peasants slept in their clothes on a heap of verminous, damp straw; if they were prosperous enough to afford it, they slept in a wooden bed. Their diet was simple and unchanging. Drinking water was often scarce and even unsafe. When they could get it, the peasants in the south drank cheap wine; the peasants in the north drank cider and beer when it was available (in years of famine the brewing of beer was forbidden in order to conserve grain). Peasants were plagued by crop failures and frequent epidemics. Life on the manor was rather monotonous, although there were times for entertainment and merrymaking. Books were scarce; in any case, virtually no peasants could read.

The parish church and the priest, usually a peasant, played an important role in the village community. The priest depended on the peasants for his living. Theoretically, he received a *tithe* (one tenth) of the produce of each peasant, paid in corn, wool, fruit, honey, fish, cheese, meat, and other produce. The tithe was to be used for his support and the maintenance of the church, especially the sanctuary, and possibly for social assistance to his parishioners. But if the lord wished (and he often did), he could seize this revenue for his own use, granting only part of it to the parish priest.

The parish church was very important to the life of the village. It often owned the bull, ram, and stallion by the villagers for breeding their livestock. When possible, the Church made an attempt to mitigate the hard life of the peasants. For religious reasons, and possibly to ease the life of the peasants, the Church demanded that they do no work on holy days, which were numerous. The parish church and churchyard constituted the public meeting place and

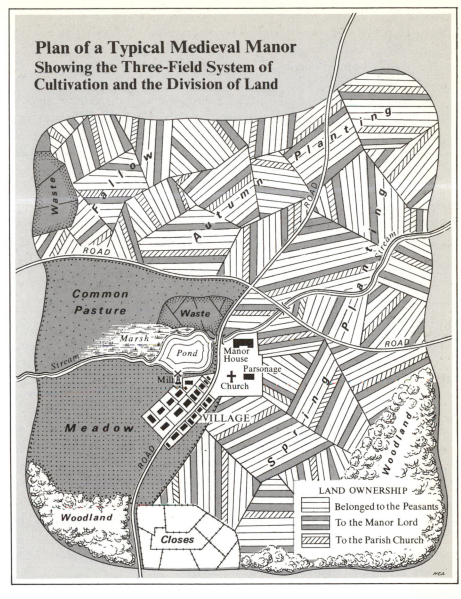

Plan of a Typical Medieval Manor
Showing the Three-Field System of Cultivation and the Division of Land

Waste

Fallow

Autumn Planting

ROAD

ROAD

Stream

Spring Planting

Common Pasture

Waste

Marsh

Pond

Stream

Mill

Manor House

Parsonage

Church

Meadow

VILLAGE

ROAD

Woodland

Woodland

ROAD

Closes

LAND OWNERSHIP

Belonged to the Peasants

To the Manor Lord

To the Parish Church

A plan of a typical medieval manor shows the three-field system of cultivation and the division of arable land. White strips belonged to the peasants, gray to the lord, and diagonally striped to the parish church.

center of social activities. On feast days the people congregated in the church-yard to dance and sing, subject of course to ecclesiastical regulations. Dice games might also take place, though the Church frowned upon gambling. From the twelfth century onward religious plays, scenes from the life of Christ, were presented there.

It was a real hardship to the village if the priest were mentally or morally inferior. What little instruction the peasants got (and it was hardly any) was imparted by him. The Church sometimes made attempts to moderate the gross superstition of the times—belief in evil spirits, devils, fairies—but it was always an uphill fight. On the other hand, both the Church and the people believed in the miracles of the saints. One can imagine the people loved hearing stories about miracles, especially if the story had a humorously pious slant, such as the one about the fly that kept the place for a saint as he read in the Holy Book!

Manorial Taxes and Dues

The number and kind of manorial taxes and dues varied considerably from manor to manor. In the multi-volume medieval Latin dictionary composed by Ducange, no less than twenty-seven columns are devoted to the types of taxes collected by lords from peasants. Most common was the *taille,* paid every year in produce by serf, villein, and perhaps the few freeholders. The *taille* was paid by the family as a group. The serf was usually *taillable à merci* ("taxable at the mercy" of the lord), but in the case of villein and freeholder a "customary" sum was paid instead. The lord also levied a type of indirect tax by requiring his peasants to use (and pay for the use of) his mill, bakery, and smithy—public utilities we might call them—over which the lord had a complete monopoly, and which each peasant had to use under threat of severe punishment. In addition, the serf had to pay his lord for the right to marry into another estate and, like the lord himself, to inherit his father's property. The lord had the right, when traveling through the area, to board and lodge himself and his retinue at the expense of the villagers. Most hated by the peasant was the *corvée,* or forced labor, mentioned earlier.

Not all lords were as cruel to their peasants as discussion of the system might imply. Some peasants, however, finding life too hard and exacting, might escape to the forest and there live the life of an outlaw. (The legendary Robin Hood was an outlaw of this sort.) The forest itself was considered the private preserve of the lord, and anyone caught hunting (poaching) there was subject to a severe penalty, sometimes death.

In this period, when the margin of living was very narrow, weather conditions could produce terrible havoc and mean the difference between life and

*The Luttrell Psalter includes numerous pictures of fourteenth-century rural life
in England. Here plowing with a team of oxen is depicted, together with the new,
heavy-type plow. Note, however, that the new type of harness invented for horses is
not used. (Reproduced by permission of the British Library Board)*

starvation. Communications were tenuous, even between nearby areas, and it
was not too uncommon for there to be plenty in one area and starvation less
than a hundred miles away. What food there was, of course, was primarily
consumed by humans. There was rarely any surplus. The livestock were thin
and scrawny, and many of them could not survive the winter.

What I have described is typical of peasant life in Western Europe, extending from England to the eastern areas of Germany and down to the Adriatic. As I have noted, however, custom and practice varied widely from region
to region, and even from manor to manor, but the general characteristics of the
system and manner of life were similar almost everywhere. The basic characteristics of the manorial system existed for centuries without drastic change down
to the late Middle Ages. Social position and relationships for both noble and
peasant were static. Contributing to this was the generally accepted belief that
no one should aspire to change his status, for his place in society had been ordained by God Himself.

The Papacy and Byzantium

The institution that most exemplified Western Christendom in the
Middle Ages was the Papacy. Today the Papacy is still important, but its territory is physically limited to the few blocks of Vatican City in Rome, and its
temporal power has to a great degree vanished. In the thirteenth century, how-

ever, when the Papacy reached the height of its power, it had great control, direct or indirect, over all of Western Europe, and even for a time over large segments of Eastern Europe. It was in many respects, particularly in the High Middle Ages, the most powerful and important institution in the Christian world. The origins of its power may be found in the early medieval period.

Despite the invasions of the German barbarians, the idea of Roman imperial unity was never entirely lost in the West and continued to exist in one institution in particular, the Church. In this sense the Church, at least in the West, was the heir of Rome. In the reign of the Emperor Justinian (527–565) the Papacy was still to a considerable degree under the control of the Byzantine emperor, who, through his governor of Italy, the exarch at Ravenna, in effect selected each new Pope. The Lombard invasion and conquest of large portions of the Italian peninsula provided the Papacy with the opportunity to achieve independence from Byzantine domination. With the emperor far away in Constantinople, and the exarch also a considerable distance away, the Pope was the one official in the city of Rome to whom the population could look for protection, especially when the Lombards, as repeatedly happened, attacked Rome. Thus, by the end of the sixth century the Pope had become the virtual ruler of Rome.

Pope Gregory the Great

The Pope most closely associated with this period is Gregory I, called the Great (reigned 590–604). As a monk Gregory was sent to Constantinople as Papal ambassador. But Gregory disliked what he considered the worldliness of the Byzantine clergy; apparently he even refused to learn Greek. On his return to Rome his patron, the Pope, died, and Gregory was named his successor by popular acclamation, the first monk to achieve this high office.

During his pontificate Gregory established important, long-lasting precedents in many spheres of ecclesiastical life. In the first place, although Gregory considered himself a faithful subject of the emperor, he tried (but not always with success) to prevent imperial interference in what he considered strictly ecclesiastical affairs. As an administrator (800 of his letters giving instructions to his assistants on every conceivable subject are extant) it was his task to govern the lands of the Roman Church, which were referred to as the "Patrimony of St. Peter." Gregory used the great wealth of the Papacy for many projects other than maintaining the Church itself—to aid the poor, rebuild the city walls of Rome, to carry on missionary work, and to feed, in his "soup kitchens," thousands of refugees fleeing the Lombard advance. During his reign Gregory was angered by the assumption of the title "ecumenical" (roughly, "universal") by the patriarch of Constantinople. Gregory's response, intended by contrast to indicate his own humility, was to sign himself *servus servorum Dei* ("servant of the servants of God"), a title to be adopted by all subsequent Popes, and still in use today.

In Gregory's pontificate certain developments took place that marked the beginnings of the Papacy's temporal power. Occupied in the East with the aggressive Persians and with other enemies, the Byzantine emperor could spare few troops to guard Rome from the Lombard advance. Without Byzantine aid, therefore, Gregory had to defend Rome and attend to the needs of the refugees. He even managed to gain a certain influence over the Lombards, converting some of them from Arianism to Nicene Catholicism. His successor Popes have been accused by certain modern scholars of opposing at any cost a Lombard takeover of Rome, despite the Lombards' conversion to Catholicism. This thesis is based on the theory that the Popes did not want to give up the temporal power they had gained during this conflict.

Pope Gregory's attitude influenced and at the same time reflected the decline of interest in classical learning. A contemporary of Gregory of Tours but better educated, Pope Gregory, too, believed that classical learning was not conducive to leading a good Christian life. Regarding his own Latin style (which was not very refined), Pope Gregory is supposed to have said: "I know I sin against [the grammarian] Donatus, but I care only if I sin against God."

Gregory's most influential work is the *Pastoral Care,* a handbook of practical rules to help bishops and priests in the administration of their flocks. It was the guidebook for the clergy of the Western Church for centuries. Another work usually attributed to Gregory is *Dialogues,* a series of stories about the miracles of Italian saints, especially the famous monk Benedict. The sixth and seventh centuries were the golden age of hagiography (literature on saints' lives). Gregory's work had great influence on this literary genre, which was very popular in a highly credulous time. Gregory tells about saints who became invisible to their enemies, stopped stones in midair, changed water into oil, and even raised the dead—typical of the stock miracles that in this period were assigned indiscriminately to one saint or another.

Gregory's most intellectual work was the *Moralia,* a commentary on the Book of Job. It was Gergory's purpose to show his flock, frightened by the Lombards at the gates of Rome, that their salvation, like that of the ancient Hebrew Job, lay only in faith—blind faith—in the will of God. Indeed, all of Gregory's theological thought emphasizes the total acceptance of the authority of the Church, with no doubting whatsoever permitted to the faithful.

Gregory lacked a metaphysical turn of mind, theologically speaking. Rather, he reinterpreted the abstruse, often complex doctrines of St. Augustine in a manner simple enough for the people of his time to understand them. As the Church had earlier done, he too rejected Augustine's extreme views of predestination, attributing some role also to human merit in the attainment of salvation. Gregory was the first to formulate and define the Catholic ideas on purgatory. His descriptions of purgatory were vivid and terrifying, but he did offer comfort by reminding Christians that the soul's stay in purgatory could be alleviated by an appropriately penitent attitude on the part of the sinner.

Pope Gregory was greatly concerned with missionary work. In 596 he sent the monk Augustine to Britain with twelve men to convert the heathen Anglo-Saxons. Although Augustine's mission had only a limited success, it led ultimately to conversion of all of Britain. At Canterbury Augustine built what became the mother church of England, Christ Church. Gregory's psychological insight is revealed in his exchange of letters with Augustine. He wrote that the newly converted pagans should not be forced at once to abandon their pagan customs; rather, a Christian significance should gradually be attached to those customs. This assimilation of pagan practices became a papal policy in conversion that is reflected today in the customs of the Yule log, Christmas tree, and mistletoe, all of which originally were pagan customs later adopted by Christianity.

Gregory greatly increased the authority of the Papacy, creating or renewing papal ties with the kingdoms of Gaul, Germany, England, and other regions. For his remarkable influence in all these various spheres of spiritual and temporal authority, Gregory earned his appellation "the Great," the founder of the medieval Papacy. He was also, as noted in Chapter 1, the last of the four principal Latin Fathers of the Church.

After the death of Gregory in 604 the Papacy did not experience a steady growth of power. In the period following his pontificate, and especially during the late ninth and early tenth centuries, the Papacy was not even able to control the various churches of the West. Two significant events, however, did occur that helped substantially to increase the spiritual and temporal authority of the Papacy—its acquisition of the exarchate of Ravenna (756), and the pontificate of Nicholas I (858–867).

Ecclesiastical Authority and Corruption

The Byzantine imperial policy of iconoclasm (see Chapter 5), the attempt to rid the Church of holy images, and the vigorous imperial attempts to enforce this policy in Italy alienated the Popes and the Italian population. Primarily this dissatisfaction, together with the weakness of Byzantine power in Italy, induced the Papacy in 751 to reorient its policy of dependence on the Byzantine emperor to seek aid from the Frankish king, who became the Pope's new protector against the Lombard princes. One result of this Frankish-Papal alliance was the Donation of Pepin in 756 (Chapter 3). The Donation was renewed by Charlemagne in 774, thus assuring the Papacy's claim to the block of territories roughly consisting of the old Byzantine exarchate of Ravenna.

These lands, cutting across central Italy, were thereafter known as the Papal States. The origins of Papal temporal power date from this period.

The Popes were well aware that the Donation was legally insufficient to give them the right to exercise full authority over the exarchate. Therefore, in the years *c.*780 to *c.*800—some scholars would say several decades earlier—a forged document appeared in Rome to legitimize the Papal position. This document, known as the "Donation of Constantine," is the most famous forgery in history. It stated that the Emperor Constantine, grateful to Pope Sylvester I for curing him of leprosy (he suffered from no such disease), turned over to the Pope's authority Rome, Illyricum (the Balkan peninsula), south Gaul, and the islands around Italy—almost the entire Western half of the Roman Empire. The document thus provided a convenient juridical basis for the Pope's claim to the exarchate. Whatever the Popes may have envisioned regarding a further increase of their temporal power, however, their aspirations were short-lived. For Pepin's son Charlemagne assumed the title of king of the Lombards and, despite Papal temporal claims, incorporated into his empire all of Italy north of and including Rome.

Except for its triumph in gaining the old exarchate, the Papacy after the high point of Gregory's pontificate was caught up in the political and social disorders of the period and could not control affairs in Rome itself, let alone in the outlying churches of Europe. For a time the Papacy was so dependent on the support of Charlemagne that it was even obliged to shut its eyes to his inclination toward iconoclasm. During the grave disorders of the ninth and tenth centuries when the institutions of feudalism began to emerge, the Church, under the pressure of economic and political necessity, differed little from other great landowners of Europe in its adoption of feudal practices. The Church's land as well as its organization was thus little by little caught up in the developing feudal network, and finally, by the end of the tenth and first half of the eleventh century, there was grave danger that the Church and even the Papacy would fall totally under the domination of secular feudal lords.

From Carolingian times laymen, in return for special payments, held and disposed of great blocks of ecclesiastical land. In this period it was quite acceptable for a layman, when founding (as often happened) a church or an abbey, to reserve for himself the right to approve the appointment of bishops or abbots. To head such bishoprics or abbeys, relatives or friends were frequently appointed who, more often than not, were completely unworthy of such office. Some bishops and abbots (especially in Germany), without reference to Rome, were able to gain for themselves the position of feudal lord with "governmental" control over great ecclesiastical territories that they could pass on to their heirs, much in the same manner as the secular lords. Such a procedure was directly contrary to the canon law of the Western Church, which prescribed (unlike the early Church and the Eastern Orthodox Church) celibacy for *all* clergy. In the tenth century it was not uncommon for the clergy to get around the injunction of celibacy by taking concubines, unmarried women with whom they had sexual relations. (Children of such unions had no *legal* status as heirs.) Also widespread was the practice of buying and selling Church offices—bishoprics, abbacies, and so on. This was termed *simony* after the sin of Simon Magus, who, according to the Acts of the Apostles, had attempted to buy St. Peter's powers of conferring the gift of the Holy Spirit by the laying on of hands.

But before I condemn the Western Church too harshly, its morality should be judged in the context of the total ethic of the period. Indeed, in this age of widespread corruption the churchmen were generally not so bad as the laymen; the trouble was that society expected more of them.

The increasing localization and difficulties of communications with Rome made the bishops of Western Europe more and more self-dependent. Thus, they fell increasingly under the influence of tyrannical local lords—often helplessly so. What the Church could have used but could not get was support from the Papacy. At the same time, certain higher archbishops began to try to control the bishops under them without reference to Rome. In an effort to remedy the situation, certain other documents were forged, possibly in Gaul, in the mid-ninth century. These documents are included in what are known as the *Pseudo-Isidorean Decretals*, some of which are genuine. Drawn up to provide legal justification for appeals of local bishops directly to Rome over the heads of the often tyrannical archbishops, these documents at the same time provided a further basis for the theory of Papal control over all Western churches. Indirectly, too, they gave support to the ecclesiastical desire for freedom from lay control. The Decretals purported to show that from the very beginning the Pope had legislated for the whole Church, and that he therefore controlled the Frankish Church.

Pope Nicholas I: The Photian Schism with Byzantium

Pope Nicholas I (858–867) was the first to implement such claims of universal ecclesiastical jurisdiction. Nicholas is an example of how much a powerful personality could exalt the prestige of the Papacy. Accepting the Pseudo-Isidorean Decretals as valid, Nicholas devoted his whole pontificate to an attempt to bring under his effective control all the ecclesiastics of the West. He also sought in certain ways to extend Papal control over laymen and even claimed jurisdiction over the Eastern Church.

Three conflicts stand out during Nicholas' pontificate. In the first of these, involving Photius, the famous patriarch of Constantinople, Nicholas attempted to intervene in the internal affairs of the Eastern Church and thereby give substance to his claim of Papal world jurisdiction. A grave conflict had broken out in the Byzantine Church over who was the rightful patriarch, Ignatius, whom his supporters claimed had been illegally deposed, or Photius, who had earlier been a brilliant teacher of philosophy at the higher school (or "university") of Constantinople. Conflict between supporters of the two men became serious, and finally the adherents of Ignatius appealed to Pope Nicholas for support. The ambitious Nicholas eagerly intervened and, after an exchange of caustic letters, proceeded to excommunicate Photius. Photius responded similarly. Photius then drew up a list of charges against the Roman Church concerned mainly with certain innovations instituted among the Bulgars by German missionaries sent by Nicholas. The most important of these accusations was that the Papacy had changed the meaning of the creed as it had originally been pronounced at the Councils of Nicaea and Constantinople by adding to it (in the Latin text) the phrase *filioque,* meaning that the Holy Spirit, the third person of the Trinity, proceeds from the Father *and from the Son.** The difference, though today considered far less important by theologians, was to become the greatest doctrinal stumbling block between the Greek and Roman Catholic churches.

An important point all too frequently overlooked is that the rivalry between Photius and Nicholas can be understood fully only in the broader context of the rivalry between the Papacy and Constantinople for conversion of the Bulgars, a newly emerging Balkan people. For the Papacy the conversion of the Bulgars was a matter of further disseminating its influence over a barbaric people, but for the Byzantines conversion and control of the Bulgars were absolutely essential, situated as the Bulgars then were in Thrace, on the very doorstep of Constantinople. In this conflict, though the Bulgar ruler reversed his allegiance more than once, the Byzantines finally prevailed. Like most of the Slavic peoples, the Bulgars (originally a Turkic people) thus accepted Christianity from the Greeks instead of from Rome (see Chapter 12).

The so-called Photian schism, the result of mutual excommunications, was healed a short time later. (Contrary to what many scholars have until recently understood, no second papal excommunication was launched against Photius.†) But the basic issues of the *filioque* and of Papal claims to jurisdiction over the East remained unresolved. Because Photius launched the charge of heresy against the Roman Church, Rome has for centuries considered him the archheretic responsible for the schism that later developed between the two churches. For the Greeks, on the other hand, Photius is a kind of Byzantine national hero, the champion of the independence of the Greek Church from the claims of the Papacy to rule the entire Church.

A second problem during Nicholas' reign was his claim to be moral ar-

---

* The addition of the *filioque* to the creed, first introduced by a council of Spanish bishops in the sixth century in an effort to root out Arianism from among the Spanish Visigoths, was only in the twelfth century officially accepted by the Papacy as valid dogma.

† This is important because the two churches were thus in communion when the schism of 1054 occurred. See Chapter 9.

biter over kings. Excommunicating King Lothair of Lorraine, Nicholas forced that monarch to take back his lawful wife whom he had discarded for his mistress. By using the weapon of excommunication to enforce the claims of morality over the highborn, the Pope thus further strengthened the precedent set earlier by St. Ambrose that even a monarch, as a Christian, is subject to ecclesiastical judgment.

In a third conflict Nicholas successfully (if temporarily) asserted the papal claim to rule all the Western bishops. The powerful Archbishop Hincmar of Reims had severely disciplined a Frankish bishop, who then appealed to Rome. In pronouncing that only the Pope could condemn a bishop, Nicholas cited in support of papal authority the Pseudo-Isidorean Decretals. Hincmar had his doubts about the authenticity of the Decretals. Insisting that he had never before heard of them and calling them "a mousetrap to catch the unwary bishop," he nevertheless yielded.

The "Pornocracy"

Between the pontificates of Gregory the Great and Gregory VII (1073–1084), the reign of Pope Nicholas I may be considered the high point. Soon after Nicholas' death in 867 the Papacy, together with the Western Church in general, plunged into the worst anarchy and corruption it was ever to experience. The Arabic invasions disrupted Italian life. The Church fell increasingly under the domination of the lay lords. The Papacy itself, with the strong hand of Charlemagne removed from Rome, became involved in the sordid local politics of the city. Morally the Papacy became very corrupt. The body of one Pope, Formosus, was exhumed, tried by his opponents for his "crimes," convicted, and then dumped into the Tiber. Eight Popes reigned in eight years, and two women, mistresses of virtually all, controlled the Papacy. Finally Alberic, son of one of these women, became ruler of Rome. Because of the corrupt conditions, this period, extending over the late ninth and the first part of the tenth century, has been called by modern historians the "Pornocracy" (rule of the whores).

With the almost complete degradation of the Papacy in Rome, the clergy in the various Western areas were now on their own, lacking papal support or direction. Many ecclesiastics were forced to raise armies to protect themselves, and much Church property was secularized. Naturally, as the clerics became increasingly involved in the feudal network, they neglected their spiritual duties. Conditions became worse and worse. But hope for the Church was sustained in one of its institutions—the monastery. A few of the monasteries—although their estates, too, were the object of secular cupidity—maintained a high morality and were thus able to escape the worst evils of lay control. It was in the monasteries during the tenth century that a reform movement was prepared that would ultimately save both Western Church and Papacy from complete submergence in the feudal system.

FOR FURTHER READING

Bloch, M., *Feudal Society,* trans. L. A. Manyon, 2 vols.* (1961). The masterwork on feudalism, especially of the French type, from the viewpoint of its effect on all segments of society.

Boissonade, P., *Life and Work in Medieval Europe: The Evolution of the Medieval Economy from the Fifth to the Fifteenth Century,* trans. E. Power (1927; 1964). Emphasizes the social history of the West.

Cheyette, F., ed., *Lordship and Community in Medieval Europe* (1968). Acute analysis of institutions.

Coulton, G. G., *Medieval Village, Manor and Monastery** (1960). Focuses on England.

Duby, G., *Rural Economy and Country Life in the Medieval West* (1968). Important work.

Dvornik, F., *The Photian Schism: History and Legend* (1970). A very important, revolutionary work, putting the schism between Patriarch Photius and Pope Nicholas I in proper historical perspective and "rehabilitating" Photius for the West.

Ganshof, F. L., *Feudalism,* trans. Philip Grierson, 2nd English ed.* (1961). A study focusing on the legal aspects of feudalism.

Kempf, F., Beck, H., Ewig, E., *The Church in the Age of Feudalism,* in *Handbook of Church History,* trans. A. Biggs (New York, 1970). Fine chapter in a collaborative work.

Lopez, R. S., *The Tenth Century: How Dark the Dark Ages?** (1959). Source problems on the Dark Ages by a distinguished specialist.

Neilson, N., *Medieval Agrarian Economy* (1936). An excellent introduction to the subject of manorialism.

Painter, S., *Mediaeval Society** (1951). A good, brief introduction.

Seignobos, C., *The Feudal Regime* (1902). A standard work.

Stephenson, C., *Mediaeval Feudalism** (1967). A very clear introductory treatment.

Wallace-Hadrill, J. M., *The Barbarian West: The Early Middle Ages, A.D. 400– 1000 * (1952; 1962). Standard, brief work on the period.

* Asterisk indicates paperback edition available.

In the last three chapters I have concentrated to a great extent on the Western, Latin-speaking segment of the old Roman Empire. The history of the Eastern, also Christian portion of that empire—which has been very much neglected until recently by Western historians—constituted what we call the Byzantine Empire. This, too, was a successor civilization to Rome; and it derived its cultural uniqueness from and was centered in the Greek East. When the West fell to the Germans in the fifth century, Byzantium continued to exist for almost a thousand years more, until 1453 when its nerve center and capital city, Constantinople, was finally taken by the Turks. This "Eastern" Roman Empire was not, however, merely carrying on the history and traditions of old Rome. For, although some historians, especially Gibbon and Voltaire during the Enlightenment, considered Byzantium to be hardly more than a "fossilization of an-

CHAPTER 5

Eastern Christendom and the Islamic World

tiquity," modern research has shown and continues to show that Byzantium made many valuable contributions to European culture. Indeed, for some six centuries, from about 500 to 1050, it was the only civilization in Christendom really worthy of the name.

The Byzantine World

Christian Civilization in the Greek East

Byzantium served as a buffer for the West against repeated waves of invaders from the East—Huns, Avars, Persians, Arabs, Bulgars, Mongols, and Turks—thus giving backward Western Europe a chance to revive from the low state of civilization to which it had sunk after the Germanic and Viking invasions. It also performed the extremely valuable service of preserving ancient Greek learning, the fountainhead of Western philosophy, literature, and art. Moreover, as is only now being fully realized, it made some significant and original cultural contributions of its own. These contributions—in art and architecture, in forms of Christian worship and theology, in law and statecraft, in industry and refinements of living—together with Greek culture preserved from antiquity, reflected a refined, sophisticated civilization which is very much worth studying both for itself and for its influences upon other cultures.

Virtually all of Byzantium's achievements eventually benefited the West, introduced either by Greeks themselves or by Western travelers returning from Constantinople. As Étienne Gilson, the leading modern scholar of medieval Western thought, has said, the Latin West revived philosophically only when it once again came into contact, either through the Arabs or Byzantines, with the ideas of ancient Greek philosophy. No less important was the Byzantine role in Christianizing and civilizing the Slavic peoples. For in the medieval period the Slavs (the eastern ones at least) moved primarily in the orbit of Byzantium, being influenced to a far lesser degree by Latin Christendom. Thus, for example, the greatest influence on the early civilization of Russia up to the sixteenth century is generally recognized to have been Byzantium (see Chapter 12).

Tensions Between East and West

As the medieval period progressed, Eastern and Western Christendom, though originally parts of the undivided Roman Empire, tended to draw farther and farther apart. Indeed, by the late ninth century, and certainly after the early crusades of the late eleventh and twelfth centuries, the Greek East and the Latin West had become virtually two different worlds. Of course no iron

Ivory plaque of the Byzantine Emperor Anastasius (sixth century). He is depicted as Champion of the Faith. (Cliché des Musées Nationaux, Paris)

curtain as such separated them: pilgrims, merchants, or scholars frequently crossed from one area to the other. But the customs, the political systems, and, more important, the religious traditions and standards of living had become so disparate that already in the late tenth century a citizen of Paris and a citizen of Constantinople could think of the other as completely alien. Vivid evidence of these differences (and also of rivalry over claim to the title of "Roman" emperor) is in the vituperative report of Bishop Liudprand of Cremona, written just after his return in 969 from an unsuccessful mission to Constantinople as envoy of Emperor Otto I of Germany. As he wrote to Otto:

> ... After a miserable reception ... we were given the most miserable and disgusting quarters. The palace where we were confined was certainly large and open, but it neither kept out the cold nor afforded shelter from heat.... To add to our troubles the Greek wine we found undrinkable because of the mixture in it of pitch, resin, and plaster.... I was brought before the Emperor's brother Leo ... and there we tired ourselves with a fierce argument over your imperial title. He called you not emperor, which is Basileus in his tongue, but insultingly Rex, which is king in his.

Liudprand was so incensed at his treatment that before he left Constantinople he scrawled on the walls of his quarters the following words, exaggerated to be sure but even more revealing of the growing anti-Greek attitude of many Westerners:

> Trust not the Greeks; they live but to betray;
> Nor heed their promises, whate'er they say.
> If lies will serve them, any oath they swear,
> And when it's time to break it feel no fear.

Part of this growing estrangement between East and West was the result of the religious schism that developed between the Roman and Orthodox churches. But the schism itself was symptomatic of differences that were perhaps even more deep-seated. I should emphasize here again, as I did at the start of this discussion of medieval history, not only the political problem of the two "Roman" emperors that began with Charlemagne in 800, but the different components of culture in East and West. In the Latin West the fusion of the Germanic element with what remained of Latin classical culture contrasted with the synthesis in the East, where the Oriental ethos was grafted onto ancient Greek or, more accurately, Hellenistic culture and the Roman legal and administrative tradition.

Moreover, the Orthodox Church was usually more mystical in its approach to Christianity than the Western, which was characterized by a more legalistic, sometimes more pragmatic, approach to Christianity and hence a more rigidly worked-out administrative system in the Church. It is perhaps significant that the chief Eastern holy day, at least in the later period, was Easter, celebrating the Crucifixion and the miraculous Resurrection of Christ, while in the West, Christmas, the birth of the Christ child, came to be more emphasized.

In the East, Greek rather than Latin was the common language, at least of all the educated classes. To be sure, some Roman titles were preserved in the Byzantine court, but even the vaunted Roman law which Justinian had forbidden to be translated from Latin began to be translated into Greek in the last half of the sixth century. In the West, Latin was the common tongue of clerics and whatever educated laymen remained; Greek, on the other hand, was almost completely forgotten. Thus by the sixth or seventh century citizens of East and West, with rare exceptions, literally could no longer understand one another.

Finally, until the late Middle Ages citizens of Constantinople had materially and intellectually a higher—usually much higher—standard of living than their counterparts in the West. This inevitably caused considerable jealousy and resentment.

Constantinople

I have noted the origins of the new capital Constantinople, named after its founder Constantine who established it on the site of a much older Greek city, Byzantium. Constantinople had perhaps the most strategically advantageous location of any city in the medieval world. Situated on a little strip of land, surrounded by water on three sides and by a massive triple land wall with 192 towers (eventually), Constantinople was virtually impregnable. Its situation commanded the bridge between Europe and Asia; land and water routes from the Danube, Black Sea, Asia Minor, and Aegean Sea converged there, making it an admirable location for trade. Already in the early Middle Ages it had become the world's most important emporium. For the Greeks of that entire period, and even today, it was known as "the City" (the modern Turkish name Istanbul is probably a corruption of the Greek words "to the city"), while for the Slavs of Russia and the Balkans it was Tsargrad, the city of the emperor. It may be said without exaggeration that for at least 700 years, from the fourth to the eleventh or twelfth centuries, Constantinople was the real capital of all Christendom, probably the most powerful state in the world politically, economically, and at times militarily. After the twelfth century, and until the fourteenth and even the fifteenth century, it continued to be an important cultural center. In fact, the Byzantine émigrés scholars who fled to the West before and after Constantinople fell to the Turks in 1453 played a primary role in furthering the great cultural movement of the Renaissance (see Chapter 14).

Earlier I discussed the reigns of Constantine and his sons, then of Julian the Apostate, Jovian, and Theodosius the Great; the latter helped solve the German problem and brought about the definitive triumph of Christianity. Although Odovacar's deposition of the boy-emperor Romulus Augustulus in 476 technically brought the Roman Empire in the West to an end, this fact seems to have struck few in the West as of any particular political importance at the time. Zeno continued to rule from Constantinople as the emperor of what the Byzantines considered the one undivided Roman Empire.

Nevertheless, after the reign of Justinian (527–565), and with certain exceptions, Byzantium and the West pursued more or less separate courses until the beginning of the crusades in 1095. Westerners then began to converge upon Byzantium and Islam, and from then on their history must be treated together, showing the interaction of the three worlds of East and West. But first it is important to examine the Byzantine state and its culture during the reign of the great Emperor Justinian, a high point in the early history of Byzantium and one which was in many ways characteristic of the entire Byzantine development.

The Reign of Justinian

In the early sixth century the Byzantine Emperor Justinian made a persistent and in some ways successful attempt to reconquer the Western areas of the old empire. It was a Byzantine principle never legally to recognize territorial losses, for the "sacred" empire had been bestowed on the emperor by God and therefore could not be alienated. This principle is demonstrated by the grant of honorific titles to many of the German kings. So when the Greek East became stronger and richer after the basic financial and monetary reforms of Emperor Anastasius (491–518)—he fixed the ratio of copper to silver to gold—one of his successors, the ambitious Justinian, decided to reconquer the West.

Justinian, like all Byzantine emperors, was considered the king of kings (*Basileus*)*, the sole ruler of the world (*Autocrator*), the vicegerent of God. He was the absolute ruler of the state and, so at least it seemed to a Westerner, of the Church as well, though occasionally in the early and more often in the later centuries, the patriarch was able to put up an effective opposition to the emperor's claim to control over spiritual matters. Nevertheless, the emperor should not be considered purely a secular ruler but a kind of semi-priestly figure as well, who drew his power directly from God and was able to perform certain functions reserved only to the priesthood. For instance, he could preach in church during religious services, cense the congregation, and even take communion from the cup with his own hands. But he could not on his own alter ecclesiastical dogma (only an Ecumenical Council could do that) or administer the sacraments. His authority over the Byzantine church was not then "Caesaropapistic" (total) as many scholars used to affirm.

Justinian, a controversial figure to historians (though undoubtedly one of the greatest of Byzantine emperors), insisted, in accordance with a tradition that prevailed throughout the Middle Ages, on the religious unity, the "orthodoxy," of his empire. Hence his expedition against the West may in a sense be considered a kind of crusade against the heretical Arian Germans. In fact, some Western Catholic Christians, including the Pope, had already sought the aid of the Roman emperor in Constantinople against the Germans.

At his accession Justinian's empire consisted of Illyricum (the Balkan peninsula), Asia Minor, Egypt, Syria, and Armenia. Egypt and Syria were still rich provinces, with the Greek-speaking cities of Alexandria and Antioch as capitals, while Asia Minor grew to constitute the heartland of the Byzantine Empire, dotted as it was with Greek cities celebrated from biblical and patristic times such as Ephesus, Smyrna, Philadelphia, Tarsus, and Nicaea. No Turks were then in Asia Minor; they did not arrive until the mid-eleventh century. Nor were there as yet Arabs in Egypt or Syria.

* The title was not formally adopted until the Emperor Heraclius assumed it in the early seventh century after the Byzantine defeat of the Persian Empire.

Celebrated Byzantine mosaic of Emperor Justinian and his court in the Basilica of San Vitale, Ravenna. There is a purposeful lack of perspective and frontal positioning of the figures, in order to give the impression of the after-life in heaven.
(Alinari/Scala)

Reconquest of the West

Under the generals Belisarius and Narses, Justinian's troops waged several wars against the Germans in what was to be the last effort to reunify the Mediterranean lands of old Rome. The Byzantine armies reconquered North Africa from the Vandals, Italy from the Ostrogoths, and southern Spain from the Visigoths. All these wars were long and extremely costly, and Justinian's strong focus on the West permitted the Persians, Byzantium's most deadly enemies, to advance on Asia Minor, Egypt, and Syria. Meanwhile, on the Danube frontier, invasions of a Turkic people, the Avars, and of a people new to the Romans, the Slavs, took place, though Slavic tribes in larger numbers did not enter the Balkans until a century or two later (see Chapter 12).

What permitted the Byzantines to reconquer such distant areas as Vandal Africa and southern Spain was the superb organization of the Byzantine army, partly a carry-over from old Rome. The science of tactics was well developed by the Byzantines; formal texts on strategy later were written by emperors themselves; and a sense of command and discipline was strongly inculcated. Unlike most Western armies of the medieval period, the Byzantines had very efficient supply lines and auxiliary services such as corps of engineers, ambulances, stretcher bearers, and doctors. The navy too was a potent weapon; from the eighth century on it even possessed a secret weapon in the famous Greek fire, a combustible mixture fired from copper tubes that would burn even on water.

The catholic population in Carthage, the North African capital, welcomed Belisarius' army joyfully, and fortresses were built nearby to protect catholic Africa. Except for the westernmost part, North Africa was held by Constantinople for some two hundred years, after which it fell to the Arabs. The Byzantine armies could take only a part of Spain, the southeast part around Cordova; however, later this also fell to the Arabs.

The conquest of Ostrogothic Italy was more interesting and important. Under Theodoric the Ostrogothic kingdom had been strong and prosperous, but his successors were not of his stripe. Nevertheless, it took Justinian's troops twenty years—in a war costly and destructive to the economy of Italy and Byzantium as well—to destroy Ostrogothic power. The extensive devastation eased the advance of the Lombards when they began to descend into Italy from the northeast in 568. The Italian lower classes (not the ecclesiastics and great secular landlords) favored the Goths, who had in general pursued a tolerant, liberal policy from both social and religious points of view.

After the first Byzantine commander, Belisarius, was recalled on charges of treason, the eunuch general Narses was dispatched to Italy. The Ostrogoths finally succumbed under the hard blows inflicted by Narses and then virtually disappeared from history. Under Narses the great cities—Rome (where the Pope still recognized the emperor in Constantinople as his political superior), Naples, Ravenna—were all retaken, with Ravenna now becoming the Byzantine capital in Italy and the seat of the imperial governor.

Once again the Mediterranean was Roman; the empire extended from the Pillars of Hercules (Gibraltar) to the Euphrates in Mesopotamia. Only the provinces of Gaul and Britain in the West remained unconquered by Byzantium.

But Justinian's conquests in the West were accomplished at the price of Persian advances in the East. The Byzantine-Persian rivalry was partly political, partly economic. It involved the trade in silk, precious stones, and spices between the eastern Mediterranean and China and the East Indies. The Persians, situated between the Byzantine eastern possessions and the Far East, cut into much of this trade during the reigns of Justinian and his successors, and under the latter the conflict was more severe than ever. In 540 the Persians sacked the great Byzantine city of Antioch, in Syria. The historian Procopius has accused Justinian of ruining the East in order to satisfy his megalomania for retaking

ΚΑΙΤΟ ΜΕΝ ΡΩΠΙ ΚΟΡΕ ΝΤΩ ΠΛΟΚΟΔΑΡΤΑΧ ωοαμοέ ται · ΚΑΙ ΠΩ χΩρίω προσορ μὴ ἵετου ΤΟΟ βΝεν
ΟΣΩΡ · ΕΚ ΤΕΡ ΤΗ ΚΟΡ ΤΑ ΚΑΙ ΤΡΙΑ Κοοι ωρο οωι ΔΑ ΜΕΡ ΟΝ ΠΛΟί ωΝ · ΠΟΛΕ ΜΙ ΚΩΡ π ΚΑΙ ΤΩ φο ΛΟΝ   οἱ
ΔΕ ΤΟΝ βΑΣΙ ΛΙ ΚΟ ΥΛΟ ΥΚΑΤΑΡ ΧΟΝ ΤΕΣ · Π ΚΡ ΤΟΥ ΠΩ ΡέΠΑΗ σΟΚΟ ΠΤΟΣέ λΔΟΙΝ · ΜΩΚ ΤΟΣέ ΩΙ Πῖ ΠΕΡ ΤΑΙ ΡΑΝ
λο χΩ ΙΩΙ ΤΟΙΣ έ ΡΑΗ ΠΟΙΟ · ΚΑΙ ΤΩ οΑΙ φΝΙ ΖΙ ω ΚΑ ΤΑ Πλη Ξ ΑΜ ΝοΙ · ΠΟΛΛΑΟ ΜΕΝ οΑΝ ΤΑΝ ΔΡΟ Μέ ΟΝ ΡΩ
Π ΩΝΝ ΚΩΝ · Η ΡΑΝ ΔΕ ΚΑΙ ΤΩοΚΛΑΣ Ω ΤΗ Ω ΠΟ ΛΟ ω ΠΠΥ ΡΙ

φΟ ΛΕς ΡΩ ΜΑΗ   ΠΥ Ρ ΠΟΛ   ΤΟΝ ΤΩΝ έ Ν ΗΑΗ ΤῚ φλΟΝ ·

Ω λίχΩΝ ΠΑ ΠΤΗ χΩ οέ ξ ω γχΝΟ μέ Ν ωΝ ΠΟΝ ΤΟΝ Πλο Ιοι · ΚΑΙ Π Τ ΠΡΟΣ ΤΟΝ ΚΟ΄λ ΠΟ ΝΤΟΟ Ν βλΑ Χέ ρ ΝΩ ΚΑ ΤΑΡ ΑΙ ΔΟΣ

A fourteenth-century manuscript illumination depicting Greek fire in action.
The mixture used probably contained saltpeter, sulphur, and naphtha. Greek
fire burned even on contact with water. (Biblioteca National, Madrid)

the West. Whatever the truth may be, these vast campaigns brought a period of
near economic collapse to the Byzantine East at Justinian's death and permitted
the Lombards in the West to take most of Italy (see map, page 133).

Law

There is no disagreement about the significance of Justinian's work
in certain other spheres, especially in legislation. The greatest contribution of
Rome to Western civilization was unquestionably its law. More practical and less
theoretical than the Greeks, the early Romans, when they came into contact
with the Greeks, absorbed more and more of Greek culture and philosophy. In
particular, the precepts of Roman law became leavened by the broader, more
humanitarian outlook of such a philosophy as Stoicism.

By the time of Justinian, the emperor was considered to be the fountainhead, the sole source of Byzantine law. But, unfortunately, the imperial edicts of

his predecessors had fallen into disorder, producing a veritable chaos of codes and interpretations. Justinian appointed a special commission under the lawyer Tribonian to codify the various collections of Roman law. Four great works were published. The first, the *Codex Justinianus,* was a collection of all the imperial edicts; the commission reconciled them if contradictory and eliminated the obsolete. Even more significant was the *Digest,* a collection of the opinions of famous jurists or philosophers of the law. For, as is true today, more important than individual legal decisions is the reasoning, the philosophy, behind them. A handbook, or summary, of law for students, the *Institutes,* and the *Novellae,* the new laws issued in Justinian's reign, completed the commission's undertaking. Scholars of Byzantine history often point out that while the first three codes mentioned were in Latin, the *Novellae* were drawn up in Greek because the people of the empire no longer understood Latin. The empire was becoming "Byzantinized."

The influence of these books of law, together called the *Corpus of Civil Law* (*Corpus Iuris Civilis*), has been profound. Roman legal techniques, combined with the spirit of pagan philosophic equity and the Christian principles of Byzantium, have influenced the law codes of many nations, especially with respect to laws of inheritance, marriage and divorce, manumission of slaves, and above all the principle of the existence of the state as an entity before the law. Roman law, in large part beyond the grasp of most of the medieval West as a result of the German invasions, would begin to be restored only in the eleventh century and later—a long process of revival that was of great importance for Western civilization. Today most of Western Europe, the Balkans, Latin America, even Russia—that is, almost half of the entire world (with certain exceptions, notably Britain and all but Louisiana in the United States)—have as the basis of their legal codes the Roman law of Justinian.

Byzantine Civilization

Religion and the Church

Even more than in Western Christendom, Christianity permeated all aspects of Byzantine life. The Eastern type of religion was a deeply mystical faith that was able to weld together all the diverse aspects of Byzantine culture and provide that culture with its greatest distinctiveness. The unique ethos of Byzantine piety was expressed best in the Eastern liturgy, a vivid ceremonial in which the worshiper could experience a kind of mystical foretaste of the life of the hereafter. This mystical quality of the religion must be clearly understood

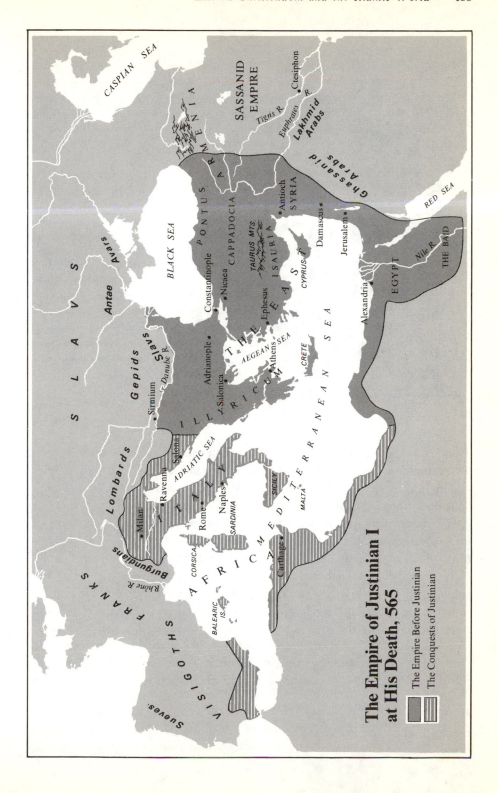

The Empire of Justinian I
at His Death, 565

The Empire Before Justinian
The Conquests of Justinian

*This twelfth-century
manuscript illumination
represents the Church
of the Holy Apostles in
Constantinople, which
contained the imperial
tombs. (Bibliothèque
Nationale, Paris)*

if one is to appreciate the various aspects of Byzantine culture—art and music,
for example—which were all so deeply conditioned by the Orthodox religion.

In Justinian's reign the conflict over Monophysitism—that is, over the relationship of the two natures, divine and human, in Christ—broke out with even
greater force than before (see Chapter 1). Many theological views were expressed earlier, but the solution to the problem was not provided until the statement of the dual nature of Christ in the creed defined at Chalcedon in 451.
Nevertheless, the Monophysites of the East (Egypt, Palestine, and Syria) who
emphasized one rather than two natures in Christ, were not at all satisfied and
continued to insist on the truth of their own doctrine. Declared heretics, they
were persecuted by the state. There is reason to believe that the "nationalist"
tendencies of these various Eastern areas, together with the religious persecution and the domination by "upstart" Constantinople over their earlier established patriarchates of Alexandria and Antioch, played some part in arousing
their fanaticism.

Several of the Byzantine emperors, aware of the danger inherent in this
situation when the Persians and later the Arabs were poised at their borders,
made determined attempts to placate the Monophysites. Justinian, whose own

St. Mark's Basilica in Venice was built by Byzantine workmen in the eleventh century. The famous church of Venice is modeled exactly on the Church of the Holy Apostles in Constantinople. (Bernard G. Silberstein/Rapho Guillumette Pictures)

wife, Empress Theodora, was a Monophysite supporter, tried by every theological means at his disposal, as would his successors (especially the Emperor Heraclius), to find a suitable formula for agreement. Heraclius (610–641) even proposed to by-pass the question of two natures in Christ by substituting one energy or will, a solution that he hoped both sides, Orthodox and Monophysite alike, could agree to. But, like Justinian, Heraclius had also to contend with the intransigent orthodoxy of the Pope. In Rome, far from the eastern Mediterranean, the Pope cared little for Eastern political and military exigencies and could therefore pursue a more or less independent policy. Justinian himself had made several attempts to induce the Popes to accept a solution acceptable to the Monophysites. He personally convoked the Fifth Ecumenical Council at Constantinople in 553, seeking to make changes in the creed (in the process revealing his own near-absolute control over the church). But all was in vain. The emperor might control the formal ecclesiastical machinery, but he could not enforce a compromise in dogma. Neither Monophysites nor Orthodox would give in. Religious tensions as well as oppressive taxation led the Monophysite population in Syria, Egypt, and Palestine even to welcome the Persians and later the more tolerant Arabic invaders, whom the Monophysites often preferred to what they called the "heretic" Orthodox Greeks.

Byzantine Commerce and Guilds

I have noted that Justinian's reign was characterized by the spread of Byzantine commerce over the entire Mediterranean, now almost entirely under Byzantine control. Most of what Western commerce there was in this period was in the hands of the Syrians, Jews, and Greeks, who brought to the West such prized products of the Byzantine East as silk and linen cloth from Syria, wine from Gaza, papyrus from Egypt, furs from Cappadocia, slaves and salt from the Black Sea area, and from the Far East, spices, precious stones, and Chinese raw silk. Much of this great trade passed through Constantinople, the world's busiest entrepôt.

Under Justinian, as told by a Byzantine chronicler, the Persian stranglehold on the silk trade was finally broken, though in an unexpected way. A monk visiting in China brought back, in a hollow cane, silkworm eggs, and from then on silk was manufactured in Byzantium. But Justinian made it a state monopoly, keeping strict control over the export of raw silk and silk products. Gifts of silken garments or products were often used by the Byzantine emperors as instruments of diplomatic policy when they wished to impress or ingratiate themselves with foreign rulers.

Byzantine commerce was based on the Byzantine gold coin, the *nomisma* (called *bezant* in the West). By the sixth century this had become the standard gold coin of a large part of the world, even to some extent in the Far East. It could be called the dollar of that age; hoards of Byzantine gold coins have been discovered in such distant areas as Scandinavia and even the East Indies. A famous sixth-century Byzantine geographical work, that of Cosmas Indicopleustes (meaning "the traveler around the Indies"), relates that in the Far East it was a standard of exchange.

The Byzantine government taxed all trade coming through Constantinople, and state custom houses dotted the Bosporus and Black Sea regions. In this period, when regular revenues were not available to the Germanic rulers of the West, the Byzantine emperor could depend on a huge income from regular taxation. State monopolies also brought revenue. At first only the palace could manufacture silk, under stringent regulation, with the imperial color red being reserved for the emperor's own garments. Besides silk there was an imperial monopoly on arms and other products. Minute regulations, in fact, controlled all industry and commerce in Constantinople in behalf of the state. Constantinople developed a rather complex guild system with specific provisions governing all aspects of trade, industry, and manufacture. Some of the regulations, such as those against bad merchandising, cornering the market, and so on, sound very much like the later Western guild regulations. It is likely, though of course similar needs may have led to similar developments, that some inspiration from the Byzantine system may have influenced the West (see Chapter 6).

Byzantine Administration

State control over many aspects of life—corporatism one might call it —was more or less typical in Byzantium's long history. This kind of control was necessary if the state were to survive, for Byzantium was constantly in danger, perpetually threatened by external enemies from almost every side. In times of repeated crises it was necessary that the emperor, as absolute ruler, be able to draw immediately upon all the energies and resources of the state.

A remarkably developed civil service aided the emperor in administration. This group of officials, trained primarily at the "University," or rather "higher school," of Constantinople,* was organized in a hierarchical arrangement with intersecting competencies much like our present-day civil service. As is also true today, the government became plagued by excessive bureaucracy, but on the whole it functioned very well. Taxes were collected regularly, justice was administered, armies were raised and put into the field, and the functions of the state adequately carried out. In its period of great power the Byzantine government, despite all its faults—its excessive love of pomp and protocol, its bureaucratic tendency, and its frequent venality—functioned more effectively for a longer period of time, from the administrative reforms of Diocletian and Constantine in the early fourth century to the Byzantine apogee in the mid-eleventh, than any other state in history. From the economic viewpoint, also, historians generally agree that Byzantium's record of non-depreciation of gold coin for some six centuries surpasses the record of any other coinage in the annals of history.

A further word about Byzantine administration. The empire itself was reorganized beginning with Heraclius in the early seventh century. Altering the Diocletianic-Constantinian framework, he established new divisions (called "themes") for the provinces, especially in Asia Minor. Each theme was put under a military governor who could act immediately, when called upon by the emperor, to thwart an invader. And indeed Asia Minor was repeatedly invaded —in the sixth century by the Persians, in the eighth to the tenth repeatedly by the Arabs, who several times besieged Constantinople itself—and from the late eleventh to 1453 by the Seljuk and Ottoman Turks.

---

* Our modern Western universities and their institutions are descended from the medieval Western rather than the Byzantine "higher schools."

Society

Unlike the feudal Western world, Byzantine society lived under the rule of public law, where the emperor as head of the state could make law as he saw fit. To be sure, in the early period he had at least technically consulted the Senate (a body of men who held or had held administrative offices) but in reality his will remained law. Theoretically the throne was elective, but in practice it gradually became dynastic, with certain families for generations occupying it through heredity. Medieval Western society came, certainly by the twelfth century, to be characterized by a more or less rigid class system in which one not born a noble found it impossible to become one. In Byzantium, however, despite its own class structure, it was not too difficult to move from one social group to another. Basil I, the great ninth-century emperor, was originally a stable boy who had found favor with his predecessor and later managed to attain the throne itself.

Besides a noble class, Byzantium also had a large commercially employed middle class and, of course, many peasants in the countryside. All Byzantines were, at least theoretically, required to belong to one church, sharing the common faith and the common Greek language and culture. Many peoples aside from Greeks—Armenians, Bulgars, Georgians, Syrians, Egyptians, Jews—lived at various times within the empire, and it is therefore somewhat misleading to speak of a Byzantine "nationality" as such. But there is no doubt that all these peoples (with the exception of the Jews and heretics) had a strong allegiance to "Romania," as they called their state, and to the Orthodox faith. Over both state and religion, as head of the government and protector of the faith, ruled their emperor, the representative of God.

Art and Literature

In the history of Byzantine art the reign of Justinian is often referred to as the "First Golden Age." Today Byzantine art is recognized as one of the supreme creations of the aesthetic spirit. It is much in vogue not only because of its richness of color and subtlety of line, but also because of its idealized, semi-representational character. Rather than attempting simply to reproduce nature photographically, it sought to express the inner, more mystical feeling of the other world. This is well exemplified by the Byzantine mosaics at Ravenna, executed during and before Justinian's reign, or even more so by those of Hagia Sophia in Constantinople, done throughout the centuries. These mosaics were composed of small pieces of glass or stone, set together at various angles in order to refract the light and produce a depth of expression similar to the effect of stained-glass windows in Gothic cathedrals. As will later be noted, the theory has been put forth that Western stained-glass was preceded in time by the work of Byzantine window glaziers and that Western stained-glass therefore was influenced by the latter.

In architecture Justinian's greatest contribution was the cathedral of Hagia Sophia (the Church of Holy Wisdom, that is, Christ), perhaps the most impressive, though not the largest, Christian church ever built. In its construction the architects Anthemius of Tralles and Isidorus of Miletus, through the use of the device known as pendentives, solved for the first time the difficult engineering problem of how to place a large dome over a square surface. The cathedral is of unparalleled magnificence; Justinian, like other medieval rulers, despoiled the marble of ancient temples to enrich it. When the church was completed in 539 Justinian is quoted as saying: "Solomon, I have surpassed thee!"

There are many medieval testimonials to the impressiveness of Hagia Sophia. One of the most striking is provided by the so-called Russian *Primary Chronicle,* which states that when emissaries of the Kievan Prince Vladimir in the late tenth century were contemplating which religion to adopt, their presence at a liturgical ceremony in Hagia Sophia persuaded them to become Orthodox. They exclaimed, "we knew not whether we were in heaven or on earth; for on earth there is no such splendor or such beauty.... We only know that God dwells there among men...."

The supreme masterpiece of Byzantine architecture was the cathedral in Constantinople of St. Sophia. Built by Emperor Justinian in the sixth century, its interior was incomparably impressive with its mosaics, marbles, and especially the great dome that appeared to be "suspended from heaven." (Marburg-Art Reference Bureau)

Under Justinian and his successors the art of historical writing, carried on in imitation of the ancient Greeks Herodotus and Thucydides, continued in Byzantium. Byzantium's entire thousand-year history is in fact illuminated by historical works, some of the first rank. This is again an example of the cultural tradition the Byzantines carried on from ancient Greek and Hellenistic times. But the Byzantines were so enamored of the literary accomplishments of their ancient forebears that they usually contented themselves with merely imitating them, sometimes servilely, permitting little literary creativity. (The remarkable religious hymns, among the most original of Byzantine creations, are an exception, as is the epic poem *Digenes Akritas* of the tenth century, which may be compared to the *Chanson de Roland* of the West.) What impeded, often even stultified Byzantine literary creativity was that the Greek normally used for literary writing was an imitation of the Hellenistic Greek form, while the Greek spoken by the ordinary Byzantine citizen was something rather different, simpler and more like the Koine of the New Testament. One scholar, perhaps with exaggeration, has compared a Byzantine attempting to write the artificial literary Greek to an American seeking to write in the Chaucerian idiom of fourteenth-century England. But, on the other hand, this problem facing Byzantine scholars was probably little more difficult than that facing a Western scholar in the Renaissance trying to write in the "learned" Latin, not in his own vernacular tongue.

The Four Periods of Byzantine History to 1095

Byzantine history, as I have pointed out, extended for more than a thousand years. For the sake of convenience, its development up to the First Crusade in 1095 may be divided into four periods. The first extends from the foundation of Constantinople in 330 to the accession of Leo III in 717. In this period, after the troubles with the Arian heresy and the Germans, there took place the Monophysitic struggle and the conflict with the Persians, resulting in the loss of the rich Eastern provinces of Syria and Egypt, first to the Persians and ultimately to the Arabs. In the next period, 717 to 867, the primary preoccupation of the emperors was the grave Arab danger. After many vicissitudes this threat was finally contained, but only at great cost and sacrifice. Meanwhile, the Bulgars were converted to Orthodoxy and a great conflict (iconoclasm) took place over the problem of images. In the third period, from 867 to about 1025, the Byzantine Empire reached its height. Gathering its forces, it was now able to carry the offensive to the Arabs, in the process recovering much territory in the East and becoming even more powerful politically and economically. At the same time the Slavs of the Balkans, Russia, and other areas were converted and brought into the Byzantine orbit, if not always into the empire itself.

In the fourth period, from 1025 to 1095, many important events took place:

altercations with the Papacy and Holy Roman Empire in the West; the advance of the Normans and their conquest of Byzantine southern Italy; depreciation of the Byzantine gold coin for the first time in six hundred years; invasions by the Turkish Pechenegs; and, worst of all, the entrance of the Seljuk Turks into eastern Asia Minor, climaxed by their victory at the battle of Manzikert in 1071.

During the period from 1025 to 1095 Byzantine power declined, slowly at first, culminating in the near collapse of the empire in the last quarter of the eleventh century. It is difficult to determine all the reasons for its decline, but it was partly owing to the internal decay of state authority and the emergence to power of the great landowners. As I have emphasized, in contrast to the West a key element in Byzantium's great strength was the centralization of the power of the state in the emperor. The growth of local authority on the part of the Byzantine nobles, a kind of incipient "feudalism" that tended in some areas to loosen the ties between the central government and the provinces, in the long run fatally weakened the authority of the state (see Chapter 12).

Byzantium Versus Persians and Arabs

To return to events after the death of Justinian in 565, the empire was then almost bankrupt and lay open to the advance of the Persians. Approaching through Asia Minor, they besieged Constantinople itself. But when Emperor Heraclius came to the throne in 610 he was able to marshal Byzantine strength, then to mount a counteroffensive in the seesaw struggle with the Persians. At one point Constantinople had to oppose a Persian fleet on the Asiatic side and at the same time beat off a great army of Slavs and Avars from the European shore. But the threat was averted, the Byzantines believed, by the miraculous aid of the Virgin, their divine protectress, acting through the instrumentality of her holy icon, the Hodegetria. (See p. 395.)

The able Heraclius recaptured all the eastern provinces lost to the Persians; before he died, however, a new and far greater danger erupted from Arabia. Indeed, in the incredibly short period of a few years all the eastern provinces as well as North Africa, Crete, Cyprus, and Rhodes were taken by the Arabs. It looked almost as if they would conquer all of Europe. In the early eighth century their victorious advance was checked in the West at Tours (732) by the Frank Charles Martel, and in an even more decisive encounter, in the Byzantine East (717) by Emperor Leo III with the aid of the new secret weapon, Greek fire.

During this time of Persian and Arab incursions in the first historical period the empire was reorganized. Martial law was established; military commanders were given joint military and civil authority, especially in Asia Minor where the provinces were given the new name of "theme," a word probably derived from the term referring to the military unit stationed there. In this period, in order to increase revenues the old taxation system of Byzantium, originally established by Diocletian and Constantine, was overhauled. Heavy, sometimes crushing, taxes were levied on the peasant villages, and if a villager could not pay his tax it was decreed that his neighbors would have to contribute. This naturally produced many complaints and a good deal of social discontent.

Iconoclasm

During the second period, that of the Arab danger, the celebrated iconoclastic conflict broke out. This resulted originally from an order of the Emperor Leo III in 726 that all holy images (icons) of Christ, the Virgin, and the saints in the empire should be destroyed. The reasons for his order are not entirely clear, though it is certain that many of the more ignorant Byzantines were in effect worshiping the images rather than simply showing them appropriate Christian reverence. To almost all Byzantines (and the Western church as well), veneration of the icons was an important aspect of their religious life, one deeply rooted in church tradition and popular piety. As a result a storm of opposition was raised, especially in Italy by the Pope, and in Greece proper. Monks, the special guardians of the faith, were severely persecuted by the emperor, and finally, after the whole empire had been convulsed, the images were restored by two women: first in 787 by the Empress Irene at the Seventh Ecumenical Council, and then in 843 by the Empress Theodora in a ceremony still commemorated annually by the Greek Church as the "Feast of Orthodoxy."

The conflict left its scars, however, for in the course of it the Pope excommunicated the Byzantine Emperor Leo III. Leo in turn removed from Papal authority the provinces of south Italy, Sicily, and Illyricum, which he proceeded to hand over to the jurisdiction of the Constantinopolitan patriarch. The Popes never forgave the emperor for this Act. A veritable revolution broke out in Italy as a result of the iconoclastic persecution, which at least in part led the Popes, as I have shown, to turn away from Byzantium (the emperor was still the Popes' superior, politically) to a new protector in the West, the Franks.

Apogee of Byzantine Power

Meantime, in the early part of the third phase of its history before 1095, from 867 to 1025, Byzantium was able to recover its strength and to take the offensive against the Arabs. The Byzantines penetrated almost as far as Jerusalem, even annexing Armenia, which had acted hitherto as a buffer state between Byzantines and Arabs. Under the imperial governor the Byzantines in Italy attacked (unsuccessfully) the Arabs of Sicily, who, in 826, had taken that strategic island. At the same time the Byzantines exerted a certain control over the small Lombard states of south and central Italy. In southern Italy, however,

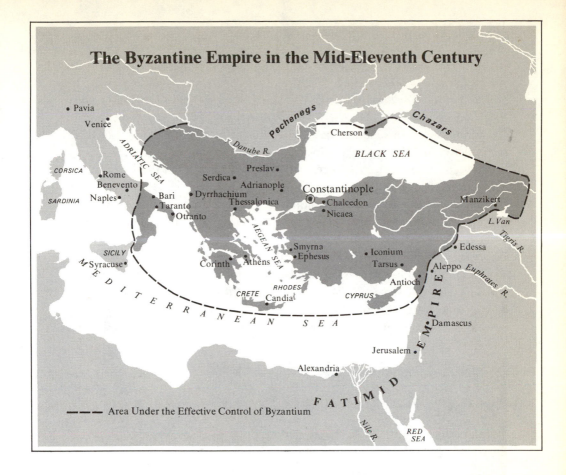

The Byzantine Empire in the Mid-Eleventh Century

Map labels: Pavia, Venice, CORSICA, Rome, Benevento, SARDINIA, Naples, Bari, Taranto, Otranto, ADRIATIC SEA, Danube R., Pechenegs, Serdica, Preslav, Adrianople, Dyrrhachium, Thessalonica, Constantinople, Chalcedon, Nicaea, Cherson, BLACK SEA, Chazars, Manzikert, L. Van, Tigris R., SICILY, Syracuse, Corinth, Athens, AEGEAN SEA, Smyrna, Ephesus, Iconium, Tarsus, Antioch, Edessa, Aleppo, Euphrates R., EMPIRE, CRETE, Candia, RHODES, CYPRUS, MEDITERRANEAN SEA, Damascus, Jerusalem, Alexandria, FATIMID, Nile R., RED SEA

– – – Area Under the Effective Control of Byzantium

they not only consolidated their own control, but instituted an administrative reform, organizing Calabria and Apulia into the "theme" of Langobardia under a Byzantine *strategos*. In this third period, 867 to 1025, Byzantium was the strongest and richest power in Europe and the Middle East militarily, diplomatically, and economically.

Bari and Manzikert (1071)

But though the Byzantine areas in southern Italy were made safe from Arab attacks (aided by the Venetian fleet), they soon became, in the early part of the fourth period, 1025 to 1095, exposed to an even more formidable enemy, the Normans. Taking advantage of the internal difficulties of the Byzantine Empire, its troubles with Rome, and later and above all the advance of the Seljuk Turks into eastern Asia Minor, the Normans ultimately (by 1071) took all of southern Italy from the Byzantines, Sicily from the Arabs, and even launched two expeditions against Constantinople itself.

The leader of the Normans was Robert Guiscard, younger son of the family of Hauteville in Normandy (France). He attracted around him other Norman adventurers. They first worked (from 1030 onward) as mercenaries for Byzantine armies in southern Italy. Then, gaining confidence, on their own they attacked several Byzantine fortresses. Finally, with the aid of a fleet Guiscard had assembled with his brother Roger, Robert launched an attack on Bari, the Byzantine capital in southern Italy. After a siege of three years the city finally surrendered in 1071 to Robert Guiscard. Byzantine control over Italy was forever ended. Robert's brother Roger with Norman forces then took the island of Sicily from the Arabs. Fired by ambitions of mounting the Byzantine throne, Robert launched a full-scale expedition across the Adriatic, landing in present day Albania, aiming to attack Constantinople itself. But his opponent was the great Emperor Alexius Comnenus, who decisively defeated the Norman forces before they even reached Thessalonica. We shall later see Alexius defeat Robert's son Bohemund in his invasion of the Balkans, also aimed at Constantinople.

The Norman subjection of southern Italy did not destroy Byzantine influence in southern Italy. Guiscard and his successors (notably his relative Roger II, who in 1130 was crowned King of Sicily, including southern Italy, at Palermo

A twelfth-century mosaic in the Martorana church of Palermo, Sicily, showing the Norman King Roger II being crowned by Christ. Note the Greek letters above ("Rogerios") and that Roger is dressed completely as a Byzantine ecclesiastic. (Alinari/Scala)

in the robes of a Byzantine emperor: see picture on p. 144) preserved the Byzantine administrative organization in the conquered districts, issued official documents in Latin, Greek, and Arabic, and acted as patrons of the numerous Greek monasteries in the area. Generally speaking, the Norman conquerors and the conquered Byzantines for some time lived side by side without merging, maintaining their own languages, customs, and habits. In southern Italy, in fact, Greek continued to be spoken for many centuries, and from that area Byzantine cultural influences continued to radiate to the West. As we shall see later (Chapter 9), during the Norman penetration of southern Italy, the ecclesiastical episode of 1054 marked the schism between the Greek and Roman churches.

In the East, the Byzantines were defeated at Manzikert (in Armenia) in 1071 by the advancing armies of a new invader, the Seljuk Turks, under the Sultan Alp Arslan. This defeat, even more serious than the one at Bari, was in the long run fatal for Byzantium, for henceforth the Byzantine heartland of Asia Minor would suffer constantly from the incursions of the Turks—first the Seljuks and later the Ottomans, who in 1453 finally took Constantinople itself.

At Manzikert the Seljuks captured the Byzantine emperor in battle, and, advancing all the way across Asia Minor, they established their capital at Nicaea. The situation looked bleak for Byzantium until Alexius Comnenus ascended the throne. A brilliant diplomat and general, he not only staved off the Turks but in the process got deeply involved in the First Crusade. But the story of that vast movement will be discussed later. Suffice it to say that in its long history Byzantium managed to hold off enemy after enemy, a power of resistance due not only to its superior military tactics, the great defensive walls of Constantinople, and the stability of its currency, but also to the steadfast belief of its people in the purity of their Orthodox religious faith and the divine origin of their empire. When Asia Minor, from which the empire drew much of its strength, began to fall to the Seljuk Turks in the late eleventh century, the end seemed near. But under capable emperors Byzantium revived and for over four hundred years, with various ups and downs, clung tenaciously to life and produced a remarkable record of cultural and artistic achievement which had considerable impact upon its Western Latin, Slavic, and Arab neighbors.

The Arabs and the World of Islam

Muhammad and the Origins of Islam

To the south and east of Latin and Byzantine Christendom lay the Christian world's greatest political, religious, and cultural antagonist, Islam, the third successor civilization to the ancient and undivided Roman Empire. Like the Latin West and the Byzantine East, the Islamic world, despite its great diversity of peoples, was also united in religion, language, and, for a considerable period, in politics as well. The rise of the great Islamic Empire in the seventh and eighth centuries, extending from Spain in the West across North Africa to the Middle East—with the ensuing, centuries-long struggle between the Muslim Crescent and the Christian Cross—was to have important and enduring effects on the development of medieval European culture. Nevertheless, modern historians of both the Christian West and East sometimes still tend to underestimate or even to overlook these Islamic influences.

For centuries before the advent of Muhammad in the sixth century, the primitive Bedouin tribes of Arabia had pursued their uneventful lives, interrupted at times perhaps to serve as minor allies of the Persians or Byzantines in their struggles with one another. Why this people, originating in the Arabian peninsula—unorganized, disunited, and backward—would one day be able to overthrow the great Persian Empire and wrest from Byzantium some of its choicest provinces is one of the great questions of medieval history. The principal dynamic that brought the Arabs to the fore was the new religion of Muhammad, a faith that provided not only religious inspiration but also incentive for expansion.

Besides the primitive Bedouins of the peninsula, whose life before Muhammad was characterized by nomadic wanderings and perpetual tribal strife, other, more civilized Arabs lived in the caravan cities. These urban Arabs were in some ways even more important for the development of Arabic civilization than the Bedouins. Their main cities were situated in Palestine, Mesopotamia, and along the western coast of the Red Sea. Of these cities, Mecca was the most important. A significant trading center, Mecca drew many pilgrims to its religious shrines, the most famous of which was the Kaaba. It contained the revered Black Stone, which, according to Islamic legend, was sent down from heaven to Abraham and Ishmael. Much of the city's prosperity came from its position as the center of Arabia's polytheistic religion (though, to be sure, all Arabs revered Allah, along with other gods, as an abstract, creative force). Mecca, through Muhammad, became the birthplace of Arabic monotheism and the holiest city of Islam.

Of humble origin, Muhammad, the founder of Islam, was born in Mecca about 570. Orphaned at an early age, he found work as an agent for a wealthy widow, guarding her caravans and managing her business. During the course of his travels, it has been speculated, Muhammad came into contact with educated Christians and Jews of Palestine and Syria. It seems likely that these contacts, particularly with Syrian Christians, had much to do with the development of his religious thought.

The marriage of Muhammad to his wealthy employer enabled him to cease working and spend his time in meditation. According to the *Koran,* on one of his frequent visits into the desert he had a vision in which the Archangel Gabriel appeared and instructed him to preach God's Word. However one may choose to explain the frequent visions of Muhammad, it is clear that he sincerely believed that God had commissioned him to reform his polytheistic fellow Arabs. Muhammad believed that in the past God had revealed himself to many prophets—to Abraham, then to Moses, to Christ, and now, in the final consummation of revelation, to himself. Although Muhammad denied the divinity of Christ, he insisted on the divine inspiration of both Christ's and the Old Testament prophets' teachings. He considered Christ the greatest of the "prophets" of the past, and ranked his teachings second only to his own.

The central theme of Muhammad's religious teaching was its strict and uncompromising monotheism. Muhammad, in fact, warned against any attempt on the part of his followers to deify him. "There is no God but Allah, and Muhammad is his prophet." Such strict monotheism obviously allowed no place for a belief such as the Christian Trinity. The oneness of God is the cornerstone of Islam (literally, "submission to God's will"), the name that Muhammad gave to his new faith.

Muhammad prescribed five duties to be followed by all Muslims: 1) pray five times a day as they kneel toward Mecca, 2) believe in the "oneness" of God, 3) give alms to the needy, 4) fast during the holy month of Ramadan, and 5) make a pilgrimage to Mecca at least once in their lives. (According to some authorities this last injunction was a concession to the Meccan aristocracy, who would thereby be enabled to preserve their lucrative pilgrim trade by transforming pagan pilgrimage into an Islamic act of faith.) In addition to these duties were certain moral prescriptions: gambling, the eating of pork, and the drinking of alcoholic beverages were forbidden. The excessive polygamy of earlier times was checked; Muslims were now allowed only four wives (although, of course, few could afford even that many). It may be noted that the assimilation of Christian customs into pre-Islamic religious practices was much more pronounced than the somewhat analogous assimilation by Christianity of pagan Greco-Roman and German practices.

Muhammad's precepts were written down in Islam's holy book, the *Koran*. These precepts are believed to be those revealed to Muhammad by God and are thus considered sacred and the highest expression of God's will. The *Koran*, which was actually collated after Muhammad's death, is arranged according to the length of its chapters ("Suras"), the longest coming first, the shortest last. It is important to note that the Koranic teachings are not only religious in scope, but also form the basis for *all* Muslim law, secular as well as religious.

Muhammad first preached his new religion in Mecca, gathering around him a small group of converts, the so-called "Companions of the Prophet," who were to have great influence in the years following his death. As the Prophet became more outspoken in his criticism of Meccan polytheism — which, as observed, the Meccans feared would result in loss of the pilgrimage trade — the leaders of the city began to persecute the followers of Islam. But the northern city of Medina, after summoning Muhammad as an arbiter between warring tribes, offered him and his followers refuge, ultimately accepting not only the Islamic religion but Muhammad as its leader. Before Muhammad left for Medina, the Meccan aristocracy, alarmed at this turn of events, plotted his assassination, whereupon he fled from Mecca to Medina. The date of his flight (called *hijra* in Arabic) on September 24, 622, is taken to mark the initial date of the Muslim calendar, as Christ's birth is the central point of reference for Christian chronology.

At Medina, Muhammad, as the Prophet of God and the executor of his will on earth, established a strong government. He then launched a series of campaigns against the Meccans and other Arab tribes, which culminated ten years later in his triumphant return to Mecca and the establishment of an Islamic, theocratic state under his leadership. Soon afterward, most of the tribes of the peninsula, at least nominally, accepted Muhammad's rule and religion. Meanwhile, the Prophet also instigated, or at least approved of, the raids being made by his followers on certain Persian and Byzantine border provinces. Whether

Muhammad choosing Ali as his successor, as recorded in the Islamic Shiite tradition. The depiction of Muhammad is exceedingly rare in Islamic art. (Edinburgh University Library)

these raids were the result of a deliberate policy of extending the faith, or were merely plundering expeditions, is difficult to say. In any event, only after Muhammad's death in 632 did these raids evolve from the usual nomadic forays for plunder (*razzias*) into full-fledged conquests.

Rise of the Islamic Kingdom

Muhammad's death caused a crisis for the Islamic state. Since no provision had been made for the succession, many Bedouin tribes began to break away from the unity imposed by Muhammad. To stave off collapse, a caliph (literally, "successor" to the Prophet) was elected to act as civil and religious leader of all the faithful. It became Muslim belief that all law, civil as well as religious, derived from God (Allah) through his prophet, Muhammad. Thus, however despotic, the caliph, in contrast to both the Western pope and the Byzantine emperor, was never theoretically able to assume the role of legislator or doctrinal innovator. His duty, technically, was to enforce the already existing and complete holy law revealed to Muhammad as interpreted by Islamic legal scholars and, as such, he was the supreme religious and temporal leader. Nevertheless, many Western historians, in view of the great authority invested in the caliph, consider him to have been at once a kind of Muslim pope and emperor combined.

The reign of the first caliph, Abu Bakr (632–634) was concerned with suppressing the Bedouin "apostates," who had reverted to their old tribal independence. After Abu Bakr's death, the new caliph, Umar (634–644), and his great general, Khalid, permitted the foreigns wars of his predecessor to continue as a diversion for Arab energies. Contrary to commonly held opinion, Islam did not seek the conversion of all infidels throughout the world. Other monotheistic traditions such as Christianity, Judaism, and Zoroastrianism were tolerated. Instead, the main factors in the remarkable Arab expansion that ensued were the collapse of trade as a result of civil war after Muhammad's death, the pressure of an expanding population (a factor unacceptable to some scholars), and a continuation of the pre-Islamic practice of raids for booty, but now on a larger scale. To these economic and social factors was added the militant ideal of the self-identification of the Arab tribes within the larger Muslim-Arab community.

Whatever the causes of the conquest, within the amazingly brief span of ten years all of Palestine, Syria, and most of the Persian Empire were vanquished. Between 640 and 646, Egypt, with its great naval base at Alexandria, was taken from the Byzantines, and the Arabs now began to push across North Africa, seizing Byzantine territory as far west as Tripoli. In the mid-seventh century civil wars among rival caliphs and a more determined resistance on the part of the Byzantines interfered with Arab expansion. But under the first caliph of the new Umayyad dynasty, Muawiyah (661–680), expansion resumed.

By 720 all of the Middle East except for Asia Minor, all of North Africa, and most of Spain had been overrun and conquered.

The phenomenal victorious drive of the Muslim armies was checked by the Byzantines only in 717 after a prolonged blockade of Constantinople itself, and, as I have shown, in 732 by a Frankish army at Tours under Charles Martel. Of these two dates, 717, though less familiar to Western historians, is probably of greater ecumenical significance. For, as the historian J. B. Bury affirms, had the Arabs taken the great fortress city of Constantinople, they would probably have conquered the weaker west as well, and all of Europe would have become Islamized. Some historians have suspected that the Arabs had planned to concert their drives in the East and West, ultimately meeting somewhere in central Europe. These two defeats marked the high point of Muslim expansion, and the areas around the Mediterranean subjected to the Muslims (with the exception of Sicily, Crete, Cyprus, Sardinia, and the Iberian peninsula) ultimately became largely Muslim in religion and Arabic in language and culture.

The Umayyad Caliphate

A civil war broke out in the mid-seventh century between the fourth caliph, Ali (cousin and son-in-law of Muhammad), and the governor of Syria, Muawiyah (of the old and important Meccan family of Umayyad), which resulted in the establishment, under Muawiyah, of the Umayyad dynasty. Muawiyah, in fact, in 660 moved the capital of Islam from Medina to Damascus in Syria. The significance of this event for Europe is that from this time onward the Muslims began to absorb even more of the Greco-Byzantine culture of Syria and to graft it onto their own. After Muawiyah's death in 680, another revolt broke out between his son and another claimant to the throne belonging to Ali's family. This revolt marked the beginning of a schism within the Islamic world between the Sunnites, who accepted the authority of the Umayyad caliphate, and the Shiites, who insisted that only a descendant of Ali, Muhammad's son-in-law, could be the legitimate ruler. This schism is of prime importance for Islam and was responsible (along with a growing desire for equality on the part of non-Arab converts to Islam), for the overthrow of the Umayyads in 750. Shiism was to act as a disruptive force within Islamic society throughout the entire medieval period; even today Iran is still basically Shiite in religion.

The revolt that led to the destruction of the Umayyad dynasty broke out in Iraq in 747 and was led by Abu-al-Abbas, a great-great-grandson of one of Muhammad's uncles. Shiites as well as other malcontents rallied to the Abbasid cause and in 750 the last Umayyad caliph was defeated in battle and killed. Abbas then systematically exterminated the entire Umayyad family. Only one escaped, Abd-er-Rahman I, who fled to Spain and there founded the Umayyad emirate (later caliphate) of Cordova. The first political—though not yet religious—breach in Islamic unity had been created.

The Abbasid Caliphate

The Abbasid revolution was more than a change of dynasties. Under the Umayyad caliphate the empire was essentially Arab-dominated, with non-Arabs, Muslim or otherwise, occupying an inferior position. Under the Abbasids, however, all Arabs and non-Arabs were considered equal, a fact that facilitated the fusion of the Arab and non-Arab peoples, and helped to produce an Islamic culture that was a mixture of Arab, Persian, Syrian, and Greco-Byzantine elements. Moreover, the caliphs greatly emphasized the religious aspects of their rule and sought to acquire the attributes of an Oriental "divine right" despotism.

As a sign of the changed regime the capital itself was moved to Baghdad (762), a new city built on the Tigris River. This marked the start of a new and more glorious period of medieval Islamic history and culture. Baghdad (near the site of Sassanian Ctesiphon), a city fabled in both Byzantium and the West, reflected the power and prestige of the Abbasid caliphs. Its luxury was unequaled in the Latin West; its only rival in all of Christendom in terms of size, commercial activity, and material and cultural civilization was Constantinople. It has recently been estimated that in the twelfth century, when Paris had a population of about 20,000 to 50,000, Constantinople had about 700,000 to 800,000 inhabitants and Baghdad somewhat less—figures that provide some sense of the relative urbanization of the three societies.

Although the caliphate itself endured until 1258, the period of genuine Abbasid greatness lasted only about a century (754–861). This period included the reigns of Harun al-Rashid (786–809), well-known from the legends of the *Arabian Nights,* and al-Mamun (813–833). Compared to these great caliphs, their successors are less worthy of notice, for, withdrawing from governmental affairs and caught up in palace intrigue, they became in effect figurehead monarchs, actual power being exercised by "viziers" (a kind of prime minister) and the commanders of the palace guards. (This reminds one of the Merovingian monarchs of Gaul who were in fact termed *roi-fainéants,* that is, "do-nothing kings.")

Under the later, weak Abbasid rulers the Muslim Empire slowly fell apart. In 929 the emir of Spain, which under the descendants of the Umayyads had never recognized Abbasid rule, proclaimed himself caliph, thus establishing a rival caliphate in the West. It is tempting to compare this event to a similar one occurring earlier, in 800, in the West, when Charlemagne was crowned Roman emperor, thereby establishing two Roman emperors in Christendom. But such a comparison is not entirely valid, for Eastern and Western Islam differed less, culturally and linguistically, than did Eastern Byzantine and Western Latin Christendom. (Indeed, the primary source of Spanish-Islamic culture remained Iraq and Baghdad, in contrast to the growing cultural separation between the Byzantine and Latin halves of Christendom). Moreover, the establishment of

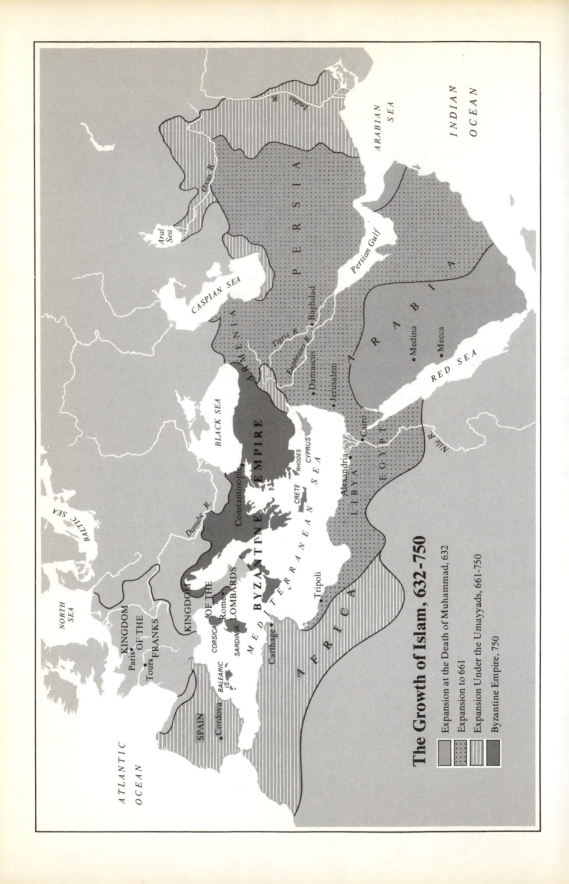

The Growth of Islam, 632-750

Expansion at the Death of Muhammad, 632

Expansion to 661

Expansion Under the Umayyads, 661-750

Byzantine Empire, 750

ATLANTIC OCEAN

NORTH SEA

BALTIC SEA

KINGDOM OF THE FRANKS

Paris

Tours

SPAIN

Cordova

BALEARIC IS.

CORSICA

SARDINIA

Rome

LOMBARDS

Carthage

MEDITERRANEAN SEA

AFRICA

Tripoli

Danube R.

Constantinople

BYZANTINE EMPIRE

BLACK SEA

CRETE

RHODES

CYPRUS

Alexandria

LIBYA

EGYPT

Cairo

Nile R.

Jerusalem

Damascus

ARMENIA

CASPIAN SEA

Aral Sea

Oxus R.

Indus R.

PERSIA

Tigris R.

Euphrates R.

Baghdad

Persian Gulf

ARABIA

Medina

Mecca

RED SEA

ARABIAN SEA

INDIAN OCEAN

the Western Caliphate was essentially a political phenomenon, although it had social and cultural implications comparable to those of Charlemagne's accession in the West. Nevertheless, later political events prevented the Western Caliphate from developing an independent civilization such as Charlemagne's.

Despite the defection of Umayyad Spain, most of the other provinces did not repudiate Abbasid rule. While becoming autonomous, *de facto,* Tunisia and northern and eastern Persia continued to recognize the theoretical control of Baghdad. In the tenth century, however, Syria, Arabia, and Egypt fell completely under the control of dynasties sympathetic to Shiism. Even the Abbasid house itself was now dominated by a Shiite family, the Iranian Būyids, who for more than a century (945–1055) proceeded to depose and elevate captive Abbasid caliphs at will.

The greatest of these independent states was Egypt, which, under the family of the Fatimids, who claimed to be descendants of Ali, set up a rival caliphate in denial of the legitimacy of Sunnite Baghdad. Ultimately the Fatimids controlled all of North Africa, Arabia, and for a time even Palestine and Syria. The Fatimid caliphs established a new capital at Cairo in 969 which gradually came to surpass the old Abbasid capital of Baghdad in both wealth and power.

It appeared therefore for a time that orthodox Sunnism would be politically submerged by Shiism. But in the eleventh century a new force appeared in Islam, the Seljuk Turks. Semi-barbarian and strongly Sunni, the Seljuks, who had pushed west from the steppes of central Asia (Turkestan), ultimately restored Sunni political primacy and a kind of Islamic unity. The Abbasid caliph was rescued from his Shiite captors only to become the tool of the Turkish sultans. In the eleventh century the Seljuks were able to unite under their rule Egypt, Syria, Persia, and parts of western and central Asia Minor (the latter taken from Byzantium). But the story of the Seljuk conquest of Byzantine and Fatimid territories and the later breakdown of their empires belongs properly to the period of the collision of the Latin, Byzantine, and Islamic worlds in the era of the crusades, beginning in 1096. I shall therefore deal with these matters in Chapter 9.

Islamic Civilization

The golden age of Islamic culture was the period of the late Umayyad and early Abbasid caliphates. During this era Islamic civilization was far more advanced than that of the West and in some ways equaled, in a few respects even surpassed, that of Byzantium. Islamic civilization, especially during the eleventh, twelfth, and thirteenth centuries, had a considerable, even critical, influence on Western culture.

The political unity imposed on the Near East by the Islamic conquest contributed to the mobility of its inhabitants and the therefore easy exchange of ideas. And, of course, the universality of the Arabic language within the entire Muslim world also facilitated the transmission of knowledge. In addition many of the Caliphs were themselves active patrons of arts and letters.

It is particularly significant that from the seventh and eighth centuries on, the Arabs came into direct contact with the more highly civilized Byzantine and Persian populations, and when Byzantines and Persians in great numbers became subject to them, the Arabs were able to borrow heavily from these more advanced cultures. Strong Byzantine and Persian influences are found in medieval Islamic culture, though of course in this cultural mix the Arabic and Islamic strains became dominant. In politics the Islamic form of government and political thought was largely Persian in origin. Among the best studies of political science in the Islamic world were the *Art of Government* by al-Māward and also the *Treatise on Politics* composed by Nizam-al-Mulk, the Persian Grand Vizier of the Seljuk Malik Shah (d. 1092).

The chief influences on the development of Arab philosophy and science, however, were the ancient Greek and, to a far lesser extent, the Byzantine writings. Islam in fact shares with Byzantium the role of preserver and transmitter to the Latin West of ancient learning, in particular of Greek philosophy and science. The beginnings of translation from the Greek (as well as from Syrian, Indian, and Persian texts) into Arabic occurred under the later Umayyads and the Abbasid Caliph Harun al-Rashid. But the reign of al-Mamun (813–833) may well mark the height of Islamic intellectual activity. Under al-Mamun a university was founded at Baghdad, an astronomical observatory was built, and, perhaps most important, the great works of Greek and Oriental (primarily Indian) science and philosophy were translated into Arabic. By the year 900 Arabic translations of almost all the works of Aristotle, plus some of Plato's, and other great Greek thinkers', were available to Islamic scholars. After Aristotle's, the works most eagerly studied by Muslim philosophers were those of the Greek Neoplatonists, such as Plotinus, many of these in order to combat the dualist, Manichaean tendencies current within the Islamic Empire.*

Islamic-Byzantine Cultural Interaction

It is not easy to establish the specific mutual influences between the Byzantine and Islamic civilizations. Indeed, the almost permanent state of war between the Arab and Byzantine states would seem at first glance to have pre-

---

* The Manichaeans were extreme dualists who believed in a good and an evil God. Their views reverted to ancient times. See pp. 250 and 365.

cluded the possibility of any extensive cultural influences. Recent scholarship, however, has rendered this task easier by indicating the existence and significance of an Arab "enlightened" class as a counterpart to the group of humanist-minded Byzantines who always existed in Byzantium. The filtering of classical Greek philosophy and science to the West by way of Islam was made possible precisely because there had previously been transmission of this learning to the Arabs from Byzantium, the repository of this Greek learning. The most fertile period of cultural transmission from Byzantines to Arabs (after the Arab conquest, that is) occurred in the ninth and tenth centuries when Byzantium was recovering from a period of near anarchy and disorder and laying the groundwork for its own political and cultural revival.* In the eastern Islamic reception of learning, as it was already observed, under such caliphal patrons as Harun al-Rashid (785–809) and al-Mamun and Al-Mutasim (d. 843) the greatest progress in translating from Greek texts were made—work closely connected with Gondi Shapur, near Baghdad in the Persian (Sassanid) kingdom.

Despite the prevailing atmosphere of conflict between Byzantines and Arabs, economic, social, and cultural contacts seem actually to have been rather considerable through intermediaries such as diplomatic messengers, merchants, border traffic, prisoners of war, refugees, and renegades all of whom contributed to a certain cultural interaction. A Byzantine story tells of how the learned tenth century Byzantine Emperor Constantine VII sent to the Arab Caliph of Cordova in Spain the gift of an illuminated Byzantine manuscript of the most important Hellenistic writer on drugs, Dioscorides, and offered, along with the book, the services of a monk-translator.

Byzantium's connections with the Western Islamic world, though more sporadic than in the East, were usually warmer owing to mutual enmity on the part of both states toward Baghdad.

But Byzantine relations with the Muslim worlds of East and West were characterized also (though to a far lesser degree) by Byzantine reception of certain aspects of Arab culture. In literature the only surviving Byzantine epic, *Digenes Akritas,* clearly reflects a certain symbiosis on the part of the Byzantine and Arab populations on the easternmost Byzantine border—that between Byzantine and Arab territory. (The idea of racial hatred, especially toward the Arabs—whom the Byzantines considered to be their only equals, politically and culturally—was foreign to the Byzantine mind.) The *Digenes Akritas* gives some idea of Byzantine attitudes to the Arab religion and customs. The father of the hero of the epic is an Arab warrior, who on a raid into Byzantine territory abducts the daughter of a Byzantine strategos (general of a Byzantine province or "theme"), makes her his bride, but then himself converts to Christianity. It

---

* Most basic, of course, is the contact resulting from Islamic conquest of learned Byzantine cities such as Antioch and Alexandria.

Dome of the Rock (Mosque of Omar), Jerusalem. This late seventh-century mosque was built by Caliph Abdel-malik. Note the Byzantine-style dome. (Israel Government Tourist Office)

is the issue of this mixed marriage, Digenes ("two blooded"), who becomes the border fighter (*Akritas*), a kind of national Byzantine hero.

In art, the Arabs adopted certain late classical as well as Byzantine artistic elements. The Mosque of Omar in Jerusalem contains mosaics in the style of those in contemporary Byzantine Christian churches. And the dome of the same mosque, entirely Byzantine in form, was in fact probably constructed by workmen from among the conquered Byzantine population of the area. Another famous mosque, that of the Ummayads in Damascus, contains a special type of figureless art typical of the Byzantine Iconoclastic period (when representation of human figures was forbidden in Byzantium)—a Byzantine art form which was subsequently largely lost or discontinued but which still found favor in the Islamic world due to Islam's own discouragement of pictorial representation. On the other hand we may note the influence of Arab ornamentation in Byzantine art works such as enamels. In various Byzantine churches in Greece

St. Sophia is the greatest Byzantine church. The cathedral of Constantinople, built by Justinian in the sixth century, is most famous for its remarkable dome, erected on pendentives. This dome served as the model for other Islamic and Western domes (see the Dome of the Rock and St. Mark's). (Marburg—Art Reference Bureau)

belonging even to later periods, the Arab origins of their tile work is unmistakable.

To return to the more purely intellectual field, initially the Arabs (like the early medieval West) knew Aristotle only as a logician. Such works of his as the *Categories, Early* and *Posterior Analytics,* and *Organon* were turned into Arabic, and Aristotle's works on rhetoric and poetics were included by the Arabs under the rubric of logic. But it was Al-Kindi (of the later ninth century) who first revealed to the Arabs the true scope of Aristotle's philosophic work, even though certain beliefs of Aristotelian philosophy (his view of the eternity of the world, that is, of matter, and the lack of a doctrine of resurrection) clashed with the teachings of the *Koran* (as they did, also, with those of the two other "religions of the book," Christianity and Judaism.) Thus subsequent Arab commentators, both Aristotelian and Neoplatonic (such as al-Farabi of the tenth century) sought, as also did their counterparts in the West and in Byzantium, to reconcile the contradictions between classical Greek philosophy and their own "revealed" religion.

Concurrent with the Aristotle translations, Arab versions appeared of Greek mathematical, astronomical, and medical texts. Included were works of Euclid on geometry, Ptolemy on astronomy (his *Mathematike Syntaxis,* which the Arabs considered the chief astronomical text, was known to the Latin West almost exclusively by its Arab title, *Almagest*), and also Galen and Hippocrates on medicine. Although the ninth century marked the period of greatest Arab activity in translating Greek works on science coming through the Byzantines, it was in the tenth century that translations were also made of ancient Greek (or Byzantine) *commentaries* on Aristotle and on other Greek works of mathematics and natural science.

Islamic Cultural Influences on the West

With the Spanish Christian conquest of Muslim Toledo in 1085, a Spanish Christian school of translators was established, and to this intellectual city flocked many Western Latin scholars, thirsty for knowledge of ancient Greek learning. In many instances the Jews of Spain performed the role of translators. Here was made available to Western Christendom in Arab guise, a large body of Aristotle's writings even before the West was able to secure the original Greek texts from Christian Byzantium. Indeed, because of the contemporary Western prejudice against the Byzantines, the West for a long time preferred the second- and even third-hand Arab versions to the original Greek texts of Byzantium.

Like Byzantine and Latin Christianity, when the Islamic religion first came into contact with ancient Greek philosophy, it too had been confronted with the problem of trying to reconcile its faith—enshrined in religious law drawing on the teachings of Muhammad and the *Koran*—with human reason. But unlike the medieval West, some Islamic scholars for a time were interested entirely in pure *philosophy* without reference to Islamic *theology*. Indeed, Al-Kindi, and especially Avicenna of the tenth century, developed philosophical systems based essentially on pagan Aristotelian and Neoplatonic ideas. And later the Spanish Muslim Averroës of the twelfth century wrote many significant commentaries on Aristotle. The adoption of some of Averroës' ideas by Latins, notably his emphasis on the eternity of matter and the concept of the "double truth," led to the emergence in the medieval West of a philosophic school, the Latin Averroists. These "Averroists" of the West completely divorced philosophy from theology and, as a result (like Averroës in the Islamic world), created a grave problem for the Latin church and its Scholastic theologians (see Chapter 10).

Fourteenth-century Islamic manuscript painting depicting "automata" (mechanical devices) in the form of animals and singing birds, whose origins revert to the Hellenistic East. The Byzantines made use of them in court ceremonies to impress foreigners. See Liudprand's report on p. 125. (Metropolitan Museum of Art, Bequest of Cora Timken Burnett, 1957)

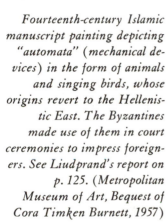

In Islam, much as in Byzantine society (but rather unlike the later medieval West), there existed, theoretically, no really clear-cut division between secular and religious law. Yet Islamic law, originally based on the *Koran* and the words and deeds of the Prophet, was expanded through continuing interpretations made by Islamic legal scholars. This legal study, and the study of theology which in time proceeded out of it, constituted the core of Islamic intellectual endeavors throughout much of Islam's medieval history, though without exerting any appreciable impact on the Latin West or Byzantium.

Some of the Arab advances made in pharmacology over the ancients—the Arab treatment with drugs was the most advanced in the medieval world—were brought to the West. Moreover, the number of words in Western scientific terminology derived from Arabic—for example algebra, alcohol, zenith, cipher—testifies to the importance of the Muslim scientific achievement.

A few Islamic contributions to Western music may also be noted here. Spanish music and rhythms in fact still bear the imprint of Moorish (Spanish Muslim) influence. Western musical terminology also bears witness to Muslim contributions in such words as fanfare, lute, guitar, tambourine, and the English Morris (Moorish) dance, all derived from Arabic roots.

The importance of Arab contributions to Western literature has long been debated by historians. The Muslim world had a long tradition of Arabic poetry dating back to the time before Muhammad. This poetry often concerned unrequited or frustrated love affairs, and many scholars, given the close contact between Spain and southern France in particular, look to Islamic poetry as one of the main sources for the medieval Western troubadour and courtly love tradition. An obvious Islamic contribution to Western literature is the famous *Arabian Nights,* comprising stories told to the Caliph Harun al-Rashid, which include Hellenistic, Jewish, Indian, as well as Arab legends. Finally, one modern scholar has proposed the theory (which some do not accept) that the sources and the inspiration for Dante's great poetic masterpiece, the *Divine Comedy* (a work describing an imaginary journey of a Christian through Hell, Purgatory, and Heaven), are to be found in certain Muslim legends regarding Muhammad's journey through the various realms of the afterlife.

The numerous examples of Islamic cultural achievement noted in this chapter and the interplay of Islamic with Byzantine and Latin cultures attest not only to the high level attained by medieval Arab culture, but also to the age-old and intricate Mediterranean game of cultural give-and-take among the three great medieval civilizations. In this process, as we have seen, Islamic, Byzantine, and Western cultures interacted with, and, in greater or lesser degree, fertilized each other to the benefit of all. But in the Middle Ages it was the more retarded Latin West which profited most. As we shall see in later chapters, the Latin West, through a process of internal ferment, would be able to build upon its own resources in addition to those borrowed from Islam and Byzantium, to lay the foundations for the unique Latin culture of the High and Later Middle Ages.

FOR FURTHER READING

Arnold, T., and A. Guillaume, eds. *The Legacy of Islam* (1931). A collection of essays emphasizing the Islamic impact on Western culture.

Bury, J. B., *A History of the Later Roman Empire,* 2 vols.* (1957). The standard work on the subject.

Cambridge Medieval History, vol. IV, pts. 1–2 (1966). Essays by specialists.

Constantine Porphyrogenitus, *De Administrando Imperio,* trans. R. Jenkins (1962). Byzantine treatise on government.

Daniel, N., *The Arabs and Medieval Europe* (1974). Good, recent introduction.

* Asterisk indicates paperback edition available.

Diehl, C., *Byzantium: Greatness and Decline,* trans. N. Walford * (1957). Valuable introduction to the subject.

Digenes Akritas, trans. J. Mavrocordato (1956). First English translation of the sole surviving Byzantine epic.

Downey, G., *Constantinople in the Age of Justinian** (1960). A fine, brief survey of life under Justinian, emphasizing the religious and intellectual aspects.

Geanakoplos, D. J., *Byzantine East and Latin West: Two Worlds of Christendom in Middle Ages and Renaissance* (1966). Careful, detailed discussion of relations between the medieval East and West, especially cultural and religious. Chapter 1 deals by subject with the Byzantine cultural impact on the West.

Geanakoplos, D. J., "Byzantium," in *Perspectives on the European Past,** ed. N. Cantor (1971). Stimulating essay on Byzantine culture and its contributions to Slavic, Arabic, and Latin cultures.

Geanakoplos, D. J., *Interaction of the "Sibling" Byzantine and Western Cultures in the Middle Ages and Italian Renaissance (330–1600)* (1976). First half of book on Byzantine culture to 1453. An original treatment of the subject, combining historical and sociological approaches.

Geanakoplos, D. J., *The Byzantine Empire and Its Civilization: A Source Book with Commentary* (in press). English translation of sources.

Gibb, H. A. R., *Mohammedanism: An Historical Survey,* 2nd ed.* (1962). Excellent short treatment of the career of Muhammad and the evolution of his ideas in Islam.

Haussig, H., *A History of Byzantine Civilization* (1971). Adequate general survey of the field.

Hitti, P. K., *A History of the Arabs,* 8th ed. (1963). A long survey of Arab history.

Hodgson, M., *The Venture of Islam* (1974). Fine recent survey.

Hussey, J. M., *Church and Learning in the Byzantine Empire, 867–1185.*

Lewis, B., *The Arabs in History,* 3rd ed.* (1956). Short but accurate.

Liudprand of Cremona, *The Works of Liudprand of Cremona,* trans. F. A. Wright (1930). Portrays the anarchic state of tenth-century Italy; especially a Western prelate's view of Byzantium.

Lombard, M., *Golden Age of Islam* (1975).

Moss, H.St. L. B., *The Birth of the Middle Ages, 395–814* * (1935; 1964). A provocative though rather sketchy work on the early period attempting to cover both East and West.

Ostrogorsky, G., *History of the Byzantine State,* trans. J. Hussey (1969). The best historical synthesis available, focusing on political, social, economic, and ecclesiastical history, but omitting the intellectual and cultural aspects.

Procopius, *Secret History,* trans. R. Atwater (1961). Scurrilous account of Justinian and Theodora by disgruntled contemporary official of Justinian.

Rosenthal, E. I. J., *Political Thought in Medieval Islam** (1958). A valuable essay on a difficult question.

Vasiliev, A. A., *History of the Byzantine Empire, 324–1453,* 2 vols.* (1958; 2nd ed., 1968). A standard scholarly account of Byzantine history, including cultural aspects.

Von Grünebaum, *Classical Islam: A History, 600–1258* (1970). Good short survey.

PART II

The High
Middle Ages

PART II *The High Middle Ages*

Western World	Byzantine and Slavic World	Islamic World
910 Cluny monastery founded		
911 Conrad I elected King of Germany		
	922ff. Byzantine emperors first legislate against power of great landowners	
		929 Umayyad Emir of Cordova takes title of Caliph
c.950ff. Western agricultural revolution (heavy plow, horse collar, three-field system)		
c.950–1050 "Peace" and "Truce of God" established		
c.950–1000 Ottonian "renaissance"		
955 Otto I crushes Magyars at Lechfeld		
	962 Nicephorus Phocas recovers Crete from Arabs	
962 Otto I crowned emperor in Rome		
	969 Antioch falls to Nicephorus Phocas	969 Fatimid Caliphate established in Egypt
	976–1025 Zenith of Byzantine power	
987 Hugh Capet elected King of France		
	989 Vladimir and Rus nation converted	
c.1000–1150 New villages and "bourgs" founded		

1009 Jerusalem taken by Hakim

1055–1058 Seljuks occupy Baghdad, control Caliph

1071 Seljuk Turks defeat Byzantines at Manzikert

1085 Spanish Christians take Toledo

1002 Venice aids Byzantium to defend Bari against Arabs

1030 Norman conquest of Byzantine south Italy begins

1054 Death of Rus Jaroslav the Wise
1054 Schism between Byzantine and Latin churches

1059 Pope makes Normans his vassals (Melfi)

1071 Catastrophic double Byzantine defeat: Bari and Manzikert

c.1081 Alexius I devalues Byzantine coinage
1082 Venice secures trade concessions in Constantinople under Alexius I

1096 First Crusade army passes through Constantinople

1039–1056 Emperor Henry III: height of "Holy" Roman Empire
1049 Leo IX, reform pope

1059 Decree regulating papal elections
1066 Normans conquer Anglo-Saxon England

1074 Gregory VII's "Dictatus Papae"
1077 Henry IV humbled at Canossa

1095 Urban II at Synod of Piacenza: Alexius asks military aid
1095 Urban preaches "First Crusade"
1096 First Crusade at Constantinople

PART II *The High Middle Ages*

Western World	Byzantine and Slavic World	Islamic World
1099 Jerusalem falls to army of First Crusade	1099 Jerusalem falls to Western Crusade army	1099 Jerusalem falls to Western armies: Crusade kingdom of Jerusalem established
c.1100 University of Bologna founded c.1100–1200 Champagne Fairs prosper c.1100–1200 Cistercians clear forests	1107 Norman Bohemund launches invasion of Byzantine territory	
1109 Death of Anselm 1122 Concordat of Worms 1140 Gratian codifies canon law		1141 Peter the Venerable visits Muslim Spain: leads to first Latin translation of *Koran*
1142 Death of Abelard		1144 Fall of Edessa to Turks 1147 Second Crusade
1147 Second Crusade preached by St. Bernard	1147 Roger of Sicily attacks Thessalonika; Second Crusade passes through Constantinople: Manuel I, emperor	c.1150 Toledo becomes center for Western translations of Greek from Arabic; Adelard of Bath translates Euclid and Arab mathematics into Latin
1158 Diet of Roncaglia 1163 Cathedral of Notre Dame begun	1167–1196 Stephen Nemanya, founder of Serb state	1169–1193 Saladin reigns

1174 Battle of Legnano

1180–1223 Philip II, "architect" of modern France

1187 Saladin captures Jerusalem— leads to Third Crusade

1200–1300 Italian gold coins minted; heyday of guild system
1204 Frankish and Venetian forces seize Constantinople

1208–1223 Albigensian Crusade

1214 Battle of Bouvines
1215 Fourth Lateran Council; Magna Carta signed

1268 Charles of Anjou takes Sicily

1176 Byzantines defeated by Turks at Myriocephalon

1182 Massacre of Latins in Constantinople
1187 Third Crusade passes through Constantinople

1204 Constantinople falls to Crusaders: Latin Empire established

1240 Kiev burned by Mongols

1261 Michael Palaeologus restores Constantinople to Greeks: Byzantium revived

---

1171 Saladin overthrows Fatimid caliph in Egypt

1187 Fall of Jerusalem to Saladin; death of Gerard of Cremona, most important Toledo translator of Ptolemy and Avicenna
1198 Averroës dies

1204 Death of Maimonides, Spanish Jew who "reconciled" Old Testament and Aristotle

1212 Las Navas de Tolosa: Castilian victory over Muslims

1258 Mongols take Baghdad, kill last Caliph

PART II *The High Middle Ages*

Western World	Byzantine and Slavic World	Islamic World
1270 St. Louis' Crusade to Tunis		
1274 Council of Lyons: deaths of Aquinas and Bonaventura	1274 Council of Lyons between Greek and Latin churches	
	c.1280 Ottoman Turks begin penetration of Asia Minor	c.1280 Ottomans penetrate Asia Minor
1282 Sicilian Vespers		
1290 Jews expelled from England		
1291 Acre falls to Muslims		1291 Acre falls to Muslims
1295 Edward I and English "Model" Parliament		
1297 Closing of Venetian Grand Council		
1302 Boniface's Bull, *Unam Sanctam*		
1306 Jews expelled from France		
1321 Death of Dante		
	1328 Ivan Kalita, Grand Prince of Moscow	
	1334 Jews emigrate to Poland and Lithuania	
	1341–1346 Byzantine synods approve Palamism	
	1355 Death of Stephen Dušan	
		1366 Adrianople, Ottoman capital
	1380 Russian victory over Mongols at Kulikovo	
	1389 Battle of Kossovo: Serbia destroyed	
	1396 Battle of Nicopolis: Turks defeat Crusaders	
	1402 Tamerlane defeats Turk Bayazid at Angora	1402 Turks defeated at Angora by Mongols

1422 Murad besieges Constantinople
1444 Crusade of Varna; Rus
     metropolitan named
     independently of Byzantium

1453 Fall of Constantinople to Turks
1472 Byzantine princess Sophia
     marries Ivan III

1589 Metropolitan of Moscow
     crowned Patriarch

1451–1481 Muhammad II reigns
1453 Turks capture Constantinople

1492 Spanish Kings expel Moors
     from Granada and Jews from
     Spain

In a general view of Western medieval society at the period of its lowest ebb, the ninth and early tenth centuries, almost no power or institution of any real vitality seemed to exist. During this period of the semi-barbaric "Dark Ages" it is difficult to discern even the seeds that would produce a culture which, at its height in the thirteenth century, would be worthy of comparison with almost any in history. One of the great problems confronting scholars is explaining the reasons for this remarkable revival of Western society and civilization.

Many medievalists believe that the most fundamental factor in Europe's revival was the gradual development in the West of a surplus in food supply and a population increase. No doubt there is much to be said for this view. But one may ask what underlying factor permitted, for the first time in centuries, the development of such a surplus. Bearing in mind the complexity of this question

CHAPTER 6

Economic and Social Revival of Western Europe

and the interdependency of the many factors involved, it would seem that a necessary basis for the survival of more people and the growth of food requisite for this survival was the beginning, very faint at first, of a certain order in society.

With constant invasions from without and almost perpetual warfare within, few advances in any sphere of civilization could occur. But the ending of the invasions by the mid-tenth century, the feeble beginnings of a kind of regulation of feudal warfare through the Peace of God and the Truce of God (which, as shown in Chapter 4 protected clerics and peasants and attempted to limit the days in which war could be carried on), and the gradual formation of feudal institutions themselves permitted the establishment of a certain political stability in some areas. This in turn led to the development of more peaceful pursuits, such as the extension of agricultural and commercial activities, and, still later on a higher level, even the exchange of ideas among various areas of Europe.

The revitalization of the West that occurred in the tenth to the twelfth centuries was so striking that it has sometimes been called, not without justification, the only true renaissance—that is, rebirth—in Western European history. Perhaps the most fundamental aspect of this renaissance was the economic and social revival. Indeed, by the twelfth century this had so transformed the West that for the first time since Rome's fall in the fifth century an *urban* society emerged.

The Western Medieval Agricultural Revolution

Medieval civilization, at bottom, was always agrarian, but a fundamental step in the economic revival was the agricultural improvements that enabled production of even greater amounts of food. The first important technological change was the adoption in the West of the heavy, wheeled plow equipped with a moldboard, a curved metal plate that lifted, turned, and pulverized the soil. This new type of plow was designed to meet the problems caused by the heavy wet soil of northern Europe. Extensive agrarian activity had of course been carried on in the north for millennia; surprisingly, the invention of a plow that would more satisfactorily cultivate the land does not seem to date earlier than the seventh or eighth century.

To pull this heavier plow considerable animal power was required, at least that of eight oxen. At first horses were rarely used, there being no satisfactory way to harness them; the old Roman method of simply tying a rope around the horse's neck choked him if the load were heavy. Harnessing a horse with an ox yoke also proved ineffective, since the yoke was ill placed for pulling. During the Carolingian period, however, there was an increased use of what appears to have been a new development, the horse collar. This device—originally con-

I ors descent alixands/ ius del maist doignon
o lui les·v·puceles/ qui li sont au gieron
a i su porus lindois/ qui ot cuer de lyon

A blacksmith at work with bellows and anvil. (*Bodleian Library, Oxford*)

ceived in the East, though probably developed in the West—enabled horses to pull greater loads by distributing the weight more effectively around their shoulders. Before the horse could displace the ox, however, still another innovation was required. Horse hoofs are softer and more easily broken than oxen, and in the cold, damp climate of northern Europe they deteriorated rather rapidly. The adoption of a simple but extremely important invention—the nailed, iron horseshoe—obviated all this. When horses could be shod with iron shoes and harnessed with a horse collar, they gradually supplanted the ox as the most important draft animal in the West. (It is interesting to note that in the last decades of the ninth century, horseshoes appeared almost simultaneously in such widely distant areas as China, the Byzantine East, and the West.)

What advantages would a horse have over an ox? A horse eats more and has a shorter life expectancy, nor can it usually be fattened up for food once it becomes too old to work. On the other hand, the horse can pull a greater weight than the ox and possesses more stamina, allowing it to work two or three more hours per day. Of course, the horse is much faster, so much so that, according to calculations, if the same load were to be pulled by horse and ox, the horse would put out fifty foot-pounds more per second. Further, since with the horse the peasant could work his land more efficiently and reach the outlying fields more quickly, he could put more land under cultivation. Striking testimony of how much more the medieval peasant valued the horse than the ox as a draft animal is the fact that land measurements in some areas were often based on the amount of land *two* oxen or *one* horse could plow in a day.

The combination, then, of three important new factors—the use of the heavy plow, the employment of horsepower, and the development of the three-field system (Chapter 4), which reduced the amount of agricultural labor and at the same time increased the total harvest—led to the production of more food and thus the creation of a surplus. At the same time, medieval peasants began to increase their cultivation of vegetables, especially beans. Beans not only brought more nutritive value to their diet (containing more protein than grain), but, since legumes release nitrogen into the soil, their increased cultivation tended to make the land more fertile as did the increased use of animals, which provided more manure for fertilizing the soil. These various agricultural and diet improvements, juxtaposed with rudimentary political organization, all served in turn to stimulate the growth of population—a factor often considered the ultimate key to the rebirth of Western Europe.

In the course of time the old villages found that they could not adequately support or employ the growing population. New farm lands became necessary. And so the increase in population itself became in turn a causative factor for the cultivation of new lands. Gradually, especially during the eleventh century, huge hitherto uninhabited areas of Western Europe—forest and wasteland— were cleared and placed under cultivation by means of the new type of plow, which could more efficiently till marginal lands. Not without justification has this phase of agrarian development been termed the "expansion" or the internal "colonization" of Western Europe.

In the eleventh and twelfth centuries entire new villages began to spring up everywhere in Western Europe. In France, for example, hundreds of towns named *Villeneuve* (new town) appeared. In the Low Countries marshes were drained and dikes erected to hold back the sea. In Central Europe, with the clearing of forests, Germans in great numbers flocked eastward, beginning what has been viewed by historians as a "national" drive to the East against the Slavs —a movement sometimes compared to the westward expansion of the United States. In this opening up of new lands, there were few individual "pioneers." The most practical, and often the only, manner of attaining economic and political security was through the joint action of a village community acting under the aegis of a feudal lord who would authorize a group of his peasants to till hitherto uncultivated lands. These lands then became part of his manor, with the peasants often being granted certain exemptions from customary assessments.

Special mention must be made of the role of the Church, particularly the monasteries, which were often among the earliest to adopt the new developments in agriculture. It is possible that the three-field system was in fact first adopted in the German monasteries established in the eighth century by Boniface at Fulda and elsewhere. Evidence indicates that some monasteries in the medieval period, especially the Cistercians of the later period, experimented with livestock breeding. The Cistercian monks, who first appear in the twelfth century, were well known for clearing and tilling many wilderness areas. This was a concomitant, however, of their primary objective of seeking solitude or converting the heathen of remote, uncivilized areas. In the over-all picture of medieval agriculture, at least up to the thirteenth century, the manors belonging to the Church were, as a rule, the best managed, the most productive, and, as a result, the most prosperous farmlands of Europe.

The development of new lands for cultivation had significant ramifications for the social order. The increased yield meant that the population could continue to expand, so that by the end of the eleventh century a slight surplus of food and increase in population existed in Western Europe for the first time since antiquity. The economic advantages stemming from the recovery of Europe provoked various responses from the landlords. Some, hoping to gain through the sale of surplus goods collected from the serfs on their lands, tended to clamp down on the traditional dues and services owed. Others soon enough saw the advantage of letting the peasant sell his own surpluses and pay his obligations to the landlord in cash. The latter approach was particularly advantageous for landlords who wanted to secure laborers to open up and settle new lands.

A major although unintentional result of the opening of new lands was the gradual emancipation of the serfs. In seeking to recruit serfs to emigrate to new lands, landholders gave special privileges to those doing the arduous work of draining swamps or clearing forests. The privileges often included a significant diminution of the manorial dues customarily paid by a serf to the lord. The lord might, for example, exempt the serfs from certain tolls or services, or grant a charter restricting the amount of rent to be imposed on each serf. The general result of all these conditions, by the late twelfth and thirteenth centuries, was not only the gradual freeing of the serfs from their most onerous manorial obligations but, ultimately, from their servile status itself. New villages with such names as *Freiburg* and *Villefranche* (German and French for "free town") testify to this lessening of restrictions. The more ambitious of the peasants often fled to such new lands, and often the lords of the manors, fearing the depopulation of their older villages, were forced to grant similar privileges to those serfs who remained. Gradually, then, the number of freemen began to grow, and as their number increased, serfdom, manorialism, and to some extent even feudalism were weakened.

The Revival of Commerce

The increase in the supply of agricultural products and the steady increase in population density and mobility in turn stimulated the rise of trade and commerce. As noted, the increased population was at first siphoned off in developing new lands, but as time went on and the new lands filled up, an in-creasing number of people had to turn to other, nonagricultural pursuits, the most important of which was commerce. It was the commercial revival, fostered in part by this demographic change, that ultimately brought about the emer-gence in the West of the medieval town. But before we examine the question of town origins let us first discuss trade, the lifeblood of towns, and merchants, the agents of trade.

Trade with Byzantines and Arabs: Rise of Venice

In 1935 a book entitled *Mohammed and Charlemagne* by the Bel-gian historian Henri Pirenne began a protracted debate among historians about the nature of the decline and subsequent revival of the Western economy. Al-though his theories have been seriously attacked, the "Pirenne thesis" still serves as a useful starting point for discussing the early development of Western Europe's economy. The essential core of his thesis is that the economic life of Western Europe depends fundamentally on commercial activity. Pirenne em-phasized long-range trade with the East as a fundamental factor in the decline and revival of Western commercial activity. He sought to show that long-range trade continued until the closing of the western Mediterranean by the Arabs in the eighth century, and that only then did Western Europe turn in upon itself, to relapse into a self-sufficient, almost totally agrarian, economy. But Pirenne, as later historians have demonstrated, did not adequately stress that an *internal* decline in commercial activity among the inhabitants of Western Europe had already taken place before the eighth century. And in pointing to the Western trading activity carried on by traveling Syrian, Jewish, and Greek merchants before the Arab invasions, it appears that he failed to realize this trade was of a relatively minor nature. In answering Pirenne, then, historians have affirmed that to look for the beginnings of a revival of commerce focus must not be ex-clusively on the resumption of long-range trade with the East but, no less im-portant, on the stirrings of commercial activity within Western European society itself. Further, they point out, Pirenne overemphasized the effect on long-range trade produced by the Arab conquest of the western Mediterranean, for, on the contrary, rather brisk commercial contacts seem to have existed between some areas of East and West even after the conquests of the Muslims.

From the fourth century up to about 1100 the Byzantine Empire was the greatest commercial power in Christendom. Through the Byzantine capital of Constantinople passed the silks, spices, and precious stones of the East, and to a lesser extent wool, timber, and produce of the West. Despite the conquest of the western Mediterranean islands by the Arabs, the Byzantines, in the ninth century, still maintained contacts with Italy by way of Venice and of the Byzan-tine or Byzantine-influenced cities of Bari and Amalfi in southern Italy.

Through these Italian cities a certain amount of Eastern trade was thus also transmitted to northern Europe.

Another Byzantine contact with northern Europe was by way of Russia, via the so-called "Varangian route." As already noted, in the eighth and ninth centuries a group of Swedes moved eastward into Russia. They established trading centers in northern Russia, later moving down into the central plain, where they set themselves up as princes of Kiev. In time they came into contact with the Byzantines, and soon the "Rus," as these originally Swedish princes of Kiev were called, came to accept Christianity from Byzantium. The Byzantines carried on a flourishing trade with the Russians, the latter even securing a small trading depot of their own in Constantinople around the church of St. Mamas. In exchange for timber, furs, honey, and slaves, the Byzantines sent luxury goods—silks, spices, gold, and other items—to Kiev, the developing center on the Dnieper River. From there the Russian merchants (the Rus were noted for both their trading and fighting abilities) shipped these goods north to the Baltic Sea area. The island of Gotland appears to have been a great trade center for these goods; great hoards of Byzantine coins have been discovered there. From there the products of Byzantine commerce were then often carried to areas of Scandinavia and even to northwestern Europe.

But it was the Italian cities that, after 1100, began to dominate the Eastern trade. In this development Venice and, to a somewhat lesser extent, Genoa and Pisa, played the most important roles. During the eleventh, twelfth, and thirteenth centuries these cities were to become bitter commercial rivals for the control of the lucrative Eastern trade.

From about the eighth century until well into the period of the Renaissance, Venice remained the most important Western center for long-range trade between East and West. The city had been founded at the mouth of the Po River in the fifth century by refugees from the ancient Roman city of Aquileia, who were fleeing the Hunnic advance into Italy. The area was marshy and dotted with islands, ideal for defense.

Venice early turned to trade and commerce for its livelihood; indeed the location and the lack of good farm lands nearby necessitated this. From the beginning its citizens engaged in salt and fish trading. By the tenth century the city dominated the Adriatic Sea and thus had easy access to the East, particularly Byzantium.

Venice always remained an Eastern-oriented city and up to at least the early thirteenth century moved in the Byzantine orbit. Even after Charlemagne revived the imperial title in the West in 800 the Venetians preferred to remain subjects of the Byzantine emperor. For, under nominal Byzantine suzerainty, the city was able to maintain itself as an essentially independent republic. The Venetian cathedral of St. Mark's (constructed in the late tenth and eleventh centuries) was modeled after the Church of the Holy Apostles in Constanti-

This view of Venice, 1338, shows the city's busy commercial life. By the fourteenth century Venice was becoming the West's leading center for trade from Italy to Germany and the North, and from Constantinople to the West. (Mansell Collection/ London)

nople and probably built by Byzantine workmen. The Venetian dialect contained many Greek words; the doge even held the Byzantine title of *protosevastos* ("first honored"). Strikingly enough, in 1204, after Constantinople had been captured by a combined Venetian and crusading force, the Venetians even discussed moving their seat of government to Constantinople. And as late as the fifteenth century a Greek, the statesman and Cardinal Bessarion, could still call Venice "another Byzantium."

Almost the entire Venetian population was in one way or another connected with trade—as sailors, artisans, or merchants. No genuine serfdom as we have described it developed in medieval Venice. The social structure was based on commercial activity rather than land tenure, and the significant class of the aristocracy was composed not of lords of manors trained as knights but of the wealthiest merchants. This aristocracy ruled the city through two councils: the Council of Ten (a kind of executive council), and the Great Council (Maggior Consiglio). A doge, elected for life, acted as chief executive and head of state, but in time his power became more and more circumscribed by the aristocratic councils.

In the tenth century the Venetians built a fleet which they were soon called upon to use to aid Byzantium. In 1002 they helped the Byzantines expel the Muslims from Bari. More important, in 1082 their naval assistance was decisive in repulsing the Normans of Sicily, who were then attacking the Byzantine possessions in the Balkans. In return for such services the Byzantine emperors granted the Venetians exemption from the payment of export and import duties within the Byzantine Empire, a privilege, significantly, not granted even to Greek merchants. Finally, Venice received a sizable quarter along the Golden Horn in Constantinople itself, and its citizens living there were granted extraterritorial status; thus Venetians within Constantinople were in effect subject to Venetian rather than Byzantine law. With the decline of Byzantine power, beginning in the late eleventh century after the disasters of the battles of Manzikert and Bari, the Venetians came increasingly to take over much of the commerce of the Byzantine Empire. And by the late twelfth century the Venetians had established commercial bases in all strategic areas of the Byzantine East.

Neither Venice nor the southern Italian merchant towns of Bari and Amalfi had any scruples about trading with the Saracens. Venice, especially, carried on a huge traffic with them in slaves. From Dalmatia and the north the Venetians exported young Slavic girls and boys to the Arabs of Egypt and North Africa. (The word "slave," incidentally, is sometimes said to be derived from the word "Slav.") And they sold to the Muslims such products as timber and iron, despite their value to the Arabs for the construction of ships that were all too often launched against the Christians.

In contrast to Venice, the rise of Pisa and Genoa to commercial and political power was more closely tied to the Christian struggle to drive the Saracens out of the western Mediterranean and still later from the Holy Land. Pisa was pillaged twice, in 935 and 1024, by Muslims based in Sardinia and Sicily, and Genoese ships or outposts suffered repeatedly from Muslim raids. In the eleventh century, however, the tide began to turn; in revenge the Genoese and Pisans launched expeditions, sometimes jointly, against the Muslims and ultimately succeeded in driving the Arabs out of Sardinia and Corsica. The two cities even penetrated to the Arabic capital of Palermo in Sicily. The Pisans used the rich booty gained from this successful raid to help build and ornament their new cathedral. When, in the late eleventh century, the Normans finally succeeded in ousting the Muslims from Sicily itself, the entire Tyrrhenian Sea was irrevocably lost to Islam. Now, far more freely than before, Christians could carry on sea trade with all areas of the Mediterranean.

It was the movement of the crusades (to be discussed in Chapter 9), however, that firmly established Genoa and Pisa as serious commercial rivals of Venice in the East. At the end of the First Crusade the Genoese and Pisans played a large role in transporting men and supplies to the newly established Christian states in the Holy Land. Indeed, from the Second Crusade on, every subsequent crusading expedition was launched by way of the sea route, accordingly increasing the importance of Pisa and Genoa as shippers of men and supplies. As a result the Pisans and Genoese (and later the Venetians) early established trading posts in Syria and Palestine. Even after 1187, when Jerusalem was retaken by the Saracens, these Italian cities were able to maintain their bases, a fact that gave them a monopoly of trade in the Holy Land. Thus by the end of the twelfth century the Italian cities controlled most of the trade carried on in the areas extending from Constantinople, Syria, and Palestine across to Gibraltar. The French city of Marseilles and the aggressive Catalan port of Barcelona also entered into this trade, although at a later date and playing a more minor role than that of the chief Italian cities. In the twelfth century the Mediterranean had in effect become a Christian lake over which long-range trade between the most distant corners of the Mediterranean had become commonplace.

Internal Commerce in Western Europe

As noted earlier, Pirenne believed that the resumption of long-range sea trade between Italy and the East in the eleventh century, the result of the Christian reconquest of the Mediterranean from the Arabs, was primarily responsible for reawakening commercial activity in the West. Nevertheless, as we have seen, trade routes to the East, though greatly diminished, had not in fact been entirely cut off by the Arabic conquest of the western Mediterranean. A few Italian towns and the Baltic Sea area continued in contact with Byzantium and the East throughout the period of Arab Mediterranean hegemony.

An almost equally cogent explanation of the revival of Western economic life after the so-called Dark Ages may well be found in the development of the essentially internal aspects of the Western European economy. During the Dark Ages Western Europe had had little or nothing to offer in exchange for Eastern products. Wars, depopulation, and especially the breakdown of order had necessitated recourse to a subsistence, almost totally agricultural economy even before the Arabic conquests of the Mediterranean in the eighth and ninth centuries. There was therefore little market for Eastern goods in Western Europe; nor did the Western areas have the energy, time, or manpower to produce products for exchange. Had direct trade between much of the West and the East been really profitable, it seems likely that more merchants would have found effective ways to get through or around what Pirenne describes as the Muslim "blockade." (Another related factor of some significance was the very strong position of the Byzantine coinage up to the early eleventh century that made Byzantine goods —which were highly prized throughout the Mediterranean world—extremely expensive in terms of the depreciated coinage of the early medieval Western merchant, and, to a lesser extent, also in the Islamic East.)

As I have emphasized, the increase in food supply and population, beginning in the late tenth century, altered all this. Surplus food—grains, wines, and so on—now became commodities of exchange within the West. The increasing labor supply also began to be used to fell trees for timber, to work mines, to manufacture goods, and carry on trade—all activities that led to an increase in the wealth of Western Europe. For the merchants a potentially great and profitable market had now been created.

In contrast to the sharp commercial rivalry of the Italian cities, trade in the north of Europe seems to have been more interdependent, at times even characterized by a measure of cooperation. A good example is the wool trade, which linked England with Flanders and Flanders with Germany and Italy. From English sheep came the finest raw wool of Europe. But the English did not have the necessary equipment to weave their wool into cloth; the raw wool therefore had to be sent to Flanders, which had specialized in the manufacturing of textiles since late Roman times. Flemish woolen cloth was of such fine quality that it was sought after all over the world. For it Germans would exchange iron, timber, and perhaps furs from the Slavic areas. Italian merchants also would come north, bringing with them goods from the East, which they would then exchange for wool. In Italy, too, spurred by growing markets not only locally and overseas but north of the Alps as well, a number of inland cities such as Lucca, Siena, and Florence began to develop some manufacturing, especially of textiles. Overland commerce northward from the Lombard cities began to flourish in the late eleventh century. It was the Italians, then, who served as agents to connect the internal trade of the West with the long-range commerce with the East. For, after purchasing the wool, the Italians might send large quantities of it to the Byzantines and the Arabs even farther to the east. Thus the development of internal Western trade itself served to stimulate long-range commerce.

An example of commercial cooperation in northern Europe was the formation, in the later medieval period, of a union of merchant guilds of German cities located on the North and Baltic seas, called the Hanseatic League. Although formally organized only in the fourteenth century, the Hansards (merchant guildsmen) had earlier drawn their towns into a loose association. Most important of these cities were Lübeck, Hamburg, and Danzig, though the league was eventually connected with such distant towns as Novgorod and London, where the Hansards had trading posts. The league imposed on its mem-

Grapes, and especially wine, were an important agricultural product for much of medieval Western Europe. (Reproduced by permission of the British Library Board, Royal ms. 2. B. VII, f. 79v)

bers stringent regulations whose main purpose was to maintain a monopoly of trade in certain commodities throughout the region, to reduce competition among the members, and to provide mutual protection. The Hanse ships and merchants, in their heyday in the fourteenth century, linked north Germany with England, Scandinavia, Flanders, and Russia. At one point, in 1370, no less than seventy-seven Hanse cities dictated a peace to their vanquished enemy, Denmark.

As noted earlier, the major product of this northern trade was Flanders wool. The county of Flanders was perhaps the earliest area of medieval Western Europe to develop an industry. As with most of Europe's manufacturing, the primitive Flemish cloth industry almost disappeared during the anarchy of the so-called Dark Ages. In the tenth century, with the restoration of the beginnings of order, the manufacture of wool revived. From the geographical viewpoint Flanders was ideally located for trade. It formed the apex of a triangle linking it with Germany and Scandinavia in the East and England in the West. Demands for raw wool from England increased with the growing market for Flanders woolens in Germany, France, and Italy.

With the passage of time the economy of Flanders became geared primarily to the production of woolen cloth, and agrarian pursuits tended to recede into the background. By the twelfth century almost the entire population of Flanders was in one way or another involved in the production of woolen cloth. The concentration of workers and the increased volume of trade helped to aid the growth of such Flemish merchant towns as Ghent, Bruges, Ypres, and Lille.

Proto-industrial centers also began to develop in other areas of Europe, each dependent essentially on the production of one marketable product. Thus Toledo became famous for steel (particularly for its swords, which were in demand all over Europe), Florence for wool finishing and silk, Arras for lace. The growth of industry also stimulated the growth of towns as more and more people settled in certain areas in order to carry on trade or manufacturing. I shall take up shortly the origins, development, and rise of urban centers.

The distribution of goods throughout Europe was, in the thirteenth century, facilitated by the growth of the great fairs, from which our present county and state fairs are descended. The most famous of these Western fairs were those of the region of Champagne in northeastern France. At specified times of the year merchants from Italy bringing luxury goods from the East, merchants from Flanders with cloth, from Spain with leather and steel, from Germany and England with still other products, would gather together at Troyes or other areas in the county of Champagne and set up booths to display their wares. From all the surrounding areas merchants came to these festive expositions to browse and to buy goods, finding the fair a good place not only to trade but to make arrangements for future exchange of goods or to settle old accounts. Champagne was ideal for this purpose, located as it was almost midway between Flanders, Italy, and Germany. The counts of Champagne promoted commerce by granting passes of safe conduct to merchants. There were other fairs in Western Europe, too, such as that at St. Denis near Paris and at Ghent in Flanders. The chief fair in the Byzantine Empire was at Thessalonica, in Greece, which in the twelfth century perhaps attracted an even greater number of merchants than the Champagne fairs. Most of these fairs lasted for weeks at a time; the Champagne fairs ultimately continued throughout most of the year.

Rise of Money and Banking in the West

With the increase in trade, money, to use Pirenne's phrase, "now began to travel with the merchants." And, indeed, one of the most important consequences of the revival of trade was the quickening of a money economy. During the Dark Ages the use of money did not completely cease, but at times the coin circulation was almost negligible. Actually in the primitive feudal and manorial system there was little need for quantities of coin. Land, not specie, constituted wealth. Rewards and payments were made in land, and feudal and manorial dues were paid with produce and services.

With the increase in the volume of trade in the eleventh and twelfth centuries, however, the circulation of money was greatly stimulated. Up to the eleventh century the Byzantine gold coin, the *nomisma* (called *bezant* in the West), was the standard monetary unit in West as well as East. But in the later eleventh century, owing to the decline in Byzantine military and political power, the bezant began to depreciate in value. At the same time the increased demand for money in the West and the near exhaustion of Byzantine silver mines meant that there were not enough Byzantine coins to meet the need. In the twelfth and thirteenth centuries, therefore, new Western coins—copper, silver, and more important, the first of gold—began to be minted in ever-increasing quantities. Thus the French tournois appeared (not always of gold), the Venetian gold ducat, and most important, the Florentine florin.

Along with the circulation of money it was inevitable that the practice of lending money and the extension of "credit" would develop. The Western Church had long sought to discourage, indeed it forbade, the charging of interest on loans; in an economy virtually lacking in liquid capital and in which land was the primary source of wealth, the charging of interest, prohibited by Scripture as usury, was considered morally reprehensible. In the early medieval period the Church, with its vast wealth in all areas of Europe, was itself the principal moneylender. But the Church did not ordinarily charge interest. With the growth of the Western economy and the dependence on money, however, the practice of moneylending for interest became more and more widespread. The Church's ban was often circumvented by listing the loan as greater than the sum actually borrowed. Ultimately, the Church was forced to modify its position and allow for charging interest. This, however, was allowed only in cases where the lender shared the risk involved with the borrower, and even then only at a rate commensurate with the degree of risk. Although excessive interest rates were forbidden, once interest was "legalized" in the eyes of the Church, rates continued to spiral upward. By the thirteenth century the Church had ceased to be a major source for loans. It could not evade its own prohibition of usury and, more important, it lacked the great amount of liquid capital needed to meet the increasing demand for credit. The Church itself was, in fact, often forced to borrow money from the newly developing banking houses or from Jews.

Although the role of Jews as moneylenders has been exaggerated, it is true that until the development of the great Christian banking houses of fourteenth-century Italy (and later of Germany and France), Jews perhaps constituted the largest single group of moneylenders in Western Europe. As non-Christians, Jews were not subject to the Church's prohibition against usury. One Pope is, in fact, recorded as being unfavorable to the conversion of certain Jews because it would curtail their lending service to him. But there is no doubt that the periodic outbursts of anti-Semitism occurring in the West were in part caused by the lending activities of rich Jews. Debtors often incited riots against the Jews. Shakespeare's unfavorable depiction of Shylock has been taken to reflect the attitude of many toward what they saw as the grasping Jewish money-lender. (For the treatment of the Jews as a social minority see Chapter 11.)

The Commenda.   As a result of the enormous expansion in the volume and value of commerce, the cities of Italy began to develop what has been called "commercial capitalism." The risk involved in sending ships to distant ports was still great. Pirates, Muslim and Christian, lurked everywhere, both on land and sea. Storms were particularly dreaded. To lessen the risk of possible loss and, even more, as a means of making a profit, various commercial practices developed. By far the most important was the *commenda*. The *commenda* was an agreement, a notarial contract, between a person with capital (money), who remained at home, and a travelling merchant, who supplied the labor. One-fourth of the profits usually went to the merchant (the "worker") and three-fourths to the investor, the supplier of capital who bore all of the monetary risk.

The origins of the *commenda* are still being debated, but have been attributed to the Byzantine practice of the *chreokoinonia* (dating from Greco-Roman times), the Islamic *qirad,* and even the Jewish practice *isqa*. Though the influence of all three is in varying degree probably involved—customs of the sea were easily spread by sailors throughout the expanse of the Mediterranean—perhaps the Byzantine practice of the *chreokoinonia* played the dominant role. In any event, the almost simultaneous emergence in the eleventh-century Italian towns of Amalfi, Venice, and Genoa of the commercial instrument of the commenda is the result not only of the crystallization of earlier common Mediterranean practices, but, even more, of the response to the expanding commercial needs and opportunities of the period.

In Genoa and Venice the hey-day of the commenda was the eleventh through the thirteenth centuries. The commenda began to decline in the fourteenth century, when a more complex form of commercial organization developed in which a wealthy individual (or often his entire family), by retaining salaried agents in various trading ports, was able to dispense with the need for travelling merchants and the commenda contract.* (See Chapter 13, for example, on the Bardi family and others).

Practices such as the commenda opened the way to riches for individual merchants; moreover, the contacts of the merchants with many areas fitted them to carry on what may be called banking activities. Especially active throughout Europe were the north Italians, referred to indiscriminately as the "Lombard" bankers. (Lombard Street in present-day London still bears testimony to the widespread activities of these late medieval financiers.) Florentine merchant-

---

* The *commenda* continued in use in smaller trade ventures in more peripheral Mediterranean areas.

bankers, in particular the houses of Bardi and Peruzzi, established branches all over Europe in the early fourteenth century.

One of the most important functions of a banking house was to act as an agency for the exchange of a new financial instrument, the letter of credit. The latter had been developed to obviate the need for merchants to carry large sums of cash around with them. With a letter of credit—roughly comparable to the modern check—an exchange of goods could be arranged without the need for actual transfer of cash over long distances. Letters of credit were especially common at the Champagne fairs, which served as a great clearinghouse for the payment and cancellation of debts. So powerful were some great banking houses that they came to control the finances of Europe, collecting taxes and revenues due to princes and prelates, lending money to Popes and kings (kings were so notorious for reneging on debts that the interest rates charged them were as high as 50 percent), as well as serving as agents for the deposit and transfer of funds.

Interestingly enough, one of the chief "banking" institutions in the later Middle Ages did not originally develop for commercial enterprises. The order of the Knights Templar had been founded as a crusading order of knights organized along monastic lines, whose primary purpose was to guard the Temple in Jerusalem. But nobles of the crusading armies began to use the different branch houses of the Templars for depositing and transferring money from one place to another, particularly from East to West. And thus as time went on, and particularly after the conquest of the Christian states of the Holy Land by the Muslims, the original purpose of the order was lost sight of and it functioned primarily as a financial institution. (On the destruction of the Templars in France see Chapter 8.)

The emergence of a genuine money economy from the eleventh century onward served gradually to transform Western society. Peasants began to receive money for the surplus produce of their fields sold in the local markets. They in turn paid money to the lords rather than rendering payment in kind or in services. Indeed, many lords, anxious to acquire the new luxury products of the East, began to "commute" services and payments in kind—that is, to convert them into monetary equivalents. Increasingly the serfs tended to become what we might call "tenant farmers," and many purchased their freedom outright. Payments to lords in money came to be crystallized by custom, a fact which in the long run (by the late thirteenth century) was to become an embarrassment and disadvantage to the nobles, who in time of inflation could not increase the rates of payment and thus were often ruined. On a higher level of society, kings also began demanding financial payments instead of the customary knight's service or other duties required of their vassals. Instead of the old feudal levy of troops (who by tradition would serve only forty days) the kings now preferred to hire mercenary soldiers, who could of course besiege a castle for as long as the royal funds held out. By the fourteenth century the military significance of the nobility, so important because of the nobles' dominant position in society, declined, thereby shattering one of the foundation stones of the feudal system. Thus the total effect of these beginnings of what might be termed a proto-capitalist economy was to weaken or transform both the old feudal and manorial systems and hence to contribute to the emergence of modern society.

The Emergence of Western Towns

Perhaps the most revolutionary element in the entire social and economic history of Western medieval society was the development of towns. The town injected a dynamic element into a social structure that had been essentially static. Its growth meant not only the movement of considerable population from rural to urban areas, but also a new organization of society from the economic, social, and political points of view. Simply put, the emergence of towns meant that the customary medieval stratification of society into two general classes, nobles and serfs, was now disrupted by a third and powerful new class, the medieval townsmen. Unlike the nobles and peasants, the townsmen (or burghers), consisting of merchants, craftsmen, and artisans, had little dependence on the land. For them money, not land, constituted wealth.

It is difficult to imagine Western Europe without cities. But during the period of the Dark Ages urban centers had virtually disappeared. Some of the nuclei of the Roman cities still remained in Paris, Rome, London, Cologne, and especially in Italy and southern France. But they were only shadows of the old Roman towns. They did not constitute cities in the modern sense of the word; they were, essentially, the sites of fortresses or of episcopal sees. They were usually inhabited only by the bishop or secular lord and his servants. These old settlements lacked any substantial group of merchants or artisans and were in consequence largely dependent on the local agricultural economy. Paris, for instance, consisted only of the Île de la Cité, a small fortified island in the middle of the Seine, where the royal residence, the episcopal palace, and the cathedral were the most important buildings. Rouen, the capital of the duchy of Normandy, was centered on the ducal palace, the bishop's residence, and a great monastery. To be sure, some merchant-craftsmen of the peddler type sold their wares in nearby regions where protection could be secured. And local markets existed in virtually all major concentrations of population. Their number and importance, however, were negligible, their purpose being only to serve local needs.

The Western Townsmen

In the tenth and eleventh centuries as conditions became more settled, peasant (and also noble) families often grew too large to find support for all their members on the manorial lands. Some, of course, were employed to cultivate new areas, but many others, unable to find sufficient land for themselves, simply left the manors to become wanderers. To earn a living some became mercenaries who sold their services and traveled about looking for places where war was taking place. Others joined organized bands of robbers. Many also turned to trade, earning their livelihood by transporting and selling the surplus of one area to another. (It should be noted, however, that the distinction between the legitimate merchants and the bandits was, in this early period, not always clear.) Hence the great growth of trade and commerce must be attributed not only to an increase in the products and wealth of Western Europe, but, it seems obvious, to the increasing number of men who turned to commerce to make a living.

There were enormous profits in trade, and many of these early merchants became quite wealthy. But there was danger too. Travel was very difficult; in winter the trails were almost impassable. Even more dangerous were some lords who were themselves little more than brigands, and who looked upon merchants, with their expensive wares, as fair game. As the merchants moved about they needed places to rest or to set up permanent or temporary bases of operations. They sought locations that were geographically advantageous, such as at the confluence of two streams or the point where a river ceased to be navigable. The most important stops were fortified castles, episcopal centers, or monasteries. (Monasteries often served as hospices, being duty bound to grant "hospitality" to travelers.) And many merchants established permanent residence at these fortified centers.

Soon enough, however, the space available to the merchants inside episcopal centers or castles was no longer sufficient. Hence the merchants were forced to settle outside the walls. In order to protect themselves they built new walls surrounding their settlements, connecting them with the old castles. The word for "castle" in German is *burg* (*bourg* in French), and thus these merchant settlements were called *faubourgs* ("outside the bourg"). Today we would call all such settlements "suburbs," a term that describes an area "at the foot of" the walls of a citadel situated on a hill. The city of Paris today consists, in part, of what in this early period was the merchant faubourg. An examination of the building of new walls in the German city of Cologne clearly reveals the growth of its merchant community, and, indirectly, of the rapid increase of trade and commerce from the tenth century onward. At Cologne, by the end of the tenth century, a large settlement of merchants had interposed themselves between the old Roman wall and the Rhine River; a new wall was built to enclose this new

The Garisenda and Asinelli towers in Bologna belonged to rival families. Italian urban strife for economic and political reasons in the thirteenth and fourteenth centuries led wealthy and powerful families to construct such towers for defense—the higher, the better. (Alinari/ Scala)

community. In the eleventh century another wall, completely surrounding the old Roman wall, was constructed, and in the twelfth century still another, encircling that built in the eleventh century.

Those living in these newly walled settlements surrounding the old fortified centers of Europe thus came to be called "burghers" (*bourgeois* in French). In due time these merchant settlements came completely to overshadow the original nucleus—the old castle or episcopal "city"—and thus, as Pirenne maintains, the medieval town (and hence the modern urban center) may be said to have emerged from the faubourg, or suburbs, rather than from the old "city."

Other reasons for the growth of towns include the expansion of certain kinds of manufacturing. A main example is that of textile centers in Flanders, where the increasing markets promoted the specialization of labor to the extent that each step in the process of manufacturing woolen cloth was controlled by a guild of master craftsmen. Such guilds helped both to protect and to control the life of the craftsmen, and, up to the thirteenth century, provided an adequate framework for the expansion of manufacturing. Since preparation of woolen cloth involves not only weaving but also cleaning of the raw wool, card-ing, spinning, dyeing, fulling, and other steps, it is clear that where all these specialized processes could be drawn together in a single place not only would the production of more and better woolens result but the urban population would be greatly expanded.

The earliest urban development took place in Flanders and in Italy, but the growing concentration of labor began to develop in many regions throughout Western Europe. Artisans began to leave the great estates to congregate in towns, where a larger supply of customers could be found and greater profits made. By the twelfth century all but the most backward areas had local manufacturing centers in which some amount of cloth, leather, ironware, and so on, was produced. Some towns became famous for the high quality of their products. I have already noted that the steel swords and other weapons of Toledo were in wide demand. Cordova became famous for its leather goods, Florence for silk and woolen cloth, and Hildesheim, Nuremburg, and Dinant in Flanders for metal products.

The size of these growing urban centers was, however, very small by modern standards—the population of most Flemish towns was only ten to twenty thousand inhabitants.

The following quote from a twelfth century chronicler's account of King Philip II gives an indication of a Western ruler's attitude toward the development of one medieval Western town, Paris:

> [Philip] was strolling in the great royal hall thinking over affairs of state and came to the palace windows from where he often looked out on the River Seine as a diversion. The horse wagons, crossing the city and cutting up the mud, stirred up a stench which he couldn't stand and he decided on a difficult but necessary piece of work which his predecessors had not dared to initiate because of the crushing expense. He summoned the burgesses and the provost of the city and ordered by his royal authority, that all the roads and streets of the city should be paved with strong, hard stone.*

But even local market areas of a more limited scope had an important impact on the economic life of medieval Europe. A sharp difference increasingly appeared between the functions of rural and urban areas. The rural came primarily to produce only food; the urban, manufactured goods and imported luxuries for the well-to-do. Each area now began to specialize in what it was best fitted for, and the old system of manorial manufacturing declined. Thus the rural self-sufficiency began to disappear, to be replaced by an interdependency of town and country.

---

* From Ch. Petit-Dutaillis, *The Feudal Monarchy in France and England: From the Tenth to the Thirteenth Century* (London: K. Paul, Trench, and Trübner, 1936), p. 199.

It is important to note, however, that the ordinary burgher was not a wealthy merchant who engaged in long-range luxury trade or owned large industrial enterprises. Even in Italy he was typically a baker, cobbler, smith, or weaver, not a dealer in silks and spices.

Indispensable to the merchants and craftsmen of the towns was the freedom to come and go at will for trading purposes and, consequently, relief from the exactions and dues of the feudal lords. How could a merchant be subject to the *corvée* and still carry on his trade effectively? The townsmen in the newly established merchant communities thus soon were demanding more autonomy. In medieval society, where every individual, whether vassal, lord, or serf, owed allegiance and service to some higher person, this demand for recognition of group freedom and self-government constituted a genuinely revolutionary element. But how did the townsman achieve his aims?

As discussed earlier, some feudal lords were willing to free their men from services provided they received monetary payments in exchange. For the same reasons, they would frequently be willing to grant charters of government to merchant communities. Nevertheless, the merchants often aggressively took the initiative. As people at the time of the great invasions had organized themselves for protection, so too the burghers now formed associations called *communitates* (communes) for the purpose of opposing the lords and asserting their demands. There was tremendous opposition to the rising communes from the privileged classes, for many of the nobles and at times the great ecclesiastics, not without justification, saw in the communes the seeds of the destruction of their society. Indeed, to them the commune had all the sinister implications that the word *communism* has or recently had in capitalist societies today. To them it represented anarchy, the destruction of their privileges and vested interests. In the course of great struggles the communes forced nobles or ecclesiastics in many areas of Europe to recognize them and even to grant them charters affirming their privileges.

A bitter enemy of the rising communes was the local bishop, who might at the same time be the feudal lord of the city, but whose episcopal palace and diocesan duties bound him inextricably to the town. Historians know that in thirteenth-century Cologne, for example, the burghers, banding together, revolted against the authority of the archbishop, lord of the city. The archbishop was forced to grant them self-governing status, which in effect gave them control of the city.

As might be expected, feudal customary law, agrarian and military in scope and often slow to administer justice, was usually incompetent to judge affairs of the merchants. Hence the burghers developed their own commercial or town law in order to take care of their own specific needs. Ecclesiastics, however, even those residing within the city, were as a rule not subject to the duties or civil law of the townsmen. Even if a cleric committed murder, according to canon

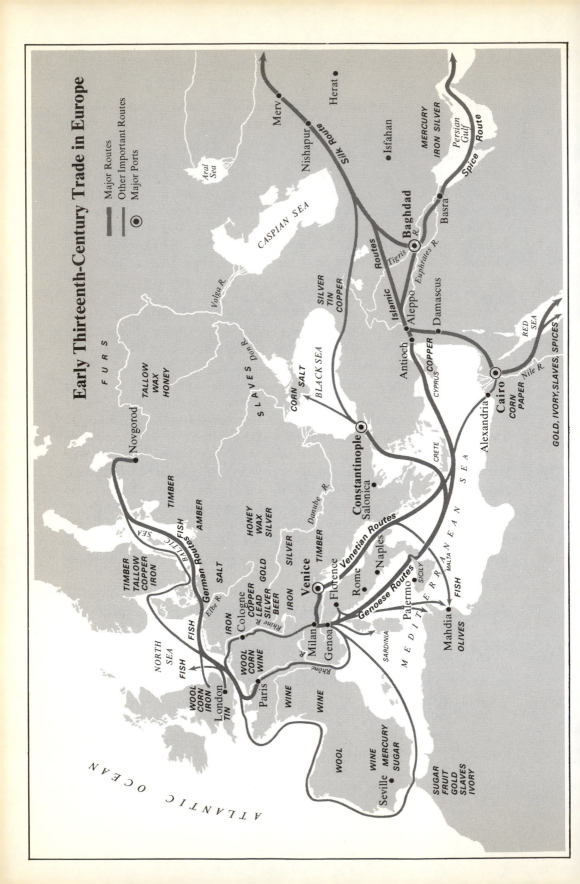

Early Thirteenth-Century Trade in Europe

Major Routes
Other Important Routes
Major Ports

ATLANTIC OCEAN

FURS

TALLOW
WAX
HONEY

Novgorod

Aral
Sea

CASPIAN SEA

Merv

Herat

Nishapur

Isfahan

Silk Route

Baghdad

Basra

MERCURY
IRON SILVER

Persian
Gulf

Spice
Route

Volga R.

Don R.

SLAVES

CORN
SALT

BLACK SEA

SILVER
TIN
COPPER

Islamic
Routes

Tigris R.

Euphrates R.

Aleppo

Damascus

Antioch

COPPER

CYPRUS

RED
SEA

Nile R.

Alexandria

Cairo

CORN
PAPER

GOLD, IVORY, SLAVES, SPICES

TIMBER

AMBER

FISH

BALTIC SEA

HONEY
WAX
SILVER

Danube R.

Constantinople

Salonica

CRETE

TIMBER

German Routes

SALT

Cologne

COPPER
LEAD
SILVER
BEER

GOLD

SILVER

IRON

Rhine R.

Elbe R.

Venice

TIMBER

Venetian Routes

Naples

Genoese Routes

SICILY

MALTA

TIMBER
TALLOW
COPPER
IRON

IRON

NORTH
SEA

FISH

FISH

WOOL
CORN
IRON
TIN

London

Paris

WINE

WOOL
CORN
WINE

Milan

Genoa

Florence

Rome

Palermo

Mahdia

OLIVES

FISH

MEDITERRANEAN SEA

SARDINIA

Rhône R.

WINE

WINE

WOOL

WINE

Seville

MERCURY
SUGAR

SUGAR
FRUIT
GOLD
SLAVES
IVORY

law he could not be tried by any secular courts. The class of clerics included not only bishops, priests, and monks, but any who were tonsured (that is, shaven-headed). Thus even secretaries of bishops and students were considered "clerics." This situation created deep resentment among the townsmen, who came to regard many of the clerics as privileged parasites. One of the most dramatic struggles, lasting even up to modern times, concerned the attempts of the burghers to deprive the ecclesiastics of their jealously guarded clerical immunities.

With the acquisition of autonomy or near autonomy, towns became corporate entities with legal personalities of their own. As a unit a town often might be required to perform military service for a lord, much as if the town were a feudal vassal. In time, however, the townsmen as a group gained a special status in feudal law. However grudgingly, they came to be recognized as a new class in society, their members in fact being considered outside the customary law. Indeed, the custom arose that if a serf who escaped to a town lived there for a year and a day without being apprehended he became a free man. As the famous saying put it, "Town air makes a man free."

Gradually the burghers developed municipal institutions to govern themselves. Although some towns never threw off outside control—Paris, for example, was always ruled by the king's agents—by the thirteenth century most towns had a mayor and a council whose functions were to represent and administer the town. The mayor and the council kept the town seal, saw to the maintenance of buildings, markets, bridges, roads, and, in general, handled relations with their lords. The municipal government usually levied taxes on its markets and business transactions, not on landed property as in the manorial systems. All townsmen had to aid in its defense, help build and repair the wall, and fight in the town militia.

Western Guilds

It might seem at first glance that the spirit of the medieval Western town was democratic. But this conception is certainly false; far from wishing to extend their rights to others, townsmen, once they had achieved their privileges, formed exclusive, regimented organizations with the aim of preserving these rights for themselves alone. First organized to provide group protection to merchants in their travels, and, later, to preserve the local rights of merchants and craftsmen, these associations, or guilds, quickly became monopolistic, sharply curtailing individual liberty. An analysis of the Western guild system will provide us not only with a key to the understanding of the organization and structure of the medieval town, but will reveal as well the manifold aspects of town life.

A guild may be defined as a sworn, voluntary association of men organized for protection and mutual aid. There were many kinds of such associations. The medieval university and the town itself each constituted in fact a kind of guild. But for the moment let us turn to the *merchant guild,* which was probably the first to appear and constituted the nucleus for the organization of the towns. As early as the late tenth century merchants formed associations for the protection of their horses, wagons, and goods when travelling. A heavy guard, sometimes even mercenaries, flanked the caravan to protect the tradesmen and their merchandise. Regulations governed the caravans, and after the trip was completed the merchants split the costs and profits in proportion to their investment.

Apparently the systematization of guilds came about at roughly the same time as the towns themselves developed. Often in fact a merchant guild would found a town—of only a few people, to be sure—but with both organizations having the same or parallel structure. With the increasing specialization of industry, however, there soon emerged another kind of association, the *craft guild,* a group of artisans engaged in the same occupation—bakers, cobblers, stone masons, carpenters, and so on. With the further growth of manufacturing, these craft associations became even more important than the older merchant guilds, and their leaders often took over, or at least demanded a share in, the leadership of the town. Soon no one within a town could practice a craft without belonging to the appropriate guild association.

By the thirteenth century to become a guildsman one had to go through three successive stages. The lowest was that of apprentice, then journeyman, and finally, at the top, the master craftsman. The apprentice was a youth who was learning his craft. After a two-week probationary period he was accepted as an apprentice for a seven-year term. During this time the master lodged and fed him and taught him the trade or craft. If the apprentice fled or complained about his treatment, an inquiry was supposed to be held. At the end of his period of apprenticeship the young man was released to become a wage earner, or journeyman. As a journeyman he attempted to improve his skills, and if he could produce a "masterpiece" that would meet the standards of the local guild, he became a master craftsman and a member of the guild.

If for some reason an apprentice who had served his term could not become a master (he might, for example, lack the capital to set up his own shop), he remained a journeyman, a paid worker who hired himself out to a master. In an expanding economy the working conditions were usually fairly good for a journeyman. He was the companion of the master; moreover, as soon as he raised enough capital he could fairly easily rise to the status of master. By the early fourteenth century, however, growth was coming to an end and the status of the journeyman declined. Attempts to raise wages were often opposed either by the masters or sometimes even by the Church.

The masters, of course, ran the guilds. A master had his own shop, usually with one or two apprentices and perhaps a journeyman or two to assist him. It was forbidden for a master to lure away another master's journeyman by the offer of a higher wage. With the increasing number of men seeking to achieve mastership, thereby lessening profits and even weakening the power of the old masters within the guild, the latter became more and more jealous of their status. Because they made entry into the mastership very restrictive (by the late thirteenth century many apprentices found it difficult to rise above the status of a journeyman), the masters increased the number of journeymen and made it easier to hold down their wages. The journeymen formed a kind of incipient urban proletariat, and because of poor working conditions, particularly in Italy and Flanders, they sometimes rioted and went on strike. Newly organized guilds composed of disgruntled journeymen entered into price competition with old guilds in spite of the expected (often only theoretical) practice of charging only a "just price." But the basic problem, probably not appreciated at the time, the surplus of labor, was to be altered considerably in France by the ravages of the Black Death (1348) and military devastation.

To understand the aims and methods of the guilds, the system should be examined from the economic, social, and political viewpoints, aspects of town life all affected by the guilds. The primary purpose of the guild was economic— to regulate competition among the members and to protect its monopoly over a particular craft. In so doing, it not only protected its own members but the consumers as well. There were many craft guild regulations to prevent poor workmanship. Each article had to be examined by a board of the guild and stamped as approved. To help avoid inferior craftsmanship, work at night was prohibited. In Florence the number of vats used by the dyers was prescribed exactly; in the Byzantine guilds in Constantinople and elsewhere the measurements used in making garments were strictly set forth. In other places it was forbidden to sell pigs fattened by a barber-surgeon for fear they had been fed on sick people's blood! Fraud was to be avoided; in Venice, for instance, it was forbidden to sell plated metalware.

To regulate competition between members the guild forbade advertising; they even forbade any attempt on the part of the guildsmen to gain the attention of another's customer by such acts as sneezing! All prices were strictly regulated, and "price-cutting" was expressly forbidden.

In order to preserve its monopoly a guild would forbid the sale of foreign artisans' work within the city. The most important processes used in manufacturing were jealously guarded. In Florence the secret of making silk brocade (derived earlier from Byzantium) was so zealously protected that for a long time silk brocade could be procured only in that city. In Venice it was a law that if a worker in possession of trade secrets fled for any reason to a foreign territory, he must be tracked down and killed, lest he divulge his information.

There was monopoly even within the individual guild. I have already noted the attempts of the masters to limit their number. Membership in guilds became virtually hereditary. Yet within set limits fair play and honest competition were stressed. No member was ever allowed to corner the market, that is, to purchase a large supply of a product or commodity so as to be able to fix its price. In the woolen industry, where each guild specialized in only one step in the process of manufacturing, the guild officials often acted as middlemen and bought in behalf of their members.

The guild also provided for virtually the entire social life of its members. One of its most important aspects was its "social" or "welfare" work, aspects of which were no doubt a carryover from the guilds of Roman times. Money was supplied for funeral expenses of the poorer members and aid was given their families. Dowries were granted to poor girls. Members were covered by a kind of health insurance. Each guild often had its own provisions for care of the sick, even a hospital. Periodically during the year the guild held great banquet festivities for the entertainment of its members. It also built chapels or donated windows to the town cathedral and at times helped in the actual construction of the building.

More than this, the guild watched over the morals of its members, punishing those indulging in gambling and usury. It provided schools for members' children, important for their contribution to the emergence of Western lay education. Previous to this the only schools in existence in the West had been monastic or cathedral schools for the training of clergy. In effect, then, from a social point of view all members of the guild were confrères, brothers helping one another and presenting a united front to outsiders.

From the political viewpoint, however, the guild was neither absolutely sovereign nor unrelated to society outside the guild and town organizations. In time the guilds became accommodated to the feudal system. As a collective unit the guild, like an individual, might owe allegiance as a vassal to a bishop, lord, or, as in Paris, to the king. Yet the degree of vassalage or independence of the guild depended to a great extent on the degree of independence of the town in which it was located.

Within the town itself there was a close connection between the city authority and the guild. In the event of trouble between guilds, the mayor and council would intervene to preserve order. The council also could establish the hours of work, fix prices, and establish weights and measures. In addition, municipal custom required each guild to perform public services such as policing the streets (the guilds took turns at this, one being responsible one week, another the following) and helping to construct public buildings and walls to defend the city. On the other hand, guild officials themselves often were appointed, by town charters, to serve in the town government, since the guilds usually voted as a unit in elections, raised troops for the town militia, and paid taxes as a group. The Florentine craft guilds, for example, often controlled the nomination of city officials.

This painting by Ambrogio Lorenzetti depicts Siena in the fourteenth century.
(Alinari/Scala)

In Florence, where the guild system was perhaps most highly developed, guilds were ranked by law according to importance, the highest possessing special privileges. Professional men were members of the top-ranking guilds; manual laborers (who were allowed to form guilds only once—after the Ciompi revolt of 1378—see Chapter 13) were at the bottom. Judges, merchants, and painters were the most privileged; bakers, butchers, and carpenters belonged to the lower group. One even walked on the street according to his rank in a guild: the privileged walked nearest the wall, where balconies and overhanging structures afforded some protection from the heaving of garbage and the emptying of chamber pots out of upper-story windows directly onto the unpaved street below.

Byzantine Guilds

The possible influence of the Byzantine guild system or its practices on the guilds of the West should be noted, since the Byzantine guilds long preceded those of the West and almost constant economic contacts between East and West existed. We learn of the Byzantine system primarily from the late tenth century Greek *Book of the Prefect*—in effect from the "mayor" of Constantinople. Although on the surface Byzantine and Western guilds seem to have been quite similar, there were several basic differences. Unlike the West where by the tenth century the authority of the central state had virtually disappeared, in the East the Byzantine guild system was not intended to serve the interests of the producers and merchants but was primarily to promote governmental control of economic life in the interest of the state. The Byzantine guilds had carefully delineated and even more fully detailed regulations than in the West—the Byzantine dealing for example with at least eight kinds of silk merchants and manufacturers as well as with cattle traders, carpenters, notaries, and others. But the increasingly monopolistic practices of the Western guild system remained in sharp contrast to those of Byzantium where the central government strictly regulated the guilds for the corporate interests of society as a whole rather than for the benefit of any specific merchant or craft guild. Given these fundamental differences in the two guild systems, whatever Byzantine influences on the West existed were probably more a matter of secondary significance than of any fundamental importance.

Evaluation

In attempting to analyze the merits and flaws of the Western guild system, noting the protection it gave the consumer against bad workmanship and fraud is important. The system also helped him by keeping prices "just," that is, at a stable level (or, as we would say, helping to prevent inflation) and at a point where normal production and market would provide a subsistence income. On the other hand, the strictness of regulation tended to stifle progress by cramping initiative on the part of the producers. Improvements designed to speed up work and production were discouraged by all except the very largest guilds. And taste as a factor in manufacturing was too often disregarded. Admittedly a great deal of protection was afforded to guild members, but in general those outside the organization, the consumers, were at the mercy of the guildsmen.

Why did the emergence of modern capitalism destroy the medieval guild system? The answer to this question lies perhaps in the guilds' restrictions on production and prices and their monopolistic character. It is notable that when town loyalty began to be displaced by allegiance to the larger national unit, significant change took place in the guilds. Nevertheless, the guild organization as such continued to exist for a long time in Western Europe. In France its last vestiges were finally destroyed only as late as the French Revolution in 1789. But long before the guilds themselves ceased to exist, they had decayed from within and by the fifteenth century had lost much of their former importance.

In the economic revival of Western Europe, the development of towns and municipal organization depended on the rise of trade and commerce, caused by the gradual increase in population beginning in the late tenth century. The increase in population had been made possible by improved agricultural methods —practices brought into wider use only after a certain measure of peace and order had been established. As each factor developed, then, it in turn stimulated the others. It is not easy in this long process to single out a "first cause," nor can a rigid series of causes and results be set up. Rather, the remarkable revival of Western Europe from the late tenth century onward must be viewed as a kind of circular chain in which each link was necessary for the support of the other links. The pendant of this chain was the medieval town.

FOR FURTHER READING

Duby, G., *Rural Economy and Country Life in the Medieval West* (1968). Outstanding work.

Genicot, L., *Contours of the Middle Ages* (1967). Social factors in culture.

Havighurst, A. F., ed., *The Pirenne Thesis: Analysis, Criticism, and Revision** (1969). A collection of essays analyzing the Pirenne thesis on Arab influences on the early medieval West.

Herlihy, D., *Pisa in the Early Renaissance: A Study of Urban Growth* (1958). Important study of Italian town life.

Lopez, R. S., *The Birth of Europe** (1972). An original work by an important scholar.

Lopez, R. S., *The Commercial Revolution of the Middle Ages* (1971). A concise, stimulating treatment.

Lopez, R. S. and I. W. Raymond, eds., *Medieval Trade in the Mediterranean World** (1967). A valuable collection of translations of medieval economic documents.

Marongiu, A., *Medieval Parliaments: A Comparative Study* (1968). Focuses on Italy.

Mundy, J. H., and P. Riesenberg, *The Medieval Town** (1958). A collection of sources.

Pirenne, H., *Economic and Social History of Medieval Europe* (1937; 1956). A standard short history of economic and social life by a famous scholar.

Pirenne, H., *Medieval Cities** (1925, 1956). The standard work on the emergence of the medieval city; a thesis accepted by most scholars.

Pirenne, H., *Mohammed and Charlemagne** (1955). A celebrated but highly controversial work proposing the thesis that the Arabs were largely responsible for bringing about the Western Dark Ages.

Power, E., *Medieval People,* 10th rev. ed. (1963). A collection of biographies of Western personalities and a Carolingian peasant.

---

* Asterisk indicates paperback edition available.

Pryon, J. H., "The Origins of the *Commenda* Contract," *Speculum,* vol. 52 (1977), pp. 5–37. Summarizes the various views.

Rorig, R., *The Medieval Town* (1967). Focuses on German towns.

Stephenson, C., *Borough and Town: A Study of Urban Origins in England* (1964). A specialized study.

Waley, D., *The Italian City-Republics* (1969). Good, brief analysis of communes' development.

White, L., Jr., *Medieval Technology and Social Change** (1966). Valuable survey of the relationship of technology and society; the only work of its kind in English.

As seen in Chapter 3, Charlemagne's reestablishment of the "Roman" Empire in the West seemed to promise order and prosperity to the people of Western Europe. What are today France, Germany, northern Italy, and parts of the Slavic lands were brought under the rule of one emperor. The influence of religion grew hand in hand with the power of the state, and the Carolingian revival of learning seemed to presage a general uplifting of cultural standards. But Charlemagne and his successors were unable to maintain the order he had imposed on so vast an empire. The Carolingian organization therefore soon broke down, and by the beginning of the tenth century no one even bothered to claim the shadowy imperial title. In East and West Frankland dukes and counts now ruled virtually as free agents, while northern Italy was torn by intrigue and civil war. In the ninth century the West was also plagued

CHAPTER 7

Rise and Decline of the Holy Roman Empire

by the terrible devastation wrought by Northman, Slav, and Magyar. Thus at the beginning of the tenth century a condition of near anarchy prevailed in most of Western Europe.

The decline and disintegration that beset the Carolingian Empire was, however, less evident in the eastern, more Germanic areas than in the western, a phenomenon which became increasingly apparent by the mid-tenth century. Indeed at this time it seemed possible that Germany rather than France would develop into a strong, unified state and become the leader of Western European civilization. Poorer, less Romanized, and at the same time more isolated, the old territory of Louis the German had been left more or less alone by the Viking marauders. Moreover, the Germans of this eastern area seemed more warlike and hence better able to repulse such invaders as the Magyars (Hungarians). No less important, there soon arose in Germany a dynasty able to exert effective sway over the dukes and at the same time to end the anarchy of Italy by incorporating the latter once again into the German realm.

Under this dynasty, called the Ottonian (after the first emperor, Otto the Great) or Saxon (after the ducal House of Saxony), a strong monarch was again able to build up a supra-national state and reassume the title of Roman emperor. As an ally (more exactly, an instrument) of the crown the German Church prospered, and, as under Charlemagne, a certain revival of learning took place. Later, however, in the eleventh and twelfth centuries, this German-based Roman Empire declined when a mighty conflict between Pope and emperor arose. When this contest was finally resolved, the Empire had virtually collapsed. And by the thirteenth century the Pope was able to emerge not only as the supreme spiritual authority but, in effect, even as arbiter of temporal affairs in Europe.

The Saxon Dynasty

In the late ninth and early tenth centuries five well-defined duchies began to emerge in the kingdom of East Frankland (modern Germany): Saxony, Franconia, Swabia, Lorraine, and Bavaria, each under the rule of a duke. Originally the homelands of the great German tribes (except for Lorraine), these duchies had been organized by Charlemagne and his successors into military districts for the purpose of defense. With the breakup of Charlemagne's empire, however, the king lost much of his authority over the dukes, and by the death of the last Carolingian king of Germany, Louis the Child (d. 911), the dukes had become virtually independent. Reasserting the ancient German right of election, the dukes now chose one of themselves as king, Conrad I, Duke of Franconia (911–918). But the weakness of Conrad's rule permitted a further development of the duchies into semi-independent principalities.

At Conrad's death the Duke of Saxony was chosen king, as Henry I (919–936).* With Henry's accession (he is known to history as Henry the Fowler because he supposedly was bird hunting when notice came of his election) the leadership of the House of Saxony over Germany began. Henry the Fowler was the first German king to establish as a definite policy the famous German drive to the East (*Drang nach Osten*) against the semi-nomadic Slavs of that region. This German push eastward was to continue for many centuries, even up to our own day, and in fact constituted a factor in the background to the beginning of the Second World War. Henry began a piecemeal conquest of the nearby Slavic areas, adopting a policy of displacing the conquered Slavs with German colonists. More significant for his reign were his victories over the Magyars, whose annual marauding raids through Central Europe still constituted a severe threat to Germany. Despite the added prestige these successes over foreign enemies brought to the monarchy, Henry did not try to curb the power of the dukes, being satisfied with technical overlordship and instead concentrating his attention on strengthening his own duchy, which constituted the true basis for his royal power.

The reign of Henry's son, Otto the Great (936–973), marked the high point of Saxon power. At the Battle of Lechfeld in 955 Otto administered the decisive blow which finally and decisively checked the Magyars. Further inroads from Hungary were thwarted by the establishment of garrisons along the frontier. Although I question one modern view that in its larger implications the Battle of Lechfeld was as important for European history as that of ancient Marathon, it cannot be denied that Otto's victory did serve to end forever the Magyar threat to Western Europe. The Magyars abandoned their nomadic raids and settled down permanently on the great plain of what is now Hungary, thus driving a permanent wedge between the Slavs of the Balkans and those of the north and east in Poland and Russia.

Determined to reassert royal authority over the whole kingdom, Otto spent the first two decades of his reign in constant struggle with his rebellious dukes. In order to check their power, he revived Charlemagne's policy of forging a close relationship between German church and state. Indeed he so expanded the alliance that it became his greatest source of strength. Judiciously drawing into his administration ecclesiastics appointed by himself, he utilized them as counterweights to the authority of the dukes. Although he depended primarily on this alliance with the Church, Otto also gained a large measure of control over the duchies by military victories, by binding the dukes to him through marriage alliances, or by supplanting the lords of certain areas with his own relatives. A prime example of Otto's policy toward church and state was the

---

* After 962, it became the practice that in order to become Emperor, the King of Germany had to be crowned in Rome by the Pope.

appointment of his brother Bruno as first the archbishop of Cologne and then duke of the important but turbulent duchy of Lorraine.

The use of clerics in the royal administration brought many advantages to the king. In this period, when ecclesiastics were invariably better educated than lay lords, clerics made far better administrators. Moreover, since they, in effect, owed both their religious office and temporal authority to the king, they were generally more trustworthy. As yet the monarchy had no central institutions, no professional bureaucracy, and only inadequate finances; therefore, churchmen throughout the empire came to constitute the king's most valuable officials. Moreover, they often provided him with revenues from the Church lands and even supplied him with some of his best-trained troops. Not to be overlooked also is the fact that because churchmen could not legally pass on lands to their sons (if they had any), the king retained ultimate control over their lands.

But such a policy of royal dependence on the Church, however useful at the time, was in the long run to prove disastrous to the German crown. For despite the effective control Otto himself was able to exercise over his bishops, as the power of the papacy increased in the time of Otto's successors, the bishops became far less compliant to the imperial will. Thus when a prolonged struggle broke out between Pope and Emperor the alliance between the German king and church gradually crumbled. Otto, of course, could hardly have foreseen this development. Given the conditions of the time, his most expeditious policy was to ally himself with the German Church. And indeed, far from damaging the monarchy, ecclesiastical support made the German king the strongest monarch in Western Europe in the tenth century.

In the latter part of his reign Otto turned his attention to the conquest of Italy, a policy some have tried to explain in the light of his alliance with the German bishops. With his kingdom so dependent on ecclesiastical support, it was perhaps judicious to seek a measure of control over the supreme head of the Church in Rome as well. Otto seemed consciously to have emulated the example of Charlemagne. He had himself crowned king of Germany at Aachen, and he probably dreamed of his own coronation in Rome as Roman emperor. It was probably for all these reasons that Otto spent ten of his last twelve years in Italy.

Otto's first intervention in Italy occurred in 951, ostensibly to rescue a damsel in distress. Adelaide, the widow of the last (nominal) Lombard king of Italy, had appealed to Otto for aid against a petty lord who was trying to marry her in order to gain the crown of Italy. "Thus," as Hrotswitha (a tenth-century nun of Gandersheim) cogently says, "seeing a fitting means of joining the Italian Kingdom to his own," Otto came to Adelaide's rescue and married her himself. He then returned to Germany.

At the time of Otto's intervention, both Italy and the Papacy were in a state of political and moral chaos. Primarily as a result of the collapse of the stabilizing influence of Carolingian rule, Northern Italy was torn by intrigue and civil war, with the nobles constantly struggling among themselves for the crown of Italy. And in Rome itself the Papacy had become the pawn of rival noble factions that, by violence and treachery, were often able to elevate and depose popes at will. As seen in Chapter 4, the Papacy itself was virtually controlled for a time by two mistresses of the Popes, leading some historians to refer to this period of moral degradation and disorder as the "Pornocracy."

Revival of the Empire

Descending into Italy a second time (961), Otto succeeded in bringing some order to the affairs of that chaotic land. He gained effective control over the north and saw to the installation on the Papal throne of men of good character. Like Charlemagne he was summoned by a Pope (John XII) embroiled in conflict with a noble faction. After Otto's triumphal entry into Rome in February of 962, the scene of Charlemagne's coronation of 800 was re-enacted in St. Peter's. Once more there was a Roman emperor in the West.

Historians know little about the circumstances leading to this famous event, but it seems probable that Otto had made as a condition of his aid to the Pope his coronation in Rome. Otto's awareness of the turbulence of the Roman popu-

This plaque from a tenth-century altar shows the Holy Roman Emperor (probably Otto I, reigned 962–973) offering a model of the Magdeburg Cathedral to Christ. Scenes of a ruler offering a model of a city or church were common in Byzantine art. (The Metropolitan Museum of Art, Gift of George Blumenthal, 1941)

lace is indicated by the contemporary German chronicler Widukind, who relates that Otto directed his sword bearer to stand by him in St. Peter's during the ceremony and not to leave his side for any reason whatever.

Otto's coronation was not simply the re-establishment of Charlemagne's empire. Indeed, though Otto may have claimed to be the successor of both Constantine and Charlemagne, his empire was really a new political organism. Lacking Gaul, it was essentially a union of Germany and two-thirds of Italy. It was less Roman, less Pan-European than that of Charles. It was not indeed until later, in the twelfth century, that the empire came officially to be known as the "Holy Roman Empire of the German nation." After Otto, election to the kingship of Germany by the German nobles constituted, in practice, election to the imperial title as well, though in legal theory the title had to be confirmed by the ceremony of papal coronation in Rome. Although the Ottonian Empire was weaker than that of Charlemagne, it still bore the great name of Rome, a name which in the minds of some people summoned up memories of the glorious days of ancient Rome.

In exchange for Papal coronation Otto confirmed the Donation of Pepin. But at the same time he insisted (reminiscent of Byzantine practice) that all future Popes must be approved by the emperor. When Pope John XII appeared recalcitrant, Otto showed his determination to exert his authority by summoning a synod of Italian bishops and persuading them to condemn and depose John for immoral acts. John's political crime, of course, was defiance of the imperial will. In John's place Leo VIII, Otto's nominee, was elected. By these acts the precedent of imperial control over the Papacy was firmly established, and it was to last for a century.

After the eventful reign of Otto the Great that of his son, Otto II (973–983), seems anticlimactic. As might be expected, the new emperor had first to suppress an attempted uprising of the dukes, in the course of which he divided up Bavaria, splitting off the eastern part (East Mark), which became the nucleus of modern Austria. Turning to Italy, Otto II made a rash bid to take southern Italy from the Byzantines, but he was defeated. He died soon afterwards.

Theophano and Byzantine Influences. Otto II's son and successor, Otto III (983–1002), was a fascinating figure but rather ineffective as a ruler. His reign began with the regency of his mother, the Byzantine princess Theophano, who, after lengthy negotiations, had come to Germany with a large Greek retinue to marry Otto II. The ambitious Theophano turned her son's head with Byzantine ideas of imperial power and glory, and it became young Otto's dream to reunite the Eastern and Western empires into one great reunified Roman Empire.

This dream of course would remain far from being realized. Nevertheless, the court of Otto, even if only superficially, reflected certain aspects of Byzantine cultural influence. For instance Otto used Byzantine titles such as Logothete ("minister") in his administration and borrowed ideas from Byzantine political theology for the creation of certain art works. But despite these Byzantine-oriented tendencies, Otto's political ideology remained essentially faithful to the ideal of his Western imperial predecessor Charlemagne. Thus in the year 1000 he had Charles' tomb in Aachen opened and that great monarch's ring of authority removed for his own use.

Despite, or perhaps in part because of, his dreams, Otto III's reign was rather ineffectual, and against him the nobles once again reasserted their power. Only in his relations with the Papacy did he achieve any real success, for he and Pope Sylvester II worked together in harmony. This is not surprising since Sylvester, who was the celebrated scholar Gerbert, had been young Otto's tutor and was, in fact, elevated to the Papal throne by Otto himself. Together they worked tirelessly to extend the boundaries of Latin Christendom eastward, converting the Hungarians and most of the Poles to Catholicism. The famous crown of St. Stephen (whose construction reveals a good deal of Byzantine workmanship) was sent to the first Hungarian king by Pope Sylvester in 1000.

At the death of Otto III in 1002 it seemed as if the great work of his grandfather Otto I would be undone. Since Otto III left no heir, the nobles elected as king Henry of Bavaria (1002–1024), a cousin of Otto III and the last male representative of the Saxon dynasty. Revolts now broke out in both Germany and Italy. Henry was able to restore his imperial prestige, however, only by neglecting affairs in Italy in order to concentrate on Germany.

Like his predecessors, Henry II relied on ecclesiastical support to bolster the authority of the monarchy. Sincerely interested in the welfare of the Church (the Roman Church has in fact named him a saint), Henry encouraged the great monastic reform movement of his time that was to revive the Church and, ironically, enable it ultimately to throw off imperial control. For his support of ecclesiastical reform Henry has been accused of unwittingly preparing the way for the destruction of his own empire. But of course in his time, when the German bishops were still loyal allies of the crown and were kept under strict royal supervision, Henry, like the other Saxons, could not foresee that the Church under the leadership of the Papacy would one day become the great enemy of the Empire.

The Ottonian Renaissance

Under the Saxon emperors a revival of learning, primarily centered in Germany and to a lesser degree in northern Italy and France, took place. This revival has been called, with some exaggeration, the "Ottonian Renaissance." As had been true in Charlemagne's time, the leaders in the Ottonian revival were churchmen, and thus there was a revitalization of monastic and cathedral schools. In the sphere of art, too, in connection with illuminated manuscripts,

Henry II (1002–1024), last Emperor of the Saxon dynasty, is shown here being crowned by Christ. Note the strong Byzantine influence on the dress of the Emperor and the strictly Byzantine gesture of Christ. (The faces show little Byzantine influence, however.) Henry II was the successor of Otto III, whose mother was the Byzantine princess Theophano. (Bayerische Staatsbibliothek, Munich)

and particularly in sculpture and stone and bronze work—at Hildesheim Cathedral, for example, there was increased activity.

Unlike their Carolingian predecessors, however, the Saxon emperors did not take such a personal role in fostering scholarship. To be sure, under the influence of Otto I's brother, Archbishop Bruno of Cologne, the imperial chancellory instituted a school to train administrators for the government and the Church, but there was less emphasis on training in the liberal arts than there had been among the scholars of Charlemagne's court at Aachen. Emphasis was placed, instead, on the revitalization of monastic and cathedral schools such as those at Cologne, Liège, and Hildesheim. Although some Ottonian scholars—for example, Gerbert—may have been as erudite as their Carolingian counterparts, the Ottonian Renaissance produced no speculative thinker comparable to Johannes Scotus Erigena.

Historical writing in the form of chronicles delineating yearly events and concerned with monasteries and the deeds of princes and bishops flourished at this time. A prime example is the work of the Saxon monk Widukind, a turgid though informative account of the deeds of the Saxons up to the imperial coronation of Otto I in 962. Biography, too, was a favored type of writing, especially of the careers of leading bishops. The value of such biographical accounts is considerable, for, in contrast to the naive credulity of earlier hagiography, far less mention of the miraculous is made than of day-to-day political events.

Liudprand and Byzantium.   The best known of Ottonian historical writers is Liudprand of Cremona (d. 972), a north Italian bishop in the service of Otto the Great. Among the most learned men of his day, Liudprand was one of the very few who knew Greek. His *Antapodosis,* which covers the period of Italian history before and after the intervention of Otto I, provides a vivid picture of the anarchic conditions in Italy during the time of the Pornocracy. And his *Gesta Ottonis (Deeds of Otto)* describes the trial and deposition of Pope John XII. As envoy to Constantinople for Otto I, Liudprand has left us a remarkable account of his reception by the Byzantines. His *Legation to Constantinople* is, to be sure, highly biased against the Greeks, but it does provide us with a good picture of court life in Byzantium. As pointed out in Chapter 5, his work vividly demonstrates the increasingly hostile attitude of the Byzantine and Western emperors toward each other, each denying to his counterpart the title of Roman emperor. Berating the Byzantines for their military impotency in the West during the entire period of the Pornocracy, Liudprand scornfully declares to the Greek emperor:

> Your [Byzantine imperial] power . . . was fast asleep then; [as was] the power of your predecessors who in name alone are called emperors of the Romans, while the reality is far different. If they were

powerful, if they were emperors of the Romans, why did they allow Rome to be in the hands of harlots? Who of your emperors... troubled to punish so heinous a crime and bring back the holy church to its proper state. You neglected it; my master [Otto] did not.... In accordance with the decrees of such Roman emperors as Justinian, Valentinian, Theodosius, etc., he [Otto] slew, beheaded, hanged, or exiled.*

On another occasion Liudprand records a comment of the Byzantine emperor which reveals similarly Byzantine scorn for Western military might:

> [The Greek ruler] asked me many questions concerning your [Otto's] army. And when I had replied to him consequently and truly, "Thou liest," he said, "the soldiers of thy master [Otto] do not know how to ride, nor do they know how to fight on foot; the size of their shields, the weight of their breastplates, the length of their swords, and the burden of their helmets permit them to fight in neither one way nor the other." Then he added, smiling: "Their gluttony also impedes them, for their God is their belly, their courage but wind, their bravery drunkenness. Their fasting means dissolution, their sobriety panic. Nor has thy master a number of fleets on the sea. I alone have a force of navigators; I will attack him with my ships, I will overrun his maritime cities with war, and those which are near the rivers I will reduce to ashes. And how, I ask, can he even on land resist me with his scanty forces?

One of Liudprand's missions to Constantinople was to arrange the marriage-alliance between the Byzantine princess Theophano and the son of Otto the Great, Otto II. Theophano's arrival in the West, accompanied by an entourage of Byzantines, brought to the West, as shown earlier, a momentary awareness of certain Byzantine customs and way of life. In his writings, however, Liudprand above all reflects the widening breach between the Byzantine and Western worlds of Christendom.

Other literary figures of merit lived during Otto I's reign, including Ekkehard, a monk of St. Gall, who wrote the Latin epic poem *Waltharlied,* describing the escape of a German hostage from the camp of Attila the Hun. This poem ranks as one of the best Latin epics of the medieval period. Another writer, the nun Hrotswitha, who belonged to the convent of Gandersheim in Saxony, wrote several stories about early saints as well as historical pieces in verse form. The best-known writings attributed to her by some scholars, however, were her plays, probably the first full-length dramas to appear in the Western medieval period. While imitating the style of the ancient Roman

---

* Both excerpts are from *The Works of Liudprand of Cremona,* trans. F. A. Wright (1930).

NORTH SEA

DENMARK

BALTIC SEA

Elbe R.

POMERANIA

Vistula R.

NORTHERN MARCHES

Boundary

DUCHY OF
SAXONY

Hildesheim

Oder R.

Indefinite

DUCHY OF
POLAND

THURINGIA

D. OF
Liège
LOWER LORRAINE

Cologne

Aachen

Rhine R.

DUCHY OF
FRANCONIA

DUCHY OF
BOHEMIA

MORAVIA

Worms

DUCHY
OF UPPER
LORRAINE

Meuse R.

Danube R.

KINGDOM OF FRANCE

DUCHY OF
SWABIA

Lechfeld

DUCHY
OF
BAVARIA

EASTERN MARCHES

K. OF
HUNGARY

Saône R.

Cluny

D. OF CARINTHIA

KINGDOM OF BURGUNDY

Rhône R.

LOMBARDY

MARK OF VERONA

Venice

REPUBLIC OF VENICE

CROATIA

SERVIA

KINGDOM

Po R.

Canossa

OF

Ravenna

ITALY

TUSCANY

ADRIATIC SEA

CORSICA

Spoleto

DUCHY OF
SPOLETO

Sutri

PATRIMONY
OF
ST. PETER
(Under Papacy)

Rome

BENEVENTO

APULIA

CAPUA

Naples

SALERNO

SARDINIA

TYRRHENIAN SEA

CALABRIA

The Holy Roman Empire, 919-1125

German Duchies
Border Lands
Other Kingdoms Under German Rule
Boundary of the Holy Roman Empire
Area Conquered by Normans
Byzantine Areas Before Norman Conquest

SICILY

dramatist Terence, she put them in a Christian setting. For her contribution many German critics have called her the founder of German drama.

Gerbert and Muslim Spain. The greatest scholar of the Ottonian era was the ecclesiastic Gerbert of Aurillac, whom I mentioned earlier in this chapter. Of humble origin, he rose through the ranks of the clergy from simple monk to the eminence of the Papacy itself. Educated at the monastery school of Aurillac in southern France, Gerbert, who was fascinated by what he had heard of the more advanced Arabic culture of Spain, went there and spent two years studying Arabic science. His travels throughout Western Christendom and especially to Muslim Spain reveal not only a certain element of mobility in society but indicate the growing intellectual exchange between the Muslim and the less advanced Western civilization.

On his return the young scholar astounded both the Pope and Otto I with his learning. Otto then appointed him tutor to his son, but later Gerbert went to Reims for further study. So rapidly did he progress that he became master at the cathedral school there. His pupils included the future King Robert of France (son of Hugh Capet) and Fulbert, who founded the cathedral school at Chartres, later to become celebrated for its literary activities. After a period as tutor to young Otto III, Gerbert was elevated to the Papal throne in 999 as Sylvester II (the first French Pope) by his student.

Gerbert's scientific knowledge was so far advanced over that of his contemporaries that common belief branded him a wizard who had sold his soul to the devil in exchange for magical powers. Gerbert is credited with introducing to Western Europe the use of Arabic numerals (not the zero, however) and the abacus. Advocating direct observation of the heavenly bodies, he designed various instruments for this purpose. His scientific interests led him also to the study of music. A proficient performer, he personally constructed several organs; he is praised by one of his pupils (perhaps exaggeratedly) for making music popular again in France after long neglect.

In the field of Latin letters Gerbert displayed remarkable knowledge. His correspondence was filled with quotations from ancient Latin writers, and he had almost a mania for procuring copies of ancient manuscripts. Strikingly enough, unlike Alcuin (who, while admonishing his pupils to *use* classical works as an aid to understanding Christianity, warned them against *enjoying* them), Gerbert recommended the reading of the classics for the sheer pleasure and enlightenment to be derived from them. He expressed his interest in literature, including the more practical benefits to be derived from it, in the following letter, which also reveals a certain "humanistic" interest on his part:

> I have always added the fondness for speaking well to the fondness for living well, although by itself it may be more excellent to live

well than to speak well, and if one be freed from the cares of governing, the former is enough without the latter. But to us, busied in affairs of state, both are necessary. For speaking effectively to persuade, and restraining the minds of angry persons from violence are both of the greatest usefulness. For this activity, which must be prepared beforehand, I am diligently forming a library.*

However limited in scope and knowledge the Ottonian Renaissance may have been, it had certain consequences of undeniable significance. First, in the wake of the ravages of the new invasions (which occurred in the period we have called the "Second Dark Age") Ottonian scholars were able to preserve the classical learning transmitted from the Carolingian period and even to circulate it more widely. Moreover, in this period old cathedral schools were revitalized and some new ones founded in Germany and France, a fact which helped raise the cultural level of the clergy in parts of Western Europe. At the same time a certain amount of ancient Greek scientific learning now entered France and Germany from Islamic Spain and Italy (see Chapter 5). We should not overlook the influence on the court of Otto III, though seemingly rather ephemeral, of the Byzantine princess Theophano and her entourage. Most important, however, the Ottonian Renaissance, by achieving at least the beginnings of a synthesis of German, classical Latin, Islamic, and in considerably lesser degree certain Byzantine influences, provided the foundations for the later twelfth century "Renaissance" of Western learning.

The Salian Dynasty and the Cluniac Reform

Under the Salian dynasty, which succeeded the Ottonian, events led rapidly to a confrontation between emperors and Popes, as a result of which the empire began to decline and the Papacy finally emerged as the preeminent power in Western Europe. The Salian dynasty came to the throne in the person of Conrad II (1024–1039), Duke of Franconia, who was chosen king at the death of Henry II. Conrad seemed to abandon the old traditional policy of alliance with the Church. Instead he deliberately strengthened the hereditary titles of the lesser nobles in order to balance their authority not only against that of the great nobles but, more important, against that of the great ecclesiastics, whom he apparently mistrusted. To some extent he even dispensed with ecclesiastical services in his administration, weakening the bishops by detaching monasteries from their control. Thus he sought to substitute for the bishops a

* *The Letters of Gerbert,* trans. H. P. Lattin (1962).

hereditary class of crown servants drawn from the lesser nobles. But since no really central governmental institutions as such yet existed, a delicate balance of forces was created which could crumble at any moment. Even more than was true in the reigns of the Ottonians, authority now depended on the ability of the individual monarch.

Some historians believe that the medieval German Empire reached its height under Henry III (1039–1056). A capable monarch, Henry was able to reap the rewards of the work of his predecessors. But the inherent weaknesses of the empire were now becoming clearer. Like Henry II, Henry III supported the aims of the ecclesiastical reformers. Nevertheless, though he himself was able to control the German ecclesiastics, his policy in the long run only aided the Roman Church in breaking away from the authority of his successors. But in order to trace the beginnings of the historic rupture that ensued between church and state it is first necessary to discuss the reform movement itself.

In the tenth century, owing to the widespread state of ecclesiastical corruption, reformers such as St. Dunstan in England, Bruno of Cologne (Otto the Great's brother) in Germany, and, a little later, Peter Damian in Italy and St. Nilos, a Byzantine monk, in southern Italy, took steps to institute a program of reform in the monasteries. The reform movement, which came to overshadow all others, however, was centered in one monastery—Cluny, situated in French Burgundy.

Cluny was founded in 909 or 910 by Duke William of Aquitaine, who intended it to be an ideal monastic community. By placing the monastery directly under the Pope, William ensured that it would escape the potential dangers of both lay and episcopal control. Since no secular lord or local bishop could then interfere with the management of the house, it would not become a political pawn and could therefore devote itself exclusively to religion.

The monks of Cluny rapidly gained a reputation for austerity and piety, and its abbots were called upon to aid in the reorganization of other monasteries. For example, Odo (927–942), the second abbot of Cluny, almost singlehandedly reformed a vast number of institutions in France and Italy. As time went on, more and more monasteries came under the control of the mother monastery at Cluny. Thus the Cluniac order of monks became a powerful organization comprising thousands of monks in hundreds of monasteries all over Western Europe.

The Cluniac reform movement, as it came to be called, was at first aimed primarily at enforcing in the monasteries strict observance of the Benedictine Rule as it had been reinterpreted by Benedict of Aniane (d. 821), the spiritual adviser of Louis the Pious. De-emphasizing manual labor, the Cluniacs spent more time in liturgical and spiritual activities. Further, unlike earlier monastic institutions, Cluny would accept no one in its schools who did not intend to become a Cluniac monk. Earlier Benedictine houses had been more or less independent of each other, but the Cluniacs maintained a highly centralized organization of all their monasteries. There was only one abbot and one mother house for all. The dependent houses, which were under the authority of priors, reported directly to the abbot at Cluny, who in turn owed allegiance only to the Pope.

Until recently scholars associated almost every phase of the general ecclesiastical reform movement of the tenth and early eleventh centuries with Cluny. And, to be sure, the weight of Cluniac influence was thrown against the two major abuses of the secular clergy—simony (the purchase or sale of Church office), and concubinage (habitual cohabitation of a cleric with a woman). Actually, however, an independent but simultaneous movement of monastic and cathedral reform, centered in northern Lorraine and patronized by the emperor and the bishops, perhaps had greater influence in Germany than did the reform movement of Cluny. For in Germany, where the monarch and the Church were so mutually dependent, the Cluniac ideal of freedom from lay and episcopal control was less encouraged. In other respects the German reform movement paralleled the ideals of Cluny.

Nevertheless, though modern research has tended to reduce the significance of Cluny's role in reforming the Western Church in general in the eleventh century, its ideals took root throughout Europe; the abbey was for a long time looked upon as the great model of monastic virtue. Nevertheless, Cluny was not the sole source of ecclesiastical reform in the period. The role of men such as the Emperor Henry III and Duke William of Normandy in their own territory is not to be discounted. Undeniably, however, Cluny was for a time the most prominent spiritual influence in the reform movement and, particularly by its insistence on monastic freedom from outside authority, helped to pave the way for the ultimate independence of the Catholic Church from lay control.

Reform of the Papacy

After the strong support of the Saxon monarchs had been removed, the Papacy in Italy again fell into the morass and corruption of local Roman politics. Scandal-ridden and controlled in turn by factious Roman nobles, the Papacy in 1044 fell into the hands of Benedict IX. Benedict, however, soon tiring of his office, proceeded to sell the crown of St. Peter to his successor, Gregory VI (1045–1046). Paradoxically, Gregory was a sincere reformer who, despite this initial act of simony, hoped to reform the Papacy. But the unpredictable Benedict soon reasserted his claims, and as a result Henry III marched down into Italy in 1046 and summoned a council at Sutri to straighten out the tangled Papal affairs. There the rival claimants were deposed, and Henry employed what he considered to be the old imperial prerogative by pressing on the Roman populace and nobles his own candidate for Pope, a German bishop. When the latter died, Benedict IX once again briefly usurped the Papal throne. Henry then appointed his own cousin, the able Bruno, bishop of Toul, who was elected to the Papacy in 1049 under the name Leo IX.

Leo IX (1049–1054), one of the great medieval Popes, was an ardent supporter of reform. Indeed, he accepted the Papacy only on condition that his nomination be formally approved by the Roman clergy and populace, in the old canonical manner. Leo's program, undergirded by the ideas for zealous reform espoused by the monks Peter Damian and Humbert of Lorraine and by the Papal secretary Hildebrand, aimed primarily at rooting out the practices of simony, concubinage, and marriage of the clergy (which was then not uncommon). To achieve these aims throughout the Church, Leo felt it first necessary to reestablish Papal authority north of the Alps, where it had been almost forgotten during the tenth-century disorders.*

Leo called a great council at Reims, at which only one-third of the French bishops appeared—an indication of the weakness of Papal authority. The French king himself objected to the council. Leo thereupon showed his determination to bring the bishops into line by taking the drastic step of excommunicating all absentee bishops. Supported by Henry III, he took up the question of simony. He found many French bishops guilty of simony and deposed them; at the same time he forced married priests to choose between giving up their wives and families and being unfrocked. The success of Leo's actions within the Church, coupled with the spread of the Cluniac reform program, now led some ecclesiastics to believe that perhaps it should be free of *all* lay control, even that of the emperor. In line with this view, which began to take root after the deaths of Pope Leo and Henry III, Pope Nicholas II in 1059 promulgated a decree designed to regulate Papal elections. The decree prescribed that the cardinals (the clergy in charge of the chief churches in Rome) should meet in a body to elect the Pope. Although aimed primarily at ending the influence of the Roman mob, the new procedure also had the significant effect of stripping the German emperor of his power over the choice of Pope. Thereafter, Popes have been elected by the College of Cardinals, which remains even in our day the central organization of Papal administration.

The Church, so long passive, had now revived. Henry III's support of Church reform, completing the work of the Ottos, had freed the Papacy, at least for a time, from the mire of Roman politics. Now the Pope no longer needed the aid of the German king; as a result of Leo IX's work, the Papacy was finally in a position to effect its age-old claim to control the Church in the West. Con-

---

* On Pope Leo's important role in the schism of 1054 between the Greek and Latin churches see Chapter 9.

sequently, some ecclesiastical reformers, especially Cardinal Humbert, now began to insist that churchmen, in particular those of Germany, should serve the Pope, not the emperor. But the implementation of such a policy would, of course, undermine the entire structure of imperial power as it had developed during the last century.

Now began what was the most significant, and at the same time the most dramatic, conflict of the Western Middle Ages—the struggle between the Popes and the emperors for supremacy in the West. In its initial phase the Church sought only to secure its freedom from secular control. But, soon enough, it aspired to the direction of all of society itself. This grandiose ideal was to find its fullest implementation in the thirteenth century when all, or virtually all, of Christendom was united in the framework, however loose, of one great Christian commonwealth directed by the Pope.

Emperor Versus Pope

Henry IV and Gregory VII

In Germany young Henry IV (1056–1106) succeeded his father, Henry III, on the throne. In the civil war that took place during the boy king's minority, Henry was passed from hand to hand, and royal authority was greatly diminished as the nobles struggled among themselves for control of the regency. When Henry finally reached his majority, he determined to take control himself. Desperately in need of aid, he turned to the Pope and, in a reversal of tradition, addressed a letter to the throne of St. Peter humbly beseeching aid against his recalcitrant vassals. But the reform leaders, who were now in control at the Papal court, recalled the former imperial interference in Church affairs and showed little eagerness to aid the German monarch.

The Pope who received Henry's letter was Gregory VII, perhaps the ablest, certainly the most iron-willed of medieval Popes. While still a monk, Hildebrand (Gregory's name before he assumed the Papal office) had been strongly imbued with the ideals of ecclesiastical reform and was one of the leaders in the Papal Curia. Indeed, scholars generally affirm that long before 1073, when he became Pope, he was the real power behind the throne. Although perhaps not a Cluniac monk himself, he was to some extent inspired by the aims of the Cluniac program. His own plan for reform, once he became Pope, far surpassed that program. Gregory envisioned not only a moral uplifting of the Church as a whole but a Papacy whose spiritual authority, as the chief custodian of salvation for men, would be supreme over all of society, from the emperor down to the serf. In this quasi-theocratic ideal, the Pope and emperor would retain their independent authority over spiritual and secular matters respectively. But the Pope, by virtue of his higher responsibility for men's souls, would by implication also possess an indirect right to intervene in political matters.

In 1074 Gregory drew up a subsequently celebrated document, the *Dictatus Papae,* which set forth sweeping claims in behalf of papal power. According to the *Dictatus,* within the Church the authority of the Pope was supreme with respect to both ecclesiastical officials and Church councils. Regarding temporal matters, it was clearly implied that since the aim of all life was salvation, and the clergy, headed by the Pope, held the keys to salvation, the Pope was therefore supreme over all men—including secular rulers. He alone was to judge kings and emperors, and if they were found morally sinful, he had the authority to depose them. In the words of the document: "The pope can be judged by no one."

Such claims had never before been made by the Papacy, certainly not in so explicit and all-inclusive manner. It should be emphasized that the *Dictatus* was never officially issued by Gregory, because it was essentially only a draft of ultimate goals of papal power—aims Gregory may or may not have considered possible to attain. In any event, the Pope's claims to authority seem fundamentally based on the theory that as chief of the clergy he was accountable to God for men's souls, his political power therefore being only a logical extension of this God-given responsibility.

As Pope, Gregory at once launched an attack on clerical immorality throughout the Roman Church, reiterating Leo IX's order that married priests separate from their wives and children or lose their parish. This demand met with violent opposition, especially in the North, where clerical marriage long had been an accepted practice. But the order succeeded mainly because lay opinion, tired of ecclesiastical corruption, was now ready to accept such reform as necessary. It was quite different, however, when Gregory sought to free bishops and abbots from the control of lay rulers and to exert papal authority over them. Here Gregory focused his attack on one particular aspect, the widespread practice of investiture, that is, the investing of a cleric with his ecclesiastical office (including the lands attached to it) by a layman.

Gregory and Lay Investiture

In this period it was a generally accepted practice that kings conferred on bishops their authority over the lands attached to their bishoprics (what we term their "secular" authority), while exacting from them an oath of fealty as a vassal. But—and this was the real evil in Gregory's eyes—secular rulers also invested the bishop with the ring and staff, the symbols of his *spiritual* authority. This meant that in appointing bishops and abbots to their clerical office, the kings too often chose whom they wanted without particular regard for the cleric's qualifications for spiritual duties. What Gregory therefore now sought was to strip the kings of this power to invest ecclesiastics with spiritual authority—in effect to remove lay control over the appointment of bishops and abbots.

It is possible that Gregory meant to go even farther, to remove lay control even over the lands churchmen held in fief from the lay lords. Undoubtedly he thought that if the Church were to become truly independent, lay investiture must be forbidden. Increasingly the Church had been caught up in the expanding feudal network and was in danger of becoming completely feudalized. In this period every government was, of necessity, more or less dependent on the men and resources of the Church. Ecclesiastics acted as judges, served as envoys, and provided military service, sometimes even in person at the head of troops.

Gregory's decree against lay investiture struck hardest at the emperor. When Henry IV first heard of it (through a letter from Gregory), he had just crushed a rebellion and was in no mood to put up with papal defiance. Henry was especially angered by the salutation of the papal letter: "Bishop Gregory, servant of the servants of God, greetings and benediction to Henry *if he obeys the Apostolic See* as becomes a Christian king." In response Henry summoned a council of German bishops which went so far as to disclaim any obedience on their part to the Pope. Henry and his council now sent a letter to Gregory, addressing him contemptuously as "Hildebrand, now no pope but false monk," and declaring that Gregory had set himself wrongfully over the whole Church and the German ruler. The document ended: "Come down, come down, to be damned throughout all eternity." But could the German bishops defy the wishes of the Pope, who claimed to be their spiritual leader? And could the German king successfully overrule what was in effect the Papacy's declaration of independence from imperial authority?

In answer to Henry, Gregory now took the grave step of excommunicating the German king and releasing his subjects from their obedience to him. "I declare Henry," the bull of excommunication read, "deprived of his kingdom in Germany and Italy because he has rebelled against the church." This was an unprecedented statement, the implication of which was that the real question at issue was no longer lay investiture per se but who was supreme in Christendom, emperor or Pope. With the rebellion of Henry against the Church and the counter-release by the Papacy of Henry's subjects from their political allegiance to the Emperor, the struggle between the two great antagonists had now become a bitter conflict over universal political supremacy.

The Pope then launched a barrage of propaganda against Henry, piously stressing the spiritual nature of his reforms and the necessity of removing a man who would morally contaminate his subjects. Most of the nobles in Germany, usually at odds with the monarch, were delighted to find any excuse to rebel against royal authority. But it was the papal excommunication, which declared

Henry a heretic, that really brought him to his knees. In the eyes of the great clerics, the chief props of the monarchy, the nation could hardly support a ruler expelled from the Church and in danger of eternal damnation. The whole structure of the kingdom—the personal bonds between king and vassals—was threatened. In this epoch excommunication was an extremely powerful weapon that no ruler could defy without running the risk of being excommunicated himself. To be excommunicated was in effect to be an outcast from society.

The German nobles met in conference to discuss Henry's deposition and ruled that if within a year he were not free of the papal excommunication he would have to forfeit his crown. Observing the general agreement of the German princelings and clerics on the question of his deposition, Henry became desperate to save his throne. One flaw, however, existed in the papal position that alone might save Henry. As a Christian priest the Pope could not refuse absolution—that is, the lifting of the sentence of excommunication—to any sinner who appeared to be truly penitent. And so Henry rushed toward Italy to intercept Gregory before the latter could reach Germany, where he intended to confer with the German nobles.

Fearing an attack by Henry, Gregory had retreated to the castle of Canossa in Emilia (Italy), an area that belonged to his faithful supporter, the Countess Matilda. Henry proceeded to the fortress and made a show of humbling himself. Barefoot and in wretched penitent's garb, Henry remained outside the gates of the castle for three days, standing in the snow. In the end, Gregory, his political aims forced to the background by his religious duties, was compelled to lift the sentence of excommunication. In a letter later addressed to the German princes Gregory half-apologized for his actions, blaming his reversal on outside pressures:

> All were amazed at the unwonted hardness of our heart and some even declared that we were displaying not the austerity of apostolic severity, but, as it were, the cruelty of tyrannical ferocity.... At last, overcome by the sincerity of his [Henry's] compunction and the persistent supplication of those who were there, we loosed the chain of anathema and received him back into the grace of communion.*

This event, one of the most dramatic in medieval history, was certainly for Henry a great personal humiliation. From another, more immediate point of view, however, he gained a diplomatic victory. For by forcing the Pope to revoke the excommunication he had, at least for a time, saved his throne.

But from the viewpoint of Christendom in general, Canossa was a tremendous moral victory for the Pope. Henry was forced to his knees to beg forgive-

* J. H. Robinson, *Readings in European History* (1904).

ness in the manner of a common sinner. More important, the event marked the triumph of the spiritual over the temporal power, the first major step in the West in the realization of the ideal of a theocracy under the Papacy. Henceforth, for some two hundred years, no secular ruler would be able, in a test of strength, to withstand the power of the Pope. Thus the episode at Canossa (from which comes our phrase "going to Canossa") became a symbol of the humiliation of the civil power by the ecclesiastical. It was not soon forgotten.

But Gregory, aware of the many implications involved and wanting a complete political as well as moral victory, insisted that Henry's case was not settled. Despite the damage done to Henry's opponents by the lifting of his excommunication, the more stubborn of the German nobles and clergy now proceeded to elect an antiking, who promised to respect the rights of the nobility. In the acute civil war that ensued, Henry slowly prevailed, despite his being excommunicated a second time by Gregory. But since the first had ultimately failed, this second excommunication had far less impact.

His power increasing rapidly, Henry now marched on Rome and drove Gregory from the city, even installing as antipope Guibert, archbishop of Ravenna, who had crowned Henry emperor.* As for Gregory, with the fortunes of war now turned, he took refuge in Salerno with a group of Norman adventurers from northern France engaged in conquest of the Byzantine areas of southern Italy. But the Normans proved strange allies; in the process of saving Gregory from the Germans, they unmercifully sacked Rome. Gregory died the next year (1085) at Salerno. His last embittered words were, "I have loved righteousness and hated iniquity. Therefore I die in exile."

Henry's victory was in the end to prove ephemeral, for the newly won prestige of the Papacy in Christendom could not be destroyed so easily. Moreover, along with the German nobles, those perennial enemies of imperial power, Henry's family turned against him. And so, when even his son, the future Henry V, deserted him, Henry abdicated. He died in 1106, his corpse for a long time denied burial in sacred ground.

The reign of Henry IV, despite certain triumphs, dramatizes the weakness of the German monarchy during this period. The king was still too dependent on the great German ecclesiastics. When he alienated them he had no bureaucracy to replace them. And whenever the Church withdrew its support, the emperor could hardly preserve his title to the throne.

Henry V and Paschal II

Young Henry V (1106–1125) decided upon a shift in policy: he would give way to his magnates in order to combat only the Pope. Crossing the

---

* An antipope was a bishop uncanonically installed as a rival to the legitimate pope.

Alps he moved against the new Pope, Paschal II, who in a weak position now offered a remarkable compromise. He proposed that in Germany the Church give up all the possessions of lay nobles which it held. The feudal lords, including the emperor, would then have no cause to interfere in the selection of ecclesiastical personnel, and the ecclesiastics, in turn, would owe no feudal services. Thus in this area the Church would become independent, and Henry himself would gain large territories. Though agreement to this effect was actually reached, a riot among the clerics broke out in St. Peter's on the very day that Paschal was to crown Henry emperor. Not surprisingly, the ecclesiastics balked at giving up some of their lands. Anticipating this reaction, Henry seized the Pope and cardinals and held them prisoner until Paschal reaffirmed his right to invest German prelates.

At the first opportunity Paschal repudiated the concessions wrung from him by force. Relations between Pope and emperor became more and more strained until, at last, the solution to the investiture conflict was found. By a historic compromise, the Concordat of Worms (1122), Henry pledged to give up the imperial right of investing prelates with the ring and staff, their insignia of spiritual authority. Lay investiture, technically at least, was thus abolished. But with respect to an even more basic issue, control of appointment to Church offices with the lands attached thereto, the emperor still retained some of his power. It was decided that in Italy and Burgundy there was to be no imperial representative, which implied imperial pressures to elect a prelate agreeable to the emperor. It was also required that bishops had to take an oath of fidelity to the emperor *before* consecration. Thus, in general, it was clear that in Germany the monarch still had a large measure of control over the election of bishops, together with the imperial fiefs received by these prelates.

After Worms, however, the German emperors never again had the same unlimited control over clergy and Church resources possessed by the Ottos. For now the Pope also demanded obedience of the German prelates, and in the long run it was safer for them to remain on the papal than on the imperial side. The technical question of investiture was settled, but the basic reason for conflict still existed. Worms did not end the struggle for supremacy between Pope and emperor; it merely transferred it to other fields.

Frederick I Barbarossa and Henry VI

The conflict between Pope and emperor now became, more clearly than before, a struggle for power. The question was often posed: Who holds the supreme authority on earth? The Pope based his claims to supremacy on his position as head of the Church and hence the holder of the keys to salvation. Since the ultimate aim of human life was salvation, the Papal supporters maintained that all, including the emperor, must be subject to the Pope's authority.

The emperor, on the other hand, as the political heir of both Caesar and Charlemagne, insisted that his temporal authority was outside the scope of papal spiritual authority. Papal supporters responded that the power of the Pope, essentially spiritual in nature, was more sacred and hence superior to that of the emperor. But imperial theorists quoted the fourth-century doctrine formulated by Pope Gelasius. According to this theory, God had established two powers ("two swords") on earth, the spiritual represented by the Pope, the temporal represented by the emperor. Both Pope and emperor were to work in harmony for the good of human society, but each was to be supreme within his own sphere.

Papal theorists were able to shape Gelasian theory to their own purposes and made the reply that though there are indeed two swords in the world the emperor was to wield his for and in defense of the Church. Appealing to old Roman tradition, imperial supporters began to cite passages from Roman law as codified by the Byzantine Emperor Justinian—law which clearly exalted the emperor (not the Pope) as the head of the Christian community. Moreover, to emphasize that imperial claims were on the same sacred plane as the Holy Roman Church, the emperors' supporters came increasingly to call the empire the *Holy* Roman Empire.

But the struggle between the two powers was more complicated than a difference between political and religious theory. Besides the question of the allegiance of the German nobles, lay and ecclesiastical, another factor was the involvement of foreign powers, especially in Italy. For in order to make good his claim of supremacy over the Pope the emperor had to control Italy. Here he had to face more than papal opposition. From mere marauders the Normans had become the rulers of Byzantine southern Italy and Arabic Sicily, and now the powerful Norman kings of Sicily tried to block attempts by the German emperor to establish imperial power as a rival in Italian politics. The Byzantine emperors, too, as we have seen, were never able to become reconciled to the idea of another emperor in the West. Thus both Byzantium and Sicily did not hesitate to give aid to the Pope in his struggle against the German emperor.

The strongest obstacle in the path of the emperor's goals in Italy, aside from his vassals in Germany, was, however, the defiance of the rich north Italian cities, now rising to prominence. Although from the time of Charlemagne these cities had been fiefs of the Western emperor, they had in practice long enjoyed virtual independence. Thus when the Emperor Frederick I attempted to regain effective control over them, most of these rich towns threw in their lot with the Papacy.

At the death of Emperor Henry V (1125) civil war again broke out in Germany over succession to the throne. Henry V's closest male heir was his nephew Conrad, Duke of Swabia, who had taken Hohenstaufen as his family name, from a favorite castle of his family. But Conrad was passed over by the German princes who hated the Salians for their attempts to curtail their power. Consequently, for the first time since 911, hereditary claims were brushed aside and the nobles, reasserting the old right of election, chose Lothair, Duke of Saxony, as the king of Germany.

As a result of this election the celebrated rivalry developed between the two famous families of Guelphs (Lothair's party) and Ghibellines (the Hohenstaufen), a rivalry that disrupted Italian as well as German political life for centuries. In general, the Guelphs were partisans of the Papacy, the Ghibellines supporters of the emperor. In Germany these two warring factions disappeared about a century later, but in Italy the names continued to remain labels for factions within each city long after the death of the last Hohenstaufen in 1268. At Lothair's death in 1137, the Hohenstaufen Conrad III was elected king, but Lothair's relative, Henry the Lion of Bavaria, continued the Guelph opposition.

Conrad was succeeded by one of the best-known and perhaps most highly regarded of all German emperors, Frederick I (1152–1190), known as Frederick Barbarossa ("Red Beard"). Frederick's election held out hope for the conciliation of the Guelph-Ghibelline rivalry, since his father was a Ghibelline and his mother a Guelph. Moreover, his own personality inspired confidence; he was young, energetic, and handsome. Frederick's first task was to conciliate the Guelph faction in Germany—a feat he seemed for a time to accomplish, pacifying its leader Henry the Lion by granting him the duchy of Bavaria. Frederick also hoped to extend his authority over his powerful vassals. His first step in this direction was his attempt to build up a royal domain on the Rhine, particularly by favoring the wealthy Rhenish cities and granting them commercial privileges. He also gained control of the resources of many rich monasteries by taking them under his protection. And by establishing royal officials in castles on crown lands throughout the realm, Frederick sought to make his presence felt as the most powerful feudal lord in Germany. Although he achieved a measure of success in his various objectives in Germany, by now the princelings had become so strong that when he and his successor became deeply involved in Italian affairs, the nobles were able to regain most of the privileges they had lost.

What was the fascination of Italy for the German monarchs? Since the time of Otto the Great they had been traditionally drawn to Italy for the sake of the imperial title. Moreover, the Italian cities, much richer than those of Germany, could provide greater revenues. The towns of northern and central Italy were then disunited, torn not only by external rivalries but also by internal factional strife. Impatient with his slow progress in Germany, Frederick may have seen an easier victory in Italy. And the power he gained in Italy he could use against his German vassals. Finally, as had been the case with Frederick's predecessors, the Papacy itself appealed to Frederick to intervene. The Pope sought the young emperor's aid to crush the chronically rebellious Roman populace, this time led by a renegade cleric, Arnold of Brescia.

Symbolic twelfth-century depiction of the Emperor (in this case Constantine I) lead-ing the horse of the Pope (here Sylvester I). In the same period, Emperor Frederick Barbarossa was compelled to observe the Western tradition of an Emperor leading the mule of a Pope (Hadrian) in the great square in Venice in order to show the subservience of Emperor to Pope. (Alinari/Scala)

Arnold, an idealist who protested vehemently against the temporal power and wealth amassed by the Church as the root of all evil in society, had put himself at the head of a popular revolt against papal authority. Under his lead-ership the Romans drove out the Pope and in 1145 established a popular govern-ment, choosing Senators to govern the city. The ultimate aim of the Roman populace, however, was the restoration of the ancient glory of their city as a self-governing republic under the high authority of the emperor, not the Pope. Hence, like the Pope, they too appealed to the Holy Roman Emperor for sup-port.

Frederick, however, distrusted the Roman mob, and when he led his army into Italy he formed an alliance with the Pope. In exchange the Pope crowned him emperor in St. Peter's. But the two allies succeeded in seizing all of Rome only after the Pope, invoking one of his powerful spiritual weapons, laid the city under interdict. This meant that within Rome no religious services could be performed, and hence the souls of the citizens were placed in mortal jeopardy. The interdict also had the effect of cutting off the lucrative pilgrim trade to Rome. Owing to both economic and spiritual pressures, the Roman populace was finally forced to submit. Arnold was sacrificed to Frederick, who had the cleric burned at the stake in 1155 and his ashes strewn over the Tiber.

The Papal-imperial cooperation, however, did not last long. From the very first meeting at Sutri of Frederick Barbarossa and Pope Hadrian IV (the only Englishman ever to become Pope) there was friction. Frederick refused to hold the bridle and stirrup of the Pope's horse while Hadrian mounted and dismounted. This traditional ceremony, the proud young monarch felt, would seem to place him in the subservient position of the Pope's "groom." Frederick grudgingly gave in when it became evident that the Pope would not otherwise crown him emperor. More difficulties arose after Arnold was burned. In 1157 Hadrian sent a letter to the emperor which implied that Frederick was his vassal. Frederick, furious, thereupon sent his own vassals an open letter not only denying these papal claims but asserting that, as emperor, he held his power from God by virtue of his election by the German princes. Sensing that German public opinion, including that of the ecclesiastics, favored Frederick, Hadrian hastily explained that what he had meant was that the emperor received "benefits," not the fiefs of a vassal (*beneficia*) from the Pope. The incident was closed, but an atmosphere of deep suspicion had been created. Hadrian now viewed imperial intervention in Italy as a threat to papal temporal power. Frederick, on his side, became convinced that he must neutralize papal power if he were to control Italy.

The result was to lead to open warfare between the north Italian towns and the emperor, in which the Italian communes, in order to preserve their independence, allied themselves with the Pope. For the Papacy such an alliance offered a number of advantages. The towns were wealthy and possessed well-organized militias. Moreover, the Pope could use the hostility between the towns and the German emperor and nobility (both of whom despised the townsmen as pretentious, low-born upstarts) to play off one side against the other.

Frederick attempted to assert his authority over the communes by an appeal to Roman law. Accusing the Italian towns of usurping his regalian (royal) rights, he held a Diet at Roncaglia (1158) in northern Italy. Frederick summoned to the meeting professors of law from the University of Bologna, where, since the beginning of the twelfth century under the noted scholar Irnerius, there had been a revival of the study of Roman law.

These scholars of Roman law, with its ideas of imperial exaltation, especially the concept of the emperor as in effect head of *both* church and state, fitted in well with Frederick's own attitude. The lawyers defined, in particular, Frederick's "regalian" rights, which they affirmed had been usurped by the towns during the last centuries. The emperor alone, they declared, had the right to coin money, levy certain tolls, and collect dues as well as to enter and quarter his army in the towns. Frederick insisted that these towns could legally exercise such privileges only if they had secured a charter from one of his imperial predecessors granting them that right and that, in any case, an imperial governor (*podestà*) must be appointed over each town.

Frederick Versus the North Italian Towns.   The towns had no such documents, but they would not give up their newfound freedom. A severe conflict broke out between them and the emperor, with Milan at the head of the alliance of the communes. Hoping to break the back of the alliance, Frederick besieged Milan for three years. When he finally took the city, in his fury he ordered it leveled to the ground, seizing its most important citizens as hostages. But far from ending the resistance, the fate of Milan convinced the communes and the Pope of the need to resist Frederick at any cost. Meantime, the Italian communes formed a stronger alliance; they created the Lombard League (1167–1168) to oppose the empire and rebuilt Milan in defiance of Frederick, who had to return to Germany.

To crush this resistance Frederick again led his army into Italy, where he faced troops of the Lombard League as well as some from Byzantium sent by the Greek Emperor Manuel I, who secretly (though unrealistically) hoped to regain control of Italy. Finally, in 1176 at Legnano, the despised town militia were able to inflict a crushing defeat on the imperial forces. This event marked the complete triumph of the Pope and the communes. And, from the military point of view, it constituted the first major defeat of feudal cavalry by infantry.

Frederick, however, was clever enough to play on the antagonisms among the communes in order to secure more favorable peace terms. At the Congress of Venice (1177) and later by the Peace of Constance (1183) he made peace with the Papacy, and the excommunication against the emperor was lifted by Pope Alexander III. Although forced to recognize the virtual independence of the Italian communes with their claim to regalian rights, Frederick did manage, technically, to retain a vague kind of imperial suzerainty over them. They were not to exercise their rights outside the town walls, and town officials had to take an oath of allegiance to the emperor. Nevertheless, Frederick's dream of subduing Italy and reducing the Pope and communes to subservience had failed.

The last years of Frederick Barbarossa's reign were marked by successes in Germany. There he even managed to dispossess his great rival, Duke Henry the Lion of Bavaria. Henry had been summoned to appear before the emperor to answer charges. When he refused to appear, Frederick pronounced him a contumacious vassal—one who refused to obey the terms of his feudal contract. He declared Henry's possessions forfeit and, after civil war, defeated him. Through such feudal means Frederick sought to control all of his German vassals and thereby strengthen royal authority. But his efforts to implement the claims of

Frederick I Hohenstau-fen ("Barbarossa") was the enemy of the papacy. He died in Asia Minor while on the Third Cru-sade in 1190. (Marburg —Art Reference Bureau)

the monarchy had begun too late. Barbarossa's successors were either too weak or too occupied in Italy to carry on his work, and the attempt to centralize royal power in Germany did not therefore succeed as it was to do in France and England.

Frederick's greatest diplomatic coup, according to his contemporaries, was arranging the marriage of his son Henry VI to Constance, heiress to the Nor-man kingdom of Sicily. What Frederick had failed to accomplish—the control of Sicily through conquest—he was now able to obtain for his family through marriage. Sicily, consisting not only of the island but also of most of the Italian mainland south of Rome, was then a great maritime state, culturally and eco-nomically advanced.

For the Papacy, such a marriage was an unmitigated disaster. With Ger-many and south Italy in the hands of one hostile power, the Papal States were caught in a vise that could threaten papal independence. The Pope consequently refused to crown Frederick's son Henry co-emperor, and the Papacy prepared itself for a desperate struggle for survival as an independent political power.

Frederick himself did not live to participate in the even more bitter duel between Pope and emperor that resulted from the acquisition of Norman Sicily. For, though realistic, in his final years he was still imbued with enough idealism to lead the German expedition in the Third Crusade. On his way to Jerusalem Frederick drowned in a river in Asia Minor (1190). After his death he became a legendary figure, the emblem of German unity, the emperor par excellence. According to one tradition Frederick still sleeps in a cavern high in the mountains of Berchtesgaden, and when Germany has real need of him he will again return to lead it.

Henry VI

Frederick Barbarossa's son Henry VI (1190–1197) inherited his father's dreams of imperial glory. With Germany secured by his father, and Sicily, he assumed, secured through marriage, he seems to have planned an expedition to conquer Byzantium, thus taking up the old Norman aspirations against Constantinople.

According to a modern view, in the reign of Henry VI the real crisis of medieval Germany occurred. This view holds that Henry's attempt to join the completely different, culturally and politically more advanced, state of Norman Sicily to the Germanic Holy Roman Empire brought about a strain—a strain so severe that it led to the complete collapse of imperial power under Henry's son and successor, Frederick II. For sixty years, in fact, between 1190 and 1250, the Hohenstaufen attempt to incorporate Sicily absorbed all the imperial energies. The struggle of the emperor with the Papacy became even more bitter, for, with Sicily and Germany both under the same ruler, the Papacy's very existence was threatened. To preserve itself in the struggle, the Papacy destroyed the Hohenstaufen dynasty and in effect permanently crippled the German kingdom. Medieval Germany was never to recover from the blow.

Henry's abilities were revealed at his accession when he was able to crush simultaneous rebellions on the part of the Sicilian nobles and the German Guelphs. Using the lavish ransom he extorted from King Richard of England (who had been captured as he returned through Germany from the Third Crusade), he prevailed over the German and Sicilian nobles, and in the process even forced Richard to declare England a fief of the empire. But in 1197, while in the midst of preparations for his expedition against Constantinople (a continuation of the ambitions of his Norman predecessors), Henry died suddenly in Sicily at the young age of twenty-three. He was the last ruler who might successfully have held together the disparate regions of Germany. Thereafter, for about two decades two rival kings ruled in Germany, and it was during these years that the Papacy strengthened itself as it prepared for its final struggle with the Holy Roman Empire.

Frederick II, "Wonder of the World"

At the death of Henry VI the previous election of his infant son Frederick II was ignored; the old Guelph-Ghibelline rivalry again broke out. Two new kings were elected, Philip of Swabia, the brother of Henry VI, and Otto of Brunswick, son of Henry the Lion and the leader of the Guelph party. During the bitter civil war between the two, the great German nobles and ecclesiastics skillfully used their promises of support to wring concessions—with the end result that they became almost completely independent of the crown.

Meantime in Sicily, too, there were uprisings against Hohenstaufen hegemony. The dowager Queen Constance was hard pressed to hold the kingdom for her infant son Frederick, for the Sicilian nobles also wished to repudiate him. Desperate, Constance appealed to the Hohenstaufen's mortal enemy, the Papacy, which was the suzerain, that is the overlord, of Sicily. For papal support the queen had to pay the price of relinquishing the rights previously gained by Norman monarchs over the Sicilian Church. At her death she even named the Pope, Innocent III, her son's guardian. It was an ironic situation, to say the least, but it was the only possible solution to her difficult position. Constance knew that although Innocent would strive to keep Sicily separate from Germany, he would preserve the kingdom of Sicily for her son.

The most powerful of all medieval Popes now sat on the papal throne, Innocent III (1198–1216). His goal was to preserve the independence of the Papacy by preventing at any cost the union of Sicily and Germany. At the same time he hoped to cripple the Holy Roman Empire so that it could never again be a threat to papal authority. First he enlarged the Papal States, seizing southern Tuscany and Spoleto. His reasoning was that by extending the papal territories across the Italian peninsula, from the Adriatic to the Tyrrhenian Sea, the Papacy would drive an effective wedge between Sicily and Lombardy.

Innocent was not displeased at the continuing civil war in Germany, which greatly weakened the empire. He took advantage of the situation by asserting his right to decide the imperial succession by choosing the most suitable candidate. But he put off his decision as long as possible. As was to be expected, Innocent decided, in 1209, in favor of the Guelph candidate, Otto of Brunswick. In return Otto had to pay a heavy price. He renounced all the lands claimed by the Papacy, thus in effect declaring the Papal States free of imperial control. Otto also gave up the rights reserved to the emperor by the Concordat of Worms, thereby losing control over the selection of German bishops.

Once crowned, however, Otto IV fell heir to Frederick I's imperial ambitions. His demands for the return of the territories he had earlier conceded to the Pope led Innocent to bring forth a new candidate, the young Hohenstaufen Frederick II. Frederick, then a lad of only sixteen years, knew that he owed the preservation of his crown in Sicily to Innocent. In return for Papal support of his candidacy for the German crown he made elaborate promises to respect the Pope's rights. Chief among his promises was a vow never to unite Sicily and Germany and in fact to renounce the southern Italian kingdom as soon as he could establish himself in Germany.

Backed by the Ghibelline party and the Papacy, Frederick soon had Otto of Brunswick on the defensive. Otto, on his part, made an alliance with King John of England, who at the time was at war with Philip II of France. Philip naturally threw his support to young Frederick, and a great battle resulted, one of the most decisive of the Middle Ages. In 1214, at Bouvines in the Lowlands, the French and Ghibelline German troops crushed Otto's invading army. The victory gave Frederick undisputed claim to the Holy Roman Empire. More significant, it led in England to the signing of the Magna Carta and, on the Continent, to virtual French hegemony (Chapter 8).

At the time of Innocent III's death in 1216, he believed that he had at last achieved the old papal dream of a subservient emperor. How wrong he was! For from the death of Innocent III to that of the last Hohenstaufen in 1268, the history of Italy and Germany was dominated by a fight to the finish between the Papacy and the Hohenstaufen Frederick II and his heirs.

To answer satisfactorily the question of why Frederick II turned against the Papacy, despite the solemn promises he had made and the debt of gratitude he owned Innocent III for his protection, the character and aspirations of this remarkable man must be examined. Even the circumstances surrounding Frederick's birth were unusual. Queen Constance, his mother, was almost too old to bear a child when Frederick was born. To obviate any suspicion concerning the birth of the imperial heir, it was arranged that she be delivered of her child in public. In Jesi, in southern Italy, a royal pavilion was set up in the public square, and there the queen gave birth to her son.

Frederick was orphaned at the age of four. Innocent III, too busy to be an effective guardian, intervened only occasionally to preserve his ward's rights. At the court in Sicily Frederick grew up in neglect, with no regular regency to look after his welfare. Normans and Germans constantly quarreled over possession of the boy, passing him from hand to hand and using him as a tool in their struggle for power. Brought up in such an atmosphere of palace intrigue, with few friends and knowing little affection, Frederick learned at an early age all the uses of trickery and deceit. He trusted no one and ignored the advice of others—failings that no doubt were the product of his early environment. Of a restless, passionate nature and handsome physique, the boy was brilliant and versatile, though at times cruel and unstable.

Frederick had a great love for learning and an avid mind. His education was excellent; he could read and speak German, French, Italian, Latin, Greek, and Arabic fluently. He was especially devoted to science and delighted in posing difficult questions to scholars whom he gathered at his court. To ascertain the existence of the soul after death he once locked up an old man in a large wine cask to see if the weight remained the same before and after the man's demise. An interest in the processes of digestion induced him to order the dissection, alive, of two condemned criminals, one who had slept after eating, the other who had not. Frederick also wrote courtly love poetry, and his treatise on falconry (he was very fond of hunting) remains one of the best ever composed.

In Frederick's eyes the imperial title, however exalted, held few tangible benefits. It offered no financial or military power, only prestige. The kingdom of Sicily, on the other hand, was the center of his power—the only part of his domains where he could exercise effective authority. Therefore, despite his vow to Innocent III, Frederick would not renounce Sicily. Innocent's immediate successor, Honorius III, a mild and kindly man who had once been Frederick's tutor, gave Frederick little trouble on this score. But with the accession, in 1227, of the strong-willed Pope Gregory IX, the situation changed. The Papacy became alarmed at Frederick's successes in Sicily and particularly at the young monarch's revival of imperial claims to Lombardy. Gregory feared for the independence of the Papal States. He could foresee the possibility of the Papacy's being reduced to a state of dependency on the emperor, perhaps not unlike that of the patriarch of Constantinople.

At his coronation as emperor, Frederick took the vow to go on a crusade. In this he was probably sincere, but the need to establish himself first in Italy and Germany held all of his attention. When Frederick seemed to revive his dynasty's ambitions, Gregory demanded that he prepare at once to take the cross. Although the young monarch was unable to fulfill his pledge to go on the Fifth Crusade (his army was racked with plague), Gregory excommunicated him. Later, as I shall discuss in Chapter 9, Frederick, though still under the ban of excommunication, did lead the so-called Sixth Crusade in 1228, which, through negotiation, succeeded in regaining Jerusalem. The Pope, however, not only disclaimed this diplomatic victory by Frederick, labeling it a "sell-out" to the Muslims, but laid the Holy City itself under interdict. After Frederick's return to Italy, Gregory preached a crusade against the emperor himself. Because of circumstances, however, Frederick and Gregory signed a peace treaty in 1230. But it was an uneasy truce; both sides were merely biding their time.

Sicily and Frederick. Frederick now turned his attention to the kingdom of Sicily, the favorite area of his inheritance. In sharp contrast to today, this region was then in many ways more advanced than the rest of Italy. Its administrative institutions had been established soon after the Norman conquest, though the first Norman king, Roger II, had drawn on elements from the preceding Byzantine and Arabic periods of rule. In the Norman period, in fact, it was prescribed that the laws of Sicily be drawn up in Greek and Arabic as well as in Latin. Indeed, so well had the Norman kings built on the more advanced Byzantine and Arabic foundations as well as their own Latin tradition that it may be said that in the twelfth and early thirteenth centuries Sicily was culturally and economically the most highly developed state in Western Europe.

The civil wars that had taken place in Sicily during Frederick's minority, however, had wrecked the Norman institutions of government. Frederick realized that to dominate all Italy he had first to restore royal power in Sicily. After crushing noble opposition, he issued the famous "Constitutions of Melfi" (1231), whose aim was to centralize all authority in the person of the king. He forbade private feudal wars, removed criminal jurisdiction from the hands of the great feudatories, placed the towns under the jurisdiction of royal officials, and established a uniform royal coinage. To reduce clerical influence in temporal affairs, he removed from the jurisdiction of the Church courts virtually all cases involving laymen. He even forced the clergy to pay taxes and give up the holding of public office. These were advanced measures; neither France nor England were to achieve such a state of centralization for at least another two centuries.

With the resources of Sicily at his disposal Frederick could now intervene effectively in northern and central Italy and hope ultimately to control all Italy. He relied heavily on the influence of Ghibelline towns such as Pisa, the great rival of Guelph Florence. He also found support among the petty tyrants of the Italian towns who were involved in difficulties over problems of papal jurisdiction.

The primary obstacle in Frederick's aim to control Italy was the Papal States separating the emperor from his Lombard supporters. The real trouble between Frederick and the Pope perhaps lay not so much in Frederick's dual possession of Germany and Sicily as in his influence in Lombardy which, because of its proximity, was a dangerous threat to papal power. With Frederick's territory and supporters closing in on all sides, the Papacy found itself faced with the most dangerous political threat of the entire medieval period.

Following the policy that had proved so effective earlier, the Papacy once more formed a league with the north Italian communes. In 1237 Frederick inflicted a crushing defeat on the communes at Cortenuova, a victory which made it clearer than ever that he intended to subdue all of north Italy. The communes and the Pope were forced into an even closer alliance and again the Papacy excommunicated Frederick, absolving his subjects from their allegiance.

The combat between emperor and Pope had repercussions over all of Europe. Both sides appealed to public opinion, circulating pamphlets and send-

NORTH
SEA

DENMARK

BALTIC SEA

C. OF
HOLSTEIN

DUCHY OF
POMERANIA

KINGDOM
OF
POLAND

Vistula R.

FRIESLAND

C. OF HOLLAND

Elbe R.

M. OF
BRANDENBURG

DUCHY OF
SAXONY

M. OF
LANSBERG

M. OF
LUSATIA

Oder R.

DUCHY
OF
SILESIA

Bouvines •

DUCHY OF
LOWER LORRAINE

Rhine R.

L. OF THURINGIA

M. OF
MEISSEN

VOGT-
LAND

DUCHY OF
FRANCONIA

KINGDOM
OF
BOHEMIA

M. OF
MORAVIA

DUCHY OF
UPPER
LORRAINE

Danube R.

DUCHY
OF
BAVARIA

DUCHY OF
AUSTRIA

DUCHY OF
SWABIA

DUCHY OF
STYRIA

KINGDOM
OF
FRANCE

Saône R.

C. OF
BURGUNDY

C. OF
ARLES

C. OF
TYROL

D. OF CARINTHIA

M. OF
CARNIOLA

KINGDOM
OF
HUNGARY

Danube R.

C. OF SAVOY

KINGDOM OF

Rhône R.

LOMBARDY

M. OF
FRIULI

Cortenuova
Milan •
• Lodi
Roncaglia

M. OF
VERONA

M. OF
VERONA

Venice •

M. OF
ISTRIA

REPUBLIC OF VENICE

CROATIA

BOSNIA

Po R.

ROMAGNA

C. OF
PROVENCE

Pisa •

Florence •
TUSCANY

M.
OF
ANCONA

ADRIATIC SEA

K. OF
SERVIA

Sutri •

PATRIMONY
OF
ST. PETER

D. OF
SPOLETO

• Rome

CORSICA

KINGDOM

Naples •

SARDINIA

TYRRHENIAN SEA

OF THE

The Holy Roman Empire, 1138-1254

TWO SICILIES

SICILY

☰ Area of Conflict Between Papacy and Hohenstafens
▬ Boundary of the Holy Roman Empire
█ Controlled by Hohenstafens from 1186

ing messengers to all the courts of West and East, including even Byzantium. Neither, of course, discussed the real issue, political control over Italy. Rather, the Pope stressed Frederick's impiety and misdeeds, while Frederick warned other monarchs that if the Pope managed to crush the Holy Roman Emperor, their turn would be next.

Since the excommunication had little effect on Frederick, Pope Innocent IV resorted to a desperate expedient. He proclaimed a "holy" crusade against the emperor. But in the long run the Papacy was to find such use of the crusading ideal a two-edged sword. It brought the Papacy some military support, but, on the other hand, the use of religious weapons for obviously political reasons—and against the emperor at that—helped no little to decrease the moral prestige and authority of the Papacy itself, alienating even the pious King Louis IX of France.

At the time of Frederick's death in 1250, the struggle between Pope and emperor had reached an impasse. Nevertheless, in the long run the emperor had really lost. In many ways Frederick's reign had been brilliant, for he was both an astute diplomat and a successful general, yet hindsight indicates that he blighted almost everything he touched. Sicily, the jewel of his domains, was bled of its wealth to support his campaigns and rapidly declined. More significant, engrossed as he was in Italian affairs, Frederick ruined the German Empire. He himself admitted that he loathed Germany with its "long winters, somber forests, muddy towns, and rugged castles." Of the thirty-eight years of his reign Frederick spent only nine in Germany. Unlike his father and grandfather, Frederick seems, knowingly and intentionally, to have sacrificed control over Germany in favor of Sicily and Italy. He probably realized that in the last analysis the conflicting requirements of Italy and the empire could no longer be reconciled. The last remnants of imperial authority in Germany were sacrificed when he granted charters to the great German princes, which further confirmed their virtually independent status in their own lands. Henceforth, for the next seven hundred years, until it was to be unified in the latter part of the nineteenth century, Germany remained a loose confederation of petty states.

An explanation for Frederick's ultimate failure can be found in his mental and emotional constitution. As noted, he trusted no one. He ruled through fear and never was able to gain the wholehearted support, not to speak of the love, of his subjects. He was a man out of step with his time. Skeptical in an age of belief, he even wrote (it is said) a treatise on Moses, Jesus, and Muhammad, calling them mankind's greatest deceivers. Nor did his ideas of absolutism correspond to the prevailing ideas of feudal restrictions on monarchy. People were awed by him. They called him "Stupor Mundi" ("Wonder of the World"), but they were never quite convinced of the righteousness of his cause.

Frederick's descendants reaped the whirlwind he had sown. Pope Innocent IV now vowed to "exterminate this viper breed of Hohenstaufen." In Germany, after the short reign of Frederick's son Conrad IV (1250–1254), the

Papacy once more stirred up controversy over the imperial title. And in Italy the Pope took measures against Frederick's able illegitimate son Manfred, who had laid claim to Sicily in an attempt to carry on his father's policies. As a supreme measure to crush the Hohenstaufen hold on Sicily once and for all, the Papacy called forth a new champion, Charles of Anjou, the brother of King Louis IX of France, promising to invest him with the Sicilian crown once he had wrested it from Manfred. In 1266, at the Battle of Benevento, near Naples, Charles defeated and killed Manfred, thereby putting an end to the last serious threat to the Papacy from the Hohenstaufen house. Two years later the Papacy achieved its aim of exterminating the family: Conradin, the grandson of Frederick II, attempted to seize Sicily, was defeated by Charles of Anjou, and was publicly beheaded in the great square in Naples.

The temporal power of the Papacy had risen to the greatest heights it was ever to attain. No future emperor would again seriously threaten papal authority. The medieval German Empire had ceased to be a power to be reckoned with.

FOR FURTHER READING

Barraclough, G., *The Origins of Modern Germany,* 2nd ed.* (1946; 1963). The best recent treatment of medieval Germany.

Brooke, Z. N., "Lay Investiture and Its Relation to the Conflict of Empire and Papacy," *Proceedings of the British Academy,* Vol. XXV (1939). The best, brief analysis of the reasons behind the investiture contest.

Bryce, J., *The Holy Roman Empire*￼ (1961). The classic work on the subject, if dated on certain points of interpretation.

Butler, W., *The Lombard Communes* (1969). One of the few works in English on the northern Italian communes as a whole.

Cantor, N. F., *Church, Kingship and Lay Investiture in England, 1089–1135* (1969). An acute analysis of a "great crisis" in history.

Davis, R. H. C., *A History of Medieval Europe: From Constantine to St. Louis,* rev. ed. (1971). Includes a good chapter on the empire.

Gregory VII, *Correspondence,* ed. E. Emerton (1966). Selected letters of perhaps the greatest Pope.

Kantorowicz, E. H., *Frederick the Second, 1194–1250,* trans. E. O. Lorimer (1957). An excellent, scholarly work, if at times too imaginative.

MacDonald, A. J., *Hildebrand, a Life of Gregory VII* (1932). A biography of the great Pope.

Painter, S., *The Rise of the Feudal Monarchies*￼ (1951). A short analysis of the reasons for the emergence of strong Western monarchies in the feudal structure.

* Asterisk indicates paperback edition available.

Tellenbach, G., *Church, State, and Christian Society at the Time of the Investiture Contest** (1970). A scholarly, readable work on various ramifications of the investiture conflict.

Tierney, B., *The Crisis of Church and State, 1050–1300* (1964). Good, illustrative selections.

Van Cleve, T. C., *The Emperor Frederick II of Hohenstaufen: Immutator Mundi* (1972). Good, recent biography.

Williams, S., ed., *The Gregorian Epoch: Reformation, Revolution, Reaction* (1964). Collection of readings from sources.

One basic problem in the study of Western medieval history is the emergence toward the end of the medieval period of large, unified nation states—states which, surprisingly enough, emerged out of the small local units of the old feudal order. As I have shown, in the early medieval period, and especially during the anarchy of the ninth and early tenth centuries, central government and political loyalty to anything other than local authority had virtually disappeared. Yet by the end of the thirteenth century and the beginning of the fourteenth, certain areas of Western Europe—notably France, England, and to some extent Spain—saw the development of institutions of centralized government and at least the beginnings of a feeling of "nationalism" among their inhabitants.

CHAPTER 8

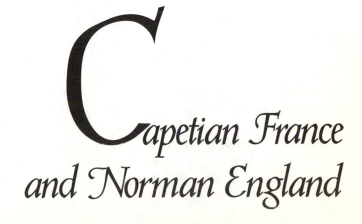

Capetian France
and Norman England

Why did these areas develop along the lines of a nation state, while others, particularly Germany and Italy, did not? In the tenth and eleventh centuries the Holy Roman Empire seemed on the way to becoming the most powerful, and in certain respects the most centralized, state of Western Europe. Yet this promise was not fulfilled. Instead, the German-based empire lapsed into anarchy. On the other hand, France and England, neither of which then seemed to be fertile ground for the development of strong government, slowly emerged from 1000 to 1300 as the leading states in Western Europe.

This development of centralized institutions of government in the long run took two principal forms. In France authority gradually became concentrated in the person of the king. Finally, in the seventeenth century, this centripetal tendency culminated in absolute monarchy, a system that eventually character- ized most of the nations of the Continent. In England, however, where after 1066 the king had gained considerable power over the whole kingdom, the monarch was gradually forced to share his authority with a rival, the nascent Parliament (perhaps more accurately, "community of the realm"). Ultimately, in a development sharply contrasting with that of France, his authority was almost entirely overshadowed by that of Parliament.

To trace this process in two of the most important Western countries, France and England, let us begin with events that mark the appearance of new dynasties in those kingdoms: the ascension in 987 of the Capetian house to the French throne, and the conquest of Anglo-Saxon England in 1066 by William the Conqueror, Duke of Normandy.

France: The Capetian Dynasty

Tenth-century France, unlike Germany under the Ottos, witnessed the disintegration of monarchical power. The descendants of Charlemagne— men either weak or involved in circumstances beyond their control—could not effectively maintain royal authority: two Carolingian kings were deposed by their strong vassals, and the others had to live under the threat of deposition. Thus in 987, when the last Carolingian king of France died, the country had become a patchwork of duchies, counties, and innumerable petty baronies held precariously together only by a common oath of fealty to the king.

Linguistically and culturally, as well as politically, there was little cohesive- ness in France. Southern France, for example, comprising for the most part the vast duchy of Aquitaine in the southwest and the county of Toulouse in the center and southeast, was more closely linked culturally, and to a lesser extent linguistically, with the antique Roman culture of Italy and Spain than with northern France.

French politics were dominated by the great principalities lying north of the Loire—Anjou, Brittany, Normandy, Flanders (now part of Belgium)—and by the counties of Champagne and Blois, and, most significant of all, the Île-de-France, or County of Paris. Centered on Paris, the Île-de-France was to form the nucleus of modern France. It should be noted that Alsace, Lorraine, and the kingdom of Burgundy (the latter today constituting the southeastern part of France and containing cities such as Lyons, Besançon, and Marseille) were not then part of France but provinces of the Holy Roman Empire.

These territories belonged to lords who originally had been vassals of the Frankish kings but had in time become virtually independent. Some lords were the descendants of Carolingian counts; others were magnates who had risen to local prominence, finally gaining recognition from the king. In some of these territories a considerable degree of internal cohesion on a local basis had been achieved by the opening years of the eleventh century, sharply contrasting with that of the Île-de-France under the king.

The two territories that were to play the most important role in French history were the possession of the Robertian dukes of Paris, and that of the dukes of Normandy. The duchy of Normandy had come into existence as the result of Viking raids. In 911 Charlemagne's descendant Charles the Simple, unable to resist the invading Northmen, granted to the Viking chieftain Rollo the area around the mouth of the Seine River, which came to be called Normandy (after the Northmen). Rollo's descendant William, Duke of Normandy, crossed the Channel in 1066 and laid the foundations of Norman England.

The Robertian dukes of Francia (Paris) gained prominence when they successfully resisted the attempts of the Northmen to capture Paris. For a short time, in the late ninth and early tenth centuries, this family usurped the French throne from the Carolingians, and later, in 987, one of its descendants, Hugh Capet, gained the French crown for his family. Thus the famous Capetian dynasty was established which, in the direct line, ruled France for over three hundred years and, through cadet branches of that family, until the French Revolution.

To gain supporters in their frequent disputes with their great vassals, the tenth-century Carolingian kings often found it necessary to yield some royal prerogatives to the nobles. These prerogatives—rights today of national governments, that is, of the "state"—were then termed *regalian* (royal) rights. By acquiring (sometimes actually usurping) these regalian rights, the great nobles of France thus came increasingly to gain authority in matters such as the coining of money, the administration of justice within their own territories, and the maintenance of their own private armies.

Hugh Capet

Upon the death in 987 of the last descendant in direct line from Charlemagne, the great nobles of France reasserted the old Germanic principle of election of a king. Their choice was Hugh Capet (987–996), Duke of Francia, whose election finally realized the old Robertian ambitions. Despite his selection as successor by the dying wish of the last Carolingian ruler and his strong support from the bishops, Hugh's position as king was not strong. Several of his great vassals—the Duke of Normandy and the counts of Flanders, Anjou, and Champagne in particular—were more powerful than the king himself. Even Hugh's personal possessions, his patrimony as Duke of Francia, were smaller than those of the great magnates.

Nevertheless, Hugh did have some advantages. The royal domain, the Île-de-France, though small in comparison to the other great fiefs, was compact, situated in a central position in France, and easily accessible to all areas. Moreover, its location between the lands of the ambitious and powerful Duke of Normandy and the Count of Champagne made it possible for him to play one off against the other to his own advantage.

The kingship itself, however weak it may have seemed in practice, possessed several theoretical advantages denied to other magnates. At his coronation the king was blessed by the Church through the ceremony of consecration and anointment by a bishop. Thus, while dukes and counts owed their authority to inheritance, the king's authority was believed to be sanctioned by God. Furthermore—and this was only fully realized in the next two centuries—the king was the supreme overlord of the kingdom. All fiefs, even if held indirectly, were considered ultimately to derive from the royal authority. The monarchy, accordingly, had a mystique of its own, which exalted the king above all other nobles of the realm.

The kingship therefore provided the Capetian dynasty with two important bases on which to build its power: the position of supreme overlord (at the apex, so to speak, of the feudal pyramid), and the sacred nature of kingship itself. The history of the rise of the Capetian dynasty to authority over all France is largely the exploitation and manipulation of this twofold advantage.

Little is known of Hugh Capet and his immediate successors, since the sources for the first century of Capetian rule are relatively meager. We do not even know what Hugh looked like. In any event, he had some ability, for despite the weakness of the monarchy he was able to maintain the royal dignity and to pass the crown on to his son without baronial opposition. Hugh's son, Robert II, called the Pious (996–1031), is somewhat better known, largely because of a biography left by a monk. Here, as might be expected, Robert's piety and generosity toward the Church are emphasized, whereas his political career is somewhat neglected. Robert's son Henry I (1031–1060), is again a rather

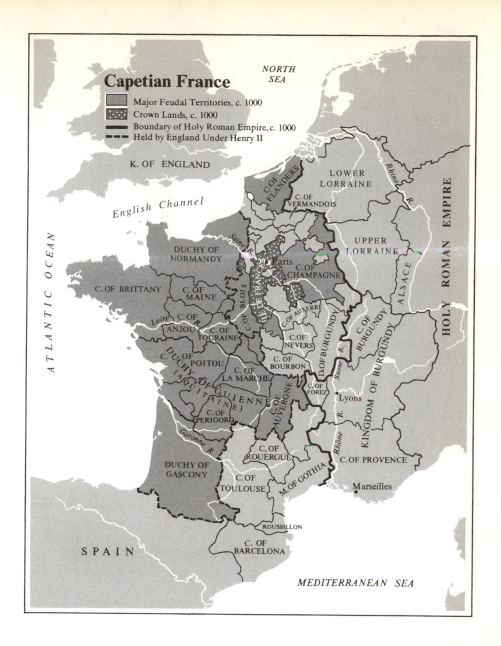

Capetian France

- Major Feudal Territories, c. 1000
- Crown Lands, c. 1000
- Boundary of Holy Roman Empire, c. 1000
- Held by England Under Henry II

NORTH SEA

K. OF ENGLAND

English Channel

ATLANTIC OCEAN

C. OF FLANDERS

LOWER LORRAINE

Rhine

C. OF VERMANDOIS

UPPER LORRAINE

HOLY ROMAN EMPIRE

DUCHY OF NORMANDY

Seine R.

Paris

C. OF CHAMPAGNE

ALSACE

C. OF BRITTANY

C. OF MAINE

C. OF BLOIS

ILE DE FRANCE

C. OF AUXERRE

Loire R.

C. OF ANJOU

C. OF TOURAINE

C. OF NEVERS

D. OF BURGUNDY

C. OF BURGUNDY

KINGDOM OF BURGUNDY

C. OF POITOU

DUCHY OF GUIENNE (AQUITAINE)

C. OF LA MARCHE

C. OF BOURBON

Saône R.

C. OF FOREZ

Lyons

C. OF AUVERGNE

C. OF PERIGORD

Garonne R.

Rhône R.

DUCHY OF GASCONY

C. OF ROUERGUE

C. OF PROVENCE

C. OF TOULOUSE

M. OF GOTHIA

Marseilles

SPAIN

ROUSSILLON

C. OF BARCELONA

MEDITERRANEAN SEA

shadowy figure, whose reign, according to one modern scholar, marked the nadir of Capetian fortunes. What little information we have about his successor, Philip I (1060–1108), is largely unfavorable, because the major sources for his reign are ecclesiastical, and Philip frequently clashed with the Church.

Despite the meagerness of source material, it is clear that under these monarchs certain tendencies emerged that may be considered characteristic of the entire subsequent three centuries of Capetian rule. One cannot, however, speak of a "Capetian policy," since there seems as yet to have been no carefully conceived, over-all plan of action. Rather, each succeeding Capetian continued along the same general lines found useful by his father. The strength of the dynasty hinged in no small measure on two contingencies: first, in every single case the eldest son was able to succeed his father; and, second, the reign of each king was consistently long, averaging no less than thirty years. Each ruler without exception was able to produce a male heir to succeed him. And to ensure his son's succession each Capetian, before the thirteenth century, saw to the coronation of his son and his son's association in the government during his own lifetime. This latter procedure provided the dynasty with a remarkable continuity, a fact that made the danger of baronial revolt less likely and frequently enabled each new king to ascend the throne with some experience in governing.

It was only natural that the first objective of the Capetian house was to impose its jurisdiction more securely over its sometimes recalcitrant vassals in its own domain, the Île-de-France. With an eye to profiting from their position as feudal overlord, the kings paid much attention to the prescriptions of law. Infractions of the feudal code by a vassal of the king could be used as an excuse for royal intervention, an intervention that almost invariably worked to the advantage of the king and the detriment of the vassal's power.

Nevertheless, the early Capetians, in particular Philip I and Louis VI, realized their weakness before the power of the great feudal princes of the kingdom and, unlike the last Carolingian kings, did not attempt to exert royal authority over the feudal magnates outside the Île-de-France. Thus, while these early monarchs quietly built up and consolidated their power within their own territory, they were not yet forced to meet determined baronial opposition on the part of powerful nobles from without.

Louis VI and Louis VII

The first Capetian king about whom we have a good deal of information is Louis VI, known as Louis the Fat (1108–1137). The nickname was no doubt fitting: at the age of 46 he was too corpulent to mount a horse unaided. Indeed, because of his love of food one English chronicler characterized him as a "worshipper of the belly." Louis, nonetheless, was possessed of great energy and no small measure of sagacity. To his credit it may be said that he was the first king who was able to master all the rebellious vassals within the Île-de-France. Repeatedly he sallied forth to protect monasteries and towns of the royal domain from the depredations of petty tyrants. In this effort he gained not only the support of the clergy but of the common people as well. As his biographer and chief minister, the Abbot Suger, put it, "Louis studied the peace and comfort of plowmen, laborers, and poor folk, a thing [which had been] long neglected."

Louis VI succeeded in raising the administration of his royal domain up to the level then prevailing in the more advanced principalities of France. From the Church he secured able and trusted officials such as Abbot Suger; others he drew from the ranks of the petty nobility. These servants of the crown were much more dependent upon the king than the great lords (who at this time paid little attention to the king) and therefore were more loyal. Through their efforts Louis's court began to assume the appearance of a regular instrument of government. Indeed, during his reign the court even heard a few cases brought to it from outside the royal domain, an indication of the advancing prestige of the monarchy.

Shortly before his death in 1137 Louis secured a major, if ephemeral, acquisition for the French crown. He arranged the marriage of his son and heir, the future Louis VII, to Eleanor, the heiress to the vast duchy of Aquitaine. Thus for a short time a large bloc of southern France was joined to the royal domain. But events forced Louis VII to seek an annulment and relinquish this large territory, for which French historians have castigated him, branding him weak and overly pious. He was pious, to be sure. (Eleanor is once supposed to have remarked, "I thought I married a man; instead I married a monk.") Yet it would be unjust to brand the annulment of his marriage, with the resulting loss of Aquitaine, as completely misguided. For Eleanor failed to present him with a male heir, and in Louis's eyes this failure might have plunged the country into chaos.

Louis VII had other reasons for getting rid of Eleanor. In 1147 when the royal couple went on the Second Crusade (Chapter 9), the uninhibited Eleanor, reared in sophisticated southern France and rather more prone to unusual modes of conduct than her husband, created a scandal by her actions. Gossip of the time had it that in Antioch she engaged in an illicit affair with her own uncle. The incident was smoothed over, but Louis remained deeply suspicious of his wife.

During Louis's absence on the crusade the able Abbot Suger acted as regent of the kingdom. An invaluable servant of both Louis VI and Louis VII, Suger carefully built up the royal finances and sternly suppressed all disorders. As long as this energetic cleric lived he was, guided by concern for the crown, able to dissuade Louis from putting aside his wayward wife. But with Suger's death this restraining influence was removed.

New rumors of his wife's amours, this time with the young Prince Henry of Anjou (later Henry II of England—whom she had actually not even met!) further embittered Louis, who had already begun the process of having his marriage dissolved on the grounds of consanguinity (close blood relationship). Almost immediately after the grant of annulment Eleanor married Henry, bringing to him as dowry the vast territory of Aquitaine.

This loss of Aquitaine may not have been as detrimental to Capetian power as some historians have believed. The monarchy was in reality still too weak to subdue the vast, turbulent duchy, and any such attempt might have led to the exhaustion of the Capetian house. As yet the resources the king could draw upon from his newly pacified royal domain were slender, and the great vassals might well have taken advantage of royal preoccupation with Aquitaine to wring new concessions from the crown. The loss of the duchy, and even more important, the marriage of Eleanor with Henry, embroiled the Capetian monarchy in a long struggle with the Norman kings of England—a struggle that led to one of the gravest crises ever to face the dynasty.

The threat posed by the English kings to Capetian hegemony over France was the direct result of the conquest of Anglo-Saxon England in 1066 by a vassal of the French king, William the Conqueror, Duke of Normandy. Under the descendants of the Viking chieftain Rollo, the duchy of Normandy had become the most powerful and centralized territory in all of France. And by now the duchy had become a virtually independent principality.

With the conquest of England in 1066 by the duke, these dangerous Norman vassals of the French king gained the added prestige of a royal title and the resources of an entire kingdom to draw upon. From this date onward, although the English king remained technically the vassal of the French king for his lands in France, he tended to treat these lands as parts of a kind of Anglo-Norman kingdom. Thus what before had been only a dangerous and powerful vassal now became a "foreign" power intent on maintaining and expanding his control over French territory.

When, in 1154, William the Conqueror's great-grandson Henry II ascended the English throne, he ruled not only the duchy of Normandy and the county of Anjou but also, through marriage to Eleanor of Aquitaine, all of southwestern France. The kings of France were thus confronted with a vassal who in fact ruled more French territory than they themselves. The conflict that ensued between France and England over the English possessions in France would last up to and even beyond 1453. And it was in the course of this three-centuries-long struggle that the French state became unified under the king, and the French nation was formed.

Recent scholars have tended to look more benevolently on Louis VII, crediting him with being the first Capetian ruler to venture outside the realm on campaigns, thus laying the groundwork for Philip Augustus.

Philip Augustus: Founder of the French State

The monarch who did most to create the modern French nation was Philip II (1180–1223). He was called Augustus (from the Latin *augeo*, "to increase") because during his reign the kingdom greatly expanded. Philip not only successfully ended the Angevin threat to Capetian power, but was also able to seize for himself the great fiefs of Normandy and Anjou. Thus at one stroke he made the power of the French king for the first time greater than that of any other French lord.

One-eyed and suddenly becoming bald halfway through his reign, patient, shrewd, and often unscrupulous (one modern scholar terms him a "nit-picking legalist"), Philip Augustus devoted his whole life to extending the royal domain and perfecting the royal government. He constantly strove to manipulate the feuds within the Angevin family in order to weaken the English position on the Continent. Philip first supported Henry II's sons in revolt against their father, and after Henry's death he exploited the rivalry between Henry's two surviving sons, Richard the Lion-Hearted and John. During King Richard's absence on the Third Crusade Philip plotted against him with John, who was then acting as regent in England. And when Richard, upon his return to Europe from the Holy Land, was held for ransom in Germany, Philip conspired with John in an ultimately unsuccessful attempt to bribe the German king to retain Richard permanently in captivity.

Once he had gained his freedom, Richard launched a series of campaigns that seriously threatened Philip. But, fortunately for the French king, Richard, an able general and alone capable of standing up to Philip, died in 1199 as the result of a minor wound received during a siege. When John then succeeded to the English throne and to the Angevin, however, Philip was prepared to support John's claim to certain French lands (notably not Brittany) if John made it worth his while—which John did with a large payment of 20,000 marks relief.* Meantime, for dynastic reasons John had his rival, his young nephew Arthur, murdered (*c.*1203).

Through a series of brilliant political maneuvers lasting over a number of years, Philip ultimately was able to strip John of Normandy and Anjou. Always careful to cloak his actions with the appearance of legality, Philip sought to pose as the champion and protector of the rights of John's French vassals. When John married a young lady already betrothed to one of his vassals, Philip, on the appeal of the vassal to him as John's overlord, summoned John to court to answer for this breach of feudal custom. John refused to appear, and Philip, seeing an opportunity to turn law against his English rival, declared him a contumacious vassal and all of his French fiefs forfeit. Legally fortified, Philip at once marched into Normandy in order to carry out his sentence against John before the latter could act, paying troops with John's relief.

By 1204 the French king had stripped the English monarch of Normandy, the most administratively advanced area of northwestern Europe, Brittany, Anjou, Maine, and Touraine. By the addition of these Angevin territories (except for Brittany, which was to remain in the hands of its count) Philip had trebled

---

* Relief was the sum paid by an heir on securing possession of a fief.

the area of the royal domain. Aquitaine alone remained in English hands; it would later become a cause of the Hundred Years' War.

In a last-ditch attempt to recover his lost territories John made an alliance with the Guelph emperor of the Holy Roman Empire, Otto of Brunswick. In a countermove Philip allied with the rival Hohenstaufen (Ghibelline) party in Germany. Philip also shrewdly secured papal sanction, for both Otto and John were at this time at odds with the Pope, Innocent III. The climax came, as I have shown, at the famous Battle of Bouvines, fought in Flanders in 1214 (Chapter 7). Here Philip won a resounding victory over John's allies and shortly after over John himself, thus confirming the French king's possession of the Angevin lands north of the Loire. The king was now indisputably the most powerful lord in all of France, and no vassal could muster enough resources to defy him successfully in open warfare. French predominance in Western Europe dates from this victory. The defeat of the German emperor, on the other hand, led to civil war in Germany and the ultimate decline of the Holy Roman Empire. Not Germany but France was to become the strongest nation on the Continent.

While Philip Augustus was gaining military and political victories, he was at the same time effecting administrative reforms. Though less spectacular than his military achievements, these reforms were no less important for the growth of monarchical power.

Previous to Philip's reign French kings had strengthened their authority through alliance with the Church, notably by using clerics in the government and by appointment of high ecclesiastics. Not infrequently the monarch went to the defense of bishops and abbots attacked by neighboring secular lords. The effectiveness of his policy was limited, of course, by the actual ability of the king to provide security and thus to extend his jurisdiction.

Increasingly the growing towns too sought royal protection, for in order to carry on trade—upon which the existence of the towns depended—peace and order were indispensable. And against the depredations of local lords, the townsmen could turn only to the king for protection. The king granted many royal charters that guaranteed rights to the municipalities and at the same time served to establish a legal basis for their existence. While these charters served to grant privileges to the towns, they often also served to bind the townsmen closer to the monarchy.

These two groups—the clergy and the townsmen—Philip exploited as much as he could. In the expanding royal administration he used the Templars (for banking and finance), members of the urban middle class, and especially the *petite noblesse* (minor nobility) of the Île-de-France. Thus a more professional, specialized "bureaucracy" began to emerge.

Under the early Capetians royal rights and privileges had been enforced by local agents called *prévôts* (provosts). But by the time of Philip's reign these officials had become hereditary officeholders whose interests merged with those

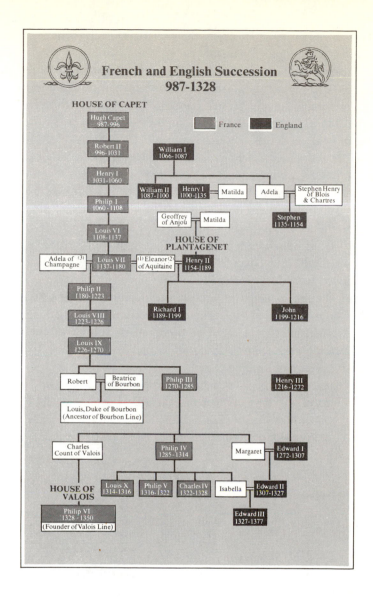

**French and English Succession
987-1328**

HOUSE OF CAPET

- Hugh Capet 987-996
- Robert II 996-1031
- Henry I 1031-1060
- Philip I 1060-1108
- Louis VI 1108-1137

☐ France ■ England

- William I 1066-1087
  - William II 1087-1100
  - Henry I 1100-1135 — Matilda
  - Adela — Stephen Henry of Blois & Chartres
  - Stephen 1135-1154

- Geoffrey of Anjou — Matilda

HOUSE OF PLANTAGENET

- Adela of Champagne (3) — Louis VII 1137-1180 — (1) Eleanor (2) of Aquitaine — Henry II 1154-1189
  - Philip II 1180-1223
  - Louis VIII 1223-1226
  - Louis IX 1226-1270
    - Robert — Beatrice of Bourbon
      - Louis, Duke of Bourbon (Ancestor of Bourbon Line)
    - Philip III 1270-1285
    - Richard I 1189-1199
    - John 1199-1216
      - Henry III 1216-1272

- Charles Count of Valois
- Philip IV 1285-1314
- Margaret — Edward I 1272-1307

HOUSE OF VALOIS

- Louis X 1314-1316
- Philip V 1316-1322
- Charles IV 1322-1328
- Isabella — Edward II 1307-1327

- Philip VI 1328-1350 (Founder of Valois Line)
- Edward III 1327-1377

of the rest of the aristocracy. In order to tighten royal control over the administration Philip created the new office of *bailli* (in English, "bailiff"; "seneschal" in southern France), who looked after a large territory and supervised the work of several *prévôts*. He also collected the king's revenues and saw to the administration of royal justice. Philip required the *baillis* to report directly to him. He paid them a regular salary rather than, as in the case of *prévôts,* allowing revenues from specific royal holdings to be farmed out to them. In this way he hoped both to preserve the loyalty of the *baillis* and keep them from becoming part of the hereditary landed aristocracy.

The steady accretion of land to the Capetian domain brought increased revenues to the king. But the corresponding increase in royal authority required the outlay of proportionally greater funds for government than had been the case under Philip's predecessors. Custom forbade any kind of taxation and therefore, to squeeze out the necessary revenue, Philip was forced to find ways to manipulate the feudal machinery. In his efforts are seen the glimmerings of the modern concept of direct taxation. Exerting pressure on foreign groups such as the Jews and Italian bankers, he forced them at his "request" to grant him large loans. Whatever feudal dues were owed to him as suzerain he insisted on collecting to the letter. More important, he was able to benefit from some "extraordinary" (that is, non-customary) revenues, although a special tax levied to support his crusade (the Saladin Tithe) was not actually collected. In lieu of military service from his vassals, Philip now began to demand a money payment. Thus, though it would be an exaggeration to say that Philip instituted modern methods of taxation—his demands at bottom were based on the concept of feudal dues—his manipulation of his prerogatives as high suzerain freed him from complete dependence on haphazard feudal levies and secured for him a more uniform system of royal revenues.

Philip Augustus' reign is generally considered by historians to mark the true beginnings of the development of centralized monarchy in France. Succeeding Capetian kings like St. Louis and Philip IV were to make great contributions, but they were only completing the work that Philip had begun.

Heresy: The Albigensians

The beginning of royal efforts to subdue the southern French county of Toulouse occurred in the brief reign of Philip II's son, Louis VIII. Toulouse (part of Languedoc) differed in culture from the rest of France north of the Loire, being more urbanized and sophisticated. This distant county had a long tradition of almost complete independence from the crown. But Languedoc became the center of religious heresy, and the attempts of the French kings and their northern vassals to extirpate this heresy brought about the eventual annexation of the area to the royal domain.

Most important of the heresies that took root in Languedoc was Albigensianism, based on an ancient Eastern dualistic sect believing in the complete antithesis of spiritual good and material evil. Although it did not initially derive from Christianity—it had begun in the third century A.D. in the teachings of Persian Zoroastrianism and Manichaeism—it was regarded as a Christian heresy. The tenets of Albigensianism spread early from the Near East to the eastern part of Asia Minor in the Byzantine Empire (where it was known in Greek as "Catharism"). From there it later moved westward through the Balkans (known in Bulgaria as "Bogomilism") and northern Italy, finally penetrating into southern France in the eleventh century. By the beginning of the thirteenth century the cult had gained so strong a foothold in Languedoc that the Papacy feared Christianity would entirely disappear in the area.

The Albigensians believed in a curious blending of Manichaean and Christian doctrines; they asserted the existence of two principles, one good and the other evil, both eternally struggling to win men's souls. Many of the religion's adherents, disgusted at the worldliness and corruption of the southern French clergy, denounced the Catholic Church as the instrument of Satan. Despite the Papacy's efforts to put an end to the heresy peacefully, it continued to spread, especially among the lower and middle classes, and even to the nobility. The Count of Toulouse himself, if not openly favoring the religion, at least showed great reluctance to move against its followers. Finally, in 1208, when the papal legate to Toulouse was murdered (perhaps with the connivance of the count himself), Pope Innocent III decided to take more drastic measures. He proclaimed a holy crusade against the Albigensian heretics and declared that any noble who participated in the expedition would be rewarded with lands seized from the southern French supporters of the heretics.

The Albigensians offered violent resistance. Indeed, they were even aided by many of the orthodox Christians of the area, who themselves feared that they would be stripped of their lands. For the northern nobles (derisively called "foreign French invaders" by the people of Languedoc) made little distinction between the heretics and true believers. The papal legate, in fact, when asked how to distinguish the good Catholics from the Albigensians of a town under siege, is reported (probably exaggeratedly) to have replied, "Kill them all. God will know His own."

Increasingly the struggle in the south took on the aspect of a war to preserve southern independence. Finally in 1223 Philip Augustus, who had until then remained aloof, fearing the complete alienation of southern France and its possible despoiling by others, sent his son with an army to ensure that the territory taken from the Albigensians would go not to the northern feudatories but to the French crown. Philip's successor, Louis VIII, entered Languedoc in 1225–1226. But not until twenty years later and after many bloody massacres were the heretics virtually annihilated. Languedoc, now almost ruined, fell into the hands of the royal family through a marriage alliance arranged between Louis IX's brother and the heiress to the county of Toulouse, which was sealed at the Treaty of Paris (1229). Later, when the king's brother died without an heir, Toulouse finally accrued to the French crown. In these various ways Philip II laid the foundations for the modern French nation, thus justifying his nickname of "Augustus."

St. Louis

The most respected of all Western medieval monarchs was probably Philip II's grandson, Louis IX (1226–1270). Almost the antithesis of his opportunistic grandfather, Louis (who constantly insisted he was following his grandfather's advice), was the embodiment of the ideals of medieval kingship and chivalry. Considering himself a kind of benevolent father of all classes of the realm, Louis sought to use his royal authority for the benefit of all. Deeply imbued with the concept of knightly honor, he sought scrupulously at all times to live up to the obligations of the king. Yet, despite the limitations such a strict adherence to the law and religion would imply, his reign marked a significant growth in the power of the French monarchy. He too did much to further centralize monarchical power, but his chief contribution to France was his own character—a character that endowed the monarchy with new prestige and respect.

Louis's personal life was exemplary. He generally disdained ostentation, dressing simply and keeping a modest court, though when occasion demanded he insisted on proper splendor. Of a deeply religious nature, he sought always to follow the moral precepts of Christianity, giving alms to the poor, building hospitals, and, in imitation of Christ, even washing the feet of lepers.

Louis's biographer and close friend, Jean de Joinville, the seneschal for Champagne, has provided us with the best insight into his master's character. According to Joinville, Louis never spoke ill of any man, never swore or blasphemed, was temperate in eating and drinking, and personally made royal justice available to his subjects. Sitting beneath an oak tree in the forest of Vincennes, Louis would listen to the complaint of anyone who wished to present his case to the king. On such occasions all could expect an impartial decision. So famous did he become for fairness and punctilious regard for law that subsequent generations of nobles frequently exclaimed, "Let us return to the days of St. Louis the Just." His reputation became so widespread that he was asked to mediate quarrels both within and outside the realm—in Flanders, Lorraine, Burgundy, and even in England, where a dispute between the king and his barons had resulted in civil war.

Louis's personal life, his devotion to Christianity, and his deep concern for a crusade to recover Jerusalem distinguished him during his lifetime as a unique and saintly person. In 1297, less than thirty years after his death, Louis was canonized as a saint of the Church.

Yet Louis, though morally exemplary, was not unaggressive when he thought his royal rights were involved. Even his great devotion to the Church did not lead him to yield if he believed royal prerogatives were being threatened by his bishops or, more important, by the Papacy. When the Popes tried to secure money and men from French ecclesiastics to carry on papal military campaigns, Louis declared that French ecclesiastical property belonged to him and his realm, and was to be taxed only for the benefit of France. And when the Popes declared a crusade against Emperor Frederick II, Louis refused to have anything to do with it, considering it a perversion of the crusading ideal (Chapter 9). When he did lead a crusade of his own—finally implementing his deep-rooted desire to go to the Holy Land—he was so demanding that the French clergy appealed to the Pope against Louis's "exactions." Although a "true and loyal son of the Church," Louis would bow to no one when it was a question of the French monarch's control over the Church in his own realm.

The further development of monarchical authority under Louis was the increase in the scope of the jurisdiction of the royal courts. Owing partly to his reputation as a just king, the royal court gained in prestige and began to receive more and more cases. It became established that the decision of a baronial court could be appealed to the king. Its competence to hear cases of treason against the king was especially notable. Appeals from lower courts began to pour into the *parlement*, Louis's supreme tribunal or court of law (which is not to be confused with the English Parliament). The *parlement*, originally a council or place of discussion of the great nobles, had by Louis's time become a more specialized court of law that met permanently and was staffed by more or less professional men.

Louis at the same time managed to extend his control over the town governments. Internal conflicts had arisen between the rich merchants, who controlled the municipal governments, and the lower classes of artisans, who resented their exclusion from these governments. The crown, therefore, intervened to restore order and ensure the continued revenues due the king from the towns. Louis created a new official, the *enquêteur*. These "inquirers" were to supervise all the royal officials and report back to the monarch. Unlike earlier officials, *enquêteurs* did not have a fixed district to which they were attached. Thus it was more difficult for them to become tied to local interests and hence independent of the crown.

A key point in the long growth of French monarchical power is Louis's issue for the first time of a royal edict applicable to the whole realm without the prior consent of the great vassals. At this point it may be said that the French monarch first began to "legislate"; royal authority had become so strong that Louis no longer felt it necessary to obtain the assent of all his vassals before issuing a decree concerning them. The great example was his edict establishing a standard royal coinage for the entire realm.

St. Louis was one of the primary architects of the modern French nation. The profound respect gained for the crown through his exemplary life, administrative reforms, and canonization gave the monarchy a prestige it had never possessed, and caused the French to look to their monarch as the very symbol of the nation.

Philip the Fair: First Steps Toward Royal Absolutism

As long as St. Louis reigned, there was little danger that the ever-increasing accretions of royal authority would result in arbitrary rule. St. Louis was always careful to observe the regulations of law and custom. But under his successors, notably his grandson, Philip IV (1285–1314), this solicitude for legal customary "rights" gave way to an overt manipulation of law in order to exalt the authority of the king.

About Philip himself—known as Philip the Fair because of his handsome appearance—we have little concrete information, his character, in particular, being something of an enigma. Some scholars maintain that Philip was merely a figurehead whose ministers were the real architects of his power. Others affirm that he was a clever, unscrupulous, avaricious monarch who had a good deal to say about the policies of his reign. Recent scholarship now shows that he was a complex, able, and rather unscrupulous monarch who himself directed royal policy. Under Philip's rule the more temperate wielding of royal authority was cast aside in favor of any means that could profitably be used to extend monarchical power.

The increase of royal authority could not, of course, occur in a vacuum. In each case it had to be gained at the expense of—that is, as an encroachment on—the privileges of the nobility, the towns, or even the Church. One of Philip the Fair's primary aims was to supplant local courts with royal justice. His lawyers actively urged litigants to appeal to the crown against the judgment of lesser courts. Pressure was exerted on baronial courts to effect the transfer of cases to monarchical courts. Philip promulgated a decree stating that a case initiated in a royal court had to be completed there, even if the court was not competent to deal with such a case. It was even permitted that the judge of a "private" court, on the complaint of a litigant, could be haled before a royal justice to face charges of "malpractice." The result was that the entire system of "private" baronial justice, so typical of the medieval West, began to be displaced by a royal judicial system.

Now that royal administration had expanded so greatly, it became more and more costly. One of Philip's most pressing needs, therefore, was increased revenue, and it was in his efforts to secure more money that he was most ruthless. Beginning with Philip Augustus, French kings had permitted the nobles, townsmen, and clergy to substitute money payments for the customary military service. In order to take advantage of this practice, Philip would declare a military "emergency," and after receiving payments in lieu of military service, make a quick peace without fighting. He also filled the royal coffers by imposing additional customs dues and tolls, forcing wealthy people to "lend" the government money, and finally by debasing the coinage. (Recent scholarship affirms that twinges of conscience induced Philip, at times, to suspend these practices). But these methods were still insufficient to implement his ambitious policies, and he had to cast about for other revenues. In this way he became involved in a famous conflict with Pope Boniface VIII and launched a highhanded attack on the Knights Templar.

Philip, at war with England, attempted to raise revenues by taxing the French clergy, whereupon in 1296 Pope Boniface VIII (1294–1303), insisting on the exemption of churchmen from secular jurisdiction, forbade him to tax the clergy of his realm without papal consent. In retaliation Philip banned the export of precious metals from France, thereby cutting off an important source of papal revenue. As a result of this pressure Boniface was forced to retreat, admitting, in order to save face, the king's right to levy "taxes" on the French clergy if the king considered the situation an emergency.

A more serious conflict between Philip and the Pope arose in 1301 over the king's trial of a French bishop accused of treason. Boniface, defending the traditional ecclesiastical prerogative that clerics be tried only in ecclesiastical courts, strongly protested Philip's action. Philip, according to one important modern view (which not all scholars accept), then sent his "hatchet man," William of Nogaret, to the papal summer residence at Anagni, Italy, with no less an aim than to kidnap the Pope and bring him back to France for trial. The plan failed, but Nogaret and his men were able to seize Boniface and for a brief period held him prisoner before he was freed by the outraged townsmen of Anagni. Shocked and humiliated, however, Boniface died shortly thereafter. As a result in part of Philip's manipulations, the cardinals proceeded to elect a French Pope, Clement V. Clement moved the papal court to Avignon, in southern France, an event that marked the beginning of the so-called Babylonian Captivity of the Papacy (1305–1378) (see Chapter 13).

Having thus dealt with the Papacy, Philip then launched an attack on the Templars. This famous crusading order of knights, whose original purpose had been to protect pilgrims in the Holy Land, had become wealthy. They managed the royal finances, and their headquarters in Paris had, in fact, become a kind of bank of deposit. Philip himself had borrowed heavily from the Templars. Perhaps aiming to renege on his debt (though the issues are not entirely clear), he launched a smear campaign against the order, accusing its members of such crimes as heresy, performing the "Black Mass," and even of homosexuality. With the aid of confessions extorted under torture, he convicted the Grand Master and other leaders of the Templars and sent them to the stake. Under pressure from Philip the Pope was compelled to dissolve the order (1312). The French king tried to confiscate all the possessions of the Templars in France, but Pope Clement transferred them to the Hospitallers and, in the end, Philip did not profit that much. Steps were also taken by the monarch against other moneyed groups, such as Jewish and Italian bankers, who were expelled from France, their property confiscated.

To secure a broad base of support for his campaign against the Papacy and the Templars, and also to tap still another source of revenue, Philip almost unwittingly became the instrument for the creation of a new institution, the Estates General. Earlier kings, in accord with feudal practice, were in the habit of summoning councils of nobles and high ecclesiastics when seeking to undertake new policies. But in 1302, to gain popular support for his struggle with the Pope over the jurisdiction of ecclesiastical courts, Philip set a new precedent by also summoning to the assembly representatives from the towns. And in his later struggles with Boniface VIII and the Templars he again included municipal representatives in his summons. Here, too, his aim was to influence public opinion—to secure a "rubber stamp" of approval for his actions and to clothe them with some semblance of legality. (It should be emphasized that in Philip's summons to town representatives in 1314, a primary aim was to pressure the townsmen into granting him additional revenues.)

The meetings of the assemblies that took place under Philip—the term *Estates General* did not come into use until more than a century later—can hardly be said to have represented all classes in France. Nevertheless, the policy he initiated of summoning representatives of the non-noble classes may be said to mark the beginnings of this French version of representative government. Unlike the English Parliament, however, which managed to retain control over the levying of new taxes and thus gained a weapon to control the king, the French Estates General was to lose this right to the king. The inability of the Estates General to gain control of revenues is one important reason that no institution arose in France that was able to act as an effective check on the development of royal absolutism, once feudal restraints had been successfully removed by the monarch.

During the three centuries of Capetian rule the government became more and more institutionalized and there emerged in time a professional bureaucracy. To help the early Capetian monarchs carry on the royal business, few officials were needed, since most of the work was done by the king's own household. As Capetian territory and authority grew, however, this rather primitive method of governing gradually evolved into a system that might be called bureaucracy—though, to be sure, not in the full, modern sense of the word. As more and more business was brought before it, the royal household came to be subdivided into specialized departments. A group of officials, headed by the Chancellor, drew up and issued royal charters and edicts. Later, a *chambre du comptes* developed to deal exclusively with financial matters: it collected income and paid expenses. Even the king's so-called Great Council of nobles, originally sitting as an advisory group, now evolved into a kind of supreme court, the *parlement*. As cases became more complex, trained lawyers were called in to give advice on points of law; later these legal experts replaced the barons as judges. The *parlement* itself tended to split up into sections, and by the time of Philip the Fair there existed a *chambre des enquêtes* to supervise the activities of local courts, a *chambre des requêtes* to receive complaints and decide if a case should be brought to trial, and a *chambre des plaids* to actually hear and judge cases.

As might be expected, the ever-increasing number of professional men in the government—men who owed their position entirely to the king—became enthusiastic supporters of extending royal authority. Under Philip Augustus and St. Louis these officials worked zealously to increase the king's power. But it must be stressed again that these monarchs still thought in terms of a strong *feudal* king whose authority was more or less still limited by custom. Under their successor Philip the Fair, however, a shift in emphasis appeared. His principal legists were trained in the newly revived study of Roman law, a law reflecting the theory of a centralized state headed by an absolute monarch. Influenced by such ideas, these professional officials played an increasingly important role in shifting the theory of government from a personal relationship between king and vassal to one between the "crown" as an institution and its subjects. When this change was completed modern theories of the direct sovereignty of the state over its subjects came into being.

Norman England

Whereas in France the establishment of royal authority was a centuries-long process, in England, after its conquest in 1066 by the Normans, the development of the monarch's central authority began on a firmer basis. When William the Conqueror won Anglo-Saxon England, he managed, with some qualification, to transplant the efficient and well-organized Norman type of feudalism to his new domain. Thus in England the essential foundations for a strong monarchy were laid during the reign of one monarch. At first glance one might expect that the authority of the king of England would have developed along the same lines, and even more rapidly, than that of France. But this was not the case. In contrast to France, where the path ultimately led to royal absolutism, in England it led instead toward *limited* monarchy, in which the king was required to share his power with his subjects.

Anglo-Saxon Period

One reason for this difference in development was the characteristics of pre-Norman, Anglo-Saxon England. The barbarian invasions had produced more widespread devastation in England than on the Continent, and by the seventh century virtually all traces of Roman civilization had disappeared. The country itself came to be divided into several petty Germanic kingdoms. In time the weaker of these kingdoms were absorbed by the stronger, but before the ninth century no one king had succeeded in uniting the entire island. The larger of the Anglo-Saxon kingdoms were small when compared to the great states of Continental Europe, a circumstance that permitted their rulers to maintain closer control over them. This, together with the disappearance of the great landholders of the Roman period, militated against the emergence of powerful, semi-independent lords, though in a sense the kings of the "Heptarchy" *were* their lords.

When, in the ninth and tenth centuries, the Vikings launched their raids on Western Europe, Anglo-Saxon England proved unable to withstand them effectively; ultimately the Danes were able to crush the more important Anglo-Saxon states, with the notable exception of the expanded kingdom of Wessex in the south. The famous Alfred the Great of Wessex (871–899) managed to prevent the complete subjugation of the island by granting the Danes (after defeating them) a vast stretch of land comprising much of the northeastern areas, subsequently to be referred to as the "Danelaw." In the face of great odds, the successors of Alfred gradually conquered and reabsorbed the Danelaw until in the tenth century one king finally ruled over all England.

A new wave of invaders from Denmark soon returned, this time to conquer the entire kingdom. Their leader, Canute, who in 1016 assumed the title of King of England, ruled a supra-national state that included England, Denmark, and Norway. But this remarkable union of territories fell apart after his death in 1035. With the extinction of his family, the English throne then reverted to a Saxon family descended from Alfred the Great, while Scandinavia went its own way. Thirty-one years later England was to be conquered by the Normans, thereby becoming tied to western rather than northern Europe.

With the unification of Anglo-Saxon England under the successors of King Alfred in the late ninth and tenth centuries, a new administrative organization for the realm emerged. The kingdom was divided into shires (something like the Carolingian counties), in each of which a bishop and an earl, both appointed by the king, handled spiritual and temporal affairs. For each shire there was appointed a sheriff (from "shire" and "reeve"—a royal representative), who reported directly to the king. It was the sheriff's duty to collect the royal revenues and to preside over the shire court that met twice a year. Each shire was itself subdivided administratively into districts called "hundreds," which in turn possessed their own court.

Authority was exercised by the king through the earls, bishops, and sheriffs as well as through the officers of his household, all of whom he appointed. A council, the Witan, rather amorphous and apparently composed of all important churchmen, landholders, and officials of the realm, met on occasion to advise the king, elect, and, if necessary, depose the monarch, and at times to act as a kind of supreme court. Although the composition and function of the Witan is not entirely clear, nineteenth-century historians affirmed that the Witan marked the beginnings of representative government in England—in other words, it was the ancestor of Parliament. But put more accurately, it simply fulfilled the need to consult on the part of those present.

Like the counts and dukes on the Continent, the earls tended to become hereditary officeholders with large estates. Despite this semi-feudal characteristic, Anglo-Saxon institutions seemed more to resemble those of the earlier period of Merovingian Gaul than those of ninth- or tenth-century Europe. Revenues came from the personal estates of the king, fines imposed by courts, various tolls, and, very late in the Anglo-Saxon period, from the so-called Danegeld, a direct tax levied on all Anglo-Saxon landholders for defense against the Danes. In contrast to the rulers on the Continent in this period, Anglo-Saxon kings maintained a certain degree of direct supervision over their kingdom. Thus when William of Normandy grafted the Norman feudal system to the institutions of Anglo-Saxon England, the English kings emerged, at least for a time, as among the most advanced in Europe.

The Norman Conquest

As justification for his expedition against England in 1066, Duke William of Normandy made shrewd use of his shadowy claim of relationship to the last "legitimate" Anglo-Saxon king, Edward the Confessor. Edward, who was so pious as to take a vow of chastity along with his marriage vows, had (not surprisingly) died without issue, and the Witan thereupon elected one of its own number, Earl Harold Godwin's son, as the king. William, however, claiming the throne by "kin right" (in addition to his claim that Harold previously had taken an oath of allegiance to him), now invaded England with papal sanction. Landing at Pevensey with a Norman army composed of adventurers and land-hungry vassals, he defeated and killed King Harold at the famous Battle of Hastings. In only five years William was able to subdue the entire kingdom.

The new king, William I, displayed a veritable genius for government. He acted as though *all* the land of England belonged to himself, when it has been estimated that one-sixth was retained by him as personal estates, and the rest was alloted as fiefs to his Norman followers and the Church. And, after 1069, when the earldoms of Edwin and Moriar were forfeited, the Anglo-Saxons retained none or only a small fraction of the land. But not only were the Norman barons who acquired land required to perform all the services of vassals to the king, so were churchmen. Particularly important was the military obligation, which permitted William to augment the English army with a large group of loyal, well-trained knights.

A detail from the celebrated Bayeux Tapestry, the near-contemporary record of the events of 1066. Here William of Normandy sails to England for the Conquest with his knights seated on their horses in the boats. (From The Bayeux Tapestry *published by Phaidon Press Ltd., Oxford, England)*

By acquiring at one blow, as it were, a newly conquered country, William was thus enabled to enforce a uniform application of the feudal principles that his thirty years' experience as Duke of Normandy had taught him. It is notable that interior lands were granted piecemeal, so no one vassal was permitted to hold contiguous fiefs. The latest theory holds that since his vassals were land-hungry and the kingdom conquered slowly, William had to hand out land piecemeal to keep everyone reasonably happy. William granted large blocs of land only on frontiers, where the vassals were charged with the defense of the realm, a practice not unfamiliar from Charlemagne's day.

Some of the better features of Anglo-Saxon administration were incorporated into William's system. Though the threat of the Danes was long since past, he continued to collect the Danegeld. The practice of imposing judicial fines was retained, and on occasion the king even called up the old Anglo-Saxon militia (usually in order to gain money by commuting military service for a price). Maintaining the shire courts, he bound the sheriffs tightly to the king. Thus, through the instrument of the sheriff, the monarch was able to maintain a direct link with local government. The Norman *Curia Regis* (king's court) met at the king's pleasure and, on a very informal basis at first, dealt with matters similar to those previously dealt with by the Witan.

The most striking evidence for William's determination to maintain strong royal control over his kingdom was the Domesday Book. Begun in 1086, this remarkable document—the only one of its kind in medieval Western Europe—was intended to be a complete survey of all real property in England. A listing of all resources and a statement of ownership, both before and after the Conquest, were required of all property holders. Tenants, farm utensils, fields, forests, and waters were all very carefully listed. Also set down were the amount of Danegeld paid and obligations owed by each region to its lord and to the king. By referring to this book the English kings could quickly ascertain where more revenue could be gained and had an authoritative source in case of usurpation of property.

At the death of William the Conqueror his patrimony was for a time divided between his two elder sons. Robert, the first son (whom his father disliked), was made Duke of Normandy, and William II became the king of England (1087–1100). William's third son, Henry, who was destined to reunite the two territories, was at this time given only a cash settlement.

William II (called Rufus—the Red), an unscrupulous and grasping monarch, carried on intermittent warfare with his brother Robert in the hope of gaining Normandy. As king he was so demanding that later generations labeled him a tyrant. William's avarice was well known: he would, for instance, delay making new appointments to vacant bishoprics in order to collect the episcopal revenues for the crown (the Church was probably the largest single landholder of the realm). William's reign was cut short by a mysterious hunting accident, which, according to the latest scholarship, occurred with the connivance of his brother Henry.

The new ruler, Henry I (1100–1135), proved to be one of England's most able kings. His reputation for insistence on the royal prerogatives and for the extension of the jurisdiction of the royal courts gained him the epithet "the old lion of justice." When he found, for instance, that certain directors of the royal mints were guilty of debasing the royal coinage in order to reap a profit, Henry had their right hands cut off—a standard punishment, milder than other ones such as boiling the guilty in molten lead!

Henry I

In 1106 Henry won a decisive victory over his brother Robert, taking him prisoner and seizing Normandy. Subsequently Henry married his daughter and heiress, Matilda, to Geoffrey, the Count of Anjou. Their son was the famous Henry II, who was to pose a great threat to the Capetian monarchs in France.

Upon ascending the throne Henry I issued a coronation charter disclaiming his brother William's flagrant violations of custom. Although in practice Henry was often to violate his own charter, its issuance served as an important precedent. For by this charter he in effect recognized that custom placed definite limits on royal authority, and the more famous Magna Carta of 1215 (see below) was, from one point of view, merely an extension of Henry's earlier charter.

Under Henry I were the beginnings of a more professional bureaucracy and administration. Henry began the custom of dispatching royal judges to various parts of the kingdom, thereby initiating the system of itinerant (almost equivalent to our circuit court) judges. On the return of these judges to the king's court, they naturally compared notes, and as a result tended to render more uniform judgments for all areas of the realm. The practice of sending out itinerant justices has been considered to mark an important stage in the evolution of the great English system of common law.

As membership in the *Curia Regis* expanded and the complexity of its business increased, it became too unwieldy a body to deal effectively with the day-to-day problems of government. It thus tended to break up into separate sections. The Great Council of all members met now only to deal with extraordinary matters, and it was on the few members of the king's immediate entourage (later called the Privy Council) that the business of daily administration fell. The paperwork of government grew ever larger, and to handle it a special group of the king's servants evolved into a sort of secretariat headed by the Royal Chancellor. Many of the records of medieval England's administration are simply the records kept by this chancery. At a time when the Capetian and German kings were still carrying their records around with them, the English kings had learned the value of keeping systematic archives.

Increased revenue poured into the royal coffers from tolls, feudal dues, and rents owed to the monarch. In addition, Henry encouraged the practice of his vassals to make regular money payments called scutage ("shield money") in place of rendering the customary military service. (This was of course a further step in the emergence of modern taxation.) With the great increase in royal revenues Henry saw the need for a specialized "treasury" section to receive monies and to audit royal accounts. Because the money collected was counted out on a checkered table (a custom probably derived from Sicily), this section of the administration came to be called the Exchequer.

When Henry I died in 1135, Norman England was moving toward a system of government and administration of a type that was not to appear in France for at least another hundred years. But for a time it seemed that the gains made by the Norman kings might be lost. Since Henry left no male heir, a civil war over the succession broke out between the supporters of his nephew Stephen and those of his daughter Matilda. Stephen's party eventually won out, and Matilda was forced to flee with her husband to Anjou. Stephen, however, proved unable to maintain the position of his predecessors, a situation that permitted the nobles to reassert many of their customary prerogatives against the monarchy. Although royal authority thus almost collapsed under Stephen, the danger of England's falling into complete anarchy was averted. For Stephen, whose one heir was killed, left his kingdom to Matilda's son, the young and energetic Henry of Anjou. During his reign this forceful monarch was able to regain not only the prerogatives lost during Stephen's reign but to extend royal authority even further.

Henry II and the English Common Law

As noted earlier, when Henry II (1154–1189) assumed the English crown, he was already lord of over half of France. He was the Duke of Normandy and Count of Anjou by inheritance, and, through marriage, Duke of Aquitaine. Yet before Henry could turn his attention to his Continental lands, he had first to establish his authority in England. This moody yet energetic and often brilliant monarch set out to undermine baronial power. His first act was to force the barons to destroy all unlicensed fortifications (some reports have it that more than 1,100 such castles were thus razed). To reassert his prerogatives as suzerain, Henry insisted that all vassals implement their obligations to him to the letter. The careful accounts kept by his predecessors, especially in the Domesday Book, were now used to uncover usurpations of lands and regalian rights by the barons. The new king was thus soon able to bring his barons to heel, and revenues and business again came to the king's court.

Most important, perhaps, from our point of view, were Henry's contributions to English law, in which he built on the reforms previously instituted by his grandfather. Henry's work in this connection is so significant that he may be said to have established some of the most basic judicial practices of the English-speaking world.

Unlike today, when new laws are "legislated" into existence, medieval people believed that law already existed in the form of custom and that it was the duty of the king and his officers simply to "discover" and proclaim it. In this connection Henry I and Henry II always denied they were "innovating" (we would say "legislating") in legal matters, but claimed rather that they were adhering to the customary law existing from time immemorial. But by standardizing existing law and extending it over all England through the royal courts, these two monarchs did in effect create new law—a law that came to be called the common law of the realm (law, that is, common to all England). As is the practice today, judges, when rendering a decision, were urged to follow the precedent of earlier, similar cases. If, for example, the penalty for stealing a hog was a fine of twenty shillings in Yorkshire, a judge trying a like case in Kent was required to impose the same fine. The precedents established by judicial decisions thus acquired the force of new law.

With William the Conqueror, much of the business of the old shire and hundred courts had shifted to the private manorial courts of the lords. Henry II sought to counter this threat to royal jurisdiction by offering better justice in the

Stone effigy of King Henry II at Fontevrault. He was the great lawgiver of England and long-time opponent of Philip Augustus of France. (Caisse Nationale des Monuments Historiques, Paris)

royal courts. First, he reinstituted the practice of sending itinerant royal justices throughout the realm, who were specifically charged with receiving reports from the sheriffs and handling all cases pending before the shire courts. In each area the sheriffs were required to bring before these itinerant judges a group of men sworn under oath to report all crimes recently committed in the area and to name ("indict") the suspected offender. The latter would then be bound over for trial by ordeal. From this evolved the important modern institution of the grand jury, whose function is to review evidence and indict a suspect.

The petty jury (which is suggestive of today's trial jury) also became widespread under Henry II. When a civil complaint was lodged with the crown through the purchase of a writ, a royal official, usually the sheriff, would gather together twelve men who had knowledge of the case. After stating the facts as they knew them, the twelve would jointly reach a verdict regarding the defendant's guilt or innocence, or, more specifically, with regard to the rights of plaintiff and defendant. A fine was then paid to the Exchequer by the party losing the case. It should be noted that these juries were not yet trial juries in the modern sense. Rather, their proceedings were more in the nature of a sworn inquest or investigation. Moreover, they were used only in civil cases; the barbarian German ordeal was still employed in criminal proceedings. (After 1215, when the Fourth Lateran Church Council forbade the use of ordeals, the use of a jury in both criminal and civil cases tended gradually to replace recourse to trial by ordeal.)

Henry's practice of issuing (for a fee, of course) royal writs, documents prescribing the course of action to be followed in legal matters, had considerable bearing on the development of our modern concept of equity. (In modern law equity is a means of protecting a party or parties *before* an injustice has been committed. The writ of injunction, equity's principal instrument, prevents or enjoins, action from being taken.) To cite a hypothetical case in Henry's time: A former serf has lived in a town for the prescribed length of time needed to gain his freedom (usually a year and a day). Threatened with seizure by his former lord, he can apply to the royal chancery for a writ enjoining (preventing) the lord's action until the case has been heard before a royal court. Should the lord, nevertheless, attempt to proceed with the seizure, the lord would then be liable to face charges in a royal court.

The growing reputation for impartiality of royal justice and the ease of obtaining it led increasing numbers of Englishmen to seek the jurisdiction of royal courts. As a result, the ancient local customs of Anglo-Saxon and of baronial law were gradually supplanted by the king's new Common Law.

For centuries it had been the firm belief of the Western Church that no cleric should be tried in a nonecclesiastical (secular) court. Henry, seeking to extend the jurisdiction of royal justice over all subjects, including the clergy, came into direct conflict with the archbishop of Canterbury, Thomas Becket. Becket, although he had been the Royal Chancellor and was an intimate friend of Henry, became the champion of ecclesiastical rights after his elevation to the archbishopric.

In 1164 the king promulgated the Constitutions of Clarendon, which attempted among other things to restrict the scope of ecclesiastical courts. He left to Church courts such cases as perjury (where the breaking of an oath taken in the name of God was concerned) and marriage. According to the Constitutions, however, "criminous clerks," that is, churchmen who committed the more serious crimes such as murder and grand larceny, were to be turned over to royal justice for punishment after they had first been convicted and unfrocked by an ecclesiastical court. Becket, on the grounds that unjust "double punishment" would then be meted out, unyieldingly resisted this provision. A lasting enmity was thus created between the two former friends. After a six-year, self-imposed exile on the Continent, during which time he sought papal aid, Becket returned alone to oppose Henry. At length Henry became so exasperated at Becket's refusal to lift an excommunication imposed on the clerics who supported the king that Henry remarked, angrily and perhaps thoughtlessly, before some of his

Depiction of Thomas à Becket being murdered in the Canterbury Cathedral by knights of King Henry II. His death was the culmination of the struggle between the twelfth-century English church and state. (Reproduced by permission of the British Library Board, Harley ms. 5102, f. 32)

courtiers, "Will no one rid me of this man!" This remark was taken seriously by four men present. Crossing the Channel to England, they found Becket in Canterbury Cathedral and there cut him down at the foot of the altar.

This act brought down the wrath of the Church on Henry, and he was forced to humiliate himself by doing public penance before the tomb of the martyred archbishop. More important, the king now had to withdraw virtually all of his restrictions on ecclesiastical courts.

Most of Henry's reign was taken up by his enterprises in France. To govern Normandy, Anjou, Brittany, and Aquitaine was in itself no slight task. Moreover, Henry was faced with the almost unrelenting attacks of his Capetian suzerains. Some scholars, attributing grandiose ideas of power to Henry, have termed his vast holdings in England and on the Continent an "Angevin empire." Whatever his dream, it is certain that, in line with the policy of the greater lords of the period, he sought to consolidate his holdings in France and to secure as much independence as possible from the French crown. But the rebellion of his sons and the shrewd manipulations of Philip Augustus brought all his schemes to naught. In the end the old king died a broken and embittered man.

The reign of his successor, Richard I, "the Lion-Hearted" (1189–1199), revealed the firm foundation of Henry's governmental system. Embroiled in a crusade abroad and later in wars against Philip Augustus, Richard spent no more than six months of his entire ten-year reign in England. Yet despite his neglect of the kingdom, Richard's ministers were able to maintain royal authority through the machinery of government built up by Henry.

Magna Carta and the Royal Authority

The first real setback to the rapid extension of monarchical power in England occurred in the reign of King John (1199–1216). Though clever and ambitious, John at times acted foolishly. His flippant attitude during his investiture as Duke of Normandy (he winked at the ladies and even dropped the lance, symbol of ducal authority) scandalized the Norman barons. And his insistence on marriage to an already betrothed woman ultimately resulted in the loss of his French lands. Unfortunately for John, he was faced simultaneously with three formidable adversaries: Philip Augustus of France, Pope Innocent III, and an English nobility outraged not only by the growth of royal power but especially at John's squandering of English resources in Continental campaigns.

I have already described John's loss of all Angevin possessions in France north of the Loire. He clashed with Pope Innocent III in 1206 over a disputed election to the archbishopric of Canterbury; John proposed one candidate, the English clergy another. When the case was referred to Rome, Innocent decided to appoint his own candidate, the English Cardinal Stephen Langton. Angered at the English clergy as well as the Pope, John refused to admit Langton to England, exiled the canons of Canterbury Cathedral, and confiscated all the property of that see. Innocent retaliated by placing John's entire kingdom under the dread sentence of interdict—which meant that almost all religious services were forbidden and the administration of the sacraments so vital to salvation was curtailed. John remained intransigent after a year under interdict. The Pope took the step of excommunicating him, at the same time threatening to depose him and transfer the crown to his archenemy, Philip Augustus. Philip, delighted, began to gather forces for an expedition, whereupon John, doubting the loyalty of his own barons, capitulated (1213). He accepted the papal nominee to the see of Canterbury, returned all the confiscated ecclesiastical property, and, in order to stave off Philip, even declared England a fief of the bishop of Rome.

Although he had foiled Philip's invasion of England, John suffered a disastrous defeat at the hands of Philip at Bouvines (1214). His quarrel with his barons now became acute. The English nobility had long been smouldering under John's highhanded treatment (he often, for example, punished vassals without proper trial); they resented his and his predecessor's exactions to pay for the campaigns in France. Hence, after the fiasco of Bouvines, open revolt broke out, with fully one-third of the English nobles renouncing their oaths of fealty to John and gathering forces to oppose him. Unable to muster enough strength to crush his rebellious vassals, John met with them on June 15, 1215, at Runnymede. There he was forced to accept a document listing the barons' demands. This famous document has come to be known as the Magna Carta (Great Charter). It is often referred to as the cornerstone of English and American liberties.

Actually the document was essentially only a guarantee that the king would respect the traditional privileges of the baronage. Although most of the provisions of the charter had a temporary significance, two provisions came to take on a much broader meaning. And over the centuries these two clauses have been interpreted (or overinterpreted) as providing guarantees of certain basic rights to all English subjects. The first, a promise by John not to levy any new "aids" without the prior consent of a council composed of his vassals, came in time to mean that Parliament's consent was necessary before a new tax could be levied. This interpretation, by extension, has come to guarantee representative government. The second provision, which forbade the king to arrest, imprison, or punish any "free man ... unless by legal judgement of his peers or by the law of the land ...," has been cited as the basis for English and American ideas of personal liberty. Although the phrase "free man" had little significance in 1215, with the gradual disappearance of serfdom the application of this clause came to mean that the government could take no action against any subject, highborn or lowborn, without what we would today call "due process of law."

More significant than these two clauses, however, is the principle implicit in the very issuance of the charter. For when John sealed it he admitted that the king was subject to and bound to rule by the law. The ultimate result of the establishment of this precedent, now firmly rooted in the English-speaking world, was that no government can exercise arbitrary powers over its subjects. It should be emphasized that for John, however, who had no intention of living up to the charter, it was merely a stopgap measure until he could gather strength to crush his barons. It is worth noting that John immediately appealed to the Pope, who "annulled" Magna Carta. Thus its continuing force actually depended on its reissue by King Henry III.

Despite the efforts of King John during his last days to bring his barons under subjection and force them to repudiate the document, Magna Carta and its importance survived. Fearing heavenly penalty for his sins, especially his failure to take the cross in obedience to his earlier vows, John ordered himself to be buried in the garb of a crusader so that when the devil stalked through the graveyard examining the crypts to collect souls of the newly dead, he might be fooled by the sight of a big red cross of cloth resting on John's chest!

John's son, Henry III (1216–1272), was unduly influenced by his favorites throughout most of his reign. His mother remarried, bringing her new husband —the very man from whom John had taken her—and her French relatives to England. Henry granted these adventurers high offices and lavish gifts. His obvious favoritism for these foreign nobles and his repeated demands for more money increased the dissatisfaction of the English nobles. Thus, in 1258, when Henry asked for a substantial sum of money after a year of poor harvests, the nobility took as direct action against him as they had against his father.

The barons forced upon Henry a document known as the Provisions of Oxford, which set up a "junta" of fifteen barons to govern England and ratify every act of the king. Foreign nobles were to be expelled from England and their offices in the government given to nominees of the baronial council. But almost as soon as they had gained these concessions, the barons, characteristically, fell out among themselves. For a time Henry was able to reassume personal rule. In 1263, however, civil war again broke out between Henry and the barons, now led by the Earl of Leicester, Simon de Montfort. The French King Louis IX was asked to arbitrate, but when he ruled in favor of his fellow monarch, the barons refused to yield. Taking Henry prisoner, Simon set up a baronial administration based on the earlier Provisions of Oxford. Again, however, the barons fell to squabbling among themselves, and in 1265 Henry's son Edward crushed them, killing Simon and restoring his father to power.

When Edward I (1272–1307) came to the throne, his first task was to regain the privileges lost to the crown during his father's reign. Nobles had forbidden the royal sheriffs to enter their lands, forced their tenants to appeal to manorial instead of royal courts, and in other ways usurped royal rights. Edward, therefore, compelled every lord to produce a charter proving his legal right to exercise these privileges. If a baron could neither produce such a charter nor prove his predecessor's exercise of these rights under King Richard I, he might well be forced to relinquish his privileges. At least that is what the barons feared. In fact Edward issued the needed charters himself, though in so doing he made the point that *all* justice was royal in origin.

Royal authority by this time was being threatened by still another consideration—subinfeudation. This process, the division of and granting of land by a lord to rear vassals, had, by Edward's reign, proceeded so far that many nobles were removed from direct feudal obligation to the king. As many as six or more lords, for example, could stand between the king and the vassal who actually held the land. Such aids as scutage, payable to the monarch in place of customary military service, were therefore often considerably reduced in amount by the time they had passed through all these various hands. To combat this process, Edward promulgated a decree—significant as an early example of "statute" law applicable to the entire realm—which now allowed land to be transferred to another for money, but only if the lord of the original fief became the direct lord of the new proprietor. This statute had the effect of arresting the process of sub-infeudation. Indeed, it reversed the process so that gradually more and more vassals held their lands directly from the king. Some historians have attributed the decline of feudalism in England to Edward's efforts to stop the subdivision of land.

The royal judicial system by now had split up into two distinct courts: one, the court of king's bench, dealt with both criminal and civil cases of direct interest to the monarch (treason, breaking the king's peace, disputes involving crown lands); the other, the court of common pleas, handled only civil suits between subjects. On rare occasions the Great Council of barons still met as a tribunal, but this practice fell more and more into disuse, the council becoming more or less a court of last resort. In England today, the House of Lords—the descendant of the baronial council—can still receive appeals.

Edward's diplomatic and military policy centered on his attempts to unite the entire British Isles. Ireland had already been subdued and made subject to the English crown, the process beginning in earnest under Henry II. Henry had also partially subdued Wales. But the Welsh, becoming restless over the years, revolted against Edward's suzerainty. Crushing the rebellion, Edward annexed the territory in 1283, and had his young son proclaimed Prince of Wales, a title since that time reserved for the heir-apparent of England.

A disputed succession in Scotland led Edward in 1290 to intervene there. He proclaimed himself king of Scotland and carried off the famous Stone of Scone on which Scottish kings had always been crowned. The Stone remained at Westminister Abbey as the base for the English coronation throne. But Edward never truly conquered Scotland, and died while leading an expedition northward. His son, Edward II, was soundly defeated by the Scots at the Battle of Bannockbourn (1314), and Scotland went its own way. The two kingdoms were not to be united under one monarch until 1603, when James VI of Scotland succeeded Elizabeth I as James I of England. Throughout the medieval period these two kingdoms remained bitter enemies, with Scotland usually allying with France against England.

Edward's successor, the incompetent Edward II (1307–1327), had to face another baronial rebellion, this time led by his wife and her lover. Edward was tortured to death, his screams echoing throughout the castle. For a time the queen and her paramour ruled in the name of his son, Edward III. Since Edward III's reign marks the beginning of the Hundred Years' War, the century-long conflict with France, I shall take it up later, in Chapter 12.

Evolution of the English Parliament

From the modern viewpoint perhaps the most significant feature of Edward I's reign was the appearance of a semi-representational institution of government, the direct ancestor of the modern English Parliament. Kings, of course, had always summoned their great vassals in council when attempting to undertake new policy or to secure extraordinary revenues. Attendance at the meetings of the *Curia Regis* (roughly analogous to the old Saxon Witan) had been made compulsory by the early Norman kings, a circumstance that tended to give the barons the idea that they should play a certain role in governing the kingdom. Gradually the idea grew that the king *must* gain the assent of his Great Council when matters affecting the whole realm were involved.

During the reign of Henry III the composition of the Great Council changed somewhat. Lesser nobles, called knights of the shire, began to be summoned to the council meetings. And in 1265 Simon de Montfort, seeking support for his government when the barons were deserting him, summoned not only knights of the shire but representatives from the towns as well. Such a gathering, including the knights and townsmen as well as the nobles, did not occur again during Henry III's reign. The precedent created had a certain significance, but the "parliament" lacked legal basis because the king had not called it.

The summoning of townsmen to regular sessions of the Great Council during Edward I's reign seems to have been prompted by the monarch's ever-growing need for revenues. Previous kings had negotiated with towns on an individual basis when requesting money. Edward perhaps thought to simplify this process by gathering in one great assembly representatives from all the taxable groups—great nobles and knights of the shire as well as townsmen. Thus in 1295, when he summoned his vassals to a meeting of the Great Council, he also directed his sheriffs to send two knights from each shire, and, more important, two burgesses from each town.

This meeting of the Great Council was the first to include all the groups later to comprise the English Parliament; for this reason it has been called the "Model Parliament." It would be a mistake, however, to believe that the Model Parliament had any great significance during Edward's reign. The king did not bother to summon rear vassals or townsmen to subsequent parliaments, and, even when present, they were sometimes asked only to assent to business already considered and finished before their arrival, or simply to witness, not act on, what was done in their presence. When discussion was carried on, moreover, the townsmen and knights of the shire were completely dominated by the great nobles and the king. After Edward's reign, however, the townsmen and knights of the shire were more frequently summoned. Finding that they had more in common with each other than with the great barons, the burgesses and knights tended to work together in their not infrequent opposition to the king and sometimes the greater lords. Parliament as a result began to divide into two distinct sections—sections which later evolved into the House of Lords and the House of Commons.

At Edward's death this division had not yet taken place. But Parliament

Depiction of King Edward I during a session in Parliament. Note representation of all three classes, with churchmen on left, red-robed barons on right, and judges seated on wool sacks between them. (Society of Antiquaries of London)

had gained, or was on the way to gaining, impressive concessions. It soon became established that Parliament alone could alter or add to the Common Law of the realm. Equally important, it was in time to be clearly recognized that Parliament's consent was necessary before new taxes could be levied. Using its control over revenue as a weapon, Parliament was able to force later kings to grant it more and more authority. The result was that, in contrast to France, where the monarch *alone* was finally to emerge as the symbol of the state, the English king and his Parliament *together* came to embody the authority of the kingdom.

Why did the monarchy in France and England evolve along such different lines? Why no Magna Carta in France? Part of the answer lies in the nature of each monarchy at the advent of the Capetian and Norman dynasties. The very weakness of the early Capetian kings kept the great nobles of France from combining against royal tyranny, the monarchy having few means at its disposal to become tyrannical. William the Conqueror, on the other hand, had from the beginning bequeathed his dynasty effective means of control over the barons of England, who were thus constantly on guard to protect their prerogatives.

The Capetians normally had to face only one great noble at a time, and once the latter's territory was subdued or annexed, they usually had little to worry about from that noble's lesser vassals. For these had already been whipped into line by the machinery earlier established by the great feudatory himself. The Norman kings, on the other hand, in their very insistence that no such great estates could arise in England, had unwittingly created a situation more favorable to the organization of a series of baronial coalitions against them.

Finally, and perhaps most important of all, there is the element of chance. The Capetian dynasty was fortunate in producing a long series of monarchs of forceful personality. Little widespread baronial protest arose in France, and that which did (for example, the revolt during Louis IX's minority and the protests under Philip the Fair and his son Louis X in 1314–1316), occurred during the reigns of able rulers. In England, on the other hand, strong kings were as often as not succeeded by weak ones, and thus the English baronial reactions were opposed only by the feeble efforts of a Henry III or an Edward II.

FOR FURTHER READING

Davis, H. W. C., *England Under the Normans and Angevins, 1066–1272,* 13th ed. (1949; repr. 1957). Interesting, useful work.

Evans, J., *Life in Medieval France** (1969). A good picture of medieval French society.

Fawtier, R., *The Capetian Kings of France,* trans. Lionel Butler and R. H. Adams* (1960). Now the classic work on the subject.

Haskins, Charles H., *The Normans in European History** (1959; 1966). Aging but still valuable work.

Haskins, George L., *The Growth of English Representative Government** (1948). Well written.

Kantarowicz, H., *The King's Two Bodies* (1957). Traces ideas of kingship in history.

Kelly, Amy, *Eleanor of Aquitaine and the Four Kings** (1950; 1957). A fascinating account of one of France's most famous women.

Lewis, P. S., *Later Medieval France: The Polity* (1968). Emphasizes society and politics.

Luchaire, A., *Social France at the Time of Philip Augustus* (no date). A portrayal of social life, focusing, perhaps unduly, on its violent side.

Painter, S., *The Reign of King John* (1949). A standard account of the life of King John, by an important American specialist.

Painter, S., *The Rise of the Feudal Monarchies** (1951). See *For Further Reading,* Chapter 10.

Pegues, F., *The Lawyers of the Last Capetians* (1962). Very scholarly study. Very useful.

* Asterisk indicates paperback edition available.

Petit-Dutaillis, C., *The Feudal Monarchy in France and England: From the Tenth to the Thirteenth Century,* trans. E. D. Hunt* (1949; 1964). An excellent comparative study of the development of these two medieval monarchies.

Sayles, G. O., *The Medieval Foundations of England* (1948). The best work on the subject.

Stephenson, C., and F. G. Marcham, eds., *Sources of English Constitutional History,* rev. ed.* (1972). Legal texts with commentary, including material on early representative assemblies.

Tilley, A., ed., *Medieval France* (1964). Essays on various topics of political theory.

Wood, C. T., *The French Appanages and the French Monarchy* (1966). A careful, scholarly analysis. Valuable.

Although Western Christendom had sporadic contacts with the East in the early medieval period, it was not until the First Crusade at the end of the eleventh century that the West was able to burst out of its virtual isolation and come into closer and more protracted contact, indeed into direct collision, with the Byzantine and Arab worlds. For more than two centuries Western crusaders, taking the offensive, pushed the narrow boundaries of Latin Christendom outward—southwest into Spain, eastward to Byzantium, north and east toward Russia, and, most strikingly, southeast to the Holy Land. Latin kingdoms or principalities in the Western style were established in the Holy Land, and in 1204 the Byzantine Empire itself was conquered and occupied by Latin armies. Although the crusading movement created deep resentment between East and West, the physical barriers between Latin Christendom and the Byzantine and

CHAPTER 9

The Crusades: Latins, Arabs, and Byzantines in Conflict

Islamic worlds were let down to the extent that economic, social, and intellectual influences could flow back and forth more freely than before. In this process of cultural give and take, the Latin West gained much more than did the East; the civilizations of the two Eastern worlds—Byzantine and Islamic—up to the early thirteenth century were in many respects still more advanced than that of the Western world.

The crusades occurred within the broader context of the social, economic, and political changes described in the preceding three chapters, but once the crusades began they helped to effect some of these changes.

Ideology and Background of the Crusade

A crusade may be defined essentially as a holy war—a war in defense of the Cross (Latin *crux*)—sponsored by the Pope (who promised remission of sins to participants)* and directed toward delivering the Holy Land from the hands of the infidels. In the later medieval period the definition came to be extended to include any expedition blessed by the Papacy. Thus a crusade could be a war against any enemy of the faith—heretics (Albigensians, for example), schismatics (Greeks), unbelievers (Muslims), or even Anti-popes. Ambitious Popes tended to use the crusading idea to achieve their own political ends. As seen in Chapter 7, in the thirteenth century a crusade against the Holy Roman Emperor himself, Frederick II, was proclaimed by the Papacy.

Even before the so-called First Crusade to the Holy Land in 1095, a kind of crusade or holy war under the sponsorship of the Pope had taken place within Western Europe. Such, essentially, were the military expeditions to Spain to reconquer for Christianity Spanish lands held by the Muslims. During the late tenth century internal dissension caused the breakup of the caliphate of Cordova into small Muslim principalities. The Christian kingdoms of northern Spain, particularly Castile and Aragon (kingdoms that emerged after the Arab conquest of the eighth century), in the early eleventh century began a struggle for these Muslim states—a struggle that developed into a centuries-long program of *Reconquista,* as the Spanish called it. Slowly the conflict moved in favor of the Christians. At the time of the First Crusade this movement in Spain began to take on greater impetus—aided by French nobles looking for land and sometimes salvation, and spurred on by Cluniac monks who incited the religious zeal of the fighters.

The Byzantines, too, fought what may be called holy wars against the Muslims under the Emperor Heraclius in the seventh century and the Emperors

---

* This remission of sins was guaranteed by documents called "indulgences."

Nicephorus Phocas and John Tzimisces (John I) in the tenth century. Although the primary aim of the Byzantines was to recover territories lost to Islam in its expansion during the previous three centuries, it was also their objective to recover the Holy Land and especially the Cross on which Christ had died. Because of the latter objectives, such Byzantine expeditions may perhaps be called "proto-crusades." It should be noted, however, that unlike the subsequent crusades of the West no guarantee of spiritual rewards in the afterlife ("indulgences"), such as were promised the crusaders by the Popes, was offered to the Byzantine armies.

The motives behind the launching of the First Crusade by Pope Urban II were far more complex than a simple desire to free the Holy Land of the infidel and recover the Cross. To understand this event in its proper context we must examine the political situation in both East and West.

In fact, events taking place in the Byzantine East led directly to Urban's preaching of the First Crusade. The Byzantine state had reached its height politically and economically about 1025, at the end of the reign of Emperor Basil II. Thereafter internal decay and severe external catastrophes brought about a decline in Byzantine power. As seen in Chapter 5, in 1071 two disastrous military defeats for Byzantine arms occurred: the Norman invaders seized Bari, the Byzantine capital of southern Italy; and, even more significant, the Seljuk Turks annihilated the Byzantine army at Manzikert in Asia Minor.

After the disaster of Manzikert (where the emperor himself was taken prisoner) the Byzantines seemed unable to resist successfully the ever-increasing power of the Turks. The Seljuks, who had already conquered and reunited under their control the old lands of the Arab caliphate, now penetrated farther and conquered most of Asia Minor, the heartland of the Byzantine Empire. From their first capital, which they established at Iconium, the Seljuks took Nicaea—founding what they called the sultanate of Rum (Rome), which they considered a kind of successor-state to Byzantium.

At his accession in 1081 the new Byzantine emperor, Alexius I Comnenus, found himself in a desperate situation. Constantinople faced attack from two sides: from the sea by the Turkish pirate Tzachas and his fleet, and from the north by the savage Petchenegs, another Turkic people. To save his capital Alexius felt compelled to melt down and sell venerated church treasures, with which he bought the services of a third Turkic people, the Cumans. By skillful diplomacy he was able to avert the conquest of Constantinople.

It was formerly believed that Alexius' desperate position led him, at this time, to turn to the West for assistance. He did actually make such an appeal, but it was later, when the situation in Byzantium had become considerably less precarious. The immediate threats to Constantinople had been checked: the Seljuks were being plagued by internal dissension, and the great Seljuk Empire, stretching from Palestine to Persia, had broken up into various petty principalities. Why then did Alexius appeal to the West? Inspired by the proud Byzantine tradition, Alexius wanted to restore to his empire the vital territories lost to the Turks, especially Asia Minor, the source of most of the Byzantine revenues and troops for a long time. For this reason, then, he sent letters to the West requesting assistance—to individual Latin princes, and, more important, to the Pope, who as the spiritual head of Western Christendom might persuade Western princes to provide Byzantium with military aid.

Alexius was not the first Byzantine emperor to appeal to the Papacy for aid. His predecessor, the Emperor Michael VII Ducas, had sent messages to Pope Gregory VII requesting assistance and promising in exchange reunion of the Greek and Latin churches. Gregory had, in fact, exhorted Western princes to go to the aid of Constantinople and even had written for this purpose to his great antagonist, the Holy Roman Emperor Henry IV. As Gregory declared, "Most of eastern Christendom is being destroyed. The Christian race is being exterminated like cattle." To Pope Gregory, however, the prospect of the submission of the Greek Church to Rome was apparently the prime reason to aid Constantinople, the conquest of Jerusalem being relegated to second place. Nothing came of Gregory's plans. He became too embroiled in the great investiture conflict to spend much energy on aid for Byzantium. Yet the idea for a movement to aid the Christians of the East gained ground and helped to prepare the way for the preaching of the First Crusade by Gregory's successor, Urban II.

The First Crusade

Why did Urban turn his attention primarily to the recovery of Jerusalem? Western Christendom, to be sure, had always been concerned with the fate of the Holy Land, for the most sacred shrines of Christendom, those intimately connected with the Passion of Christ were located there. Throughout the medieval period it was an act of the highest piety for a Christian to make a pilgrimage to these shrines. With the development of the Western system of penance, pilgrimage to shrines containing relics of saints came to be considered a way to atone for one's sins. Pilgrims, for example, went in ever greater numbers to the tomb of St. James of Santiago de Compostela in Spain or to the sites of the martyrdom of St. Peter and St. Paul in Rome. Not all pilgrimages, however, were made out of purely religious motives; they might be spurred by a spirit of adventure or by a desire for economic gains. While gaining religious merit a merchant, for example, might turn a nice profit by bringing along goods that could be sold during his pilgrimage. An extreme instance of this blend of piety and practicality was the practice of certain women who, on their way to and from a shrine, would sell themselves as prostitutes in order to support their journey.

By the eleventh century pilgrimages to the Holy Land had become relatively common, with hundreds, even thousands, of people embarking on the long and arduous journey to Jerusalem. The most famous of these mass pilgrimages took place in 1064–1065 under Gunther, bishop of Bamberg, who led a group of 7,000 persons to the East. The pilgrims usually went by land, passing through Constantinople (where they were normally well treated) and across Asia Minor to Jerusalem. Neither the conquest of the Holy Land by the Arabs nor its conquest later by the Seljuks interfered for more than brief periods with these pilgrimages. Muslims had long been fairly tolerant of Christians, particularly of pilgrims. Most pilgrims, in fact, came unarmed, bearing in their hands the traditional pilgrim's staff.

Historians used to think the Seljuk conquest closed the Holy Land to pilgrims and thus directly brought about the First Crusade. But although the Seljuks were generally less tolerant than the Arabs, this view is too simple. No doubt the advance of the Seljuk Turks played some part in the launching of the crusades. Reports by Western pilgrims returning from the Holy Land that Christianity's holiest shrines were in the hands of the infidel deeply stirred Western Europeans and contributed to the idea of a holy war to free Jerusalem from "Muslim pollution."

At a synod called by Urban II at Piacenza early in 1095 to discuss the question of reform in the Western Church, envoys from Alexius appealed for aid against the Turks. The Byzantine envoys shrewdly associated their plea for aid with an explanation of the need for an expedition to liberate the Holy Land— an expedition that would traverse Asia Minor and, in so doing, would help Alexius to recover this former Byzantine territory. Later in the same year, Urban summoned a council at Clermont in southern France. Here, before a vast multitude of clergy and nobles, he delivered a stirring, impassioned address that set in motion the First Crusade:

> From the confines of Jerusalem and from the city of Constantinople a grievous report has gone forth and has repeatedly been brought to our ears; namely, that a race from the kingdom of the Persians[!], an accursed race, a race wholly alienated from God, "a generation that set not their heart aright, and whose spirit was not steadfast with God," has violently invaded the lands of those Christians and has depopulated them by pillage and fire. They have led away a part of the captives into their own country, and a part they have killed by cruel tortures. They have either destroyed the churches of God or appropriated them for the rites of their own religion. They destroy the altars, after having defiled them with their uncleanness.... The

kingdom of the Greeks is now dismembered by them and has been deprived of territory so vast in extent that it could not be traversed in two months' time.

On whom, therefore, is the labor of avenging these wrongs and of recovering this territory incumbent, if not upon you—you, upon whom, above all other nations, God has conferred remarkable glory in arms, great courage, bodily activity, and strength to humble the heads of those who resist you?

Let hatred therefore depart from among you, let your quarrels end, let wars cease, and let all dissensions and controversies slumber. Enter upon the road to the Holy Sepulcher; wrest that land from the wicked race, and subject it to yourselves. God has conferred upon you above all other nations great glory in arms. Accordingly, undertake this journey eagerly for the remission of your sins, with the assurance of the reward of imperishable glory in the kingdom of heaven.*

At the end of this speech, certainly one of the most effective in all history, Urban's audience was so moved, we are told, that the cry arose spontaneously from thousands of throats, "God wills it!" The Pope took it up and called upon all those who undertook the crusade to make it their battle cry and also to wear a cross of cloth on their garments.

Urban molded his speech to appeal to all sides of the Western character. Promising heavenly reward to all who would go to fight the infidel, arousing religious indignation against the "atrocities" of the Muslim Turks, flattering in particular the vanity of the French knights, he at the same time subtly suggested the opportunities for wealth and power open to those who conquered the Holy Land. He also probably sought to reduce the destructive internecine wars and saw the crusade as a means of channeling the disorderly belligerence of feudal barons into a holy war against the enemies of the faith.

This speech, however, did not reveal all of Urban's motives in preaching the crusade. Some of his thoughts obviously could not be stated publicly. French by birth and a Cluniac monk, Urban had been an intimate of Pope Gregory VII and knew of his intention to aid Constantinople in exchange for submission of the Greek Church to Rome. As successor to Gregory, Urban strongly desired to enhance the newly won prestige of the Papacy and establish its claims to universal supremacy. From the beginning of his pontificate, Urban had enjoyed cordial relations with the Byzantine emperor, and he hoped to prevent Alexius from entering into an alliance with the Pope's archenemy, Henry IV. For his part, Alexius maintained close contact with the Pope in hopes of preventing an invasion of Constantinople by the latter's ambitious Norman vassals, now masters of formerly Byzantine southern Italy.

* As reported by Robert the Monk, from J. H. Robinson, *Readings in European History,* 1904.

The emotional enthusiasm of those present at Clermont soon spread to Italy, Germany, and England; the result was the assembling of great hosts of crusading knights and a vast movement of armies to the East. The direct responsibility for the shaping of the First Crusade thus lies primarily with Urban II, who was able to combine in his own thinking the needs of the East, the ambitions of the Papacy, and, above all, the religious fervor of eleventh-century Western Europe—the latter emotion, however, only too soon sullied by Western nobles and merchants in their desire for political and commercial gain.

Before the main armies could get under way, however, early in 1096 a motley throng of peasants, vagabonds, and landless knights was gathered together and led east by a fanatical French preacher, Peter the Hermit. Pillaging as it marched through the Balkans, this "horde" reached the gates of Constantinople. There the Emperor Alexius, alarmed at the excesses committed, had it ferried across the Bosporus to Asia Minor. Ill-equipped, badly led, and militarily inexperienced, this ragtag army was quickly cut to pieces by the Seljuks. The incident was one of the first in a long series of incidents that drove a wedge between the Byzantines and Latins. The Latins placed the blame for the fate of Peter the Hermit and his followers directly on what appeared to them as treachery on the part of the Byzantine emperor.

A few months later the main force of crusading knights converged on the Byzantine capital. Led by some of the most powerful nobles of Europe—Godfrey of Bouillon, Duke Robert of Normandy, Count Robert of Flanders, Stephen of Blois, Count Raymond of Toulouse, and from southern Italy Prince Bohemond, the son of Duke Robert Guiscard—it was a formidable army, though loosely organized under the nominal command of Urban's legate, the bishop of Le Puy. Not one Western monarch participated in this crusade. The kings at this time were involved in conflicts with the Church—William II of England with Archbishop Anselm of Canterbury, Philip I of France under excommunication because of his notorious personal life, and Henry IV of Germany at odds with Urban II in the investiture conflict.

Role of Byzantine Emperor Alexius

One can imagine the consternation of the Emperor Alexius upon seeing this army of knights massed before the gates of Constantinople. Instead of the mercenary troops for whom he had hoped, he had received first a band of looters and now dangerous and powerful armies of haughty knights. And he had good reason to fear them, especially the ambitious Bohemond—his father, Robert Guiscard, had only recently tried to conquer Byzantium, and Bohemond himself apparently was scheming to seize Constantinople if the opportunity presented itself.

Alexius agreed to aid the Western armies in their campaign against Jerusalem. At the same time, he not only insisted that the crusaders hand over to him all Greek territory reconquered in Asia Minor, but also that their leaders swear an oath of allegiance to him as their feudal overlord, in the Western manner. The crusaders and Alexius apparently had different ideas about the meaning of the oath of fealty. Whereas Alexius probably envisaged permitting them to administer certain lands in something of the manner of Byzantine officials, the Western knights tended to view him as merely a nominal "suzerain," thus leaving them with the kind of feudal independence to which they were accustomed at home. This is only one example of the misunderstanding between the Byzantine emperor and the Western crusaders that led to hostility between them. As time went on, each believed that the other was not living up to the agreements and branded each other treacherous.

With Byzantine troops Alexius assisted the crusaders in their siege of Nicaea, the first city in Asia Minor to be retaken from the Turks. According to previous agreement, this city, with its Greek population, was now turned over to Alexius—but not, however, before causing a rift between the crusaders and the Byzantines. Alexius forbade the crusaders to plunder the city, a privilege of conquest usually awarded to victorious armies; although he granted lavish gifts to the crusade leaders, the incident served to generate mistrust.

Latin-Byzantine Mistrust.   The crusading host then advanced toward the Holy Land. One of its leaders, Baldwin of Flanders, retired from the expedition after the conquest of Edessa in northern Syria and established himself as count of that city, founding the first Latin principality in the East. After a prolonged and exhausting siege of Antioch, followed in turn by a Turkish siege of the crusaders then ensconced in the city, new difficulties arose between the Byzantines and the Latins. Alexius had not sent aid to the besieged crusaders at Antioch; to be sure, in accordance with the agreements, he had given provisions and guides, but he had not committed any substantial forces to the campaign. Spurred on by the ambitious Bohemond, the crusaders were persuaded that Alexius had failed to carry out the agreements, and accused him of perfidy and collusion with the infidel Turks. At that point a Latin knight discovered what some believed to be the Holy Lance—the spear that had pierced the side of Christ—and the crusaders, encouraged by this apparent sign of divine favor, were able to drive back the Turkish army. Bohemond, in direct violation of his agreement with the Byzantine emperor, thereupon seized Antioch for himself. Future relations between Latins and Byzantines were to be marked increasingly by suspicion and, soon enough, by outright hostility.

Muslim Distrust of Latins.   The remaining Latin leaders and their depleted armies now moved southward against Jerusalem. After a long and bitter siege the Holy City, in June of 1099, fell to the crusading host. An incredible slaughter

A Western army assaulting city and walls of Jerusalem in 1099, bringing the First Crusade to a successful conclusion. (Bodleian Library, Oxford)

of Muslims and Jews followed. One account tells us that Jews and Muslims, seeking refuge in their houses of worship, were burned alive when the buildings were set on fire. The slaughter was so great, records another Western source, that "the knights rode in blood up to their horses' knees." Similar excesses against Christians had not previously been committed by the Muslims, who had generally been tolerant of the Christians of the East. After the First Crusade, however, this spirit of tolerance changed to one of bitter hatred for those whom the Muslims now regarded as the "arrogant and bloodthirsty Franks." Muslim intolerance can be dated from this event as accurately as from any other.

Latin Kingdom of Jerusalem

The problem now facing the crusaders was how to maintain themselves in the Holy Land, an alien country surrounded on all sides by enemies. Even before the capture of Jerusalem their forces had been reduced to some 20,000 men when Baldwin and Bohemond chose to remain in Edessa and Antioch. And now a considerable number of the 20,000 having fulfilled their pilgrim vows and grown tired of their ordeal, returned home. In order to provide for the defense and administration of the newly conquered territories, the crusaders therefore organized the feudal kingdom of Jerusalem, with Godfrey of Bouillon, as a mark of respect for the sacredness of the area, elected Defender of the Holy Sepulcher; at his death his brother, Baldwin of Edessa, was crowned king. The Assizes of Jerusalem, a collection of Western administrative and legislative edicts establishing the organization of the kingdom, constitutes a remarkable source for medieval feudal and political institutions.

Territorially the kingdom consisted of a narrow strip of land (at places only fifty miles wide) stretching along the Syrian and Palestinian coast and including such important ports as Acre, Tyre, Beirut, and Sidon, as well as the inland cities of Edessa and Antioch. The king of Jerusalem was the feudal suzerain of these territories; his authority was limited by feudal law and by the privileges of certain groups such as the Venetians, Genoese, Templars, and others. In the cities the local political organization was left intact. The crusaders, probably following Pope Urban's policy of conciliating the Greeks, for a time recognized the authority of the Greek patriarchs at Antioch and Jerusalem. Soon enough, however, the Latins installed their own patriarchs in these cities.

In view of the enemies surrounding them, the crusader states had to turn to the West, especially maritime Italy, for economic aid. The Genoese fleet had carried provisions across the Mediterranean to aid in the conquest of Jerusalem. To ensure the continuing services of the Genoese, the crusaders granted them vast commercial privileges in the Holy Land—special trading rights, exemption from taxes, and a residential quarter in each city for their nationals. Pisan and Venetian merchants soon gained equal privileges. The resultant rivalry among the Genoese, Pisans, and Venetians led to disorders and even riots within the crusader states. Worse than this, the Italians, especially the Venetians, motivated by the desire for material gain, did not hesitate to trade with the nearby Muslim enemy and, on occasion, plot with the Muslim princes. The foothold gained in the Holy Land as well as in Byzantium by these Italian city states was a basic cause of their rise to great wealth and power.

To guard their lands the crusaders built massive castles in such strategic locations as Acre and Krak. Some still exist today. Whether or not they improved their technique of castle fortification as a result of Byzantine or Arab influence, there is no question that Latin castle architecture, both in structural techniques and military design, was greatly improved in this period. The feudal levy was insufficient to defend the area, the lordly vassals of the king of Jerusalem sometimes refusing to serve and even conspiring with the Muslims against him. Recourse to native mercenary troops also proved unsatisfactory. Hence the repeated Crusader appeals to the West for new infusions of men and supplies.

The best soldiers were provided by the Templars and Hospitallers, knights organized under the discipline of a monastic community whose main purpose it was to fight for the faith. Members of these religious military orders took vows of poverty, chastity, and obedience, as well as the vows of the Western knights. The order of the Knights Templar, whole rule was drawn up by the great St. Bernard and adopted in 1128, was originally formed to protect pilgrims; the name was derived from the location of its headquarters near the site of the Temple of Solomon. Early in the eleventh century a group of Amalfitan merchants established a hospital in Jerusalem to care for pilgrims and to nurse wounded crusaders. This institution developed into the religious military order of the Hospitallers. Later, at the time of the Third Crusade, still another group, that of German knights, was organized into the order of the Teutonic Knights.

Each of these orders possessed branch houses throughout Europe for the purpose of recruiting men. The branch houses were under the control of the order's Grand Master, whose authority was similar to that of the abbot of Cluny over his dependent houses. Like Cluny, each order was responsible only to the Pope, an independence that often led to clashes with local authorities as well as with one another. Bequests were left to the orders, all of which in time became wealthy. The orders continued to exist even after the Muslims retook the Holy Land. The Templars, as I have observed, soon became involved in banking activities (Chapter 6). The Hospitallers transferred their activities to the Aegean island of Rhodes, then later to Malta. The Teutonic Knights left the Holy Land after the loss of Jerusalem and established themselves in northeastern Europe as semi-independent rulers of a portion of northern Poland; they later became a thorn in the side of Poland's kings.

The creation of the crusader states wrought great changes in the map of the eastern Mediterranean. The four small Latin states of Jerusalem, Antioch, Edessa, and Tripoli now became the foes of Byzantium. Open conflict between Alexius and Bohemond broke out over possession of Antioch. To secure reinforcements against Alexius and the Turks, Bohemond returned to Italy, where he received a hero's welcome. He began a vicious propaganda campaign against the Byzantines and succeeded in gaining the support of Pope Paschal II for his plan to launch an attack on Constantinople itself. After a disastrous campaign at Durazzo (in present-day Albania) the defeated Bohemond was grudgingly reconciled to Alexius. Swearing another oath of fealty to the Byzantine emperor on the Holy Cross and other sacred relics and promising to fulfill his feudal obligations, Bohemond was re-enfeoffed with Antioch. Humiliated, Bohemond died soon thereafter. As for Alexius, as a result of the First Crusade he had achieved a triumph of diplomacy. Not only had he warded off a grave Western threat to his capital but he had also managed to make use of the crusaders to restore much of Asia Minor to his empire.

Had the First Crusade fulfilled the hopes envisioned for it by Pope Urban II? From the point of view of delivering the Holy Land from the hands of the Muslims the crusade was a sensational success. If Urban's goal, moreover, was to enhance papal prestige through the crusade, this too had been achieved. But if, as some scholars maintain, Urban had hoped that the crusade would foster closer relations with the Byzantine East and ultimately bring about religious union with the Greeks under papal authority, the First Crusade must be considered a failure. Indeed, though East and West had been brought into closer contact, such a wedge of animosity had been introduced between the Latin and Greek halves of Christendom that the effects would be felt even up to modern times.

The Second and Third Crusades

The hostility generated between East and West by the First Crusade and the internal dissension created among the crusaders themselves kept the Byzantine and Latin Christians of the East from uniting their forces against the threat now posed by a resurgence of Muslim power. A factor that had contributed to the success of the First Crusade had been the dissolution of the once great Seljuk Empire. In 1144, however, a Muslim prince of one of the numerous Turkish states in Syria seized Christian Edessa and started the process of reuniting all the old Seljuk territories. His son and successor, Nureddin, was able to unite the Muslim areas of Mesopotamia, Syria, and Palestine and, thus strengthened, to make an attack on the Fatimite caliphate of Egypt.

The fall of Edessa removed a buffer state between Christian Palestine and the Muslims, and Nureddin's subsequent successes became a threat to the existence of the other Latin crusader states. Appeals to the West for aid against the new Muslim threat launched the Second Crusade.

Since the Pope at this time was involved in conflict in Rome with Arnold of Brescia (Chapter 7) enthusiasm for the Second Crusade was stirred by the famous Cistercian monk St. Bernard of Clairvaux (1090–1153). Bernard's fiery preaching inspired both the French King Louis VII and the German King Conrad III to take the cross. Though it would seem that the presence of two leading Western rulers on the expedition would guarantee its success, the rivalry of the German and French kings created such discord within the crusader host that the failure of the expedition was almost inevitable.

Manuel I and the Crusaders. Once again massed Western armies appeared before Constantinople. Manuel I Comnenus, grandson of Alexius I, though an admirer of Western customs such as tournaments and twice married to Western princesses, did not underestimate the Latin threat to Byzantium. His suspicion was not at all alleviated by the report that Louis VII, on his way to Constantin-

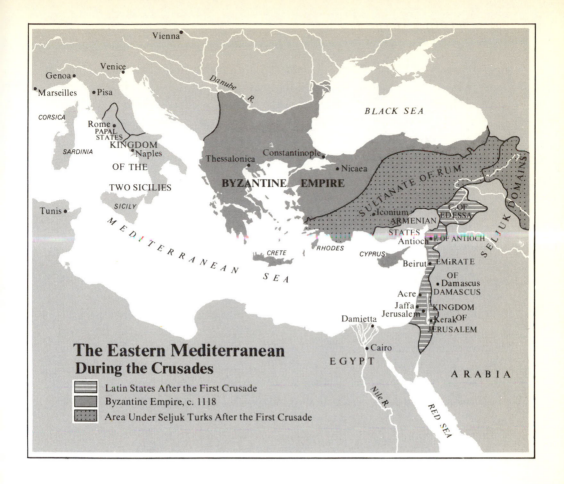

The Eastern Mediterranean During the Crusades

Latin States After the First Crusade

Byzantine Empire, c. 1118

Area Under Seljuk Turks After the First Crusade

ople, had stopped off in Sicily to confer with Byzantium's archenemy, the Norman King Roger II. To be sure, by his own marriage to Conrad's sister, Manuel had a nominal ally in the German king, but this bond was somewhat weakened by East-West rivalry over the imperial title and Manuel's dreams of controlling northern Italy.

In 1147 the German contingent of crusaders arrived before the walls of Constantinople, which had recently been fortified by Manuel. Like Peter the Hermit's followers, these crusaders had pillaged the Balkan areas en route. Manuel, as his grandfather had done, provided ships to transport the German crusaders as quickly as possible to Asia Minor before the French troops could arrive. The Germans were badly mauled by the Turks, and again the West blamed the defeat on the Byzantine emperor.

Upon the arrival of the French armies and the return of the surviving German troops, Manuel became even more alarmed. Perhaps he had learned of Louis's temptation to take Constantinople. According to Odo of Deuil, the chaplain of the French king, Louis and his staff had discussed this possibility. Meanwhile, the Norman King Roger II attacked Greece and devastated the islands and the mainland.* But Louis did not attack Constantinople. Manuel's diplomacy was so adroit that the French king was induced instead to pledge allegiance to him as a vassal in the manner of the earlier crusaders' pledge to Alexius. The crusade, however, eventually met with a disastrous end when Louis and his knights and Conrad, with his remnant of forces, were routed by the Muslims at Damascus. Louis then returned home. Conrad departed for his own realm, stopping on the way at Thessalonica to meet with the Emperor Manuel and reaffirm their alliance against the Normans. Thus the Second Crusade, so brilliantly begun, ended in complete failure. As a result, the Muslims gained confidence, more intensive strife broke out between the Franco-German armies and the Palestinian Christians, and the Byzantine-Latin antagonism was further exacerbated.

Most significant, the Second Crusade marked the beginning of what might be called the secularization of the crusades, that is, the decline of religious fervor and the emergence of more clearly political motivations for such expeditions. In particular, the alliance between Conrad III and the "schismatic" Greek Emperor Manuel so angered the Normans, the French, and the Papacy that there was talk of a new campaign, this time against Byzantium itself, to break the alliance. But the death of Conrad III in 1154 and the accession of the ambitious Frederick Barbarossa in Germany obviated this possibility. As already noted, Frederick and the Byzantine emperors clashed frequently over claims to universal imperial authority.

Manuel's initial successes against the Turks in Asia Minor and his reconquest of Antioch apparently aroused in him the dream of restoring imperial authority over the old territories of Byzantium. As I have observed, in order to combat the claims of Frederick Barbarossa to Italy, Manuel sent troops to aid the Lombard communes against the Western Emperor (Chapter 7). But the end result of this policy was only to unite Western opinion against Byzantium. The marriage of Frederick's son, Henry, to Constance, heiress to Sicily, which united two of Byzantium's deadliest foes, presented a further grave threat to the Byzantine East.

At home, also, Manuel's policy had adverse consequences. Engrossed in Western affairs, he could pay little attention to his eastern borders, and in 1176 at Myriocephalon in central Asia Minor a disastrous defeat of Byzantine arms at the hands of the Seljuks sealed the fate of Asia Minor, closing most of it forever to Byzantine authority. Some scholars, in fact, believe that this defeat decided the destiny of the entire Near East.

Manuel's Latinophile policy of adopting certain Western customs and awarding high posts in the government and special commercial privileges to

---

* From Greece Roger brought back expert silk workers to his capital city of Palermo, which resulted in the stimulation of the silk industry in the West.

Westerners served only to anger his subjects. Almost immediately after his death their resentment flared, in 1182, into a massacre of those Latins living in Constantinople. The West, especially the Venetians, who suffered most, was never to forget this episode and harbored thoughts of revenge.

Muslim Resurgence Under Saladin. After the vain Second Crusade the situation of the Latins in the Holy Land became much more serious. The Palestinian Christians now faced the grave external threat of a resurgent Egypt, where the clever and ambitious Muslim ruler Saladin (1169–1193) began a program of conquest of the Syrian and Palestinian areas. Saladin took Syria and Mesopotamia, thereby completely surrounding the little kingdom of Jerusalem. At the same time he seized the vital Christian ports of Beirut and Jaffa, thus cutting off Western supply lines from the sea. Finally, in 1187, Saladin took Jerusalem itself; in contrast to the earlier Christian conquest, however, no mass slaughter occurred. The Holy City had fallen again into the hands of the infidel, and a new crusade was called to recover it for Christendom.

The three most powerful monarchs of Europe, Richard I of England, Philip II of France, and the Emperor Frederick Barbarossa, now took the cross at the exhortation of the Pope. But, as previously, no general policy was agreed upon by all participants, and internal discord, particularly between Philip and Richard, made cooperation almost impossible.

Saladin, in contrast, had been carefully preparing for the coming of the crusaders, studying the character of the Western leaders and their typical military tactics. Legend has it that to observe his opponents at firsthand, he had traveled in disguise to the West. Saladin appealed to the Muslims to meet the crusaders by launching a holy war, a *jihad*, against the Christians. The conflict now assumed the character of a true religious duel between Christianity and Islam.

Barbarossa led his troops by the traditional land route through the Balkans to Constantinople. One can imagine the consternation of the Byzantines at the sight of the armies of their most bitter opponent before the gates of Constantinople. A Greek source relates that "the whole city of Constantinople shivers with fright, thinking its destruction and the extermination of its populace are at hand." Small wonder that the Byzantines formed an alliance with Saladin against Frederick! From the political point of view this was a necessary, if bold, stroke of diplomacy. But from the religious point of view, at least in the eyes of the Latins, such an act was a heinous piece of treachery that proved conclusively that the Greeks were cowards, deceivers, and enemies of the true faith. Frederick seriously contemplated seizing Constantinople, but later accepted the Byzantine offer to transport his forces to Asia Minor. There Frederick drowned while crossing a river. Most of his troops returned home; the rest proceeded to the Holy Land to join the French and English armies.

Meanwhile, the two armies of Philip Augustus and Richard the Lion-Hearted had arrived in Palestine by sea from Sicily. On his way, however, Richard had stopped off at Cyprus, seized it from the semi-independent Greek governor, and handed it over to the exiled king of Jerusalem, Guy of Lusignan. Thus another Latin state was established in the East. After reaching the Holy Land the French and English kings besieged and captured Acre and slaughtered the hostages turned over to them by the town when the ransom demanded was not paid.

The sole tangible result of the glamorous Third Crusade was the capture of a few ports. Philip II did little, constantly engaged as he was in bickering with the English king, against whom he even intrigued with the German contingent. Finally Philip, little animated by chivalric virtues, returned with his troops to France. Alone, Richard was unable to capture Jerusalem; embittered, he even refused to go to the top of a hill and gaze upon the city. He and Saladin, however, agreed to a truce which, though it left Jerusalem in Muslim hands, gave to Christian pilgrims peaceful access to the city. The ports captured by Richard were retained by the Christians.

Thus, in terms of its objective the Third Crusade, too, was a failure. Many factors were responsible. Notable in comparison with the earlier crusades was the lack of religious motivation on the part of the leaders, particularly of Philip II, who had been maneuvered into participating by Richard. The bitter rivalry between Philip and Richard, in fact, created grave discord between the French and English armies, a discord that enabled the united Muslims more easily to check the crusaders. Moreover, the Byzantine-Muslim alliance against Frederick Barbarossa and the Byzantine fear of a sudden Latin attack against Constantinople strained still further the already deteriorating Greco-Latin relations. The result was the destruction of the Byzantine Empire itself by a crusading army and the opening of the road to Western Europe to future Turkish advances.

The Fourth Crusade

The period of the first three crusades witnessed the development of an ever-widening mistrust between Byzantine East and Latin West. This antagonism, especially on the part of the East, would be transformed into an overt hostility, even hatred, as a result of the Fourth Crusade. For now Western crusading armies, diverted from their goal of recapturing Jerusalem, would lay siege to and capture Constantinople, carve up the Byzantine Empire, and in its place establish a Latin state. At the same time "Roman Catholicism" would be imposed upon the Greek Orthodox population. To understand why the crusaders attacked the Christian city of Constantinople instead of going to combat

An illustration from the Luttrell Psalter, c. 1340, showing a symbolic duel between King Richard of England (left) and the Muslim ruler of the Holy Land, Saladin, during the Third Crusade. (General Research and Humanities Division, The New York Public Library, Astor, Lenox and Tilden Foundations. Reproduced by permission of the British Library Board.)

the Muslims holding the Holy Land, the background leading to the estrangement of Eastern and Western Christendom must be examined in greater detail.

Even when united in the one great political organism of the Roman Empire, East and West had on the whole spoken different languages. Later, with the establishment of the Germanic kingdoms in the West especially the revival of the imperial title by Charlemagne in 800, a "political schism" between East and West was created. Most historians have fixed on 1054 as the date when the definitive religious breach between Eastern and Western Christendom occurred, a date when legates of the Roman Pope Leo IX and the Byzantine Patriarch Michael Cerularius excommunicated each other.

But certain religious differences between East and West had been developing as early as the Patristic age: the West, for example, adopted Latin as its liturgical language in contrast to the Greek of the East; the Eastern clergy, unlike the Western, were allowed to marry (before ordination); and the East used leavened bread instead of the Western unleavened bread (or wafer) for the Holy Eucharist. Doctrinally, the greatest stumbling block was the dispute over the Western addition of the phrase *filioque* to the Nicene Creed. As formulated in the officially accepted creeds of Nicaea (325) and Constantinople (381), the third person of the Trinity, the Holy Ghost, was defined as proceeding *from the Father*. In the early sixth century, in order to combat the Arian heresy then strong in Visigothic Spain, the Catholic clergy had added to the creed the phrase *filioque,* thereby making it read that the Holy Spirit proceeds from the Father *and the Son.* To the Greeks any addition to the officially proclaimed creed was tantamount to heresy; the Latins, however, believed that the addition was a necessary clarification of dogma. Whether or not the addition was canonically right or wrong, a vital point of doctrine was involved. The Greeks maintained that the addition of *filioque* actually changed the original meaning of the creed by implying that there were two first principles or sources for the Holy Spirit (that is, in effect, two Gods). The Latins, on the other hand, maintained that the Greek view seemed unduly to subordinate the Son to the Father, thereby making the persons of the Trinity no longer co-equals. We have already seen the first formal appearance of the *filioque* difference in the conflict beginning in 867 between Pope Nicholas I and Patriarch Photius. See Chapters 4 and 12 for the rivalry of the two churches over conversion of the Bulgars, which was the context for this first contest over the *filioque*.

The Schism of 1054

What brought these various differences between Greek and Latin Christianity into sharper focus was the ecclesiastical rivalry that had existed between the patriarchates of Rome and Constantinople since antiquity. This rivalry reached a head in the mid-eleventh century with the Norman conquest of Byzantine southern Italy and the attempts of the Popes, especially Leo IX, to assert universal jurisdiction over the Church. Leo insisted that the southern Italian Greeks, who owed ecclesiastical allegiance to the patriarch of Constantinople, forswear that allegiance and instead accept the Latin ritual with insertion of the *filioque* clause into the creed. A sharp clash developed between Leo and the patriarch, and Leo finally sent three legates, headed by the intransigent Cardinal Humbert, to Constantinople. The equally strong-willed Patriarch Michael Cerularius received them scornfully. The result was that on July 16, 1054, the papal legates entered the cathedral of St. Sophia in Constantinople during the service, deposited a bull of excommunication against Cerularius "and his followers" on the main altar, and, departing haughtily from the church, "shook from their shoes the dust of the heretics." The Greek clergy were at first astounded, then angered, at this unexpected act. Michael, in retaliation, immediately convoked the synod of Greek bishops in Constantinople and anathematized the legates. This event has traditionally been thought to mark the definitive schism between the Greek and Roman churches.

Yet at that time the religious schism of 1054 did not seem to have any far-reaching effects on East-West relations. Most pilgrims and individual crusaders, if not the massed armies, of the first three expeditions continued to be received cordially in Constantinople, though to be sure, a spirit of mutual mistrust grew gradually. Also significant is the fact that in 1054 the papal legates excommunicated only Cerularius and his immediate followers; they praised the orthodoxy of the emperor and his subjects as a whole and the Greek synod excommunicated the papal legates, not the Pope. Whatever the situation at the time, subsequent tradition in both churches has pointed to this event as marking the formal beginning of the schism; and from that date to the fall of Constantinople in 1453 many Popes and emperors sought to reconcile the religious breach. What really served to confirm the schism, turning it into complete alienation of East and West politically and ecclesiastically as well as psychologically, was the Fourth Crusade of 1204.

One of the circumstances leading to this event was the marriage of Frederick Barbarossa's young son, Henry VI, to Constance, heiress to the Norman kingdom of Sicily. The marriage united the two deadliest enemies not only of the Pope but of the Byzantine emperor as well. Once he had pacified his new domain in Sicily, Henry, in the manner of his Norman predecessors, turned covetous eyes on Constantinople and prepared a crusade that seems to have been aimed as much at Byzantium as at the Holy Land. The Byzantines, noting the extensive preparations of their formidable opponent, were so alarmed that citizens had to pay a special tax called the *alemanikon* (German tax) in order to strengthen Byzantine defenses. At this critical juncture the Pope took the side of the Byzantines. As one scholar put it, "for the first time in history the Greek problem lost for the Papacy its religious character and became exclusively political." * For with Henry's possessions threatening the Papacy on both north and south and with the possibility looming of the addition of the Byzantine Empire to Hohenstaufen possessions, the power of the Hohenstaufen would become overwhelming and the Papacy doomed, politically, to impotence. This was the first step in the drama leading to the capture of Constantinople. But just as his fleet was ready to sail, Henry died. The Pope no less than the Byzantines breathed a sigh of relief.

Upon the election of Innocent III as Pope in 1198, the Papacy made preparations for the launching of a new crusade to recapture Jerusalem. At the same time, it was Innocent's aim to unite the Greek and Latin churches under his authority. Virtually all the monarchs of the West were involved in conflicts at home, but the more important Western nobles, particularly those of northern France, Flanders, and Germany, took the cross.

The crusader host assembled at Venice. But its leaders found themselves without funds to hire ships for transportation to the Holy Land. The Venetians, seeing an opportunity to use this army for their own purposes, offered to supply the necessary ships if the crusaders would first help them to conquer the nearby Dalmatian city of Zara. Zara, a Christian city, was accordingly stormed and sacked by Western troops wearing the badge of the cross. Innocent III, infuriated at this use of a crusading host, excommunicated the entire body of crusaders.

During the siege of Zara there suddenly appeared in the crusader camp a

---

* W. Norden, *Das Papsstum und Byzanz* (Berlin, 1903), p. 122.

young Byzantine prince, Alexius Angelus, whose father, the Emperor Isaac, had recently been deposed. In exchange for crusader aid to restore his father to the Byzantine throne, Prince Alexius promised funds and troops to aid the crusaders in retaking Jerusalem. He also promised to bring the Greek Church under the authority of the Pope. Alexius' proposal, which would result temporarily in diverting the crusade from the Holy Land to Constantinople, was a tempting prospect—one that may well have coincided with the intentions, latent or overt, already in the mind of the Venetian Doge Enrico Dandolo and perhaps even in the minds of other Western leaders. The eighty-year-old Dandolo, the central figure of the Fourth Crusade, energetic and fanatically devoted to Venice's aggrandizement, had little love for the Byzantines. As a youth he had spent some time in Constantinople where, as punishment, he had been partially blinded. Moreover, he recalled bitterly the massacre of Venetians that had occurred there in 1182. Dandolo may have harbored thoughts of taking Constantinople not only for revenge, but more tangibly because rival Pisan and Genoese merchants had been seriously cutting into the profits of the Venetians in the lucrative Byzantine trade.

After agreement of most of the crusader leaders to attack Constantinople, in June 1203, the crusader fleet appeared before the walls of Constantinople. According to Villehardouin, a noble French participant and chronicler of the Fourth Crusade, the city with its hundreds of churches, glittering riches, massive towers, and enormous size was greater than the Western knights had ever imagined. "Never in all the world," he wrote, "was there so rich a city as Constantinople."

The Latin Empire of Constantinople

After a brief siege the city fell, and Alexius and his father were restored to the Byzantine throne. But they were unable to maintain power. A popular revolution of the citizens of Constantinople brought about their deposition in favor of an emperor hostile to the Latin crusaders. Angered and accusing the Byzantines of treachery, the crusaders, who were encamped outside the city walls, decided to take the city. After drawing up a detailed treaty that divided up the empire among themselves, they stormed the walls while the Venetian fleet attacked from the sea. The city's defenders, demoralized by the first siege, the recent revolution, and now a fire that consumed almost one-third of the city, were unable to resist for long. Constantinople succumbed on April 13, 1204.

The crusaders were granted by their leaders the customary three-day period of sack, which resulted in an unparalleled looting of the city, raping of women, including nuns, and the destruction of many manuscripts and priceless works of art (including masterpieces of ancient Greek statuary) that had been in Constantinople since its founding. In St. Sophia the crusaders trampled upon the

The Aegean World, 1214-1254

Latin Empire and Fiefs

HUNGARY

BOSNIA

CROATIA

SERBIA

BULGARIA

Danube R.

BLACK SEA

EMPIRE OF
TREBIZOND

Dyrrachium

THESSALONICA

LATIN EMPIRE

EMPIRE OF
CONSTANTINOPLE

Constantinople

Nicaea

EMPIRE OF NICAEA

DESPOTATE

OF

EPIRUS

AEGEAN

SEA

SULTANATE OF KONIA OR ICONIUM
(RUM)

IONIAN

SEA

D. OF ATHENS

LESSER ARMENIA

PRINCIPALITY OF
ACHAIA   Mistra

NAXOS

RHODES

CYPRUS

CRETE

MEDITERRANEAN   SEA

sacred books and icons, drank wine out of the sacred chalices, and even seated a prostitute on the patriarchal throne. After three days of pillage the city, then Christendom's greatest center of civilization, was a shambles, its population demoralized. As one Byzantine chronicler bitterly put it, "Even the Saracens would have been more merciful."

Many works of art that were spared were shipped to the West by the Venetians, who appreciated the value of such things more than did the Western knights. The four bronze horses that now grace the façade of St. Mark's of Venice were taken from the Hippodrome of Constantinople at this time. Innumerable relics sacred to early Christianity—the crown of thorns, the head of John the Baptist (one Byzantine belief was that at his decapitation a second head had appeared to replace the first!), parts of the "True Cross"—were sent to embellish many Western churches, particularly those of France. (Most of these relics were later destroyed during the French Revolution of 1789.) So great was the amount of booty sent West after the sack of Constantinople that its enumeration and analysis fill three entire volumes.

The task now facing the Western knights was the organization of their newly conquered territories. Count Baldwin of Flanders, after some dispute, was awarded the imperial title. The empire itself was reorganized along Western feudal lines: the emperor became feudal suzerain and received five-eighths of the city of Constantinople; the rest of the nobles secured lands on the mainland of Greece as fiefs of the new Latin emperor. Some of these principalities were to remain Latin long after the reconquest of Constantinople by the Greeks in 1261. Indeed, those centered at Athens and Mistra (ancient Sparta) became splendid Latin courts.

To the Venetians, however, fell the lion's share: they secured the remaining three-eighths of Constantinople (including St. Sophia), fortified ports in Greece, and numerous islands in the Aegean Sea. They were even exempted from swearing allegiance to the Latin emperor. Controlling the most strategic areas of the empire, the Venetians held a stronger position than the Latin emperor himself. As a direct result of the Fourth Crusade the great Venetian colonial empire came into being; it appeared that Venice would completely eclipse its commercial rivals, Genoa and Pisa.

The capture of Constantinople put Innocent III in a difficult position. Although he angrily re-excommunicated the crusaders upon hearings the news of Constantinople's sack, he later relented, rejoicing that the "schismatic" Greek Church had at last "returned to the bosom of the Roman see." Soon a "Latinization" of the Greek Church was attempted. Greek bishops were forced to adhere to the Latin rite or relinquish their posts; Greek priests had to take oaths in the Latin manner; and, perhaps most odious to the Greeks, the *filioque* was inserted into the creed. The majority of Greeks, however, refused to accept this attempted Latinization; they rebaptized their children and cleansed the "polluted" altars of the churches after a Latin service. Those few Greeks who accepted the Latin rite were reviled by their compatriots. For the Greeks, their religion now became equated with their heightened sense of "nationality," and any real hope of reconciliation between the Greek and Roman churches, as history has shown, disappeared. The antagonism and suspicion generated among the Greeks by the earlier crusades were transformed into an almost implacable hatred for the Latins.

Not all areas of the Byzantine Empire were conquered by the crusaders. Three small, independent Greek states arose from its ruins—Epirus, located south of and including part of present-day Albania; Trebizond, on the northern coast of Asia Minor; and, most important of the three, Nicaea, centered around that city in northwestern Asia Minor and situated between the Latin Empire and the Seljuk Turks. Though rivalrous, all three states remained faithful to the Byzantine tradition and the Greek Church. Ultimately, in 1261, the ruler of Nicaea, Emperor Michael VIII Palaeologus, was able to retake Constantinople to restore the heart of the Byzantine Empire to the Greeks (see Chapter 12). But the empire was never to regain its former prestige. After the reign of Michael the empire became essentially a small Balkan power, though it still retained enough strength and the diplomatic skill to resist the pressure of the advancing Turks until 1453.

The Later Crusades

Although in Latin eyes the Fourth Crusade had restored the Greek Church to the jurisdiction of the Pope, it had nevertheless failed to recover Jerusalem or to provide aid for the Christians in Palestine. Therefore a new plea went out from Innocent III for the organization of another crusade to retake the Holy City. The result was the Fifth Crusade. This time the crusaders decided on a new strategy—first, to seize the city of Damietta in Egypt and then to negotiate with the Muslims the exchange of Damietta for Jerusalem. In 1218 the first stage of the plan succeeded with the capture of Damietta. But this success made the crusaders greedy, and when the Muslims offered Jerusalem in exchange, the papal legate refused and instead encouraged the crusaders to march on Cairo, the Egyptian capital. The knights, however, did not reckon with the flooding of the Nile; after a disastrous defeat on its banks, they were forced to abandon Damietta to save their lives.

The dismal failure of the Fifth Crusade brought into sharp focus the tendency of the new crusaders to refuse to cooperate with the Palestinian Christians. The descendants of the original crusaders from long years of contact had learned to respect the Muslims, even to adjust to their way of life. But the newly arrived crusaders, haughtily refusing to deal at all with the infidel, ignored the advice of the Palestinian Christians who had warned against an attack on Cairo. This discord between the old and the new crusaders was an underlying factor in the failure of the crusading movement as a whole.

Before the launching of the Fifth Crusade one of the most bizarre and tragic episodes in all medieval history occurred—the so-called Children's Crusade. The failure of the first four crusades had given rise to the belief that the Christian misfortunes were due, at least in part, to the sins and excesses of the crusaders themselves. And so now in 1212 a teenage boy in France and another in Germany went about preaching that the Holy Land could be delivered only by innocent children. The German children reached Genoa. Unable to find anyone to transport them across the sea, some began the long and arduous journey back home. Others remained to find a livelihood in Italy. The French children met a more tragic fate. Gathering together a host ranging in age from about six to twenty, the young French leader marched them to the Mediterranean, expecting its waters to part before them and open a path to the Holy Land as the waters of the Red Sea had parted for Moses. Some died en route. Upon reaching the port of Marseilles, they were promised passage by unscrupulous merchants, who instead transported them to Egypt and sold them into slavery. But the merchants did not long enjoy their ill-gotten gains, for the children's plight touched the heart even of the cynical German Emperor Frederick II, who seized the merchants and hanged them. (Recent scholarship questions the number of children sold into slavery.)

The Children's Crusade reflects many facets of the crusading movement as a whole. On the one hand, it reveals an underlying religious fervor and faith in the crusade on the part of the common people of Western Europe. On the other hand, and perhaps more important, it demonstrates an increasing disillusionment with the actions of the crusading knights, whose motives and actions were looked upon with increasing cynicism.

If the Fourth Crusade was a perversion of the crusading ideal, the Sixth Crusade (1228–1229) was an almost complete secularization of the movement. The story of the Sixth Crusade reads like a comic opera. We see an excommunicated ruler recovering Jerusalem without striking a blow, only to have the Pope refuse to accept his gift of the city and even lay Jerusalem under interdict. When he embarked on the Sixth Crusade, Emperor Frederick II was still under sentence of excommunication for his failure to go on the previous crusade. Arriving in the Holy Land with his army, Frederick, always friendly to the Muslims, soon concluded a treaty with the sultan of Egypt by the terms of which the Holy City was restored to the Christians. Both the Muslim and Christian worlds, however, were shocked at the treaty. Frederick was accused of being in league with the infidel. As he was being crowned king of Jerusalem, the Latin patriarch of the city suddenly appeared and, in accordance with papal instructions, interdicted the city.

The events of the Sixth Crusade demonstrate the changing attitude of the Papacy toward the crusading movement. The Pope could not accept Jerusalem from the hands of his greatest enemy, for in so doing he would, in a sense, have granted Frederick a moral victory. More concretely, to accept Jerusalem the Pope would have had to lift the sentence of excommunication and recognize Frederick as a dutiful son of the Church—two acts that would have effectively nullified any justification for the Papacy's conflict with Frederick. To the contrary, the Papacy now proclaimed its war against Frederick a crusade in itself, granting to those taking up arms against the Hohenstaufen the same indulgences awarded those fighting the infidel. This policy of the Papacy, when viewed together with its earlier proclamation of a crusade against the Albigensians of southern France, caused many now to look upon the crusading movement as a political tool of the Papacy to be used against any and all who defied the Roman Pontiff.

After Frederick's departure from the Holy Land, civil war broke out there, with the nobles at each others' throats, Venetians combatting Genoese, and even the Templars fighting the Hospitallers. Finally, in 1244, Jerusalem fell again to the Muslims. This event called forth the Seventh Crusade, led by King Louis IX of France.

St. Louis, a deeply religious man who from his youth had burned with a desire to lead a crusade, took the cross in 1248 and conducted a force against the Egyptian city of Damietta. For a second time Damietta was taken; but again the

A miniature of the fifteenth–sixteenth centuries depicting St. Louis of France about to leave his kingdom to go on a Crusade to the East. (Giraudon)

knights, heedless of the advice of the Palestinian Christians, marched up the Nile against Cairo. This time the results were even more disastrous than those of the Fifth Crusade. Louis himself was taken prisoner; he not only had to surrender Damietta, but he also had to pay a huge ransom for his freedom. This was to be the last major crusade directed against Jerusalem. Louis led still another crusade in 1270, but it never reached the Holy Land; it was directed instead, for reasons not entirely clear, against the Muslim city of Tunis in North Africa. There Louis succumbed to disease, dying before the walls of the city. Louis's death marked the end of the last real crusade in the traditional sense of the word. And after the fall of Acre to the Muslims in 1291, the Christians no longer held any important stronghold in the Holy Land.

The Spanish Reconquista: Christians Against Muslims

The failure of the crusades in the East was in part balanced by gains made at the other end of the Mediterranean during the Spanish crusades. In the early eleventh century the small Christian kingdoms in the north of Spain—

Castile, León, Navarre, and Aragon—began their long struggle to reconquer the Spanish peninsula from the Muslims.* Slowly the Christians gathered strength and resolution. The Papacy proclaimed the expeditions against the Spanish Muslims to be crusades and granted participants the same privileges awarded those going to the Holy Land. Many foreign knights, especially from southern France, came to aid the Spanish kings. By the early thirteenth century, owing in no small part to a great victory in 1212 at Las Navas de Tolosa, the way was finally opened for the Christian conquest of the south of Spain. A series of victories finally extended the central kingdom of Castile to the Mediterranean Sea. Meantime, the kings of Aragon conquered the Balearic Islands, off the eastern coast of Spain, and on the mainland they pushed to the south. Soon all that remained of the former Muslim states was the small principality of Granada on the southern edge of the peninsula. That stronghold did not fall to the Christians until 1492.

As a result of the long duration of the *Reconquista* many problems were created in Spain. In the areas retaken from the Muslims there had for centuries been an interpenetration of Christian and Arabic civilizations. The product of the mingling of these two cultures was the so-called *Mozarabic,* that is Arabized Christian, culture, whose liturgy had a special Mozarabic rite used in the entire Iberian peninsula until the mid-eleventh century. In the areas newly conquered by the Christians, however, a large minority of Muslims and Jews remained. (The Jews, in particular, though regarded as second-class citizens in the Muslim and Christian civilizations, played an important role and continued to do so until their expulsion by Ferdinand and Isabella in 1492. On the treatment of Jews see pp. 360–65.)

The centuries-long crusades of the northern Christian Kingdoms of Spain (Castile, Leon, Navarre, Aragon) against the Muslims of Spain were given a final and decisive impetus in the later fifteenth century by the "Catholic Kings," Ferdinand of Aragon and Isabella of Castile. In fact these rulers made use of the crusading spirit and the enthusiasm it engendered to develop an almost fanatical Catholicism that they transmuted into an incipient Spanish "nationalism." Hence in Spain the Christian Crusades against the Muslims became in time one of the factors that led to the unification of the country.

Islamic Influence on Christian Spain

Even after the Christian reconquest, Islamic influence on Spanish civilization remained strong. Spanish art, literature, and music still bear the imprint of the long centuries of Arab domination. But in the medieval period the

---

* The great Spanish epic poem, *The Cid,* commemorates the heroic deeds of the most famous Spanish hero of this period, El Cid (d. 1099).

The famous mosque in Cordova, capital of Islamic Spain. Byzantine craftsmen were sent to Cordova in the tenth century to furnish the Mihrab wall and the dome chambers within with mosaics. (Spanish National Tourist Office)

most significant intellectual contribution of the Muslims of Spain was probably the transmission of texts of Aristotle in Arabic translation with commentary to the scholars of the West.* The focal point for transmission of these translations (often turned from Arabic into Latin by Jewish intermediaries) was the Moorish capital of Toledo, especially after its conquest by Christian Castile in 1085. Latin scholars came to that city from France, England, and other Western areas seeking access to ancient Greek scientific and philosophic writings, especially Aristotle's. The subsequent appearance of these versions of Aristotle's works in Paris and other cultural centers of the West created a sensation, a genuine crisis of thought, culminating in the theological and philosophical writings of St. Thomas Aquinas, who made the most successful attempt to "reconcile" the methodology and thought of Aristotle with Catholic Christianity (for fuller explanation of this important phenomenon see Chapter 10).

---

* These Aristotelian (and other Greek) texts were already in the Greek centers such as Antioch, Damascus, and Alexandria when the Arabs invaded them, or were later secured from Constantinople. From the Islamic East they were taken to Islamic Spain; for, despite political rivalry between the two Caliphates, intellectual relations were not disturbed.

Effects of the Crusades

Some years ago scholars considered almost everything that happened in the West in the later Middle Ages—the development of trade and the growth of towns, the decline of feudalism and the formation of national monarchies, the emancipation of the lower classes, even the intellectual revival—as more or less direct results of the crusading movement. Today, however, the pendulum has swung to the other extreme, with a few scholars maintaining that the crusades resulted in virtually nothing except ridding Western Europe of troublesome knights. Actually the truth lies somewhere between the two extremes, though it will probably never be entirely clear what was caused by the crusades or developed concurrently, what influenced the crusades or was in turn influenced by them.

If the crusading movement is viewed as an attempt to save Eastern Christendom from the Muslims, the entire episode must be judged a vast fiasco. At the beginning of the movement Byzantium stood as the great Christian bastion, but at the end of the crusading period Eastern Christendom had been gravely weakened or had fallen into the hands of the Muslims. Some spectacular successes were certainly achieved, such as in the First, and to a lesser degree, the Third Crusades. Of course, much greater cultural contact between the Byzantine and Muslim East and the Latin West resulted from the crusades. From the long-range point of view, when the crusades began, Western Europe had barely emerged from the "Dark Ages"; when they came to an end, the Italian Renaissance had begun. But the precise role the crusading movement played leading to this Renaissance is very difficult to ascertain. Even Arabic science and learning—so important for the formative intellectual growth of Western Europe (see pp. 329–30)—did not come from the Holy Land but rather through Spain and Sicily. The rather striking lack of any real intellectual stimulus from the Holy Land may perhaps be attributed to the fact that the Christian society of that area was composed mainly of soldiers and merchants, who were not really interested in learning or intellectual matters. It is undeniable, however, that the crusades did affect the development of popular and romantic poetry in the West. Numerous troubadors who went on crusades brought back fascinating stories in the form of songs about the brave deeds of crusading knights or the sad fate of those captured by the Muslims. And from such tales the popular romances of the chivalric deeds of figures such as Richard the Lion-Hearted and Saladin developed.

Life in the society of the East had considerable influence on those crusaders who remained in the Holy Land and Byzantium. They were quick—too quick, according to their Western confrères—to adopt the more refined and luxurious living habits of the East. Knights adopted Eastern garb, delighted in rich Eastern foods, and built castles, many with round towers in the Byzantine style.

Some kept harems. On the whole, however, the effect of the crusades on the West still remains an area for research, since cause and effect are inordinately difficult to establish in this centuries-long movement. The revival of trade and commerce, for example, had begun at least a century before the crusades, yet there is no doubt that the crusading movement, with the greater influx of Eastern goods from the conquered areas, at least hastened the development of commercial activity in the West. The crusades may also have had some effect, if only indirectly, on the development of stronger monarchies in France and England. The first direct "tax" in Latin medieval history (aside from the Anglo-Saxon Danegeld)—the "Saladin tithe"—was levied by the French and English kings to meet their needs for funds to combat the Muslims in the Holy Land. Western Europe's exodus of nobles for crusading expeditions often relieved the kings of their more turbulent vassals, as well as diminishing the destruction caused by feudal warfare. Finally, the cost of going on a crusade and the more expensive tastes acquired in the Byzantine and Arab East financially ruined many nobles.

The role of the crusades in heightening the power and prestige of the Papacy is indisputable. Since it was through papal initiative that most of the crusades began, the Popes became the spiritual heads of an international movement of tremendous scope. The unexpected success of the First Crusade, especially, greatly enhanced papal prestige. When the ancient Byzantine patriarchates of Antioch, Jerusalem, and Constantinople all fell under the sway of Rome, it seemed that papal claims to universal jurisdiction over the entire Church might become a reality. Moreover, the Papacy now enjoyed the fruits of a new source of revenue—the tithe collected from the Western clergy for support of the crusading movement.

But the crusades also served, in the long run, to harm the Papacy. When the Popes began to use them for their own political ends, such as the bitter crusade against the Holy Roman Emperor Frederick II, many Western Christians were aghast at this perversion of the idea of a holy war. Against such a policy even St. Louis of France raised his voice in protest. As a result, the Papacy lost a good deal of its moral prestige. It is not entirely coincidental that at the time the crusading ideal was losing its appeal, the moral authority of the Papacy over Western Christendom began to decline.

FOR FURTHER READING

Altamira, R. A., trans. M. Lee, *A History of Spain* (1949). Competent survey from beginning to today.

Atiya, A. S., *Crusade, Commerce and Culture* (1962). Useful.

Brand, C., *Byzantium Confronts the West, 1180–1204* (1968). Careful and comprehensive.

Charanis, P., in K. M. Setton and H. Winkler, *Great Problems in European Civilization,* 2nd ed. (1966). Good translations of Greek and Latin source materials.

Comnena, Anna, *The Alexiad,* trans. E. A. Dawes (1966). A biography of the great Emperor Alexius Comnenus, by his daughter. Deals with the First Crusade.

Fulcher of Chartres, *Chronicle of the First Crusade,* trans. M. E. McGinty (1941). One of the basic contemporary accounts of the first expedition to Jerusalem.

Gabriele, F., ed. *Arab Historians of the Crusades* (1969). Islamic viewpoint.

Geanakoplos, D. J., *Byzantine East and Latin West: Two Worlds of Christendom in Middle Ages and Renaissance* (1966; 1976). Essays treating the Byzantine cultural interaction with the West, especially during the crusades. New points of view.

Geanakoplos, D. J., Chapters 2 and 3, on "Byzantium and the Later Crusades," in *A History of the Crusades,* ed. K. Setton, Vol. 3 (1974), pp. 27–103. First systematic study of the later crusades and Byzantium.

Geanakoplos, D. J., *Emperor Michael Palaeologus and the West, 1258–82: A Study in Byzantine-Latin Relations* (1959; 1973). Emphasizes the aftermath of the Fourth Crusade and Byzantine efforts to respond to Western attempts to reconquer Constantinople. Comprehensive.

Geanakoplos, D. J., *Interaction of the "Sibling" Byzantine and Western Cultures in the Middle Ages and Italian Renaissance* (1976). Original, inter-disciplinary study of historical and social aspects of cultural interaction between the two Christian worlds.

Geanakoplos, D. J., *The Byzantine Empire and Its Civilization: A Source Book with Commentary* (in press). English translations of sources.

Krey, A. C., ed., *The First Crusade: Accounts of Eyewitnesses and Participants* (1921). A successful attempt to piece together in one narrative the contemporary accounts of the First Crusade.

LaMonte, J., *Feudal Monarchy in the Latin Kingdom of Jerusalem* (1932). A careful work on Latin rule in Jerusalem.

Mayer, H., *The Crusades* (1972), trans. J. Gillingham. New survey of Crusades, Western viewpoint.

Memoirs of the Crusades, trans. F. T. Marzials* (1933). Includes Villehardouin's chronicle of the Fourth Crusade and Joinville's of the life and expedition of St. Louis.

Munro, D. C., *The Kingdom of the Crusaders* (1935). Old work describing the Latin Kingdom of Jerusalem.

Newhall, R. A., *The Crusades* (1949; rev. ed. 1963). A very brief introductory account of the crusades.

O'Callaghan, J., *A History of Medieval Spain* (1975). One of very few textbooks on the period in English.

* Asterisk indicates paperback edition available.

Prawer, J., *The Crusaders' Kingdom: European Colonialism in the Middle Ages* (New York, 1972). Valuable recent scholarly work.

Runciman, S., *A History of the Crusades,* 3 vols. (1951–1954). A comprehensive account of crusading expeditions up to 1291.

Setton, K. M., ed., *A History of the Crusades,* 3 vols. (1955; 1962; 1974). Authoritative essays by specialists in each field.

Smail, R. C., *Crusading Warfare, 1097–1193* * (1967). An interesting analysis.

William of Tyre, *History of Deeds Done Beyond the Sea,* ed. E. H. Babcock and A. C. Krey, 2 vols. (1943). Excellent translation of the history of the Latin Kingdom of Jerusalem.

The most distinctive characteristic of the medieval period in both the Christian East and West, distinguishing it most from ancient and modern history, was the permeation of all aspects of society by religion. This emphasis is most clearly seen in the intellectual and cultural life of the period. Medieval education, music, art, and architecture were motivated by, permeated with, or channeled into religious goals. Indeed the most highly regarded branch of learning—the "Queen of the Sciences," as it was called—was theology, the study of doctrines concerning God. Up to at least the thirteenth century Western education was almost the exclusive province of the clergy. Painting and sculpture dealt mainly with religious subjects. The most magnificent, most costly buildings constructed were churches and cathedrals. Even chivalry, the conduct and ethic of the warlike knightly class, came to be associated with religious ceremony

CHAPTER 10

Church and Culture in the Latin West

and sought to secure the sanction of the Church. For the medieval period, then, the Latin phrase *ad maiorem Dei gloriam* ("to the greater glory of God") was meaningful and relevant for all activities.

The Papal Zenith

One of the most striking manifestations of this religious emphasis was the rise of the Papacy to a position of spiritual, and in some ways, temporal, supremacy in the period of the High Middle Ages. For several centuries the Pope, recognized as the head of Western Christendom, became in effect the arbiter of Western Europe and, for a brief time, even of the Greek East. An understanding of the extent to which papal influence came to dominate Western Europe—a point difficult for the more secular, modern Western mind to grasp—will aid in a fuller comprehension of the degree to which medieval civilization was shaped by religious ideals.

Pope Innocent III

The supremacy in ecclesiastical and, by implication, temporal affairs claimed by Pope Gregory VII at the end of the eleventh century (see Chapter 7) achieved its fullest realization under Innocent III (1198–1216), perhaps the greatest of all medieval Popes. Certainly he was the most successful in achieving his ecclesiastical and most of his political aims. Not only had the Pope gained firm control of the administrative machinery of the entire Western Church in this period, but under Innocent III Western Europe with its various states came very close to constituting the one Christian commonwealth led by the Pope that Gregory VII's pronouncements had seemed to many so boldly to envision. Innocent did not, however, exercise *direct* control over the political affairs of Europe. Rather, he held the position of a kind of arbiter or supreme judge to whom appeals could be carried from the various monarchs and princes, though in political matters, he was not always able to secure the implementation of his decisions. It should be emphasized, moreover, that the directives or decisions rendered by the Pope were based, at least in principle, on the moral implications of the political conduct involved or on the possible infringement of ecclesiastical rights. In addition, the Pope had temporal powers over his own vassals in the so-called Papal States of Italy and for a time became the actual suzerain over several Western monarchies.

Innocent III, scion of a noble Roman family and trained as a canon lawyer, was elected Pope at the age of thirty-seven. At his accession he determined to make good the Papacy's claims to universal jurisdiction, to be the head of Christian society. This passage from one of his many letters expresses his political ideology:

> No king can rule rightly unless he devoutly serves God's Vicar [the Pope]. . . . As God, the Creator of the universe, set two great lights in the firmament of heaven, the greater light to rule the day and the lesser light to rule the night, so He set two great dignities in the firmament of the universal church, . . . the greater to rule the day, that is, souls, and the lesser to rule the night, that is, bodies. These dignities are the papal authority and the royal power. And just as the moon gets her light from the sun, and is inferior to the sun in quality, quantity, position, and effect, so the royal power gets the splendor of its dignity from the papal authority.

Innocent's comparison of the kingship to the moon is particularly significant, for medieval man believed that the light of the moon was only the pale reflection of the sun. (The most recent interpretation of this passage, however, takes it to be less radically intended by Innocent than it would seem to be at first glance.)

One may wonder, in view of his struggles with the Holy Roman Emperors, why the Pope, in claiming universal jurisdiction, did not take what would seem the logical step of assuming the imperial title himself. If any Pope had ever seriously contemplated such a measure—and there is no evidence to this effect—he would have been well aware of the great opposition it would have aroused in Europe's monarchs. Such a step was completely opposed to the long medieval tradition of the existence of two distinct powers in the world—the ecclesiastical and the secular (*sacerdotium* and *regnum*). Nevertheless, the Pope certainly realized the necessity for having his own political power base; hence the constant insistence on the independence of the Papal States in Italy. Moreover, with political power the Popes could better enforce their primary religious, spiritual authority.

The Papacy found it could better achieve its various political aims by acquiring, in the political and social context of the time, even an overlordship over many of the princes of Europe. Already in the tenth century a Polish prince had become the vassal of the Pope, and by the time of Innocent III's death in 1216 the kings of Poland, Aragon, Hungary, Denmark, Bohemia, Sicily, Jerusalem, Albania, Portugal, and even of England, plus the Latin emperor at Constantinople, had all at one time or another sworn oaths of fealty to the Papacy. It should be stressed again, however, that these ties had a rather loose structure. For, impressive as they may seem, Innocent did not demand the same secular services from these various rulers that they normally demanded of their vassals. Yet, at least theoretically, the Pope was the feudal overlord of much of Europe.

Not only did the Papacy under Innocent III reach its zenith in temporal affairs, it also achieved the full limits of its power in the ecclesiastical sphere.

More than previously, the Pope was now viewed as the "monarch" of the Church with rights of jurisdiction over all bishops and abbots. In terms of canon, that is, ecclesiastical law, this meant that the Popes now possessed complete administrative, judicial, and financial powers. The Pope was the supreme judge over the Church, and the decision of a lower ecclesiastical court could be appealed to Rome for ultimate judgment. All ecclesiastical officials were in effect considered to be appointees of the Pope, though of course he usually did not interfere in local affairs unless he was asked or felt it necessary to do so. The Pope exercised the right to investigate all offices held by the clergy throughout Europe; he alone could depose the higher clergy, transfer a bishop from one see to another, or at least supervise the filling of an episcopal vacancy. It should be noted, however, that despite papal assertions not a few bishops still owed their position to lay influence.

The Fourth Lateran Council

A convenient way to consider the problems of Innocent's pontificate and to appreciate the full extent of his power is to focus on the Fourth Lateran Council. This council, convoked in 1215 by Innocent to discuss the questions of Church reform and the launching of a new crusade, was the greatest ecclesiastical assembly yet held in the West. It was attended by 400 bishops, 800 abbots and priors, and by envoys from virtually every European monarch—rulers with little intention of abiding by all of the papal regulations. Aware that ecclesiastical influence over laymen was in some areas waning (partly as a result of the decline of the crusading ideal and the inroads of heresies such as Albigensianism), the Council, under Innocent's leadership, decreed that henceforth clerics were to demonstrate greater piety, observe stricter discipline, and be better educated. Bishops were ordered to appoint only competent, well-trained men to parish duties. Priests, bishops, and abbots were admonished to provide a good example to their flocks by avoiding ostentatious luxury and eschewing such pernicious practices as gambling and frequenting taverns.

Relics.　The old ecclesiastical abuses of the Middle Ages—simony (the buying of a church position), pluralism (the holding of more than one ecclesiastical office for more revenue), and absenteeism—were once again forbidden. Interestingly, the sale of relics was then also prohibited. Since the sack of Constantinople by Western armies in 1204 the West had been inundated with relics from the conquered Byzantine Empire: bones of saints, pieces of the "True Cross," the Crown of Thorns (for which St. Louis of France built the architectural gem of Sainte Chapelle in Paris), and, reflecting the mixture of coarseness and credulity so typical of the age, even the Virgin's milk! The sale of such relics had become a profitable business, involving a good deal of fraud. Although Innocent, through the Lateran Council, attempted to put a stop to such fraudulent practices, the decree had little effect.

Another act of the Council forbade priests from officiating at or taking part in trials involving ordeals or judicial combat, the principal methods of proof in feudal law. The Council thus forced reliance on rational proof and evidence, in other words, on testimony. Though this prohibition took a long time to implement, its success had the ultimate effect of strengthening royal power by removing cases from the courts of the lords and placing them instead under the jurisdiction of the king's courts, where the new type of proof was more acceptable.

In the dogmatic sphere, at the Fourth Lateran Council the sacraments of the Roman Church were first formally defined and fixed at seven, and "transubstantiation" was proclaimed to be official doctrine of the church (the view that the bread and wine of the eucharist actually become the body and blood of Christ though the physical form of the bread and wine remain). Annual confession and communion were now required of all Catholics (two requirements still in existence); more explicitly than ever, the means of salvation were placed in the hands of the Church.

Bases of Papal "Power"

What were the bases for the great power exercised by Innocent? The Pope possessed no sizable army—only his personal bodyguard and the limited number of troops he could call up as suzerain of the Papal States. Yet, in the investiture conflict the Pope had won a great victory over his rival, the Western emperor. Moreover, the leadership the Pope had exercised over the crusading movement had brought him additional prestige. Nor can we forget the energetic personalities of certain Pontiffs preceding Innocent—iron-willed men such as Gregory I, Nicholas I, Leo IX, Gregory VII, Alexander III—whose every act seemed to have been motivated by the religious conviction that they must exalt the prestige and authority of their high office. Of course the increase in papal power was greatly facilitated by the attitude of medieval man toward life, an attitude which saw life in this world essentially in terms of a pilgrimage to eternal salvation in the hereafter. As the head of the Church, as the successor to St. Peter, the Pope was the keeper of the keys to salvation with all that this implied.

By the period of Innocent III far more appeals, ecclesiastical and political in nature, poured into Rome. To handle this the Papacy developed an elaborate administrative machinery. The papal court (*Curia*) was probably the best organized in all of Western Europe, with special sections to deal with matters of ecclesiastical justice, finance, and the mass of daily correspondence. Papal revenues were extensive: money poured in from tithes and other taxes on Church properties, monastic dues, feudal "aids" from papal vassals, fees for services from the papal chancery, and the like. The collection of these monies was usually entrusted to the Templars, and later, to the Lombard bankers, who received a commission in return for their services. This activity helped to build up great banking empires such as those of the Florentine families of the Bardi and later of the Medici.

As every state had its body of law, the Church, too, in the medieval period developed its own elaborate, at first confused, but later well-organized system called *canon law*. Canon law consisted of the decrees of general and local councils, opinions of the early Church Fathers, and papal decrees (called *decretals*). Several early attempts had been made by churchmen to codify this vast and often confusing corpus, but the first really systematized collection of Church law was that of the Bolognese lawyer Gratian. About 1140 Gratian published his *Concordia discordantium canonum* ("Concord of Discordant Canons"), in which he sought to reconcile the discrepancies or contradictions that had inevitably arisen in ecclesiastical law over the centuries. His method was first to state the differences in each case and then to reach a decision through appeal to reason and/or authority, with the most recent papal or conciliar decision usually taking precedence. Ecclesiastical law dealt with almost every conceivable subject: with the problems of "divorce," wills, heresy, oaths, and ecclesiastical organization. Church courts were under the jurisdiction of the bishops, who now tended to delegate their authority to lawyers trained in canon law. From the judgment of these courts appeal was always possible, leading up through the court of the archbishop and ultimately to that of the Pope himself, from whom there was no appeal.

The Sacramental System

The ecclesiastical function that most directly touched the everyday life of each person—and took up most of the priest's time—was the administration of the sacraments. A sacrament is a ceremony or act through which divine grace, which is necessary for salvation, may be received by a Christian. These sacraments, the number and significance of which had been frequently debated in earlier centuries, were in the West first formally defined and fixed at seven by the Fourth Lateran Council; they marked the most significant phases of life from cradle to grave and are still important in the life of the modern Catholic church: 1) *Baptism,* usually administered to an infant, washed away the stain of original sin, which was inherited by all people from their common father, Adam; 2) *Confirmation,* originally part of the baptismal ceremony, was administered by a bishop to the child at the age of twelve, symbolizing the entry of the recipient into the full enjoyment of the responsibilities and privileges of membership in the Church; 3) *Holy Eucharist,* the central part of the mass and (with baptism) the chief sacrament; it enabled the communicant by partaking of the bread and wine, now miraculously transformed into the body and blood of Christ, to enter into a mystical union with Christ;* 4) *Penance* enabled sinners to be forgiven for their sins. After confession to a priest, penance (the reciting of special prayers, going on pilgrimages, fasting, and so on) would be set and absolution (forgiveness) given; 5) *Marriage* bound husband and wife together in a sacred union. Since marriage was considered indissoluble, divorce was not permitted. A marriage could be "broken" only through annulment (that is, an ecclesiastical declaration that the marriage had been originally invalid), only obtainable on such grounds as consanguinity (too close a blood relationship); 6) *Holy orders* conferred the authority of a priest upon the receiver, and, once received, could not be revoked. Priests of course could be defrocked or suspended from office, though, theoretically, they never lost their power of administering the sacraments and offering mass; 7) *Extreme unction* was given to persons on the point of death, the priest anointing the believer with chrism (holy oil) and preparing the dying person for divine judgment. It should be emphasized again that it was the common medieval view that salvation was doubtful if not impossible without the sacraments. The Church, however, as the agency of divine authority, administered or withheld them as it chose. Thus the Pope, as head of the Church, indirectly affected the personal life of every person in Western society.

Interdict and Excommunication.   The Papacy had at its disposal two spiritual weapons with which to admonish and punish those who defied the wishes of the Church. The first of these, the interdict, was a sentence that could be levied upon a city or province, or in extreme cases, even on an entire country. Once the sentence was pronounced, the sacraments could not be administered within the area interdicted, though exceptions, especially in the case of infant baptism, might be made. The interdict was often employed against a government to force it, by means of public pressure, to capitulate to the wishes of the Papacy. The fact that the papal interdict ceased later to be effective is suggested by its failure when used against King John of England and Emperor Frederick II in the early thirteenth century, both of whom managed for years to hold out against papal pressures.

Excommunication, on the other hand, was a device directed against an individual. It was the most severe sentence the Church could pronounce, depriving a person of the benefit of the sacraments, thus endangering the soul. The condemned person became virtually an outcast from society. There were several gradations of excommunication, the most fearful being the anathema, or damnation, which not only denied one the sacraments but doomed one's soul to

---

* By the thirteenth century the laity of the Western Church no longer received both bread and wine, the wine being reserved for the clergy alone. In the East the laity received both.

perdition. Its severity is demonstrated by the following passage contained in one such anathema: "May the excommunicate be seized with jaundice and smitten with blindness—suffer a wretched death and everlasting damnation with the devil—and may the worm that never dies feed on his flesh, and the fire that cannot be quenched be his food and sustenance eternally." Besides placing the excommunicates' souls in jeopardy the effect, as early as the twelfth century, was also to impose civil liabilities upon them. The courts would refuse to hear their case, and in most areas their property would be confiscated. On pain of contamination, even their best friends would avoid them. Were the excommunicate a noble or a king, all oaths of allegiance to him were declared dissolved, and his vassals were considered justified in rebelling against him. Little wonder that excommunication was such a potent weapon!

Protest and Reform

As the power of the Western Church grew and its wealth increased, its officials became more and more immersed in secular affairs. Even monasticism, which had arisen originally as a protest against the involvement of Christians in affairs of the world, was affected as time went on, or, to the medieval mind, became "corrupted by the world." Thus it is not surprising that at various times during the medieval period movements of reform arose that sought to restore a more rigorous adherence to the earlier monastic ideal. I have already discussed the Cluniac reform movement of the tenth and eleventh centuries and the parallel reform waves that tended to merge with it (Chapter 7). But Cluny, too, with its amassing of wealth and prestige, gradually lapsed into a less rigorous form of monasticism, so much so that by the twelfth century the Cluniacs themselves had become the target of a new reform movement.

One of the principal changes wrought by this new wave of reform in the eleventh and twelfth centuries was the effective regulation of the cathedral "canons," priests assigned to cathedral churches. Previously these priests had been subject to little discipline, but now they were organized into cathedral chapters with *regulae* (rules) modeled after the Benedictine, constituting a semi-monastic organization of secular priests. As their rule was formulated largely on the basis of precepts set forth by St. Augustine, the cathedral canons were known as Augustinian, or "canons regular."

Cistercian Monks, Bernard, and Arnold of Brescia

The most significant monastic reform, however, was that of the Cistercian monks, who protested not only the laxness that they believed pervaded the older Cluniac and Benedictine houses but also the ranks of the secular clergy as well. The first Cistercian monastery was founded in 1098 at Cîteaux (Burgundy) in east-central France. The rule adopted was that of St. Benedict but, in contrast, and probably as a reaction to the Cluniacs, the Cistercians did not have a centralized organization, though they had annual meetings of representatives from each of their monasteries. As they grew in number and influence, the Cistercians came gradually to owe allegiance only to the Papacy. The missionary zeal and emphasis on manual labor by the monks themselves led them to establish many Cistercian houses in the new Slavic lands of the East and in deserted or wild areas of Western Europe. Thus the Cistercians played an important role in the agricultural revolution and expansion of Western Europe.

A good deal of credit for the Cistercian success must go to St. Bernard of Clairvaux (1090–1153), the greatest religious figure in the first half of the twelfth century and probably the most influential man of his time. Almost single-handedly Bernard, through his fiery preaching, launched the Second Crusade. He also wrote the *regula* for the Knights Templars. Through his extensive correspondence he advised and admonished various kings and princes of Europe, and even stepped in to resolve a disputed papal election. Deeply religious, Bernard as a young man had first entered the monastery at Cîteaux accompanied by thirty companions, a testimony to his early powers of persuasion. From Cîteaux he soon went forth to found the abbey of Clairvaux, over which he presided as abbot until his death. But though Bernard railed eloquently against the growing worldliness of the Church, one of his most violent conflicts was with Arnold of Brescia, an Italian cleric whose reform program, like Bernard's, concentrated on attacking the laxity and wealth of the Church. The fundamental disagreement between Bernard and Arnold was, however, over the nature of the Church and its role in the world. Bernard might sympathize with Arnold on the question of apostolic poverty (that is, that in imitation of the life of the Apostles the Church should possess little or no property), but unlike Arnold, he had no quarrel with its hierarchical organization, or, more important, with the Church's exercise of power in worldly affairs. Indeed, to Bernard it was right and proper for the superior moral authority of the Church to be exercised in helping to regulate the affairs of mankind. To Arnold, on the other hand, who might be termed a precursor of the modern idea of complete separation of church and state, the Church should renounce all claim to temporal authority and abandon all pretensions to worldly power. The fate of Arnold I have already described—a brief period of success in Rome followed by ultimate defeat and death at the hands of Pope Hadrian and Frederick Barbarossa (Chapter 7).

Later movements to reform the Church reflected something of the rivalry between Bernard and Arnold. The careers of both men evidence the increasingly critical attitude of the time toward laxness of the religious life. But Bernard, called by one modern scholar "the self-appointed conscience of the Church," was

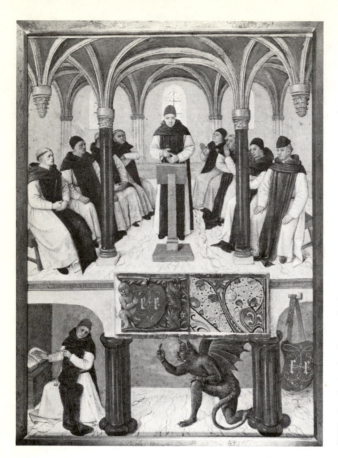

This depiction of St. Bernard, the greatest religious figure in the West in the early twelfth century and launcher of the Second Crusade, shows him teaching his Cistercian disciples in Paris. (Giraudon)

a very conservative reformer who sought to work *within* the structure of the Church, primarily through monastic reform. Arnold, on the other hand, was a revolutionary whose ideas, if implemented, would in effect have destroyed the institution of the Church as the Middle Ages knew it, depriving the clergy of all political and economic power.

Arnold's radicalism nevertheless did not die with him, for even more extreme movements arose insisting on drastic change within the Church. Earlier, in the first half of the twelfth century, a mob had burned the French preacher Peter of Bruys, who advocated scrapping the entire organization, the ceremonial, and even much of the dogma of the Church. The significance of Peter should not be exaggerated, but his career was certainly symptomatic of an ever-increasing current of criticism against the Church. The resurgence of heresy, which was to trouble the Church and, during the late thirteenth century and increasingly in the fourteenth and fifteenth centuries, shake it to its very foundations, I shall leave to Chapters 11 and 13.

The Dominicans and Franciscans

The forces of protest described above generally followed a negative pattern. But in the same context a protest movement arose that made a positive contribution to Church reform and ended by strengthening the Church. This group of reformers, to be sure, also advocated the leading of a purer life but, unlike medieval monasticism, they preached service to man within the world and not withdrawal from it in order to serve God. The result was the foundation of the two great Mendicant orders, the Franciscan and the Dominican. Certain precursors of these two orders had already gained ground in the second half of the twelfth century, among them two groups of laymen—the Waldensians of southern France and the Humiliati of Italy, who also were interested in service within the Christian community. But these two groups were destined to cross over the sometimes tenuous line between orthodoxy and heresy and thus to end up by suffering persecution themselves. The Waldensians, after their founder Peter Waldo, were at first a group within the Church who wanted essentially to read the Bible for themselves in ordinary French and live by its precepts. Later they came to reject certain practices and doctrines of the Church —infant baptism, the administering of sacraments by priests in a state of sin, the mass, indulgences, and purgatory. They also rejected the institution of the Papacy. The Humiliati of northern Italy, who came into contact with the Waldensians, underwent a somewhat similar development.

The Dominicans and Franciscans appeared on the scene almost simultaneously: their founders, St. Dominic (1170–1221) and St. Francis (1182–1226) were contemporaries. In a sense the basic aim of the two men was the same: to convert heretics and the infidel Muslims. Their methods, however, differed. Though both Dominic and Francis required their followers to be mendicants (that is, to beg for their subsistence from their fellow man), Dominic emphasized learning and preaching in the aim of convincing the unbeliever of the truth of Christianity. Francis, on the other hand, seemed to distrust learning, placing his confidence instead in evangelistic preaching and service to the poor. Both, however, advocated service *within* the world in contrast to the traditional monkish withdrawal from human affairs.

St. Francis of Assisi, Italy, is one of the most fascinating and probably the most loved saint of the Western church. After a dissolute youth he gave up the fortune he was to inherit from his wealthy merchant father in order to go among the poor and administer to their needs. For him all creatures were sacred. With a simplicity, a complete lack of sophistication that is today not easy to understand, he preached to the birds and the wolves as well as to men, considering all living creatures his brothers. Although he had no intention of founding an order, the magnetism of his gentle, sincere personality soon attracted a large following. He resisted the establishment of a formal order as long as he

Pope Innocent III is shown receiving St. Francis in this painting by Giotto, who is the key figure in the transition from Western medieval to early Renaissance art. (Alinari/Scala)

could, but after a meeting with Pope Innocent III, Francis was induced to draw up a rule. Displeased at the turn of events, however, he retired to the background as a new leadership emerged which forged the Franciscan order into the form that still characterizes it today.

In his last will and testament Francis left the following inspiring directions to guide the conduct of his followers or, as he always called them, his brothers:

> The Most High himself revealed to me that I ought to live according to the model of the holy gospel. Those who presented themselves to follow this kind of life distributed all they might have to the poor. They contented themselves with one tunic, patched within and without.... I firmly desire that all the other brothers work, for this makes for goodness. Let those who know no trade learn one [so that they may] flee idleness.... Let us resort to the table of the Lord, begging our bread from door to door. Let the brothers take great care not to accept any buildings erected for them, except as all is in accordance with the holy poverty which we have vowed.*

* J. Dahmus, *History of Medieval Civilization* (1964), from J. H. Robinson, *Readings in European History* (1904).

In short, a Franciscan was to live in imitation of Christ and the Apostles, abandoning material things and, for Christ's sake, going forth to minister to his fellow man. Above all he was to consider all men his brothers.

One of the simplest, most appealing (and psychologically sound) prayers ever written is the following by St. Francis:

> Lord make me an instrument of thy peace.
> Where there is hatred let me sow love
> Where there is injury pardon
> Where there is doubt faith
> Where there is despair hope
> Where there is darkness light
> Where there is sadness joy.
> Divine master, grant that I may not so much seek to be consoled as
>   to console
> To be understood as to understand
> To be loved as to love
> For it is in giving that we receive
> It is in pardoning that we are pardoned
> And it is in dying that we are born to eternal life.

St. Dominic (1170–1221) was born into a wealthy Spanish family. He began his career as a preacher in southern France, where he strove to reconvert the heretical Albigensians to Christianity (see Chapter 11). More prone to involvement in worldly affairs than Francis, he admonished the southern French clergy and papal legates: "If you want to convert the Albigensians, dismount from your horses, dress in simple clothing, and walk among the people like the Albigensian *perfecti*." (The *perfecti* were the highest type of the Albigensians— their "holy" men who were noted for their extreme self-denial of worldly things.)

Dominic, too, attracted a large following, and the result again was the creation of a new order. Since it was founded primarily to combat heresy, the Pope placed the order in charge of the Inquisition, which was to ferret out and punish heretics.

Previous to the Albigensian crusade, heresy had been handled by the ecclesiastical courts of the local bishop. Under Innocent III and later Gregory IX, however, the Papacy set up in the Curia a centralized organization, the Inquisition, to supervise the task of locating and eradicating heresy. Even though the Inquisition was to function in all countries, it never really secured a foothold in some, including England. Though technically an ecclesiastical tribunal of experts to assist the regular Church courts, the Inquisitorial court usually acted hand in hand with the civil authorities. Its methods of investigation, though not unusual for the period, would today often seem overly severe, even unjust:

the accused were not allowed to confront their accusers, torture was used to extract confessions, and guilt was assumed until innocence was proved. If the accused "confessed" voluntarily before trial, ordinary penance such as fasting or pilgrimage would be imposed. If during trial the accused recanted, that is, confessed and renounced their heresy, the punishment was usually imprisonment. But should they refuse to recant or, more serious, should they "relapse into heresy" once they had admitted their guilt, they were remanded to the secular authority and usually burned at the stake. The fact that the major Inquisitorial figures were Dominicans earned their order the nickname "the hounds of the Lord" (from the Latin, *Domini canes*). Its close connection with the Inquisition made the order in many areas feared and less loved by the common people than the Franciscans.

With the passage of time the Dominicans and Franciscans became wealthy and powerful orders, a development that was a deviation from their founders' original ideals. However, some organization, under papal sanction, was necessary to keep the orders under proper discipline. For unlike other, less organized, groups, such as the Waldensians and Humiliati, who ended up rejecting the institution of the Church itself, the Franciscans (except for a large splinter group, the Spirituals) and the Dominicans, by receiving the official sanction of the Papacy, remained within the Church. As time passed, certain rivalry between the two orders developed—witness, for example, the great theological opponents of the thirteenth century, the Dominican St. Thomas Aquinas and the Franciscan St. Bonaventure. But in the long run the work of the two orders in satisfying the growing popular need, especially of the townspeople, for a sense of the greater relevancy of Christianity in their lives, was able to channel much of the movement of protest against the Church into the mainstream of Catholicism, and thus to perform a great service for the medieval Western Church.

Medieval Thought and Education

Until the thirteenth century education in the Latin West was largely connected with the Church. In the early medieval period, with few exceptions, education was available only in monastic and cathedral schools. Later, in the twelfth and thirteenth centuries, even some of the great medieval universities that emerged were under the control of the Church and had many ecclesiastics on their teaching staffs. One of the few names of important lay scholars that may be cited from the time of St. Augustine in the fifth century to Dante in the fourteenth is Boethius.

Monastic and Cathedral Schools: the Twelfth-Century Renaissance

In the Western medieval period, although there were no state-supported, free elementary schools like those of today, education was not entirely limited to the upper classes. An intelligent young boy of the lower class might, if he attracted the attention of the village priest or of the abbot of a nearby monastery, obtain some formal education at a monastic or cathedral school. And in rare cases he could use this schooling to rise above his station, as did Pope Sylvester II (999–1003), who was a peasant. But the vast majority of students in these monastic and cathedral schools intended to enter the ranks of the clergy, particularly the younger sons of noble families, who at birth were traditionally destined for a career in the Church. Since the elder son was to inherit the lands and was ordinarily occupied with the long, arduous training in the use of weapons required for knighthood, he usually had no formal education. Up to about the mid-thirteenth century, he was probably totally illiterate or received only rudimentary training from the court chaplain. Even if he had the inclination to acquire any formal learning it was generally restricted to reading, writing, and, possibly, the rudiments of arithmetic—just enough to help in the administration of his estates. Girls, with a few notable exceptions, rarely learned to read and write; their training centered on what we would call "home economics."

Education at a cathedral or monastic school generally consisted of learning to read, write, and speak Latin and included some instruction in philosophy and "science" (arithmetic and a smattering of geometry and astronomy), and perhaps a bit of rhetoric and history. By the twelfth century, especially in the northern French cathedral schools, the teaching of Latin literature and rhetoric became very strong. So strong was the revival of classical Latin literature that it has been termed the "Renaissance of the Twelfth Century." But its humanism, unlike the later Italian Renaissance, was clerical. The chief scholar at the famous cathedral school of Chârtres was its bishop, John of Salisbury, whose Latin style and knowledge of Latin works was remarkable for his time. The cathedral schools of Reims and Laons also had ecclesiastics or monks conducting classes. But this intense interest in classical Latin letters gave way in the late twelfth and thirteenth centuries to an emphasis on the "new" Aristotelian logic and metaphysics discussed later. The humanist achievement of the twelfth century, however, was not lost; it was drawn upon later in the fourteenth century and played a part in the genesis of the Italian Renaissance.*

The University

Beginning in about 1100 the first universities emerged in the West. Several factors lay behind this development: the growth of cities, the rise of dis-

* On the Twelfth-Century Renaissance, see also pages 325 and 361.

tant trading, and the transmission of Greek science from the Arab and Byzantine worlds. But the most immediate cause was the growing need of Latin society for professionals in law and medicine.

The origins of the medieval university are not entirely clear. Antecedents are found in the medieval monastic and cathedral school and in the growing practice of students following a famous teacher. When a noted teacher established himself in a certain area, students might flock to him and take up residence nearby. Also groups of scholars might congregate in a particular location, a town (Paris for example) favored by prospering economic conditions or the accessibility of manuscripts. Groups of students and teachers sooner or later found it necessary to band together formally for mutual protection. In the twelfth and thirteenth centuries such scholars and students, both together or each group separately, organized themselves, often loosely, into a *universitas* (a word applying to *any* medieval collectivity, as for instance a guild).

The two most famous medieval universities were in Bologna and Paris. Bologna became famous as a center for the study of civil law through the work of the renowned Italian jurist Irnerius (d. 1130), an authority on the Justinian Code. When Bologna's schools of the arts and medicine were founded is not precisely known.

Irnerius was the creator of medieval jurisprudence, and his profound knowledge of the subject attracted students to Bologna from all over Latin Europe. They organized themselves into student "guilds" to provide mutual protection and, interestingly enough, to administer the university. By the thirteenth century the student guilds exercised extraordinary power even over the professors. The guild statute laid down strict rules and regulations that the teachers had to adhere to under penalty of fine or dismissal. Lectures must begin and end promptly; if the professor overran his allotted time, the students exercised the right to walk out on him. If the professor spent too much time on method to the detriment of content, he could be fined or dismissed. Any teacher desiring a leave of absence was required to obtain permission from the students. He had to compete with his colleagues for students, for if enrollment fell too low, he faced dismissal. To counteract these rigid demands made on them by the students, the professors were finally forced to organize themselves into a faculty group called "the college of doctors," and ultimately control over the university passed into the hands of the professors (or masters) who were the more permanent element.*

The University of Paris was administered quite differently. Here it was the teachers who were first organized into a guild, under the authority of the chancellor of the cathedral school of Notre Dame, and they prevented the students

---

* Our modern university is based on medieval Latin rather than the Byzantine university or "higher schools."

from seizing control of the expanding university. The studies offered at Paris were the arts, theology, canon law, and medicine. Paris became the prototype of the developing universities of northern Europe; southern universities, especially the Italian, were modeled after Bologna.

In the medieval universities all instruction was in Latin. The subjects studied in the arts curriculum were divided into two groups: the *trivium* (grammar, rhetoric, logic) and the *quadrivium* (arithmetic, music, geometry, astronomy). Though the scope of these "seven liberal arts" today appears limited, under the general rubric of grammar were the ability to read and understand Latin, instruction in spelling and writing, composition, and the rather elementary study of Latin literature, both prose and poetry. Music, which was considered a mathematical science, also entailed some higher mathematics. Experimental sciences were not taught, though in the thirteenth century a few rare individuals, especially among the Franciscans, such as the English friar Roger Bacon (1214–1294) and his older contemporary Robert Grosseteste (1168–1253), seem to have advocated a more or less experimental approach to certain of the sciences such as optics.

Medieval universities in the West began the practice of conferring academic degrees. After prescribed study—usually four years—and proper examination, a student became a bachelor—the equivalent of a journeyman in a craft or merchant guild. With his bachelor's degree in arts (the baccalaureate), he received a limited right to give lectures and, when he had studied enough, to qualify for his licentiate. When he had passed his examinations for the licentiate, he was given a license to teach. Only after an elaborate and expensive ceremony of inception for the licentiate was he declared a full master of the master's guild and accorded the title of master of arts. Some universities at first used the titles of master and doctor interchangeably, the difference being in which of the various faculties of the university the candidate had qualified—that is, master of arts, but doctor of law, medicine, or theology.

Of the three professional fields of study offered in the western universities —law, medicine, and theology—the University of Paris became preeminent in theology and Bologna in law.* For the study of medicine students went to Bologna, or Salerno in Italy, or to Montpellier in southern France.

Most of the students lived in residence halls (*collegia*) collectively rented by them or endowed by philanthropic patrons. At first these were merely student dwelling places. Later, however, masters began to give courses in the residence halls, and thus the latter became specialized schools ("colleges," in our sense), since those who pursued the same area of study tended to live together.

---

* At Paris the chief text was Peter Lombard's *Sentences,* containing propositions on doctrine systematically arranged. In Byzantium law was taught at the government's "higher school" (university); theology was taught at the separate Patriarchal School.

A typical day's work in the life of a medieval student is shown in the following quote from an order of the Duke of Burgundy in 1476 for the University of Louvain in Flanders:

> The tutors shall see that the scholars rise in the morning at five o'clock, and that then before lectures each one reads by himself the laws which are to be read at the regular lecture, together with the glosses.... But after the regular lecture, having if they wish, quickly heard mass, the scholars shall come to their rooms and revise the lectures that have been given, by rehearsing and impressing on their memory whatever they have brought away from the lectures either orally or in writing. And next they shall come to lunch.... After lunch, each one having brought to the table his books, all the scholars of the Faculty together, in the presence of a tutor, shall review that regular lecture; and in this review the tutor shall follow a method which will enable him, by discreet questioning of every man, to gather whether each of them listened well to the lecture and remembered it, and which will recall the whole lecture by having its parts recited by individuals. And if watchful care is used in this, one hour will suffice.*

Student life was similar in many respects to that of today. Friction existed between "town" and "gown." Students often played pranks on the townsmen and sometimes engaged in fights with them. Since all students—at least in schools north of the Alps—were considered members of the clergy, they were not usually subject to local municipal authorities. For entertainment and merry-making they engaged in hazing, songfests, and drinking parties. Letters home asking for money evidence occasional financial troubles.

In the twelfth and thirteenth centuries groups of wandering French, English, or German students called Goliards (after their mythical hero, "Bishop" Golias) wrote highly satirical but eloquent poems against the Church and often in praise of wine and riotous living. Condemned by the Church, they were weakened only when they were denied the "privileges of clergy."

Scholasticism and Aristotelian Philosophy

Theology, the study of Christian thought and dogma, was the most esteemed branch of learning. At the same time, an integral part of medieval education came to be the classical Latin literature inherited from the ancient

* H. Rashdall, *The Universities of Europe in the Middle Ages*, rev. ed. (1960).

world. Indeed a strong thread of "classicism" ran throughout the medieval intellectual "thought world," although during the long period of the so-called
Dark Ages the corpus of the classical Latin works was for the most part neglected. Early medieval theology was based primarily on faith—that is, acceptance without logical proof of the basic tenets of Christianity (such as the
existence of God, the Trinity, and the divinity and humanity of Christ). The
emphasis of classical learning, on the other hand, was on human reason as the
means to truth. These two approaches to knowledge, faith and reason, if juxtaposed can produce considerable disagreement. Therefore, when, for example, in
the twelfth-century French cathedral schools there was an important revival of
classical Latin learning, the conflict between classical reason and Christian
dogma, which had for so long been implicit, opened up.

Earlier there was evidence of this conflict in the attempts of the Fathers of
the early Church to reconcile their Christian beliefs with Greco-Roman philosophy. We have seen it too in Pope Gregory I's distrust of classical learning and
in the beginnings of a compromise as shown in the attitude maintained by the
Carolingian scholars. Their solution to the problem—not entirely new with
them, to be sure—was as one scholar put it, "to *use* classical Latin works but to
try not to *enjoy* them." Once the Carolingian "compromise" was made, it was
almost inevitable that the thought barriers against reading more of the classical
works would begin to break down. Thus under the impact of the renewed
study of the classics, which became more pronounced in the twelfth century,
reason began to be applied more extensively to the articles of Christian faith. A
few scholars began to rationalize that, since both revelation (faith) and human
reason come from God, they cannot contradict each other. They must both be
true. If not, our understanding must be at fault. The truth of the most basic
premises of Christian dogma—the existence of God, the mystery of the Trinity—
was still, however, almost never questioned, reason instead being applied to
show logically the validity of these already accepted truths. Whatever the advances of the Western mind in the period of the twelfth and thirteenth centuries—and they were considerable—a true and all-pervasive "rationalism" did
not prevail. There were set limits to the use of reason, which to some degree
restricted speculation. But within these limits the Church did not prevent, indeed it sometimes encouraged, the exercise of a certain freedom of thought. The
result may be seen in the development of more than one theological system
acceptable to the Church.*

Aristotle.   The great crisis in Western medieval thought occurred in the mid-
twelfth century when the many heretofore unknown works of Aristotle, the

---

* The same kind of crisis in faith and reason (most often based on Aristotle) occurred in the
Byzantine and Islamic "thought worlds."

great ancient Greek philosopher, scientist, and logician, as transmitted through the Muslims of Spain, began to appear in the West. Medieval scholars were here confronted with a completely rational explanation of the universe, an explanation that had no recourse to Christian revelation. Moreover, on some points (such as the eternity of matter and denial of the existence of a personal God) Aristotle's theories were in direct contradiction to Christian teachings. How to reconcile these two views of the cosmos was the problem facing the medieval thinkers of the late twelfth and thirteenth centuries. It is testimony to the mental agility of two scholars, Anselm and Abelard, that their efforts were to be climaxed by the remarkably sophisticated synthesis of Aristotelian philosophy and Catholic Christianity finally worked out by St. Thomas Aquinas.

Anselm

Anselm of Canterbury (*c.*1033–1109) was the precursor of the renaissance of theological-philosophic thought, though it probably reverted back even earlier to Gerbert of Aurillac, who had even studied in Arabic Spain. Anselm was born in northern Italy and was made abbot of Bec in Normandy in 1078. Under his rule the monastic school at Bec became a major school of learning in the West. Later, Anselm became archbishop of Canterbury, wherein he did much to extend Gregory VII's reform program to the English clergy. Anselm believed that it was almost always possible to explain Christian faith rationally. But he was also convinced that Christian truth first had to be believed before it could be understood. With more than a little insight he argued that the unbeliever, that is, one without faith, could not truly understand dogma, in the same way that "the blind man cannot conceive of light, nor the deaf man of sound." To quote his famous phrase, "I *believe* in order that I may *understand*."

St. Anselm attempted to prove the existence of God by reason alone. Starting with a definition of God—"God is that than which nothing greater can be conceived of"—Anselm reasoned that this "greatest thing" must of necessity exist in reality as well as in the mind. For if it did not, it logically cannot be that greatest thing. By this ontological definition, therefore, God *must* exist. The monk Gaunilo took issue with Anselm by arguing that a concept such as that, for example, of the "blessed isles" *can* exist in our minds though these perfect, imaginary isles do not exist in reality. Gaunilo was not questioning Anselm's premise that God exists, only his reasoning. Nevertheless, from the viewpoint of strict logical argumentation without recourse to outside empirical observation, Anselm's demonstration of God's existence is, as the modern scholar Étienne Gilson puts it, "the triumph of pure dialectic operating on a definition." * For

* E. Gilson, *History of Christian Philosophy in the Middle Ages* (New York, 1955), p. 133.

his contribution to the dialectical method of later medieval thinkers some authorities have considered Anselm the direct precursor of Scholasticism.

Nominalists Versus Realists

The philosophical speculation of Anselm leads to the problem of the universals, the most basic and difficult intellectual problem of Western medieval philosophy. The question posed by the medieval philosophers was what kind of concrete reality corresponds to the abstractions or concepts existing in the mind. The problem of the universals then underlies the question of the nature of reality and of certitude: How do we really know what we think we know, or, in other words, what is the relationship of what we think to the world of reality? Today we accept as "certitude" primarily only what can be determined by scientific observation, by experimentation. But in the Western Middle Ages, when the notion of empirical proof was still alien, indeed almost unknown, "truth" was accepted as definitively shown by the use of logical argument alone. Thus, relatively unimportant as the problem of the universals may seem to us today, this question for medieval philosophers remained, in a broad sense, the fundamental issue in their *logical* attempt to explain reality in this and the other world.

The conflict over universals had its roots in the philosophical differences between the ancient Greek thinkers Plato and his pupil Aristotle. In the Middle Ages the distillation of their differences by Western theologians resulted in two major points of view. One, that of the *Realists* (supporters of Plato and his successors), maintained that universals (concepts) have a genuine existence or reality of their own, being reflections of "forms" in the mind of God. The other view (in part derived from Aristotle) held that the universals exist only in the mind; they are only mental classifications of like things and have no independent existence of their own. According to this latter group of thinkers, called *Nominalists,* knowledge of a universal results only through the mental process of categorizing and arbitrarily "naming" the data perceived through our senses. According to the Realists, on the other hand, the universal exists antecedent to the individual things that, in turn, depend upon the universal for their own existence.

The first genuine Nominalist was the monk Roscellinus (d. *c.*1125) of northern France. In a clash with Anselm, Roscellinus maintained the extreme view that universals are only words, which to many implied, shockingly, that even the concept of the Trinity was only a name. Such a position smacked of the heresy of tritheism—the doctrine that the Father, the Son, and the Holy Spirit are, in effect, three separate Gods.

Abelard

In the late twelfth and thirteenth centuries most scholars, among them Peter Abelard (1079–1142), in some respects the most original Western thinker of the medieval period, tended to take a modified Realist position. Abelard formulated a theory concerning universals that came to be known as Conceptualism. The word *concept* signifies a universal idea as distinct from particular objects. For example, one may see many chairs and abstract from these the general idea of "chair." Abelard in effect saw the universal only as a concept. He believed that, while universals do in a sense have a kind of existence, this is *only* in the mind of the person who observes the similarities among members of a group—similarities that exist outside the mind.

Abelard studied with Roscellinus, and also in Paris under the leading Realist of his time, William of Champeaux. Contentious and often arrogantly intellectual, Abelard took a certain delight in ridiculing his teachers. As he wrote, when describing his response to a challenge to debate on the part of one of his teachers (whom Abelard had already provoked to the point of exasperation): "I was all unprepared to do so but, trusting in my genius, I began to speak and was very successful." *

Abelard's most celebrated work, *Sic et Non* (*Yes and No*), reveals his critical turn of mind. In this work he demonstrated what some probably had suspected but never dared to point out: that certain passages in the writings of the Church Fathers sometimes contradict one another. Abelard had the misfortune to incur the wrath of the most powerful religious figure of his century, the intransigent St. Bernard of Clairvaux. Bernard, who regarded faith as unquestionably the highest form of "knowledge," believed that Abelard's essentially rationalistic approach to theology was dangerous to the Catholic faith. For if carried to extremes such reasoning might well imply that any doctrine that could not logically be demonstrated was not to be believed. As Bernard (somewhat exaggeratedly) put it: "Abelard is trying to prove everything so that no one will have to believe anything." Under Bernard's influence certain of Abelard's works were condemned. Driven to desperation, Abelard finally had to find refuge at the monastery of Cluny.

Abelard's influence on subsequent medieval thought, despite his rather unorthodox attitude for his time, was profound. His method of marshaling authorities pro and con, as set forth in *Sic et Non,* and above all his method of doubting, of questioning the validity of almost everything, were to have an important influence on the formulation of the Scholastic method, the standard of thirteenth- and in large part of fourteenth-century Western religious and philosophic thought.

---

* In the *Historia Calamitatum,* which one leading scholar now claims is a forgery.

Influence of Aristotle from Islamic Spain and Byzantium

It is important to note that Abelard worked *before* the influx from Arabic Spain and Sicily of most of the Aristotelian treatises mentioned above—the treatises primarily responsible for bringing about the crisis in Western intellectual thought. Western scholars were literally dazzled by this vast new corpus, for Aristotle had written on virtually everything: on natural science, law, ethics, philosophy, rhetoric, politics, even on the theory of poetry and drama, though some of his works were not to be introduced to the West until brought by Byzantine scholars in the Italian Renaissance. Nevertheless so much new material was now available, so different an approach to the problem of the world and the universe, that merely to assimilate this information was no mean task. The new Aristotelianism was in certain ways directly in conflict with traditional Christian teachings. To Aristotle the deity was an impersonal "prime mover," not the personal Christian God who actively intervened in the world. Further, it would seem that "*the* Philosopher" (as medieval scholars called Aristotle) did not believe in the immortality of the *individual* soul, rather in that of the *world* soul. Finally, his argument that matter was eternal directly contradicted the Christian belief in God's creation of the world out of nothing. Little wonder that the Papacy for a time in the early thirteenth century forbade the teaching of works of Aristotle at the West's preeminent theological school, the University of Paris.

Western Reactions to Aristotle

Such a prohibition, however, was almost impossible to implement because Western scholars were too fascinated with the great wealth of new data and the new approach. In the main there were three reactions to this "New Learning" primarily provided by Aristotle: 1) One school of thought simply admitted that contradictions existed between Aristotle and Christian doctrine but insisted that each was true *in its own sphere*. This group was called Averroist after the similar view—known in the West as that of the "double (or twofold) truth"—held by Averroës, the twelfth-century Arabic commentator on Aristotle. 2) Another group, which we might call traditionalists (they derived their inspiration primarily from St. Augustine), insisted that in case of conflict Revelation should always take precedence over Aristotelian logic. And finally, 3) the most significant position—dominated by two Dominicans, Albertus Magnus (*c.*1206–1280) and Thomas Aquinas (1225–1274)—which accepted the philosophy of Aristotle but attempted wherever possible to reconcile his theories with those of Christian teaching. Where this could not be done Aristotle of course was shown to be wrong. This last group, later called Thomists, loomed largest in Latin thought during the thirteenth century, the intellectual apogee of the Western medieval period.

Thomas Aquinas

The foundations for St. Thomas's great work were laid by his teacher Albertus Magnus, a learned German scholar who taught at Cologne and Paris. Albertus's ambition was to write commentaries on all of Aristotle's treatises then known. Albertus had a particular penchant for natural science and at times displayed something of an empirical attitude. Advocating observation of natural phenomena, he even rejected certain conclusions of the ancient scientific writers because, as he wrote, "they do not agree with experience." An important accomplishment of Albertus was to utilize in his commentaries more accurate Latin translations of the texts of Aristotle—translations based primarily it seems on Arabic translations from the Greek or possibly directly on the original Greek texts.

But the one who did the most to bring the original texts of Aristotle to the attention of Western scholars was the Latin Bishop William of Moerbeke, who resided in the Greek East (in Latin-held Corinth) after the Western conquest of Byzantium in 1204. Moerbeke conceived the idea of making a revised, literal translation, directly from the original Greek, of as many of Aristotle's works as were available (including those on logic, natural science, aesthetics, and the political treatise, the *Politics*). In fact these translations of Moerbeke and other minor figures for the first time made available to the Latin West not only the original versions of certain hitherto unknown writings of Aristotle, but also gradually replaced Latin translations of previously known Aristotelian works, themselves based on second- and third-hand translations from the Arabic.

The impact of the reception of all this "New Learning" coming from the Greek East and earlier from Arabic Spain (and also former Byzantine-held Sicily) was tremendous. For the reception of Aristotle's works in particular brought with them not only Aristotle's rational view of the universe, but also myriads of new facts, new data about the world. No wonder, as one historian has well put it, Western scholars of the twelfth and thirteenth centuries were "dazzled."

As this huge mass of new information was digested, Western theologians began not only to sort out its inconsistencies with respect to Christian beliefs but, in keeping with the synthesizing intellectual tradition of the time, sought to formulate a single, all-embracing explanation of the universe that would harmonize the new learning with Christianity. Such a systematic all-embracing synthesis of Catholic theology and Aristotle was most thoroughly and effectively accomplished by Albert's great pupil and contemporary of Moerbeke, the Dominican Thomas Aquinas.

Born of a noble family near Naples, Thomas (*c*.1225–1274) was educated as a boy at the famous abbey of Monte Cassino. Later he studied at the newly established University of Naples. After becoming a Dominican friar, Thomas set out for Paris to study theology. According to one story (possibly apocryphal), on his way there his brothers seized him, hoping to dissuade him from his objective. Thomas was locked up in a tower, and after all their efforts had failed, his brothers tried to tempt him from his goal by sending a strumpet into his room to seduce him. Thomas, however, seizing a burning brand from the fire, drove the girl from the room and burned a cross on the door. His brothers grudgingly gave in, and Thomas went on to Paris. There he studied with Albertus Magnus and later taught theology in the university. His extreme seriousness and slow, careful analysis of problems led his fellow students at the beginning to regard him as rather dull witted and ironically they nicknamed this man, one of the finest intellects of his time, the "Dumb Ox."

In his great *Summa Contra Gentiles* (directed primarily against what he considered the non-Christian Latin Averroists) and his *Summa Theologica* (a text for theological students), Thomas established a clear line between philosophy and theology. Each had its own sphere, but both together formed a great whole, a unified synthesis of faith and reason. Theology he defined as "science" (knowledge) based on revelation from God. Philosophy was the logical explanation of nature. And all truths regarding God, the universe, and man that could be discovered by experience and unaided reason belonged to the sphere of philosophy.

Thomas believed that since both reason and revelation are gifts from God it was logically impossible for them to contradict each other. But reason, to Thomas, was not always sufficient as a means to truth, since it was limited by man's finite nature. Yet insofar as reason could go, it would never deny truth; it would merely explain it. The *Summa* was a stupendous work of systematic logic that used or sometimes even reshaped Aristotle's theories so that they could be reconciled with Christian beliefs. As the great modern Thomistic scholar Gilson has said, "Thomas uses the language of Aristotle everywhere to make the Philosopher say that there is only one God, Creator of the World, infinite and omnipotent, intimately present to all his creatures, especially to men, every one of whom is endowed with a personally immortal soul naturally able to survive the death of its body." Aquinas did, then, "metamorphose the doctrine of Aristotle into Christian principles."

In his time St. Thomas was considered by many to be a dangerous modernist; indeed, some wanted to condemn his work, and for a time the Bishop of Paris and the faculty of that University actually did. To these more conservative theologians Thomas had so reduced theology to a logical scheme that he was endangering the mysteries of the faith itself. Their position in fact was to predominate for hundreds of years.

Occam and Duns Scotus

Other opponents, while approving Thomas's methods, attacked his premises or conclusions. A contemporary of Thomas's was the Franciscan mystic Bonaventura, who, though somewhat influenced by Aristotle, remained *within* the traditional Augustinian framework. But Thomas' two leading opponents, not surprisingly, came, subsequently, from the rival Franciscan order—Duns Scotus and William of Occam. Scotus, whose theological views were closer to Thomas's than Occam's, in contrast to Thomas emphasized the primacy of the human will over human intellect, since, as Scotus believed, it was more important to *love* God than to *understand* him. In addition Scotus carried the Scholastic use of the syllogism to what many believed to be excessive limits.

But William of Occam's extreme nominalism, with its emphasis on the existence of the particulars and denial of the reality of the "universal," led to the shattering of the carefully wrought Thomistic synthesis of faith and reason. (Thomas's synthesis was in fact shortly to disappear completely from the Church, not to reappear until centuries later when his clear definitions were needed by the Council of Trent in 1563 to combat the Protestants.) To Occam matters of faith should be accepted unquestioningly for, in contrast to Aquinas, he believed that any attempt to understand God through reason would be futile. Through automatic acceptance of the Church's theological tenets the followers of Occam believed they were now free to shift their attention from theology to the natural world. Occam had in effect "divorced faith from reason."

Though Occam's views were of critical importance for theology, they were even more meaningful for medieval society in general. For by drawing men's attention away from theology, they could not help but lead to increased emphasis on the worldly and material, that is, to what we would call "secularism." (This result, incidentally, was actually opposed to what Occam had originally intended.) On Occam (d. 1349) see Chapter 13.

Nevertheless, for the Latin High Middle Ages Thomas's *Summa* truly "summed up" virtually all knowledge then available and reconciled it with the Scriptures and the dogmas of the Church. It was the most impressive system of theology produced in the Western Middle Ages and offered the thirteenth century in particular what it seemed increasingly to be looking for—a new and "scientific" support for Christian belief. With certain changes, the theology of Thomism, or Neothomism as it is now called, has remained the standard system for the Catholic Church.

Medieval Arts

If the phrase *ad maiorem Dei gloriam** expresses the highest ideal of medieval civilization, the aspect of medieval culture that most graphically expresses this theme is in the arts—architecture, sculpture, painting, and music. It may well be an exaggeration to say that the usual anonymity of medieval artists and architects was primarily due to a desire to labor for God alone. (In recent times such persons have been increasingly identified.) Nevertheless, such artistic creations as the Gothic cathedral remained mainly community endeavors, efforts by the town as a whole to build and ornament the house of God.

Architecture

In a medieval town the public buildings—the town hall, guild halls, parish churches—were generally the product of joint undertaking by the various artisan guilds. The jewel, the building on which the greatest amount of time, money, and artistic effort was lavished was, however, the town cathedral. Even today when one speaks of Paris, Chartres, or Cologne, the celebrated cathedrals of each of these cities come to mind.

Not only was the cathedral the center of religious activity, it was also the public gathering place of the community, where townsmen congregated during weekdays within the building or on the square before it to conduct business, meet with friends, find shelter during a storm, or meet with one's lover. These more "profane" activities were not considered reprehensible, provided a certain moral restraint was exercised. The church was long the main center of entertainment, where on feast days plays were performed and dancing and feasting were carried on in the churchyard. The church was wise to permit these activities, for not only could it thereby impose a certain supervision on the revelers but more than ever draw their activities into the sphere of the faith.

Of course community rivalry also motivated the construction of cathedrals, with each town striving to build a more impressive edifice than its neighbor. Even within the town itself, the various guilds competed in creating lavish works of art. Yet overriding these more mundane factors was the citizens' desire to provide an external expression of their faith. The Abbot Suger of St. Denis reveals this spirit when describing the transporting of columns to the construction site for the great church of St. Denis (*c*.1137) near Paris:

> Whenever the columns were hauled down from the bottom of the slope with knotted ropes, nobles and common folk alike, would tie their arms, chests, and shoulders to the ropes and, acting as draft

---

* This phrase was used in the sixteenth century, but it is applicable to the medieval period.

A French medieval cathedral in the process of construction. (The Bettmann Archive)

animals, drew the columns up; and in the middle of the town the diverse craftsmen laid aside the tools of their trade and came out to meet them, offering their own strength against the difficulty of the road, doing homage as much as they could to God and the Holy Martyrs.

In the last analysis, the cathedral was built to glorify God on earth and to help medieval people to achieve their main objective: salvation of their souls.

The religious theme was dominant even in the basic layout of the church building. The distinctive feature of the Western cathedral was its cruciform (cross-shaped) floor plan. The statues, paintings, carvings, and the beautiful stained glass windows, all of which we today value for their artistic beauty, were in the medieval period much more than mere decorations: they served, through their remarkable expressiveness, not only to heighten feelings of piety in the faithful but also to illustrate biblical stories and the traditions of the Church to a largely illiterate population. Medieval people could learn something of the faith from the ornamentation of their cathedral.

Two basic architectural styles developed during the medieval period: the first, called *Romanesque,* led to the second, *Gothic,* which became the prevalent style of the High Middle Ages, especially in the North. The Romanesque style, which developed and prevailed during the eleventh century and first half of the twelfth, bore certain similarities to classical Roman architecture but was actually a new style. Romanesque was characterized by round semicircular arches and had a stone vaulting raised over the top of the church, over both the nave and the aisles. A well-integrated structure, the Romanesque church emphasized spatial organization. Its construction was dictated by the early medieval building materials. The walls were required to be thick enough to support the great weight and outward thrust of the heavy stone barrel-vault of the roof. What few windows existed in the side walls were very small, often mere slits. This tended to give a poorly designed Romanesque building an almost fortresslike appearance.

A technological improvement, the pointed arch, combined with the use of the ribbed vault, enabled the medieval architect to free himself from these restrictions. This technique enabled the weight of each section of the roof to be distributed along masonry ribs and to be supported by pillars at the four corners, thus permitting the construction of thinner walls with large openings for windows and greater overall height of the buildings. (Beauvais, the highest of the Gothic cathedrals, measures about 155 feet from floor to the ceiling.) The addition of flying buttresses—placed as a prop high against the external walls— further facilitated the construction of buildings of greater height with even more

The Romanesque cathedral of St. Ambrose in Milan was built in the late eleventh to early twelfth centuries. The heavy walls and thick pillars work as supports in contrast to the much slimmer pillars and greater height (supported by flying buttresses) of the Gothic cathedrals. (Alinari/Scala)

window space. The result, finally, was the emergence of the great Gothic cathedral, with its high towers, lofty vaulted ceilings, and magnificent and numerous stained glass windows—"vaulted glass cages," as they have been called—soaring upward toward the heavens.

Since these buildings were the product of several generations of craftsmen (some cathedrals took centuries to complete), variation in style inevitably crept into the architecture. A church may have begun as a Romanesque building, but, with the development of the new Gothic style, subsequently evolved into a Gothic structure. As the Gothic style itself became more elaborate, even completed buildings became more ornate. Nevertheless, despite a mixture of styles, the Gothic cathedral—a few exaggerated cases excepted (the cathedrals of Milan and of Cologne for example)—always possessed a basic organic unity that made it immediately distinguishable from any other architectural type.

Painting, Sculpture, Stained Glass

Other fine arts—painting, sculpture, stained glassmaking—were mainly adjuncts to the construction of churches. The statues and carvings, for instance, designed to blend with the architecture of the building, were used to

Cathedral of Amiens, one of the greatest French Gothic churches. (Courtesy French Consulate)

decorate archways and spires or to fill in niches. Nor were wall decorations to be viewed apart from the building. Paintings on the surface of the walls and mosaics (consisting of small pieces of colored glass and stones set into plaster at various angles) were the only Western forms of wall decoration. And of course the magnificent creations of stained glass, with the sense of depth and mystery they evoked, had the primary function of serving as windows.

Medieval Western art—with the exception of Gothic sculpture—was not what we would call "realistic." There was little attempt to depict nature photographically. Art was semi-representational, essentially symbolic, attempting to portray the mystical quality of the divinity of Christ, the holiness of the saints, the dogmas of the Church. Medieval Madonnas, a common subject for artists, were very stylized; the infant Christ-child usually was portrayed with the face of a man, not that of a child, in order to stress the eternal wisdom of the Savior.

Stained glass windows exhibited the qualities of symbolism to a high degree. Using pieces of colored glass the artisans fitted them together with leaden framing to form a mosaic. The process by which Western craftsmen produced the remarkably translucent blues, reds, and yellows of these windows has unfortunately been lost, and we have not yet been able exactly to reproduce the quality of the colors.

Byzantine Influences

In style and technique Western medieval art (except Gothic sculpture and architecture) owed much to the Byzantine East. Most of the West, particularly Italy, up to at least the thirteenth century was an artistic province of Byzantium. We know of Greek mosaicists decorating the Western-style cathedrals built by the Normans in Sicily and of Byzantine workmen connected with the building of St. Mark's in Venice, itself a copy of the Byzantine Church of the Holy Apostles in Constantinople. There are fewer examples of Byzantine artists working in the North, but the style of the North, like that of Italy, often directly copied or was at least influenced by Byzantine works: for instance, the manuscript illumination of the Irish monks, the bronze doors of Charlemagne's palace chapel at Aachen, the art works produced in the Ottonian Renaissance, and certain works of art at Monte Cassino and Cluny. It has even recently been suggested that the Western craft of stained glass received its initial impetus from the work produced earlier by Byzantine window glaziers.* Whether this is true or not, Byzantium, of course unlike the West, did not exploit the full aesthetic potential of this type of art.

---

* The evidence is the broken pieces of stained glass from the Pantocrator Monastery in Constantinople. See D. Geanakoplos, *Interaction of the "Sibling" Byzantine and Western Cultures* (1976), p. 115.

These column statues at Gothic cathedral at Chartres are good examples of the development of Gothic sculpture. (Courtesy French Tourist Office)

But some believe that the greatest artistic achievement of the West, aside from stained glass windows, is the beautifully illuminated manuscript, laboriously copied and decorated by monkish hands. Certainly the best of these manuscripts, replete with brilliant color and elaborate design, are among the greatest masterpieces of world art.

Medieval Music

The most significant music to come down to us from the Western medieval period is the liturgical music of the Church, to which verses taken from the Scriptures were set. Perhaps inspired by the Byzantine chant, the Western Gregorian chant (or plain song) had its beginnings in the sixth century and may be connected with the reforms of Pope Gregory the Great. Originally "monodic" music, that is, music in which all voices sing in unison the same melodic line, plain song grew increasingly complex, gradually changing into a more ornate form. This growing complexity of composition demanded a means of notation less vague than plain song had used. Tradition has it that in the eleventh century the Italian monk Guido d'Arezzo invented modern notation. Actually his work (connected rather with "tablature") is the culmination of previous developments. At any rate, by his time names were given to the first six notes of the scale—*do, re, mi, fa, sol, la*—and, more important, a musical staff of four (later five) lines was developed. Still another invention in the medieval period was the system for indication of the duration of musical notes. After these three inventions, contrapuntal music began to develop. Two, three, even four antiphonal choirs would now by turn or simultaneously sing independent but harmonizing melodies. A favorite technique was to have one choir sing, and another respond. By the fourteenth and fifteenth centuries, however, the music had become so florid and complex as to be almost unintelligible to any but a trained musician. (Pope John XXII actually for a time forbade the complexities of this period's polyphony.)

Latin and Byzantine Hymns

Magnificent hymns were composed in the medieval period, such as the well-known *Dies Irae* and *Stabat Mater*. The theme of the former is the Last Judgment. Even the form and style of the hymn (consisting of a series of three-line stanzas) has a sonorous quality and majesty that inspire a feeling of fear and awe in the listener. How expressive are the lines,

> Oh, what trembling there shall be,
> When the world its judge shall see,
> Coming in dread majesty.

And by contrast, after this verse, how moving is the hope offered to the believer in the next line,

> Oh Jesus, on that day remember me!

The *Sabat Mater,* on the other hand, evokes feelings of compassion and mourning as it describes the very human emotions of the Virgin Mary on witnessing the tragic crucifixion of her son:

> Next the cross in tears unceasing,
> Worn by sorrow much increasing,
> Stood the Mother 'neath her Son.
> . . . .
> Hard the man his tears refraining,
> Watching Mary uncomplaining

> Bear a sorrow like to none.
> Hard the man that shares no sorrow
> With a Mother fain to borrow
> Every pang that writhes her Son.

Different in ethos from these Western masterpieces was the greatest Byzantine hymn, the *Akathistos Hymnos,* where the aim was not to evoke the human emotions of this world, but rather the more spiritualized, sublime emotion of the celestial world above.

> To thee, protectress, leader of my army, victory!
>
> I, thy city, from danger free, this song of thanks
> Inscribe to thee, Mother of God.
> Since thou hast an unconquerable power,
> Free me from all danger
> That I may sing to thee:
> Hail! Mother undefiled!
>
> . . . .
>
> Hail! by whom gladness will be enkindled;
> Hail! by whom the curse will be quenched,
> Hail! righting of the fallen Adam;
> Hail! ransom of Eve's teachers.
> Hail! height unscaled by human reasonings;
> Hail! depth inscrutable even to angel's eyes.
> Hail! for thou art the king's seat;
> Hail! for thou bearest him, who beareth all.
> Hail! thou star that makest the sun to shine;
> Hail! thou womb of God's incarnation.
> Hail! thou by whom all creation is renewed;
> Hail! thou through whom the Creator became a babe.
> Hail! Mother undefiled!

It should be noted that translation is much less satisfying for the Greek hymns than Western since most of the Byzantine technical effects used to produce the lofty effect of sublimeness are lost, for example, the internal rhythm of the lines, repetition of key phrases, chanting in special intonation, and the acrostic starting of each line with a consecutive letter of the Greek alphabet. One important difference between Western and Byzantine liturgical music is that the Latin developed harmony, while the Byzantine did not—its aim was to reproduce the "simplicity and purity of the eternal in heaven."

Our knowledge of medieval Western *secular* music up to the twelfth century is extremely scanty. Certainly from time immemorial ballads in the vernacular had been sung by peasant and noble alike. The great eighth-century Anglo-Saxon epic *Beowulf,* for example, was most likely meant to be sung. But it was

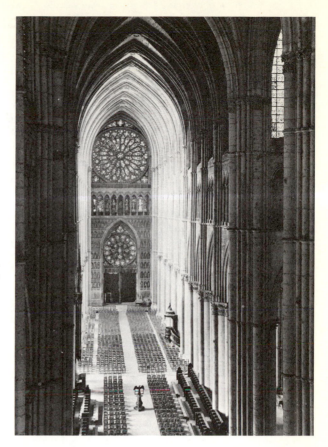

View of the nave interior of the Gothic cathedral at Reims. Compare with the picture of the interiors of the mosque at Cordova (p. 300) and the St. Sophia in Constantinople (p. 138). (Giraudon)

not until the time of the minstrels, the troubadors of the late eleventh and twelfth centuries, that composition of a good deal of truly secular music developed, such as songs by the Crusader King Richard the Lion-Hearted. The real advances in medieval Western music, however, were not to be made until later in the fourteenth century.

Dante and the "Medieval Synthesis"

Medieval Western civilization reached its height in the thirteenth century, which perhaps with a certain justification has been called "the greatest of centuries." Under Pope Innocent III and his immediate successors Western Europe became virtually the *unum corpus Christianorum* so often envisioned by the political theorists. In the person of St. Louis of France was realized the highest ideal of medieval kingship.

The greatest synthesis of medieval philosophy and theology was produced by St. Thomas Aquinas, who managed to reconcile the new, "scientific" ideas of Aristotle with Catholic dogma and beliefs. At this time also the great flowering of Gothic art and architecture occurred, which culminated in the magnificent cathedrals of France, reaching almost to heaven and so religiously inspiring as to be called "sermons in stone." Each achievement in its own way expressed some aspect of medieval life. But what perhaps best gathered everything together in one grand synthesis and reflected all aspects of the Western medieval mind and ethos, was a literary masterpiece that appeared at the beginning of the fourteenth century, the *Divine Comedy* by the Florentine poet Dante Alighieri (1265–1321).

Technically, the *Divine Comedy* advanced from a kind of pluralism to a unity of the entire universe in God. From another point of view, however, the work clearly expresses the dualistic outlook so important to medieval man—the view of this life on earth as essentially a preparation for the spiritual life of the hereafter. Specifically, the burden of the poem portrays the journey of a soul (Dante's) through the three realms of the afterlife: Hell, Purgatory, and finally Paradise, where the beatific vision of God, the ultimate end and meaning of life, is experienced.

In the *Divine Comedy* strains of medieval mysticism, Scholastic thought (particularly that of Aquinas), and classical learning are all blended together, serving to portray the entire range of the medieval "thought world." The actions of men, all their sins and virtues, are judged and their souls rewarded or punished accordingly. From the viewpoint of literature, too, the poem is a masterpiece, written in *terza rima,* rhyming three-line stanzas (symbolic of the Trinity), and possessing an architectonic form of astounding proportions. The work was the first, or one of the first, literary endeavors to appear in the Italian vernacular, and so greatly did its style influence subsequent writers that Dante has been hailed as the creator of modern literary Italian.

At the beginning of the poem, Dante is met at the gates of Hell by the Latin poet Vergil, who guides him through Hell. Significantly, Vergil and other virtuous pagans, including Aristotle, Plato, Cicero, Caesar, and even the Muslims Averroës and Saladin, are not relegated by Dante to eternal punishment; their souls, rather, reside in Limbo, a place of rest situated within the realm of Hell but not really part of it. Since they are non-Christian these pagans cannot hope to be united with God, but neither, in view of the nobility of their lives, are they deserving of everlasting torment. To Dante, as to other medieval intellectuals, the wisdom of the ancients possessed *some* of the truth but, lacking Christian revelation, their wisdom alone was insufficient to achieve salvation in Paradise.

Dante's Hell, composed of nine concentric circles, contains the souls of those who have sinned, ranging from the least important of sins down to the most grievous. In the ninth and lowest circle, frozen in a lake of ice, are the souls of traitors, headed by Lucifer himself, "the emperor of all the realms of woe." The three faces of Satan contain three ugly mouths with which Satin gnaws upon the three archsinners of all time—Brutus and Cassius, the murderers of Caesar, and the supreme traitor, Judas Iscariot, the betrayer of Christ. As he passes through Hell, Dante speaks to many people (some, like Paolo and Francesca, made famous by inclusion in the work), here tormented by punishment meted out in accordance with their sins. Dante's protest against ecclesiastical corruption is revealed when he sees Pope Nicholas III, the nepotist, thrust downward into a pit of fire. The sins represented—lust, sloth, theft, suicide, murder, treason —are, typical of Scholastic philosophy, conceived of in a hierarchical order.

In Purgatory Dante meets those souls whose sins are forgiven but for which they have not yet atoned. Here, unlike in Hell, though souls undergo punishment, they can look forward to eventual admission to Paradise. The expectation of the souls in Purgatory is to be contrasted with the famous, despairing motto placed over the entering gates of Hell, "Abandon hope all ye who enter here!"

Dante is conducted through Paradise by Beatrice, a young woman whom he had loved in real life but from a distance—a love that transforms and transcends, as in the medieval courtly love tradition. In Paradise Dante meets the souls of the great medieval saints, Benedict, Bernard, Albertus Magnus,

Fifteenth-century bronze bust of Dante Alighieri, whose Divine Comedy *expresses in many ways the essence of medieval Western thought.* (Alinari/Scala)

Aquinas. Here the planetary spheres are arranged in the geocentric system of the Greek Ptolemy, and the angelic spheres are ordered in the hierarchy set forth in the mystical writings of the Byzantine, Pseudo-Dionysius the Areopagite (believed, in the West, though wrongly, to have been an Athenian who was one of St. Paul's converts and the first bishop of Paris). The highest and outermost ring is the abode of God himself. Here Dante at last gains the mystical experience of a glimpse of the Divine, the Vision of God.

The whole journey is projected in the form of a grand allegory, representing, as the poet himself later wrote in a letter to a friend, the idea that "mankind, as by its merits and demerits, in the exercise of its free will, exposes itself to the rewards or punishments of justice." The entire universe is arranged hierarchically, ranging from the vilest evil in the pit of Hell through the more minor sins, then through Purgatory, and ultimately through the ranks of the blessed up to God Himself. Medieval life and thought in every aspect are reflected here—virtues and vices, Scholasticism, mysticism, superstition, literary and artistic form, classical learning—all within the massive framework of the medieval Ptolemaic system, which (by Latins, Byzantines, and Arabs alike) was thought to bind the entire universe together. The *Divine Comedy* was truly a summation of the Latin Middle Ages, and, above all, of salvation. At the same time, in its use of vernacular Italian (instead of Latin), its allusions to classical figures, and the unique appreciation of nature, the work also points ahead to the emerging world of the Italian Renaissance.

FOR FURTHER READING

Adams, Henry, *Mont Saint-Michel and Chartres** (1963). Popular account of Western religious thought and architecture in the early twelfth century.

Baldwin, M. W., *The Medieval Church** (1973). A good brief treatment.

Copleston, F. C., *Medieval Philosophy** (1961). Sound treatment.

Crombie, A. C., *Medieval and Early Modern Science**, 2 vols., 2nd rev. ed. (1959; 1961). A handy, praiseworthy work.

Dante, *Divine Comedy,* ed. L. G. White (1948). One of the best English translations of this masterwork; in blank verse.

Evans, J., *Monastic Life at Cluny* (1968). Interesting treatment of the eleventh-century religious revival.

Gilson, E., *Heloise and Abelard** (1960). One of the world's famous romances, now possibly damaged by a recent scholar's claim that Abelard's so-called *Historia Calamitarum* is a forgery.

* Asterisk indicates paperback edition available.

Gilson, E., *History of Christian Philosophy in the Middle Ages* (1955). Best work on the subject, focusing on the West, by the master in the field.

Grant, E., *Physical Sciences in the Middle Ages* (1970). Fascinating analysis.

Haskins, Charles, *The Renaissance of the 12th Century** (1927; 1957). A masterwork whose thesis almost revolutionized study of the Italian Renaissance.

Hughes, P., *A History of the Church*, vol. 2, rev. ed. (1949). History of the medieval church by a very objective, Catholic historian.

Knowles, D., *Religious Orders in England*, 3 vols. (1948–59). Authoritative treatment.

Kuttner, S. G., *Harmony from Dissonance: An Interpretation of Medieval Canon Law* (1960). Authoritative.

Leclercq, J., *The Love of Learning and the Desire for God* (1961). Penetrating analysis of monastic life.

Leff, G., *Medieval Thought* (1960). Brief, neat survey.

Lloyd, R., *Peter Abelard: The Orthodox Rebel*, 2nd ed. rev. (1947). Old but still informative.

McIlwain, C. H., *Growth of Political Thought in the West* (1932). One of the best works on the subject.

Noonan, J. T., *The Scholastic Analysis of Usury* (1957). Careful analysis.

Packard, S., *Europe and the Church Under Innocent III* * (1927). Brief survey. Old and "popular" but informative.

Sabatier, P. *The Life of St. Francis*, trans. L. S. Houghton (1930). A standard work of the life of many peoples' favorite saint.

Simpson, O. von, *The Gothic Cathedral* (1956). Useful study though a bit dated.

Southern, R. W., *The Making of the Middle Ages** (1953). A fine work of synthesis and interpretation.

Steenberghen, F. van, *Aristotle in the West* (1955). The reception of Aristotle.

Taylor, H. O., *The Mediaeval Mind*, 4th ed., 2 vols. (1959). A celebrated work emphasizing not only the thought but the emotions of Western medieval figures.

Tellenbach, G., *Church, State, and Christian Society at the Time of the Investiture Contest* (1970). Scholarly and readable on aspects of Western society.

Ullmann, W., *The Growth of Papal Government in the Middle Ages*, 2nd ed. (1970). A standard work in the field, if controversial on some points of interpretation.

Waddell, H., *The Wandering Scholars*, 7th ed. (1968). The best work in the field of medieval Latin lyric poetry. Slightly dated.

Workman, H. B., *Evolution of the Monastic Ideal* * (1913; 1962). A fine synthesis tracing the development of the monastic ideal from withdrawal of the monk from the world to service within the community.

Wolf, M. de, *Philosophy and Civilization in the Middle Ages** (1922). A very readable, scholarly study integrating philosophy and general culture. Brief.

By the mid-thirteenth century Western society had developed three distinct classes—the feudal aristocracy (including the high clergy), the peasants, both living on or deriving income from the land, and, now increasingly important, the middle class of the towns, for whom money was the most essential commodity. While religion continued to play a pervasive role in everyday life, there began at the same time to emerge, if only slowly, a more worldly side to the culture. This secular tendency, to be sure, had always existed in some degree, but as segments of society became more urbanized and complex, secularity took a more pronounced form.

Medieval men, though basically religious, were probably even less inhibited than we are today, and probably gave way more easily to the demands of their

CHAPTER 11

Medieval Lay Society

"bodily appetites." And in the attempts of the Church and secular authorities to restrain man's aggressive and often lusty nature, as well as to provide ideals to strive for, certain modes or rules of conduct developed.

Life of the Western Noble: Chivalry

Chivalry is the term for the way of life of the feudal nobility. The word derives from the Latin *caballus,* horse—an apt expression since the noble knight was a mounted warrior. The product of a long development, chivalry by the late thirteenth century had become crystallized into a knightly or aristocratic code of conduct prescribing elaborate ceremonies and formal observance of a set of ideals. This knightly ethic grew increasingly fixed as the nobility became more and more class conscious. As the kings began to extend their political authority, as the liquid capital of the merchants became more prized, and as rulers began instead to rely on mercenaries, the noble class tended to become less significant politically, economically, and militarily. And so, aware of the challenge to its long-standing supremacy, the nobility now closed ranks in the aim of preserving its social prestige and aristocratic privileges, especially against the inroads of the upstart merchants. By emphasis on observance of the chivalric code and way of life the nobility thought it could best emphasize and preserve its social status, prestige, and indeed its very identity as a distinct and unique class. Chivalry may be considered from three points of view: 1) *feudal chivalry,* which stressed the virtues of a warrior; 2) *religious chivalry,* which emphasized the duty of a knight to the Church and to his fellow man; and 3) *courtly chivalry,* which accentuated the more romantic, genteel aspects of knightly conduct.

Feudal Chivalry

The first of these types, feudal chivalry, was certainly the oldest. It stressed the warlike qualities of a knight. A good knight was above all to exhibit prowess, the courage and ability to best others in knightly combat. A *prud'homme* (in effect, one brave and proud) should also be a loyal knight. This meant primarily allegiance to his immediate lord, but also implied loyalty to his fellow knights, to the Church, or in the case of courtly chivalry, to his chosen lady. "Largesse," lavish giving, sometimes to the point of ruinous generosity, was also considered the mark of a true knight. As loyalty to class developed, courtesy toward other knights became still another virtue. A courteous knight did not attack a wounded man, kept his word in tournaments, and if captured on the battlefield and held for ransom, was, simply on the strength of his word (*parole*), allowed to go free in order to raise the money. Finally, all knights aimed to cover themselves with glory, to be publicly honored as brave, true, and mighty warriors.

Western knights are shown jousting in this fourteenth-century ivory. Jousting in tournaments was a favorite pastime of the upper classes in the High and Later Middle Ages. (The Walters Art Gallery, Baltimore, Maryland)

By the twelfth century, however, the feudal knight had less opportunity to put these knightly virtues into action. Private warfare had been reduced; therefore, though often prohibited by kings and the Church, the institution of the tournament developed, a festive occasion when mock battles were fought and knights pitted their skills against one another. At these tourneys the virtue of knightly courtesy was probably first emphasized and later extended even to the battlefield. During the Hundred Years' War, in accord with this knightly code, King John II of France returned himself to captivity when the ransom demanded by his captor, the English king, was not raised. Tournaments relieved the boredom of the life of the nobles now that they had less chance to exercise their vocation of fighting as a result of the use of mercenary troops. But the code of chivalric conduct retained such a hold on the nobility of Europe that tournaments were held far into the sixteenth century, long after the mounted knight had ceased to be of real significance in military terms.

Religious Chivalry

Not surprisingly, in view of the emphasis in society on religion, the Church came to exert an increasingly important influence on the chivalric ethic. It sought to mitigate the excessive violence among the nobility and at the same time to channel the activities of knighthood to its own purposes. This latter tendency (the roots of which may be found in the Peace of God, which the knights at first resisted), some scholars have called "religious chivalry." Knighthood, like the priesthood, was said to be an institution ordained by God, the knight being expected to come to the aid of the needy and unprotected and to wield his sword in defense of the Church. Even the ceremony of knighthood became a quasi-religious service. On the day before his dubbing, the knight fasted throughout the night; he kept the "vigil of arms" in the castle chapel, his sword and armor having been consecrated and placed on the altar, while the knight-to-be prayed over them. In the morning the young man was garbed in his armor, his golden spurs were put on, and finally, kneeling before his lord, he was dubbed a knight (i.e., struck on each shoulder with the flat of the sword blade). The knighting of a young man became an occasion of festivity, with tourneys and feasting lasting for days following the ceremony.

The religious ceremony aside, few knights seemed actually to have lived up to the precepts of religious chivalry. To be sure, individuals were strongly influenced, such as the Western feudal ruler par excellence, St. Louis of France. But religious chivalry (witness the knights of the Fourth Crusade) did not seem basically to alter the behavior of the knightly class. In a sense, the entire movement of the crusades may be considered motivated by ideals set forth by churchmen; nevertheless, at least through the twelfth century, more knights looked for damsels to distress than in distress and churches to raid than to aid!

Courtly Chivalry: Role of Noblewomen

The third type of chivalry, courtly chivalry, is closely bound to the role of the aristocratic noblewoman and her position in medieval society. In general the principal function of the noblewoman was the management of the household economy. Specific information on this activity is unfortunately scanty. From the eighth and ninth centuries onward, however, some Western "documents of practice" (leases, donations, inheritances, records, etc.) exist that offer clues on the place of the noblewoman in the household. Her husband, the lord of the manor, tended to matters of war and, in connection with his steward, looked after such aspects of his property as the care of herds and outlying lands. To the noble's wife, however, belonged the supervision of the household, including the care of clothing, spinning, weaving, brewing, the garden, and yard animals. Functions of this kind on the part of women were important for all classes, but especially for the wives of warriors and married clergy (before Pope Leo IX's prohibition of clerical marriage in 1049).

Legally and socially, women were considered inferior, though the influence of the church may have helped to protect them from undue physical violence at the hands of their husbands. At the same time, the church, recalling the story

An influential noble-woman of the Western High Middle Ages, Countess Matilda of Tuscany (seated). She is shown with Emperor Henry IV kneeling before her, beseeching her intercession (and that of the Abbot of Cluny, left) in his dispute with the Pope. (Vatican Library)

of Adam and Eve, looked upon women as the source of evil. In many areas, and at least up to 1230 in France, the noblewoman was completely subject to her husband's will, and, when she married, whatever property she possessed passed legally into his control, unless of course he cast her out. In that case he would have to restore her dowry and face the wrath of her relatives. Nevertheless, the noblewoman was the unquestioned mistress of the castle and as such was much more than a chattel, though certainly less than a matriarch.

From the mid-eleventh century onward the status of noblewomen seems gradually to have improved. This was owing, in part at least, to the greater mobility of the male population in the wake of the crusading movement and of other military campaigns—expeditions which could take husbands far away from home and on which they often perished. The wife, mother, or infrequently the daughter, was left to care for the family property. Male caretakers or "seneschals" to oversee the property were available, but the lords naturally tended to place more trust in their wives.

Thus the factors that aided in the long run to improve the status of noblewomen were not only the moral influence of the church and its canon law, but also the practical requirements of household management in an age of increasing absence of men on military expeditions and of an expanding economy (see

Chapters 6 and 9 on Western economic advances and the crusading expeditions). Both considerations not only helped to ameliorate the lot of women but
occasionally to bring them to a position of greater prominence. It goes without
saying that at all times certain individual women of unique gifts, status, great
beauty, or, above all, of strong personality (queens or abbesses of convents, or
female mystics, for example) could and did play a prominent role in political
and religious affairs, especially after about 1050. Among such personalities are
Queens Eleanor of Aquitaine and Blanche of Castile (the mother of St. Louis),
Countess Matilda of Tuscany, and the mystic, Catherine of Siena.

As might be expected, in the subsequent period of the Later Middle Ages
or Early Renaissance, especially in Italy, with the increasingly secular attitudes
pervading noble and merchant-class society, women became even more "eman-
cipated," particularly in their conduct and mores, than had been the case in all
of the preceding medieval centuries.

Courtly Love.   While the clergy tried to preach their ideas of knighthood to the
nobles, the ladies (of France, in particular) carried on a more effective campaign in behalf of *their* concept of the ideal knight. This third type of chivalry
was exemplified by what has been called the "code of courtly love." * The ladies
helped to stimulate the development of such a "code" through their propagan-
dists, the minstrels, who, traveling from castle to castle, entertained noble households with ballads of the deeds of brave knights and their romantic attachments
and love affairs.

The ideal of courtly love seems first to have been formulated in the eleventh
and twelfth centuries by the troubador poets of southern France, although some
scholars think the troubador ideas originated in the Arabic lyric poetry of Spain.
Others limit the Arabic influence on troubador poetry only to such technical
matters as meter and rhyme scheme. The main theme propagandized by the
troubadors was romantic love; the true motivation for an ideal knight should be
love for a lady (usually *not* one's own wife). For his "mistress" he should win
battles and tournaments, he should conduct himself as a gentleman, carrying
out her desires in all things. In southern France the emphasis (at least at first)
was on what we would call "platonic love," the knight expecting no sexual relationship with his lady. He was, so to speak, to love her from a distance. In
northern France, however, among the *trouvères,* as the court poets in that region were called, the mutuality of love was stressed, with the result that some
trouvères, such as the famous Chrétien de Troyes (twelfth century) came even
to condone adultery. The stories of the adulterous affairs of Sir Lancelot and
Queen Guinevere and of Tristan and Isolde are products of this tradition. This
ethic of courtly love, which glorified romantic passion, not only served to some

* The existence of a formal "code" of courtly love has recently been severely attacked.

A Latin knight and his lady in a garden—a visual representation of a favorite scene in the literature of Courtly Love. (Reproduced by permission of the British Library Board, Harley ms. 4431, f. 376)

degree to improve the status of noblewomen, but, more important, became so firmly rooted in the traditions of Western literature and life that its effects may still be seen in our emphasis on marriage for love as opposed to the medieval idea of a union for economic or political advantage.

Medieval chivalry of the twelfth and thirteenth centuries, then, was the result of a combination of three sets of ideals—the warrior, the Church, and "courtly love." To implement the requirements of the chivalric ideal, it is interesting to note that a higher standard of living soon became necessary, entailing refinements in castle living, table service of silver, expensive plate armor, luxurious clothing—all of which contributed by the fourteenth century to the economic depression of the nobility. On the defensive against economic ruin, facing the constant encroachments of royal authority, the challenge of the middle class, and the burgeoning cost of living, the noble class found as its only effective weapon its intransigent insistence on the preservation of what it considered the privilege of birthright. It was therefore through its devotion to the complex knightly ethic developed in the High Middle Ages that the nobility was long able to preserve at least its social prestige and, in some individual cases, even its economic well being.

Burghers

While the aristocracy was declining in importance, the status of the townsmen in the thirteenth century was rapidly rising. Economically the townsmen were becoming wealthy owing to the rapid increase of trade and manufacturing. Politically, too, the bourgeoisie became a force to be reckoned with; now for the first time they began to appear (though not regularly) at national assemblies called by the kings and were increasingly employed to staff the royal administration.

Indeed, for the first time in the medieval period, Western civilization began to take on some of the characteristic traits of the middle class. The pursuit of wealth and its advantages, the growing sophistication of town life, even a growing skepticism with regard to rewards in the afterlife—all of these traits were gradually transforming the medieval ethos—particularly in Italy, where the nobles of some areas were abandoning their estates to move into the towns. The number of educated laymen sharply increased: townsmen began to secure training in medicine, law, and accounting. The profit motive was more clearly and unashamedly acknowledged, thus preparing the way for changes in, and still later even the destruction of, the guild system.

This fifteenth-century market scene depicts the life of the Western urban middle class. (Cliché de Bibliothèque Nationale)

The example of luxurious townhouses possessed by rich merchants made the nobles wish to emulate them. For instance, rugs imported from the East first graced the homes of rich burghers; nobles then began to follow suit and replaced the straw covering their floors with handsome imported carpets.

On the other hand, some of the ideals of noble chivalry began to attract the burghers, at least those of northern Europe. For the wealthy merchant, to enhance his prestige, sought if at all possible to enter the ranks of the nobility. He might marry his daughter to an impoverished noble, the bride bringing her husband a lavish dowry, or buy the estate of a bankrupt noble, hoping thereby to gain a patent of nobility from the king, or enter the service of the king and gain what was later to be called the rank of *noblesse de robe*. Such practices were, of course, bitterly resisted by the old aristocracy, which was naturally contemptuous of these *nouveaux riches* tradesmen.

Peasants

For the peasantry, too, economic conditions improved during the twelfth and thirteenth centuries. By this time many serfs, especially in France, had been freed of the worst abuses of the manorial system and were not yet subjected to the new tyranny of the royal tax collector and the banker. Except in England in the thirteenth century, the number of serfs and the corresponding labor services due the lords of the manor diminished with increasing rapidity. Peasants could now save the money they earned from selling the surplus of their fields to the towns. By this time, therefore, many peasants were paying rent for their land instead of performing feudal services. Since prices for produce continued to rise, while the rents remained fixed, many peasants grew prosperous and were able to buy the land of their less fortunate peasant neighbors.

We have inadequate sources of information on peasant life for this period. Most contemporary accounts take peasants for granted, listing them as one of the essential classes in society, yet deeming them unworthy of further attention. The other classes, it is clear, disdained the peasant, the townsmen perhaps somewhat less than the clergy and the nobility. In general, however, the life of the peasant class probably changed less in the thirteenth century than that of the other two classes. Though the peasant might grumble at tithes and at the sight of a well-fed, lazy cleric, he still accepted the leadership of the Church. It should be emphasized, finally, that, though the life of the peasant was somewhat improved, it was still restricted by illiteracy and above all by lack of economic and political power.

Living Conditions

Housing

Western society was divided into three major classes, and each was distinguished by its manner of living. Not even the nobles' abodes would be pleasant for us today. Their castles (which did not become common until the thirteenth century) were dank and dark, with little ventilation. Windows consisted only of slits in the massive stone walls. Castles were cold in the winter; the only heat was provided by huge stone fireplaces. On the walls tapestries were hung as much to prevent drafts as for decoration. Floors were strewn with straw, which was changed only twice a year when the odor became too rank. In a small castle there was usually only one bed, a huge affair placed in the chamber of the lord, and shared by the lord, his wife, and sometimes even by the lord's mother. When guests came they were given the bed, but the lord still slept in the room, on the floor. Servants slept where they could, in corners or even on the stairs.

From the late thirteenth century onwards, it was usually the rich burghers in the towns who lived in the most comfortable homes. These often contained spacious glass windows to let in light. As noted earlier, imported carpets often covered the floors and luxurious tapestries decorated the walls. Interestingly enough, rubbish was often put underneath the flooring to serve as insulation. Life in the crowded cities was hazardous, however, because of the constant danger of fire.

For most of the Western peasants, despite certain economic gains, living conditions did not change substantially over the earlier centuries of the medieval period. A peasant's cottage usually consisted of only two rooms, one for the family and one for the animals. The house had a packed-dirt floor, and a hole in the thatched roof to let smoke escape from the fire. A wealthier peasant might (but often did not) have a fireplace, but danger of fire here too was always present.

Health Conditions

In the West during the Middle Ages cleanliness was not next to godliness. Personal hygiene and public sanitation left much to be desired. Baths were taken infrequently, sometimes only once or twice a year. The middle class tended to be somewhat more fastidious and the peasantry naturally less so. Bathtubs and latrines in castles were flushed out with water, but the sewage was washed into leaky cisterns or more often into the moat—which did nothing to improve sanitary conditions. In the towns, chamber pots were emptied out of the upper-storey windows into the street below, often accompanied by the per-

This picture of the burial of plague victims at Tournai shows the hasty burial by the people, since professional gravediggers were unable to handle all of the work. The picture also probably reflects the people's extreme fear of contamination. (Bibliothèque Royale Albert 1er, Bruxelles)

functory warning "look out below." (Such dangers may be behind the long-established modern custom of a gentleman walking on the outside near the street when promenading with a woman.)

Plague: The Black Death

In view of such conditions of filth and carelessness, epidemics often swept through the countryside and could easily decimate the crowded towns. The most devastating epidemic of which we have record was the so-called "Black Death," a form of bubonic plague carried by rat fleas. Originating in the Orient, it was brought to Constantinople and from there in 1348 transmitted to the West, probably on Genoese ships.

The Black Death, unprecedentedly destructive (though such a general plague or "pandemic" had apparently occurred in the West six centuries before, in 747 to 750), did not strike once but repeatedly throughout the late fourteenth century. Demographers have in fact established that virtually every year after 1348 for over a half century this plague raged in one area or another of Europe. The effects of this European (possibly even world) pestilence had serious psychological as well as economic and social ramifications for Western Europe.

Besides the horrors of disease—in some towns such as Avignon over half the population died—and the uncleanliness, the main effect was the huge decimation of the population and the attendant repercussions. It is now estimated that as much as one-fourth of the inhabitants of Western and also of Eastern Europe died. The many deaths not only in the towns but especially in the rural areas meant a great diminution in the food supply, thus leaving fewer laborers to work in the fields. On the other hand, as the most recent scholarship has shown, the population so decreased that those who survived were able to eat a lot better. Nevertheless, broadly speaking, the principal economic consequence was a prolonged depression throughout most of Western Europe—an economic crisis that became especially severe in the later fourteenth century.

Medical Practice: Byzantine and Islamic Influences

Western medical practice, at least up to the thirteenth century, was quite primitive. A common method of treatment for practically every ailment was bleeding by leeches or at times by the use of the knife. On rare occasions even a warrior weak from loss of blood as a result of a wound suffered in battle might be bled further in order to restore him to health! In one area the West was in a sense rather advanced: sometimes a disease was diagnosed by means of urinalysis. One story related that when a noble, as a joke, presented his doctor with the urine of a pregnant woman for examination, the physician responded: "Either milord has substituted another's specimen or he is about to be brought to bed with child." On the other hand, magic charms and curious drugs were prescribed—for example, the drinking of urine for its supposedly beneficial qualities.

Western medical diagnosis in particular began to improve from the twelfth century on, when the medical knowledge of the ancient Greeks began to seep in from the Arabs of Spain and Sicily and was used in such famous medical schools as Salerno and Montpellier. From the Greeks (sometimes by way of Byzantium) the West learned cleanliness, cauterization of wounds, and diagnostic techniques; from the Arabs, pharmacology and optics. Indeed the works of the ancient Greeks Hippocrates, Galen, and Dioscorides, as well as of the Arab Avicenna, were still used as medical textbooks in the West up to the fifteenth century and later.

Amusements

What did Western medieval people of the twelfth and thirteenth centuries do for amusement? Their sports and games tended to be of a rather rough nature. The nobility, besides tournaments, enjoyed hunting, hawking, and gambling. Bear baiting and bull baiting (teasing the animals until they became enraged) were favorites of all classes. The English bulldog, with its power-ful undershot jaw, was developed especially for bull baiting; the jaw enabled the dog to bite down on the bull's neck and hold on tightly. A rough-and-tumble form of soccer was also very popular, especially among the lower classes. In England this rough sport became so widespread that in the thirteenth century Edward I outlawed the game lest it maim too many of his potential soldiers. Swimming was relatively rare. Skating was not uncommon but was not enthu-siastically practiced.

More refined entertainment took place at the feasts of the great nobles: min-strels sang, jugglers and perhaps mimes performed, and usually gentlemen and ladies of the court indulged in rather elaborate, formal dancing. At these noble feasts, which could last for hours, a variety of foods was served: different kinds of meats, vegetables, and pastries, all elaborately prepared. Swans, for example, were cooked, then served with the feathers replaced. Meat, roasted over the open hearth, was preferred charred on the outside and almost raw at the center. Since preservation of meat was difficult, the spices of the East (especially pepper) were sought after as much to hide the taste of the spoiled meat as to preserve it. At table people were seated in pairs: a lady and lord usually shared a cup and plate. Spoons were provided, but forks, though known, were not yet common. (Forks were introduced to Venice from Byzantium in the eleventh century.) Each diner provided his own knife. At the elbow of each couple stood a page-boy to refill their cup and serve the different courses.

Peasants were not permitted to hunt, for forests were the exclusive preserves of the lord. Any serf caught "poaching" was subject to severe penalties—maim-ing or even death. Fishing was done from necessity (for survival and fast days, that is), not for enjoyment. On feast days the peasants would gather in the churchyard to enjoy various forms of entertainment. Feats of strength such as wrestling matches, tugs of war, and quarterstaff fighting were common on such occasions. Feast days took on a carnival atmosphere with much eating, drinking, and rustic dancing. Sometimes (especially in the towns) rather crude plays were performed, either inside or outside the church. They usually had a religious set-ting, but as time went on some of these became so coarse that the Church finally refused to allow their performance on church property—a prohibition that some scholars believe contributed to the emergence of secular drama.

Religion played a far more intimate and direct role in medieval life than in ours. But this close adherence to religion often led to some disrespect. There were parodies of religious services, such as the Feast of the Ass, which was cele-brated in a few towns of northern France and supposedly instituted in honor of the donkey that carried the Virgin Mary to Bethlehem. The lower clergy of the cathedral took over the services, performing a mock mass, burning shoes in the censer, and at the very moment of the consecration of the Host, braying three times to commemorate the "holy" donkey. At the Feast of Fools (this was condemned in England by Bishop Robert Grosseteste of Lincoln in the thirteenth century and later in the fifteenth by the Council of Constance), a prostitute was led into the cathedral and seated on the bishop's throne, and a mock mass was then held. But the highlight of the day was the choosing of the mock king by the lower classes. He was usually the town idiot, who on that day was feted with exaggerated, false deference, the real purpose being to poke fun not only at him but at higher authority.

The Church and civil officials generally looked the other way when such festivals occurred, as long as no real destruction of property took place. These mock ceremonies were generally viewed as harmless, as a means for the lower classes to let off steam without endangering the vested interests.

Minority Groups

Having discussed the constituent parts of Western lay society and the conditions of life for each class, it would be useful to concentrate for a time on minority groups, especially on the Jews, who, though living in the midst of Western society, were never really "accepted." Because of the Jews' rejection of the established faith they were forced to remain on the fringes of Christian society. Of all medieval minority groups the Jews were the most conspicuous, and the changing treatment accorded them in Western as well as in Arabic and Byzantine societies therefore deserves particular attention.*

The Jews

The exclusion of the Jews from the mainstream of the medieval Western social structure was owed not only to their adamant refusal to accept conversion but also to the common Christian belief that they were responsible for Christ's death. As non-Christians (though *not* heretics) they were considered unassimilable. This view seems understandable, at least from the legal viewpoint: since medieval law and procedure depended on Christian oaths and ordeals, all normal law was therefore inapplicable to Jews.

Jewish communities had been established in many areas of eastern and western Europe since Roman times. After the Germanic invasions of the fourth to sixth centuries, with their accompanying dislocation and unrest, a forced con-

---

* The usual one or two pages allotted by medieval textbooks to the Jews is another reason for the ampler treatment provided here.

version of Jews to Christianity became common, extending from Constantinople and reaching Arian Visigothic Spain. In contrast, the Arab conquerors of North Africa and Spain allowed the Jewish communities to maintain their religious convictions.

Jews in Islamic Spain. The Moors of Spain in the Umayyad dynasty exhibited a remarkable degree of toleration, subjecting the Jews to comparatively minor restrictive measures (payment of a special tax, exclusion from public office, and the like). The linguistic and financial talents of the Jews nevertheless carried some of them to high places in the Arab administration and even secured them entrance to the learned professions. Indeed many Jews became socially (though not religiously) almost assimilated to Arab culture. One example is the twelfth century Jewish physician, philosopher, and Talmudic scholar of Cordova, Moses Maimonides, who, in the manner of the earlier Arab philosopher Averroës and of the eighth century Byzantine John of Damascus before him— not to forget the later Thomas Aquinas in the West—achieved a synthesis between his faith—Judaism—and Aristotelian philosophy.

The relatively tolerant Moorish attitude toward the Jews was, with certain exceptions, continued by the expanding Christian kingdoms of Spain during the tenth and early eleventh centuries. In the twelfth and thirteenth centuries in particular, Spanish Jews translated important Arab works for Christian rulers (especially King Alfonso X of Castile) and not infrequently collaborated with Latin scholars who came to Spain seeking ancient Greek and Arabic knowledge. (Adelard of Bath and Gerard of Cremona were two of the most important Western scholars involved in the translation of ancient Greek writings from Arabic to Latin.) In this activity, which centered in Toledo in Spanish Castile, the Jews acted primarily as "middle men," translating the Arabic versions into "Romance," * while the Latins translated the versions made by the Jews into Latin. As already noted (in Chapter 5), this activity of translation was part of a very important phase in the interaction of the Arabic and Western Christian cultures. More significant, it constituted a critical advance in the broadening of, and arrival to maturity of, medieval Western culture.

During this same period in Spain and also in other areas of the West, the Jews, besides being active in the learned professions of medicine and astronomy, achieved importance in mercantile and financial affairs. A basic reason for their success in finance and commerce was their exclusion from the developing Western social and economic system with its rigidly compartmentalized social order, a circumstance that pushed the Jews away from the soil and into commerce. Forbidden to engage in most occupations, Jews could do little else but engage in

* Referring to a form of early Spanish based on medieval Latin.

business. Recent scholarship has tended to show that the stock image of the rapacious Jewish moneylender is in general inaccurate, and that he did not as a rule charge excessive rates, considering the degree of risk involved.

Jews in the Early Crusades and Later.   A new phase in the treatment of Jews in the West was marked by the launching of the First Crusade in 1095. The former, generally tolerant attitude to Jews now gave way to a general persecution which began essentially as a consequence of a sudden awareness on the part of Christian Western Europe of a sense of Christian "community," and of a resulting antipathy (almost xenophobia) not only toward Jews but all outsiders (including Byzantines and Muslims). At this time the first in a long series of massacres of the Jewish population began in the Rhineland (where Jewish communities had existed since Carolingian times), in the wake of the dramatic Crusader attempt to free the Holy Land from Islam—a venture which all too readily reminded Christian Europe of what they believed to be the Jewish role in Christ's Passion.

After the early Crusades, the next wave of persecution occurred following the convocation of the Fourth Lateran Council in Rome in 1215 (see Chapter 10). A policy was enunciated against heresy, aimed especially at the Albigensian heretics of southern France. Jews, as non-Christians, were in the popular mind now associated with such heretics and thus became a special target for persecution. In order to exercise control over the Jews and their activities, the Church began to impose restrictions upon them (such as special dress, prohibition of eating with Christians and of intermarriage). These regulations against Jews did not, of course, appear everywhere at once nor were they consistently enforced. (In both Muslim and Christian Spain, for example, the earlier attitude of toleration toward Jews continued to prevail.) Yet the screws were gradually tightened throughout most of the West and persecutions were no longer a rarity. Persecution broke out particularly in time of adversity—war, starvation, or plague. And fiery Western preachers, alarmed especially by the Albigensian movement, increasingly inveighed against heresy. As a result, attempts were often made by religious authorities to censor or confiscate Jewish books, or to force Jews to attend religious disputations held with Christian theologians in the aim of demonstrating the "falsity" of Jewish beliefs.

From the early Crusades on persecutions became more frequent and severe and were renewed on the slightest pretext. The most incriminating charges against the Jews were ritual murder and desecration of the host. Ignorant Christians believed that at Passover Jews killed a Christian child whose blood would be used in the Jewish ritual performance, or that Jews desecrated the Christian communion cup. Meantime, the emergence of a class of north Italian merchants (the Lombards) in northern Europe made the formerly dominant Jewish position in finance unneeded, thus leading them to the baser calling of pawnbroking.

The growth of Christian commerce and the development of urban centers throughout Western Europe rendered the wealthy Jews increasingly subject to suspicion. The result, finally, was their complete expulsion from various areas of the West. This was often connected in each country with the growth of incipient "nationalism," in particular with royal attempts to unite all the elements of a nation's population. The Jews, of course, as an unassimilable element, were prime candidates for attack.

In England, the last country of the West to receive Jewish immigration (after the Norman conquest in 1066), the lot of the Jews had become tolerable, though they were accorded a markedly second-class status. There, too, however, this policy of relative tolerance, marked by an occasional outbreak of persecution, gave way to the general hostility generated by the First Crusade. Later, in 1290, England, under the strong king Edward I, became the first country to expel the Jews completely. Their expulsion from France followed shortly thereafter, in 1306, under another forceful ruler, Philip IV. Germany, perhaps partly because of its lack of political unity and the variety of policies among its many regions, saw no general expulsion of the Jews, even though it possessed a substantial Jewish community. Yet it was in Germany that the Jews in the fourteenth century began to undergo a severe persecution.

A climax was reached with the outbreak of the Black Death in 1348–1349, when the ravages suffered by Western Europe made the population of certain countries (France in particular) accuse the Jews of committing crimes against society, such as poisoning wells used by the community at large. Some Jews now with great difficulty emigrated to Italy, where they were usually treated with greater moderation. (The Popes in particular generally viewed the Jews with tolerance in the medieval period, in part perhaps because of a need for Jewish services in banking.) Later, large numbers of Jews emigrated to the vast areas of Poland, invited there in 1334 by King Casimir.

Even in Spain, where for centuries Jews had been treated without harshness, the growth of "national" and religious feeling brought a wave of persecution. Beginning in 1391, this culminated in several massacres of Jews. Many Jews now took the extreme step of seeking to escape persecution by undergoing Christian baptism. But such conversions were in many cases superficial, as the religious and civil authorities clearly realized. Later, in the late fifteenth century, under Ferdinand and Isabella, the ecclesiastical machinery of the Spanish Inquisition was introduced to ferret out false Jewish converts to Christianity (called *Marranos*).

The Christian conquest of all Spain after the fall of Moorish Granada in 1492 brought banishment for all Spanish Jews. Many refugees managed to make their way to Islamic areas of the eastern Mediterranean, to Constantinople, or to other former Byzantine areas today constituting part of Turkey, to which the Sultans encouraged them to come. Under the Sublime Porte many Jews attained high office (notably a certain Joseph Nasi, who for his services was created Duke of the Greek island of Naxos).

During the fourteenth and fifteenth centuries anti-Jewish sentiment in Western Europe decreased, but sporadic outbreaks continued. A tragic phase in the life of the Jewish community of western Europe began with the Catholic Church's reaction to the Protestant Reformation. Hitherto reasonably tolerant to Jews, the Catholic Church now prescribed ghettos for them to live in, decreed regulations for the wearing of special badges by Jews, and sponsored hortatory sermons urging the Jews to convert. But the Papacy, in contrast to European popular opinion, never accepted the charges of ritual murder and desecration of the host. Nonetheless the end result of all these developments was the exclusion of Jews from all honorable professions.

In sum, the treatment accorded the Jew in medieval western Europe was the tragic consequence of two basic circumstances—the necessity felt by the authorities of church and state for keeping Jews isolated from what was really a closed Christian society (closed that is to non-Catholic Christians) and the deep ignorance throughout most of the period on the part of Christian society in general of the beliefs of Judaism. Of significance also was the fact that the Jews, who in earlier years had not infrequently assumed good positions as merchants and bankers—professions necessary to the developing Christian economy but which on canonical grounds were forbidden to Christians—were later almost completely replaced by the rise of Christian merchants active in these same fields.

The ambiguous position of Jews in Western society as a group, tolerated on the one hand yet often violently persecuted on the other, was almost inevitable. Unlike heretics such as the Albigensians, who could expect death, and unlike the earlier pagans who were forcibly converted, the Jews were usually not killed. After all, the Jewish faith of the Old Testament was the direct precursor of the monotheistic Christian religion, and its sacred book was second in importance only to the New Testament itself.

Jews in Byzantium.   In Byzantium the treatment accorded Jews differed from the West mainly in degree. There too they were not considered to be an integral part of society and, to a lesser extent, were subject to governmental restrictions. The Byzantine rulers, as guardians of the Orthodox faith, considered it a special duty to arrange conferences between bishops and rabbis in the aim of converting the Jews. The Islamic religion, in contrast to Judaism, was viewed by Byzantine theologians (at least at the beginning) as a Christian "heresy." This attitude toward Islam was first expressed by John of Damascus who knew Arabic and worked in Damascus under the Abassid Caliph (see Chapter 5). John in the eighth century wrote the first important Christian treatise against Islam, using the original text of the Koran.

After the seventh century, the Jews, though allowed to work in Constantinople, had to live in their own quarter (the "Braka"). Yet the Jews, even if isolated by imperial command, were never faced in Byzantium by the violent, sometimes well-organized persecutions of the Latin West. Nor did Byzantium have the excuse of "usury" with which to persecute the Jews, since moneylending was a recognized function of the guild of Byzantine bankers and moneylenders. Yet, theoretically, if not culturally, the Orthodox Church, even more than the Western, condemned any liturgical practices (use of the *azyma,* unleavened bread in the eucharist for example) that might reflect Judaic practices.

Heretics

In the West after the end of the Arian controversy in Spain in the sixth century, very little persecution of heresy occurred owing, in part at least, to the lack of any really definitive ecclesiastical pronouncements on newly arising theological questions. The pontificate of Innocent III, and in particular the Fourth Lateran Council of 1215 was the watershed, for it first clearly provided dogmatic definitions so that the more recent heretical beliefs could more easily be uncovered and uprooted. Before that, as we have seen in Chapter 10, the Waldensians had appeared, but persecution of them became systematic now only in the thirteenth century. The heresy most persecuted in the Western medieval epoch—Pope Innocent III even proclaimed a crusade to extirpate it—was Albigensianism of southern France. (Its roots, it may be recalled, were to be found in the Byzantine East.) To combat the surprisingly great strength of the Albigensian movement the Papacy created the instrument of the ecclesiastical Inquisition which juridically established clear-cut procedures for the definition and prosecution of heresy.

In addition to the Waldensian and Albigensian heretics, there were other more minor heretical figures and groups such as Arnaldo of Brescia, or the Humiliati, "poor people," of northern Italy and southern France who sought primarily a feeling of more immediacy with God. Although groups such as the Humiliati diverged from Catholicism only in the sense of insisting on a much stricter adherence to Christian ideals by both Christian clergy and laity, they were sooner or later rejected by the Church as heretics and as a result alienated not only from the Church but also from Christian society. It may accurately be said, then, that heretics and Jews were the two largest "minority groups" excluded from the mainstream of the Christian community.

Social "Deviance"

Still other groups, whose beliefs or practices conflicted directly with the moral teachings of the Church, were explicitly condemned by both religious and secular authorities. Such were those who engaged in or committed acts of homosexuality, rape, or prostitution. Bastardy was of course a phenomenon apart from these.

Homosexual practices, the sin of "unnatural lust" between men, were emphatically condemned by St. Paul and many Christian Fathers, Latin as well as Greek.* But the Roman law code of the sixth century Byzantine Emperor Justinian specified new and stringent measures against homosexuals (castration, for example, or, as the historian Procopius indicates, exile). The severity of the penalties in Justinian's code may have been as much due to the belief that homosexual practices would endanger the state by provoking God's vengeance (recall the example of the Old Testament) in the form of famine, plague, or earthquake, as to the Church's view of the immoral nature of the act. Justinian, nonetheless, exhorted homosexuals first to penitence and then, only when the law was spurned, were harsh penalties to be imposed. Through his famous code, then, Justinian played an important part in determining the Byzantine attitude to homosexuality. And, with the beginning of the reception of Roman law in the West in the late eleventh century (earlier the Theodosian code had influenced certain Germanic codes), its attitude had some effect on the West as well.

The actual incidence of homosexuality, especially in the West, is of course another matter, extremely difficult to estimate since we hear about it almost exclusively from such sources as the legal codes of Germanic peoples, records of the Inquisition, and most emphatically of all, from certain anti-monastic or anti-papal tracts attacking the morals of monks or clerics. Evidence of the practice also remains in sermons of religious reformers or fanatics, for example of the fourteenth century Waldensians, the Spiritual Franciscans, and others.

Perhaps the most notable tract against homosexuality in the entire medieval period, West or East, was written by the eleventh century Italian monk, Peter Damian, whose *Liber Gommorhianum* reflects his alarm at the spread of this unnatural vice among clergy and monks. Especially horrifying to him was the incidence of such acts between a monastic "spiritual" father and his "spiritual" son.

A supposed marked increase in homosexuality in late eleventh century England is often attributed to the Norman invasion. But this view has been shown to be exaggerated and based primarily (if not almost solely) on the conduct of William the Conqueror's homosexual son, William Rufus, whom all the contemporary chroniclers castigate for his "unnatural lust." But apparently few of the rank and file of the English clergy and monks of the time were involved or affected. Another view is sometimes adduced that an eleventh-century Church Council in Paris condemned Arabic paraphrases from Aristotle's works on the

---

* Lesbianism, or "unnatural lust" between females, has left very few traces in the medieval sources and I therefore shall not discuss it here.

grounds that they reflected too strongly his teacher Plato's approval of homosexual love. This view has recently also been shown to be ill founded.

A more pragmatic modern view on medieval sexual mores holds that the intense opprobrium attached to homosexual acts committed in the Middle Ages by males was, in considerable part, owing to the medieval view (based directly on Old Testament belief) that male semen was a precious fluid that should not be wasted.

In view of the violence of the age *rape* was not uncommon in the medieval West, though stringent penalties were usually imposed. A noble, so reads an English ordinance, "who covers a maid without her thanks," was subject to a very heavy fine. Adultery on the part of a nobleman was, however, a generally accepted practice. *Prostitution,* though probably as widespread as today, was practiced less openly. The Church was often lenient toward "Magdalenes," for often, in order to atone for their profession, they gave lavish gifts to the Church. In turn, the Church sometimes provided homes for reformed or retired harlots. Interestingly, it was the bishop of Lincoln who, for the purpose of regulation, first licensed the brothels in London. Of course streaks of moral austerity did appear, but efforts to proscribe prostitution proved futile. King Louis IX, for

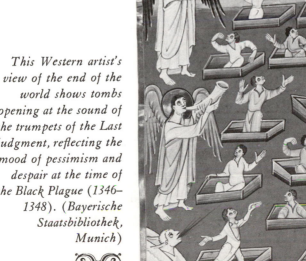

This Western artist's view of the end of the world shows tombs opening at the sound of the trumpets of the Last Judgment, reflecting the mood of pessimism and despair at the time of the Black Plague (1346– 1348). (Bayerische Staatsbibliothek, Munich)

example, outlawed the practice but only two years later the burghers of Paris, who complained that now it was unsafe for their daughters and wives to walk the streets, forced him to rescind the order.

Medieval people, though religious, were at the same time lusty, and the Church was able to do little other than try to mitigate their excesses. Illegitimacy was common, more among the nobility than any other class. *Bastardy* did not stigmatize one socially, though a bastard was subject to legal privations—he could not, for example, inherit property. Many heroes of famous literary romances were illegitimate (King Arthur, according to one tradition), and William the Conqueror was a bastard.

It seems then, that the moral conduct of medieval Western people (and Byzantines as well) was probably no better and probably no worse than that of today. Yet unlike today they *did* usually aspire to a strict and exemplary moral code based upon the precepts of Christian teaching (though it should be noted that not a few of their beliefs and practices were the result of sheer superstition). One must not, however, regard medieval people as hypocritical because of the discrepancy between their ideals and practices. Though they did not always live up to their professed standards, they were acutely aware of their sinfulness. They were not saints, but they realized this only too well and hoped fervently that God in His mercy would forgive their sins at the Final Judgment.

FOR FURTHER READING

Bailey, D. S., *Homosexuality and the Western Tradition* (1955). One of the few scholarly works on the subject.

Bridenthal, R. and C. Koonz, *Becoming Visible: Women in European History* (1977). Chapters 4–6 on medieval women.

Chenu, M. D., *Nature, Man and Society in the 12th Century,* trans. by L. Little (1968). Good introduction.

Duby, G., *The Early Growth of the European Economy . . . Seventh to Twelfth Century** (1978). Remarkably perceptive study.

Genicot, L. *Contours of the Middle Ages* (1967). Social factors in culture; important.

Herlihy, D., "Land, Family and Women, 701–1200," in M. Haskell, ed., *Women in Medieval Society* (1971). Excellent, unusual study.

Lea, H. C., *A History of the Inquisition of the Middle Ages,* 3 vols. (1955). Old, but still standard.

Leff, G., *Heresy in the Later Middle Ages* (1967). A standard work.

Painter, S., *French Chivalry** (1940; 1957). The best short treatment of the various types of chivalry, especially in France.

* Asterisk indicates paperback edition available.

Roth, C., and H. Levine, eds., *The Dark Age: Jews in Christian Europe 711–1096* (1966). Most exhaustive work on the period.

Roth, C., *A Short History of the Jewish People* (1948). Brief, informative.

Southern, R. W., *The Making of the Middle Ages** (1953). A very fine work of synthesis and interpretation.

Stuard, S. M., ed., *Women in Medieval Society* (1976). One of the best recent collections of studies by various authors.

Tellenbach, G., *Church, State, and Christian Society at the Time of the Investiture Contest* (1970). Scholarly and readable.

Turberville, A. S., *Medieval Heresy and the Inquisition* (1964). One of the standard works on the subject.

Prior to the First Crusade Byzantium was the leading power in Christendom. Its only rival for world hegemony had been the Arab Caliphate of Baghdad, which reached its height in the early ninth century and was now in the later medieval period in a state of collapse. About 1025 contemporaries everywhere would have concurred in recognizing Byzantium's preeminence; yet barely half a century later it was clear that the Byzantine state was in real trouble. And less than two hundred years later (1204), as we have seen (Chapter 9), it was overthrown by armies of Western crusaders. Although Byzantium regained its independence in 1261, its political and military history for the next three centuries was characterized by a protracted decline, ending with the Turkish conquest of Constantinople in 1453.

CHAPTER 12

Eastern Christendom: Byzantium and the Turks, the Slavs

The Byzantine Decline

Why great states such as Byzantium seem at one moment to be un-assailable and within only a few decades of the same century to have lost a good deal of their vitality is a basic question for the historian. In the late eleventh century Byzantium had to face two formidable new enemies: in the East the Seljuk Turks, who were penetrating Asia Minor; and in the West the Nor-mans, operating out of their base in the newly conquered Byzantine areas of southern Italy and Sicily. In the same year, 1071, both powers inflicted crushing defeats on Byzantine arms, the Turks at Manzikert and the Normans at Bari. But these reverses are not the whole answer to the question of the Byzantine decline. Internal decay of the central administration, that is, the decline of im-perial authority over the provincial areas, had begun even before these military disasters and had resulted in conflict between the military aristocracy of Asia Minor and the civil bureaucracy of the capital—a conflict that reflected basic economic and social disorders. These internal factors help to explain what ap-pears to be the sudden decline of Byzantine strength in the mid-eleventh century and, to a great extent, the complete collapse, in 1204, of the Byzantine Empire.

Although at first glance the Byzantine emperor seems always to have exer-cised absolute power, it cannot be denied that internally, from the mid-eleventh century on, this power in certain respects was becoming circumscribed. Local magnates, especially those of Asia Minor, waxed more and more powerful as a result of the disorders attendant on the continual invasions from the East. At the same time the peasant class was falling increasingly under these lords' authority, sometimes voluntarily in order to escape the crushing burden of state taxation by handing over their lands in exchange for the lord's protection. More often, the lords simply sequestered the lands of peasants unable to pay their debts. The result of this phenomenon, which in some blocks of territory substi-tuted the jurisdiction of the local magnates for that of state authority, was the emergence of a servile peasantry and a class of quasi-feudal landlords. The pro-cess continued until the late thirteenth century when, during the reign of Michael Palaeologus, certain lands (though relatively few compared to those of the feudal West) were declared *legally* to fall under the hereditary authority of the great lords. This meant that to all intents and purposes the imperial author-ity was now unable to enter these territories in order to exercise the duties of the state (collect taxes, dispense justice, etc.). The result was that the centralized authority of the Byzantine state itself was weakened.

These forces of internal weakness did not of course go unnoticed by the emperors, a few of whom, like Basil II and Nicephorus Phocas, enacted strin-gent laws to limit the growing power of the great landlords. But these measures were mainly unsuccessful, and the Latin invasions of Byzantine territory during the first three crusades rendered their task even more difficult. The *coup de grâce* for Byzantine imperial authority came in the Fourth Crusade of 1204 when the empire itself was destroyed and replaced by the so-called Latin Empire of Constantinople.

Byzantium and Sicily

After the half-century occupation of Constantinople by the Latins the Byzantine Empire was in 1261 re-established by Emperor Michael VIII Palaeologus (1261–1282). But his restoration of Greek rule did not end the Western threat to the existence of Byzantium. Indeed, in the face of the dangers confronting him from all sides it is a tribute to Michael's diplomatic skill that he was able to thwart what was to be the last and greatest Latin attempt to reconquer Byzantium. In the process of countering this Western aggression, however, Michael, by an irony of history, almost ruined the empire.

The destruction of Hohenstaufen power in southern Italy and Sicily by the papal champion Charles of Anjou, the brother of Louis IX, only resulted in Charles falling heir to the traditional ambitions of the Sicilian Normans to take Constantinople. Shrewd and energetic, Charles set out to build up a vast coalition of forces against Michael, ultimately winning to his side almost all the Balkan rulers—the Serbs, Bulgars, various Greek renegades, the Latin princes of Greece—even Venice with its powerful fleet. (Venice was anxious to regain its old possessions in the Greek areas, especially the trading concessions lost to the rival Genoese when Michael retook Constantinople.) Only the Popes remained to be won over to the Angevin cause.

For fifteen years, from 1266 to 1281, Michael, through the exercise of consummate diplomacy, was able to prevent the implementation of Charles's designs. Realizing that only the Pope, Western Christendom's most powerful figure and the feudal overlord of Sicily, was in a position to block the Eastern ambitions of Charles, Michael dangled before the Papacy the promise of ecclesiastical union with Rome. But the price was high: subordination of the Greek Church to Rome with all that it implied for the Greek population.

The protracted negotiations between the Popes and Michael culminated, in 1274, in the famous Second Council of Lyons, at which time the union was signed by the representatives of Michael and the Pope. For Michael the proclamation of union at Lyons was a veritable diplomatic triumph. It saved Constantinople from the danger of imminent Latin invasion and gained him the support not only of the Pope but, at least nominally, of a council as well.

In the eyes of most Byzantine people, on the other hand, the Council of Lyons was fraudulent. For the Greeks the validity of a general council depended on the presence of all five patriarchs—including the patriarch of Rome and the four of the Greek East.* The Greeks therefore believed that the union of Lyons, signed only by representatives of the emperor and the Pope, was not binding on the Greek Church and people. More fundamental for the Greeks than the legal technicality involved was their psychological, almost paranoid aversion to the Latins. The memories of the sack and looting of their capital in 1204, the destruction of their empire, and, not least, the enforced conversion of the Greek clergy and people to Roman Catholicism still rankled. Even those Greeks who were able to realize that Michael's policy of union was essentially one of expediency—that is, lip service to be paid to the Pope until the threat of Charles of Anjou had subsided—even these refused to have anything to do with the union. To most Greeks union with Rome was tantamount not only to loss of the independence of their church but even to the beginnings of a Latinization of their culture and religion. The rabble in Constantinople greeted Michael's envoy on his return from Lyons with the taunt, "By accepting the union you have become a Frank." The conflict became so heated that a virtual civil war broke out in Byzantium.

Michael's diplomatic maneuvering with the Papacy continued to stave off Charles's projected expedition. Finally, however, in 1281 Charles succeeded in securing the election of his own papal candidate, Martin IV. Martin almost at once declared Michael excommunicate and proclaimed Charles's expedition a holy crusade against the "Greek schismatics." On March 31, 1282, at almost the very moment Charles's powerful fleet was gathering in the southern Italian ports to begin the invasion of Byzantium, a revolt broke out in Sicily against his authority. In this rebellion of the "Sicilian Vespers" (it began at the hour of Vespers), Michael, together with the Hohenstaufen party in Sicily and King Peter III of Aragon, played a significant role. For years Michael had been pursuing a highly complex diplomatic policy of building alliances against Charles. He had subsidized the dissident Hohenstaufen elements in Sicily and also the king of Aragon who, through his wife, the daughter of Manfred, had claims to the Sicilian crown.

The conflict of the Sicilian Vespers effectively ended Charles's authority on the island of Sicily (but not in southern Italy) and, by occupying all of his attention, thwarted his plans for an assault on Constantinople. Michael had saved his empire, but in the process of warding off this Western peril and buying off potential enemies, he drained Byzantium of its financial resources and brought about internal religious dissension. Even more serious, while engrossed with the West he had to neglect the defense of his eastern borders against the now rapidly advancing Ottoman Turks. Through his policy of offering ecclesiastical union to Rome in return for political and military aid, he bequeathed to his successors

* With the Muslim conquest of three of the old Byzantine patriarchates in the East, those patriarchs or their vicars often resided in Constantinople.

a precedent that was to be used repeatedly in time of danger and thereby to cause serious division within the empire until the fall of Constantinople in 1453. If during Michael's reign the Greek East was still able to play an influential part in European diplomacy, it was largely due to the finesse of his statecraft. Under his generally less able successors Byzantium was no longer a world power. It became instead a Balkan state, but one which, recalling its great legacy, tenaciously clung to the trappings and traditions of empire.

The Rise of the Ottoman Turks

During the reign of Michael VIII Palaeologus a new group of Turks appeared in Asia Minor, the Ottomans. Gradually displacing their Seljuk predecessors, the Ottomans were ultimately to fulfill the old Muslim aspirations of taking Constantinople. The Seljuk Empire of Rum (Iconium) in Asia Minor had been seriously weakened by the attacks of the Western crusaders. It soon fell into smaller fragments, emirates situated mainly on the central and southeast coast of Asia Minor; the rest of the territory was divided among the Byzantines, who recovered a few of their former territories, the Armenians, and the heirs of the Western crusaders.

The entire political complexion of Anatolia became dislocated in 1243, when the Mongols, still another people from Central Asia, advanced westward, striking decisive blows at the Seljuk sultanate of Rum. The sultanate disintegrated. One of the small emirates that emerged belonged to a Turk named Othman, whose father had earlier been granted certain lands in fief by the Seljuk sultan.

From this insignificant beginning as ruler of a frontier march against the Byzantines and Mongols, the family of Othman or Osman (after whom the Ottomans are named) began its remarkable rise to power, a phenomenon which in the sixteenth century would bring its forces to the very gates of Vienna. By 1301 these Ottoman Turks had penetrated into the Byzantine province of Bithynia in northwestern Asia Minor. Their advance had been rendered easier by Michael Palaeologus' preoccupation with his Western rival, Charles of Anjou.

In the beginning the Ottomans were simple cattle herders, but they soon settled down and learned to farm. They had with them, it seems, some Christian advisers. Owing to the poverty of their language and culture, they borrowed certain Greek words and practices and other aspects of civilization formerly unknown to them. This small group of Turks became gradually assimilated by the numerically far greater Greek population surrounding them. On the other hand, some Greeks, more than is usually believed, were converted to the Ottoman religion, Islam. Indeed, one may say that the Ottoman Empire—and thus by extension the people of the modern Turkish state—was in large part the result of a fusion of the native Greeks of Asia Minor, the Seljuks, and these new Turkish invaders, the Ottomans.

The Ottomans continued to advance, and by 1337 Nicaea, Brusa, and Nicomedia in western Asia Minor had fallen into their hands. Rather than exterminating the defeated Greeks, the Turks in this early period seemed tolerant of the practice and organization of the Greek religion. Byzantium, of course, became increasingly alarmed at the threat to its existence by this piecemeal Turkish conquest of Asia Minor. But involved in civil wars, engaged in conflicts with the West, and, above all, now lacking Asia Minor as a base for the recruitment of soldiers and revenues, Byzantium could offer little effective opposition to the advancing Turks. The Greek emperors made repeated appeals for aid to Western rulers. But whatever help the latter provided was primarily to serve their own interests: it was directed mainly against the maritime Turkish emirates of Asia Minor or Egypt to safeguard their Eastern commerce or to regain the Holy Land.

The abilities of Michael VIII, the last truly great sovereign of Byzantium, served to mask the weakness of his empire. Under his son, Andronicus II (1282–1328), the internal weakness of the state now became more clearly visible. Not only was it threatened by a struggle between the emperor and a pro-Latin party under the leadership of his wife, the Western princess Irene of Montferrat (she wanted, in the Western manner, to divide up the Byzantine Empire among her sons), but by an even more serious menace, the progress of what might be called incipient "feudalism"—a development that now reached the point of gravely undermining the strength of the state itself.

The Last Years and Collapse of Byzantium

Once the Angevin threat to Constantinople had been overcome, Andronicus' first act as emperor was to denounce the union with Rome and punish all those pro-unionists who had been active under his father. To save money he began a drastic reduction of the military forces, almost disbanding the Greek navy while becoming dependent on Genoese naval support. Worse, a financial crisis now gripped the empire. The Byzantine gold coin, the *nomisma,* for over seven hundred years the entire medieval world's standard and most solvent monetary unit, underwent a severe devaluation. This depreciation, to be sure, had first begun in the mid-eleventh century, but the coin had meanwhile recovered 90 percent of its value. By the late thirteenth century, however, it was gravely weakened and finally displaced in the economy of Europe by the newly minted Italian gold coins, especially the Florentine florin and the Venetian ducat.

To raise revenue (the nomisma now possessed only half of its former value)

Andronicus took the step of increasing taxes. To add to his woes, a religious conflict broke out between a radical group of ascetics and a more moderate group of ecclesiastics who often favored a pro-Western orientation in political affairs. Meantime the Venetians and Genoese, by now virtually in control of Byzantium's economic life, were able to interfere constantly in imperial affairs; their rivalry caused considerable disorder. Affairs worsened and by 1300, as a result of the weakness of the state, almost all of Asia Minor had fallen to the Turks.

Prolonged civil war now wracked the Byzantine areas, the result of a family feud between Andronicus and his grandson, the latter supported by a powerful noble, John Cantacuzene. Cantacuzene became the power behind the throne and, to fight for him in his struggles against his rivals, he even summoned across the Dardanelles Turkish mercenaries. This marks the first appearance of the

Islamic painting of Byzantine prisoners, led by ropes, being brought before Ottoman Sultan Orkhan (fourteenth century), seated on a throne. (Courtesy of Mr. H. P. Kraus)

Ottoman Turks in Europe. Finally, Cantacuzene secured the throne for himself.

Events became more complicated by the outbreak of the Hesychast conflict. The Hesychasts, a group of monks from the monastic community of Mt. Athos in northern Greece, held the mystical view that in this life on earth one could, through contemplation, achieve a kind of union with God. Their views often came to symbolize the aspirations of the Greek "nationalist party" backed by Cantacuzene against those of their opponents whose views were often equated with the pro-Latin faction. The intermittent civil war now took on a kind of religious as well as a political character, a fact that served to embitter the conflict all the more.

The political and economic situation of Byzantium appeared almost hopeless. It seemed as if the capital would fall to anyone. Yet, until the very end, the empire showed an amazing tenacity for life. Paradoxically, even in this period of ruin Byzantium was able to undergo a remarkable cultural revival in the fields of art, literature, philosophy, and learning in general—showing that, although the state was bankrupt, its civilization was still vigorous and viable. Indeed, it would seem that the political reverses made some of its population turn, almost as an escape, to intellectual pursuits.

The West, which had hitherto failed to give aid to the Byzantines despite repeated appeals, began at last to recognize the peril to itself from the Turkish successes in the Balkans and to take an interest in the fate of Byzantium. But it was the Slavs of the Balkans who first confronted the Turkish advance. In 1389 at the Battle of Kossovo the Serbian army was destroyed by the Turks. With the Bulgars previously subjected, this meant that the entire Balkans, except for parts of Greece, had fallen to the Ottomans. The Byzantine Empire was now reduced to the environs of Constantinople, the Peloponnese, Thessalonica, and one or two islands. The emperor himself was forced to become a vassal of the Turkish sultan and to pay a yearly tribute.

Despite notable military successes, Turkish civilization did not seem to undergo much development. The vigor of the Ottoman advance—a problematical question for historians—is sometimes explained not only by the strength that the Ottomans drew from their subject peoples and the swiftness of their campaigns, but also by the inspiration provided by two remarkable Turkish brotherhoods, the Akhi, a kind of monkish group that managed to imbue some of the ruling group with its ascetic ideals (it is possible that Sultan Murad was their Grand Master), and the Ghazi, Muslim "holy" warriors zealous to fight Christianity. But whatever their influence, once the Turks crossed the Dardanelles into Europe it seems to have diminished.

The Turkish army was by this time perhaps the best in Europe. Its core was the famous contingent of Janissaries, personal, expertly trained and educated soldiers of the sultan, who had been taken as children by the Turks from among their Christian subjects. Carefully instructed from boyhood, they were fanatically

Growth of the Ottoman Empire

- Byzantine Empire, c. 1389
- - - Ottoman Empire, 1355
- Ottoman Empire, 1453
- Areas Under Ottoman Influence by 1453

loyal to the sultan. The Janissaries were extremely well equipped and constituted probably the most elite corps of soldiers in Europe.

After the Battle of Kossovo the able Bayazid I (1389–1402) ascended the Turkish throne as sultan. A few years later the Byzantine throne came to be occupied by one of the most gifted Greek rulers of this later period, Manuel II Palaeologus (1391–1425). Lofty minded and well educated, Manuel was faced with the almost impossible task of preserving the independence of Constantinople, now isolated in a sea of Turkish conquests. During Bayazid's sultanate Constantinople was almost in a constant state of seige. Blockaded on the land side by Turkish armies, only its great walls saved it. The lone access to the city was by sea.

When Hungary became threatened by the Turkish advance, the West at last affirmatively answered the Hungarian king's appeal for a crusade against the Turks. In 1396 an army of Burgundians under John the Fearless, of Frenchmen under Marshal Boucicault, and of Hungarians under King Sigismund met the Turkish troops under Bayazid in a famous battle on the plain of Nicopolis, in modern Bulgaria. The result was a complete debacle for Western arms. Ten thousand knights were captured; King Sigismund himself barely managed to escape seizure.

The road to Constantinople seemed completely open. Now Manuel, on Boucicault's advice, decided to go to the West in person to seek aid. He visited Paris and London, where the people were curious to see this emperor from the East whose ancestry harked back to the days of ancient Rome. One English chronicler, on seeing Manuel "begging" for aid, reported: "My God! Where art thou, ancient glory of Rome?"

Manuel was received everywhere with great pomp and ceremony but was unable to secure any effective aid. The West was still too engrossed in its own problems: France and England in the exhaustive Hundred Years' War, the Italian city states in their internecine rivalries. But Byzantium, now in deadly peril from Bayazid, was granted a respite of several decades, ironically enough not by Christians but by the defeat of Bayazid at the hands of another Turkic people, the Tatars, led by the bloody conqueror Timur the Lame (known also as Timurlenk, and, in English literature, as Tamerlane). At the Battle of Angora, in 1402, the vaunted Turkish Janissaries were cut to ribbons by the Tatar host; Bayazid himself was captured and carried around by Tamerlane in a cage. With Bayazid in captivity the Ottoman Empire momentarily collapsed. Tamerlane, however, did not advance much farther westward, and at his death the Ottomans began to recover their former power.

At the glorious news of Angora Manuel jubilantly returned to Constantinople, where he made every effort to prepare his tiny empire for the long-awaited Turkish onslaught. On the advice of the Byzantine Neoplatonic philosopher Gemistus Pletho, he erected a protective wall across the Isthmus of Corinth; he also repaired the walls of Constantinople and built up his army. A more formidable antagonist came to the fore in the person of the Ottoman Sultan Murad II who, after killing off his rival brothers, was able to restore the unity and power of the Ottoman Empire. When Murad, in 1422, laid siege (unsuccessfully) to Constantinople, the new emperor, John VIII Palaeologus (1425–1448), realized he must now make a supreme effort to bring the armies of the West to his aid.

After considerable negotiating with individual Western rulers, especially with Pope Eugenius IV, John decided to go personally to the West to attend a great council summoned to discuss the problem of union between the Greek and Roman churches. Like previous emperors, John expected to receive effective Western military aid in return for bringing about union.

The Council of Florence.   In 1438, accompanied by 700 ecclesiastics, scholars, and court officials, John reached Venice and proceeded from there to the city of

The Byzantine Emperor John VIII Palaeologus and his Patriarch at the Council of Florence (1438–1439). Note their beards, flowing silk garments, and Asiatic-type hats. This is a detail from the "Miracle of San Bernardino," attributed to an anonymous painter from Urbino. ("La nicchia di S. Bernardino," Electa Editrice, Milano 1963)

Ferrara, where the opening sessions of the conclave were to be held. Shortly thereafter, however, the council reconvened in Florence. For many months the Latins and Greeks wrangled over the ecclesiastical differences separating them: differences of rite, church organization, and especially dogma. An even more basic issue was the question of the papal claim to jurisdiction over the Greek Church, a primacy that the Greek ecclesiastics vehemently denied. But the most acrid disputes occurred over the doctrinal issue of the *filioque,* a dispute deriving from two different approaches to the doctrine of the Trinity. As I have already noted (Chapters 4 and 9), the Latin clergy, in contrast to the Greek, maintained that the Holy Spirit, the third person of the Trinity, proceeds from the Father *and the Son* (in Latin, *filioque*). At Florence the Greeks contended that an addition of any kind to the original wording of the creed was tantamount to heresy. To this contention the Latins answered that the "addition" was not doctrinal innovation but rather clarification of dogma. After months of complicated and tortuous argument a compromise solution was finally arranged which could be accepted by both sides, namely that the Holy Spirit proceeds from the Father *through* the Son. On the more basic issue, that of jurisdictional primacy over the Church, the wording of the decree of union was marvelously vague, asserting papal supremacy over the whole Church but "reserving the traditional rights of the Eastern patriarchs." As Gibbon so cogently put it in his *Decline and Fall*: "To satisfy the Latins without dishonoring the Greeks...they weighed the scruples of words and syllables till the theological balance trembled with a slight preponderance in favor of the Vatican."

On July 6, 1439, in the cathedral of Florence, under the magnificent new dome of Brunelleschi, the solemn ceremony of union took place. But despite the promises of the Greek delegation, on its return to Constantinople the union was repudiated by the great majority of the Byzantine people. The popular opposition was owing not only to the belief that the union had been obtained under duress but, more important, to the Byzantines' deep-rooted mistrust and their nearly fanatical hatred of the Latins. The memory of the atrocities committed in 1204 still rankled, and they feared that through union with Rome not only would the Greek Church lose its independence but the Greeks would in time lose even their political identity. So vehement, in fact, was the Orthodox opposition to the union that it persisted until the very capture of Constantinople by the Turks in 1453. Some anti-unionists were so extreme in their fear of Latin influence that they openly declared their preference for "the turban of the Turk in Constantinople to the tiara of the pope."

As for the Latins, their historic antagonism toward the Byzantines was further inflamed by the Greek repudiation of the Florentine union. As a result Byzantium secured no effective aid from the West. The final determined attempt to help Constantinople was made only by Eastern European powers. The Poles and Hungarians, acting in concert, attempted to launch a crusade against the Turks. But at the Battle of Varna in 1444 the Turks routed this army, effectively ending the last hope of Byzantium. Thus by 1453 East and West were cut off from each other almost as much by mutual antagonism as they were to be by the Turkish conquest of Constantinople itself.

When the new Ottoman sultan, Muhammad II ("the Conqueror"; 1451–1481), came to the throne, he was already consumed by an overpowering ambition to take Constantinople. One Byzantine historian tells us that "by night and day, going to bed and getting up, he turned over in his mind the military actions and means by which to seize Constantinople." Carefully studying the terrain of the capital city, Muhammad even sought the advice of Greek renegades. His first step was to build a castle on the European side of the Bosporus (Bayazid had already erected one on the Asiatic side), studding this fortress with cannon in order to cut off the approach to the city from the Black Sea area. Finally, after intensive planning, the sultan began his attack in early April 1453, massing a huge Ottoman army of more than 150,000 men against the 4,000 or 5,000 military defenders of the city. Muhammad had at his disposal the first real artillery in history, heavy cannon (cast by a renegade Hungarian) with which he constantly bombarded the walls. By the stratagem of transporting Turkish vessels overland he managed to corner the Greek fleet in the Constantinopolitan harbor of the Golden Horn, behind the great defensive chain stretched across the mouth of the harbor. The bombardment lasted for fifty days; it exhausted the defenders, who each night would rush to repair the damaged walls. Muhammad, exasperated, ordered a final assault. Anticipating the attack, the Greeks, on the night before what was to be the death of their capital city, gathered together in St. Sophia for divine services. It was to be the last Christian service in Christendom's most beautiful cathedral, "a liturgy of death before the last agony of the empire," as one scholar has put it. The Byzantine historian Sphrantzes wrote later that "even a man of stone could not help weeping that night."

On Tuesday, May 29, about one o'clock in the morning, the final assault began. After two attacks had been repulsed, Muhammad stormed the weakened gate where the Emperor Constantine XI Palaeologus was fighting. Making a breach, the Turks poured in through the walls. Constantine himself died fighting; his body was never found.

For three days the Turks looted and pillaged the city. All of the churches were robbed, holy images were burned, and many old and valuable Greek manuscripts were destroyed (including, for example, certain tragedies of Euripides which had survived from the ancient world and are now no longer extant). Muhammad rode his horse into Hagia Sophia and, ordering the walls to be whitewashed in order to cover the mosaics (like the Jews, Muslims are forbidden to have depictions of people in their houses of worship), the Conqueror converted the historic cathedral into a mosque.

Truly the fall of Constantinople marked the end of an era, a millennium.* Not only was it the end of one of the Middle Ages' most important political organisms; it was, technically, the end of the Roman Empire, which hearkened back in an unbroken line to the reign of Augustus. Realizing that Constantinople's fall removed a chief barrier to the Turkish advance, and moved by the plight of the Eastern Christians, several Popes later attempted to raise armies to go on a crusade to recover Constantinople. But their efforts were fruitless. Nonetheless, the Eastern concept of the "Roman" Empire never perished. For the idea of a "third Rome" to replace the fallen Byzantium was now taken up by distant Moscow. In 1472 the niece of the last Byzantine emperor, Sophia Palaeologus, married Prince Ivan III of Moscow, bringing with her Byzantine cour-

---

* Though Constantinople had fallen to the Turks, Byzantine culture continued to influence the West and the Slavic areas (see Chapters 12 and 14).

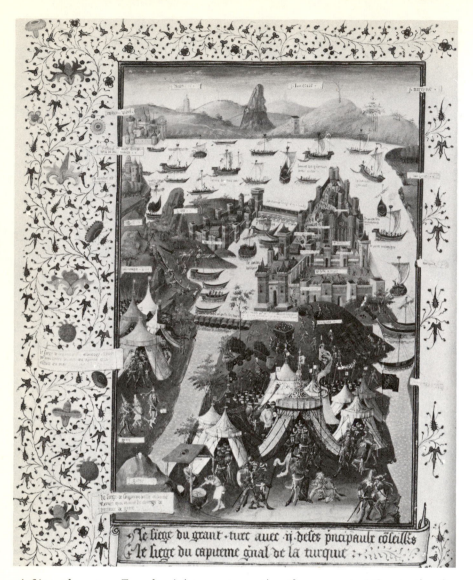

*A fifteenth-century French miniature representing the conquest of Constantinople
in 1453. In the foreground are tents of the besieging Turkish forces; before the city
walls are cannon and siege equipment. (Bibliothèque Nationale, Paris)*

tiers and the Byzantine court ceremonial. Ivan IV soon assumed the title Tsar
(Caesar) and adopted the Byzantine double-headed eagle as his crest. As the
greatest surviving Orthodox power, Moscow now lay claim to be the protector
of all the Eastern Orthodox. Thereafter, as the inheritor of the mantle of By-

zantium and rulers of the "third Rome," the Russian tsars were to be consumed by a desire to gain control of the old imperial city of Constantinople.

The Slavs

Slavic Origins and Expansion

When did the Russians become Orthodox? Why did they consider themselves part of the Greek Orthodox rather than of the Latin, Roman Catholic world? To answer these questions we must turn back and trace the development of the early history of the Slavs—a history in which the influences of Byzantium played a prominent, if not the most formative, role.

Despite the continuing research of historians and archaeologists the earliest history of the Slavic peoples is still very obscure. One thing is certain: the Slavs were an Indo-European people native to Eastern Europe, and as the various Slavic tribes grew in size they assimilated other peoples—peoples less numerous who had themselves migrated to Eastern Europe from Central Asia or Scandinavia, in the North. The Slavic tribes began to disperse quite early, and as a result three major groups of Slavs may be distinguished: the East Slavs, today found primarily in Russia; the South Slavs, now located in the Balkans, especially in Yugoslavia and Bulgaria; and western Slavic groups such as Poles, Czechs, and Slovaks, all of which are scattered throughout Central and Eastern Europe.

The original habitat of the Slavs was probably either in the forests and steppes of western Russia, near the city of Kiev but probably no further west than the Vistula river. Little information is available on the process of Slavic expansion from the original homeland. But by the turn of the eighth century Slavic tribes occupied lands near the Baltic Sea and extending southward into areas of the Balkan peninsula. The word Balkans almost automatically brings to mind the Slavs, but before the early sixth century few if any Slavs had penetrated south of the Danube. It is in fact not until they entered this Byzantine-held Balkan area that we begin to have any precise knowledge of the Slavic tribes.

The Slavic tribe that was later to give its name to all Slavs was known to the Romans as Sclavenes. In the sixth century the nomadic Sclavenes and another tribe, the Antae (probably also of Slavic origin), roamed the area north of the Danube. From the reign of the Byzantine Emperor Justin I (518–527) individual Slavs were infiltrating across the Danube; later, along with other primitive tribes appearing in the area, such as the Bulgars, they came in force to raid Byzantine territories south of the Danube. What finally provided the Slavs the opportunity to settle permanently in the Balkan area was the wars of the Avars against the Byzantine Empire. A barbaric Turkic tribe related to the Huns, the Avars had earlier moved through the steppe corridor from Asia into the Slavic areas. And, conquering some of the Slavic peoples (including the Antae), they soon built up a huge empire, which, at its greatest extent, stretched from the upper Elbe eastward to the Volga and southward to the Danube.

To ease the pressure on his northern frontier from the constant Avar-Slavic raids, the Byzantine Emperor Justinian, in 558, made peace with the Avars in exchange for the payment of a yearly subsidy. The Avars, in turn, agreed to help stop the raids into the empire of their Slavic subject-allies. After 578, however, the Avars once again began to raid in conjunction with the Slavs. Attacking the frontier Byzantine fortress city of Sirmium (near present-day Belgrade) and appearing in 580–581 in large numbers before the Long Walls guarding the approaches to Constantinople, the Avars and Slavs virtually managed to paralyze Byzantine power in the Balkans. The Byzantines were at that time involved in a deadly struggle with the Persian Empire in the East—a struggle so engrossing that they had little time to devote to the Balkans. By the end of the sixth century the Slavs had become so firmly lodged in the northern Balkan areas that they could not be dislodged.

In the early seventh century, under the Emperor Heraclius, the Slavs, again in conjunction with the Avars or perhaps the Huns, continued their depredations in the Balkans, their aim being the Greek port city of Thessalonica, the terminus of the easiest passage extending from Sirmium on the middle Danube to the Aegean Sea. But these invasions were repeatedly hurled back; the pious Byzantine citizens of Thessalonica attributed the preservation of their city to the personal intervention of their patron saint, St. Demetrius.

The most famous attack of the Avar-Slavic hordes against Constantinople took place in 626 during the absence of the Emperor Heraclius, then campaigning in eastern Asia Minor. To make matters worse, a Persian army encamped on the Asian side of the Bosporus and hurled itself against the capital's defenses. The courage of the people was inspired by their Patriarch Sergius, whose leadership, together with a timely Byzantine naval victory, saved Constantinople. This was the last serious Avar threat to the Byzantine Empire.

But the Byzantines were incapable of stemming the increasing flow of Slavs into the Balkan provinces. Indeed by the mid-seventh century the Balkan peninsula, except for the coastal areas, the Albanian mountains, and Thrace, had become more or less thickly settled by Slavic peoples. In this period the Byzantine state had to face a variety of enemies from the east and north: the Huns in the fifth century; the Avars in the sixth and seventh centuries; the Bulgars in the seventh century and later; the Magyars, Pechenegs, and Cumans in the ninth and tenth centuries. All of these peoples, except for the Slavs, were Asiatic— that is, they were Turkic nomads who lived a pastoral life as they moved swiftly on horseback from one area to another attacking and subjugating other peoples.

As among other primitive Indo-European peoples, the foundation of early Slavic society was the family. Clans and tribes were made up of groups of families. The land with all its products was considered to be the common property of the whole community. Despite this communal aspect of their early tribal society, the Slavs were by nature democratic and had a very loose social and governmental organization. Procopius, the sixth-century Byzantine historian, an important source for the history of the early Balkan peoples, described their political organization as follows: "The Slavs do not live under the regime of one man, but in democracy and that from old times. Therefore all profitable or damaging things are common to them." With their very loose governmental structure and extremely democratic tendencies, the Slavs did not find it easy to cooperate and set up a central organization—that is, to take the fundamental step of turning their petty tribes into nations. Indeed, the repeated subjugation of the Slavs by non-Slavic invaders during this early period has led some scholars to characterize them in general as a rather docile people. At any rate, viable political organization of the various Slavic tribes (except that of the Antae) seems to have come as the result of outside stimulus. Thus in the seventh century a renegade Frank named Samo molded the western Slavs of the German areas into a kingdom. The Slavs of the northwest, however, had to wait two centuries to develop into states: Moravia and, later, the duchies of Bohemia and Poland. But even their existence was to some degree due to the stimulus provided by the nearby Germans.

In the Balkan areas the Slavs were even more disorganized, and here the Byzantines were presented with a unique opportunity. If the Slavs could be conquered and civilized, they might be absorbed into the Byzantine Empire before they could become too nationally conscious. As always in the medieval period, the first step in this direction was conversion to Christianity—a conversion that would have wide implications not only with regard to religious beliefs but to social and political organization as well.

The entrance of the Slavic invaders into the Balkan areas extinguished much of the Christianity of the area. To be sure, individual Slavs subject to Byzantine influence had become converted to Christianity. But the first mass conversion of a Slavic tribe occurred in connection with the Moravians (863), a people who lived in present-day Czechoslovakia. Their conversion was followed very soon thereafter by that of a people who were originally not Slavic at all, the Hunnic tribe of the Bulgars. Entering Eastern Europe from their homeland in Central Asia, the Bulgars, on the decline of the great Avar Empire, established themselves on the north shores of the Black Sea. By the end of the seventh century they had penetrated into the northeastern part of the Balkan peninsula just south of the Danube, in the process conquering the more numerous Slavic tribes already settled there. As time went on, however, the Bulgars were gradually absorbed by the conquered. By the tenth century the Bulgars had become completely Slavonized. It is interesting that today in modern Bulgarian there remain not over ten words of Hunnic origin.

Bulgars and Moravians Converted by Byzantium

The Bulgars first provided a political organization for the Slavs of the Balkans, and soon the rising Bulgar state even began to challenge Byzantine power. In a great battle in 811, the khan (ruler) of the Bulgars, Krum (803–814), crushed an imperial army; the Emperor Nicephorus himself was killed. Krum's ambitions extended not only to the conquest of all the Balkans but to the capture of Constantinople itself. In this effort he failed, but his achievements were considerable. Not only had the Bulgars under his rule become permanently established in the Balkans; they had secured an untrammeled passage into Macedonia, in the process uniting Pannonia—where Charlemagne in 796 had crushed the Avar power—with Balkan Bulgaria. Looking to the internal development of his nation, Krum made a simple codification of laws and, with the aid of imported Greek architects and artisans, built great royal palaces. Because of the lack as yet of a Bulgar alphabet, Greek was used for royal inscriptions. By the time of his death the Bulgarians had become not only an important European power but were permanently settled in Thrace and Macedonia, on the very doorstep of Constantinople.

The still barbaric tone of Bulgar life, however, is reflected in Krum's action of taking the skull of the defeated Emperor Nicephorus, plating it with silver, and using it as a drinking cup. Nevertheless, Bulgar-Slavic society, partly through Byzantine influence, was becoming less primitive. It had reached the stage of requiring better political organization and, more important for that period, a more advanced type of religion. Paganism was out of date; not long thereafter the Bulgars converted to Christianity. But though it was perhaps inevitable that the Bulgars adopt the religion of their neighbor, the powerful Byzantine state, the Bulgar leaders and boyars (nobles) for a time held off adoption of Christianity because they feared that along with the Greek religion it would bring not only imperial propaganda but Byzantine political encroachment. The Bulgar feelings of "attraction" and alternately "repulsion" toward the Byzantine state and culture in varying degrees characterized the relations of virtually all the Slavic peoples with the Byzantines, especially when the Slavs moved so close as to have their very "national" identity as a people threatened by the superior Byzantine culture and power.

The process of the Slavic conversion to Christianity, as noted, began elsewhere, farther to the West in Moravia. Rastislav, ruler of the Slavic Moravians, controlled a large state that had reached a stage of development somewhat similar to that of the Bulgars. But Moravia was situated next to powerful German neighbors, the Eastern Franks, who had already made their influence felt on the Moravians through the activities of Frankish missionaries. Fearing to fall under German political domination, Rastislav, in 862, set in motion the process which was to lead ultimately to the conversion of all or most of the early Slavic peoples and to bring many of them into the Byzantine orbit.

Rastislav sent an embassy to Constantinople, requesting the dispatch to Moravia of a Greek missionary who could preach Christianity to his people in their own Slavic tongue. For Rastislav, as was to be the case with other Slavic rulers, Christianity could bring advantages. Not only were Greek Christianity and culture then more splendid than the Frankish culture of the neighboring Carolingians, but no less important, Rastislav wanted a Byzantine alliance in order to counter the real possibility of being outflanked by a Franco-Bulgar coalition. Moreover, it also seems likely that he wished to reap the benefits of Byzantine political and religious theory. As vicegerent of God on earth, the Byzantine emperor not only controlled church and state but was considered the absolute ruler over all classes, including the nobles. For a Slavic ruler of absolutist ambitions, whose authority was impeded by the "democratic" influences which were characteristic of early Slavic society, such a theory could prove most useful.

Two Greek monks from Thessalonica, the brothers Cyril and Methodius,* still venerated as the "Apostles to the Slavs," were now sent to Moravia by the Greek Emperor Michael III. Cyril, a very learned man, formerly professor of philosophy at the patriarchal school of Constantinople, was, like his brother Methodius, skilled in the Slavic language, in particular the dialect spoken around their native city of Thessalonica. Cyril may have been a member of a Slavic "institute" that the Greek Patriarch Photius seems already to have established in Constantinople, probably with the aim of proselytizing the Slavs. At any rate, when Cyril and Methodius went to Moravia they put into use for the Slavs (who as yet had no written language) an alphabet developed by them— one based essentially on Greek cursive letters (that is, handwritten characters joined by strokes) but with the addition of a few letters from Hebrew to represent non-Greek sounds. Most scholars now identify this alphabet with the so-called Glagolitic, which is therefore to be considered the earliest Slavic alphabet. But this was later displaced by another alphabet developed under Byzantine influences in Bulgaria, probably by disciples of the two brothers. It was again based on Greek but with uncial (that is, handwritten *capital*) letters. And it is this latter alphabet, termed Cyrillic after Cyril, which is essentially still in common use among the Russians, Bulgars, Serbs, and others. The brothers brought

* Cyril did not become a monk until on his deathbed. His given name was Constantine.

with them the Bible and other liturgical books, which they translated into the dialect of the Macedonian Slavs. Their translations and writings of ecclesiastical works in Slavic—a remarkable innovation for the age—constitute the beginnings of Slavic literature. Indeed the language they employed, now termed "Old Church Slavonic," became standard for the liturgy of the Orthodox Slavic churches.

Byzantium and the Bulgars

Meanwhile, Boris of Bulgaria, alarmed at the formation of the Byzantine-Moravian alliance, sought in defense to create a Franco-Bulgar alliance. He therefore asked for Christianity from the Germans, writing in 866 to the Roman Pope for this purpose. Boris posed many questions as to the practical, everyday problems that would face a newly converted prince: Could the Bulgar people continue to wear trousers? What about sexual relations on Sundays and holy days? For the primitive Slavic peoples Christian conversion meant not only a change of religion but a change in the whole context of everyday life. The crucial point that finally persuaded Boris to turn from Rome to Constantinople for conversion was the greater liberality of the Greek emperor and the Orthodox Church in granting him virtual ecclesiastical autonomy. Rome refused to grant him an independent church of his own. Hence in the 860s, after sharp rivalry between missionaries of the Byzantine Patriarch Photius and the Roman Pope Nicholas I to convert the Bulgars (see Chapter 4), the Byzantine Church triumphed, and the attempt of the Bulgars to reap the diplomatic benefits of conversion from the more distant West proved fruitless. The consequences were profound for all of subsequent Slavic history.

The Papacy, furthermore, refused to sanction the use of liturgical works in the Slavic vernacular, insisting instead on the use of Latin. The Byzantine policy of fostering the Slavonic liturgy in the Slavic territories was therefore a crucial factor in the adhesion of the Eastern Slavs to Byzantium rather than to Rome. On the other hand, the work of the Byzantine missionaries among the Moravians did not long survive. Despite the valiant efforts of Cyril and after his death of Methodius in converting many and spreading the new Slavic liturgy, the Frankish influence proved overwhelming in Moravia. With the complete destruction in 906 of the independence of the Moravian state by the Magyars, the Roman form of Christianity finally triumphed there.

Despite the Frankish dominance, the work of the two Greek "Apostles to the Slavs" was not entirely lost. Some of the newly Christianized Moravian clergy managed to flee to the Balkans, to Bulgaria and Croatia, bringing with them the Slavic "Byzantine inheritance." To be sure, in Bulgaria "Byzantinization" had as yet occurred only on the surface, but the effects were soon to be felt even among the common people. Not all Bulgars were in favor of conversion. Indeed, on several occasions the Bulgar nobility revolted, opposed as they were to the growing absolutism of the khan. They favored a return to paganism.

When Boris's son Symeon came to the throne he moved the capital from Pliska to Preslav and organized the Church structure in Bulgaria, even establishing a patriarchate. The use of Slavonic was now confirmed in the liturgy. But Symeon, who had been educated in Constantinople, was more ambitious than his father. He aimed at using the Bulgar throne as a steppingstone to mount the Roman throne of Constantinople. A real collision thus developed between Symeon and Byzantium—partly owing to his aggressive ambitions and his desire for the glitter of Constantinople, and partly to the growing trade monopoly exercised by Greek merchants in Bulgar territory. When Symeon undertook a military campaign against Constantinople, the Byzantines, in their typical diplomatic fashion, summoned to their aid a counterpoise, the Magyars. This marks the first appearance of the Finno-Ugrian Magyars (the modern Hungarians) in civilized European affairs. The Bulgars, on their side, appealed for aid to still another Turkic people in the area, the Pechenegs.

Deeply involved with the Arabic danger in Asia Minor and the East, the Byzantines could not stem Symeon's advance. He burned the suburbs of Constantinople, and only the negotiations of Patriarch Nicholas Mysticos were able to save the city. At Symeon's repeated insistence the patriarch even seems to have agreed to the coronation of Symeon as emperor, for Symeon now styled himself "Emperor of the Bulgars and Romans." But the Byzantines never really granted him the titles of both basileus and autocrator, which were reserved for the senior emperor. At his death in 927 he left a great state extending from the Black Sea to the Adriatic and from the Danube almost to Thessalonica. His reign marks the first attempt to replace Byzantine domination of the Balkans by Slavic domination.

A period of forty years of relative peace now ensued, made possible largely because of the diplomatic success of Byzantium in calling upon its former enemies, the Pechenegs, to oppose the still ambitious Bulgars. Moreover, the Bulgars themselves were now divided between anti- and pro-Byzantine parties.

Symeon's successor, Peter, was given a bride of the imperial house and an annual subsidy by the Byzantines. But underneath these appearances of Bulgar success, the important fact was that with the adoption of Byzantine titles, ceremonies, and concepts of Byzantine political theory and theology, Byzantine influences at the Bulgar court were penetrating deeper and deeper. Nevertheless, the lower class, especially the peasantry, was undergoing a reaction against what they considered foreign, Greek influences.

The long peace between Bulgars and Byzantines ended in 966. But by then the Bulgar state had become a weak mass of territory, and Byzantium, now at the very apogee of its power, decided once and for all to crush this rival to its ecumenical claims.

In 965–966 the Byzantine Emperor Nicephorus Phocas provoked a fight with the Bulgar ruler and called forth as his ally Sviatoslav, the chieftain of the barbaric "Rus" or Russians. (This marks the first use made by the Byzantines of the Russians as a military ally.) Crossing the Danube Sviatoslav and his troops soon overran northern Bulgaria. As his strength increased, Byzantium, now changing tactics, allied with its erstwhile enemy, the Bulgars. This shifting of alliances clearly reveals the growing power of the Russians. When Peter of Bulgaria died, Sviatoslav on his own once again invaded Bulgaria, this time capturing the entire Bulgar royal family. His expedition might be termed the first "Russian" imperialist venture in the Balkans.

Phocas was murdered within a year and his successor, Emperor John I Zimisces, was faced with the problem of the growing Russian danger. John, an able general, managed to capture Pereiaslavets, which was then in Russian hands, massacring in the campaign many of the Russian troops. Negotiations for peace resulted in a conference on the Danube between the two rulers, a meeting that has remained famous because of the accounts left by the Byzantine historians. On his way back to Russia Sviatoslav was killed by the Pechenegs.

Zimisces returned in triumph to Constantinople, leading the captured Bulgar ruler, Boris, on foot behind him. Eastern Bulgaria was now turned into a Byzantine province. Soon, however, a new family, the Comitopouli, came to the fore in the almost inaccessible mountains of western Bulgaria. Samuel established an independent Bulgar Church in that area and set up his capital at Ochrida. The final struggle between Bulgarians and Byzantines now began, with Samuel, after overrunning eastern Bulgaria, pushing his territory east to the Black Sea and west toward the Adriatic. Samuel's opponent, Emperor Basil II, however, was no less able and enjoyed the advantage of superior Byzantine resources and military organization. Taking personal command of his troops, Basil crushed the Bulgar army in 1014, capturing 14,000 men. Of these he blinded 99 out of every 100, leaving one eye to each 100th soldier so that he could guide his comrades back to Samuel. At the sight of his pitiful troops Samuel suffered such a shock that he died of a stroke. Basil, on his part, though destroying the independence of the Bulgar state and earning for himself the title *Bulgaroctonus* (Bulgar-Slayer), wisely did not abolish the Bulgar ecclesiastical organization. He permitted the Bulgar Church to remain autonomous under the archbishop of Ochrida. After this there were sporadic Bulgar revolts but with no genuine success. They nevertheless showed that a Bulgar national consciousness was not dead.

Basil had delivered the knockout blow to the Bulgars, but his very success was to prove almost fatal for Byzantium. The long war had required the expenditure of enormous treasure and manpower, a fact which led to the exhaustion of the state and the near collapse of Byzantium in the mid-eleventh century. Nevertheless, the conversion of the Bulgars by Byzantium instead of by Rome, and the Bulgar assimilation of much of the Cyrillic legacy, with its vernacular liturgy and literature, served to tie the Bulgars and hence, later, the Serbs—who were to derive their Christianity from the Bulgars and Byzantines—to the Byzantine orbit and not to that of the Latin West.

Early Russia

The most important state to emerge from among the Slavic peoples was that of the Russians, or "Rus" as they are called in the sources.* From earliest recorded history the steppes of southern Russia had served as a bridge between Asia and Europe. Repeatedly Asiatic invaders—Scythians, Sarmatians, Huns, Avars, Bulgars—had entered Europe through the open plains north of the Black and Caspian seas. Aside from the Greek settlements hugging the Black Sea coastline, the first important state organized between the Don and Volga rivers was that of the Khazars. A Turkic people, they established themselves in the Caucasus (their capital was at Itil on the lower Volga) in the latter half of the seventh and early eighth centuries. In time they came to control a vast area between the Black and the Caspian seas extending northwestward to Kiev on the Dnieper. In this general area, traversed by great rivers—the Dnieper, Volga, Don, and Dvina—that flow southward into the Black or Caspian seas and northward into the Baltic, commerce took place largely by water. The Khazars, situated near the Byzantine and Arabic territories, were able to take full advantage of their position and develop a flourishing trade. What they are perhaps most remembered for, however, is their conversion to Judaism, perhaps the sole people outside the Hebrews themselves to adopt this religion. (Some scholars believe, probably wrongly, that the modern Polish and Russian Jews, the Askenazy, are descendants of the Khazars.)

As already seen, the Slavs, a large, rather amorphous mass of people, were already by the sixth century settled in the area west of the Khazars, overrunning present-day western Russia. But the Slavs of this huge area do not emerge as a genuine political force until the late ninth century. In that period, according to the earliest Russian source, known as the *Primary Chronicle,* a group of Scandinavian Vikings under the Swede (some scholars believe the Dane) Rurik

---

* "Rus" was a term apparently used by the Finns, neighbors of the Slavs, to refer to these early Scandinavians. "Varangian," another term used in the sources, especially the Byzantine, comes from the Scandinavian "Var," meaning an oath of a brotherhood of troops. In the sources it is used to refer to the Rus or to the Scandinavian mercenaries from the Kievan state who served in the Byzantine army.

settled in 862 in the Slavic town of Novgorod, in northern Russia. Rurik, the *Chronicle* states, came in answer to a Slavic summons. According to the *Chronicle,* conditions in the Slavic areas were anarchic, there being

> no law among them, but tribe against tribe. Discord thus ensued among them, and they began to war one against another. They said to themselves, "Let us seek a prince who may rule over us and judge us according to the law." They accordingly went overseas to the Varangian Rus ... and said, "Our whole land is great and rich but there is no order in it. Come to rule and reign over us." *

Whether the Rus actually came in response to a summons or simply as conquerors is not possible to know. Nor is it certain that Rurik was Scandinavian. Some modern Russian scholars, in fact, deny his Scandinavian origin, or that he even existed. But most scholars of Europe and America are convinced that the Rus are not of Slavic stock, that they are rather Scandinavian, and that, therefore, the state of Kiev which came to be established in the late ninth century was carved out and ruled by the Scandinavian Rus. Though one may, then, accept the Scandinavian origin of the Rus and attribute the first political organization of the Russian state to them, it should at the same time be realized that the great mass of people of this state were Slavs. Thus, despite the origin of the ruling class, the institutions of the Kievan state that emerged must to some degree at least have been based on those of the indigenous Slavic population. The legendary account of the Russian *Primary Chronicle* cannot explain, on the basis alone of the coming of a few barbaric Rus, how the Kievan state could so suddenly have emerged in the form it did. We may perhaps make a useful comparison with the Scandinavian invaders of England or France in the same period whose rule was based in no small degree on the well-established local social and economic institutions of the conquered peoples.

The Kievan State

In the sixth decade of the ninth century Rurik's fellow countrymen, Dir and Askold, and later Oleg of Novgorod, moved southward along the Dnieper to capture the important settlement of Kiev (capital of the modern Ukraine). Situated on the Dnieper overlooking the whole of the fertile steppe area, Kiev (a city founded earlier) became under the Rus the center of a rapidly expanding state whose chief activity, along with agriculture, was trade. Loosely organized politically, the territory nevertheless began early to exhibit the warlike, aggressive tendencies of its Viking overlords. And thus there occurred in 860 the first of a series of Rus expeditions against Byzantium.

* S. H. Cross, ed., *The Russian Primary Chronicle* (1930).

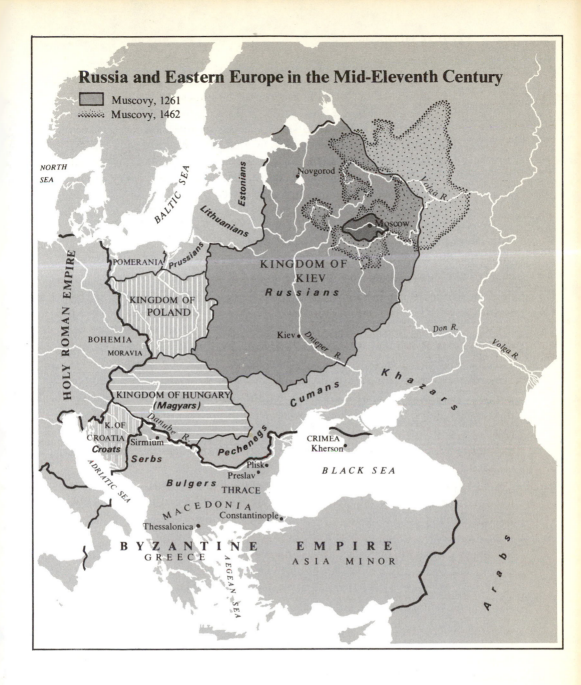

Russia and Eastern Europe in the Mid-Eleventh Century

▢ Muscovy, 1261
⣿ Muscovy, 1462

NORTH SEA

BALTIC SEA

Estonians

Lithuanians

Novgorod

Volga R.

HOLY ROMAN EMPIRE

POMERANIA

Prussians

KINGDOM OF KIEV

Russians

Moscow

KINGDOM OF POLAND

BOHEMIA

MORAVIA

Kiev

Dnieper R.

Don R.

Volga R.

Khazars

KINGDOM OF HUNGARY
(Magyars)

Danube R.

Cumans

K. OF CROATIA

Croats

Sirmium

Serbs

Pechenegs

CRIMEA
Kherson

Plisk
Preslav

THRACE

Bulgers

BLACK SEA

ADRIATIC SEA

MACEDONIA

Constantinople

Thessalonica

B Y Z A N T I N E   E M P I R E

GREECE

ASIA MINOR

Arabs

AEGEAN SEA

The appearance at this time of some two hundred barbarian warships before Constantinople brought panic to the citizens of the capital. The attack has been described by the Patriarch Photius, who attributes the repulse of the savage Rus warriors and fleet to the divine intercession of the capital's protectress, the Virgin, through the instrumentality of her mantle and of her icon of the Hodegetria.

> As the whole city was carrying with me the Virgin's robe for the repulse of the [Rus] besiegers and the protection of the besieged, we offered freely our prayers and performed the litany, whereupon with ineffable compassion she spoke out in motherly intercession: God was moved, His anger was averted, and the Lord took pity on His inheritance. Truly is this most holy garment the raiment of God's Mother.... For at once, as the Virgin's garment went around the walls, the barbarians [Rus] gave up the siege....*

Several other Rus attacks followed in the next century, all of which the Byzantines managed to repulse. What the Russians sought besides booty was close economic ties with Byzantium, especially greater concessions to their merchants in the great emporium of Constantinople. Evidence has remained (in Russia) of two tenth-century trade treaties negotiated between the emperor and the rulers of Kiev.

Trade between the Rus areas and those of the Byzantines became brisk indeed and was of value to the Byzantine world as well as to the Rus. The Rus served as intermediaries between Byzantium and the Baltic and North Sea areas of northern Europe, carrying goods in their boats up the Dnieper and connecting by portage with other rivers flowing into the northern seas. In exchange for the manufactured Byzantine luxury goods, such as spices, cloth, metal objects, glassware, and wine, the Rus brought to Constantinople their furs, wax, honey, hides, timber, and slaves—merchandise that the Greeks were very eager to obtain.

The real founder of the state of Kiev is generally considered to be the Rus Oleg. According to legend, his occupation of Kiev, which finally ended the Khazar domination, occurred in 882. Spreading his rule over several neighboring eastern Slavic tribes, he began the peaceful process of fusing the Scandinavian upper class with the Slavs. It was during his reign that the first Russian commercial treaty of which we have record was made with Byzantium (911).

Oleg's successor, Igor (913–945), possibly Oleg's nephew, is the first historically significant ruler of Kievan Russia. Under his rule Kievan territory was further expanded. He again waged a major campaign against Constantinople, devastating even its suburbs. The Byzantine navy, however, defeated his fleet largely because of its use of the celebrated Greek fire. As before, similar commercial agreements were entered into, though now less favorable to the Rus merchants.

The Christianization of Russia by Byzantium

The key event in early Russian history was the conversion of the Rus of Kiev to Byzantine Christianity. No doubt as a result of the contacts between

* From C. Mango, *The Homilies of Photius* (Cambridge, Mass., 1958), p. 102.

Rus and Byzantine traders, individual Rus from an early period had become converted to Christianity, either because of the allure of the superior Byzantine civilization and society or simply as a result of the conviction that their own gods were false. Indeed, the second trade treaty in 944 reveals that some of the Russian envoys had already abandoned their pagan gods for Greek Christianity; in the document they swear "by the Holy Cross" that they will carry out the provisions of the treaty.

The first significant step in the conversion of the Russian *people* is associated with the Princess Olga, wife of Igor. She visited Constantinople in 957 (perhaps also earlier in 955) and was baptized there (although according to another tradition she was baptized in Kiev), with the emperor and/or empress acting as godparent. But as had happened among the Bulgars, members of the Rus noble class began to oppose the rising Byzantine influence resulting from the penetration of Greek Christianity into Kiev. To placate them embassies to offset this influence were now sent from Kiev to the West, to the German Emperor Otto I, asking for German missionaries, who soon arrived in Kiev. But this German attempt at conversion of the Kievans failed, and Byzantine influences continued to infiltrate among the Russians.

Olga's son Sviatoslav was called upon by the Byzantine Nicephorus Phocas to aid him against the onslaught of the Bulgars. But Sviatoslav, whose ambition it was to conquer the Bulgars for himself, was killed by the Pechenegs on his way back to Russia. The fate of the Rus was to be decided by his son Vladimir, who was later canonized because it was under him that the entire Rus people were converted.

According to the story recorded in the *Primary Chronicle,* Vladimir, feeling the inadequacy of the old faith but uncertain which religion to adopt, sent envoys to several peoples—to the Jewish Khazars, the Muslims, and the Greeks of Constantinople. At this point the Russian *Chronicle* speaks for itself. The envoys responded to Vladimir:

> When we journeyed among the Muslims, we beheld how they worship in their temple, called a mosque.... There is no happiness among them, but instead only sorrow and a dreadful stench. Their religion is not good. Then we went among the Germans, and saw them performing many ceremonies in their temples; but we beheld no glory there. Then we went to Greece [Byzantium] and the Greeks led us to the edifices where they worship their God, and we knew not whether we were in heaven or on earth. For on earth there is no such splendor or such beauty.*

The result was that shortly afterward Vladimir accepted Christianity from Byzantium. In accordance with a previous agreement, Vladimir had pledged to

---

* S. H. Cross, *op. cit.*

send his military guard to aid the Greek Emperor Basil II to suppress a pretender to the Byzantine throne. In return Vladimir was to secure the hand of Anna, sister of the emperor. Though Vladimir carried out his part of the agreement and the Byzantine pretender was defeated, Basil refused to send his sister to Kiev. Whereupon Vladimir, in 989, seized the Greek city of Kherson, in the Crimea, refusing to return it until Anna was handed over to him. Whatever the exact sequence of these events—the sources, Greek, Russian, and Arabic as well are not in agreement—it is certain that in connection with them Vladimir, either in 987 at Kiev, or after 989 in Kherson, was himself baptized and at the same time or shortly thereafter compelled his nobles and people to be converted to Greek Christianity. He had the pagan idols flogged, we are told, and in the course of a single day had his entire people baptized in the waters of the Dnieper.

It seems likely that the (probably already existing) Greek archbishopric of Kherson was now given supervision over the newly converted Rus. Another view of this event, however, holds that the Kievan Church that now came into being was from the start autocephalic, that is, independent of the Greek Church of Constantinople. At any rate, fifty years from the time of Vladimir's conversion events become much clearer and we know definitely that the primate of the

The Virgin of Smolensk, one of the most famous Russian icons of the Virgin and Child. This icon is attributed to the greatest Muscovite painter, Andrei Rublev, disciple of the Byzantine Theophanes. (Courtesy of A La Vieille Russie, New York)

Russian Church, the metropolitan of Kiev, was henceforth appointed by the patriarch of Constantinople and, except for two known cases, seems always to have been a Greek. The lesser clergy were virtually all Slavic. The important fact in all these controversial questions is that the accounts reveal the many influences to which the people and state of Kiev were then exposed. And there can be little doubt that the Christianization of Kiev by Greek clergy was owing primarily to the impressiveness of Byzantine power and to the benefits, political or in the way of prestige or culture, that such a conversion would bring to the Kievan ruler and his state.

Byzantine Cultural Influences. Conversion wrought many changes in the Kievan way of life. The extent to which the Rus could absorb the Byzantine cultural influences was naturally conditioned by their ability to assimilate such

Byzantine Icon from Grottaferrata. The prototype for all Byzantine and Russian portraits of the Virgin and Child was the famous Hodegetria of Constantinople. (Fototeca Unione Roma)

influences, given their views toward life, which in many ways were so different from those of the Byzantine. Rus society was still rather primitive with respect to morals, family affairs, and law. The concept, for example, that the state should punish those guilty of committing a crime now only slowly began to displace the older Rus view that punishment of the guilty was a matter of personal revenge. The most immediate effect of the conversion, of course, was the destruction of the old idols and the emergence of a new and important power in Kievan society, the Church. The clergy formed an influential new social class and, with the land that soon accrued to it, also became an important economic force. As in Byzantium, the Church began to exercise a pervasive influence on society and morals. Byzantine canon law was adopted, which brought directly under the jurisdiction of the Church matters pertaining to morals, marriage, and divorce, as well as questions of worship. Churches and monasteries began to appear in all the cities and in time even in the rural countryside, where the peasants were more prone to preserve the old religious customs and beliefs.

Byzantine artists and architects now began to be imported from Constantinople to produce icons and buildings in Kiev and to teach their techniques and style to native Kievan artists. The chief architectural creation of the period was the cathedral of St. Sophia in Kiev, named and partly modeled after its prototype in Constantinople. Kiev, and through Kiev, Novgorod, especially, produced a remarkable school of Byzantine-inspired icon painters; the climax came later, in the late fourteenth and early fifteenth centuries, with the painters Theophanes the Greek from Constantinople, and the Muscovite Andrei Rublev, who was influenced by him.

For the first time formal education was now established in Kiev and widespread use was made of the Cyrillic alphabet. A Slavonic literature, already partially prepared as a result of the inheritance from Moravia and Bulgaria, made its appearance. To be sure, the literature that came from Byzantium was almost entirely ecclesiastical in scope. Scores of translations made in Kievan Russia of Byzantine works still remain, works almost all of a religious character —canon law collections, saints' lives, psalters, homilies, and other liturgical matter. What is most significant, however, is that while adopting the Byzantine form of Christianity the Slavs, those of Russia among them, did not at the same time adopt the inheritance from the classical Greek world that Byzantium had preserved. The plays of the tragedians Aeschylus, Sophocles, and Euripides, the philosophy of Plato and Aristotle, the ethical and rhetorical works of Plutarch and Hermogenes, and the epic poems of Homer were all but unknown to Kievan readers. Although there are a few exceptions, in the main it may be said that the Rus, though securing the benefits of the Greek Orthodox religion, did not secure the other important benefits—from a cultural point of view, that is— of ancient Greek philosophy, literature, and thought in general. The reasons for this are probably that the Greek clergy going to Russia were almost always monks, who were often inspired by the typical monastic suspicion of classical learning and emphasis on ascetic works. Important, too, is the Byzantine permissiveness with respect to the liturgy in the Slavonic tongue. Though, as has been noted, this was a fundamental contribution to the formation of Russian civilization (and hardly less, later, to the development of a sense of Russian ethnicity), it also meant that the Slavic clergy had no need to learn Greek, so that the treasures of the classical Greek world were generally closed to them.

The Kievan state in the eleventh and early twelfth centuries, at the height of its civilization, included several important urban centers. Indeed, the contrast with the West, with only the beginnings of an urban society in the eleventh century, is quite striking. Western clerics, however, especially the monks through their knowledge of ecclesiastical Latin, had a key to the understanding of the works of Latin classical literature and also of the writings of the Latin Church Fathers, themselves students of the rhetorical education of ancient Rome. These clerics could, if they wished, read Vergil, Cicero, and other authors who, while they may have known nothing of Christianity, served to give them a sense of style and at least an awareness of a more sophisticated and cosmopolitan way of life.

In contrast, the Rus, with very few exceptions, did not learn Greek. Hence they were cut off from the beneficial influences of classical Greek civilization, a fact which certain modern Western historians believe retarded the growth of Russian culture up to the seventeenth century. In reviewing the causes of this later Russian backwardness, especially in the sixteenth and seventeenth centuries, one should not overlook the terrible havoc and disorganization caused by the Tatar invasions of Russia earlier in the thirteenth century—invasions which brought about the destruction of the Kievan state itself. In any event, there is no doubt that from the tenth to the thirteenth centuries Byzantine culture played so dominant a role in civilizing the Rus that, second only to the native Russian element itself, the Byzantine contribution may justifiably be considered the most significant component in the Russian cultural synthesis.

Kievan Social Structure

The assimilation of the old Scandinavian conquerors by the Slavic population was relatively rapid, becoming reasonably complete by the mid-eleventh century. In the twelfth century the population of the Kievan state, it has been estimated (perhaps exaggeratedly) was between seven and eight million people. At the top of this society were the prince and his family (in a sense representing the Byzantine Emperor, or at least constituting, theoretically, a member of the imperial "family of princes") with his military retainers, the *druzhina*. The fusion of the retainers of the prince and the local aristocracy, both of which comprised the noble class, produced the *boyars,* who were to become so important in modern Russian history.

The bulk of the population, the so-called *smerdy,* belonged to the lowest class, the agricultural population living in the countryside. At the beginning of the Kievan period most of the peasants were free, and this free peasantry (unlike in the Western medieval period) remained an important element in the history of the Kievan state. At the same time, however, several kinds of bondage were gradually appearing. Bondage often resulted from the inability of a person to repay loans to a landlord, forcing him to accept a dependent position. The peasants in the countryside paid "hearth" taxes and these constituted the principal taxes in Kiev.

Kiev, in contrast to the West up to the eleventh century, possessed an important middle class. Because of its location and intensive trading interests the Kievan state early developed a number of wealthy towns. I have already described the principal articles of commerce between Kiev and Byzantium. Rus traders were often organized in associations similar to Byzantine (or later Western) guilds; indeed, mercantile activity, including financial transactions, enjoyed a comparatively high development in Kiev. The Kievan people carried on an extensive internal trade for their own immediate needs, but no less important was the long-range international "Varangian" trade (discussed in Chapter 6), carried on by way of the great network of rivers. There was a rather wide circulation of money, starting with the reign of Vladimir in the late tenth century when silver coins were minted. In general, the active commercial Kievan cities resembled Constantinople or Baghdad much more than Paris or London. Agriculture was always basic to Kievan Russia but trade too was very important. Indeed, in the eleventh and very early twelfth centuries, Kiev, proportionately, may have had more of a money economy than Western Europe which was, economically, then somewhat less advanced.

The democratic tendencies characteristic of the Kievan people were seen in the Veche, an assembly which consisted of the heads of all households. Later, in the period of the breakup of Kievan power and afterward, the Veche, especially in the cities of Novgorod and Pskov, came to play an even greater role. In the earlier Kievan period, however, the town councils of the Kievan areas were only *ad hoc* assemblies with no clear definition of powers. But gradually the assembly of the Veche came to have authority to decide on such basic issues as war and peace, emergency laws, and conflicts with the prince of the realm or between various contending princes.

The ruler of the whole state was the prince (Kniaz), who was above both the Veche of each town and above his council of boyars, the Duma. The Kievan state itself, rather loosely organized, was ruled by a number of lesser princes, with the one in Kiev retaining a special position. From the twelfth century on, he was called the Grand Prince. His duties were to lead in time of war, to dispense justice, and to head the administration. In wartime he depended on his druzhina and on soldiers gathered from the important towns. Chief judicial and administrative responsibilities were his, but at the same time he worked with the elected officials and those appointed by himself, correlating their efforts with the local elements. The government by princes was, it should be noted, a somewhat later development that was superimposed on the local political institutions such as the towns. The law of Kievan Russia, known especially through Jaroslav the Wise's code, *Russian Justice* (eleventh century), reveals the considerable degree of development of Russian society in the field of commerce.*

The boyar Duma expanded with the development of Kievan Russia, the higher clergy now sometimes also meeting with it. Its chief function was to meet with and advise the prince and his immediate retainers. Conditions varied from city to city, but, as a whole, the institutions listed above were typical of the various principalities composing the Kievan state. These institutions worked reasonably well. One internal weakness, however, was so pronounced that it often left the state confused in the face of outside danger. This was the lack of any definite regulation for succession to the throne of the princes, especially that of the Grand Prince. To make matters worse, it was the practice of the great princes to divide up the land of the state among all their sons and heirs, as if it were their own private property. This fragmentation of the state, which increased the more as the families grew in size, brought constant internecine warfare to the state after the death of Jaroslav the Wise in 1054. Indeed, since the state was never *completely* centralized politically—though of course it always strove for unity—this situation finally led to the destruction of the state in 1240, when Kiev was faced with attack by the Mongols. Despite Kiev's collapse the tradition of the unity of the Russian people as exemplified in the Kievan state and church was to remain vivid in the memories of the Russians and an example to which patriots in later centuries would point with pride and nostalgia.

The Second Bulgarian Empire and the Serbs

Several revivals of Slavic power later occurred in the Balkans among the Bulgars and the Serbs. In the later twelfth century and subsequently during the period of Latin rule over Constantinople (1204–1261), a Vlach family arose to lead the Bulgars. (The Vlachs, a people primarily of herdsmen, are the ancestors of the modern Romanians, presumably descendants of Romans who, in the mountain strongholds of Dacia, had managed to survive in the face of all the depredations of Goths, Turkic peoples, and Slavs.) In 1187, under the two Asen brothers, the so-called Second Bulgarian Empire was established, which made a

---

* Only the first ten articles of the *Russian Justice* are attributed to Jaroslav, the rest to his sons. (An extended version belongs to a later time.)

serious but unsuccessful attempt to conquer Constantinople from the weak Latins. It was under John Asen II (1215–1241) that Bulgar hegemony reached its height. At his court at Trnovo—where imposing ruins remain—John ruled with Byzantine pomp and ceremony by means of a bureaucracy formed in imitation of the Byzantine. The civilization was in fact basically Byzantine but adapted to conform to the character of the Balkan Slavs. After John's death his empire practically fell to pieces under the impact of a new Slavic power, Serbia.

Serbia and Byzantine Culture.   The Serbs, largely under their first important ruler, Stephen Nemanya (1168–1196), had also accepted Christianity from their powerful eastern neighbor, Byzantium. The work of Stephen's son, St. Sava, is most important; he reorganized the Serbian Church and won recognition of its autonomy from Byzantium. In the thirteenth century Serbia was still overshadowed by the neighboring Bulgars, but in the early fourteenth century the Serbian state began to surpass its rival, reaching its zenith under its greatest ruler, Stefan Dušan (1331–1355). Like so many medieval Balkan rulers he too was fascinated by the glamor of Constantinople and dreamed of becoming "Roman" emperor. He managed to conquer all of Macedonia, except for Thessalonica, and, in the course of his reign, to culturally Byzantinize his people. His law code, based in part on the Byzantine, is notable, and Serbian churches and buildings are essentially Byzantine in style and feeling. But his empire depended too much on his personal abilities and after his death in 1355 it quickly crumbled. With the steady advance of the Turks into the Balkans, the fate of the Bulgars was finally sealed at the Battle of the Maritza in 1371 and, shortly after, that of the Serbs at Kossovo in 1389.

Western Influence on Kiev

I have focused essentially on Byzantine influences on the state of Kiev. But during the medieval period there were also significant Western influences penetrating into the Russian areas as a result of marriage alliances, trade with Western countries, travelers, and German missionaries who sought to draw the Kievan Church away from the Byzantine and into the sphere of papal influence. Influences from the West became stronger in the thirteenth and fourteenth centuries in the extreme western portion of the Kievan state, which gradually fell under the influence of Poland and Lithuania. In 1386, when the two princely houses of Poland and Lithuania were joined together, previously pagan Lithuania adopted Roman Catholicism, and, as a result, the western Russian territories became subject to stronger Latin influences. The penetration of Polish Catholicism into Russia, an element that clashed with native Russian Orthodox tendencies, made it difficult for the rulers of Poland, Lithuania, and western Russia successfully to consolidate their territories.

The state of Kiev, as noted, had been declining in power since its political and cultural apogee under Jaroslav the Wise who died in 1054. In 1167 this decline was especially marked by the removal of the seat of the Grand Prince for political reasons from Kiev northwestward to the city of Vladimir (near present-day Moscow). In 1169 and 1203 Kiev was even sacked by other rivalrous Russian princes. All these factors helped to bring about the breakup of Kievan territory and made it harder for those in authority to meet the constant threat from nomadic tribes. There are economic reasons also for the Kievan decline. As a result of the cutting of the long-used Varangian trade route by invading nomadic tribes such as Cumans, and the Latin capture of Constantinople in 1204, trade between Kiev and Latin Constantinople virtually came to an end. (Some ecclesiastical contacts, however, continued between the Orthodox areas of the East.)

The Tatars and Kiev.   What brought the final downfall, the actual destruction, of the city of Kiev, was the invasion of the Tatars. A new Mongol people advancing from central Asia, the Tatars established a tremendous empire extending from the China Sea all the way to Eastern Europe. Their raids fanned out in all directions. One group of Tatars, later called the "Golden Horde," after earlier incursions finally succeeded in 1240 in taking Kiev, which they razed to the ground. The domination of the Tatars over Russia in the subsequent two centuries is the most salient fact in the history of this late medieval period. Tatar domination was not a true occupation, however. Its main features were the levying of a heavy tribute but only a general supervision of the politics and affairs of each area through control of the ruling princes and officials. (Occasional raids of destruction and pillage on the part of Tatars did certainly occur.) Nevertheless, according to most scholars, the Tatar domination was a highly disruptive factor in Russian society and was certainly one, if not the main, cause of the stagnation of Russian culture and economic and political life in the thirteenth and fourteenth centuries. The Tatar hegemony ended only with the rise of a new Russian state, Muscovy.

Although many Western historians have deplored what they believe to be the "isolation" of Russia from Western Europe owing to the Tatar conquest, it seems more true to believe that the Tatars did not inhibit Russian contacts with the West. Rather the cutting off of Russia from the West was due more to the mutual hostility engendered by the Latin conquest of Orthodox Constantinople in 1204 and the crusade of the German Teutonic knights into the lands of the Baltic area. One exception to Russia's growing isolation, however, was the city of Novgorod in northwestern Russia which was never devastated by the Tatars, and continued to have close commercial relations with the West, especially with the German cities of the Hanseatic League.

In general, the Mongol peoples were at first tolerant of all religions. They exempted the Orthodox Church from the payment of tribute, which led to the rapid expansion of Church landholdings. Several late thirteenth- and fourteenth-century Popes made efforts to convert the Mongols to Christianity and thereby to secure an alliance against the advancing Ottoman Turks. Papal envoys were sent even to distant Peking for this purpose, and accounts they wrote of their experiences exist. It was in this period, when Western Europe came to know more about the Far East, that the Venetian Marco Polo made his fabulous journey to China. Polo's remarkable experiences at the court of Kublai Khan in Peking and other areas of the Far East may be read in his work known as *The Book of Messer Marco Polo of Venice* (probably composed in 1296 to 1299), which is a remarkable example of the linking of widely scattered cultures in the Middle Ages.

The existence of the huge Mongol Empire made communications between Western Europe and the Far East relatively easy. And conditions remained so until the conquest of the Middle Eastern territories, especially Constantinople, by the Ottoman Turks in 1453, as a result of which a kind of iron curtain was rung down between the Far East and the West. Thus in the later fifteenth century, before the voyages of Vasco da Gama and Columbus, Western Europe knew less about the Far East than it had a hundred years before in the period of the Mongol Empire.

The Rise of Muscovy

Principal credit for the expulsion of the Tatars from Russia goes to the princes of Moscow. Moscow, located in northeast Russia in the Volga-Oka basin, originated as a princely village or settlement sometime before 1147. A chronicle entry for that year reveals that the Prince of Suzdal invited his ally of Nizhnii-Novgorod "to come to Moscow." In the next decade, the chronicle tells us, the Grand Prince Iurii Dolgoruki "laid the foundations of the city of Moscow," a statement evidently referring to the construction of the city wall. In the thirteenth century the area around Moscow was still "frontier" territory, in which the chief political authority lay in the hands of the various local princes. But it was at Moscow that a line of able princes emerged, who finally managed to cast off the old, debilitating Kievan custom of dividing the state among all the princely heirs, and who, through clever diplomacy in their relations with the Tatars, were appointed the latter's agents for the purposes of tribute collection.

We have very little information on the early period of Moscow's history; almost all we know definitely is that in the course of warfare it was destroyed in 1237 by the Mongols. One celebrated name, however, dates from this obscure period—that of the hero Alexander Nevskii, Prince of Novgorod, who in 1240, on the banks of the Neva River, managed to stop the invasion of the neighboring Swedes. Later he became Grand Prince and secured possession of Moscow, which he added to his territorial possessions. Under his son Daniel (1283–1304) Moscow acquired a separate prince of its own who now resided there permanently and concentrated all his efforts in strengthening his principality. Daniel is usually regarded as the real founder of the Muscovite principality.

Like medieval France, Muscovy may be said to have developed through territorial accretion, that is, by adding the surrounding territories, one by one, to its nucleus, the city of Moscow. After conquering the entire extent of the Moscow River, the Muscovite princes, for almost two centuries, engaged in a struggle with the Grand Prince of Tver. Moscow's victory in 1375 meant that Muscovy would be the leader of Russia and unite all the Russian people.

In 1318, through his marriage to the sister of the khan of the Golden Horde, Daniel's son Iurii received from the latter the title of Grand Prince. This was only temporary, however. After much intrigue on the part of the Tatars and the several Russian princes, the Prince of Moscow, Ivan Kalita, was finally confirmed in the title of Grand Prince in 1328.* Ivan increased the territory of Muscovy severalfold through purchasing territory and by warfare and intrigue. No ecclesiastical center had as yet emerged to replace Kiev, the cradle of Russian Christianity. But in 1328 Ivan Kalita persuaded the Orthodox metropolitan (who still belonged to the hierarchy of the Byzantine church) to settle permanently in Moscow, and from then on "the metropolitan of Kiev and all Russia," as that ecclesiastic was called, resided in Moscow. This event made Moscow not only the spiritual center of Russia, but added considerable prestige to its princes who now again had a direct ecclesiastical connection with Constantinople.

By the second half of the fourteenth century the Golden Horde, which ruled over Russia, was in decline. And the Muscovite princes now became emboldened to cast off the Mongol yoke. Leading roles in the advancement of Muscovite power against the Golden Horde and also against Moscow's Russian rival, the Grand Prince of Tver and the latter's ally, Lithuania, were played by the Metropolitan Alexis and the Muscovite Grand Prince Dmitrii. In 1378 the latter defeated the Mongols in battle and replaced the wooden walls of the Kremlin with walls of stone. The Mongols, however, allied themselves with Lithuania in the aim of jointly invading all the Russian territories. Crossing the Don River quickly with a large host, Dmitrii, at the Battle of Kulikovo in 1380, succeeded in crushing the vaunted Mongol cavalry. This great victory finally laid to rest the legend of Mongol invincibility. Many of the other Russian princes now rallied against the common enemy in an undertaking blessed by the Russian Church. After this victory Moscow was to play an even more significant part in Russian history.

---

* For a time the title, technically, was "Grand Prince of Vladimir." But though he held this title, Ivan Kalita and his successors resided in Moscow.

Vasilii I (1389–1425), who now came to the throne, successfully continued the Muscovite policy of enlarging the principality and looking to its welfare. He also waged a continuous struggle against Lithuania for the western Russian territories. After Kulikovo, the Mongols, though notably weakened, were able for a time to reassert their power and even again to sack Moscow. But the last real evidence of Mongol strength came a century later, in 1480, when they tried, unsuccessfully, to extract tribute from the Muscovite lands. Henceforth, the yoke of the Mongols was formally and finally cast off.

Moscow, Byzantium, and Rome

In the reign of Vasilii II (1425–1462) in Moscow, Russia was deeply affected by events in the West involving Byzantium and the Roman Church. At the Council of Florence in 1439 (see earlier in this chapter), in order to gain Western aid against the Turks for their beleaguered capital of Constantinople, the Greek emperor and representatives of his clergy signed an abortive agreement with Rome, recognizing papal ecclesiastical supremacy. The metropolitan of Russia, the Greek prelate Isidore, on his return to Moscow from Florence, was imprisoned by the displeased Prince Vasilii II for signing the decree (Isidore later managed to escape to the West where he was appointed a cardinal of the Roman Church by the Pope.) In 1443 a council of Russian bishops formally condemned the ecclesiastical union and deposed Isidore. And, finally, in 1448 the Russian bishops elected their own metropolitan (Jonah) but without benefit of consecration from Constantinople. This marked the formal end of the centuries-long dependence of the Russian Orthodox Church on the Byzantine (but not their connection). After the Council of Florence the Russians regarded the Greeks as traitors to their common faith, the purity of which, in the eyes of the Russians, had been violated by the Greek signing of union. For the Russians, Orthodoxy was now preserved inviolate only in Russia.

The fall of Constantinople in 1453 to the Turks came to be looked upon by the Russians as a sign of God's judgment and punishment for the act of impiety committed at Florence. Thus the ties between Russia and the Greeks of Byzantium and the Slavs of the Balkans, both of whom had so greatly influenced the Russians in the religious, cultural, and ideological spheres, were now weakened. Sporadic influences, however, would continue, especially when Greek scholar-refugees or ecclesiastics (such as Maxim the Greek) would come from Orthodox monasteries on Mt. Athos or be summoned to Moscow for political or ecclesiastical reasons. To Moscow's dislike of the West was now added its violent disapproval of the Greeks. Moscow thus became xenophobic and tended more and more to withdraw into itself, to become more parochial.

Nevertheless, Russia could not completely reject the roots of its religion and culture. And so in 1472, when the Pope tried to arrange a marriage between

Ivan III, Prince of Moscow, and Sophia, the niece of the last Byzantine emperor, Constantine XI (who in 1453 had perished on the walls of Constantinople fighting the Turks), Ivan was glad to accept. In proposing this marriage between Ivan and Sophia, who had fled to Rome after 1453 and converted to Catholicism, the Pope hoped to bring about religious union with the Russian Church and then to launch a joint crusade against the Turks. But Ivan III turned the event to his own profit.

Late Byzantine Influences on Muscovy

At this time a new imperial ideology was being devised in Moscow. Part of this, especially in its religious and theological aspects, was derived from the Byzantine tradition and another part, the more secular, represented the Muscovite rulers' consciousness of being successors to the Tatar khans. Ivan III assumed the Byzantine title of autocrat and also of tsar (which, interestingly enough, had also been applied to the Tatar khans by the Russians). When Sophia arrived in Moscow (where she at once reverted to the Orthodox faith), she brought with her a large entourage of Italians and Byzantines. And it was possibly under her influence and certainly because it served his own political purposes that Ivan now began to use the titles of Tsar and Autocrat and adopted as his emblem the Byzantine double-headed eagle.* Ivan also developed a complex court ceremonial based in part on the Byzantine pattern and in part on the Tatar. Finally, in true Byzantine fashion, he had himself crowned in solemn ecclesiastical rites.

While the adoption of these new titles served to give the Grand Prince of Moscow added prestige, his position was further enhanced by the emergence in this period of various legends, especially that of Moscow as "the third Rome," the successor to Byzantium. This legend stressed that Christianity had been first brought to southern Russia by St. Andrew, one of the Twelve Apostles, who was believed to have founded the see of Constantinople. It even claimed that the Muscovite princes were descended from the brother of Augustus, the first Roman emperor, and that Emperor Constantine IX Monomachus of Constantinople in the mid-eleventh century had sent a crown to the ruler Vladimir Monomach in Kiev. Ivan III himself now seemed to act like a Byzantine ruler; he rarely consulted his nobles, preferring to make his decisions by himself. It has been suggested also that he emulated the Byzantine emperors in his ceremonies and in building a great palace set apart from other buildings in the Kremlin. It was under his successor, Ivan IV, however, that these Byzantine political ideals, with their belief in the absolute power of the emperor as derived directly from God, were explicitly formulated.

* A recent view holds, rather, that the double-headed eagle, though originally Byzantine, probably came to Russia by way of the Holy Roman Empire.

The growing political and theological ideology of a Russian absolutism in the Byzantine manner found remarkable expression in the writings of the monk Philotheus of an Orthodox monastery situated in Pskov. In a letter of his dated at the beginning of the sixteenth century we read:

> [Our ruler] is on earth the sole emperor [tsar] of the Christians, the leader of the Apostolic Church, which stands no longer in Rome or in Constantinople but in the blessed city of Moscow. She alone shines in the whole world brighter than the sun. All Christian empires are fallen and in their stead stands alone the empire of our ruler in accordance with the prophetical books. *Two Romes have fallen but the third stands and a fourth there will not be.**

With the Greek Church in bondage to the Muslim Turks, Moscow, according to this ideology, was the only Orthodox monarchy remaining and therefore should assume a protective role over Orthodox Christians everywhere. The Russian tsar who, to be sure, had also learned something from the autocracy of the Tatars, had now been transformed, at least from the Russian (and many other Orthodox) churchmen's point of view, into a Byzantine basileus.

The culmination of the Russian rise to high prestige in the Orthodox world came in 1589, when the metropolitan of Moscow was promoted to the rank of patriarch, receiving his crown from the hands of Jeremiah, the Greek patriarch of Constantinople himself, who had been summoned to Moscow for this purpose. In the charter of installation when the metropolitan was elevated to the patriarchate "of all Russia," the words of Philotheus were reaffirmed:

> Because the old Rome has collapsed on account of the heresy of Apollinaris,† and because the second Rome, which is Constantinople is now in the hands of the godless Turks, thy great kingdom, o pious Tsar, is the third Rome.... Thou art the only Christian sovereign in the world, the Master of all faithful Christians.‡

FOR FURTHER READING

Dvornik, F., *The Slavs in European History and Civilization* (1962). The best account of this complex subject by the leading scholar in the field. Emphasizes Byzantine influence.

Eversley, G., and Ghirol, V., *The Turkish Empire, Its Growth and Decay* (1969). Interesting, rather recent work.

---

* N. Zernov, trans., *The Russians and Their Church* (1945).

† The view that while Christ possessed the human body and soul, the Divine Logos replaced in Him the human spirit.

‡ Zernov, *The Russians.*

Florinsky, M. T., *Russia: A History and Interpretation*, Vol. I (1953). An excellent treatment of early Russian history.

Geanakoplos, D. J., *Byzantine East and Latin West: Two Worlds of Christendom in Middle Ages and Renaissance* (1966). Treats in synthesis the relations of the Greek and Latin worlds. Includes an essay on the Council of Florence. Valuable work.

Geanakoplos, D. J., Chapters 2 and 3, "Byzantium and the Later Crusades," in *A History of the Crusades,* ed. K. Setton, Vol. 3 (1974). Sole account to focus on the Byzantine role in the later Crusades.

Geanakoplos, D. J., *Emperor Michael Palaeologus and the West, 1258–1282: A Study in Byzantine-Latin Relations* (1959; 1973). The crucial reign of Michael Palaeologus, emphasizing his diplomacy with the West, religious union of Lyons, and the Sicilian Vespers.

Geanakoplos, D. J., *Interaction of the "Sibling" Byzantine and Western Cultures in Middle Ages and Italian Renaissance* (1976). A unique historical-sociological analysis of cultural relations between East and West.

Gibbon, E., *The Decline and Fall of the Roman Empire,* ed. J. Bury (1914). A classic work, if dated.

Gibbons, H. A., *The Foundation of the Ottoman Empire* (1968). An authoritative work.

Kritoboulos, *The History of Mehmed the Conqueror,* trans. C. F. Riggs (1954). The life and career of Muhammad I, written by a Byzantine.

Lane, F. C., *Venetian Ships and Shipping of the Renaissance* (1934). A valuable analysis of the shipbuilding of Europe's then greatest maritime power.

Lopez, R. S., and Raymond, I. W., eds., *Medieval Trade in the Mediterranean World* * (1967). A valuable collection of translations of medieval economic documents.

Miller, W., *The Latins in the Levant: A History of Frankish Greece, 1204–1566* (1964). A standard work on the subject.

Nicol, D., *The Last Centuries of Byzantium, 1261–1453* (1972). Detailed, political-ecclesiastical survey.

Obolensky, D., *The Byzantine Commonwealth: Eastern Europe, 500–1453* (1971). Fine survey of Byzantine influence on the Slavs.

Pears, E., *The Destruction of the Greek Empire and the Story of the Capture of Constantinople by the Turks* (1969). A fascinating account, though now a bit dated in spots, of the last century and a half of Byzantium's troubled existence. Political in scope.

Runciman, S., *Byzantine Style and Civilization* (1975).* Valuable on art.

Vacalopoulos, A., *Origins of the Greek Nation, 1204–1461* (1970). Fine synthesis, stressing growth of modern Greek nationalism.

Vernadsky, G., *Kievan Russia* (1948). A standard work, analyzing especially Kievan institutions.

* Asterisk indicates paperback edition available.

Vryonis, S., *The Decline of Medieval Hellenism in Asia Minor and the Process of Islamization from the Eleventh through the Fifteenth Century* (1971). Very careful analytical study of Turkish takeover of Anatolia.

Wittek, P., *The Rise of the Ottoman Empire* (1971). A significant work stressing the forces behind the emergence of Ottoman power.

Zenkovsky, S. A., ed. and trans., *Medieval Russia's Epics, Chronicles and Tales** (1963). A valuable collection of translations from early Russian sources.

The Later Middle Ages:
The Early Renaissance

PART III *The Later Middle Ages: The Early Renaissance*

Western World	Byzantine and Slavic World	Islamic World
	c.1270–1453 Palaeologan Renaissance in Byzantium	1301 Ottoman Turks penetrate into Bithynia, control most of Asia Minor
1302 Boniface's Bull, *Unam Sanctam* 1305–1306 Giotto paints in Arena chapel 1305–1378 Avignonese "captivity" of Papacy	1311 Catalans defeat Franks of Morea at Cephissus 1320s Civil wars in Byzantium 1328 Metropolitan of Kiev settles in Moscow c.1337 Theophanes "the Greek" paints at Chora in Constantinople, later in the Kremlin	1337 Nicaea becomes Ottoman capital
1338–1453 Hundred Years' War 1348 Black Plague	1348 Black Plague 1351 Hesychast theology accepted by Greek Church 1355 Death of Stephen Dušan	
1356 Battle of Poitiers	1360s Civil wars in Byzantium	
1361 Pilatus gets Greek chair in Florence		

1377 Gallipoli first European capital of Turkey

1389 Battle of Kossovo

1394 Turkish blockade of Constantinople

1402 Mongols defeat Ottomans at Ankara

1422 Turks besiege Constantinople

1367 John V accepts Catholicism in Rome
1371 Battle of Maritza
Civil wars in Byzantium

1380 Battle of Kulikovo—Moscow defeats Tatars

1389 Battle of Kossovo
1391–1425 Manuel II rules in Byzantium

1396–1397 Chrysoloras sent West for aid against Turks

1399–1402 Manuel II in West seeking aid

1409 Cretan Peter Philarges elected Pope at Pisa (Alexander V)

1422 Turks besiege Constantinople

1378 Disputed papal election: Great Schism begins

1381 Peasants' rebellion in England

1394 Petrarch dies

1396 French crusaders defeated at Nicopolis
1397 Chrysoloras begins teaching in Florence

1402 Giangaleazzo Visconti dies in Milan
1409 Council of Pisa

1410 Bruni translates Chrysostom's *Advice to Young*
1414 Council of Constance
1417 Great Schism ends: Martin IV Pope

1428 Masaccio dies in Florence

PART III *The Later Middle Ages: The Early Renaissance*

Western World	Byzantine and Slavic World	Islamic World
1431–1449 Council of Basle	1430 Thessalonica falls to Turks	
1434 Cosimo de' Medici takes power in Florence		
1438–1439 Council of Florence: Union of Greek and Latin churches	1435 Greek colony at Naples established	
	1438–1439 Council of Florence	
1447–1455 Nicholas V, Pope	1444 Battle of Varna	1444 Battle of Varna
	1448 Russian Bishops elect Metropolitan independently of Constantinople	
		1451–1481 Muhammad II reigns
c.1453 Printing with movable type appears	1453 Fall of Constantinople	1453 Turks take Constantinople
	1453ff. More Greek scholar-refugees flee to West	1454 Peace of Lodi
1457 Gutenberg Bible	1460 Mistra falls to Turks	
1462 Platonic Academy established in Florence		
1463 Chalcondyles inaugurates Greek studies at Padua		
1468–1470 Ficino finishes translating Plato	1472 Marriage of Ivan III and Sophia in Moscow	
1469–1492 Lorenzo "rules" in Florence		
1476 First Greek book published	1494 Legal recognition of Greek colony in Venice	
1492 Columbus discovers America		
1494–1510 Aldine Academy flourishes		
1494 France invades the Italian peninsula		
1494–1498 Savonarola in power in Florence		

Four or five decades ago, when they were more prone to periodization, historians tended to view the Middle Ages in the West as ending rather abruptly and distinctly during the middle or latter part of the fifteenth century. According to this simplistic view, Italy, under the influence of rediscovered writings of classical antiquity, discarded the civilization of the "moribund" Middle Ages and experienced a rebirth or "Renaissance" of ancient culture that resulted in the emergence of new institutions, new social and cultural values, and above all, a new, more secular way of looking at the world. Although historians still find the term *Renaissance* useful as a label for certain developments in fourteenth- and fifteenth-century history, no reputable scholar would today maintain that a new and radically different civilization suddenly emerged in

CHAPTER 13

*T*ime of *T*ransition: Politics, Economics, and Religion in Western Society

Italy, much less in northern Europe. Rather, most historians now tend to view the "Early Renaissance" era of the fourteenth and fifteenth centuries as a period of transition from medieval to modern times, the twilight of one era, the medieval, and the dawn of another, the *early* modern—during which older ideas and institutions continued to exist or, especially in Italy, were in the process of being transmuted by the development of an increasingly sophisticated urban society.

In this chapter I shall discuss various historical phenomena of the fourteenth and fifteenth centuries, focusing on ecclesiastical, political, and socioeconomic developments, many of which exhibited characteristics still essentially medieval and others which, in their newness, belonged rather to the "Renaissance" era. In Chapter 14 I shall concentrate particularly on "high culture," that is, on intellectual, artistic, and aesthetic attitudes and achievements in Italy and northern Europe, the creative impulses of which emerged from, or are to a large extent to be found in, the socioeconomic, religious, and political milieus of society discussed here.

Besides analyzing the *internal* forces making for cultural change within the societies of Italy and the North, I will, in Chapter 14, take care to point out the impact on the West of *external* cultural influences coming from the Byzantine East, which was in the final process of political and social dissolution, yet at the same time undergoing an astonishing cultural "Renaissance" of its own. Many of the fruits of this late Byzantine Renaissance were brought to Italy by Byzantine exiles from their captured homeland.

A word of warning to the reader: generalization is difficult in the best of circumstances but probably even more so for the transitional period of the Later Middle Ages or Early Renaissance. The conditions to be described were not the same in all parts of Western Europe nor were the cultural and social changes equally rapid in all areas. Indeed, in some instances it may even seem that society, rather than "advancing," was becoming more "medieval" than ever.

The Decline of Clerical Influence

If one were to select the clearest manifestation of the decay or alteration of the medieval ethos that took place in the fourteenth and fifteenth centuries, one would probably choose the decline of clerical influence in society. In less than a century the far-reaching moral and temporal authority of the Papacy, which Gregory VII and Innocent III had so tirelessly worked to establish, lost much of its efficacy. The Papacy underwent humiliation at the hands of a secular prince, suffering, finally, the degradation of a schism that rent all of Western Christendom and during which two and for a time three Popes simultaneously claimed to be the true successor of St. Peter. It is a testimony to the vitality of the Papacy that it managed to survive in the face of the repeated reverses it suffered during this period.

At the very beginning of the fourteenth century the Papacy received the blow from which it was never fully to recover. Only fifty years before, the Popes had destroyed their greatest political antagonists, the Hohenstaufen emperors. But, imperceptibly at first, after this high point, the influence of the Papacy as the international arbiter of Western Christendom began to be undermined by a growing allegiance on the part of Western peoples to the rulers of the emerging nation states. And it was in open conflict with the kings of the two leading states, France and England, that the head of the Church was defeated.

I have already mentioned the clash of Pope Boniface VIII and King Philip IV of France (Chapter 8). Here is a summary of the main events in the history of that quarrel, concentrating on its ramifications for the Papacy. The first dispute arose over the claim of the French and English kings to tax their clergy without papal consent. But this episode was only a prelude to a larger struggle between the kings, who were attempting to extend their authority over the churchmen of their realms, and the Pope, who was equally determined to maintain his control over these same churchmen. The first phase was won by the kings, who, by their prohibition of the export of monies from their kingdoms, forced Boniface to retreat and grant the monarchs the right to tax their clergy in time of need. The second phase involved an even more fundamental question: the claim of the king to try a cleric in a royal court, in defiance of canon law and ecclesiastical tradition.

The unscrupulous Philip IV of France had seized a French bishop and held him for trial on the charge of treason. Pope Boniface ordered Philip forthwith to send the cleric to Rome for trial. The wording of the papal bull *Ausculta Fili* ("Listen, My Son,"), accusing Philip and his advisers of transgressions against the Church, was subtly altered by Philip's "henchmen" in order to arouse French public opinion against the Pope. At the same time Philip, to manipulate public opinion further, convoked what has been called the first Estates General. Even French clerics felt compelled by a sense of outrage to protest against Boniface.

The Pope, misjudging his adversary and the strength of French opinion, now put forth in his bull *Unam Sanctam* what is often taken to be the most extreme statement ever made of papal claims to supreme power. He affirmed that there are two swords in the world, the temporal and spiritual, both of which belong to and are wielded according to the will of the Pope. The bull closed with the statement, "It is absolutely necessary to salvation that every human being be subject to the Roman Pontiff."

Thereupon Philip and his agents decided to go to Rome, arrest Boniface, and bring him back to Paris for trial. They actually laid hands on the person of the Pope, but Boniface was freed by the citizens of Anagni, where the violence took place. Shocked and humiliated, the aged Boniface died soon afterward.

At this point the fate of the medieval Papacy depended on Boniface's successors. Europe might well have been horrified at the actions of Philip's agents had an energetic and shrewd Pope played up the incident. But the newly elected Pope, Benedict XI, old and weak, did not seize the opportunity to arouse public protest against the French king. Instead, Benedict even began the process (completed by his successor) of absolving Philip of any blame in the affair, although he refused forgiveness to his agent, Nogaret. In less than a year the new Pope was dead, and after a long deadlock among the cardinals a French archbishop was enthroned as Pope Clement V (1305–1314). There is no direct evidence, but it would seem that the new Pope owed his election to French influence.

The Babylonian Captivity and the Great Schism

Clement made a decision fateful for the future of the Papacy, when, stopping in Lyons on his way to Rome, he soon made it clear that he had no intention of proceeding to Italy. Subsequently, in fact, Clement established permanent residence in Avignon in southern France. Though a Papal possession, Avignon was surrounded by imperial territory and was in effect French in culture. Clement's decision was the result of a variety of reasons: fear of the unruly populace in Rome, his natural affection for France, and political pressure from Philip IV. For the next seventy years Clement and his successors remained at Avignon under what many modern historians take to be the influence of the French crown. This period from 1305 to 1378, reminiscent of the Hebrew bondage under Nebuchadnezzar, was called by the humanist Petrarch the "Babylonian Captivity" of the Papacy. During this time the Papacy lost much of its moral prestige in Christian Europe and, particularly in Italy, a good deal of its temporal authority as well.

Meanwhile Clement, under pressure from Philip IV, gave in on every important point on which Philip had clashed with the late Boniface, even to the extent, it appears, of absolving Nogaret of excommunication. More significant, Clement declared that Philip had shown "praiseworthy zeal" in accusing Boniface. This amazing declaration marked the end of the medieval Papacy as such. The remarkable thing about this whole episode is not that the Pope was successfully ambushed, but that the Papacy now actually had to apologize to the sacrilegious king. The Church had lost its political leadership; gone were the days when it could command the kings of Western Europe.

Installed at Avignon, the Papacy, attempting to meet the danger of the rise of strong secular governments, began to reorganize the financial and judicial structure of the Church, and to centralize it even further. In so doing, however, it only weakened its spiritual authority all the more. For public opinion, whether justified or not, began more widely than ever to criticize what appeared to be the Papacy's venality.

The difficulties of the situation were epitomized in the pontificate of John XXII, who so effectively squeezed out revenues from his subordinate clerics that contemporaries not infrequently called his administrative practices "financial extortion." Clerics bitterly complained about the heavy fees they had to pay to the Papacy, the different kinds of fees for taking office, and even echoed the charge of some laymen that the Popes were "selling salvation."

The Italian humanist Petrarch, a good Catholic who lived for a time at the court of Avignon, termed the Papacy the "whore of Babylon" and constantly raised his voice to insist on the Papacy's return to Rome. Protests became so widespread that the Popes themselves finally realized that they must abandon their magnificent new palace at Avignon and once again take up residence in Rome. Urged on by St. Catherine of Siena and others, one Pope actually set out for Rome, but the chaos of local Roman politics forced him to return.

In 1378, after Pope Gregory XI had finally returned to Rome, a very noteworthy papal election took place. The cardinals at Rome, under pressure from the Roman mob to elevate an Italian, proceeded to elect Urban VI. But some cardinals, fleeing the pressures of the Roman populace, changed their minds and chose instead a Frenchman, Clement VII. Clement established his court at Avignon. Each Pope, Urban at Rome and Clement at Avignon, excommunicated the other and his supporters. The so-called Great Schism, a rupture in the Catholic Church which was to last almost half a century, from 1378 to 1417, had now begun. At the death of each Pope his college of cardinals chose a successor, perpetuating the schism.

All of Europe became divided over the question of who was the legitimate Pope. And in this period, when salvation was still so important to people, one can imagine the significance of the problem. Political rivalries, however, usually determined the Pontiff whom a particular ruler would support. The French naturally gave allegiance to Clement VII, while the English supported Urban VI.

Papal authority in the hands of two, and at one time three, Popes, each hurling anathemas at the others, reached its lowest ebb during this Great Schism. At one point the Roman Pope even proclaimed a holy crusade against the French Pontiff. So confused were events that the Roman Church itself has never officially pronounced on the legitimacy of the various incumbent Popes, although the unofficial preference is clearly for the Roman line.

With the papal authority in such a state, many people, especially the intellectuals, looked for leadership in religious matters to the theological faculty of the University of Paris. Paris in fact now became the center of discussion as to how best to heal the schism. This talk gave impetus to the "conciliar" theory that had been in the air for some time and that called for the convocation of a great ecclesiastical council, as the early Church had done, to settle questions involving the Church as a whole. In its full-blown form the conciliar theory called in effect for the substitution of a kind of representative form of Church government to replace the monarchy of the Pope. This reflected, and was in a sense an attempt to apply to the Church, a parliamentary form of government, or, more accurately, a kind of "corporatism," paralleling a similar development in the governments of the leading nations of the West.

The schism was only compounded, however, when in 1409 a council held in Pisa attempted to depose the two incumbent Popes and a new Pontiff, the Greek Alexander V,* was elected. Neither Pope would accept this decision, and so for a time there were three. With all of Europe becoming increasingly aroused, the conciliar theory gained support despite the failure of the Council of Pisa to end the schism.

At a new council, convened by the Emperor Sigismund at Constance in 1414, it appeared that the conciliarists would triumph. This council constituted a veritable congress of Europe, lay representatives attending as well as ecclesiastics. The growth of a sense of "nationality" in Europe was evidenced by the division of the representatives into four "nations"—Italian, French, German, and English. At Constance the Pope of the Roman line (John XXIII, Alexander's successor) was prevailed upon to resign, but before he did so, he called a new council validating by Roman canon law that his was the true papal line. At any rate, with the papal throne now vacant, a new Pope was elected, and a series of decrees aimed at subordinating papal authority to that of the council. The decree *Frequens* affirmed that a general council, with or without papal approval, must be convoked every seven years to discuss matters of importance to the Church at large.

But the auspicious triumph of conciliarism at the Council of Constance proved ephemeral. The new Pope elected there, Martin V, was himself a strong-willed man who exercised what he claimed was his right as Pope under canon law to dissolve the council. He thus began to reassert papal authority. The need for reform of clerical abuses, however—from an international viewpoint to heal the "Great Schism," and on the more local level to abolish the scandals of clerical immorality and multiple benefices—still existed. In 1431 a council was once again called—this time by Pope Martin—to meet at Basel in Switzerland, to discuss ecclesiastical reform, and to seek a solution to the war between the emperor and the Hussite heretics. The struggle between the Pope (now Eugenius IV) and the conciliarists broke out anew, with the conciliar party seek-

---

* Alexander, born of Greek parents in Venetian-occupied Crete, had early become a Franciscan, then professor of theology at Paris, Archbishop of Milan, and finally Pope.

ing further to circumscribe papal authority, and Eugenius (1431–1447) attempting once and for all to quash the conciliar movement.

The struggle now became three-cornered, for at this point the old question of the reunion of the Greek and Latin churches came up again. Seeking aid against the Ottoman Turks, the Byzantine Emperor, as I noted in the last chapter, now offered to negotiate for union of the two churches in exchange for military support from the West. Both the conciliarists and the Pope hoped to use this offer of union to defeat the other.

By this time Eugenius had pronounced the council dissolved and the conciliarists, in return, had declared Eugenius deposed. Offers were sent by both parties to Constantinople, but the Greeks chose rather to negotiate with Eugenius. The success of Eugenius in bringing a Greek delegation to Italy and actually pronouncing religious union at the Council of Florence (1438–1439) was a major factor in securing his victory over the conciliarists. Many clerics at Basel, including the respected Nicholas of Cusa, now came over to Eugenius' side; the remainder lost the support of most of the secular rulers of Europe. The Pope was able to come to terms with individual Western rulers but had to surrender control over Church personnel in their realms in return for their support. Thus the Papacy had finally triumphed over conciliarism, but in so doing it lost to the rulers of Europe during the Babylonian Captivity and Great Schism its claims to temporal jurisdiction over the West.

Anticlerical and Heretical Movements

The degree to which clerical influence over society had declined in the period of the Babylonian Captivity and the Great Schism can be partly seen in the growth of anticlerical and heretical movements during the fourteenth century. In England an Oxford professor and priest, John Wycliffe (*c.*1328–1384), expressing a growing discontent among the people, began a movement that subsequently became known as Lollardry. This heresy denied much of the Pope's authority over the Church and in civil affairs and castigated the Church for its unseemly wealth and corruption. Ultimately Wycliffe repudiated the central Catholic doctrine of transubstantiation and challenged the role of the priesthood in the attainment of salvation. Wycliffe himself had powerful patrons and therefore was not persecuted. The strength of Lollardry came largely from the lower classes, who were becoming more and more resentful of the exactions and growing material possessions of the Church. Just before Wycliffe's death the movement became involved in the great Peasants' Revolt of 1381 and its force was to a considerable extent diminished.

Wycliffe's ideas, however, found root on the Continent, especially in Bohemia, the western part of modern Czechoslovakia. The rector of the University of Prague, John Hus (*c.*1369–1415), studied Wycliffe's writings and soon was preaching similar ideas of reform. Hus was summoned before the Council of Constance, where he appeared under the protection of a safe-conduct granted by the Emperor Sigismund. Hus refused to recant his "errors" and was condemned as a heretic. His safe-conduct proved little protection since the Council held that a promise made to a heretic was not considered binding on the Church. He and his chief followers were burned at the stake.

But Hussitism was not dead. For the Czechs, Hus became a martyr, and in Bohemia their fanaticism aided them to defeat every army sent against them. A certain "nationalism" was clearly evident among the Hussites, who looked with resentment at their King, the German emperor, as a "foreigner." The war between the Hussites and the German emperor thus took on something of the character of a "national" revolution as well as a religious war. The Hussite problem was finally solved by the Council of Basel (1431–1449), which, despite the opposition of Pope Eugenius IV, continued to sit until 1449. Certain concessions, including the right of laymen to take communion in both bread and wine,* were granted to the Czechs, which brought most of them back into the Catholic Church.

Political Problems of the Papacy in Italy

After the end of the conciliar problem, the Popes, though reaffirmed as head of the Church, were beset by so many problems that they were unable to affirm their former claims to universal leadership of society. Thus in political affairs the Papacy began to conduct itself in much the same manner as the Italian secular princes—seeking to build up a centralized papal state and even, as with the della Rovere and the Borgia families, to found a dynasty in central Italy. When that became the case, the Papacy lost still more of its moral authority and, in view of an increasingly corrupt Church, proved almost completely ineffectual in reforming the Church from within.

The chief political problem facing the Popes was the re-establishment of their authority over the patrimony of St. Peter—the territory cutting diagonally across central Italy that had long been under papal suzerainty. During the period of the Captivity and the Great Schism, petty lords of surrounding areas had constantly encroached on these lands, usurping the papal rights over them. Meanwhile the noble factions in Rome and the Roman populace—both always unruly—had succeeded in circumscribing papal control over the city of Rome itself. To compound the problem, the powerful Italian princes of Milan and Naples, to the north and south of the Papal States, now looked with covetous eyes on these territories.

After 1450 a series of politically able Popes managed to regain control over

---

* Called *Utraquism.*

the territory of the Papal States. They restored Rome as the hub of central Italy and at the same time turned the city into a center of art and learning. Popes Nicholas V (1447–1455) and Pius II (1458–1464) were accomplished scholars and patrons of the arts. Under these two Pontiffs an extensive program of building and beautification was undertaken in Rome. The greatest builder was Julius II (1503–1513) who gathered at his court such renowned artists as Raphael and Michelangelo and began the construction of the present basilica of St. Peter's.

Most successful in regaining sway over the states of the Church were Popes Alexander VI Borgia and Julius II della Rovere. The underlying aim of the Spaniard Alexander VI (1492–1503) seems to have been to carve out of the Papal States a principality for his son, Caesar Borgia. Every means was employed by father and son to achieve this goal—treachery, military action, even assassination, most commonly through the use of poison. So feared was the Borgia reputation that some of those going to dine with them took the precaution of making their wills before attending. Tradition has it that Alexander VI himself died after mistakenly eating a piece of poisoned fruit intended for one of his dinner guests. Caesar, though he lived on for another four years, was unable to secure the election of a pliant Pope and steadily lost influence. Thus evaporated the Borgia plan to turn the patrimony of St. Peter into a dynastic principality and, in the process, possibly even unite all of Italy.

Alexander's successor, Julius II (1503–1513), who had somewhat similar political aspirations, earned his epithet, "the warrior Pope," by personally leading his troops into battle. The temporal ambitions of the Popes were cut short, however, by the rivalry for control of all Italy that broke out between the great powers of France and Spain after the French invasion of Italy in 1494—an event that ushered in international political conflicts marking, in a sense, the end of the medieval period and the opening of the early modern era.

Papal Corruption

The papal programs of reconquest and beautification of Rome were costly. Popes from Nicholas V to Leo X were, therefore, in constant need of money. Often neglecting their spiritual duties in favor of temporal objectives—especially of gaining greater revenues—the later medieval Popes set a sorry example for the rest of the Church, and their financial exactions were imitated by others of the ecclesiastical hierarchy. A bishop, for example, had to pay a considerable sum to receive an appointment (usually in the form of "annates," the entire first year's income from his benefice). Appointment of the same person to more than one benefice, often in different places, further alienated public opinion. Under such circumstances the Church became ridden with venality.

I should not, however, exaggerate the extent of this corruption in the Church, for not all clerics were grasping, nor were all uninterested in their re-

The Medici Pope Leo X, Renaissance patron of literature and art, being carried on his portable throne while blessing the throng. (Victoria and Albert Museum)

ligious duties. But there is no doubt that such practices were common enough to evoke the protest and disaffection of a great many of the faithful within the Church. As a result the Church increasingly lost its moral and spiritual hold over the people of Western Europe. The ultimate result was the outbreak in the early sixteenth century of the Protestant Reformation and of the Catholic Counter-Reformation.

Political Developments

The Hundred Years' War

In the fourteenth and fifteenth centuries, the governments of France and England underwent a fundamental evolution from feudal kingdom to centralized, "dynastic" monarchy—itself the prelude to the modern "nation state." This development, significant for the early modern world, had begun several centuries earlier, but in the fourteenth, fifteenth, and early sixteenth centuries the process was completed, with the king of France emerging as the master of his state and the English ruler sharing his authority with Parliament. Here two factors were most significant: first, the efforts of the kings to continue and expand policies already established by their "feudal" predecessors, and second (and this acted mainly as a catalyst), the great century-long conflict between France and England, the Hundred Years' War, during which a consciousness of "nationality," to differing degrees, emerged among the peoples of each kingdom. In England, to be sure, there had been some vague feeling of "national" consciousness since at least the twelfth century, but this was not always the case in France, where in 1350 people could, for example, still regard themselves as Parisian or Picard rather than as French. And it was even less the case in Italy where the average Milanese citizen as late as the fifteenth century felt almost nothing in common with a Neapolitan of the time—this despite "humanist" figures such as Petrarch and Boccaccio, who already had felt a certain bond of common tradition joining people of the Italian peninsula.

Thus, although certain sentiments of "nationality" began to emerge in Italy and less so in Germany, these two countries remained until the nineteenth century as divided as they had been during the Middle Ages, primarily for lack of a political focal point, that is, one dynastic, hereditary monarchy. Nevertheless, in contrast to Germany and perhaps even to all the rest of Europe, in the various Italian city states there developed—under the influence of their own political experience, economic rivalries, and emerging humanism—a sense of loyalty to the individual city state that often exceeded the vague feeling of patriotism or "national" identity existing in France or England.

In the period following the death of Edward I (Chapter 8) England experienced a steady growth of parliamentary authority and of the administrative organs of government. Edward II (1307–1327), a weak king dominated by his favorites, was ultimately deposed and murdered by his wife and her lover. During the half-century reign of his son, Edward III (1327–1377), who delighted in warfare and hunting, parliamentary power continued to increase. Almost constantly at war with France, Edward was in perpetual need of money, which he could get only from Parliament. By the end of his reign it was clear that a significant shift of authority had taken place; not only was the king's right to tax independently almost destroyed, but his power to legislate by royal decree became inferior to parliamentary statute.

In France in this same period a change in dynasty occurred. Since Philip IV's sons left no male heirs, the Valois family, the progeny of a brother of Philip IV, was now elevated to the throne. No change in policy resulted, however, for the Valois kings strove to continue the piecemeal acquisition of territory and extension of royal authority that had marked the policy of their predecessors.

From the time of the accession of Philip VI of Valois to the French throne (1328) the histories of the French and English monarchies were bound together more closely than ever before. For over a century they were engaged in the bitter conflict known as the Hundred Years' War (1337–1453). Sometimes called the first modern conflict between nations, this war brought about fundamental changes in both kingdoms. Besides generating the beginnings of a sentiment of French "nationalism," it witnessed the development of new methods of warfare that ultimately destroyed the usefulness of the heavy-armed mounted knight of the medieval world.

Causes of War.   On the surface, the cause of the Hundred Years' War was the rivalry between English and French kings, existing from as far back as 1066. At that time the Duke of Normandy, while becoming king of England, had retained his fiefs within the kingdom of France as vassal of the French king. By 1328 most of the English possessions in France had been lost except Gascony, a large area of southwestern France. Edward III had a dim claim to the French throne through his mother, the daughter of Philip IV the Fair, and, as closest male relative, thought his claim might be superior to that of Philip VI Valois, the nephew of Philip IV. But French legists then declared that a woman could not transmit rights she did not have herself, and Edward's claim was thus disallowed.

There were other causes for the enmity of the two kings besides dynastic rivalry. Most important was perhaps the conflict of interest over the rich county of Flanders. As suzerain of Flanders the French king was determined to extract his rightful revenues from that county, a determination matched by Flemish refusal to acquiesce. The Flemings, especially the rich merchants, thereupon sought help from England. They knew England would readily respond; for Flanders, as a textile center and market for fine English wool, played an important part in England's economy.

The Course of the War.   For the sake of convenience the Hundred Years' War may be divided into four phases: the first (1337–1364) was marked by the success of English arms; the second (1364–1389), a period of gradual French recovery; the third (1389–1429), a time of French civil war resulting in England's near conquest of all of France; and the fourth phase (1429–1453), during which the English were finally expelled from France and a strong French monarchy emerged.

In the first phase of the war almost complete disaster overtook the French kingdom. The English won stunning victories, notably at Crécy in 1346 and at Poitiers in 1356. In both battles (though less so at Poitiers) the English tactics were new to the French knights, accustomed as they were to the traditional cavalry charge against mounted warriors. At Crécy English foot soldiers armed with the longbow were placed in the front lines. These bows, five to six feet in length, could shoot an arrow over five-hundred yards (though with no great accuracy), with a force great enough to pierce the finest armor. Wave after wave of French knights threw themselves at the English line only to be shot down by this "rapid-fire" weapon before they could even reach the front ranks

Nicholas Oresme, the famous fourteenth-century French scholar of science, shown at the University of Paris with an armillary sphere representing the earth. (Bibliothèque Nationale, Paris)

of the English. The same held true at Poitiers, where the French king himself, John II, was taken prisoner.

These military disasters, together with the Black Death and its population decimation, brought unrest to France. After the military fiasco of Poitiers there was a serious insurrection of the Parisian bourgeoisie. The guilds of Paris took over the government, pressuring the dauphin (the heir to the throne, then regent in his father's absence) to convoke the Estates General representing all of France. Disturbed by the conduct of the war, the assembly drew up an indictment against King John, and especially his advisers. The dauphin was forced to sign the *Grande Ordonnance,* a charter that served to reduce royal power by providing that the Estates General could convoke itself, and removed much control of the bureaucracy from the king. This attempt to control royal authority failed, however, primarily because the Estates General as yet lacked a sense of unity: it was not yet representative of all the sections of the French people. The members of the Estates General tended to think of themselves only as servants of the monarch. Thus the nobility and clergy were uninterested in the program presented by the bourgeois guilds and, in fact, disclaimed their work.

After the collapse of this attempt to redress grievances and to increase the government's power, in 1358 France was wracked by a great peasant uprising, the Jacquerie. Aroused by the constant pillaging by English and even French soldiers during the campaigns, and angered by the exactions of the landlords, the peasants took up arms. Roaming the countryside, they burned down chateaux and indiscriminately slaughtered whatever nobles they could find. Though finally suppressed ruthlessly by the nobles, this bloody movement was only one in a long series of peasant uprisings that occurred in the fourteenth century—uprisings symptomatic of the deep economic and social unrest throughout Western Europe caused by the breakdown of the feudal and manorial systems and worsened by war and the intermittent debilitating plagues in Western Europe in this period. Momentary truces between France and England brought little respite to France. When hostilities ceased, always turned loose in the French provinces was the scourge of the "free companies"—mercenaries who, when unemployed, roamed over the countryside pillaging and raping. As a result, much of France now lay in ruins.

For a short time, under Charles V (1364–80), France was able to recover from the initial English successes. His reorganization of the administration and adoption of new military strategy—primarily defensive and combined with sudden, swift counterattacks—produced several victories over the English. But these gains were lost during the reign of his successor, Charles VI (1380–1422). Charles ascended the throne as a minor, and this, together with his later intermittent insanity, led to civil war between two rival factions aspiring to the regency headed by the dukes of Burgundy and Orléans. When the Duke of Burgundy failed in an attempt to gain control over the King, he joined the English, and after the historic Battle of Agincourt in 1415 (where the French knights were once again annihilated by English bowmen) England conquered most of northern France. Shortly thereafter, Charles VI, who since 1392 had been subject to fits of insanity, by the Treaty of Troyes in 1420 recognized Henry V of England as his heir.

It seemed that France would soon be united with England under one crown. But the deaths in 1422 of both Charles VI and Henry V altered the situation. The English were weakened because the new king, Henry VI, son of Henry V and Charles' daughter, was an infant. On the other hand, the French claimant, Charles VII, could not even be crowned, his capital of Paris and the city of Reims (the traditional place of the French coronation) both having fallen into the hands of the English. It was at this critical juncture that Joan of Arc (1412–1431), a peasant girl who was subject to visions in which she heard the voices of St. Michael the Archangel and St. Catherine, believed herself commissioned by God to expel the English and restore Charles VII to his throne. Appearing before the young king in 1429 she was able to persuade him to give her an army. Her astonishingly successful campaigns resulted in the restoration of many towns to Charles, among them Orléans and Reims, where in solemn ceremony the king was now consecrated and crowned (1429). But after an unsuccessful attempt on her part to capture Paris, Joan was captured by the Burgundians, who proceeded to hand her over to the English. Joan was tried as a witch and a heretic by a high ecclesiastical court under the watchful eyes of the English. Found guilty of heresy, she was burned at the stake in 1431. Her life provides a

The Battle of Agincourt (1415) was a major defeat for France by England in the Hundred Years' War. (Leiden University Library)

striking, though rare, example of the influence that an individual woman of extraordinary inspiration and ability could exercise in the predominantly male-oriented society of the medieval era.

Joan's patriotism, her devotion to France, and especially her martyrdom, served to infuse the French with a confidence and a sense of solidarity they had before lacked. And the defection of the Burgundians from the English in 1435 left the latter standing alone as the "foreign invader." Paris was soon retaken in 1436, and by 1453 the English were even driven out of Gascony. Their once extensive French possessions were reduced to the port city of Calais on the English Channel.

Italian Power Politics

Whereas in France and England during the fourteenth and fifteenth centuries the trend was toward dynastic monarchy, in Italy the particularist tendencies that characterized its politics during the medieval period continued to keep the city states from achieving any sort of political union. The only force that in the past had provided a semblance of unity in northern Italy, the Holy Roman Empire, was now an empty name. Even the Papacy in its temporal affairs (and despite its earlier claims to universal ecclesiastical, and at times, temporal, authority) was now in fact merely another small Italian state jockeying with others for position. Yet out of the morass of Italian politics, with its increasingly worldly view of society and the influence (to be discussed in the next chapter) of such humanistic figures as Bruni and Machiavelli, there emerged a way of viewing the relationship of the individual to the prince, and of one prince to another, that was to lead to our modern concept of the state, both in theory and practice. In fact, in 1324 in one of these northern Italian city states Marsilio of Padua, on the basis of his and his fellow citizens' political experience, and also influenced by Aristotle's *Politics,** wrote his famous political treatise, *Defensor Pacis (Defender of the Peace*—or "harmony"). This tract propounded a purely secular view of politics, that is, with no political role for the Church or the Holy Roman Emperor. As such, Marsilio's tract has been justifiably termed "the first theoretical formulation of the concept of the modern, secular state." †

The Italian City States

The basic political unit of Italy was not the kingdom nor, as in Germany, the petty principality descended from the feudal duchy or county of the Middle Ages. It was rather the city state, a political organism vaguely analogous to the ancient Greek *polis*. It acted as a sovereign power: that is, it had the power to tax its subjects, to legislate directly for all, to make war and conduct foreign relations. This form of polity dominated the affairs of Italy from the fourteenth through the fifteenth century.

As already noted, the sense of belonging to a political unit transcending the city state, the ideal of *Italianità*—of being an Italian instead of a Florentine or Venetian—did exist but was not by itself able to unite Italy into a "nation state." On the contrary, in the absence of a strong central monarchy, the bitter political and economic rivalries of the city states caused them to treat each other as virtually foreign powers. The first evidence in Western Europe of some of the practices of modern statecraft and diplomacy was in the relations of these Italian city states. Here developed the system of utilizing permanent ambassadors who regularly sent home detailed, systematic dispatches; the practice of forming military alliances among various city states consciously to check and balance the power of similar coalitions in order to preserve peace; and, perhaps most important, the idea of the state as being outside and above the medieval concept of the *unum corpus Christianorum*. Indeed, the political relations of the fifteenth-century Italian city states may, in many respects, be considered a kind of microcosm in which may be observed the development of diplomatic practices and techniques employed by all the great powers in later centuries.

Although a host of little Italian city states existed, five major powers domi-

---

* The *Politics* was first translated into Latin by William of Moerbeke, Bishop of Corinth, Greece, after the Fourth Crusade of 1204.
† G. Lagarde, *La Naissance de l'ésprit laïque* (1956–1957).

nated the political life of Italy: the city states of Milan, Florence, and Venice in the north; Naples in the south; and the Papal States extending across central Italy.

The Papacy.   During the fifteenth century, the Papacy undertook a new policy. Whereas earlier the Popes had attempted to establish a kind of nominal political suzerainty over all of Europe, now, as a result of the Babylonian Captivity and Great Schism, they concentrated on securing direct control over the Papal States (including Rome) in central Italy. This territory had become prey to numerous petty despots, and in order to maintain its own political independence the Papacy now found it necessary to recapture and rebuild the entire area. In the process of reconquest, the Papacy, from the political point of view, came to be considered by other European rulers as merely another Italian power—a power which, in the manner of Italian Renaissance princes, felt the need to defend and round out its territory as well as to satisfy personal or family pretensions.

Naples.   Both the kingdom of Naples, consisting of most of mainland Italy south of Rome, and the island of Sicily, played an important role in the history of medieval Europe, particularly in the rivalry between the Popes and the Hohenstaufen emperors. After the Sicilian Vespers in 1282 (Chapter 12), the island split off from the mainland: the king of Aragon ruled Sicily, and the French descendants of Charles of Anjou controlled Naples. In 1435, however, Alfonso the Magnanimous of Aragon reunited the two areas under his control, calling himself king of the Two Sicilies. At his death in 1458 the two were once again divided: Naples was given to his bastard son Ferrante (1458–1494) and Sicily to the new king of Aragon.

   Though less prosperous than under the earlier Hohenstaufen and Angevin domination, the kingdom of Naples now experienced a revival in its political and cultural life. Both Alfonso and Ferrante were lavish patrons of the arts and letters as well as shrewd diplomats who aspired to politically dominate all of Italy. Aragonese control of southern Italy persisted, and the connection with Spain was one cause of the French invasion of the Italian peninsula in 1494. With the ultimate triumph of Spain in Italy in 1559 Naples retained some of its ties with Spain, a relationship maintained until the nineteenth century.

Milan: The Rule of the Despots.   The real center of political power in Italy during the fourteenth and fifteenth centuries, however, lay not in the south but in the north. Before the wealth, military power, and organization of the city states of Milan, Florence, and Venice, the Papal States and Naples had to take second place.

   Milan, strategically located in north-central Italy at the terminus of the Alpine passes to Switzerland and France, had been an important political and economic power from as early as the twelfth century, when it had led the Lombard communes in their struggle against the German emperors. Although at first a republic, the city state was in 1277 seized by the Visconti family who, as hereditary dukes of Milan, were to rule the city for almost two hundred years. Under the Visconti Milan became the most aggressive of the north Italian states, constantly seeking to extend its territory southward and eastward. From the 1370s on it became a grave threat to the independence of Genoa and Florence. Some scholars in fact have viewed Milanese aggression (probably aimed at uniting the whole peninsula under the Visconti) as one cause for the development in Florence of what the historian Hans Baron has called "civic humanism," that is, the active participation in civic life of humanist scholars who, inspired by the concept of liberty in the ancient Roman Republic, sought through their writings to maintain and idealize freedom within the Italian communes.

When the last male Visconti died in 1447, the Milanese established a republic. But in 1450 control of Milan was seized by an energetic and able soldier of fortune, Francesco Sforza. Francesco and his successor, Ludovico il Moro, were lavish patrons of the arts who gathered about them a circle of intellectuals and artists, including Leonardo da Vinci. For a time the Sforza court was the most brilliant in all Europe and, as in Florence, reflected many of the new characteristics of the Renaissance. But Milanese greatness was soon destined to end. In 1500 (after the earlier French invasion of Italy in 1494) Ludovico was driven from the city by a French army. In 1535, as a result of negotiations for peace between France and Spain—both of which were now seeking to control the entire peninsula—Milan fell under direct Spanish rule. The proud commune, which had more than once defied the power of Frederick Barbarossa, now became only a small part of the vast Spanish Empire.

The Sforza and Visconti were among the most successful of a host of despots who usurped power over the governments of the Italian states during the period of the Renaissance. Owing to the disintegration of any kind of central authority after the defeat of the Hohenstaufen emperors by the Popes, and also to the bitter factional strife between Guelphs and Ghibellines in the cities themselves, the situation in each of the Italian communes was ripe for the emergence of one-man rule. After the thirteenth century town after town fell under the domination of a petty despot. Warring factions sometimes even invited someone (especially a citizen of another city) to restore order, or an ambitious military man might seize power on his own. The despot in a few notable cases was a *condottiere,* a leader of a troop of mercenaries, whom all Italian states in this period were in the habit of hiring to carry on their internecine wars. The condottieri tried to "milk" the towns they fought for. Naturally they sought to win battles; otherwise they would be dismissed. But they avoided truly decisive victories that would serve not only to end the war (along with their source of income) but might kill too many of their men in the process. By 1400 Italy had become dotted with little principalities headed by such despots as the Este family in Ferrara, the Gonzaga in Mantua, the Montefeltre in Urbino, the Baglioni in Bologna, and the Carrara in Padua.

These Italian princes were unlike any others of Europe at the time. They were not feudal lords. They had usurped power, and though in time their succession might become hereditary within the family (when they purchased "feudal" titles from pope or emperor), they were, as a rule, unable to inculcate in their towns a feeling of genuine loyalty to their "dynasty." Nor was the prince normally restricted by feudal custom. His will was law, his government personal. He had unrestricted executive and legislative power; he was beyond the law. Of course, he sought to give his authority some semblance of legitimacy in every way he could—by assuming the trappings of a lord, by securing an imperial diploma from the Holy Roman Emperor, his legal suzerain, or even (if possible) by gaining the consent, tacit or otherwise, of the governed.

Venice.   In Venice, contrary to the rest of Northern Italy, a nominal republic existed, but the old established oligarchy maintained control, its power existing in a virtually unbroken succession from the early medieval period. Since Venice's lifeblood was trade, its government was in the hands of the great merchants, who regulated the state to benefit commerce and, at the same time, to maintain themselves in power. Executive authority was technically invested in the doge, elected for life by the Grand Council, which exercised legislative power and presumably represented all Venetian citizens. In 1297 membership in the Grand Council was made hereditary, that is, closed to new families, thus further cementing the oligarchic rule of wealthy merchant families. But in time the legislative power of the Grand Council became concentrated in a smaller body—the Senate—made up of the most influential aristocrats. The authority of the Senate was in turn circumscribed, especially in matters of state security, by the dreaded Council of Ten. By the fourteenth century the Senate, and especially the Council of Ten, had taken over most of the old duties of the Grand Council, which henceforth met only to elect the doge and other government officials (who were, however, already "recommended" to it by the Senate). By now the doge, though still nominally head of the state, had become only a figurehead, whose main function was to preside over state ceremonies. Largely because of this tightly knit power structure, Venice maintained the calmest, most stable government of any Italian state in the entire late medieval and Renaissance period.

But aristocratic rule lay lightly on the Venetian citizenry. Despite a seemingly authoritarian regime, even the lower classes, which were quite unlike those of other Italian communes such as the Ciompi of Florence, did not feel excluded from the workings of the state. They felt they too had a real stake in the success or failure of Venetian mercantile, military, and diplomatic endeavors.

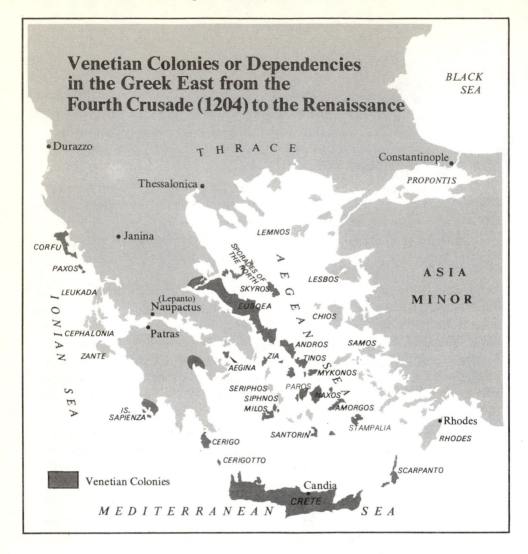

Venetian Colonies or Dependencies in the Greek East from the Fourth Crusade (1204) to the Renaissance

One may consider this an anticipation of modern patriotism, unusual for the period, for it was an allegiance directed not to a specific individual or even to his office but rather to the state, the "nation" itself. This feeling of the solidarity of Venetian society evoked the admiration of all Europe and was of course a contributory factor in the remarkable success of Venice in its continuous conflicts with its commercial rivals, Genoa and Pisa.

The systematically organized Venetian governmental machinery had many adjunct services. It possessed, for example, a chancery school in which Venetians were trained in diplomacy, certain practices of which may well have been patterned on precedents set earlier by the Byzantines, in whose capital, Constantinople, Venice had for centuries possessed a residential quarter. Indeed Venice was the first among the Western powers to establish a regular diplomatic corps that provided for the sending of frequent, systematic reports (the famous *relazioni*) to the home government by ambassadors stationed in all countries of Europe.

In a city so basically mercantile in orientation one might perhaps expect little development of culture on a high level. One of course immediately recalls the famous Basilica of St. Mark, with its impressive architecture, mosaics, and icons dating from the eleventh century. But these were essentially Byzantine or Byzantine-inspired works of art. The beginnings of Venice as a leading artistic center drawing on its own creativity did not come until the period of the later Renaissance, in the late fifteenth and sixteenth centuries (see Chapter 14). From the early medieval period Venice had attracted foreign colonists from among Greeks, Slavs, Albanians, and Jews—each group eventually establishing its own community and each adding to the cosmopolitan cultural ambience of Venice.

Portrait of a Venetian Doge by the painter Gentile Bellini (1429–1507). (Courtesy Museum of Fine Arts, Boston)

Florence.   The prosperity of Florence in the fourteenth and fifteenth centuries rested on the wealth and activities of its banking houses and even more so on the extensive marketing of textiles (especially woolens and silks) manufactured or finished in the shops of the city. For a long time the Florentine government had been more democratic than oligarchic Venice or despotic Milan. In the period after 1282 it was administered by a corporate body of the *Signoria,* six (or more) priors, two or so of whom were elected every two months (!), who really represented only the guilds (*arti*) of merchants and craftsmen, and a *Gonfaloniere* (banner bearer) of justice, originally appointed to carry out judgments against the landed nobles. In 1293 the old landed noble families in the area of Florence (magnates) were specifically excluded from the priorate.

More than any other Italian commune during the fourteenth century, Florence was wracked by factional, class struggle; the wealthier merchants' and bankers' guilds (*arti maggiori*) usually allied against the craft guilds (*arti minori*). Each group strove to attract the support of the lowest class, the laborers, though after one or the other faction managed to gain power the laborers were invariably repressed. After 1342–1343, when the government fell briefly into the hands of a despot, the greater and lesser guilds managed to compose their differences and, for some forty years, to cooperate in the rule of the city. But the workers still did not participate in the government.

As the fourteenth century progressed Florence suffered more than its share of disasters. Shortages in Flemish woolens as a result of the Hundred Years' War hampered the activities of the Florentine finishing guilds, several of the most prominent banking houses were ruined, and in 1348 the Black Death struck, wiping out, some scholars estimate, almost two-thirds of Florence's entire population. As the economic depression of the fourteenth century deepened, political and social tensions increased. Following a revolt of the lowest-class workers in the woolen and dye industries (*Ciompi*) in 1378 and the coming to power of the *arti minori,* the hold of the *arti maggiori* on the government was tightened. The evolution of Florentine government during the next half-century came to center on the struggle between the families of the great merchants and bankers.

In 1434 Cosimo de' Medici came to power in the wake of still another popular revolt against the ruling oligarchy. Head of a family that had become wealthy through banking, Cosimo developed into a shrewd diplomat. Although he wielded the actual power, he managed (as had the Emperor Augustus with the governmental machinery of ancient Rome) to maintain the forms of the old Florentine republican institutions. Cosimo himself rarely held public office, but all the officials of the government were his handpicked men (though technically selected by the people from a slate personally manipulated and chosen by him). There was of course a choice of candidates—usually between two Medici supporters! Cosimo also closely supervised the drawing up of the vital tax lists, thus

Italian City-States, 1454

SWITZERLAND

TYROL

DUCHY

DUCHY OF Milan

OF MILAN

M. OF MONTFERRAT

SAVOY

Padua

Venice

Po R.

M. OF MANTUA

Genoa

REP. OF GENOA

D. OF MODENA

FERRARA

EMILIA

Bologna

REPUBLIC OF VENICE

ROMAGNA

Pisa

REP. OF Florence

FLORENCE

ELBA

REP. OF SIENA

PAPAL STATES

ADRIATIC SEA

CORSICA

Rome

(KINGDOM

OF NAPLES)

SARDINIA

Naples

TYRRHENIAN

SEA

KINGDOM

OF THE

TWO SICILIES

SICILY

MEDITERRANEAN SEA

enabling him, financially, to weaken his opponents, in particular the powerful Albizzi family. At the same time, though himself a member of the upper class, he took particular care to favor the lesser guilds and laborers, catering to their needs and furthering a program of graduated taxation which struck particularly at the wealthy.

Cosimo's regime brought political and social stability—something that Flor-

*Relief of Cosimo de'
Medici,* de facto *ruler
of Florence (1434–
1464). (Alinari/Scala)*

entine life had for several centuries lacked. For his services to the state he was
awarded the title of *Pater Patriae* ("father of his country"). But Florence did
not reach the height of its political and especially its cultural eminence until the
rule of Cosimo's celebrated grandson Lorenzo, called "the Magnificent" for his
services as patron of the arts and letters as well as his consummate diplomatic
ability.

Lorenzo the Magnificent

Lorenzo controlled Florence from 1469 until his death in 1492, and
this twenty-three year period is often considered the golden age of the Italian
Renaissance. Like his grandfather (and father, Piero), Lorenzo remained in the
background politically but continued to control the government by arranging
that only the names of his supporters came up in the frequent "elections" held
in "republican" Florence—a fact that deceived the Florentines no more than it

did Lorenzo himself. Lorenzo was widely admired; although he was not handsome of feature, he had great charm, extremely refined manners, a way with
women, and a genuine ability to appreciate and foster talent in the extraordinary number of painters, sculptors, poets, and musicians he attracted to his
court. Lavishing money on his beloved city, he, together with other wealthy
Florentines, beautified it with magnificent palaces, hospitals, churches, and also
tombs for their families, all the work of the greatest artists of the age—Michelangelo, Brunelleschi, Alberti, and others.

Life in Florence during the fifteenth century was for the middle and upper
classes often a rich experience, with festivals, concerts, and exhibits of the finest
art works (although before 1450 the economic depression had not yet entirely
lifted). Behind much of this was the fine and discriminating hand of Lorenzo.
After his death the Medici family seemed to lose its qualities of leadership and,
especially after the French invasion of Italy in 1494, Florence itself seemed to
decay and diminish in vitality. During his lifetime Lorenzo had his detractors,
particularly his political enemies, who once even accused him of misappropriat-
ing municipal money set aside for the dowries of poor girls. More significant
was the opposition of the Papacy, which, owing to its collision with Medici ambitions in the Papal States, fomented plots against Lorenzo, one of which, the
Pazzi conspiracy (1478), resulted in the death of Lorenzo's beloved brother
Giuliano.

Lorenzo's diplomatic acumen is usually credited with preserving in Italy a
long period of relative peace during the last part of the fifteenth century. Since
the early fifteenth century the five principal Italian powers had sought to expand their commercial and political power, but this brought them into collision,
particularly in the central areas of Italy. Partly for reasons of food provision,
partly for those of commerce, or even for reasons of sheer imperialism, Milan
pushed southward toward Florence and eastward toward Venice. Florence and
Venice on their part pressed against the territory of the Milanese.

The Papacy, seeking to exert its authority over the Romagna, especially its
principal city, Bologna, was thrusting against Florence, Venice, and Milan as
well as southward against Naples. The latter had by now extended its possessions northward deep into the Papal States and by the mid-fifteenth century was
seeking, as we have seen, to dominate the entire peninsula. In this welter of conflicting ambitions, an alignment of opposing coalitions began to emerge: Venice
and Florence allied against aggressive Milan and Naples. But when the Venetians threatened to crush the Milanese, the alliances shifted—mainly as a result
of Cosimo de' Medici's machinations—and Florence joined the Sforza of Milan
against Venice. At Lodi in 1454, a key date in Italian diplomacy, an agreement
among all five powers was then engineered by Cosimo, as a result of which
peace was preserved in Italy for some forty years. This peace was maintained by
the establishment of an uneasy equilibrium among the chief Italian powers, the

Papacy excepted. (This has been termed the first application of the modern "balance of power" concept by some scholars.) Several minor crises, notably the Pazzi conspiracy mentioned above, threatened to overthrow this balance, but in the main the peace arranged primarily by Cosimo was preserved through the continuing efforts of his grandson, the dominant politician of his age, Lorenzo de' Medici.

The Lessons of Politics

The complexity of the political situation, internal and external, in each of the Italian city states forced them to work out practical, sophisticated, and in many respects new, solutions for handling their problems. The methods they used exerted a great influence on the development of virtually all other European states, especially in the realm of international relations. In particular, with respect to the conduct of diplomacy and techniques of statecraft, certain diplomatic practices arose (in Venice), such as the use of regular reports or *relazioni* sent by ambassadors to their home governments, a practice derived in part from Byzantine diplomacy. Despots such as Cesare Borgia, Lorenzo the Magnificent, and Pope Julius II were much more skilled diplomats than the Northerners until the advent of several of the "national" monarchs such as Louis XI of France and Ferdinand of Aragon who caught onto the Italian way. Indeed, from the view of sheer technical finesse, the Italians were superior. The employment by the Italian cities of the *condottieri* in place of the old feudal army or the medieval city militia, their use of spies (notably by Venice) to ferret out secrets from the leaders of enemy states even to the point of learning of those leaders' sexual weaknesses or aberrations for purposes of blackmail, the development of a more regularized diplomatic service, and finally the political acumen in discerning the precise moment to abandon one alliance and join another—the use and adoption of all these techniques and methods (with the notable exception of the use of *condottieri*) made Italy in the fifteenth century the political "school of Europe."

Nevertheless, despite the advances made by the Italians in the arts of diplomacy and politics, when in 1494 France, one of the great emerging "national" states of the north, sent an army southward to conquer wealthy Italy, it was clear that the disunited Italian cities, in military strength and resources, were no match for it. Henceforth, except perhaps for Venice, they were to be only minor actors in the great power struggle that subsequently broke out between the two super-powers of Europe, France and Spain, for control of the Italian peninsula.

Characteristic of the Italian politicians of this period was their highly realistic approach to politics, an approach that placed the interests of the state (or the ruler) above all other considerations and was almost totally lacking in, or rather disregarded, any sort of moral scruples. In contrast to the period of the Early and High Middle Ages, when political objectives, however reprehensible, were at least theoretically put in terms of the "ideal," the Italian despots of this time seldom even paid lip service to ideals. Their criterion was the completely secular *ragione di stato* (reason of state).

Niccolò Machiavelli (1469–1527), the Florentine historian and political theorist who lived during and after the rule of Lorenzo, has left us in his famous treatise, *The Prince,* what is perhaps the most acute analysis of the politics of his age. Eschewing the idealism of the medieval tradition completely, he emphasized "naked realism," imbuing the attitude of the diplomats and military leaders of his own period. For him causation of events was to be looked for not in the will of God (as was so often the case with medieval man) but in the interplay of circumstances and motivations of the personalities involved. Before acting, the "ideal" Prince should coldly evaluate all possibilities in each situation, but within the "limits of the possible." Machiavelli's analytical observations on politics—his analysis of its symptoms and disease, we might say—have become classic for the study of political theory and action in all subsequent periods of history.

Machiavelli's Florentine compatriot, Francesco Guicciardini, in some ways went even further. Guicciardini has left us (among other works) an account of the Italian politics of the period, called *History of Italy.* Unlike Machiavelli, Guicciardini was more historical than sociological in his orientation; he criticized Machiavelli in fact for being too dogmatic in his method, too ready to ascribe all action to cold calculation, and too quick to generalize on insufficient evidence. An experienced Florentine diplomat, Guicciardini was less pessimistic than Machiavelli about human nature, though probably equally realistic in his approach.

The penetrating analysis of each man provides in its way a guide to Italian power-politics of the period. But however acute in all other respects, neither man was sufficiently aware of, nor fully understood, the two emerging forces that still constitute the chief dynamics of the modern world of politics—"nationalism" and the economic interest of the state. Nevertheless, both Machiavelli and Guicciardini, in their essentially new, more pragmatic approach, transcended the traditional view of the Middle Ages and thus took a great step forward toward the political theory and political action characteristic of modern times.

Economic and Social Ferment in the Later Middle Ages

Economic Depression

Western European trade and manufacturing, which since the twelfth century had been undergoing rapid expansion, continued to increase during the thirteenth and, perhaps in a few areas, in the early fourteenth century. During the fourteenth century, however, a severe recession occurred, lasting, many think, for over a century. Only by the mid-fifteenth may we affirm that recovery and growth were such that the volume and variety of Western commercial activity could compare with that of the ancient Roman Empire or, say, of the Byzantine world in the late tenth century. One result of this expanding commercial enterprise in the West was not only the triumph of a money economy but the emergence of new techniques for carrying on business—practices that were characteristic of what may be called "nascent capitalism."

The economic depression of the fourteenth and the first half of the fifteenth centuries had many causes. Important were the chaotic political conditions and the general instability of the period. These factors were sharpened, of course, by the ravages of the Black Death of 1347–1349 (with recurrences every ten years), which carried off as much as one-fourth of Europe's entire population. Indeed, more and more scholars now think that the Black Death and its accompanying decimation and displacement of population left Europe in a state of collective shock. As a result of the shortage of labor and the havoc of military campaigns, large areas suffered severe loss of markets and reduction in goods produced for sale. Agricultural production, too, was in places almost completely paralyzed. These unsettled conditions, especially when they worsened, forced the town workers and peasants, often out of sheer desperation, to make a bid for greater freedom from the old traditional burdens imposed by feudal and guild obligations. Thus landlords and merchants, whose income was already dwindling, were often forced to grant concessions to the peasants and workers. But with the successful reassertion in some areas of medieval controls imposed by the landlords and guilds in the form of increasing rents and the limiting of wages, there was even further unrest on the part of the workers. Indeed, the fourteenth century, especially the latter part, came to be characterized by popular uprisings, both in the towns and in the rural areas—uprisings which in most cases were totally unsuccessful in the face of the vested interests of the nobility and the Church.

Interestingly enough, rather similar kinds of conflicts and ferment also characterized the Byzantine East in this period, a society in an advanced stage of decay as a result of social dislocation, intermittent plague, and civil wars. But in Byzantium, in contrast to the West where "feudalism" was becoming more centralized and led to the emergence of the "national" state, the Byzantine government was becoming so weak as to be unable, as formerly, to exercise firm centralized control over the areas remaining outside of Constantinople.

Popular Uprisings

To be sure, social unrest and popular insurrections had on occasion already occurred in the West from the middle of the thirteenth century onward: witness the remarkable uprising of the Shepherds in 1251 (an insurrection of

Wat Tyler, peasant leader, being struck down by the Lord Mayor of London (1381). This is a good example of the peasant rebellions that swept through Western Europe in the fourteenth century. (Reproduced by permission of the British Library Board, Royal ms. 18.E. I, f. 175)

obscure origins by dissatisfied French rural groups) or the internationally significant Sicilian Vespers in 1282 (see Chapters 11 and 12). But in the fourteenth century unrest and insurrections became widespread. In highly industrialized, urbanized Flanders a series of upheavals spanning more than a century involved both the poorer guilds, struggling to gain privileges from the great guilds and merchants, and the towns, which as a rule were endeavoring to break free from the political control exercised over them by the French king and the Count of Flanders. The longest and most bitter of these Flemish revolts took place between 1323 and 1328, and only with the greatest difficulty was the French king able to suppress it.

In Italy factional disputes between the greater and lesser guilds and between the great merchants and the prospering craftsmen became virtually endemic. Even in Rome, in the absence of the Popes at Avignon, the common people rose up twice (in 1347 in connection with the self-styled Roman "tribune," Cola da Rienzi, and again in 1353), establishing what they termed a "Roman Republic." But each time the movement lost its strength.

In the later fourteenth century occurrences of popular movements of unrest reached their height. I have mentioned the revolt of the Jacquerie, which swept France in 1358, and in the next fifty years France witnessed several more demonstrations of popular violence, in addition to the prolonged difficulties of the Hundred Years' War.

In England, too, in 1381, the peasants rose up in a great rebellion called the Peasants' Revolt, demanding, among other things, an end to serfdom and relief from heavy taxes. According to the confessions put into the mouths of the peasant leaders by later chroniclers, the rebels planned to drive all the clergy out of England, massacre the nobles and seize their lands, kill all the judges and crown ministers, and, after murdering the king himself, set up one of their own number to rule each county. Whatever the aims of the rebels, they were evidently extremely dissatisfied with the social, economic, and political status quo and resentful of the exactions of nobles, clergy, and crown. As in the case of the Jacquerie, however, the revolt was soon mercilessly crushed.

Not only did the peasants resort to violence to gain redress for their grievances, urban workers, such as the journeymen coppersmiths and drapers of Rouen, also revolted. And, in 1378 in Florence the Ciompi (common workmen, dyers of cloth) overthrew the government and ruled for four years, after which the movement fell apart.*

Perhaps most unusual of the revolutions that took place in Italy was that later in Florence, from 1494 to 1498, under the influence of the Dominican monk, Savonarola, after the death of Lorenzo the Magnificent. It was not only a religious and moral revolt against the conditions in the Church and Papacy but, as Savonarola saw it, a social protest against the growing laxity, corruption, and immorality of Florentine burgher society. Exhorting the Florentines to return to a stricter moral and ecclesiastical observance, Savonarola filled the vacuum created by the fall of the Medici regime in 1494, a collapse that followed the French invasion of Italy in the same year.

Taking over the reins of government, Savonarola for four amazing years ruled super-refined Florence as a puritanical theocracy. More than once under this zealous friar the citizens threw into great bonfires in the public square collections of their earthly "vanities"—rouge pots, wigs, lavish clothing, and even some "unacceptable" works of art. But, as with most fanatical reformers, Savonarola was unable to maintain the zeal of his supporters at fever pitch, and in the end was himself burnt in the public square as a heretic, having aroused the

---

* In Byzantine Thessalonica, in 1342, a rather similar kind of class war took place, in which the "Zealot" poor established an independent "commune" and seized the property of the upper class, especially landlords and merchants. But the Zealot revolt was also connected with religious factors such as Hesychasm, mystical beliefs of the monks on Mt. Athos.

Pope, the rival order of Franciscans, and others against him. The episode is, however, different from most other revolts of these two centuries. Instead of being solely a social protest, Savonarola's insistence (in defiance of the Pope) on ecclesiastical reform and the convocation of a general council to effect such reform imparted to his movement a strong element of "puritanism" and religious mysticism. It might therefore be viewed as the last vestige in Italy of medieval Christian "millenarianism." *

Most of the revolts of the transitional fourteenth and fifteenth centuries, rural as well as urban, were against the old order and were indicative of the general social unrest that was sweeping Europe. Virtually every peasant rising reflected the peasants' aversion to the old manorial dues exacted by nobles and clergy. Urban revolts sought to throw off the restrictions of the noble lords or to satisfy the demands of workers against their employers. The burden of heavier taxes and the breakdown of the medieval guild system, which created a wide gap between worker and employer, were both underlying factors contributing to the fourteenth-century uprisings. In every case, however, the lower classes were not strong enough to maintain themselves against the ruling groups. Lacking discipline and effective long-range leadership, these revolts, though in most cases dramatically successful for the moment, soon petered out and were ruthlessly put down.

The Rise of "Capitalism"

Despite the social turmoil and the economic crises, the three centuries from 1200 to 1500 saw the beginning of what is often considered a unique expression of Western economic development: capitalism. Indeed, some economic historians have gone so far as to regard the appearance in the late medieval period of great entrepreneurs, with their manipulation of vast sums of money for the sake of reaping profits, as marking the end of the Middle Ages and the beginning of the modern period. While capitalism is not actually exclusive to the West, this system of economic organization is more characteristic there than in other areas. In the territory of Byzantium during its apogee, it had been the state that usually controlled vast business enterprises. (Of course, after 1204 with vast numbers of Latins going to Constantinople, the capitalist methods of Venetians and Genoese became more common. Yet the Byzantine economy was always based much more on land than on trade.) To the contrary, in the West wealthy individuals, merchants or bankers, more often than not carried on most aspects of economic activity, and great wealth thus tended to accumulate in the hands of private individuals. Some rich Western businessmen had more ready capital at

---

* The apocalyptic belief not uncommon in the Christian West and East, of the coming of the thousand-year period before the Second Coming of Christ during which the world would be regenerated.

their immediate disposal than had the governments themselves, a fact that led many a prince to borrow heavily from them in time of need, and, inevitably and in more ways than one, placed the princes in the bankers' debt.

One characteristic of a capitalistic economic system is the concentration of large amounts of money—liquid capital—in the hands of individuals whose aim is to reinvest this money in order to create more. But what is the most essential characteristic of capitalism? Is it the existence of liquid capital in contrast to wealth tied down in landed property? Is it the profit motive, that is rational calculation combined with an acquisitive habit of mind? Or was it the greater volume of goods produced in this period that marked the transition to capitalism? During the fourteenth and fifteenth centuries all these emphases were apparent in one way or another, although certain individual characteristics had already appeared as early as the later thirteenth century. What seems best to distinguish fifteenth (and sixteenth) century capitalist development from what might better be called the "proto-capitalist" activities of the thirteenth and fourteenth centuries was (besides of course a greater "scale" of operation) a more sharply defined division of labor in the later centuries in which two quite distinct groups emerged—workers and owners. As the Marxist definition has it, when labor has become a purchasable commodity, capitalism has begun.

In line with this definition, the earlier adoption in the thirteenth century of double-entry bookkeeping with its implication of the importance of the profit motive, significant as it was, cannot be considered the chief criterion for the emergence of capitalism. Capitalism came about rather with the modification and weakening of the medieval guild system, itself characterized by strict regulation of competition and cooperation among master, apprentice, and journeyman. But the closed, static economic organization of the guilds gave way only gradually to the highly competitive, large-scale business carried on by the entrepreneur or merchant-banker in which labor was exploited for the benefit of the owner, that is, for the "capitalist" alone.

Capitalism, or rather "proto-capitalism," developed first in the most highly industrialized European areas of Flanders and Italy. By the end of the thirteenth century the weaving of woolen cloth had become "big business" in the towns of these two areas. Now, in contrast to the earlier medieval period when most produce was sold locally, a relatively small number of wealthy businessmen reaped the profits of this industry, purchasing raw wool at distant markets, employing large numbers of paid laborers to manufacture the cloth, and selling the finished product elsewhere. The medieval guild system of individual artisans was thus in some areas gradually being transformed into, or more exactly, replaced by, what began to look like the modern system of "labor and management."

Though almost no power-driven machines were invented during the fourteenth and fifteenth centuries, and most manufacturing continued to be carried on by hand in small shops or workers' homes, certain techniques were developed in a few leading industries—textiles, mining, and printing—which in some ways resembled modern methods of production. What was in a sense new in this period was 1) the increased standardization of some of the articles produced (standard in size, quality, and so on), and 2) the increasing specialization of labor. The Fuggers, the fifteenth- and early sixteenth-century German family of bankers, devised a system in their silver mines in Germany and Bohemia which organized the day into three eight-hour shifts—a technique that enabled the mines to be worked around the clock. In Florence in the fourteenth and fifteenth centuries, so specialized did the manufacturing of woolen cloth become that about twenty different types of laborers had to combine their skills to produce the finished product. Certain workers washed the raw wool, others spun it into thread, others wove it into cloth, still others dyed the cloth, and so on. And, as I shall discuss in the following chapter, the new art of printing necessitated an even more complex specialization of labor and sharp division between labor and management.

Banking. With large resources and business connections in the major cities of Europe, the great merchants almost naturally turned to banking operations. As early as the twelfth century banking practices resembling those of the modern era had begun to develop, if only on a rudimentary level. After the expulsion of the Jews from France and England and the Templars by France's Philip IV in the early fourteenth century (which led to the Templar's suppression everywhere), the Lombards (north Italians) became the leading financiers. Italian banking houses sent their well-trained agents to establish and maintain permanent branch houses in the major economic centers of the West and the East: in Bruges, London, Paris, and all over Italy in the West; and in Byzantine Constantinople, Frankish Cyprus, and Islamic Alexandria in the East. Most important in the fourteenth century were the Florentine banking houses of the Bardi and Peruzzi. In the fifteenth century the Medici even managed firmly to control the government of Florence, though, given the economic recession, they never had anything like the capital of their predecessors.

Northern European banking activities were centered in the Netherlands at Bruges and then Antwerp, with still another important center at Augsburg in southern Germany. A good example of the powerful "entrepreneur" of the fifteenth century was the Frenchman Jacques Coeur of Bourges, who became prominent during the last phase of the Hundred Years' War. Coeur, the son of a lowly artisan, built up a financial empire based on textile manufacturing, mines, and trading companies, and carried on commerce with Byzantium, Greek Trebizond in Asia Minor, and the Muslim East. He used his great wealth to influence political affairs, becoming involved in various shaky financial schemes and lending money to the French King Charles VII to carry on the final campaign against the English in the Hundred Years' War. Appointed chief financial agent of the French crown, Coeur even obtained a patent of nobility, bought up the landed estates of impoverished nobles, and erected a magnificent palace in Bourges. But Coeur aspired to too exalted a position for a commoner and thus incurred the wrath of the nobility and ultimately of the king himself. After a series of intrigues resulting in his being blamed for the death of King Charles VII's mistress, Coeur fell from royal favor and power; his wealth was confiscated by the crown, and he was exiled from France.

But the greatest example in this period of merchant-banking is the Fugger family of Augsburg. In the late fifteenth (and early sixteenth) century the Fugger brothers and their families ruled over a vast financial empire, whose wealth was primarily derived from silver, copper, and iron mines. The Fuggers had agents throughout Europe, whose task was to send back to the "main office" reports dealing not only with financial matters but with the political and social conditions of the areas in which they were stationed. During the last quarter of the fifteenth century the Fuggers made their influence felt more and more in German politics by their financial backing of the Hapsburg Duke Sigmund of Tyrol, and later the Emperor Maximilian I. Before the end of the century they had taken over a large share of the papal banking. During the early sixteenth century the House of Fugger not only dominated the financial affairs of the West but indirectly played an important role in the political affairs of the time as well. For instance, the Fuggers were probably indirectly responsible for the election of Charles V as Holy Roman Emperor. The Fuggers loaned vast sums of money to Charles, which he used to bribe the imperial electors. In a plea he later sent to Charles requesting repayment of this loan, Jakob Fugger made no attempt to minimize the effect of his financial power. Such an outlay of funds to kings, however, was usually risky business, for in this period kings too often reneged on their debts. It is reminiscent, in fact, of the activities of the Italian banking firms of the Bardi and Peruzzi, which earlier in the fourteenth century had been ruined by Edward III of England, to whom they had made loans for his campaigns against France in the Hundred Years' War and on which he defaulted.

The career of the Fuggers is a particularly striking example of the changing social and economic conditions of fourteenth- and fifteenth-century Europe. Despite humble origin, the family was able to use amassed wealth to obtain high position and power. Here, in contrast to the earlier medieval period, are examples of the great influence that money had come to play in the society of Western Europe. Yet even the Fuggers were finally ruined by ungrateful kings and jealous nobles, resentful that "lowly" commoners could achieve such great social and political influence. Money had indeed replaced land as the most effective generator of wealth. Nonetheless, society in the North had not yet become so fluid as to allow for genuine social mobility. Birth—that is, noble birth—was still the main determinant of one's status, regardless of actual wealth. In Italy, on the other hand, such a family as the Medici, of middle-class origin, could become acceptable to the upper levels of society as virtually the equal of the great noble families. But, it must be remembered, the Medici were a product of Italy, where the emphasis on birth had most tended to diminish, and they did, in the end, purchase a noble title.

The social and economic developments discussed in this section are symptomatic of a period of transition in the West of the fourteenth and fifteenth centuries with the simultaneous emergence of new institutions and decay of old ones. The urban and peasant uprisings, in particular, revealed for the first time in centuries on such a widespread scale a serious questioning of the validity of the old feudal and manorial order and even of the institution of the Church. This lack of faith in the old order, together with a corresponding growth of a more materialistic spirit in most layers of urban society, brought about the ultimate disintegration of Western medieval civilization.

FOR FURTHER READING

Brucker, G. A., *Florentine Politics and Society, 1343–78* (1962). Acute study.

Cartellieri, O., *The Court of Burgundy* (1972). A survey of life at the court of Burgundy.

Cheyney, E. P., *The Dawn of a New Era, 1250–1453* * (1936; 1962). A good treatment, though dated, of a complex period; essentially political and socioeconomic in scope.

Comines, Philippe de, *The History of Comines,* trans. Thomas Danett (1897). The memoirs of a realist adviser to French kings.

Creighton, M., *A History of the Papacy from the Great Schism to the Sack of Rome* (1882–1894). A standard history of the period (to 1527).

Froissart, Jean, *The Chronicles,* ed. W. Anderson (1964). Translation of the leading contemporary source for the Hundred Years' War; from the view of a noble knight.

Hay, Denys, *Europe in the Fourteenth and Fifteenth Centuries* * (1967). A competent, recent survey combining politics and culture.

Kempis, Thomas à, *Imitation of Christ,* trans. Richard Whitford * (1962). Apart from the Bible, perhaps the most widely published book in history; late fourteenth century.

Kerr, A. B., *Jacques Coeur* (1972). The career of the late fourteenth-century French adventurer and financier.

Lane, F. C., *Venetian Ships and Shipping of the Renaissance* (1934). Still useful and informative.

* Asterisk indicates paperback edition available.

Loomis, L. R., ed., *The Council of Constance* (1961). Source translations.

McIlwain, C. H., *Growth of Political Thought in the West* (1932). Old but still useful.

Mattingly, Garrett, *Renaissance Diplomacy** (1955; 1963). One of the few attempts at synthesis.

Pastor, L., *The History of the Popes from the Close of the Middle Ages, 1305–1799*, 40 vols. (1891–1951). A great work, based on several secret Vatican archives and others, by a distinguished scholar.

Pernoud, R., *The Retrial of Joan of Arc* (1955). Documents at the trial for her rehabilitation.

Perroy, E., *The Hundred Years' War** (1960; 1965). The best work on the subject, with much related information.

Postan, M. M., and E. E. Rich, eds., *Cambridge Economic History of Europe,* Vol. II (1952). Essays by acknowledged masters in the field.

Roover, R. de, *The Medici Bank* (1948). An authoritative work on the finances of this great financial institution.

Schevill, F., *Medieval and Renaissance Florence,* 2 vols. (1936; 1961; 1963). Very detailed; still the best general survey in English. Political in nature.

Trevelyan, G. M., *England in the Age of Wycliffe, 1368–1520 ** (1899; 1963). An authoritative account.

Ullmann, W., *The Origins of the Great Schism: A Study in Fourteenth-Century Ecclesiastical History* (1972). An important work on the grave schism in the Western Church. Good for understanding background to the problem.

Waley, D., *The Italian City-Republics** (1969). Good for earlier period up to c. 1350.

Wilks, M. J., *The Problem of Sovereignty in the Later Middle Ages* (1963). Background to Conciliarism.

In the previous chapter I examined the fourteenth and fifteenth centuries in the West from the viewpoint of political, socioeconomic, and ecclesiastical considerations, some of which reflected a continuity of development from the earlier medieval period. Yet despite this continuation of certain medieval institutions and attitudes, there is no doubt that fundamental transformations were at the same time also taking place. Change was in the air, and after 1500 Western civilization, particularly in the urbanized areas of Italy and northern Europe, had in many important respects become quite different from what it had been in 1350. The essential lineaments of the early modern world were beginning to take shape.

True, the framework of society seemed, at least superficially, to be much the same. But, almost unobtrusively at first, and much more discernibly during the

CHAPTER 14

Early Renaissance Culture: Latin and Byzantine Humanism, Philosophy, and Art

late fourteenth and fifteenth centuries, a new kind of ethos, a more secular spirit was beginning to supersede or, in some cases to co-exist with, the pervasively religious medieval outlook. Concomitant with this new lay spirit came an interest in and emphasis on the individual, which tended to make people more self-conscious, more aware of themselves and their surroundings. In this period, as already observed, there was a diminishing sense of loyalty to the old medieval spiritual and intellectual ideal of the "Christian commonwealth" and allegiance to the universal medieval institutions, the Papacy in particular. The old medieval ideal of universality was no longer operative.

This new view of the world has been termed, much too simplistically, "anthropocentric" in contrast, of course, to the more predominantly "theocentric" attitude of earlier medieval man. This is not to affirm that salvation, the gaining of eternal life in the hereafter, was no longer a significant factor in the ideals of fifteenth-century society. On the contrary, even in the worldly society of Renaissance Italy it is difficult to find anyone who actually rejected the fundamental doctrines of Christianity (except, of course, for out-and-out heretics). Nor is it easy to find genuine sceptics of the Christian religion. Nevertheless, the emphasis on religion, especially its all-pervasiveness, which had hitherto given spiritual meaning to every activity of life, was becoming less pronounced: people came increasingly and more self-consciously than before, above all in urban Italy, to view their place in the natural world as unique and to try to derive for themselves enjoyment from both nature and material things.*

The origins of this more secular or lay ethos may in large part be attributed to the socioeconomic and, perhaps to a lesser extent, the political and ecclesiastical developments discussed in the last chapter. As pointed out earlier, up to about the late tenth or early eleventh centuries the economy and society of the medieval West had remained relatively static. But with the increased contacts with the Byzantine and Arab East during the Crusades, and especially with the growth of trade and towns, a rich class of merchants emerged—such as the Bardi in the fourteenth century, and later the Medici and Jacques Coeur—whose outlook on life was molded more by the tangible objects money could buy than by concern for the traditional ideals of the medieval period. In the Italian city states, and to a lesser extent in the North, wealth came more and more to replace birth as the source of power and prestige. For the bourgeois class, as compared with the old nobility and the peasants, the strictures of tradition were now much loosened, and the new spirit of this increasingly important class came gradually, though unevenly, to filter through the entire structure of Western society, but least of all among the peasantry.

---

* The rapid turnover of wealth and the diminishing sense in general of "belonging" in turn often brought about among many an increasing sense of the uncertainty of life.

This last phase of late medieval cultural development, especially in Italy, in which this new, more emphatically secular outlook came into conflict with older, more traditional values, has been termed by most historians the "Renaissance."

Early Renaissance Humanism

For intellectual historians the most important characteristic of the new lay culture was an emphasis on humanism. The term "humanism" is sometimes used indiscriminately to apply to virtually any intellectual activity of the late fourteenth and fifteenth centuries that was not part of the Scholastic system. Actually the word derives from the term *studia humanitatis,* which in late medieval and Renaissance Italy referred to a curriculum of higher learning emphasizing the study of grammar, rhetoric, history, and moral philosophy—that is, the "humanities"—in contrast to the absorption of the medieval Scholastics in philosophy, theology, and, not infrequently, science.*

To define humanism satisfactorily is difficult. Perhaps the best approach is to consider it not so much a philosophy of life (which it came to be in the later fifteenth century), but rather as a *method* of education concentrating on the *studia humanitatis,* in particular the secular Greek and Latin classical works of antiquity that emphasized the higher sensibilities of people. Although the study of the Latin works in particular had not been at all uncommon in the medieval West, especially in twelfth-century France, the focus had been quite different, being essentially clerical-inspired and interpreted in relation to Christianity. In fourteenth-century Italy, on the other hand, the study of classical Latin and Greek literature was primarily for itself alone and without reference to the Christian religion. Thus in fourteenth-century Italy a genuinely new attitude to the pagan classics developed—an interest in the secular Greco-Roman works as a frame of reference or rationale for the humanists' own increasingly worldly society. This fascination for ancient learning continued to grow and by the mid-fifteenth century it had become a veritable mania to ferret out lost ancient manuscripts from churches, monasteries, or any place where they might have lain almost untouched for centuries.

But what accounts for this consuming interest in the Greek and Roman classics? Where did it come from? An old view, now discarded, held that Greek refugees, fleeing to the West after the fall of Constantinople to the Turks in 1453, brought with them Greek manuscripts that had the effect of suddenly opening the eyes of Western scholars for the first time in centuries to the importance of these ancient writings. But though Byzantine refugees even before

* This does not mean that humanism, especially in Italy, completely displaced the Scholastic tradition.

1453 had certainly played a significant role in disseminating *Greek* learning to the West, it must be noted that the *Latin* classics, though neglected, had been at hand throughout the entire Middle Ages. Indeed some medievalists, pointing to this fact and to the interest in the Latin classics of such twelfth-century scholars as Bishop John of Salisbury, insist that the interest evidenced in the classics during the Italian Renaissance was not new at all. And this is in a sense true, for John and other late medieval French scholars had been as conversant with most of the Latin classics as were scholars of the Italian Renaissance.

The chief difference, however, is that the Italians of the fourteenth through the sixteenth centuries, in contrast to what might be called the "clerical" humanism of twelfth-century France, developed a *new* attitude toward these pagan classics that had for so long been at their disposal. They were interested in the secular Greco-Roman heritage for its application to, or as an explanation for, their own increasingly worldly society, often even totally unrelated to Christianity. Not that Renaissance intellectuals disparaged Christianity. Most of the humanists still paid at least lip service to it. But in contrast to the intellectuals of the earlier medieval period they simply no longer attempted to view or to interpret the classics from a purely Christian point of view. They studied them rather for their intrinsic worth and, insofar as possible, in their original historic setting, attempting in many cases to apply the lessons, even the values they learned from them, to their own society. Later in Italy and still later, in northern Europe, especially with Erasmus and his followers, the so-called "Christian humanists" would attempt to use the classics precisely in order to give more meaning to Christianity. There is no doubt that the secular emphasis reflected in the Latin and Greek classics reinforced, justified intellectually so to speak, the emerging secular ethos of middle-class Italian society, and thus broke down centuries-encrusted medieval traditions and attitudes.

Petrarch

The Florentine Francesco Petrarch (1304–1374) is generally considered to be the father of humanism, though evidence exists that others in northern Italy (the lawyer Mussato and the jurist Lovato de' Lovati in Padua for example) had similar classical interests even before him. Exiled from his home city because of factional political squabbles, his family settled at the papal court in Avignon. Petrarch at first studied law but, detesting it, he later devoted himself entirely to literary pursuits. To support himself he wangled an ecclesiastical benefice through his connections in the Curia. Throughout his life he traveled widely, visiting Bohemia, France, England, and the Lowlands, finally fixing his residence at Padua near Venice. So great did his reputation as a scholar become that for a time he was considered virtually the arbiter of European letters, and his ability as a poet brought him the crown of poet laureate in both Rome and Paris, although, significantly, he accepted only Rome.

Petrarch had an unquenchable passion for ancient literature, Greek as well as Latin. Indeed, he was one of the first Westerners to realize the significance of Greek literature as a source and inspiration for Latin. At Avignon, with the aim of reading Homer in the original, he studied Greek under the Byzantine-Italian monk Barlaam. But Barlaam died before Petrarch was able to learn much Greek. As Petrarch put it: "I was always anxious to study all of Greek literature, and if Fortune had not deprived me of an excellent teacher, I might be more than an elementary Hellenist." Besides the death of his teacher, another factor contributing to Petrarch's failure to learn more than rudimentary Greek was the lack at the time of Greek grammars and lexica.

Petrarch searched all over Europe for Greek and Latin manuscripts in order to build up his personal library. His Latin style was considered excellent in his time, but it would be considerably improved upon by subsequent Renaissance scholars. Petrarch was perhaps the first man of the Renaissance to possess a genuine sense of history—he was in fact the first to "periodize" European history more or less as we know it. Fascinated by the ruins of ancient Rome, he was acutely aware that his era was very different from that of the ancient world. What caused this great difference, he believed, was the intervention of what he was the first to label the "Dark Ages," a long and presumably stagnant thousand-year period during which, as he insisted, the learning and culture of classical civilization had been lost, destroyed by the invading barbarian Germans. Enthralled by the architectural style of ancient Rome, Petrarch and his contemporary Italian humanists even scorned the magnificent medieval cathedrals as "Gothic," that is, barbaric. In addition to objecting to the increasing aridity of Scholastic education with its interminable syllogistic argumentation, Petrarch had harsh words for Scholastic theologians, especially the Latin Averroists. Thus he turned away from their worshipful reliance on Aristotle, although at the same time he did not deny the great value of some of Aristotle's works.

In his own eyes, Petrarch's best works were his Latin epic poem *Africa* (on Scipio Africanus, the Roman conqueror of Carthage) and his *Letters to the Ancient Dead,* epistles in rhetorical Latin addressed to the ancients: Seneca, Cicero, Livy, Homer, and so on. Striking a nostalgic note for the past, the letters disparage Petrarch's own age and reveal his awareness of the ancient figures' lack of Christian baptism and of the vast gulf of time separating him from the ancient world. Despite his own preference for his Latin works, scholars today seldom read them, and instead consider his sonnets in the vernacular Italian as his chief creative achievement. These sonnets, dedicated to Laura, a woman he loved only from a distance in the manner of the courtly love tradition, had a deep influence on subsequent Italian poetry and even English verse.

Petrarch's "modernity" is revealed also in his deep love of nature and his individualism. The story of how he climbed Mt. Ventoux near Avignon, not to get closer to God but supposedly simply to enjoy the view, is famous.* His *Letters to the Ancient Dead* as well as his *Letter to Posterity* (a kind of literary "time capsule") reveal Petrarch's desire for fame and glory. (Quite different from the medieval desire to glorify God.) In the latter work Petrarch, with considerable vanity, gives a description of his own "attractive" physical appearance, which he felt was spoiled by his need (at the age of sixty) to wear glasses. For his love for antiquity and nature, his pursuit of classical studies, and his individualism, Petrarch has been called the "first modern man." In a very real sense he was the archetype of the Renaissance humanist, for in his career are exemplified most of the qualities that became common to the humanists of the age.

Boccaccio

Petrarch's interests were carried on by his pupil and immediate successor, Giovanni Boccaccio (d. 1375). Like Petrarch, Boccaccio was vitally interested in Greek language and literature, and through his efforts a south Italian Greek, Leontius Pilatus, was appointed to the University of Florence as the first occupant of a chair of Greek in Western Europe. Among Boccaccio's writings is his *Genealogy of the Gods,* written under the influence of Pilatus that retells the legends of the ancient Greek and Roman deities. Here is what might be called the first work of modern classical scholarship. In this treatise the ancient gods and goddesses were for the first time discussed in the context of their original pagan setting, without any reference to or attempt at reconciliation with Christian beliefs.

Boccaccio's creative masterpiece was the *Decameron,* the forebear of the picaresque novel. Like Petrarch's sonnets and Dante's *Commedia* (the latter not a humanistic work), the *Decameron* was written in vernacular Italian, not Latin. Like Petrarch, too, Boccaccio was a little ashamed of his work, and at one time even considered burning the manuscript. The *Decameron* is really a collection of tales, many of them bawdy, told by a group of wealthy young Florentines who, having fled to the hills to escape the plague (Black Death, see Chapter 11), passed the time in telling stories. These stories are usually highly secular, dealing with thieves, whores, and vagabonds, as well as monks, all in a highly satirical vein. Boccaccio took particular relish in lampooning the clergy, especially the monks. Typical is his tale of a Jew who, when seeing the splendor and power of the papal court, decided to become a Christian on the grounds that any religion that could prosper under such corrupt conditions must be the true one. Despite

---

* Yet when Petrarch reached the summit he pulled out and began to read St. Augustine's *Confessions!*

DOMINVS · OHANNES · BOCCACCIVS

Painting of the great Florentine humanist Boccaccio, by Andrea del Castagno. (Alinari/ Scala)

the biting satire, the story actually conceals a profound religious truth and helps to explain why Boccaccio himself later came to renounce the *Decameron*. Nevertheless, the *Decameron* had great influence on future Italian literature; its language became standard for Italian prose. Its sparkling style and wit make it enjoyable reading even today.

The Rise of the Vernacular Languages

The increased use of the vernacular languages by Petrarch and Boccaccio is often taken to mark one aspect of the emergence of the modern world. The vernaculars, the popular, *spoken* languages of Europe, in contrast to the literary, scholarly Latin of the intellectual class, had begun to emerge as literary and occasionally "diplomatic" languages, however, even before the time of Petrarch and Boccaccio. But most of the humanists scorned the use of the vernaculars, fostering rather a revival of the ancient forms of Latin and Greek. Spanish, Portuguese, Italian, and French—Romance languages, as they are called—though ultimately deriving from Latin, the language of the Romans, were products of the evolution of the various local forms of Latin. The differences among the Romance languages are due not only to the distance of the area of each from Rome but also to the linguistic substratum still remaining from the languages spoken in a particular area before the Roman conquest. One reason that French, for example, differs from Spanish is owing to the differences in the languages of their pre-Roman inhabitants.

In the thirteenth century the king of Castile ordered that Castilian (the ancestor of modern standard Spanish) replace Latin as the official language for government documents. In medieval France the two dialects of north and south began to be used for literary purposes. From the twelfth century onward the poetry of the southern troubadours and the northern trouvères, many chronicles, and some documents were written in these two types of French. But with the conquest of southern France by northern knights during the Albigensian crusade of the thirteenth century, the southern dialect (the *langue d'oc*) began to disappear as a literary language. By 1400 the dialect of French spoken around Paris (*langue d'oïl*) had become preeminent as the official language of the French kingdom.

English as we know it today evolved from a combination of Anglo-Saxon and the Norman French spoken by the Norman conquerors of England. In the fourteenth century this "English" began to be extensively used as a literary language in such works as Langland's *Piers the Plowman* and Chaucer's *Canterbury Tales,* and in the same century it was officially recognized as the language of public documents. In the various German principalities, too, German began to supplant Latin as the language of official documents. During the twelfth to the fourteenth centuries German minstrels, *Minnesänger* as they were called, composed in German chivalric poetry similar in type to, and often modeled on, that of the French.

The appearance of the vernacular as a semi-official or official language reflected, perhaps even helped, the growth of a feeling of ethnicity or "nationalism." Certainly the French and English in the last phase of the Hundred Years' War were acutely aware of the difference in their languages. In Germany and Italy, on the other hand, perhaps in part because no one dialect gained the ascendancy, the use of the vernacular did not reinforce the development of "national" political units, though it did help to foster a feeling of a certain common heritage among Italians on the one side and Germans on the other. Both Germany and Italy remained divided into many little states. Yet a Saxon did tend to look upon a Swabian as a German and a Florentine to view a Milanese as a fellow-Italian.

Important as the vernaculars may have been from the standpoint of the growth of nationalism and popular literature, Latin still remained the language of scholarship and of the Church during the centuries of the Renaissance. The thesis may even be defended that humanism, with its emphasis on the Greco-Roman heritage, actually tended to retard the development of the vernacular languages as vehicles of literary expression. History and poetry might be written in the French, Italian, or German vernaculars, but no reputable scholar until the seventeenth century could hope to make an international reputation if he did not write in Latin. Thus the role of the vernacular in the *intellectual* development of what is called the Renaissance should not be overemphasized. The connection of humanism with the popular languages of the day was sporadic and tenuous at best; translations of the ancient Greek classics into the vernaculars were not made until the sixteenth century. So strong did the tradition of Latin as the scholars' language remain, even with the later triumph of the vernaculars in the late sixteenth and seventeenth centuries, that Latin would remain into the seventeenth century the international language of academic circles.

Byzantine Scholars and Greek Learning

The humanist movement in the West began as a Latin revival, but the restoration of Greek letters served perhaps more than any other single factor to expand its intellectual horizon. In the history of this Greek revival the most significant role was played by Greek scholar-exiles from the Byzantine East, men such as Manuel Chrysoloras, who were well educated in the classical Greek language and literature. Beginning in the late fourteenth and extending well into the sixteenth century, a more or less steadily increasing flow of Byzantine refugees, seeking to escape the advance of the Ottoman Turks or, later, after the fall of Constantinople in 1453, to escape Turkish domination, poured into the West. Through their work of teaching, manuscript copying, and, as I shall note later, preparing texts for the press, these Byzantine scholars contributed vitally to the advancement of Greek studies in Western Europe.

Western interest in Greek studies had been, of course, evidenced at least as early as the time of the Scholastic theologian Thomas Aquinas (d. 1274). But the interest was primarily in Aristotle—in his scientific and philosophical works, and especially in how they could be used to interpret and even buttress Western theology. After Petrarch, however, this interest not only shifted to Greek literary studies but accelerated to the point that many Italian humanists could read Greek as well as Latin.

After the deaths of Petrarch and Boccaccio the Greco-Latin tradition was given further impetus in Florence. But even there the humanist movement had its adversaries. Colluccio Salutati, Chancellor of the Florentine government from 1375 to 1406, had to defend humanistic studies against the increasing attacks of some who, in the older medieval tradition, still looked upon pagan learning with suspicion. Salutati, together with the wealthy merchant Palla Strozzi, was responsible for bringing to Florence to teach Greek the Byzantine nobleman and scholar Manuel Chrysoloras. In Florence Manuel had a phenomenal success as a teacher. Almost all the leading Florentine intellectuals of his time flocked to his lectures to learn Greek, and the tremendous impetus given to the study of Greek literature in the Renaissance may be ascribed in great part to his teaching. His *Erotemata* was the first Greco-Latin grammar to be used in the West. Through Chrysoloras' instruction in Florence (1396–1397) that city became in the fifteenth century the chief center for Greek scholarship in the Western world.

Chrysoloras' teaching at Florence opened the way to other Byzantine scholars who sought a career teaching Greek in the West. But probably the event that most strongly stimulated Western interest in Greek scholarship was the Council of Florence (1438–1439), which sought to effect a union between the Greek and Roman churches.

With the Greek delegation came some of the most accomplished Byzantine intellectuals of the last century of their empire. Mingling with the Italian humanists at banquets or at sessions of the council, they dazzled the Westerners by their firsthand knowledge of many hitherto unknown or misunderstood ancient Greek works. Gemistus Pletho (c. 1355–1450), the outstanding Platonist and scholar of the Byzantine delegation, has been credited, through the impression made by his learning, with transforming the Florentine desire for Greek learning into a virtual passion. Pletho himself was so enthralled by Platonic and Neoplatonic thought that in order to revive the collapsing Byzantine state he even proposed to disestablish Christianity, adopt as the religion of the state a philosophical type of ancient Greek paganism, and send young Greeks to the West to learn engineering and technology. His lectures on Plato in Florence attracted the attention of its ruler, Cosimo de' Medici, who, as a result, founded the celebrated Florentine Platonic Academy that made Platonism virtually a fashionable cult in Italy and later in the North.

The influence of Plato, with his use of mathematics in his *Dialogues* (in contrast to the emphasis on logic by the medieval Aristotelians), is believed by some modern scholars (a theory opposed, however, by others) to have paved the way for Copernicus' heliocentric theory of the structure of the universe. This Platonic emphasis also influenced the Renaissance philosophy of art.

Another Byzantine prominent in the revival of Greek studies was John Bessarion, whose activities in favor of religious union resulted in his being appointed a cardinal of the Roman Church. A learned scholar in his own right, he established a circle for Greek studies in the Papal Curia itself. He became the chief patron of the refugee Greek scholars in the West and, later, championed the project of launching a Western crusade to recapture the fallen Byzantium from the Turks.

This detail of a fresco by the painter Ghirlandaio in Santa Maria Novella, Florence, depicts the Byzantine and Italian humanists, Marsilio Ficino at the extreme left, Poliziano and Landino, and the Byzantine Demetrius Chalcondyles, at the extreme right. The latter explained difficult passages in Plato to Ficino. (Scala/Editorial Photocolor Archives)

Ficino, Pico, and Musurus.   But the two Italian scholars who did most to disseminate the philosophy of Platonism in the West (and gave a boost to Greek studies in general) were the Florentine Marsilio Ficino, who made a Latin translation of the entire corpus of Plato for Cosimo de' Medici, and his younger contemporary, Pico della Mirandola. So immersed did Ficino become in Platonic thought that he, as Thomas Aquinas had done with Aristotle, wrote a work, *Theologia Platonica,* in which he attempted to synthesize Platonism (or Neo-Platonism) with Catholic theology. At the Medici court, which now became the most intellectually brilliant in Italy, he taught a number of subsequently famous figures, including Lorenzo de' Medici himself and his good friend Politian, a master of Greek and Latin literature as well as Italian. Inspired by Greek tragedy, Politian wrote *Orfeo,* which some think contains the germ of modern opera.

Even more celebrated as a scholar than Ficino was Pico della Mirandola.

Handsome, rich, highborn, he studied at most of the great Western universities. At the early age of twenty he tried to summarize all human knowledge in nine-hundred propositions and offered (in the traditional medieval manner), to take on, in public disputation, anyone who cared to challenge his thesis. This opus, which like much of the work of the humanists, is today little read, nevertheless contains a remarkable preface entitled *On the Dignity of Man*. Influenced by Platonic concepts, Pico here set forth the idea that all men have within them-selves a spark of the divine—that man is not only the link in the great chain of being between material and spiritual but that each man has a certain inherent "dignity" that makes him a unique creation of God.

This type of scholarly activity, based largely on Platonism, Stoicism, and other ancient Greek philosophies, has induced some scholars to call humanism a philosophy of life. Whether or not humanism may validly be termed a philoso-phy, there is no doubt that Platonic ideas exercised a deep influence not only on Renaissance ethics, literature, and history, but on art as well.

Among other post-Byzantine refugee scholars, especially noteworthy in the early sixteenth century was the Cretan Marcus Musurus, who instructed at Padua University (1503–1509) and later taught in nearby Venice (1512–1516). So influential was he in explicating hitherto unknown or neglected Greek liter-ary texts (such as those of Euripides, Sophocles, Aristophanes, Plato, and, note-worthily, the *Rhetoric* of Aristotle and of Hermogenes) that many northern scholars flocked to Italy to study with him. As a consequence, in the last decade of the fifteenth and in the early sixteenth century Venice began to take over from Florence the primacy in Greek studies.

It should not be assumed that Greek *displaced* Latin among Western hu-manists. Latin was always much more widely known, since Greek was of course essentially a "foreign" language and had to be learned as such. Nevertheless, because Greek was viewed as the primary source of Latin literature, it always maintained its special place in the Western humanist curriculum.

The Printing Press

The emphasis on the study of Greek, the justification for which can be found in statements of the most important humanists such as Erasmus of Rotterdam, the Frenchman Budé, the Italian Politian, and the Englishman Colet, was now brought to the North not only through these pupils of the By-zantine scholars but, even more effectively, by the printing press. Whereas up to the mid-fifteenth century the dissemination in the West of classical works de-pended on manuscripts being laboriously copied by hand, with the invention of movable type a work could now rapidly be produced in hundreds of copies. The new humanistic works thus could be much more quickly circulated throughout Europe. The invention of movable type coincided not only with the fall of Constantinople—when some ancient Greek texts were lost—but occurred at the very time that humanist scholars were beginning to demand more and more texts of the ancient authors.

Printing in simple blocks apparently stemmed from an invention of the Chinese in earlier centuries. But this technique was cumbersome and unwieldy because a new plate had to be cut for each page of printing. And if a mistake was made the whole block had to be redone. It was the invention of movable type, in which each letter could be set individually, that really made possible the mass production of books. The invention of this technique is usually credited to Johann Gutenberg of Mainz in Germany. More recent scholarship, however, considers his work rather as marking the capstone of earlier developments that took place among a number of printers and in more than one area, but particularly in South Germany.

Once the technique of movable type was developed, the spread of printing throughout Europe was very rapid. By 1500 over seventy Italian, fifty German, and forty French printing presses were established, with lesser numbers in England, the Low Countries, and Switzerland. The printing industry reflected in its organization and methods the growing capitalistic system in fifteenth-century Renaissance Europe. To set up a press, a great outlay of capital was initially needed in order to purchase the expensive equipment, and only skilled workers could be employed. Clearly the organization of the medieval guild system would be inadequate here where such modern considerations of labor, management, capital funds, and marketing were involved. As printing developed further, the increasing standardization and mass production of books came more and more to the fore—characteristic also of other industries developing from the fifteenth century onward.

The most famous press of Renaissance Europe was that of Aldus Manutius of Venice. Under his guidance (1494–1515) and with the help of many Greek scholars, especially Musurus, his Aldine Press printed, for the first time, no less than thirty of the Greek classics as well as some Latin and Italian works. Virtually every major classical Greek author was first printed by Aldus, whose achievements were therefore of tremendous importance in furthering the dissemination of Greek learning in the West. In the north the most influential press was the Froben Press of Basel, which on a lesser scale than the Aldine also reproduced many classical works. The Froben Press was particularly important in publishing Latin and Greek ecclesiastical literature—the products of the northern humanists, especially Erasmus—and thus it served a vital role in the spread of Christian humanism north of the Alps.

Most of these presses, the Aldine in particular, were in a certain sense scholarly research centers. For in seeking out, editing, and publishing classical texts, printers had to employ scholars to supervise the techniques of printing and even to edit the texts, an exacting and onerous task. In this way printing presses themselves helped to further the philological study of ancient texts. And, of course, as more books were produced, more interest in Greek and particularly Latin scholarship was generated.

The printed word inevitably became a vehicle for propaganda, not only for the humanists but for Church reformers, and of course for politicians. For the first time quick and widespread appeal could be made in order to seek support for some specific program, be it ecclesiastical, political, or educational. There is no doubt that the press helped to release people from a local outlook. Now they could more quickly and easily be exposed to fresh ideas coming from more distant areas thereby gradually expanding the parochial outlook so characteristic of the medieval period. With the printing press, too, the written document sometimes even came to have an importance greater than time-honored custom. What previously had been decided by oral tradition now came increasingly to be adjudged legal by a printed document.

Humanism in Education and Critical Scholarship

With its emphasis on the method and content of the ancient classics, humanism inevitably influenced the development of many fields of thought. Humanism transformed methods of education. Indeed most humanists, Petrarch being a notable exception, were in one sense or another educators. Some humanists in fact developed plans for social reform through the use of education. Whether or not a practical application was always intended, it is clear that humanism produced the greatest concern for education of any age up to our own since antiquity.

Medieval education, though less so after the twelfth century, had been dominated by the notion of providing for an educated priesthood. And, in certain respects, formal education in the period of the fourteenth to fifteenth centuries was still associated with the Church. Cathedral and monastic schools were of course under ecclesiastical direction, and even the guild schools of the towns, though secular in origin, were in the main staffed by clergy. The primary subject in all these schools was Latin grammar—the purpose being preparation for entrance to the Church, for conducting a business (as in the guild), or for entrance into the universities. The universities, particularly of the north, were largely controlled by clerics, especially those trained in Scholastic theology. There by the fourteenth century Aristotelian Scholasticism had so come to dominate the scene that most other lines of inquiry were stifled by the nearly exclusive emphasis on dialectic (logic). The creative period of Scholasticism, that of Albertus Magnus and Thomas Aquinas, who had achieved their great syntheses of faith and reason (Chapter 10), had now given way to the nominalism of William of Occam, in which faith was sharply disjoined from reason. As a result of this divorce, faith was no longer subject to explanation and attention was more exclusively devoted to natural phenomena, thereby, as some modern scholars believe, paving the way for the advent of modern science.

With the further development of secular interests in Italy in the late fourteenth and fifteenth centuries, however, changes in the educational system began. From the twelfth century onward, the Italian universities had emphasized the secular, professional studies of law and medicine. And over these studies the Church certainly did not have the control it managed to maintain in the northern universities of France, Germany, and England. The primary emphasis on professional studies in the Italian universities certainly had something to do, at least indirectly, with the rise of humanism in Italy. Not until the late fourteenth century was theology taught in the great Italian universities. And there it was not until the late fourteenth and fifteenth centuries that instruction in humanistic studies came to exist side by side with law and medicine as well as theology.

Humanistic education began to expand as a result of the discovery or rediscovery and interest in ancient treatises on education such as those of Cicero, Quintilian, and Plutarch. And these in turn led to the development of a new approach to education in private and sometimes civic (town) schools. The emphasis of these classical works was on literary studies, not logic, with particular stress placed on the moral training of the student. Under such influences the Italian educators of the fifteenth century—that is, apart from those in the universities in general—ignoring the medieval emphasis on theology and dialectic, stressed instead the study of literature.

Important too for the humanists was the study of history as ethical philosophy, teaching by example. The ideas and practices of the ancients, they believed, could serve as guides for their own conduct. One humanist, Vergerius (*c.*1393), placed history at the head of subjects to be studied, followed by moral philosophy and then eloquence (that is, rhetoric).

Perhaps the two most significant educators of the Renaissance period were the Italians Guarino da Verona (d. 1460) and Vittorino da Feltre (d. 1446?). Both were non-churchmen; both set up secular schools at the courts of Italian princes, in which sons and even daughters of the wealthy, the nobles, and of humanists were trained. The trends these two established came to dominate subsequent humanistic education.

Guarino, who had studied in Florence under the Byzantine Manuel Chrysoloras, was so attracted by Greek learning that he went to Constantinople to perfect his Greek and to collect a library of Greek works. On his return to Italy he set up a school for the Este family, the rulers of Ferrara. Emphasizing Greek and Latin literary studies, Guarino sought to examine the ancient masterpieces for what he considered the profound moral and ethical truths expressed in them. Moreover, much like modern educators, Guarino, already in the fifteenth century, believed that the personality of each child was important and that his teaching had to be adjusted accordingly. Guarino's school, which also included a place for religious instruction of a practical nature, became famous all over Europe and was taken as a model for other humanist schools.

The teaching of Latin and Greek literature was a much more complex task for Guarino and his contemporaries than for our teachers. Only from the late fifteenth century were such fundamental tools as grammars or dictionaries composed. There were no "teaching aids." The professor of rhetoric had to possess extremely wide knowledge. As well as teacher he had to be grammarian, philologist, and historian all rolled into one. He had to comment on long passages in the ancient texts, trace the derivations of the meanings of words and, wherever possible, show the relevance of the passage to contemporary life.

Guarino's influence may have been surpassed by that of the humanist educator Vittorino da Feltre, whose early training had been in the Scholastic method at the University of Padua. Revolting against this form of learning, Vittorino turned to humanistic studies. After learning Greek he taught first at Venice and then for a time at Padua. But his fame rests rather on the school he subsequently established at the court of Mantua for the children of the ruling Gonzaga family.

At Vittorino's school, even more than at Guarino's, there was as much emphasis on character development as on intellectual development. Not only were Christian ideals and intellectual training stressed but also the Greek emphasis on athletics, as expressed in the phrase "a sound mind in a sound body." The technical organization of medieval education was retained by Vittorino, but within this context the emphasis shifted from logic to literature based on the models of the ancients. Methods of teaching were also revamped. The rules of rhetoric and grammar were no longer taught by dry memorization but through the analysis of passages taken directly from ancient literature. Vittorino's teaching was extraordinarily successful. Included among his pupils (for probably the first time since antiquity) were girls from leading Italian families. Though he left no formal treatise on education, his influence was widely felt in humanistic circles. Even after his death children from the leading families of Europe still came to study at his school.

Why was this new humanistic education as typified in the schools of Guarino and Vittorino so remarkably successful? In the first place, it tried to provide more than a mere code of manners and conduct; it sought to affect the entire ethical outlook of its pupils. Moreover, since most of the pupils were highborn, sons of princes and heads of state, they could more effectively disseminate and put into practice the ideas on education in which they had been trained. Humanist educators (like some medieval teachers before them) liked to use events of past history from which to draw lessons on moral conduct for the present. Such an emphasis was especially relevant to the Italians, since the organization and ethos of their city states in many ways resembled those of ancient Greece and Rome. Above all, then, humanist education was successful because of its social relevance, its sense of direct correspondence between the values of antiquity (as the humanists saw them) and those of Renaissance Italy.

Nevertheless, despite the success of this new type of education, I must not exaggerate the permeation of the humanist influence throughout society in general. The number of students educated by this method remained relatively small, drawn only from the noble and upper middle classes; those of the lower classes, the bulk of the population, were not affected at all. Moreover, it should be remembered that humanism did not represent *all* the major intellectual currents of the age (Renaissance Aristotelianism and science, for example, though mathematics was later "added" to the *studia humanitatis*). Yet those trained by humanistic methods included some of the leading personalities of the age, and they set the standards in education that were to prevail almost to our own day.

After Petrarch and Boccaccio, Italian humanists became more and more scholarly and technically proficient, but at the same time less creative. This tendency culminated in the sixteenth century in the writings of the Venetian Cardinal Pietro Bembo, who bragged, pedantically, that he never used a work of Latin that had not appeared in the writings of Cicero. He even had rather harsh words for the works of the Fathers of the Church, which he considered to be "vulgar" in style.

Humanism, though so learned, thus began to become sterile. Perhaps the major reason is that during the *Quattrocento* (the fifteenth century) the increasingly slavish imitation of ancient literary works tended to discourage, indeed almost stifle, any sort of free expression on the part of humanists. In a dialogue written by Leonardo Bruni, for example, his two characters complain of the absence of any good literature in their time. The first, however, observes that there is no real cause for complaint, since there are Dante, Petrarch, and Boccaccio. At which the other snorts, "I would prefer one letter of Cicero to all the works of these *Italian* writers!" Such is the sentiment that became all too often characteristic of the attitude of the later humanists. Turning away from more creative types of literature, they devoted themselves to the more technical aspects of scholarship. Little was written in the new literary language, Italian, the development of the Italian vernacular literature begun by Dante, Petrarch, and Boccaccio being for some time probably retarded by the humanists' penchant for writing more and more technically perfect Latin. Nevertheless, it was this very emphasis on "critical scholarship"—that is, the perfection of one's Greek and Latin through careful study and imitation of the ancient texts— that gave rise to the important modern discipline of philology, and through philology to the study of history as it is conceived today.

Lorenzo Valla. The work of the great Italian Lorenzo Valla (1406–1457) is generally considered to have established the foundation for modern critical scholarship. Educated in Greek and Latin in the humanist tradition, Valla worked as a court secretary, first at Milan for the Visconti, then for Alfonso of Naples, and finally at the Papal Curia. During his lifetime Valla turned out many important philological treatises, significant not so much for their literary creativity as for their textual analysis. Some of Valla's writings reveal what may be termed the "non-Christian" (rather than "anti-Christian") attitudes beginning to appear among certain Italian humanists. In his *On Pleasure,* for instance, in which he has an Epicurean, a Stoic, and a Christian debate the merits of each one's approach to life and religion, the Christian attitude is criticized as almost a danger to organized society, owing to its emphasis on humility and self-abnegation. Valla and other humanists hoped that education would result in a better society, and for progress toward this end a certain self-interest was necessary.

Valla seemed almost to have a predilection for embarrassing the Church; his best-known works in fact were textual criticisms of two famous ecclesiastical documents. In his celebrated critique of the Donation of Constantine (see Chapter 4), he struck at the heart of papal claims to temporal power. The Donation, forged in the eighth century, claimed that the Emperor Constantine the Great, grateful to Pope Sylvester I for his miraculous cure from leprosy, awarded the Pope and his successors full temporal dominion over the Western half of the Roman Empire. On this forged document the Papacy had more than once in the past relied when in conflict with Western rulers for power.

Though actually not the first to question the authenticity of the Donation— Nicholas of Cusa did so just before him—Valla was the first to prove it a forgery. He did this through philological analysis, pointing out historical anachronisms in the text, that is, language usages of a later century in a fourth-century document. Furthermore, Valla showed that there was no evidence whatever in any document contemporary to Constantine (as, for example, in Eusebius, his biographer) that Constantine had ever suffered from leprosy. In destroying the validity of this basic document, Valla became a founder of the modern historical method. It should be noted, however, that because of the growing skeptical outlook of the humanist world, his attack did not unduly startle Western Europe, not even the Papacy, though of course his exposé was immediately seized upon as a weapon by certain men of anticlerical views.

Even more influential from the viewpoint of philological and biblical scholarship was Valla's analysis of St. Jerome's Vulgate Bible. For centuries this Latin translation of the original Greek and Hebrew text of the Scriptures into the colloquial, everyday Latin of the late fourth century had been the standard version of the Bible in the West. Using humanistic techniques, Valla analyzed Jerome's version of the Greek Testament and showed in the process errors or doubtful translations. Here was an attempt, the first in the West, to analyze philologically the most basic of all Christian documents in order to see if the translation was truly accurate in meaning. The great sixteenth-century humanist Erasmus, who later published Valla's treatise, was heavily indebted to Valla's method and ideas, and he made use of them for the Greek edition he himself made of the New Testament. Critical humanism, therefore, shed light on the origins and early writings of Christianity, but it should also be noted that, through the questioning attitude it engendered, it helped to lead to the Reformation.

In his third great work, *On the Elegance of Latin*, Valla dealt with the cultivation of a good Latin style; he explained Latin nuances, synonyms, and grammar and supported the superiority, in some ways, of Latin over Greek. Erasmus considered it the best handbook on Latin style, and it remained the favorite of scholars well into the seventeenth century.

Valla was important not only because he was the founder of several modern fields and techniques of research—philology, history, and biblical scholarship—but also because he made what was probably the greatest contribution to humanist "critical scholarship" of the fifteenth (and sixteenth) centuries. Whereas Petrarch and Boccaccio had been creative humanists in the sense of originality of inspiration and subject matter, whereas Guarino and Vittorino had sought to use humanism as a means of educating various groups in society, most later Italian humanists such as Valla sought above all to achieve technical perfection—but often to the detriment of the creative spirit.

"Christian Humanism": Latin, Greek, and Hebrew Scholarship

The triumph of the Papacy over the conciliar movement did not silence the critics who favored ecclesiastical reform. Particularly vocal were those who criticized the ignorance and venality of the clergy; they protested especially against the action of such Popes as Alexander VI Borgia or Julius II, who seemed far less interested in the welfare of the Church than in their own personal fortunes and ambitions. At the forefront of those who sought reform was another group of humanists who, through the use of humanist learning and education, sought not only to improve the intellectual and moral level of the clergy but perhaps even to reform society itself.

Italian humanists seem in the main to have been less concerned with the relation between religion and humanistic studies than those of the north—although Marsilio Ficino and Pico are notable exceptions. In Spain, however, the founder of humanistic studies was a cardinal of the Roman Church, Francisco Ximénes de Cisneros (1436–1517), whose aim was more like that of the northern humanists—the furthering of clerical reform in the Spanish Church. A Franciscan, Ximénes came to power and influence after becoming the confessor of Queen Isabella of Castile. With his appointment as archbishop of Toledo and primate of Spain, Ximénes ranked second only to the monarchs King Ferdinand and Queen Isabella themselves.

In order to further his ecclesiastical reform program, Ximénes established a new university, Alcalá de Henares. There Latin, Greek, and Hebrew, as well as Scholastic theology were taught. But through the humanistic techniques of studying these ancient languages, the primary objective of Alcalá, as Ximénes envisioned it, was to train an elite corps of clergy for the Spanish Church. Humanistic learning to him, then, was not an end in itself, as among the Italians, but rather an instrument for training well-educated priests who could take the lead in the reform of the Church.

In line with this ideal, Ximénes' greatest achievement was the publication of the *Complutensian Polyglot Bible*. The *Polyglot* was aimed at correcting the errors in the Vulgate version of St. Jerome through publication of more accurate texts of both the Old and New Testaments in the original Hebrew and Greek. Greek, Hebrew, and Vulgate texts were arranged in parallel columns so that comparison of the various versions could be made at a glance. I have elsewhere shown that the original Greek text of the New Testament was edited primarily by the Cretan émigré scholar, Demetrius Ducas, who had been called to Spain by Ximénes expressly for that purpose.* The *Complutensian Bible* was actually finished before Erasmus' edition of the New Testament Greek text, but, owing to Ximénes' death, it was not issued until several years after Erasmus' version. Cardinal Ximénes accepted the new philological techniques developed by the humanist scholars but subordinated them to what he considered a higher ideal —the welfare of Spanish Christianity. Such an aim has been aptly called "Christian humanism."

Christian humanism saw its most typical development, however, in the north of Europe, in the work of scholars of France, England, Germany, and the Low Countries. Particularly important to the background of this movement was the role of the Brethren of the Common Life, a semi-monastic, quasi-mystical group which established schools in the Rhineland and the Low Countries with the intention to train young boys in Christian learning and moral precepts. The schools of the Brethren emphasized, above all, active service *within* the Christian community, that is, in the world. And though these schools did not radically change the teaching methods of the cathedral schools, their appeal to the lay student pointed up a moral way of life through study. It was in the schools of the Brethren of the Common Life that many of the more famous northern humanists were trained—Erasmus and Agricola among them.

Many northern humanists also received training and inspiration in Italy. From the fifteenth century on, Germans, Frenchmen, and Englishmen flocked to Italy for study. In Florence and Venice they came in contact with Latin or Greek scholars who aroused their interest in the original Greek and Hebrew texts of the Scriptures. And in certain cases we know that northerners (Colet, for example) acquired from Ficino a predilection for the Epistles of St. Paul. Unlike many humanists of the south, then, who focused their attention on ancient literature and history (the Florentine monk Ambrogio Traversari, with his interest in the Greek Fathers, being an exception), the northerners increasingly directed their attention to the Church Fathers and the biblical texts.

* In D. Geanakoplos, *Byzantium and the Renaissance* (1972), pp. 242–243, chapter 8 on Ducas.

Rudolf Agricola (1444–1485), generally called the father of German humanism, is a case in point. Having studied Greek in Italy under the Byzantine émigré Theodore Gaza, Agricola returned to Germany, where he was appointed professor of Greek at Heidelberg University. There he engaged in disputes with the Scholastic theologians, supporting the new humanist learning against the attacks of the Scholastics, whose increasingly extreme dialectical methods he considered to be sterile and meaningless.

More famous was the scholar of Hebrew and Greek, Johann Reuchlin (1455–1522). After study at Freiburg and Paris, Reuchlin traveled to Italy, where, in Florence, he came under the influence of the Byzantine John Argyropoulos, Pico della Mirandola, and the Platonic Academy. Pico urged Reuchlin to turn especially to the study of Hebrew, so long neglected in the West. In this field Reuchlin became a pioneer, producing a Hebrew grammar and lexicon.

In pursuing his Hebrew studies, Reuchlin was drawn into a controversy with a Jewish convert to Christianity, Johannes Pfefferkorn. Pfefferkorn, a fanatic (like many converts) insisted that all Jewish books be destroyed on the grounds that they were detrimental to Christianity. The opinion of Reuchlin, as the most respected scholar of Hebrew, was sought as to which Jewish books should be suppressed. But Reuchlin demurred, affirming that most Hebrew works had much to offer Christianity and therefore should be preserved. Pfefferkorn therefore launched a campaign of invective against Reuchlin, accusing him of heresy and betrayal of Christianity. Supported by virtually all the great humanists of the time—Erasmus, Linacre, the French Lefèvre d'Étaples—Reuchlin took up the cudgels against Pfefferkorn. The Reuchlin-Pfefferkorn controversy (1509–1519) became a *cause célèbre* in Europe. In a sense it may be taken to represent the struggle in Germany between two kinds of thought—the old traditional unquestioning acceptance of Christian teachings characteristic of much of the medieval period, and the new, more critical approach to scholarship and religion as advocated by leading northern humanists. Though some of Reuchlin's ideas were condemned by the Church, in the long run his views and those of the other northern humanists were able to pervade the intellectual thought world of northern Europe.

The clash of humanism with Scholasticism in Germany brought forth a good deal of polemical writing, notably the so-called *Letters of Obscure Men.* Written in Latin in the style of Italian humanism, these letters were essentially satires designed to discredit the Scholastics and their beliefs. Above all, the letters lampooned Scholasticism's tendency to overanalyze and its often tortuous logical methodology.

In England even more than in Germany the development of humanism emphasized a return to the original sources of Christianity, the Scriptures and the early Fathers of the Church. Particularly important to the English and

French humanists were the Pauline Epistles, written by the Apostle Paul to the various early Christian churches of Rome and the Greek East. The extraordinary interest now manifested in Paul almost simultaneously among various European humanists can be traced primarily to Marsilio Ficino and the Platonic circle at Florence.

John Colet, dean of St. Paul's Cathedral in London, studied in Florence with Ficino himself. Colet became famous for his sermons and ideas on education, especially his establishment of a boys' school in London in which instruction in Greek and Latin was given free to boys of all classes. There, as in Vittorino's school at Ferrara, ethical and moral training was emphasized as well as classical learning. The English physician Thomas Linacre also studied in Italy, at Padua and Florence, and on his return to England founded, in 1518 in London, the College of Physicians. Thomas More, lawyer, philosopher, and minister to King Henry VIII, in his *Utopia* (on the model of Plato) sets forth in satirical fashion his views of an ideal state on earth—a state in which all men are equal and each man labors for the common good, with all sharing the wealth. More's *Utopia* is not to be considered a proto-socialist work, but rather one reflecting his own judgment of contemporary society from the viewpoint of Christian principles and ancient standards. It is a product of Christian humanism as applied to the political and social spheres.

Some French scholars like to think that French humanism is entirely, or almost entirely, a product of the French genius. But there is little doubt that Italian influences were about as important in France as they were in Germany, England, and Spain. Nevertheless, France had a number of humanists who were more purely secular-minded. Guillaume Budé (d. 1540), for example, the best Hellenist north of the Alps (whose career fell largely outside our period), wrote treatises on the Roman law (*Pandects*) of Justinian, on the theory of Roman coinage, and *Commentaries on the Greek Language*. He too was interested in reform of the Church, but he felt, even more strongly than did others, that Church reform could be furthered through the instrument of classical scholarship. At his persuasion King Francis I founded the still existent trilingual lectureships in Greek, Latin, and Hebrew at the Collège de France. But the aim here, unlike Alcalá, was to educate laymen, not clergy.

Besides mentioning Étienne Dolet, the master printer of Lyons who printed classical Latin works, we should at least glance at the career of Jacques Lefèvre d'Étaples (d. 1536), whose career, though extending several decades after 1500, shows the persistence of older medieval ideals. With a degree from the University of Paris, Lefèvre went to study in Italy. On his return to Paris he became head of a circle of intellectuals whose primary interest was reform of the Church. Like Colet he wrote a commentary on St. Paul; he also emphasized Christian justification by faith alone, thus anticipating the chief tenet of Luther. Lefèvre's circle, which was at once humanistic and mystical in its interest, refused to join

Luther when the latter tried to draw the group into his movement of protest against the Catholic Church. To Lefèvre's circle the venerable medieval tradition of unity in the Church was still all-important.

Erasmus.   The chief exponent, indeed probably the greatest influence, in the development of Christian humanism was Desiderius Erasmus of Rotterdam (*c.*1466–1536), whose career, though falling in part after 1500, best sums up the moral and intellectual qualities of the Later Middle Ages and looks forward to the modern world. Erasmus is often considered the chief link between the humanism of the south and that of the north. Having studied in Italy, Germany, France, the Low Countries, Switzerland, and England, Erasmus acquired a kind of supra-national European attitude and status, looking upon himself less as a Dutchman than as a citizen of the world.

The breadth of Erasmus' knowledge was remarkable. Educated as a child by the Brethren of the Common Life, he later went to Venice and Padua, specifically to improve his Greek. In Venice the chief influence on his Greek scholarship was the Cretan émigré Marcus Musurus. Erasmus' services to Greek studies are very significant. Not only did he publish Latin translations of several plays of Euripides and essays of Lucian, but, more significantly, through his popularization of Greek letters he did more than any other scholar to disseminate appreciation of Greek literature, and of the Greek Fathers of the Church as well.

His *Adages,* the most widely read book (after the Bible) in the sixteenth century, was a collection of maxims or sayings drawn from ancient Greek and, to a lesser degree, Roman authors. Many of the Greek works from which the sayings were taken were until then unknown to Western Europe. Erasmus first learned of them through Byzantine scholars with whom he associated in the Aldine Academy of Venice and nearby Padua.

As noted, his expertise in Greek enabled Erasmus to publish the first edition (1516) of the Greek New Testament text. This work, based on relatively few manuscripts, is inferior to that of Ximénes, but it had a great influence on subsequent biblical scholarship.

Despite notable scholarly endeavors, Erasmus is best known as a satirist and reformer. He was deeply concerned with the social conditions of his time, especially the laxity of clerical morals and the ignorance and pretentiousness of lay society. In his *Praise of Folly* he lampooned with mordant wit all segments of society, as well as individual follies of human nature. Beginning with the monks, he satirized the transitory ambitions of scholars, merchants, philosophers, courtiers, even kings and Popes—all of whom he held up to ridicule, pointing out that their worst faults were influenced by "Dame Folly."

Erasmus' aim was not to destroy but, through providing a more objective view of the traditional follies and foibles of man, to correct and above all to improve Christian society. In the process, Erasmus of course aroused the ire of many groups, especially the monks of Louvain and the Scholastic-oriented clergy at the University of Paris. The program he advocated to reform society was comprehensive and the best-defined of those that we have termed Christian humanism. His influence over the humanists of Western Europe was so pervasive that Luther sought to enlist him on his side. After all, Erasmus had attacked the monks and even certain aspects of the Church itself as an institution. But Erasmus, though at first sympathetic, could not in the end bring himself to join the Lutheran revolt. For him the traditional medieval unity of Christendom was still sacred.

The Erasmian program of reform, however influential and widespread among humanists, nevertheless in certain important respects failed. It was directed to the educated and was thus over the heads of the masses. Moreover, Erasmus failed to comprehend the tremendous new forces of "nationalism" and capitalism that were bringing about the destruction of medieval civilization. In Erasmus' career we still see the lingering influences of certain medieval ideas alongside the "New Learning," humanism. Erasmus exemplified, therefore, the final stages of the intellectual transition from the late medieval to the early modern world.

Late Medieval and Early Italian Renaissance Art

Humanistic enthusiasm for classical antiquity as well as the increasingly secular outlook of the Renaissance were reflected in the fine arts. Painting and sculpture in particular underwent profound changes—not the least being the emancipation of these art forms from their subordination to architecture before the fourteenth century. In contrast to the medieval painter or sculptor who used his craft primarily to beautify and ornament the cathedral, the Renaissance artist usually wanted his work to stand by itself as an individual creation, and to gain recognition for his achievement.

Painting and sculpture also began to turn away from religious themes. To be sure the lives of Christ and the saints continued to be among the favorite, most frequently portrayed, subjects; but now, increasingly, artists also painted portraits of famous contemporaries or chose as topics the old Greco-Roman gods and goddesses. The celebrated Raphael painted not only exquisite Madonnas; among other works he also painted the great *School of Athens,* which depicts a gathering of most of the famous pagan Greek philosophers.

A new style emerged. The art of the medieval period, rich in symbolism and frequently only semirepresentational, gave way to the Renaissance emphasis on imitation of nature, on perspective, and on the depiction of more massive figures. The human figure took over the central position in Renaissance art. Artists such as Michelangelo and Leonardo da Vinci even dissected cadavers in order to learn more about bone and muscle structure. The emphasis on the human form evidenced in this new type of art only served to show more explicitly the growing interest of people in themselves and in their immediate surroundings that was so characteristic a trait of the Renaissance period.

Like most cultural developments, however, Renaissance art was the result of a long evolution rather than of a sudden abandonment of medieval for Renaissance style. The greatest artists of the Renaissance were perhaps those of the late fifteenth and sixteenth centuries: Leonardo da Vinci, Raphael, Michelangelo, Titian, and El Greco. Yet these men's works were the culmination of certain developments in painting that began to appear as early as the late thirteenth and fourteenth centuries.

Giotto, Byzantium, and Early Renaissance Painting

The problem of the origins of this new artistic style, nevertheless, is not simple, as is true of almost every phase of Renaissance development. The traditional view holds that while such Italian artists of the fourteenth century as the Sienese Duccio and the Florentine Cimabue still continued to be influenced by the Byzantine style, which still prevailed in Italy and parts of the north, a genuine revolution in painting began with the great Florentine Giotto. As Vasari, the sixteenth-century Florentine art historian, noted, Giotto freed himself from the strictures of *la maniera greca* ("the Byzantine style"). With him, it is commonly believed, the shift began in Western art from the more traditional, seemingly stereotyped Byzantine manner to realism, an attempt at a more natural representation without idealization.

But the problem is much more complicated than this. While it is recognized that Italian and almost all Western European art (except, of course, Gothic sculpture and architecture) was, up to the mid-fourteenth century, the handmaiden of the Byzantine, it has only recently been more clearly realized that in certain areas of Byzantium itself (at Mistra, Thessalonica, Constantinople, and in Serbia) a certain freedom from the older Byzantine style, a bolder and more dramatic use of color and line conducive to a greater dynamic intensity (the "Palaeologan Renaissance"), had begun to appear by the late thirteenth and early fourteenth centuries. This remarkable shift in style or intensification of feeling expressed was doubtless connected with the spontaneous outpouring of patriotism felt by the Greeks at the expulsion of the detested Latins from Constantinople in 1261 (see Chapter 12 on the Fourth Crusade and its aftermath). The climax to, or at least a distant inheritor of, this unique Byzantine artistic development is now considered by some scholars to have come as late as the sixteenth century with the paintings of the great El Greco, born Domenicos Theo-

Giotto's painting in the Arena Chapel at Padua, "The Lamentation" (1305–1306),
depicts the Virgin lamenting Christ's death. Compare with the Nerezi "Lamentation
of the Virgin" on the opposite page. (Alinari/Scala)

tokopoulos on the former Byzantine, then Venetian-held island of Crete—paintings which reflect certain "Palaeologan" characteristics: elongation of figures,
use of deeper colors, and a heightened sense of mysticism.

With these developments in Byzantine art in mind, some Byzantine art
historians have accordingly claimed that Giotto and his followers were influenced by the new Byzantine Palaeologan style. And for these scholars even the
development of Renaissance realism is to be explained as Byzantine inspired.
Granted that there was some degree of Byzantine influence on Giotto (at least
indirect), a more balanced view would be that the more dramatic, more human-
ized currents found in these late Byzantine artists and in Giotto were essentially
independent—both inspired, though in different ways, by the paintings of an-

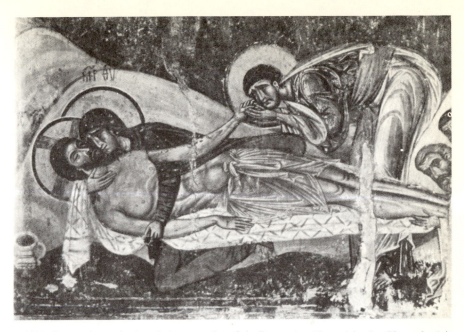

This Byzantine painting is from a church in Byzantine Nerezi (today Yugoslavia), of the mid- twelfth century. Note the remarkable similarities in the Virgin's face and in the iconography (grouping of figures) with the Giotto painting. Was Giotto influenced (and to what degree) by the Byzantine "Lamentation" of the Palaeologan Renaissance? (Courtesy of Skira and the Institution for Conservation of Cultural Monuments of Skopje City)

cient Christianity, which some artists in Italy and also in the Byzantine areas had begun to imitate. The Italian artists in particular imitated the early Christian art remains in the great churches of Rome.

Giotto (*c.*1276–1337) is generally considered to be the herald of early modern Western painting. Though still belonging chronologically to the medieval period, his character and personality were marked by the individualism, the worldliness, the versatility of Early Renaissance artists. Almost obsessed with a desire for recognition and success, in addition to painting he composed verses and coined witty phrases. He sought and received the patronage of cardinals, the king of Naples, and the rich of Florence and Padua. Once he had achieved a rather sizable fortune through his art, he became a moneylender, headed a "bill-collecting" firm, and rented weaving machines to poor workmen.

Despite the originality of his artistic genius, Giotto's style was, like that of other painters, influenced by his predecessors. Aside from the traditional rather stereotyped Byzantine elements acquired from his teacher, the Florentine Cimabue, he was perhaps also influenced by the new sculpture of Giovanni Pisano, by the realism of Gothic sculpture, by his own observations possibly formed during travels to France and throughout Italy, and, it is claimed, by viewing (in Italy) products of the Byzantine Palaeologan Renaissance.

Giotto's greatest masterpieces are the frescoes depicting the life of Christ in the Arena Chapel in Padua and those of the life of St. Francis at Assisi. In these color is perhaps the most expressive element—an element which helps to impart an almost three-dimensional quality to his work. The people portrayed here— Francis, St. Anne, even Judas—are strikingly real and alive, and seem to occupy a place in space in contrast to previous medieval painting which made little attempt to simulate depth. Giotto's artistic versatility was remarkable, though not atypical of many other Florentines of the time. Besides being a painter he was also a fine architect (he designed the famous bell tower of the Florence Cathedral) and, when he wished, could also practice the art of goldsmith and sculptor as well.

The history of Renaissance painting after Giotto is usually divided into two periods—Early Renaissance (fifteenth century) and High Renaissance (late fifteenth and sixteenth centuries). Giotto had begun the tendency to realism, to portray nature (to put it simply) more photographically. After him, during the Early Renaissance, the old medieval style tended to disappear. Prejudices against the depiction of human nudity were cast aside and perspective and foreshortening began to be employed. Most important, along with these improvements in technique there came the qualities of the Italian Renaissance: a new consciousness of the self, an awareness of the dignity of man, and a sense of his power in the universe.

The Florentine Masaccio (1401–1428) is generally considered the first true representative of Early Renaissance painting. Indeed, his influence on subsequent painting is almost the equal of Giotto's. Although he died at twenty-seven and left no real school, his investing of his paintings for the first time with what is called "atmospheric (or true) perspective," his use of more somber colors, and above all, his blending of the subordinate forms and scenery into one another so that the chief figures stand out in heroic proportions—in other words, the power and emotion expressed in his portrayals—mark him as the true founder of fully developed Renaissance painting. His best known works include the frescoes in the Brancacci chapel in Florence, in particular the famous *Expulsion of Adam and Eve* from the Garden of Eden, a painting which, according to critics, marks the beginnings of the "Grand Style" of the Renaissance.

During the fifteenth century an astonishing number of other first-class painters appeared in Italy and especially Florence, among them Fra Angelico, whose perhaps tepid spirituality nevertheless led him to perfect a refined and delicate coloration in his portrayal of important religious themes. His works include the *Death and Assumption of the Virgin* and the *Virgin's Coronation,*

"The Annunciation," by Fra Angelico (1387–1455). This painting shows both medieval and Renaissance influences. (Alinari/Scala)

paintings which, in subject matter and attitudes, seem almost a throwback to earlier medieval painting.

In Florence, under the impact of the Platonic Academy, Neo-Platonic ideas began to pervade the art of the period. Two philosophic theories were especially influential: that all creation emanates from God (a notion that particularly influenced Michelangelo), and the Platonic view of love and beauty. For the Florentine Platonists, beauty was a basic component of creation, and man, who possessed it originally when he was with God, always yearns for it. Through love man can reunite with the divine. The ideas of love and beauty were closely tied together and it was believed that the one operated, or should operate, where the other existed, though of course there were differences between higher and lower forms of beauty.

The artist whose works were most deeply influenced by Neo-Platonic concepts was Botticelli (*c.*1444–1510), the fifteenth-century Florentine whose very lyrical paintings are still the favorites of many. His greatest achievement was *La Primavera,* created for the Medici, in which he best succeeded in expressing the Platonic theories of love and beauty—a painting also characterized by a marvelous delicacy of color, tonal balance, and a certain melancholy. Another great work is the *Birth of Venus,* notable for its qualities of line as well as color. Botticelli was the last of the Italian artists of the Early Renaissance; the new phase of the High Renaissance was heralded by Leon Battista Alberti, also a Florentine.

The period of the High Renaissance, which begins in the later fifteenth century and extends through the sixteenth, in its latter development lies technically beyond the chronological limits of this book. But since the art works produced in many cases mark a direct climax to previous developments, my account, in order to avoid being cut off *in medias res,* will take brief note of the chief works of the principal sixteenth century masters, Leonardo da Vinci, Raphael, and Michelangelo.

Art of the High Renaissance

Alberti (*c.*1404–1472), though himself not a great artist, is very important for his treatises, in which he theorized on painting, sculpture, architecture (see below) and even the art of living. In these he provided for the first time a genuine rationale, a philosophy for the artists of the Renaissance. To his mind the classical principles of antiquity should guide the artist. He considered beauty a philosophical reality necessary to all life. To achieve the greatest artistic insight the artist himself should be a *uomo universale* (a universal man), at once painter, sculptor, scholar, and poet; in other words, one who, like the ancients, was interested in everything around him and through whom the peculiar sensitivities of each art form could be expressed.

The advent of the High Renaissance was marked by the gradual shift of the art capital of Italy from Florence to Rome. This event was to a great extent the result of the building program of the Popes, especially their plan to erect a new St. Peter's; they wanted the chief church of Latin Christendom to be the world's greatest basilica. Thus from all over Italy the Popes gathered masters of art.

Inspired by the ruins of ancient Rome (the newly discovered statue of Laocoön, for instance), artists developed new themes and interests. Somewhat less evident in these newly created art works of the High Renaissance was the direct delight in nature per se. Themes began to take on a grandiose, almost cosmic, quality in place of the more personal characteristics of the Early Renaissance. Abstract universal qualities were now emphasized. The apogee of this development is to be found in the mid-sixteenth century in Raphael's *Disputà,* which attempts to "depict" the doctrine of the Real Presence (transubstantiation), and, above all, in Michelangelo's *Last Judgment*.

To cite another instance: the statue of David by the Early Renaissance sculptor Donatello (d. 1466) depicts a boy charming in the quality of his youthfulness. Michelangelo's *David* of the next century, on the other hand, is rather the idealization of masculine beauty, similar in form to the idealized ancient Greek statue. The art of the later fifteenth century, as did humanism, began to turn away somewhat from the more naturalistic modes of expression to become more stylized, more analytically concerned with the imitation of classical art, and above all more heroic and grandiose in its conception. In this transformation of style older, more "medieval" elements were carefully blended with new in the creation of artistic masterpieces that seem timeless in their aesthetic appeal.

Leonardo da Vinci

Leonardo da Vinci (1452–1519) is usually considered to be the creator of the High Renaissance style in painting. Leonardo had phenomenal powers of observation and a remarkably wide range of interests—in fact, he may well be the most brilliant embodiment of the concept of the *uomo universale*. As a painter he was interested in optics and, with acute insight, understood vision as a three-way play between eye, object, and source of light. Leonardo's anatomical drawings are the first accurate depictions of the structure of the human body—the first to show the location of bones and muscles.

Leonardo was the first Italian artist to make use of the new technique of oil painting, which had been developed in the early fifteenth century in the north of Europe by Flemish painters (see below). Before this, painters had worked either in fresco or tempera. In fresco the painter applied pigment to wet plaster on the wall, which required quick work before the plaster dried and often reduced the possibilities for expression. In tempera, pigments were applied with egg white and tended to be rather opaque. Oils, on the other hand, permitted the artist to take more time and care with his work, and produced colors that were more translucent and also more permanent.

Besides exhibiting these qualities, Leonardo's paintings are noted for being the first to make effective use of *chiaroscuro* (light and shade), a perspective technique to bring certain figures into the foreground. In his *Virgin of the Rocks* he placed the human figures before the landscape, not within it as had usually been done before him.

Leonardo's *Last Supper* gives us acute insight into his style and technique. Unlike earlier medieval depictions of the Last Supper in which the group is usually shown at the moment of communion, with Judas the Betrayer isolated from the other Apostles, Leonardo daringly chose the dramatic moment when Christ announced to his disciples, "One of you will betray me." The wave of

Head of Adam by the fourteenth-century Byzantine painter, Theophanes "the Greek" (or his associates), at the Church of Chora (Kariye Djami) in Constantinople.

Theophanes later became more famous as "Feofan," painting in the Kremlin and elsewhere in Russia. His paintings are prime examples of the Byzantine "Palaeologan Renaissance" of art. (Courtesy of Dumbarton Oaks Center for Byzantine Studies, Washington, D.C.)

shock that runs around the table can be felt by the viewer. Only Judas does not gesticulate; he is apparently calm. Leonardo emphasized Christ's head by placing it in silhouette against the open doorway.

Raphael

Raphael of Urbino, who came to Florence as a young man, is best known for his supreme lyrical gift. Yet he too was master of the Grand Style. His chief works are in the Vatican, in the room called the Stanza della Segnatura, where on the ceilings and walls he represented mundane knowledge (poetry, philosophy, law), and also attempted a remarkable depiction of the truth of the dogma of transubstantiation. Perhaps his best work, again revealing the Renaissance interest in classical motifs, is his *School of Athens,* in which can be identified Plato, Aristotle, Socrates, Diogenes, Pythagoras, and other philosophers, even the Arab Aristotelian Averroës and Zoroaster.

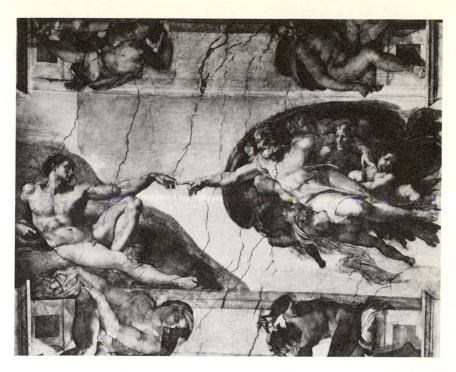

The creation of Adam by God (right) from Michelangelo's Sistine Chapel frescoes (sixteenth century). Michelangelo could not have known of the famous frescoes of the fourteenth-century Byzantine church of the Chora in Constantinople, but it is useful to compare this Creation of Adam with the picture by Theophanes. (Alinari/Scala)

Michelangelo

The artist whose work seems to bring to a climax most of the developments of Italian Renaissance art is Michelangelo Buonarotti. Representative of the extreme individualism of the High Renaissance, Michelangelo insisted that his art was his own and represented his own personality. Listening for comments on his newly finished statue, the *Pietà,* Michelangelo was irked to hear some observers mistakenly call it the work of another artist. That same day, in the dead of night, Michelangelo stole into the church and on the girdle of the Virgin conspicuously chiseled the words "Michelangelo Buonarroti."

Michelangelo's greatest work in painting is his decoration of the Sistine Chapel. It was a stupendous task worthy of his genius. Often working flat on his back on a scaffold high above the floor, he covered the walls and ceiling, including even the angles, an area of 6,300 square feet, with over six hundred figures, all part of one grandiose scheme, the depiction of God's creation of man and the world, and including the *Last Judgment.* The latter is a tour de force that has perhaps never been surpassed. In this picture (the theme of which is profoundly medieval) Michelangelo's technique seemed to summarize all Renaissance development in anatomy, perspective, composition, and line. The portrayal of God Himself, compared to previous work, is daring in the extreme: it not only depicts Him directly but imbues Him with different kinds of personalities commensurate with His activities of creation and judgment. Compare this work to that of the Byzantine artist Theophanes the Greek, over two centuries before. (See page 484.)

Remarkable as were his paintings, Michelangelo's truest talent lay in sculpture, and for this reason even his paintings give an impression of plasticity and motion, sometimes even of heaviness. His turbulent personality is reflected in his work, and it was his grand imagination and extreme individualism wedded to his advanced technique that produced the style that is often considered to be the bridge to a new phase of painting, the Baroque.

Titian and Tintoretto

Contemporary with Michelangelo is an almost equally gifted but quite different painter, Titian of Venice, whose paintings reflect the richness, pageantry, and flamboyance of Venetian life at the height of Venice's power. His special traits are the rich, deep hues of his coloration, particularly the purples and especially the red (still referred to as "Titian red"). The Renaissance came later to Venice than to other parts of Italy, but when it did, it brought a great array of painters, whose use of color and composition reflected the Venetian atmosphere and in some ways seemed to hark back to the centuries-long Byzantine connections with Venice. Titian's most famous works are *Sacred and Profane Love* (representing Venus in two aspects), *Bacchus and Ariadne,* and the *Rape of Europa.* The fame and influence of Titian, together with that of his great pupil Tintoretto, reached far beyond Italy and stimulated the painting of northern Europe in the sixteenth century.

Late Medieval Painting in Northern Europe

The Van Eyck Brothers. In northern Europe since the High Middle Ages there had existed the important tradition of Gothic art. It was the Van Eyck brothers, Hubert and Jan of Flanders, however, in the early fifteenth century, who, building on the Gothic tradition, formed a new, uniquely Flemish style. Jan and Hubert are credited with inventing the technique of oil painting—at least they were the first to use it to real effect. The paintings of the Van Eyck brothers are remarkable for their treatment of detail and their strong intensity of hue, which make the pictures gleam like jewels. More than is true of Italian Renaissance painting, every detail is meticulously delineated. The Van Eycks' masterpiece is the great altarpiece at Ghent, the *Adoration of the Lamb,* a large medieval-style triptych of some twenty religious subjects, including a nude Adam and Eve. Yet the works are more than merely photographic; they are a synthesis of infinite detail with a comprehensive theme. The style of the Van Eyck brothers should be viewed in the context of the late medieval guild system of Flanders, which so dominated the entire life of the area. It may be said that the tradition established by the brothers Van Eyck, often "medieval" in subject matter but forward looking in technique and style, was as influential in the north as was that of Giotto in the south. For over a century it dominated northern art, though some influence seeped in from Venice and other Italian areas.

Among other important northern painters, all of whom were in one way or another influenced by the Van Eycks, were Hieronymus Bosch (d. 1516), Albrecht Dürer (d. 1528), Pieter Brueghel (d. 1569), and Hans Holbein (d. 1543). Bosch typifies a northern trend toward the grotesque, almost the surrealistic (witness his *Christ Before Pilate*), and toward the use of painting for social criticism as well. Dürer, the greatest German painter, and the supreme master of the art of engraving and woodcuts, helped to develop techniques that enabled books to be lavishly and more inexpensively illustrated.

In his expression of the mentality of the lowest classes and his portrayal of peasant landscapes (of the "vulgar" genre), Brueghel outdid even Bosch. But Brueghel's paintings still possessed the fascination with the wondrous and the supernatural—a preoccupation that shows once again the different lines of development between High Renaissance Italian painting, and that of the North with its more pronounced medieval traits.

Sculpture

In sculpture Renaissance production ranks with that of ancient Greece. In the sculpture, as in the painting of early Renaissance Italy, a striving for realism in imitation of the classical style soon became evident. To be sure, Gothic sculpture in the north had achieved no little realism as early as the thirteenth and fourteenth centuries, but the element of genuine realism based directly on classical models first appeared in late fourteenth-century Italy. In sculpture, which is three-dimensional, realism might perhaps be expected to emerge before it did in other art forms.

After the work of the Italian Pisani family, father and son (influenced by the late medieval, Gothic sculpture, often found on the great Gothic cathedrals), the first great and indeed the foremost personality of the period of Early Renaissance sculpture was the Florentine Donatello (1386–1466). Painter as well as sculptor (activities often interchangeable in this period), his method of sculpture was that of low relief, which imparted a sense of intimacy, a refinement of plastic modeling. Donatello went to Rome as a boy and was influenced by the classical statues and ruins he saw there. His *Zuccone* and the youthful *David* (more delicate than Michelangelo's) are famous, as is his celebrated *Gattamelata,* the first full-scale bronze equestrian statue cast since the time of the Romans and probably even greater than any they produced. Before Donatello, sculpture in medieval Italy had made relatively little progress. But it was he who broke with the remnants of the Gothic tradition, combining a remarkable fidelity to nature with the moral grandeur of antique art.

Several decades after the death of Donatello (1466), Michelangelo produced some of the most remarkable statuary in the history of art. In the *Pietà* (done at the age of eighteen, and now in St. Peter's in Rome), the Madonna is purposely portrayed on a larger scale than Christ, and also as a young woman—distortions intended to give the effect of the mother holding her "child" and at the same time of an ever-youthful, timeless Madonna. Michelangelo added a new and important dimension to Renaissance sculpture, taking it even further from its medieval antecedents: individualism in an extreme form. His *David* is executed on a much larger scale than Donatello's and his statues for the tomb of Pope Julius II depict captives writhing in pain. Michelangelo's sculptural masterwork is *Moses,* who is shown at the moment when, returning from Sinai and observing his people's revels before the Golden Calf, he is about to shatter the tablets of the Ten Commandments given him by God. In sculpture as well as in painting, Michelangelo's work was the main bridge toward the new artistic period of the late sixteenth century, that of the Baroque with its Mannerism.

Architecture

Perhaps in no other realm of the arts is the Renaissance predilection for classicism so evident as in the field of architecture. For here there was an even greater degree of imitation of Greek and Roman forms than in sculpture. Renaissance buildings, in contrast to Gothic, were characterized by colonnades, rectangular shapes, and a feeling of solidity. Geometrical symmetry was carried through almost to an extreme, though at the same time the buildings had considerable grace and elegance.

The first and perhaps greatest Renaissance architect was the fourteenth- and early fifteenth-century Florentine Filippo Brunelleschi (d. 1446). He first attracted attention at a competition held in Florence for the design of bronze doors for the newly erected baptistery—doors to include panels depicting religious themes in low relief. Though he came in second to Ghiberti, whose magnificent doors Michelangelo later characterized as worthy to be the "gates of Paradise," Brunelleschi subsequently carried off first prize in the competition for the dome of the Florentine cathedral. He planned a dome with a span of

The cathedral Santa Maria dell' Fiore of Florence, showing Brunelleschi's great dome, which soared 308-feet high. Brunelleschi was the leading architect of the Italian Renaissance. (Rapho-Guillumette)

150 feet and soaring 308 feet high, a veritable masterpiece unrivaled in architecture except for the dome of St. Sophia in Constantinople (which had preceded it in the sixth century) and St. Peter's in Rome (which soon followed it). Brunelleschi also constructed many civic buildings for the Florentines, including the façade of the Foundling Hospital (the inspiration for which came from Roman ruins and study of the ancient, recently revived treatise of Vitruvius on architecture), a chapel for the Pazzi family, and the Franciscan church of Santo Spirito. To Brunelleschi, who carefully studied the ancient monuments, mathematical analysis provided the key to classic art, and he is credited with working out the application of the theory of perspective and proportion. It was Brunelleschi who established the norms for the Early Renaissance architecture that flourished throughout Italy.

Another significant Italian architect was the Florentine Alberti (mentioned above), whose design for St. Andrea at Mantua constitutes the first real modification of the Christian basilica form. Here he eliminated the aisles and the clerestory, while creating in the ceiling the first barrel vault of the Renaissance. But the building that perhaps most typifies the architecture of the High Renaissance is St. Peter's in Rome, built in the sixteenth century to replace the old basilica constructed by Constantine the Great. Several architects worked on the plan, including Raphael and Michelangelo. When this largest of Christendom's churches was finished, despite the changes in many details, the structure as a whole followed Michelangelo's design. Instead of medieval spires it has a classic dome, rising higher than any other, 435 feet from the floor. The round arches, heavy walls, and columns of the building all contrast sharply with the Gothic vertical style of church architecture of earlier northern Europe.

Music

New developments also came about in music during the Later Middle Ages and the Early Renaissance but, unlike humanism and painting, the lead in the field of music came first from the north, the Flemish areas in particular. One of the most influential early musicians was Philippe de Vitry (1291–1361), who in his treatise *Ars Nova* put forth precepts aimed at refining and holding within reasonable limits the growing complexity of medieval Gothic polyphony. Particularly important for him was an emphasis on rhythmic pattern in order to differentiate between the various voices.

De Vitry's main interest was still religious music; yet new developments in the secular sphere were soon to appear. During the fourteenth century, in a change of emphasis, composers increasingly turned their attention to secular music, in which the complex polyphonic form of the late medieval period was now used as the basis or setting for the creation of popular songs. This new direction was first noticeable in the north, but during the late fourteenth century it quickly caught on in Italy as well. All over Europe, in the courts of Italy, England, France, and Burgundy, lords and ladies now delighted in singing madrigals and motets—secular popular music, often bawdy, using the older forms of sacred music. (The round still sung by children today, for example, is a legacy of this transformation.)

Music came to be a vital activity in every court, royal and noble, not to mention the homes of rich burghers. In Burgundy in the north virtually all festivals included musical performances or musical accompaniments. The same held true in Renaissance Florence, Naples, and Milan. In the most important work written on Renaissance manners and etiquette, *The Courtier,* by the Italian Baldassare Castiglione (1478–1529), it was a virtual necessity for every gentleman or lady of a northern or southern court to become proficient in one of the various instruments invented or developed during the Renaissance: the viola da gamba, the harpsichord, the virginal, the more complex organ (Byzantines, Romans, and Western medieval man, to be sure, had earlier known the organ), the recorder, or the lute (the latter acquired from the Muslims of Spain by way of the French troubadors).

With the wide use of music for both secular and sacred purposes, composers began to appear in greater numbers, many of whom contributed to musical developments. But the composer who in the north occupies a position comparable to that of the Van Eycks in painting was the Burgundian Guillaume Dufay (*c.*1400–1474). For many patrons in both Church and secular courts, Dufay composed in almost every musical form of the period: masses, hymns, secular madrigals, motets. Traveling through France and Italy, he acquired new inspiration and spread his own ideas. Dufay's contribution was to emphasize the subordination of the music to the text rather than the text to the music. He thus helped to free music—both religious and secular forms were still not much differentiated—from the rather artificial, overly complex polyphony typical of the late Middle Ages. While under Dufay and his fellow composers, counterpoint, or what may be called the interplay of simultaneous melodies, continued to dominate composition, there was now a growing feeling for harmony (vertical structure) and even some incipient use of chords.

The developments that began in the north, however, reached their culmination in the work of the great Italian composer Pierluigi da Palestrina (*c.*1525–1594). Palestrina's music is indeed often considered the classical model for religious polyphony. His very moving, other-worldly masses, written for church services (and still medieval in certain respects), are among the great masterpieces of musical composition.

Patronage in the Later Middle Ages and Renaissance

The support of wealthy patrons was an indispensable factor in the remarkable flowering of intellectual and artistic endeavor during the Italian Renaissance. Were it not for men such as Lorenzo de' Medici, Ludovico Sforza, and Duke Federigo of Urbino, all willing to pay scholars and artists such as Donatello, Leonardo, and Michelangelo for their work, even to support them during long periods of inactivity, their talents might have produced far fewer results. The patronage of wealthy and powerful personages, freeing many Italian Renaissance artists from the worries of day-to-day life, enabled the latter to devote all their energies and talents to the creation of masterpieces that still survive.

Patronage, of course, was not really new; even in the High Middle Ages there were a few individual patrons such as the Abbot Suger of France, though in the different, medieval context of an entire community glorifying God through art. What is remarkable is that in the Renaissance every prince, every wealthy noble or burgher, in one way or another wanted to become known as a patron of the arts or literature. It was not only a matter of personal interest in the arts, but, no less, a way to increase one's reputation. It was thus in a real sense an expression of the new ethos of the age.

The New "Renaissance" Ethos

The Courtier of Baldassare Castiglione, the work that best explicates the values and qualities of Renaissance society, implied that the true gentleman is a devotee of arts and letters. Castiglione's appraisal of the ideal courtier affirms also that he should be of good birth, of athletic ability, fluent in several languages, and competent to discuss intelligently literature and the arts. He is to have elegant manners, display a breadth of accomplishments, and seek to preserve and extend his reputation. Notably absent among these qualities particularly stressed by Castiglione are piety and devotion to the Church. In sharp contrast to the medieval ideal (recall St. Louis of thirteenth-century France), Castiglione's gentleman is thoroughly secular; his interests are directed toward achievements in this world, and his ultimate goal is, in effect, self-glorification.

The term that best expressed the quintessence of the Renaissance ideal, for the Italians especially, was *virtù*. This quality denoted not "virtue" in the older Christian sense (humility, morality, gentleness), but rather the more pagan, now purely secular, idea of manliness (from the Latin word *vir,* "man"), the ability of one to conceive ideas and, most importantly in the political field, the capability to carry out these ideas with valor, dispatch, and style—in other words the will to power and achievement which recognized no law above itself.

This change from "virtue" to *virtù* was symptomatic of a much broader change of attitude in society which, in particular in Italy, became fully apparent by the end of the fifteenth century. The old Western medieval ideal of a "Christian Commonwealth" governed by God through natural law and in which the Church played the predominant role, had given way to the reality of a much more secular society composed of individual states and, to a considerable extent, imbued with a self-conscious and an unabashed spirit of material gain. The period of the fourteenth and fifteenth centuries, while looking forward to a new age, a new vision of the world, of nature, and of man's place in the universe, at the same time, as we have observed, carried on to a surprisingly large degree not a few of the cultural and social attitudes and forms of the late Middle Ages. The ambiguous nature of these two centuries, reflecting at once the qualities of both medieval and early modern times, marks the Renaissance as the bridge in the West between the medieval and modern worlds.

FOR FURTHER READING

Ady, C. M., *Lorenzo de' Medici and Renaissance Italy** (1966). A brief account, focusing on the role of Lorenzo the Magnificent.

Baron, H., *The Crisis of the Early Italian Renaissance: Civic Humanism and Republican Liberty in an Age of Classicism and Tyranny,* 2 vols.* (1966). An important work stressing the impetus given the development of humanism in Florence by the challenge of the Visconti of Milan.

Berenson, B., *The Italian Painters of the Renaissance** (1952; rev. ed., 1957). A work by an acknowledged master of art history.

Bolgar, R. R., *The Classical Heritage and Its Beneficiaries: From the Carolingian Age to the End of the Renaissance* (1954; 1964). A valuable study of Greek and Latin heritage, especially in the Renaissance.

Brucker, Gene, *Renaissance Florence** (1969). Fine, short treatment.

Burckhardt, Jacob, *The Civilization of the Renaissance in Italy,* 2 vols.* (1958). Old and often criticized, but still the greatest synthesis on the subject, the point of departure for all Renaissance scholarship on interpretation.

Cassirer, E., et al., *The Renaissance Philosophy of Man** (1969). Selections from works of famous Italian humanists.

Chabod, F., *Machiavelli and the Renaissance** (1958; 1965). One of the best treatments of Machiavelli's theories.

Ferguson, Wallace K., *The Renaissance* (1940). A brief but valuable introduction, emphasizing the social-economic aspects of the Renaissance.

Ferguson, Wallace K., *The Renaissance in Historical Thought* (1948). A valuable, comprehensive attempt to trace the changing attitudes toward "the problem of the Renaissance."

Geanakoplos, D. J., *Byzantine East and Latin West: Two Worlds of Christendom in Middle Ages and Renaissance* (1966). Chapters 4–6 deal with Byzantine émigrés to the West who influenced the Renaissance.

Geanakoplos, D. J., *Byzantium and the Renaissance: Greek Scholars in Venice* (1962; 1973). The sole synthesis focusing on the role of Byzantines and Cretans in the Renaissance, in Venice, especially before and after 1453. An original work.

Geanakoplos, D. G., *Interaction of the Sibling Byzantine and Western Cultures in the Middle Ages and Italian Renaissance (330–1600)* (1976). Most recent, interdisciplinary study of Byzantine and Western cultures and societies in their interaction. Comprehensive work.

Gilmore, M. P., *The World of Humanism, 1453–1519 ** (1952; 1962). A fine synthesis of this period.

Holmes, G., *The Florentine Enlightenment: 1400–1450 ** (1969). A good survey of the period.

Huizinga, J., *The Waning of the Middle Ages** (1954). A masterpiece of interpretation, viewing the fourteenth and fifteenth centuries as the period of the decline of the Middle Ages.

* Asterisk indicates paperback edition available.

Krey, A. C., *A City That Art Built* (1936). An excellent little book giving a political-social interpretation for the emergence of Florentine Renaissance art.

Kristeller, P. O., *Renaissance Thought,* 2 vols.* (1961). Excellent, provocative work by the great master in the field, focusing primarily on the significance of Aristotelianism and Platonism, and types of intellectual thought.

Martin, A. von, *Sociology of the Renaissance** (1944; 1963). A short but valuable interpretation of a complex question.

Martines, L., *The Social World of the Florentine Humanists, 1390–1460* (1963). New light on background of humanists.

Panovsky, E., *Early Netherlandish Painting* (1953). Masterful.

Rice, E., *The Renaissance Idea of Wisdom* (1958). Very perceptive analysis.

Robinson, J. H., and Rolfe, R. W., *Petrarch, the First Modern Scholar and Man of Letters* (1898). Still very useful.

Sarton, G., *The Appreciation of Ancient and Medieval Science during the Renaissance* (1955). Renaissance science interpreted by a leading scholar.

Schevill, F., *The First Century of Italian Humanism** (1970). A useful little manual of translations of early Italian humanists' works.

Vasari, G., *Lives of the Artists: Biographies of the Most Eminent Architects, Painters, and Sculptors of Italy,* ed. Betty Boroughs* (1957). The great contemporary work on Italian Renaissance artists.

Weiss, R., *The Dawn of Humanism in Italy* (1947). A brief, provocative interpretation of the origins of humanism.

Woodward, W. H., *Vittorino da Feltre and Other Humanist Educators** (1964). The best work on the subject of Italian humanist education.

The Latin West: Chief Beneficiary of Medieval Cultural Interaction

In this book I have tried to avoid the conventional, almost exclusively one-sided Western approach to the study of medieval history by discussing the origins and development of the *three* great civilizations of the medieval world—Western, Byzantine, and Islamic. Each of these civilizations, directly or indirectly, became successor to a part of the vast Roman Empire and the culture of classical antiquity. Emphasis on the three major components of medieval civilization provides a feeling for the vastness and diversity, but also in certain respects the common features of the medieval worlds of West and East. At the same time it provides a more accurate picture of the development of Western civilization, which is too often treated as the product of an historical evolution almost completely independent of influences from other cultures.

In the various forms of interaction that took place among the three societies, each culture absorbed from the other only a part of what was transmitted to it, appropriating only those cultural influences that would not conflict with the distinguishing core of its own civilization. In Islam this core was the Koranic texts and their traditional interpretation; in Byzantium, Greek "Orthodox" Christianity with its strong overlay of classical Greek learning; and in the West, Latin "Catholicism," strongly tempered (especially in the early medieval period) by the influences of the semibarbaric Germanic peoples. Anything contradictory to these core elements was considered dangerous and therefore was rejected.

All three cultures were eager to absorb ancient Greek learning, especially Aristotelian logic and philosophy, whose methodology and secular approach could readily be adapted to any religious belief. Thus, despite rather early Western acceptance of important writings of Aristotle in Arabic translation, the accompanying commentaries of the Muslim Averroës, whose doctrine of the twofold truth militated starkly against the basic tenets of Christianity, led the Catholic church ultimately to reject "Latin" Averroism.* Averroës' categories of the

---

* However, Averroism in its philosophical and scientific aspects continued to be taught at the University of Padua long after 1500.

"double truth" provided a convenient solution for using Aristotle without reference to the teachings of the Koran or the Bible. But in Islam itself Averroism was for the same reasons not accepted except by a small group of intellectuals. Nor could Western, Byzantine, or Islamic society accept the various dualistic heresies (called Catharism in the Byzantine East and Albigensianism in the West) because their beliefs were dangerous not only to the beliefs of Christianity and Islam but, if carried to their logical conclusion, would foster the disruption of organized society.

In the period of the Early Middle Ages when the West was still intellectually "retarded," it was receptive to the more advanced forms of Byzantine artistic and religious expression and spirituality such as painting and mosaics (among others), religious hymns and notions of Mariology, and, possibly, the technique of making stained glass. In the High and Later Middle Ages, however, when the West reached cultural maturity and became more confident and aggressive, it was much less receptive to Byzantine religious influences such as Hesychasm, an extreme Eastern form of mysticism that was considered heretical by the West.

Besides its core element, each culture possessed certain other unique characteristics. In Islam there was a vast amount of Persian influence, totally absent from the Western cultural synthesis and in large part also from the Byzantine. The element most unique to Western culture was probably the Germanic with its special attitudes toward society, religion, and government. Indeed, it may well have been primarily this Germanic element, in combination with other Latin factors, that provided the dynamic for Western cultural creativity in the High and Later Middle Ages. As for Byzantine culture, besides reflecting a more deeply mystical consciousness than the West, it was more importantly the sole preserver and storehouse of ancient Greek learning. In this sense Byzantium constituted the clearest continuation of ancient civilization, which may account for some of its conservatism. The effect of these additional unique elements was not only to further differentiate each culture from the others, but also to provide some of the influences which were rejected by the other cultures as unassimilable.

In the process of cultural interaction there were therefore attitudes not only of "receptivity" but also of "repulsion." Both of these reactions were characteristic as well of the cultural relations between Byzantium and the Slavic peoples. Normally eager to adopt Byzantine ways, the Slavs could react very hostilely if they felt Byzantine influences came too close to their growing sense of ethnicity. The Turks, who accepted the Islamic religion, certainly in the earlier period were too culturally underdeveloped to have any influence on either Western or Islamic civilization, though the older Islamic and Byzantine cultures affected them deeply.

After the only partly successful efforts of Charlemagne and his successors to revive Western European civilization, the West became far more divided politically than the other two great communities, despite the "universality" of its Catholic religion. In contrast to the unity of Byzantium up to the eleventh century and of Islam up to the ninth, the West, by the late ninth and tenth centuries had become politically split into a remarkable collection of feudal units. And, even before the High Middle Ages, vernacular languages emerged in every Western area. Nonetheless, out of this welter of feudal disunity there was gradually distilled in England, France, and Spain a kind of centralized feudalism leading ultimately to the "national" state of early modern times. It is likely that in this development a certain influence may have been exerted by the age-old example of Byzantium with its traditional Roman concept of the state under the rule of public law.

In the long series of encounters among the three communities, they borrowed from each other without hesitation the natural resources and commodities of trade they needed for their own economic lives—though always for a price. But capitalism took root only in the West, during the Later Middle Ages. It did not emerge as a system in the Islamic areas or even more certainly not in the Byzantine lands. In Byzantium wealth was generally invested in land that lent itself with difficulty to capitalist speculation; nor did banking and credit achieve there the advanced forms of Early Renaissance Italy. The Byzantine state itself, before its semi-collapse in the eleventh century, controlled large-scale industry and commerce primarily for the benefit and survival of the state. In the Islamic Caliphate of Baghdad, which had inherited the commercial inclinations of early Byzantium through the Arab seizure of Damascus, Alexandria, and Antioch, an early form of the Italian capitalist *commenda* (called in Arabic, *qirad*) did appear. But capitalism remained characteristic of the West alone, where a combination of factors necessary to produce the secular capitalist system occurred: increasing population, rise of a merchant class willing to take risks in long-range trading ventures, and development of an organized system of credit and banking.

By the end of the Middle Ages Western Latin society clearly had become the chief beneficiary of all this medieval cultural interaction. By 1500, the end of the epoch of the Early Renaissance, the West had secured from Byzantium, itself undergoing the remarkable "Palaeologan renaissance," the priceless gift of the whole of ancient Greek learning that it had begun to receive only piecemeal from the Byzantine East in the earlier periods. Earlier the West had acquired from Byzantium what it wanted of the more original aspects of the Byzantine ecclesiastical tradition. But in the later medieval period the West generally felt too haughty, too hostile, or even too confident vis-à-vis the Byzantines to be any further influenced by the "schismatic" Orthodox Church. The Byzantines, now in a completely defensive position due to the Turkish conquests and constant proposals for religious union with Rome—and of course mindful of the trauma inflicted by the Latins in 1204—were fearful not only of the loss of their ecclesiastical independence but, even more, of their sense of "national" identity.

From Islamic Spain the West received in the late tenth and eleventh centuries the first decisive impetus to a more sophisticated intellectual tradition, an appreciation of Aristotle, made possible by the cultural preparation of Gerbert and his successors in the tenth century. The literary efflorescence of southern France was undoubtedly influenced by Arabic Spain, less with respect to the content of French troubador poetry than the influence of Arabic poetic devices and techniques. The Western Crusaders' conquest of Islamic Syria and Palestine transmitted to the Latin West influences in food, textiles, and military science. Knowledge of scientific advances in medicine, optics, and pharmacology came from the Caliphates of Islam and from Arab Sicily, which in turn secured a good deal (though far from all) of their learning from ancient Greece via Byzantium.* Many scholars, however, believe that aside from a new style of life and themes for the popular poetry of the "romance" little of philosophical, literary or scientific value came from the Arabs to the West as a result of the Western Crusades to the Holy Land.

All of these Byzantine and Islamic cultural contributions played a very significant part in the growth of the West to cultural maturity. But the West itself assimilated and integrated these influences with the earlier, even more basic, Latin and German elements of its cultural synthesis. Thus, by the twelfth and thirteenth centuries the West was able to create a new and unique civilization.

In our survey of over one thousand years we have seen Western Latin civilization regress from the sophisticated cultural level of the later Roman Empire to the nadir of the "Dark Ages." Then, gradually grafting onto its own developing strength and vigor certain social, economic, and especially cultural influences emanating from the Byzantine and Arab worlds, the West was able to transform itself, by the time of the High Middle Ages and more so in the Early Renaissance, into an advanced society and culture. Through the vigorous cultural creativity manifested primarily in the sophisticated, now more secular life of its towns, medieval Western society may stand beside the great civilizations of human history. From the eleventh through the fifteenth centuries, the practicality of this society's institutions, originality of artistic creations, subtlety of theological formulation, and sensitivity and cohesiveness of literary and philosophic systems unmistakably marked the emergence in Western Europe of the roots, the early development, and the promise of our modern "Western" urban society and culture.

---

* In particular from the conquered Byzantine territories. Norman Sicily, too, was important.

INDEX